Police Psychology
Into the 21st Century

SERIES IN APPLIED PSYCHOLOGY

Edwin A. Fleishman, George Mason University
  Series Editor

Police Psychology
Into the 21st Century

Edited by

Martin I. Kurke
Drug Enforcement Agency (Retired)
and George Mason University

Ellen M. Scrivner
Visiting Fellow, National Institute of Justice

LAWRENCE ERLBAUM ASSOCIATES, PUBLISHERS
1995 Hillsdale, New Jersey   Hove, UK

Lawrence Erlbaum Associates, Inc., Publishers
365 Broadway
Hillsdale, New Jersey 07642

Library of Congress Cataloging-in-Publication Data

Police psychology into the 21st century / Martin I. Kurke & Ellen M.
Scrivner, editors.
    p.   cm.
Includes bibliographical references and index.
ISBN 0-8058-1344-6 (acid-free paper)
1. Police psychology. 2. Criminal psychology—United States.
3. Police—United States—Job stress. I. Kurke, Martin I., 1924–
II. Scrivner, Ellen M.
HV7936.P75P653 1995
363.2′01′9—dc20   94-24395
                                                       CIP

Books published by Lawrence Erlbaum Associates are printed on acid-free
paper, and their bindings are chosen for strength and durability.

Printed in the United States of America
10 9 8 7 6 5 4 3 2 1

Contents

V Supporting Police Operations

VI Organizational Development and Support   373

VII New Directions   417

Series Foreword

There is a compelling need for innovative approaches to the solution of many pressing problems involving human relationships in today's society. Such approaches are more likely to be successful when they are based on sound research and applications. The Applied Psychology Series offers publications that emphasize state-of-the-art research and its application to important issues of human behavior in a variety of social settings. The objective is to bridge both academic and applied interests.

Recent years have seen the development of police psychology as an important field of research and professional application. Various scientific psychological disciplines have played a significant role in our law enforcement agencies. This book brings together many of these developments. It includes chapters from individuals who have made significant contributions in law enforcement through the application of psychological science and professional practice.

The opening chapter of this book describes the development of police psychology from three distinct traditions and areas of psychology: traditional psychological service delivery to local police agencies, officers, and their families; operational support and research supporting federal law enforcement agency mission; and federal funding of behavioral science-based law enforcement technology and process development. Each of these traditions contributed to the growth of psychology as a science and as a profession and to the development of law enforcement as a professional discipline. Although each tradition-based form of law enforcement support has had its successes, and although progress has been made in integrating the results of the three traditions, the process is still far from complete.

As connoted by the title, *Police Psychology Into the 21st Century* is, in its way, a progress report on the integration effort. It describes both the state of the art and anticipates new directions that must be followed to ensure an integrated psychological support to law enforcement agencies. For this reason, the editors of this volume wisely selected a panel of 21 authors with experience at the federal, state, and local levels. Their ranks include psychologists who are or were sworn officers, federal agents, and civilian employees of law enforcement agencies, and other psychologists who provide psychological services to the law enforcement community as consultants.

It is widely acknowledged that conditions of employment in law enforcement evoke a unique set of work-related personal, family, and management problems. As a result, a police work culture has developed that often seeks self-containment and is somewhat intolerant of outsiders. Many of the authors of this book have earned their acceptance in the law enforcement community by becoming part of it. They bring to this book a body of knowledge and experience-based sharing of the frustrations and victories of police officers. They, and others like them, have broken new ground and contributed to the establishment of environments that have enabled psychologists and police officers to respect (if not always to completely understand) each other and to contribute to the bodies of knowledge of the other's profession. In my opinion, this book serves applied psychologists who work or plan to work with the law enforcement community by describing existing and emerging means of psychological support to that community as it is seen by the psychologists "in the trenches" and by those now playing management and administrative support roles.

Almost all police managers are aware of some of the psychological services that are traditionally provided by psychologists. For example, psychologists are commonly involved in police selection, training, and promotion processes; in trauma stress management; and evaluation of fitness for duty. A much smaller number of police managers have been exposed to the psychologist as a human resource expert, as a strategic planner, as a human factors (ergonomics) specialist, or as an organizational behavior expert. I suggest that this book's value to police managers should not be overlooked. It is a vehicle by which they may expand their horizons and learn of ways of applying the skills of appropriately trained psychologists to the resolution of a wide range of issues far beyond the ken of the more traditional employment of psychologists by police departments.

Edwin A. Fleishman, Editor
Applied Psychology Series

Foreword

Martin Reiser

I had the good fortune, in December of 1968, to be selected by the Los Angeles Police Department (LAPD) as the first full-time, in-house police psychologist (Reiser, 1972). I was given a small office, a salvage desk and two chairs, a new pad and pencil, a broom, and a battered Plymouth from the motor pool. The phone had a switch so that calls could be answered at the Personnel Division when I was out of the office. The broom was handy for periodic assaults on the corner dustballs indigenous to those rubber-tiled rooms. My initial job description was necessarily ambiguous and all-encompassing. I needed to provide counseling to the 9,000 sworn and civilian employees plus family members. I was expected to respond post haste to officer emergencies, barricade and hostage situations, and teaching requests at the academy. I was also responsible for psychological program development, organizational consultation, research, and addressing the gamut of other crises that might surface (Reiser, 1982b; Reiser & Sloane, 1983).

Things started slowly, with the emphasis on ride-alongs, roll calls, coffee room chatter, and trying to get up to speed in this new environment. Being accepted and gaining credibility were the first orders of business. It took about 6 months to feel more of an insider than an alien as indicators of acceptance increased. Requests for service burgeoned, as did the need for new programs and approaches as issues were identified. Gradually, the lone department psychologist was transformed into a broader Behavioral Science Services Section.

In those early years, police and mental health professionals were skeptical and suspicious if not openly hostile toward each other. Police tended to view psychologists as fuzzy-headed, cloud-nine types who had trouble finding the rest room. The watchword was that you had to be crazy to talk to a shrink. Police administrators also evidenced ambivalence toward their own psychologists—they were nice to have but not a high priority. Psychologists in turn tended to perceive the police as ham-handed rednecks, brutal, insensitive, and preferring muscle over mind. The military model, a powerful shaping influence on police over the years, helped contribute to the negative stereotypes.

Those early attitudes and judgments have been changing as police and psychologists have toiled together in the hard crucible of the police environment. Each has come to appreciate the other's unique strengths and abilities. Mutual respect has replaced old fears and anxieties, allowing for combined development of the police psychology role.

In 1972, the first internship in police psychology was initiated in the LAPD. This provided a training site for police psychologists and added sorely needed staff resources. One of the growing activities was crime-related consultation requested by detectives. This included the psychological profiling of suspects in major homicide and rape cases; evaluation of threats against celebrities, politicians, and other notable persons; and assessment of the suitability of emotionally disturbed suspects for polygraph examination (Reiser, 1973, 1982a). The use of investigative hypnosis with witnesses was piloted in a research project in 1975 and ultimately proved to be a valuable investigative tool (Reiser, 1980).

In 1981, a peer counseling program was initiated to make relevant help more available to department employees. This service evolved over 12 years with no resulting complaints, lawsuits, or other major problems. There are now 200 trained peer counselors available around the clock (Klyver, 1983). In 1983, a longitudinal research project was launched to collect stress and integrity data across the officer's career path. Factors impacting stress proneness, stress resistance, and honesty, if isolated, may allow for better understanding and utilization of the system, from the selection of recruits to how the organization contributes to the stress load of officers.

Police psychology continues to grow. A recent national survey found that in 1979 only 20% of agencies surveyed utilized these services, compared to over 50% of the departments queried in 1988 (Delprino & Bahn, 1988). Police psychology has become a full-fledged specialty with its own literature, journals, and professional organizations.

The advent of police psychology has created a vital new area of theory and practice within the purview of applied psychology. Because it deals with the everyday stresses and strains, and with the life and death conflicts affecting the police and the larger community, police psychology operates on the cutting edge of what is happening in the community.

Almost daily, the media report on and reflect the deeply held feelings people have about crime, victimization, the quality of neighborhood life, and the relationships between police and the people they serve. Police psychology often has an important impact on police operations and administration. Managers who recognize the pragmatic value of psychological insights in the welter of police-related contexts have come to view the police psychologist as a valued partner with the special expertise essential to cost-effective planning and decision making. Both professions, police and psychology, have learned much from each other in their collaborative interaction.

The police psychology venue ranges from the recruiting and screening of applicants to the retirement problems of police employees and all of the points in between. There is perennial interest in and curiosity about the police realm, the psychological aspects of police work, and the psychologists who toil behind the badge. This book provides a timely illumination of that domain.

The editors, both outstanding police psychologists, have fashioned a logical structure for this book. It starts with the history of police psychology and progresses through the key areas of involvement, from the selection process to the counseling of police personnel and families, to organizational diagnosis and development, to the kinds of support provided to police operations, to a discussion of the new directions police psychology is and will be traveling.

The individual chapters are written by seasoned police psychologists and consultants with hands-on experience in a variety of law enforcement agencies. Comprehensive in scope, this book presents the large audience of interested police and mental health professionals, researchers, legal experts, and students with an excellent overview and in-depth coverage of this evolving specialty.

The future of police psychology appears to be bright. In addition to their many areas of involvement at present, police psychologists will continue to identify and develop new opportunities for collaborative input. Work will continue on facilitating the shift from the military model of policing to a service model with emphasis on primary prevention approaches. The growing focus on community-based policing will provide fertile ground for assisting the police in achieving an equal partnership with the community as policing and police psychology move into the 21st century.

REFERENCES

Delprino, R. P., & Bahn, C. (1988). National survey of the extent and nature of psychological services in police departments. *Professional Psychology: Research and Practice, 19*(4), 421–425.

Klyver, N. (1983, November). Peer counseling for police personnel: A dynamic program in the Los Angeles Police Department. *The Police Chief*, pp. 66–68.

Reiser, M. (1972). *The police department psychologist*. Springfield, IL: Charles C. Thomas.

Reiser, M. (1973). *Practical psychology for police officers*. Springfield, IL: Charles C. Thomas.

Reiser, M. (1980). *Handbook of investigative hypnosis*. Los Angeles: LEHI.

Reiser, M. (1982a, March). Crime-specific consultation. *The Police Chief*, pp. 53–56.

Reiser, M. (1982b). *Police psychology—Collected papers*. Los Angeles: LEHI.

Reiser, M., & Sloane, M. (1983). The use of suggestibility techniques in hostage negotiation. In L. Z. Freedman & Y. Alexander (Eds.), *Perspectives on terrorism* (pp. 213–223). Wilmington, DE: Scholarly Resources, Inc.

Preface

This book presents police psychology as an evolving arena in which psychological science is applied in the law enforcement managerial and operational environments. Police psychology as we know it today is a relatively new phenomenon in the history of psychology, as it is in the history of policing itself. In this book we present a police psychology that by the last decade of the 20th century has developed a core technology consisting of psychological evaluation, counseling, and training. In addition, psychologists ply their trade in supporting police operations and by providing organizational development and support to departments. The book closes with a section devoted to new directions in which we see police psychology expanding.

Although some people date police psychology in its modern form to the 1968 full-time appointment of a psychologist to the Los Angeles Police Department, behavioral scientists and practitioners have supported the police on formal and informal bases for many years. For example, in his book, *On the Witness Stand*, Hugo Münsterberg (1907)[1] proposed applying psychology to the detection of crime. This theme still has great public appeal. As this book approaches completion, a novel by Caleb Carr entitled *The Alienist* (1994)[2] appeared on booksellers' shelves and quickly found a place on best-seller lists where it remained for many weeks. In the novel, set in 1896,

---

[1]Münsterberg, H. (1907). *On the witness stand.* Garden City, NY: Page Doubleday.
[2]Carr, C. (1994). *The alienist.* New York: Random House.

two former students of William James, along with two New York City police detectives, create a psychological profile of a serial killer and ultimately solve the case. The team was assembled by Police Commissioner Theodore Roosevelt, another former student of James. Political considerations and police hostility toward the alienist, as professionals who studied mental pathologies were then known, required the team to exist and operate covertly and unknown even to the police department itself. Since the turn of the 20th century, psychological science and practice has grown and has earned acceptance from both society and the police—which also have grown. The field of police psychology is in flux—as is the field of policing itself. As policing grows in concept and direction, many forward-looking police psychologists are applying and adapting psychology to accommodate changes in policing itself.

The careers of the 21 authors contributing to this book are testimony to this growth and adaptation. Each author is an experienced police psychologist: Some are sworn officers or federal special agents; some are civilian members of a federal, state, or local law enforcement agency; and others are consultant-contractors to the law enforcement community. As appropriate to the current state of the art, most of them have been trained as mental health experts—successors to the old alienists—but other authors have backgrounds in industrial and organizational psychology and other non-mental-health disciplines.

The editors of this volume conceived a book in which experts in different aspects of psychological support to law enforcement agencies would write on police psychology from their own idiosyncratic perspectives. For many of our authors this meant focus on the *practice* of various psychological specialty areas within a working public safety agency environment. This has resulted in a variety of approaches to the subject and of presentation styles—a sacrifice of homogeneity the editors happily made in the interest of presenting the growing heterogeneity and adaptability of today's approaches to police psychology. We believe very strongly that police psychology must continue to grow in pace, scope, and direction, and that such growth is dependent on a continuing reassessment of our *modi operandi*; and our development and inclusion of new methods and technologies in support of police officers and their families, police management, and police operations. This book is a snapshot of police psychology as we turn into the 21st century. We can hardly wait to watch and participate in its future.

Martin I. Kurke
Ellen M. Scrivner

PART ONE

OVERVIEW

CHAPTER ONE

Police Psychology at the Dawn of the 21st Century

Ellen M. Scrivner
Visiting Fellow, National Institute of Justice

Martin I. Kurke
*Drug Enforcement Administration (Retired)
and George Mason University*

This book is about police psychology—where it has been and where it is going as the public safety arena is enveloped by change. One hundred thousand new police officers are one manifestation of that change, as are factors such as violence initiatives, the health–justice interface, and the trend to community policing that may reinvent public safety. New laws and a technology-based society join forces with these factors to force an examination of the application of psychology we know as police psychology. Remarkably successful in a relatively short period of time, police psychology and its core technologies require timely examination to continue successful practice and to preclude being overtaken by events. This book provides that examination. Written by experienced police psychologists and police practitioners, the chapters describe the core technologies of police psychology and explore the issues faced by police psychologists and the departments they serve in implementing these technologies. This exploration confronts the problems that psychologists face as they apply concepts from psychology in the real-world settings of police and public safety agencies and it addresses frameworks for the future. Finally, the chapters in this volume shape an agenda for police psychology in the 21st century.

Of necessity, the agenda for police psychology needs to remain flexible and subject to modification because this fast-moving, ever-changing field is continually being shaped by current events. For example, since this book was undertaken, police psychologists have responded to major events such as the Branch Davidian confrontation at Waco, Texas, and police psychologists in Los Angeles just turned the corner on Rodney King when they had to learn to live and work amidst earthquake damage. What we can learn from them about handling situations of this magnitude and their potential to change the face of police psychology will be substantial. Unfortunately, that will have to wait for another book.

WHAT IS POLICE PSYCHOLOGY?

The last third of the 20th century witnessed the development and growth of psychological specialization, generated in large part by increasing diversity of clients for psychological services. The ability of psychologists to serve one set of clients—law enforcement personnel and their organizations—is the subject matter of this book. Psychologists provide an increasing variety of services to assist their clients, using an increasing number of methods.

Three Traditions of Police Psychology

This book proceeds with the assumption that there is a set of characteristics that define an occupational specialty that we call *police psychology*. The specialty has three traditions deriving from three distinct trends. The first tradition was created by the now-defunct Law Enforcement Assistance Administration (LEAA). As part of the Omnibus Crime Control and Safe Streets Act (1968), this Department of Justice agency provided funding for the development and procurement of police technology. Many applied experimental and engineering psychologists contributed research, development, and operational analytic results to the LEAA program and the early police selection research was developed with LEAA grants. Most of the literature produced, however, was in the form of technical reports and may be found today only in specialized subject matter archives.

Following the gradual demise of the LEAA, federal support transferred to the Department's Office of Justice Programs (OJP), where the research and development (R & D) emphasis shifted to areas other than technology development. An amendment to the 1968 legislation established OJP as the umbrella organization charged with coordinating activities of the several agencies that were designated as the research arm of the Department of Justice (DOJ). They included the National Institute of Justice (NIJ), Bureau of Justice Assistance (BJA), Bureau of Justice Statistics (BJS), Office of Juvenile Justice and Delinquency Prevention (OJJDP), and Office of Victims of Crime (OVC). The general mission of these agencies was defined as improving the criminal justice system, but agency-specific mandates were also established by Congress through the Omnibus amendment and the Anti-Drug Abuse Act of 1988. The mandates direct the agencies to support basic and applied research and demonstration projects that seek to improve federal, state, and local criminal justice systems. The agencies also collect and analyze different types of information concerning the criminal justice system, provide technical assistance based on this information, and publish national statistics and research findings with relevance for practitioners, researchers, and policy-makers. Two of the OJP agencies in particular, the NIJ and BJA, fund research and training to improve police effectiveness. Their research plans are important to the work of police psychology even though the research focus of this first tradition has shifted to that of a more practice driven-specialty.

The second tradition introduced the delivery of direct psychological services to police agencies. The next chapter, on the history of police psychological services, by James Reese notes that although behavioral scientists became involved in the law enforcement field as early as 1916, the first psychologist employed on a full-time basis by a police department did not occur until the Los Angeles Police Department hired Martin Reiser on a full-time appointment. This occurred the year after the publication of *Task Force Report: The Police*, an in-depth analysis of police issues conducted by the President's Commission on Law Enforcement and Administration of Justice (1967). Since that time, many psychologists and other mental health professionals have been employed by federal, state, and local law enforcement agencies, or have been contracted to provide for full- or part-time psychological services to law enforcement agencies. One form of service, the Employee Assistance Program (EAP), resulted from legislation that mandated federal law enforcement to establish these programs. Once established, however, the programs developed at different paces and began to differ substantially in level of sophistication and in the array of services offered. Similar trends have been observed in the programs established at the state and local law enforcement levels.

Although the 1967 task force report did not even mention psychology in its index, it reviewed issues and made recommendations in a variety of topic areas concerning police personnel, organization, and management. Many of the problem areas requiring resolution in 1967 have since been addressed. However, continued modifications and expansions occur as police psychologists learn more about the impact of their interventions in these relatively closed systems.

A third tradition of police psychology arising in the 1970s had its origins in federal law enforcement agencies, where psychologists were engaged in behavioral science-based research or policy matters related to their law enforcement agencies' missions. These psychologists were involved in the development of selection testing and assessment; in career development; program planning; and in practical application of psychological knowledge to police operations such as hostage negotiations, criminal profiling, and methods to improve witness recall. At the policy level, the growth of psychology's significance to law enforcement was demonstrated by events such as the extended secondings of one of the authors (Martin Kurke, then a Drug Enforcement Administration psychologist) to the White House to work on a series of federal law enforcement policy development studies in 1977–1978, and to the House of Representatives to serve as science officer to the Select Committee on Narcotics Abuse and Control from 1983 to 1985. Other police psychologists have been called upon to provide congressional testimony on police human resource issues that shaped subsequent legislation such as the Law Enforcement Family Support Amendment to the 1994 crime bill. Finally, police psychologists have advocated formulating professional practice and policy guidelines with police professional organizations such as the International Association of the Chiefs of Police (IACP).

These traditions demonstrate the steady evolution of an expanding police psychology that has had a major influence on law enforcement. The particular events that earmarked each tradition have strengthened the field as a discipline and have initiated a police psychology literature that makes it possible now to publish this type of book.

Integrating Traditions

FBI Conferences. Although psychologists from these three distinct traditions remain in separate areas of the police psychology specialty, the past few years evidenced a growing degree of integration and cross-fertilization. Probably the foremost stimulus to integration has been a series of week-long police psychology conferences generated by the Behavioral Sciences Unit of the Federal Bureau of Investigation (FBI), in which police psychologists supporting national and local law enforcement agencies from the United States and abroad have been invited to present experience-based papers on a variety of current issues (Reese & Goldstein, 1986; Reese & Horn, 1988; Reese, Horn, & Dunning, 1991; Reese & Scrivner, 1994). Daily presentation sessions were typically followed by small-group evening sessions devoted to special topics of common interest. Attendees had the opportunity to upgrade skills and were encouraged to interact with their peers throughout the week. This strategy resulted in an informal network of nationally recognized police psychologists with a strong sense of collegiality.

Police Psychology Organizations. Police psychologists also satisfied affiliative needs by the creation of special interest organizations, both independent of and within existing organizations. As is pointed out in several places in this book, the work of police psychologists differs in many respects from the work of psychologists in other environments. Pronounced differences in clients' problems, organizational needs, and work culture make for a client population that calls for interventions that differ significantly from those used with non-law-enforcement populations. Many police psychologists work alone or in small groups and have found it to be very beneficial to affiliate with other professionals with similar concerns. The need for peer reinforcement has encouraged the growth of local peer support networks, One example of such a group is the Law Enforcement Behavioral Sciences Association, a network of psychologists, social workers, and others who support federal, state, and local agencies in an area ranging from Baltimore, Maryland to Richmond, Virginia. Although many of the monthly meetings focus on substantive police psychology topics of common interest, meetings have been devoted to peer support relating to professional issues facing one or more of the members.

Professional Membership Associations. Other kinds of affiliation needs of police psychologists are being met by national and international organizations. Three examples of such organizations are:

* *The Police & Public Safety Psychology Section of the American Psychological Association.* The 73,000-member American Psychological Association (APA) is the largest organization representing the psychology establishment. About 190 members belong to the Police & Public Safety Psychology Section of APA's Division 18 (Psychologists in Public Service). Almost all of the members in this section are actively involved in police and public safety: About 8% are psychologists who are sworn officers, 25% are civilian employees of law enforcement agencies, and 61% are contractors or consultants to the agencies. The remaining 6% listed themselves as academics. The section meets during the annual APA convention and usually sponsors seminars on police and public safety issues. A separate miniconvention often is held concurrently in cooperation with a law enforcement agency in the APA convention host city.

* *The Psychological Services Section of the International Association of Chiefs of Police.* The International Association of Chiefs of Police is the largest association representing the police profession and its hierarchy. Full membership in IACP is restricted to active and retired sworn law enforcement personnel, and the Psychological Services Section includes law enforcement personnel who also are psychologists. Membership in this section also includes nonsworn psychologists with police connections (civilian employees and consultants) who are granted associate membership in IACP. The section meets during the annual IACP convention, and has proved to be a highly credible and influential bridge between the psychological and the police professions. Ad hoc committees of the Psychological Services Section have been instrumental in establishing standards for police-related psychological procedures, such as fitness for duty examinations, and they have provided forums for other areas of interest. An example was an analysis of the impact of the Americans with Disabilities Act on police employment screening pro-

cedures. Numerous articles pertaining to police psychology that are of interest to the law enforcement community are published in *The Police Chief,* published monthly by IACP.

• *The Society of Police and Criminal Psychology (SPCP).* SPCP is a multidisciplinary organization that brings together academicians, practitioners, scholars, and providers of services in the field of criminal justice. Most SPCP members are criminal justice faculty, practitioners, and sociologists (30%), psychologists (25%), and attorneys (20%). In contrast with the APA and IACP groups, approximately 60% of the membership of the SPCP comes from the academic world. Consultants and other private businesses such as security services constitute 30% of the membership. Only 10% of the membership are from law enforcement, corrections, and other criminal justice agencies. The society hosts an annual meeting and publishes a semiannual *Journal of Police and Criminal Psychology.* The society offers to members who sit for a written and oral examination its Diploma in Police Psychology. As of this writing, approximately 30 such diplomates have been created.

Who Are Police Psychologists and What Do They Do?

The nature of contemporary police psychology practice can be inferred from the results of recent surveys. Gettys (1990) conducted one survey to which 80 of 190 members of APA's Police Psychology Section responded. An independent analysis of the 163 entries appearing in the 1990 and 1992 directories of the APA's Police & Public Safety Section conducted by one of the present authors provided supplemental information (Kurke, 1990, 1993). Scrivner (1994) surveyed 65 psychologists who provided services to 50 of the nation's largest police departments and questioned them about the work they do in their respective agencies. The results of all three analyses confirm the viability of police psychology. Though data sources differ, they also demonstrate that in a brief span of just 3 years (1990–1993), the field has undergone some change.

Competency Areas. Approximately 85% of the individuals in the Kurke analysis identified themselves as mental health care providers, primarily clinical and counseling psychologists. Another 10% were from non-health-care specialties such as industrial or organizational, experimental, and social psychologists. The remaining respondents could not be classified based on their directory information. These data are similar to those collected by Gettys: 85% clinical and counseling psychology, and non-health-care providers (industrial/organizational, educational, and others) comprising 10% of the total. In contrast to directory listings, the Scrivner sample was comprised of clinician interviews; 75% counseled police officers and 71% provided pre-employment screening for police organizations.

Certification and Licensure. Eighty-three percent of the Kurke sample were licensed psychologists, but a number of the licensees were not licensed in the jurisdiction in which they currently practiced. The 163 directory listings cited 24 board certifications by the American Board of Professional Psychology and other certification boards.

Involvement in Police Psychology. Kurke found that one third of the respondents devoted over 90% of their time to servicing police agencies, and another tenth devoted between 60% and 90% of their time to it. About one fourth of the entries indicate devotion of 11% to 40% of their time. The Gettys survey found that when not serving police agencies, most clinical and counseling psychologists were either in private practice or were consultants in their specialty area. Non-health-care psychologists tended to be consultants to nonpolice agencies when not otherwise occupied.

Six percent of the Kurke population were psychologists who also were sworn officers, and an additional 23% were civilian employees of a law enforcement agency. Contractors and consultants constituted 57% of the population, with 7% being academics. Nearly half of the police psychologists served a single agency, and about 15% served two to five agencies. The remainder, all contractors and consultants, served more than five agencies. A small number (2%) provide service to more than 50 departments. However, Scrivner found that two thirds of the psychologists interviewed in her study were external consultants who provided services to a median of 10 departments. Grossman (1993) found that 98% of 162 agencies in the state of California used independent contractors to provide pre-employment psychological screening. Hence, police departments appear to be shifting to privatizing services and contracting for services rather than hiring psychologists onto police staffs. When they are on staff, however, another shift shows that police psychologists have gained ground in that they generally are placed at the command level. Scrivner's findings showed that 25% of the sample had achieved command staff status. Conventional wisdom suggests that these shifts are the result of diminished budgets. However, they could also be due to current market trends or to business choices of police psychologists. Whatever the reason, they clearly require evaluation if we are to know what works best and what the more appropriate service delivery systems are for law enforcement agencies.

The subject matter of this book is the rich variety of psychological services that are provided by police psychologists, either by in-house staff or external consultants. Notwithstanding the paucity of evaluations on effective service delivery, a major void in police psychology, the content of services does appear to have withstood the test of time and can be described as the core of what police psychologists do in law enforcement agencies. Perhaps it has taken this long for solid core technologies to evolve from the three traditions of police psychology and to be defined in ways that can now be evaluated.

Core Technologies of Police Psychology

This book discusses the set of core technologies that define the work of police psychology. The technologies are specified as evaluation, counseling, training, operational support, and organizational development. The different chapters discuss them from the standpoint of current trends, specific problems, and directions for the future.

Evaluation. The evaluation role has been one of the foundations of police psychology. It is credited with maintaining a stable police force and deterring the hiring of emotionally unstable officers. It also provides safeguards for police departments when concerns develop about incumbent officers. These concerns can precipitate a referral to the police psychologist who evaluates the officer and makes recommendations about the officer's fitness to carry a weapon and to perform the police function.

Scrivner found that 71% of her sample conducted pre-employment screening evaluations and 52% conducted fitness for duty evaluations of tenured officers (an added 23% referred officers they were counseling to other psychologists for fitness evaluations to avoid the inherent conflict of interests). Given this level of activity, it is not coincidental that three chapters in this book (by Flanagan, Ostrov, and Stone) address evaluation and the salient issues in what has become a legal land mine. Evaluation issues are discussed from the perspective of case law and federal regulations, in particular the Americans With Disabilities Act (ADA) and civil rights legislation (1992), and from the practice standpoint.

Counseling. Historically, formal counseling services for police personnel were initiated after pre-employment assessment was implemented, but they quickly became another primary activity of police psychology. Counseling, however, does not offer a safe harbor from legal challenges. The Tarasoff emphasis is a particular concern when clients are authorized to carry and use weapons. Confidentiality in paramilitary systems is another issue because it is always subject to challenge, and information from the critical incident counseling following on-duty traumatic incidents may be subject to subpoena by litigators in a homicide or civil rights trial. Archibald deals with some of these issues in her chapter on professional issues, but full treatment is not possible because they continue to evolve through the courts, and because state laws governing the practice of psychology are not always consistent. Given the current climate, mental health professionals who work with law enforcement are well advised to keep abreast of changes in state and federal law that apply to professional practices and to have access to private counsel who understands how public systems operate.

No particular counseling or therapy school has evolved as the most effective treatment technology for counseling police officers or their families. However, the trend seems to be in the direction of offering short-term treatment or crisis intervention for this population and there is a general focus on cognitive interventions. The police psychology literature does not present sufficient information to evaluate the efficacy of different treatment models, and the chapters here are consistent with that trend. Although the Bohl chapter on critical incidents and Hibler's treatment of the undercover officer touch on clinical issues, for the most part the subject matter of this book deals more with programmatic and philosophical issues relative to counseling.

Training. Training is developed in response to needs that come from varied experiences, not the least of which are vocal constituencies that demand better treatment for groups such as rape victims or others who show cause for training in order to change a police practice, such as reducing police brutality. Needs for training are also influenced by law enforcement trends (e.g., the use of pepper mace) or by state training commission requirements. Balancing training needs and available dollars generally falls to the budget officer who may be more involved than the psychologist in determining the training agenda. One core training area on which police and psychologists express general agreement is stress management training. In the next chapter, Reese discusses how the need for stress management training emerged. White and Honig discuss general training issues and types of training programs, such as wellness training and specific psychological skill training, that are conducted by police psychologists. The Greenstone chapter presents specific kinds of training developed for police officers. These training programs showcase skills that will become even more critical for police as law enforcement undergoes the kinds of changes addressed in the final section of the book: community policing, adapting a human resources perspective, and strategic management.

Operational Support. Practical applications of psychology to police operations have been accepted in police departments. The more traditional activities of forensic hypnosis and hostage negotiations have been augmented by different types of investigative interviewing techniques, psychological profiling, and psychological autopsies. The chapters by Greenstone, Hibler, and Gelles cover these areas and show how psychology continues to make substantial contributions to defined spheres of police operations.

Organizational Development and Support. The final technology is one that has been developing within public safety over the past few years. Traditionally, organizational support has been manifested in program development and policy consultation. Organizational development (OD), however, now focuses on strengthening the organization by building it from within. Schmuckler discusses OD activities that range from team building to strengthening strategic management, and Kirschman discusses a particular organizational development perspective. Scrivner outlines organizational development roles for psychologists that may become more prominent as law enforcement makes the transition to community policing.

Services Provided. A rich variety of psychological services are provided by police psychologists. Table 1.1 lists over 60 responses to the directory questionnaire asking what the members of the Police & Public Safety section members actually did. Services provided by police psychologists fall into three categories: clinical services to individual officers and their families (41%), program support and technical assistance (74%), and operational support (32%). About one third of the directory population reported providing services in more than one of the three categories as noted in Table 1.2.

Ethical Issues. Having a clear sense of ethics is important to all psychologists, but for police psychologists the murkiness of situations that bring threats of ethical compromise may be greater than in other facets of the discipline. The results of the analysis of APA Police and Public Safety Psychologists referred to earlier in this chapter demonstrate how the scope of professional practice could put a psychologist at variance with at least two aspects of the APA's Code of Ethics (APA, 1993). The concerns include maintaining dual relationships and risking conflict of interest, and providing professional services beyond the scope of competence.

About one third of the police psychologists appeared to provide multiple services to the same department but it was not clear from the data if they were providing both personal clinical services and support to management on decisions regarding the same officers. For example, if providing personal or family counseling, or providing psychotherapy for persons within the same organization for which they also provided evaluation services to management, such as evaluating for promotion or fitness for duty for those same clients, they could be at risk of dual relationships and conflict of interest. Should an officer suffer an adverse personnel decision as a result of advice to management arising from the dual relationship, the psychologist may be held personally liable for malpractice because psychologists are ethically prohibited from engaging in dual relationships and must avoid real and potential conflict of interest. In addition, all of the department's personnel decisions influenced by that psychologist could become subject to judicial review if a class action suit against the department is joined by officers affected by the dual relationship or their union.

TABLE 1.1
Services Provided by Police Psychologists

Individual Service
Clinical supervision
Critical incident/crisis interventions
Employee Assistance Program (EAP)
  counseling
Emergency interventions for officers &
  families
Individual counseling
Individual, marital, & family therapy
Hypnotherapy
Long- and short-term therapy
Stress management counseling
Wellness programs

Program/Technical Support
Career development program
  development/administration
Crisis intervention referrals
Critical incident debriefing
Coordination of mental health services at
  detention center
Counseling (training)
Discipline and grievance adjudicator
EAP program management
Employee performance appraisal
Expert witness concerning police manage-
  ment issues (e.g., discrimination case)
Fitness for duty evaluations
Management consultation
Management development programs
Organizational evaluation/development
Organizational policy planning board member
Peer support team training
Pre-employment and promotional screening
  and testing
Policy consultation to department
Posttraumatic incident debriefings
Program development and evaluation
Promotion screening
Psychological evaluations (for selection or
  assignment purposes)

Research on management issues and
  functions
Screening test development
Selection and physical fitness screening test
  validation
Sensitivity training for police officers
Staff adjustment counseling
Stress seminars
Team building leader
Train and coordinate peer counselor program
Training consultant
Testing/interviewing police candidates
Training/teaching (police academy or
  in-service)
Training validation research
Training supervisors and administrators

Operational Support
Active duty police officer with regular
  police function duties
Case consultation using behavioral science
  techniques
Criminal profiling
Crime scene investigation/analysis
Detection of deception (criminal
  investigations)
Domestic conflict call support
Expert witness at criminal trials
Hostage negotiation and other SWAT
  situation negotiations
Human factors and operations research on
  law enforcement equipment and systems
Interviewing suspects, victims, and witnesses
Investigative strategy consultation
Investigative hypnosis
Kidnap and homicide investigation support
Offender targeting system
Polygraph examination/interpretation
Research on operational issues and functions
Victimology and sex crime consultation

13

TABLE 1.2
Constellations of Service/Support Categories Provided

	Individual/ Clinical Service	Program/ Technical Support	Operational Support
Individual/clinical service	10 (6.8%)	32 (22.1%)	3 (2.1%)
Program/technical support		56 (38.6%)	25 (17.2%)
Operational support			5 (3.4%)
Provides all three types			14 (9.7%)

Generally, the issue arises only if the psychologist provides both types of service within the same department. Some consultant-contractor groups have attempted to avoid the dual relationship by having one or more members of the group provide only personal services to a given department, and other members provide management-oriented services to the same group; by sequestering the files of management-oriented and personal-oriented services; and by establishing a policy that the two groups of psychologists do not communicate about their work. When these practices are in place, it is suggested that the group be prepared to demonstrate the effectiveness of the policy should it be necessary to do so in litigation.

The second concern rising from the survey has to do with the issue of psychologists who may be providing services outside of a specialty area without the benefit of training. Examples include industrial/organizational psychologists who use screening instruments of a clinical nature when they have not been trained how to use them, or clinical and counseling psychologists providing job classification or task analyses for promotional processes that are not usually considered within the realm of competence of their specialties. Regardless of specialization, when a psychologist provides services without adequate cross-training they may be at risk of violating that part of the ethical code that prohibits psychologists from practicing beyond the scope of their competence, and consequently beyond the scope of their licensure. Because professional liability insurance does not cover activities beyond the scope of the insured's specialty competency, all psychologists who provide multispecialty services are well advised to assure themselves that all their professional activities are indeed within the scope of their competency, licensure, and insurance coverage. Finally, it is conceivable that any labor dispute arbitration or litigation finding that a management action was taken on the basis of recommendations of a psychologist practicing beyond his or her specialty competence limits could result in a re-opening of all prior disputes whose resolution relied on that psychologist's recommendations.

THE SCOPE OF POLICE PSYCHOLOGY TODAY

Although the vast majority of police psychologists today have been trained in psychology as a mental health discipline, police psychologists have been called upon to provide services, many of which call for competency across the broad spectrum of psychological specialties. Skills of experimental psychologists, industrial/organizational psychologists, human factors (engineering) psychologists, social psychologists, and educational psychologists contribute to the development of this occupation-based specialty. As the marketplace changes there is every reason to believe that more varied skills will be required and that some recasting of traditional interventions may occur.

Most, if not all of the ways in which psychologists can support law enforcement agencies and their personnel may be grouped into the general categories listed in Table 1.3. This table provides a framework for grouping police psychology support into five general categories.

Individual Functioning

Police work occurs in a unique environment and engenders a culture all its own. Stress arises from ordinary work pressures on the individual and the police family as well as from critical incidents that cause the officer to confront his or her own mortality. Psychologists who have been immersed in the police culture have been particularly effective in optimizing the psychological functioning and personal adjustment of police officers and their families through individual, family, and group counseling and psychotherapy. Other objectives are reduction of personal stress through training, wellness, and employee assistance programs.

Selection and Retention of Personnel

Police psychologists support police management by developing selection procedures to screen the best qualified candidates for selection or promotion, to screen out candidates with mental conditions that make them unsuitable for the job, and to conduct examinations to determine whether incumbent officers remain fit for duty. Clinical and counseling psychologists and I/O psychologists have distinct supporting roles in addressing the agency's problem of selecting, training, and retaining the best officers and support staff. Mental health psychologists have an important role in enabling officers to respond well to critical incident trauma, in conducting fitness for duty ex-

TABLE 1.3
How Psychologists Help Law Enforcement Agencies and Officers

Types of Problems to Be Addressed	Focus of Interest	Approaches to Problem Solving	Problem-Solving Objectives
How can the personal effectiveness of officers and staff be maintained or improved?	Optimizing individual functioning	Personal counseling or therapy, EAPs, personal stress reduction programs.	Optimal psychological functioning, personal adjustment, effective communications and interpersonal relationships.
How can the agency select and retain the best officers and support staff?	Optimizing Selection and Retention of Personnel. What should the officer and/or support staff be doing? What personal characteristics, skills, knowledge, and abilities are required? How does the agency select the best qualified and/or eliminate the unqualified?	Job analysis, selection and promotion criterion development, selection and promotional test development, psychological screening, performance appraisal, fitness for duty examinations, training program requirements development.	Screening out undesirable and unqualified candidates, selection of most qualified candidates, improved job performance, optimized turnover of personnel.
How can the effectiveness and efficiency of the agency be maximized?	Maximizing Organizational Effectiveness. Management, structure, rules and procedures, organizational culture, inter- and intra-agency conflicts.	Organizational development, team building, program evaluation; mediation and other alternative conflict resolution techniques.	Improved organizational structure and functioning, improved morale, organizational efficiency and effectiveness; win–win conflict resolution.
How and under what constraints and operational conditions are tasks performed? How can they be restructured or otherwise altered to improve performance?	Maximizing Job/Task Effectiveness. Characteristics of tasks, procedures, and working environment. Personnel–equipment–environment linkages as they affect job performance.	Task analysis, human factors analytic and operations research approaches; managerial-based stress reduction and workplace health improvement efforts.	Improved task and operational procedures; improved system effectiveness and safety; compliance with ADA "reasonable accommodations" requirements.
How can behavioral science be applied to enhance the agency's operational effectiveness?	Enhancing Police Operational Capabilities	Criminal profiling, psychological support to hostage and barricade situations, domestic call support, investigative hypnosis, applied research projects.	Enhanced operational capability and effectiveness

16

aminations, and in providing mental health wellness on behalf of management. Industrial and organizational psychologists are well suited for applying job analytic and other techniques to the development of selection, promotion, and job performance assessment criteria. Specialists in both fields have been asked to provide their expertise in the development and application of police training programs.

Maximizing Police Effectiveness

Suboptimal organizational structures, functions, and procedures, and suboptimal performance of those entrusted to carry out those procedures often have an adverse effect on the ability of work organizations to realize their potential effectiveness. As a general rule, organizations divide responsibility and authority for handling these concerns among separate parts of the organization. Problems with structure, function, and procedures are considered administrative or managerial responsibilities, and the ability of the staff to perform those functions and procedures are considered personnel or human resource management concerns. Psychologists have the ability to contribute in both realms.

Organizational Effectiveness. Police psychologists who are competent in organizational development and in program development and evaluation can support police managers in resolving organizational issues through reviews of the management structure, rules, and procedures. They may make recommendations concerning improvements to organizations with dysfunctional management operating in a work environment under an organizational culture that no longer facilitates the work of the organization. Tools of these psychologists may include leadership seminar workshops, other teaching or training modes, and team building sessions. Some psychologists may become involved in long-range or strategic planning, often applying group problem-solving analytic and decision-making technologies originally developed for use in military and business environments. Alternative dispute resolution techniques such as mediation also may be used by appropriately trained psychologists when intra- and interorganizational subelements appear to face insurmountable conflicts.

Performance Effectiveness. Human factors analysis and operations research approaches are employed by psychologists who address questions of how and under what constraints and operational conditions tasks are performed. They address means by which the tasks may be restructured or otherwise altered to improve performance. They consider the ergonomics of the working environment and of the technology employed in both administrative and operational procedures, and how they can be altered to improve performance and operational safety.

The state of the art of *macroergonomics*—an interdisciplinary melding of human factors psychology, industrial and human factors engineering, organizational development, and other human resource management approaches—is at present in its infancy, and has not been applied to any appreciable extent in police organizations. Its potential, however, is great and may be realized in the 21st century.

Enhancing Police Operational Capabilities

Law enforcement agencies have acknowledged behavioral sciences as a valuable resource when a criminal investigation or another police function benefits from their interventions. Psychologists fill a variety of operational support roles, many of which are listed in Table 1.1. They bring skills to police departments that lead to investigative tools and more effective technology, analytic support during hostage or barricade negotiations, and in offender profiling. Psychologists conduct psychological autopsies in equivocal death incidents, investigative hypnosis, and sex crime consultation, to name a few of their activities.

ENHANCING THE POTENTIAL OF POLICE PSYCHOLOGY

The Need for Coherence

Contemporary police psychology is not yet a coherent discipline. Present-day police psychologists represent a variety of specialty areas and for the most part they are oriented to the resolution of problems seen only in terms of the psychological specialty they brought to police work. There exists a wide range of police-related problems and issues that call for competency in more than one of the traditional areas of specialization. When confronted with pressures for solutions, however, police psychologists court the risk of confronting all problems with the tools they are most familiar with, and more effective tools familiar to psychologists trained in other specialty areas may be bypassed.

It is unlikely that the present generation of police psychologists are equipped with the competencies to work the full range of issues addressed in this book. It is equally clear that many police organizations are unlikely to bring aboard a group of psychologists with the competencies required to help them resolve the full range of those issues. Thus, psychologists would be well advised to recognize the limits of their competence and to avoid assignments beyond it, or to seek consultation from psychologists with appropriate competency configurations.

ISSUES TO BE ADDRESSED
AS WE ENTER THE 21ST CENTURY

The chapters in this book demonstrate that police psychology is becoming a multispecialty that requires varied expertise. They reflect the growth and expansion of the field, but also illustrate how some very basic issues need to be resolved as we move into the 21st century. These issues reflect professional practice concerns and the lack of academic orientation. They go to the heart of how psychologists are used in police departments and how the lack of an academic infrastructure affects police psychology.

An assessment of the current status of police psychology practices provides a reference point for beginning to address these 21st-century issues. It showed that departments do not integrate psychologists into the workings of the department but use them, instead, for crises or on an "as needed" basis (Scrivner, 1994). Consequently, departments may not get the full benefit of the range of talents and skills that the police psychologist brings to the agency. Conversely, the survey showed that 65 police psychologists provided services to 935 departments, so they may not be available for anything other than crises. Hence, police psychology may not be viewed as a resource for police problem solving and may be used only for individual interventions. If so, police psychology may risk becoming divided into narrow subspecialties, making *fragmentation of services* a strong possibility.

The trend toward privatizing services and the blurring of distinctions among service delivery models that confuse EAPs, psychological services, and peer programs may contribute to this fragmentation. Moreover, it remains to be seen how service delivery to police departments will be affected by pending health reforms and new economy concepts that encourage service delivery networks. As of this writing, it is uncertain if these changes will bring substantive improvements or sow the seeds for police psychology to become less influential. However, because 77% of police psychologists in the previously cited survey endorsed lack of coordination with police departments as the major impediment to delivery of police psychological services, anything that creates greater fragmentation stands to have a substantial effect on practice.

On a more optimistic note, Bower (1993) saw fragmentation occurring throughout psychology and viewed it as positive, inevitable, and the result of a maturing science with expanding applications. Clearly, police psychology has matured but there are strong limitations to its scientific base. A recent review of professional journals undertaken by Nietzel and Hartung (1993) revealed only a limited number of empirical studies that addressed psychology and law enforcement. Consequently, Bower's optimism may be somewhat miscast in the case of police psychology, particularly because of the lack of systemic integration of psychologists in police departments, the absence of academic programs, and the related deficits in theoretical assumptions and models of police behavior.

The themes of this book suggest that some of the long-held traditions of police psychology may be changing, and they provide some perspective for how change can be met. For example, chapter 21, by Seberhagen, incorporates significant personnel and training issues into a *human resource development approach* as one way to address change. This approach also responds to the deficiencies in systemic integration of services and is a better fit with the changing needs of law enforcement. These needs become more apparent as police agencies encounter diversity (see chap. 11) and as departments make the transition to problem solving or community-oriented policing. Moore and Stephens (1991) addressed human resource planning as a subfunction of staffing and argued that current staffing subfunctions, including selection, training, evaluation, and career development, would have to be substantially altered as policing strategies changed. Hence, police psychologists are advised to stay abreast of other literatures, such as police management or cultural diversity, in order to remain innovative and current in delivering services.

As psychology attempts to keep pace with changes in law enforcement, other changes are likely to occur in *evaluation practices.* There may be a lesser emphasis on the clinical orientation and related clinical assessment skills in pre-employment screening, and new approaches to psychological screening and validity studies will emerge as we go forward into the 21st century. In this regard, technology-based screening that tests decision making, problem solving, and people skills is anticipated, along with the use of high-performance technologies to develop valid assessment profiles.

Another component of the evaluation function, the fitness for duty evaluations, shows every indication that it may be on the way to standing on its own. Many psychologists report that wearing only one hat, in this case evaluation, provides a cleaner distinction of roles and clients and makes their career lives easier. However, because of the nature of evaluation, the legal and ethical issues that Ostrov discusses in chapter 7 will always be prevalent. A case in point is the prediction of violence potential or dangerousness. Within this context, findings from second-generation prediction research and the development of risk assessment models may hold promise beyond traditional clinical assessments, and they need to be explored more fully. Yet, a substantial debate has developed on the ethics of predictive testimony about future violence of mental patients (Grisso & Appelbaum, 1992). It needs to be followed closely to determine the relevance, if any, that the debate may have for law enforcement evaluations.

The evaluation role also touches on *critical incident debriefings*. Questions have been raised about if, at some level, debriefings become a form of fitness evaluation, particularly when an officer's return to work depends on verification that he or she has completed the debriefing process. As of this writing, the issue has not been resolved, but the question itself suggests that police psychologists need to devote careful attention to determining the parameters of their role, particularly in light of the number of peer debriefing programs that have materialized over the past few years. In these instances, stringent guidelines and clearly defined roles are needed to protect both the affected officer and the peer. Confidentiality breaches following a traumatic incident exacerbate trauma, but unsuspecting peers are also at risk when placed in vulnerable situations and unprotected by privileged information statutes, and when sworn responsibilities supersede anything they have been told about their capacity to hold information in confidence. Moreover, psychologists have to evaluate the professional risks they encounter if they elect to supervise peer programs where confidentiality may be compromised. This issue, along with the previously cited threat of fragmentation, points to the need for professional practice guidelines tailored to the rather unique needs of police psychology. This effort is best undertaken by the police psychology professional associations, which have had some success with promulgating guidelines for narrow spheres of practice. Given the scope of this project, a consortium effort might be considered.

Changes in some segments of police psychology practice may be of a more recent vintage but the need for a *stronger research emphasis* in police psychology is a long-standing issue. However, it becomes more critical now in a climate that demands accountability and evaluation of what we do. Within this same context, there is a need to determine if the information we have developed is being used to full advantage. In an information age, the capacity to collect data and make sense of it can expand the police psychology role in police departments and contribute to data-informed policy. However, and perhaps more importantly, research findings strengthen the knowledge of the individual psychologist and broaden our understanding of the interface between psychology and contemporary police issues.

There is also a need for police psychologists to develop a greater appreciation for *how legislation influences practice*, although this need is not unique to this application of psychology. In many respects, a groundwork for legislative awareness has been laid because police psychology has had to develop a well-honed knowledge of case law around screening and counseling issues. However, there are other reasons to stay abreast of major legislative issues. For example, amendments to crime legislation that provide support for training and program development relative to psychological services in police departments need to be tracked through state legislatures or Congress, and psychologists need to encourage the major professional organizations, both police and psychology, to lobby for their passage. That type of funding will become even more critical in climates of downsizing and diminished budget resources. Beyond funding, legislation can affect police psychology practice. For example, the most recent crime bill provides funds to increase the hiring and training of new officers, and to develop and utilize a police corps. Thus, there will be needs to determine how they will be used effectively. Many departments will be affected by this legislation and there will be related effects on the psychologists. Finally, legislative initiatives that support collaboration between community police-oriented law enforcement and social services through partnership grants are proliferating and stand to become a future revenue stream. Thus, events at the legislative and public policy levels may become more influential in the life of police and public safety psychology.

These issues speak to a *need for formal training programs* for police psychology that can incorporate practice, research, and public policy concerns. Not only are academic programs lacking, but it is also difficult to find a department to house a program of police psychology. One reason may be the richness of a field that does not fit well into just one academic sequence. Rather, police psychology contains interdisciplinary elements that blend psychology, criminal justice, public administration, communication, and law. *Developing academic programs* in police psychology that contain these elements would do a great deal to prepare psychologists to function in the public sector. Moreover, they would provide opportunities for cross training and strengthening competency for experienced police psychologists, and would stimulate research and theory building relative to police behavior. They would also serve as clearinghouses for databased information that is critical to the functioning of the police psychologist, and the academic focus would lend greater prestige and credibility to the field.

At the very practical level, academic programs would provide a forum to deal with issues that are unique to this field, such as the previously discussed lack of department coordination of psychological services. This concern and others related to professional practice extend beyond guild issues because their prevalence can limit the full demonstration of what psychology brings to the public safety workplace. Other issues include the unique level of exposure and related lack of protection offered by the ivory tower or consulting room. Instead, the police psychologist is in the field more often, is usually quite visible, and can be subject to ethical challenges that are less familiar to other colleagues. These challenges are frequently less clear cut than what we see in the ethical principles and can take several forms. Some examples include social invitations that are quasi-business-related and politically necessary, misinterpretations of the psychologist's casual remarks as professional opinions, pressures to give press interviews on issues that are out of one's line of expertise, and involvement in political triangles. Clearly, police psychologists need to augment professional expertise with skills that are not taught in academic settings, and these skills will be tested as frequently as professional judgment. In addition to the very practical issues, police psychology also needs to determine how the literature can be strengthened, and how an infrastructure can be built that includes academic oversight and research for police psychology. Finally, an academic program would provide the opportunity to examine police psychology within the broader geo-political framework that has become so important to our worldview.

The Post Cold War Police Workplace

Police psychology emerged as a movement significant in both the police and the psychology communities during the existence of the Berlin Wall, the most salient symbol of the Cold War. The fall of the wall in 1989 led to many changes throughout the world. National attention and resources have been shifted from averting military threats to averting economic ones. Government and industry have come to recognize a need for new norms for acceptable goods and services. Reliability of the work force is now more widely recognized as a significant influence on costs of productivity and of customer satisfaction. The survivability of business and government organizations is directly affected by the quality of an organization's products and performance. As a result, ideas concerning quality and its impact on productivity (Deming, 1982, 1986) are receiving greater attention as are needs to re-engineer corporations to become or stay competitive (Hammer & Champy, 1993). Similarly, Vice President Al Gore has proposed reinventing government in a similar fashion (Gore, 1993). In both movements, great attention is given to improving effectiveness and efficiency in the workplace, an area in which technology is almost daily becoming more complex, having a great potential for both breakdown and improvement (Potomac Chapter of the Human Factors and Ergonomics Society, 1993). Indeed, the phenomenon of complexity itself has arisen as an area of study for scientists from fields as far apart as physics, meteorology, economics, and psychology, who are conducting nonlinear mathematical experiments to simulate on a computer the dynamics of complexity that, if unchecked, leads to an inability to predict future events—a condition they have labeled *chaos* (Waldrop, 1992; Zhao & Richards, 1993).

It would be unreasonable to expect that law enforcement and other public safety agencies would not be affected by these changes in scientific, business, and governmental thinking and planning. Roles for psychology in this paradigm shift of emphasis to process–product enhanced quality were suggested by Baker (1993), who emphasized the need to apply psychology from a systems perspective. People in the system should be viewed as an independent variable with considerable influence on the quality and quantity of the system's output. Our focus should be on those interventions (such as training design, work structure, organizational change, mental and emotional status) that will improve *human performance* in the workplace. The optimization of procedures and technology in the context of the political–social environment of police organizations will provide fruitful results. Psychologists can also apply their expertise in selection and training to address the best fit of people (with their idiosyncratic characteristics) in the system. They can enhance police personnel workplace readiness by determining the best fits for people, and by task, organizational, and team restructuring.

Hunt (1993) suggested that an organization's quality can be improved if quality improvement is treated not as a program, but as a style of living. She proposed key concepts that may be applied to police organizations. First, focus on the consumer—in this case the consumers or beneficiaries of police services. Operations must be designed to meet the consumer needs, and management needs must be secondary—a rather difficult shift for any bureaucracy to make. This will require selling and involving police leadership in the program. She maintained that there is a need for participatory team efforts to create new models of leadership. There must be recognition of the need for diversity: She alleged that different perspectives add value to an organization and its performance. Finally, the organization must acknowledge and act on its social and environmental responsibilities. The challenge to police psychology inherent in these proposals for a system-oriented approach to people in the police system provides an opportunity for police psychology as we approach and enter the third millennium.

Police Psychology and Police Organizational Processes Systems

One area of potential growth in police psychology lies in a growing recognition of police personnel as a subsystem in common with two distinct but overlapping perspectives of policing as a process. Human factors psychologists tend to view goal-driven organizations such as military organizations, manufacturing plants, and more recently governmental and business entities as being driven by customer demands (Baker, 1993). In police terms, the system inputs are both continuing demands for police services such as traffic control, and event-driven demands such as crowd control and criminal investigations. These demands generate the police operational processes, and result in the delivery of public safety services to the community served by the police department. This viewpoint focuses on two component subsystems— the people who operate the system, and the devices and other tools by which the system reaches its objectives. Indeed, the growth of the human factors approach has progressed from the study of human–machine interactions to the study of person–technology–environment systems (see Fig. 1.1).

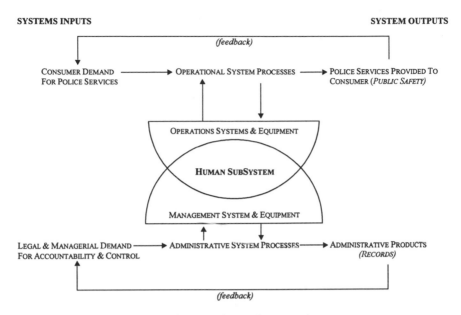

FIG. 1.1. Police organizational processes systems.

On the other hand, industrial/organizational psychologists historically have viewed personnel as they related to a system driven by managers' needs for accountability and control of the organization's processes. These inputs generate an administrative system process that provides the means by which resources are acquired, used, and controlled: Its primary product is the paperwork that ensures that legal, operational, and administrative requirements have been met. It establishes bases for acquisition and retention of resources that allow the organization to survive and grow. Like the operational system process, the administrative system process contains a human subsystem and a management system that interact to select, train, and manage the agency.

Whereas both the human factors and the industrial/organizational psychology approaches tend to view people in an organization as a subsystem in interaction with other subsystems in a police system, clinical and counseling psychologists tend to focus on the human subsystem itself. They tend to be concerned with the individuals' intra- and interpersonal relationship driven ability to function on the job. What distinguishes a good police psychologist from other mental health psychologists is an experience-generated ability to relate police personal, family, and organizational management issues to the environment in which both the police operational process system and the police administrative process system operate. They are able to provide guidance that facilitates smooth interfacing of the officer and the officer's family with both systems, which may be imposing conflicting demands on the human subsystem.

Mental health-oriented police psychologists use their skills to select, assess, and contribute to the training of police personnel with implicit and explicit reference to their suitability, often with relevance to mental health-related variables. In contrast, non-mental health-oriented police psychologists are more concerned with identifying the knowledge, skills, and abilities (KSAs) demanded by the officer's job, and performance assessment is made of the officer's demonstration of those KSAs in relation to the officer's job and task performance. Regardless of the nature of the assessment, human performance is almost always evaluated in terms of deviations from criterion standards set for speed or accuracy (how well or how correctly does the officer perform).

The job elements and the tasks they collectively define are important in the real world in terms of how they contribute to or how they inhibit acquisition of systems goals. An operational process system ultimately is assessed in terms how well its performance pleases the consumers of police services. Concurrent assessment of the performance of an administrative process system is based on how successfully it meets management's needs to control operations and accountable for acquisition and utilization of resources. In an ideal organization, assessments of performance of operational processes systems would correlate positively and highly with assessments of performance of its administrative process system. However externally imposed constraints placed on the department or dysfunctional management within the department can and frequently does generate dissonance between the two systems. The consequences of such dissonance include organizational and personnel inefficiency, ineffectiveness, and morale-related personal stress symptoms.

Because the human subsystem is an element common to both systems, a potential role for police psychological interventions may be within that subsystem and at its interfaces with both the operational process and the administrative process systems, which as already noted, place both facilitating and conflicting demands on the people who are part of both systems. Of course, psychologists traditionally intervene to help people with personal and interpersonal problems, and with management and technology interrelationships. What is proposed here are interventions that also enhance and maintain human reliability as it may be affected by the demands and pressures of both operational and administrative process systems. This may be accomplished by a blurring of psychological specialty boundaries. Mental health-oriented psychologists must develop greater sensitivity to the organization-based issues, and organizational and technology-oriented psychologists must develop improved sensitivity to personality, psychopathology, and other personal and social variables in their interventions. Because legal and ethical strictures prohibit a psychologist from practicing beyond the limits of professional specialty competence, there may be a need for police psychologists to develop multispecialty competence, or to practice in mutually supportive groups of mental health-oriented and organizational and technology-oriented specialists.

In conclusion, the following chapters provide the reader with the opportunity to see the interface of the human, operational, and administrative systems. They demonstrate the breadth and scope of police psychology, as we now know it, and bring together under one umbrella a good sampling of the state of the art. Although not tied to one viewpoint or one philosophy, the chapters clarify the activities that define police psychology, activities that may be confusing to police and public administrators and to researchers from other disciplines. Hence, one of the goals this book can accomplish is to help the police psychologist educate others, particularly police administrators, as to what it is we do, how we do it, and how professional ethics regulate our activities. Law enforcement frequently perceives all psychologists and other mental health professionals as shrinks who can be all things to all people. Frequently, they are unaware of different specializations and, consequently, expect that the psychologist can do things they have not been trained to do. Conversely, they may not be aware of the full range of resources that the psychologist is able to bring to an organization and may view them as available only for taking care of a crisis. The following chapters can help to clarify and broaden their perspectives.

The chapters are linked by a few recurrent themes. One theme is the range of skills that form the core of police psychology. A perusal of the table of contents shows what police psychologists can do in police and public safety agencies and illustrates the richness of police psychology. The individual chapters demonstrate that the skills of police psychology go far beyond the clinical interventions of "shrinks." They also show the challenges faced when applying these skills in the public sector.

Another theme is the need for adaptation to ensure that the richness does not become stale and to forestall obsolescence. This theme talks more about systemic integration of services in departments and the need for broader approaches to solve problems. It encourages police psychologists to stretch a bit and to become more creative, although not at the expense of professional integrity. This theme emphasizes strengthening human reliability, strategic planning, systems approaches, human resource planning, proactive response, and organizational interventions. This broader perspective combines the approach of servicing the dysfunctional police employee enmeshed in organizational stressors with that of using psychology as a resource to strengthen organizations and to help solve problems faced by contemporary police managers.

Still another theme calls for expanding the scientific base of police psychology by building evaluation into our work and by advocating a greater emphasis on professional training of police psychologists. This theme speaks to the need to develop an academic orientation so that research and practice needs can be met and in which the legislative and political realities that affect our work can be debated.

Embedded in these themes is the awareness that the world of work is changing and the tradition-clad police and public safety arena is not immune to change. A more culturally diverse work force, growth in the use of technology, leaner budgets, greater changes in laws governing employment, and greater accountability to the public all bring new challenges to the police psychology models of research and service delivery. As we approach the dawn of the 21st century, the time is right to re-examine our core technologies to determine how they fit with modern-day needs and to create innovative ways to respond to the changing world of law enforcement.

REFERENCES

American Psychological Association. (1993). Ethical principles of psychologists and code of conduct. In *Directory of the American Psychological Association* (pp. xxvii–xlv). Washington, DC: Author.

Baker, J. D. (1993, September). *Performance, productivity and quality: Minding your P's & Q's will make you competitive.* Presented at Human Factors Contributions to Productivity and Competitiveness, Annual Symposium of the Potomac Chapter of the Human Factors and Ergonomics Society, Arlington, VA.

Bower, G. (1993). The fragmentation of psychology? *American Psychologist, 48,* 905–907.

Deming, W. E. (1982). *Quality, productivity and competitive position.* Cambridge, MA: MIT Center for Advanced Engineering Study.

Deming, W. E. (1986). *Out of the crisis.* Cambridge, MA: MIT Center for Advanced Engineering Study.

Gettys, V. S. (1990, August). *Police and public safety psychologists: Survey of fields of study, activities, and training opportunities.* Paper presented at the American Psychological Association 98th Annual Convention, Boston, MA.

Gore, A. (1993). *The Gore report on reinventing government: Creating a government that works better and costs less.* New York: Times Books.

Grisso, T., & Appelbaum, P. S. (1992). Is it unethical to offer predictions of future violence? *Law and Human Behavior, 16*(6), 621–633.

Grossman, I. (1993). Psychological testing for pre-employment and specialty assignments in California peace officer organizations: A survey. *Journal of California Law Enforcement, 27*(1), 12–16.

Hammer, M., & Champy, J. (1993). *Reengineering the corporation: A manifesto for business revolution.* New York: Harper Collins.

Hunt, M. (1993, September). *Principles of the quality journey.* Presentation at Human Factors Contributions to Productivity and Competitiveness. Annual Symposium of the Potomac Chapter of the Human Factors and Ergonomics Society, Arlington, VA.

Kurke, M. I. (1990). *Analysis of 1990 membership of APA Police and Public Safety Section.* Unpublished data.

Kurke, M. I. (1993). *Analysis of 1992 membership of APA Police and Public Safety Section.* Unpublished data.

Moore, M. H., & Stephens, D. W. (1991). *Beyond command and control: The strategic management of police departments.* Washington, DC: Police Executive Research Forum.

Nietzel, M. T., & Hartung, C. M. (1993). Psychological research on the police. *Law and Human Behavior, 17*(2), 151–155.

Potomac Chapter of the Human Factors and Ergonomics Society. (1993, September). *Background.* Program for the Annual Symposium of the Potomac Chapter of the Human Factors and Ergonomics Society, Arlington, VA.

President's Commission on Law Enforcement and Administration of Justice. (1967). *Task force report: The police.* Washington, DC: U.S. Government Printing Office.

Reese, J. T., & Goldstein, H. A. (1986). *Psychological services for law enforcement.* Washington, DC: U.S. Government Printing Office.

Reese, J. T., & Horn, J. M. (1988). *Police psychology: Operational assistance.* Washington, DC: Federal Bureau of Investigation.

Reese, J. T., Horn, J. M., & Dunning, C. (1991). *Critical incidents in policing.* Washington, DC: Federal Bureau of Investigation.

Reese, J. T., & Scrivner, E. M. (1994). *The police family: Issues and answers.* Washington, DC: Federal Bureau of Investigation.

Scrivner, E. M. (1994). *The role of police psychology and control of excessive force.* Washington, DC: National Institute of Justice.

Waldrop, M. M. (1992). *Complexity: The emerging science at the edge of order and chaos.* New York: Touchstone Press.

Zhao, B., & Richards, L. (1993). Chaos theory and beyond: Implications for human understanding. *The Social Dynamicist, 4*(1), 1–7.

CHAPTER TWO

A History of
Police Psychological Services

James T. Reese
Federal Bureau of Investigation

Although the debilitating effects of stress have been identified in police work, the problem of helping officers in resolving these effects remains very real. Many of today's modern law enforcement agencies are meeting this problem through the use of full-time or consulting mental health professionals. However, such practice is in an early developmental stage. It is therefore important to examine the early roles behavioral scientists played in law enforcement so that the evolution and growth of psychological services in law enforcement can be documented and recorded. It would appear that the introduction and use of psychological services in law enforcement organizations in the United States represents a significant development in police work.

A number of articles have been published in the research literature and proceedings of police conferences and seminars on one aspect or another of the provision of psychological services by mental health professionals to law enforcement agencies. These studies have addressed such matters as the need for psychological services in urban police departments, the identification of problems facing mental health professionals who practice in a law enforcement setting, and the contribution of empirical findings to the body of research data on police psychologists and the psychological services they provide to police who staff law enforcement agencies in the United States. However, no research has been done which, of and by itself, traces the historical development of such services.

Police stress, as well as stress in general, has been studied from many angles. Some studies have addressed the problem of an officer's personality changing due to the stress of police work, whereas others (Morris, 1981) have advised that the personality of an officer can amplify job stress. Friedman and Rosenman (1974) examined stress from their now-renowned Type A and Type B personality approach to behavior patterns. They asserted that individuals with a Type A personality described as competitive and driven, were more susceptible to stress than were those with a Type B personality. Neiderhoffer (1967) looked at another source of stress intrinsic to the police officer's job: *anomie*. Anomie is characterized by the absence of faith in people, pride, and integrity. Other influences at work in the creation of stress in police officers are promotions, shift work, and irregular and lengthy court appearances (Cobb & Rose, 1973; Kroes, 1976; Schaefer, 1983).

Reiser (1976) indicated that change is the most common denominator to stress. Holmes and Rahe (1967), using their Social Readjustment Rating Scale, attempted to identify the impact change has on one's health. More recently, Sewell (1980), in his dissertation *The Development of a Critical Life Events Scale for Law Enforcement*, identified events that cause change in the professional life of a police officer, such as being shot or having a partner killed, thereby furthering the efforts made in identifying those events in a police officer's life that may create undue stress.

According to *Crime in the United States* (1986), in 1986 there were over 470,000 law enforcement officers and more than 12,000 law enforcement agencies in the United States. The growth of the police profession to over 470,000 police officers in today's law enforcement agencies, combined with the ever-increasing and changing role of the police officer in society, indicates a historic growth and change pattern in the profession that seems to embrace an inherent stress on people working in it. Regardless of the many roles society calls on the law enforcement officer to play, "training typically emphasizes narrowly defined aspects of the job dealing with criminal activity, understanding relevant laws, effective firearms training, self-defense, and other survival techniques" (Stratton, 1980, p. 38). Strategies for coping with job-related stress are seldom, if ever, considered. Eisenberg (1975) stated that a better understanding of stress is indeed an important requisite for minimizing many of the several dozen sources of psychological stress resulting from police work.

PSYCHOLOGY AND POLICE SELECTION

Although psychological technology has been used in the personnel field for many years, its application in selecting police personnel has covered a much shorter time (Mann, 1980). Originally, there were few guidelines for the selection of police officers. Some hiring officials were convinced that a fit body was sufficient for employment of police, whereas others believed the ability to use a revolver and the knowledge of the law constituted adequate qualification. Behavioral scientists suggested a more objective and promising criteria, minimum levels and certain kinds of personality attributes. They claimed to be able to provide these kinds of selection data through psychological assessment of police candidates.

The foundation for psychological assessment in police work can be traced to about the turn of the 20th century (Maloney & Ward, 1976). It was then that mental health professionals first became involved with some law enforcement agencies by helping them to select their police officer candidates.

Terman and his associates at Stanford University conducted one of the earliest documented studies of police selection. Terman (Terman & Otis, 1917) believed general intelligence, notwithstanding moral integrity, was the most important quality needed in a police officer, and he further believed that general intelligence could be successfully measured through psychometric instruments. His earliest attempt to do so was in 1916 and utilized the Stanford–Binet Intelligence Scale, which was the original Binet–Simon Scale, revised and translated by Terman and his associates. Using an abbreviated form of the Stanford–Binet Intelligence Scale, they tested police officers in San Jose, California, to establish their intelligence as a step toward setting criteria for police selection. Terman recommended an intelligence quotient of 80 as a minimum standard for employment for police (Spielberger, 1979).

Thurstone (1922), an influential psychologist, established valid principles for measuring intelligence, attitudes, and personality. In an article relating to the selection of police officer candidates, he reinforced the importance of intellectual ability. Intelligence continues to be a significant hiring criterion in present-day police selection.

Many psychometric instruments and examinations have been utilized through the years in selecting police officers. A major reason for using psychological tests in police personnel work is to predict job suitability of candidates for police positions. The need for testing as a precondition of hiring to find the most competent—and eliminate the disturbed—applicant was emphasized by the President's Commission on Law Enforcement and the Administration of Justice (1967): "In society's day-to-day efforts to protect its citizens from the suffering, fear, and property loss produced by crime and the threat of crime, the policeman occupies the front line" (p. 92).

The President's Commission on Law Enforcement and the Administration of Justice (1968) recommended the utilization of psychological tests in the selection of police personnel. The rationale for this recommendation was that through such examinations, the emotionally unstable individual could be identified. The Commission stated:

> Until reliable tests are devised for identifying and measuring the personal characteristics that contribute to good police work, intelligence tests, thorough

background investigations, and personal interviews would be used by all
departments as absolute minimum techniques to determine the moral character
and the intellectual and emotional fitness of police candidates. (p. 10)

In the same year, the U.S. National Advisory Commission on Civil Disorders
(1968), in its report to the president concerning the role of law enforcement,
stated that there needs to be a method or means to eliminate police officers
whose duties would be hampered by their personal prejudices. Their recommendation was that law enforcement departments use psychologists or
psychiatrists to interview applicants and have them administer a battery of
psychological examinations to determine fitness of candidates.

If there is a traditional role for psychiatrists, psychologists, psychiatric
social workers, counselors, and other mental health professionals in the
United States, it has not been one of helping law enforcement officers function efficiently and effectively. Although psychologists conducted mental
tests on law enforcement candidates as early as 1916 in efforts to select the
very best candidate for the police officer position, the literature indicates
they knew little in terms of how they might assist law enforcement in other
ways. Correspondingly, law enforcement officers did not know what type
of help they could receive from mental health professionals. An apparent
lack of communication existed between the professions.

Rogovin (1974) stated that policing and the problems inherent in the
occupation, together with the personal problems of its practitioners, were
of little interest to behavioral scientists. As testimony to this apparent lack
of interest, Neiderhoffer (1967), a noted author on the police role in society,
discovered that during the period between 1940 and 1965, the two major
social science journals of the time, the *American Journal of Sociology* and
the *American Sociological Review*, published only six articles relating even
indirectly to the police. A review of other pertinent literature confirms that
the major area of specialization by mental health professionals was that of
officer selection, not the personal problems of police officers.

Even though mental health professionals have taught police many techniques of mental health care delivery to use in assisting the public with their
problems (e.g., family crisis intervention) and have helped to provide objective assessments of the caliber and character of officers through the development of selection procedures, they still lack total acceptance within
the law enforcement community. "Psychologists, psychiatrists, forensic experts, and mental health professionals, in general, are viewed with a jaun-
diced eye by most law enforcement officers" (Benner, 1982, p. 1).

It has been only within the last two decades that law enforcement organizations started to come to terms with the occupational stress experienced
by police through services provided by mental health professionals. These
professionals tended to be consultants rather than full-time members of the
law enforcement agency. The source for such consultation in many depart-

ments can be traced back as far as the 1940s, to employee assistance programs (EAPS).

EMPLOYEE ASSISTANCE PROGRAMS

Since the 1940s, government and industry have focused on the principle that the welfare of the organization is highly dependent on the welfare of the people in the organization. Industry was first in assisting those with personal crises through its employee assistance programs. A major portion of the clients in these programs had problems with alcohol addiction. Throughout the 1960s and 1970s, alcohol education remained the major thrust of almost every employee assistance program. Later, programs evolved as an outgrowth of the assistance programs begun in the postwar years of the 1940s (Stratton, 1985).

As an example, the current Boston Police Stress Program originated in the 1950s. Initially, it was an alcohol-abuse counseling group and was modeled after the highly successful Alcoholics Anonymous Program (Donovan, 1985). By 1959, a patrolman, Joe Kelly, was assigned full time to manage the program. Fearing that the title of Alcohol-Abuse Counseling Group might make some individuals reluctant to enter the program, Patrolmen Joe Ravino and Ed Donovan expanded the program in 1973 to include any personal problem regardless of its nature or extent. Later, Donovan became president of the International Law Enforcement Stress Association.

Other early EAPS established in law enforcement were the Chicago Police Officers' Fellowship, started in 1955 for alcohol problems, and the New York City Police Department's Alcohol Program, established on May 12, 1966. The New York City program began as a counseling service by Monsignor Joseph A. Dunne, the department chaplain. Police chaplaincy, in general, has since become even more involved in the emotional and spiritual well-being of police officers as witnessed by the establishment of the International Association of Police Chaplains in 1973.

The Los Angeles County, California, Sheriff's Office initiated an alcohol program on September 11, 1975. In the same year, the Chicago Police Department established a counseling office (Wagner, 1976). Boston expanded its alcohol program on November 15, 1976, with the beginning of the Boston Police Stress Program. The San Francisco Police Department followed suit by establishing a Stress Unit on February 3, 1983.

In 1986, the major police departments in the United States had some form of stress unit, or some other means of helping officers cope with personal and occupational problems (based on professional contacts with the 10 largest police agencies). In many cases, as previously cited, alcoholism brought on the need. Whether the predication for the assistance was alcohol, brutality, civil liability, or legal decisions affecting the department (among which are notable decisions regarding "negligent retention"), the foundations for the provision of psychological services by mental health professionals in law enforcement organizations were strengthened.

PIONEERS IN LAW ENFORCEMENT
PSYCHOLOGICAL SERVICES

Among the first in the mental health profession to utilize psychological principles in a useful form for law enforcement officers was Dr. Harold Russell. In 1953, Russell worked as a psychologist with the first criminal court clinic to serve a federal court. Later, as an officer in the U.S. Army and following his retirement, Russell served as part-time consultant to numerous police departments. His utilization of psychological principles ranged from teaching officers about the use of defense mechanisms in interviewing to interpreting behavior and motivations of suspects.

Dr. James Shaw, currently of Olympia, Washington, is another mental health professional who must be considered a pioneer in the field of police psychology. He has been involved continually in police psychology since 1963 and stated, "I have had the opportunity to watch the field [police psychology] gain wide acceptance by law enforcement officials" (J. Shaw, personal communication, April 23, 1984).

Another noteworthy mental health professional, Dr. Martin Symonds, a psychiatrist, was named as an honorary surgeon in the New York City Police Department in 1965 (M. Symonds, personal communication, September 20, 1984). His function was to check on officers in his district who were sick. He was also asked to conduct examinations in connection with disability claims. In 1972 he was formally employed as the head of the department's psychological services program.

The evolution from the EAPs instituted for alcohol and related problems in police departments to the use of mental health professionals for personal problems of police officers has been slow and unpredictable. Utilized mostly on a consultation basis and largely for the purposes of police officer pre-employment screening, police psychologists had very little chance to interact with the police on a personal basis prior to the early 1970s. Several significant events in the 1960s, however, provided behavioral scientists the opportunity to counsel officers and to assist law enforcement organizations operationally.

CATALYSTS IN THE DEVELOPMENT
OF POLICE PSYCHOLOGY

This author was unable to determine when police psychology first appeared as a career in the field of psychology. Although an exact date is unknown, interviews with psychologists, as well as information from the literature, lead one to believe that this specialized occupation within the psychology profession, police psychologist, began in the 1960s.

It is believed that the specialty emerged from a series of critical incidents involving police officers. The following incidents occurred in the 1960s and are representative of those that drew police psychologists into law enforcement agencies. These incidents are deemed significant for illustrative purposes because of their national notoriety.

On a Saturday in March 1963, a night that will long be remembered in law enforcement, two Los Angeles police officers, Ian Campbell and Karl Hettinger, began what seemed to be a normal shift on patrol in the Hollywood Division. Spotting a parked car that appeared suspicious, they decided to investigate. When the police approached the car, one of the two men in the car exited the vehicle and pointed a gun at Campbell. Hettinger had his gun drawn but surrendered it on the demand of the gunman, fearing his partner would be killed if he did not. The officers were kidnapped by the two suspects and driven to a secluded onion field. Later Campbell was shot and killed; Hettinger escaped. It was 7 years before the suspects were convicted of killing Campbell. As for Hettinger, he returned to duty and continually experienced feelings of guilt about his decision to surrender his gun on that March night (Wambaugh, 1973).

Another incident that highlighted the need for the expertise of mental health professionals in police work occurred in August 1965. Two White California Highway Patrolmen stopped a Black male, Marquette Frye, following a 6-block chase. The chase ended within a 20-square-mile ghetto area called the Watts District of Los Angeles. When the officers attempted to arrest Frye for driving recklessly, he resisted. His resistance and the subsequent force exercised by the officers to subdue and get him into the patrol car were witnessed by Blacks in the neighborhood. Before the incident was over, some 1,500 Black people had gathered. This incident started the worst rioting and looting in U.S. history to that time. Unlike the Officer Hettinger occurrence, in which a mental health professional could have been of help to a police officer with respect to his resolution of postcritical incident trauma, this incident highlights the need for psychologists to train officers in interpersonal crisis management, social psychology, crowd control, and other topics that would favorably influence police officers' behavior in dealing with the public.

In 1966 a young man named Charles Whitman climbed the tower at the University of Texas at Austin and began shooting indiscriminately at people below. Within 90 minutes he had killed 16 and wounded 32 unsuspecting passersby. An off-duty deputy sheriff climbed the tower and brought the slaughter to an end by killing Whitman. In an interview with the deputy about 13 years after the incident, it was learned that there were no psychological services available for him through his employing agency. Following the shooting and after being attended to at the scene and questioned by officials, he went home to attempt to cope with his reaction to this traumatic event.

Each incident described here holds significance in its own way with regards to fostering the recognition of the need for services provided by mental health professionals in law enforcement. Collectively, they form a foundation from which the field of police psychology developed.

LOS ANGELES LEADS THE WAY

Psychological consultants have provided various services to law enforcement agencies in the United States for many years on a part-time basis. It was not until 1968, however, that a police department decided to hire a psychologist on a full-time basis. In view of the previously discussed incidents, it is not surprising that the department was the Los Angeles Police Department. The man they hired was Dr. Martin Reiser. He stated three major reasons that the Los Angeles Police Department felt a need to hire a police psychologist: (a) the aftermath of the Watts District riots, (b) reports of the President's Commission regarding improvement of law enforcement psychological services, and (c) "bad press" in the Los Angeles area due to questionable police practices (M. Reiser, personal communication, July 30, 1986).

With no models to follow or mentors to query, he blazed trails for mental health professionals to follow. Among his many functions in this new role as police psychologist were counseling and therapy for both officers and their families, teaching, research, training in stress awareness and coping, testing, hostage negotiation consultation, consultation with management about policies, and consultation with police officers about crime. Reiser is widely known as the father of police psychology.

Reiser (1972a) published a book, *The Police Department Psychologist.* Obviously aware of his pioneering efforts on behalf of all psychologists, Reiser stated in the preface that he wrote the book "with the expectation that in the future the psychologist (behavioral scientist) will be less of a rare bird in the police profession" (p. vii). Reiser has since published other books and numerous articles on police psychology.

During the early 1970s, following Reiser's employment by the Los Angeles Police Department, a large concentration of literature came from the behavioral sciences focusing on the criminal justice system and police agencies in particular (Schwartz & Schwartz, 1976). This literature, along with incidents such as those described earlier, helped to advance the cause for the provision for psychological services in law enforcement organizations:

> As a consequence of (a) the recommendation of the Task Force on the Police (President's Commission on Law Enforcement and the Administration of Jus-

tice, 1967) and (b) the lack of effective problem solvers in the criminal justice system . . . mental health professionals, particularly psychologists, have become increasingly entrenched in the criminal justice system. (Brown, Burkhart, King, & Solomon, 1977, p. 208)

Soon thereafter, the Law Enforcement Assistance Administration (LEAA), now defunct, provided money to police departments to assist in providing them with some expertise and support. The LEAA 1970 Discretionary Grant Program set money aside to fund the hiring of psychiatrists and psychologists to work with a number of medium-sized and larger police departments on a regular basis. Since that time, many departments have included funds for psychological services in their budgets. Thus, psychological services in law enforcement continued to gain support and momentum.

Reiser named the San Jose, California, Police Department as being the second department in the United States to hire a full-time psychologist (M. Reiser, personal communication, July 30, 1986). In 1971 the department hired a clinical psychologist, Dr. Michael Roberts. In spite of the fact that there were no funds available, Roberts volunteered to provide these services during the summer and fall of 1971 free of charge. During that time, he made several trips and telephone calls to Reiser to consult about his program. Later in 1971, following a fatal shooting of a citizen by a San Jose police officer, the San Jose Peace Officers Association and the Chief of Police managed to fund the psychological services program and hired Roberts.

In 1971, history was once again made in police psychology when Harvey Schlossberg, a New York City police officer, became the first policeman to earn a doctorate in psychology and become a police department psychologist (H. Schlossberg, personal communication, August 4, 1984). In May 1971, New York City Police Commissioner Patrick Murphy called Schlossberg to his office. This call was based on a computer printout within the department's personnel section that showed a patrolman, Schlossberg, with a doctorate. The Commissioner was interested to know from Schlossberg how the department could benefit from this education. In answer to this question, Schlossberg wrote a memorandum to the Commissioner stating his ideas on how he could best assist officers of the New York City Police Department. This memorandum set the stage for his eventual transfer to the medical section of the department as a psychologist. He was to set up a unit to put psychological principles to work to help policemen in their personal lives and their jobs.

It was believed that his experience as a police officer gave him an additional dimension to bring to the job; namely, firsthand knowledge of the police personality and "real world" interaction with criminals. On January 19, 1973, this added dimension paid off, as demonstrated by the following scenario. In the Williamsburg section of Brooklyn, criminals took hostages in a sporting goods store following an attempted robbery. Within minutes one police officer was dead and two other officers were wounded. This incident became known as the "Williamsburg Siege," or "Brooklyn Siege." Schlossberg was called upon to assist in the negotiations to attempt to gain the release of the hostages. He assisted in successfully negotiating the release of the hostages and soon thereafter, the New York City Police Department established a Hostage Negotiation Unit (Schlossberg & Freeman, 1974).

Up to that time, mental health professionals were used mainly for counseling and testing. Although there were isolated cases of psychologists assisting officers during hostage negotiations, nothing that attracted national attention had occurred. The operational assistance provided by Schlossberg during this hostage incident was accepted by officers and administrators alike as a natural extension of the use of psychologists beyond counseling. Thus a valuable role was added to police psychological services.

A subsequent major development in the history of police psychology occurred in 1973. James Hilgren and Paul Jacobs, clinical and industrial psychologists, respectively, began doing organizational research and some planning for the Dallas Police Department on a full-time consulting basis. In July 1973, Dr. S. Al Somodevilla became a part-time consultant teaching the Dallas officers crisis intervention. Officers soon began to come to Somodevilla with personal problems. The following April, Somodevilla became a full-time consultant and the Psychological Services Unit of the Dallas Police Department was established (A. Somodevilla, personal communication, June 10, 1981).

About the same time, Dr. John Stratton was consulting with local police departments in southern California on a part-time basis, while employed by the Los Angeles County Probation Department. He left the Probation Department later that year to accept a full-time position as Director of Psychological Services with the Los Angeles County Sheriff's Department. A prolific writer, Stratton, like Reiser, helped add numerous meaningful articles to the then-scant literature on police psychology (J. Stratton, personal communications, September 20, 1984; May 10, 1985). In the same year, units offering medical and psychological assistance to police officers were established in Boston, Chicago, and Detroit.

By 1976 the Albuquerque, New Mexico, Police Department had hired an employee assistance counselor (J. Price, personal communication, June 12, 1984). In 1977, a Police Stress Management Program was begun in the Miami, Florida, Police Department; and the Memphis, Tennessee, Police Department had hired Dr. Thomas Hickey as its police psychologist (T. Hickey, personal communication, July 8, 1986). These were but a few of the police departments throughout the United States that were among the first to contract with mental health professionals for psychological services, either on a full-time or part-time basis.

As has been discussed, psychologists have been used in police agencies for several decades; however, there were only six police agencies with full-time psychologists or counselors by 1977 to deal with personal problems other than alcohol abuse. The six departments were the Boston, Chicago, Dallas, Los Angeles, and San Jose, California Police Departments, and the Los Angeles County Sheriffs Department (Stratton, 1977). Thus, part-time consultants were still in demand. In many cases, departments could not make offers financially attractive enough to lure psychologists away from lucrative private practices. Consulting psychologists were the next best option in light of restricted department budgets.

In 1977, a Washington State Police officer, David Smith, became the first state police officer known to earn a doctorate and subsequently become the psychologist for his department (D. Smith, personal communication, December 17, 1985). Four years later, Joe Elam of the Oklahoma Highway Patrol earned a doctorate and was employed as department psychologist for the Oklahoma Department of Public Safety (J. Elam, personal communication, December 18, 1985).

Mental health professionals also found their way into the law enforcement system of the federal government. In 1980 a Psychological Services Program was established in the Federal Bureau of Investigation (FBI).

Because the police psychology specialty within the psychology profession is so new, it is understandable that in 1990 no academies or academic institutions were known to have programs that train mental health professionals to be police psychologists. Degrees are obtainable in the behavioral sciences as well as in criminal justice, but there appears to be no formal merging of the disciplines. Although there are courses dealing with psychology and the law, these usually focus on crime-related topics such as prediction of violence and mental status to stand trial.

EMERGENCE OF UNITY

Police psychology has evolved slowly since the 1960s from a relatively unknown new discipline with an uncertain future to a recognized specialty within psychology, with roots firmly planted in the criminal justice system. In the past two decades, police psychologists have become widely recognized and accepted as integral parts of law enforcement organizations by police officers and administrators alike.

This successful evolution of police psychology is a product, to a large extent, of the professionalism and tenacity of early practitioners in the field. Their professionalism was critical in that their activities with law enforcement agencies were continually scrutinized, not only by police, but by mental health professionals as well. Their tenacious efforts to provide services such as counseling and psychological testing, as well as innovative applications of psychological principles in such matters as consultation in hostage negotiations and criminal personality profiling, aided greatly in its acceptance and continued popularity.

Also assisting in the growing popularity and success of police psychology was the willingness of these early practitioners to add their views and experiences to the expanding body of literature in police psychology. Not only did they present papers detailing their successes and failures as police psychologists, but they submitted written accounts of these matters to various mental health journals and police periodicals for publication.

As police psychology matured, the one topic that drew sustained interest among its practitioners was police stress. As more literature appeared in the 1970s indicating the debilitating effects of stress and the inordinate amount of stress endured by police officers, police administrators—many of whom were familiar with some of the research reported in the various mental health and police journals—started employing clinical psychologists to assist in the reduction of job stress.

Aside from the annual meetings of the American Psychological Association (APA), when psychologists who had a mutual interest in police work made an effort to seek each other out informally and discuss law enforcement issues, police psychologists were isolated from each other. There was no established network through which they could communicate. To remedy this situation, in the early 1980s, a local group of 10 to 15 mental health professionals and law enforcement officials (the number varied from month to month) began to meet monthly to discuss their concerns, problems, and ideas about psychological services in law enforcement organizations. Among them were Dr. Ellen Scrivner, then full-time consultant to the Fairfax County, Virginia, Police Department; Dr. Paul Clavell, the provider of psychological services for the Baltimore County, Maryland, Police Department; and Dr. Harvey Goldstein, Director of Psychological Services, Prince George's County, Maryland, Police Department. Collectively they became known as the Law Enforcement Behavioral Sciences Association (LEBSA). Although these mental health professionals were from the Baltimore–District of Columbia area, they recognized that the issues they discussed were very broad and had national implications. They agreed that their effort to share data, experiences, needs, and aspirations should be extended on a national basis (E. Scrivner, personal communication, December 6, 1982).

The psychologists active in LEBSA were also members of the APA. The APA affiliation was with Division 18, Psychologists in Public Service. Division 18 brings together mental health professionals who provide assistance to public services, such as prisons and veterans' hospitals. In 1982, Dr. Harvey Goldstein, because of his involvement in LEBSA, provided the leadership necessary to form a new section within the APA's Division 18, the Police

Psychology Section (H. Goldstein, personal communication, May 17, 1984). With more than 150 members at the time of this writing, the Police Psychology Section is well-established and likely to grow.

While the debates continue concerning whether to hire a psychologist on a full-time or part-time basis, whether to have the office in the police facility or at an off-site location, and many other considerations, police psychology and psychological services are being accepted by law enforcement organizations. Many argue that full-time programs will dominate the future. Others argue that the five functional areas of psychological activities in the criminal justice system—assessment services, treatment, training, consultation, and research—cannot possibly be done well by one person (Twain, McGee, & Bennett, 1972). Perhaps the future will witness a compromise of the two positions. Reiser was correct when he stated that the net result over time will be the diminishing of the perceived distance between the psychologist and the policeman: "The birth of police psychology was unremarkable; there were no fireworks or parades. It developed slowly, out of infancy into childhood, and it obviously still has a lot of growing to do. But there is now a new specialty, with a small group of practitioners, a literature, and a future of unlimited potential" (Reiser, 1972b, p. ii).

REFERENCES

Benner, A. (1982, April). *Concerns cops have about shrinks.* Paper presented at the Symposium on Psychotherapy and Law Enforcement, San Francisco, CA.

Brown, S., Burkhart, B. R., King, G. D., & Solomon, R. (1977). Roles and expectations for mental health professionals in law enforcement agencies. *American Journal of Community Psychology, 5,* 207–215.

Cobb, S., & Rose, R. (1973). Hypertension peptic ulcer and diabetes in air traffic controllers. *Journal of the American Medical Association, 4,* 489–491.

Crime in the United States. (1986). Uniform Crime Reports. U.S. Department of Justice. Washington DC: U.S. Government Printing Office.

Donovan, E. C. (1985, February). The Boston police stress program. *The Police Chief,* pp. 38–39.

Eisenberg, T. (1975, November). Labor management relations and psychological stress: View from the bottom. *The Police Chief,* pp. 54–58.

Friedman, M., & Rosenman, R. (1974). *Type A behavior and your heart.* New York: Knopf.

Holmes, T. H., & Rahe, R. H. (1967). The Social Readjustment Scale. *Journal of Psychosomatic Research, 11,* 213–218.

Kroes, W. H. (1976). *Society's victim: The policeman.* Springfield, IL: Thomas.

Maloney, M. P., & Ward, M. P. (1976). *Psychological assessment: A conceptual approach.* New York: Oxford University Press.

Mann, P. A. (1980). Ethical issues for psychologists in police agencies. In J. Monahan (Ed.), *Who is the client?* (pp. 18–42). Washington, DC: American Psychological Association.

Morris, H. (1981, January). Police personalities: A psychodynamic approach. *The Police Chief,* pp. 49–52.

National Advisory Commission on Civil Disorders. (1968). *National Advisory Commission on Civil Disorders report.* Washington, DC: U.S. Government Printing Office.

Neiderhoffer, A. (1967). *Behind the shield: Police in an urban society.* New York: Anchor Books.

President's Commission on Law Enforcement and the Administration of Justice. (1967). *The police: The challenge of crime in a free society.* Washington, DC: U.S. Government Printing Office.

President's Commission on Law Enforcement and the Administration of Justice. (1968). *President's Commission on Law Enforcement and the Administration of Justice report.* Washington, DC: U.S. Government Printing Office.

Reiser, M. (1972a). *The police department psychologist.* Springfield, IL: Thomas.

Reiser, M. (1972b). *Police psychology: Collected papers.* Los Angeles: Lehi Publication.

Reiser, M. (1976). Stress, distress and adaptation in police work. In W. H. Kroes & J. J. Hurrell, Jr. (Eds.), *Job stress and the police officer* (pp. 17–26). Washington, DC: U.S. Department of Health, Education, & Welfare.

Rogovin, C. H. (1974). The need is now. In J. L. Steinberg & D. W. McEvoy (Ed.), *The police and the behavioral sciences* (p. 15). Springfield, IL: Thomas.

Schaefer, R. (1983, May). The stress of police promotions. *FBI Law Enforcement Bulletin*, pp. 2–6.

Schlossberg, H., & Freeman, L. (1974). *Psychologist with a gun.* New York: Coward, McCann & Geoghegan.

Schwartz, J. A., & Schwartz, C. B. (1976). The personal problems of the police officer: A plea for action. In W. H. Kroes & J. J. Hurrell, Jr. (Eds.), *Job stress and the police officer* (pp. 130–141). Washington, DC: U.S. Department of Health, Education, & Welfare.

Sewell, J. D. (1980). *The development of a Critical Life Events Scale for law enforcement.* Unpublished dissertation, Florida State University, Tallahassee.

Spielberger, C. D. (1979). *Police selection and evaluation.* New York: Hemisphere.

Stratton, J. G. (1977, May). The police department psychologist: Is there any value? *The Police Chief*, pp. 70–75.

Stratton, J. G. (1980). Psychological services for police. *Journal of Police Science and Administration, 8*, p. 38.

Stratton, J. G. (1985, February). Employee assistance programs: A profitable approach for employers and organizations. *The Police Chief*, pp. 31–33.

Terman, L., & Otis, A. (1917). A trial of mental and pedagogical tests in a civil service examination for policemen and firemen. *Journal of Applied Psychology, 1*, 17–29.

Thurstone, L. L. (1922). The intelligence of policemen. *Journal of Personnel Research, 1*, 64–74.

Twain, D., McGee, R., & Bennett, L. A. (1972). Functional areas of psychological activity. In S. L. Brodsky (Ed.), *Psychologists in the criminal justice system* (pp. 15–20). Carbondale, IL: Admark.

Wagner, M. (1976, January). Action and reaction: The establishment of a counseling service in the Chicago Police Department. *The Police Chief*, pp. 20–23.

Wambaugh, J. (1973). *The onion field.* New York: Delacorte.

CHAPTER THREE

Managing Professional Concerns in the Delivery of Psychological Services to the Police

Eloise M. Archibald
New York City Police Department

It is difficult to say with precision how long psychologists have been delivering services to police departments but it is certainly the case that their involvement began to increase to a noticeable level in the late 1960s when Dr. Martin Reiser became the first psychologist to work full-time for a police department (Reiser, 1972). As police psychologists have become more visible, working for a police agency is increasingly considered a career option for both new and experienced psychologists. However, the police psychologist must be prepared to confront and resolve a number of issues that will arise as he or she enters a non-health-related agency that is not familiar with, or necessarily sympathetic with, the professional concerns of a psychologist (e.g., confidentiality). The psychologist must maintain a sense of professional identity in this environment and adhere to standards of conduct despite pressure to do otherwise. What follows is a description of some of the concerns that can face a police psychologist and how to manage them.

DEFINING THE CLIENT

A police agency may decide to hire a psychologist for one specific job, to perform many tasks, or for purposes not totally clear even to the agency. The latter may seem like a surprising notion but not when one considers that generally police agencies are reactive entities seeking immediate solutions to problems. Thus, when faced with its first suicide of an active employee or community uproar over the death of a citizen in a police incident the agency may quickly decide to hire a psychologist with a vague sense that psychological evaluations or counseling of its employees will help, but with no clear sense of how.

One of the first duties of the psychologist may very well be to help the agency define the psychologist's role. A critical element in this process will be to define who the client will be. To fail to do so can make it difficult, if not impossible, for the psychologist to perform effectively.

Many, if not most, police agencies want the psychologist to perform some amount of individual assessment or counseling and so are looking for a psychologist with a background in clinical or counseling psychology. Yet clinical and counseling psychologists, as opposed to, say, industrial/organizational psychologists, are most likely to assume the individual employee is their client. The agency, on the other hand, may have a different assumption based on the fact that it hired and paid for the psychologist's services. Confusion and a great deal of future conflict can be avoided if it is clarified at the beginning of the psychologist–agency relationship who the client is. Once it is determined who the client will be, this affects perceptions of the psychologist by employees and management and may have implications for the amount of job satisfaction the psychologist feels. For example, will a psychologist trained in clinical psychology be happy working for a client that is an agency and the largely faceless citizenry it serves?

Of course, client definition will also have implications for the various issues of confidentiality that can arise in a police agency. The next section contains a discussion of some of the key concerns in this area.

Once the identity of the client is decided, a psychologist can move on to further defining the role he or she will play. For example, if an agency essentially wants counseling services provided to employees, will the psychologist be limited to this role, or is the agency open to the observations, thoughts, and suggestions a psychologist may have about how to improve the mental health of employees through interventions on an organizational level? A clear definition of role will not only help the psychologist decide whether working for a particular police agency will be stimulating and fulfilling, but will also hopefully prevent both the psychologist and agency from being frustrated and disappointed by a relationship that did not meet their expectations.

CONFIDENTIALITY

Confidentiality is a key factor in the psychologist–client relationship. Acknowledging the truth of this statement is only the beginning of a process in which police psychologists must struggle to apply ethical and legal standards to their unique setting.

Records

Depending on the role played by the police psychologist, the matter of records will be handled in various ways. If the police psychologist was hired to provide only confidential psychotherapeutic or counseling services to employees it should be clear to all concerned from the outset that any written treatment records created by the psychologist will not be available to those inside or outside of the agency without the written consent of the employee. However, if the police psychologist was hired to perform fitness for duty evaluations, the agency will certainly expect and be entitled to receive a report of the psychologist's findings. Here the psychologist faces a difficult task, that is, how to best summarize the evaluation in a way a lay person can understand, being careful to include enough data to support conclusions and recommendations without putting in unnecessary personal details that are unrelated to the purpose of the evaluation. The American Psychological Association (APA) addresses the latter issue when it states that in giving feedback to an agency, the psychologist should strive to include only information "germane to the purposes for which the communication is made" (APA, 1992, p. 1606).

Perhaps a more difficult problem arises regarding the issue of records when a psychologist is on the staff of the police agency and working out of the agency's offices, as opposed to serving as a consultant as part of a private practice and working out of a private office. In the latter case, it becomes fairly easy to limit the amount of information given to the agency. The psychologist can make only a report available, keeping confidential interview notes, test data, and so on. However, when a psychologist works in the agency's offices, the agency will often claim ownership of any psychological records created there and, in fact, demand the records be kept on file within the agency. The question of record ownership and who will decide who has access to such records was previously discussed by the author (Archibald, 1991). It is not sufficient to conclude that the agency owns any psychological records the psychologist creates for them. Professional considerations demand that the psychologist advise the agency on record security as well as who should be able to access the records. Of course, the psychologist's advice may be ignored, resulting in an agency head inappropriately authorizing the release of sensitive information to internal affairs investigators, administrators without a so-called "need to know," and so on. This state of affairs creates a dilemma for the police psychologist, who in the course of conducting a thorough, accurate evaluation, will gather a great deal of personal information not directly related to the employee's job performance. If the psychologist will not have control over release of information, he or she must decide what information to include in records. The temptation is to omit from the record all information not directly related to work performance, even though such data did contribute to the final clinical impression and recommendations. The danger in this approach is that it would be difficult for anyone to review the clinician's evaluation should that become necessary in the future for any reason. Review would be necessary if the psychologist's finding were challenged legally or otherwise and another mental health professional was enlisted by the challenger to obtain a second opinion. Review would also be useful if the employee entered treatment at some point and the treating clinician needed access to as much information as was available. Some psychologists would argue that the solution is simple: Keep two sets of records—one for the agency and one more complete set of records for a private, confidential file of the psychologist. This solution could create legal and ethical difficulties especially if the psychologist is not open with the agency and employee about the existence of two sets of records. A more desirable way out of this dilemma is for the police psychologist to work closely with an agency head in setting a strict written policy that clearly describes who can access agency psychological records and under what conditions.

A problem increasing in frequency in recent years is that of judges allowing detailed psychological information on police officers to be considered as evidence in trials. As attorneys are becoming aware of the fact that police departments hire psychologists to perform entry-level and fitness for duty screenings, they are obtaining subpoenas for any and all psychological records on an officer. The kinds of trials in which this can happen run the gamut from a civil lawsuit brought after an off-duty officer behaves inappropriately causing injury to another person, to a criminal trial wherein an arresting or witness officer is due to testify for the prosecution and the defense attorney hopes to undermine the officer's credibility. In these situations the police psychologist can be invaluable in advising a police agency and its lawyers when a request for psychological data is irrelevant and inappropriate and, therefore, should be resisted. Often an agency's lawyers can at least obtain an in camera review by the judge. If the judge sees the psychological data as irrelevant to the case, he or she will rule that the record cannot be entered into evidence.

To summarize, the psychologist must strive to prevent unnecessary invasion of the employee's privacy through inappropriate release of psychological records, also working with the agency to meet their need to know the emotional fitness of its officers.

Counselor Versus Evaluator

The role played by a psychologist in an agency will determine in large part what degree of confidentiality will be afforded an individual employee. This is not to say that a psychologist should assume the agency and employee share

his or her ideas on confidentiality. Rather, the guidelines in this area mu
clearly formed and articulated at the beginning of the relationship bet
psychologist and agency, between psychologist and employee, and be
employee and agency. Generally speaking, when a psychologist is func
as a counselor or therapist to an employee, information obtained in th
of that relationship should be held confidential from the employer (an
unless the employee specifically gives permission to release certair
tion or unless there are statutes that require the psychologist to br
dentiality (e.g., in cases of child abuse). On the other hand, if a p
is performing fitness for duty evaluations, it is generally the c
psychologist will provide some feedback, verbal or written, to
regarding the employee's emotional health and how it im
performance. Of course, any limits on confidentiality must l
plained to the individual being seen before the evaluation or tre.
Although most psychologists would agree with these general rules,
psychologist often finds the situation more complicated. The author p.
viously discussed some of the issues confronting psychologists performing the
roles of both counselor/therapist and evaluator (Archibald, 1986, 1991).

There is no doubt that professional considerations are less complicated
when a psychologist fulfills only one role in the police agency. However,
small agencies, especially in areas where there are few well-trained psychologists, may not have the luxury of hiring different psychologists for the
various needs they have —counselor/therapist, clinical evaluator, educator,
and so on. Thus, one psychologist may be asked to perform all these roles.
Because having more than one relationship in and of itself is not unethical
(APA, 1992), a psychologist can consider accepting such an assignment. If
the psychologist is to be a therapist for some employees and an evaluator
of others, it becomes crucial for all parties (psychologist, agency, and employee) to be clear about which role the psychologist is to have in each
particular case. If the psychologist is asked to be both therapist and evaluator
to the same employee, this must be approached with extreme caution and
ideally avoided altogether. When the same employee is being seen for two
purposes it becomes difficult, if not impossible, to determine who is the
psychologist's client. Related questions are whose interests must be of primary concern in the case of conflicting interests, what the confidentiality
guidelines should be, who will pay the psychologist, and so on. In this
author's opinion, if it is decided that the agency will be the client of a
psychologist seeing an employee in treatment, the psychologist should decline to attempt this relationship. Because a key factor in effective therapeutic
relationships is trust, the person being treated should know that his or her
best interests are paramount, not those of the employer. If this condition of
trust does not exist, therapeutic benefits will be severely limited if they occur
at all.

screening will be conducted. Uppermost in the psychologist's mind should be the fact that he or she will ultimately be held responsible legally and ethically for the psychological evaluation. Given this, he or she must always feel secure that professional standards have been met. This is not to say that the psychologist cannot listen to administrators and take their concerns and needs into consideration. In fact, that should be done. Psychologists may very well decide to adjust the number and type of tests given to meet an agency's financial and time constraints, while not seriously compromising their ability to do a professionally sound assessment. However, if all attempts at negotiation fail and the psychologist is pressured to screen in a way that is professionally unsound, he or she must be prepared to decline the assignment. This last resort should not occur frequently, because psychologists should always be familiar with the work of other psychologists conducting similar evaluations so they can be cited for support. Resistant agencies are more likely to bend if confronted with a body of literature outlining acceptable practices in the field as opposed to just being presented with one psychologist's opinion. (This is especially true of agencies sensitive about legal challenges.)

Mandated Findings

Even if police psychologists do not find themselves being told how to conduct their assessments, they can find themselves being told what their conclusions and recommendations should be in particular cases. For example, in the area of preappointment screening, if an agency has a limited number of applicants and many jobs to fill, the psychologist may be pressured not to find any problems in the applicants screened. Although an agency is free to hire despite a psychologist's findings, they would be open to vicarious liability lawsuits should they hire someone the psychologist found to have significant problems and later these problems are shown to have resulted in inappropriate and harmful behavior on the part of the police officer. For this reason, the agency would want the psychological record of employees not to document any significant problems.

Another example, in the area of fitness for duty evaluations, can occur when an agency wants to terminate the employment of an officer who is a problem employee but one who cannot justifiably be fired because of rule violations. The psychologist may be pressured to conclude that this individual has serious emotional problems that are not likely to improve in the near future and, therefore, the employee should be separated from the service (via disability retirement or whatever means a particular agency has to handle such cases).

In such cases, psychologists must be careful not to give an untrue professional opinion to please the agency, keep their job, and so on. The opinion given must truly reflect the psychologist's thoughts and conclusions after an appropriately conducted assessment. To not do so not only violates the rules of ethical practice, but destroys the credibility of the individual psychologist and hurts the credibility of the entire field.

Psychologist as Weapon

Related to the previous issue but distinct from it is the problem that arises when an agency uses referral to a psychologist to punish an employee. This can occur when the employee is considered an administrative problem but the usual disciplinary means at the agency's disposal either cannot be used in a particular case (e.g., employee never quite "crossed the line") or have not been effective in modifying the employee's behavior when used in the past. Because many police officers associate seeing a psychologist with being "crazy" or "a psycho," it is no wonder that referral to a psychologist is often an alarming event that triggers strong emotions of fear and anger. The fear can be not only of being viewed as crazy by others, but also of actually being so. There can also be legitimate concerns that one's career will be damaged or terminated because of the referral. Anger is usually directed toward those in authority within the department (including the psychologist) for putting the individual in such a threatening position. It is easy to see, then, how an administrator may decide to punish problem officers by referring them for psychological evaluation. Administrators need not consciously intend to punish, but rather tell themselves that perhaps the employee has emotional problems for which help is needed. However, the reasoning is really something like this:

> I do not like this officer. He's always been an irritant but he hasn't yet done anything I can get him on. I'll send him over to the shrinks. That will get him so upset maybe he will straighten out and even if he doesn't maybe they will find out he has got problems and they will transfer him or "psycho" him out (i.e., separate on psychological grounds).

Psychologists have to be alert to this kind of referral—one where there is no genuine concern about someone's emotional health, but rather ulterior motives behind the referral. If a referral is not legitimate and made in good faith, the psychologist should decline to do the evaluation and thereby not be a party to this type of behavior. It is also the responsibility of the psychologist to point out when a referral is not appropriate and thereby attempt to change a system that can damage the credibility of an individual psychologist as well as the field.

CONCLUSION

As can be seen from this discussion, police psychologists have to face many professional issues in the course of their duties. As in all jobs there are temptations to compromise professional standards to make the job easier, please the client, or avoid loss of income. However, if compromise leads to unethical or illegal behavior or to substandard work, then everyone, client and psychologist alike, suffers. In addition, when providing services to police agencies there is always another client present—the public. The public has a vested interest in having only emotionally healthy officers serving the community. Anything short of this is dangerous because of the special role police officers fill. They are given a great deal of authority, a firearm, and permission to use deadly force when necessary. Psychologists working with the police, whether they are screening, counseling, teaching, advising organizations, or performing other functions, have a tremendous responsibility to use their training and experience to provide the highest quality of service.

REFERENCES

American Psychological Association. (1992). *Ethical principles of psychologists and code of conduct.* Washington, DC: Author.

Archibald, E. M. (1986). Confidentiality when the police psychologist is evaluator and caregiving practitioner. In J. T. Reese & H. A. Goldstein (Eds.), *Psychological services for law enforcement* (pp. 215–217). Washington, DC: U.S. Government Printing Office.

Archibald, E. M. (1988, Summer). Developing a post-critical incident counseling program. *Public Service Psychology, 13,* 9.

Archibald, E. M. (1991, August). *Police psychologist as evaluator* and *caregiving practitioner: Ethical problems.* Paper presented at the 99th Annual Convention of the American Psychological Association, San Francisco, CA.

Reiser, M. (1972). *The police department psychologist.* Springfield, IL: Thomas.

PART TWO

THE CORE TECHNOLOGY OF POLICE PSYCHOLOGY: EVALUATION

CHAPTER FOUR

Ensuring Personal Reliability Through Selection and Training

Neil S. Hibler
Levinson, Ltd., Alexandria, VA

Martin I. Kurke
*Drug Enforcement Administration (Retired)
and George Mason University*

THE NEED TO ENSURE PERSONAL RELIABILITY
IN LAW ENFORCEMENT AGENCIES

The Human Reliability Approach

Law enforcement officers are entrusted with powers to lawfully confront, question, and search citizens, and where justified, use deadly force. No other profession in our society has authority as intense or intrusive. Those entrusted must be able to fulfill their responsibilities without risk to others, or in failure, risk to themselves. Law enforcement professionals must be able to objectively perceive their environment, use good judgment in deciding to execute their authority, and be able to effectively carry out the required tasks. In a word, law enforcement personnel must be reliable.

As used in this chapter and several other chapters in this volume, the term *human reliability* is used as a systems rather than as a statistical concept. Moray (1994) defined it as "the obverse of the tendency of a human to make an error." In this context errors are categorized as *slips*, in which a person correctly assesses a need and acts accordingly but errs in carrying out the correct intention; *mistakes*, in which a person fails to make a correct judgment about what needs to be done; and *violations*, in which a person deliberately chooses to act in a prescribed way.

When the objective of psychological consultation is to ensure human reliability, a number of factors must be considered. In fact, no single factor accounts for actual performance; outcome behavior is the cumulative result of a number of influential factors that combine naturally. To expect any single factor to account for performance would be to misunderstand the inseparable interactions that account for behavior. Consider the following reality.

A recent FBI report on officers killed in the line of duty demonstrates a consistent pattern—a "deadly mix" of factors—that combined to explain the officer's loss of control, and as a result, the officer's death. These factors included the killer as being of a virulent personality disorder, the officer being easygoing or good natured and conservative in the use of force, and a procedural miscue, such as improperly approaching the suspect's vehicle (Uniform Crime Reports Section, 1992).

This example demonstrates how even employees who are selected to stringent standards could be overcome by failure to train to achieve competency, failure to have suitable guidelines or policy, be supervised effectively, and/or be properly equipped. Accordingly, psychological efforts to enhance reliability should account for as many influential factors as possible.

This chapter directly addresses two recognized areas of influence, namely selection and training. Other influences are discussed because behavior is the consequence of multiple, interactive factors.

THE MODEL: A COMPREHENSIVE
PSYCHOLOGICAL SUPPORT PROGRAM

Selecting the Fittest for the Job

In order that no single influence on performance is mistakenly over- or underemphasized, a model is proposed to conceptualize the multifaceted interventions that can, in the aggregate, best assure the law enforcement response. In this model, the influences include the multitude of personnel, managerial, and organizational factors, including equipping, regulating, and supervising individual officers. In the micromodel, an individual's psychological factors are isolated so that professional behavioral science support may be addressed. The key concept addressed is *suitability* as a psychological concept that addresses human reliability by focusing on personal factors. This distinction emphasizes a conceptual difference between the necessary outcome (reliable human behavior) and the characteristics necessary to achieve the needed outcome (suitability). Psychological suitability is simply the presence of personal factors that effectively contribute to human reliability, and the absence of those that would be at risk to reliability. Everything comes back to the need for reliable performance and this is the criterion by which all efforts are measured. In brief, selection is picking the fittest (for the specific job). Yet sustaining reliability requires more than selection.

Monitoring to Ensure Performance

Even good people, the very best in fact, can have problems. To "keep the force fit" there needs to be monitoring to assure that readiness is sustained. Sokol and Reiser (1973) devised an Early Warning Model for use within the Los Angeles Police Department. Their concept was simple—a stitch in time saves nine—and they used it to legitimize tending to the needs of officers before major difficulties developed.

Such an effort requires the support of senior management, the services of counselors, and training for the officers, to sensitize them to the goals and the indicators of distress. Senior leadership needs to be committed to supporting good officers who righteously struggle with bad challenges. This means not just support for employee assistance services, but a close working relationship with counselors so officers are not withdrawn from duty simply because they acknowledge a problem.

Intervening Benevolently to Keep the Force Fit

Under an effective monitoring plan, distressed officers are supposed to seek assistance; the program has to be corrective, not punitive. The goal of early problem recognition (and effective intervention) means that leadership must be willing to face previously unrecognized difficulties. For example, on implementation of the program they need to be prepared to deal with their own frustration over the fact that their people were more troubled than had been suspected. Leaders must support officers who had hidden their problems, and they should become involved in situations that had been visible, but were neglected because the circumstances were awkward.

Once senior management buys into the concept it must be explained and supported among midlevel and first-line supervisors. The street force will use the program only after they are convinced that they will not be imperiled by using the resource. Sustaining the credibility of an effective monitoring and intervention program requires continuous oversight; the first benevolent intervention will bring others, the first one that becomes punishing will stem the flow.

This chapter focuses on selection as a process that includes a variety of information sources, including work histories, education, and other factors not directly psychological in nature. It begins with what police work requires and how selection procedures need to build in validity and eliminate adverse impact. In sum, the selection process includes a broad range of information that combines to contribute to the effective assessment of applicants based on how their ability, skills, attributes, and emotional steadiness meet the requirements of the tasks that must be performed. The chapter then examines how training is both a continuation of selection and preparation to reliably accomplish those job requirements.

PERFORMANCE REQUIREMENTS: ASSESSING WHAT IS NEEDED

Psychological Suitability

Requirement for Stable, Unimpaired Personnel. Police work demands personnel who are well able to understand their circumstances and effectively deal with them in the course of executing their duties. The first priority is for people with psychological integrity, the second is for those people to effectively deal with a wide range of demands that are made on them in the course of serving the public. Not only must there be emotional stability, there must be interpersonal skills with which to deal with a wide range of emotional states. Together, these features make a collection of personality characteristics that is quite dynamic because features interact to compensate and offset one another.

"Whole Person" Considerations, Compensating Factors. The fact that criterion behaviors can be achieved by varying quantities of a variety of personal and skill attributes makes identifying the merit or risk of any particular component very difficult. For this reason the concept of the "whole person" has been developed. It is an attempt to see all of the factors that contribute and as well as those that detract, and to formulate a selection decision based on the entire array of factors. Consider the individual with very modest intellectual potential who would be challenged by a highly competitive training program. Some knowledge of prior educational commitment and success may well provide an understanding of how the applicant commits his or her energy and the consequences of such dedication. Therefore, well-developed study skills, self-discipline, and strong motivation would be potent antidotes for what might otherwise appear to be a potential academic failure. This is just one example of how training was selected as a vital component to ensuring selection. Training is the test bed, a trial period where, in fairness to applicants, they can be provided the opportunity to demonstrate that necessary skills are within their grasp.

The whole person model also compensates for the many shortcomings of the selection process. It is an attempt to qualify those who are deserving; an individual's desire and achievement may well make the difference in bridging the gap between educational or cultural disadvantages of their past and their opportunity to be successful in the future.

The Domains of Human Reliability. Table 4.1 details a number of domains that contribute to overall failure to perform reliably. As the table shows, the sources of unreliability are multifaceted. They are not independent, but interactive. Accordingly, selection is a dynamic process that seeks to define what matters, and then uses multiple, overlapping methods to assess the

TABLE 4.1
Ensuring Human Reliability Through Personnel Screening

Source of Reliability Degradation	Screening Factors
Health and physical fitness deficits that impede performance of work	Inability to perform essential job functions/meet performance standards with or without reasonable accommodation due to incapacitation: illness, injury, nutrition, physical condition, substance abuse, mental health, emotional instability
Personal history impedimenta	Social, cultural, and legal history; integrity and ethics issues; relevant education and work experience
Educational/intellectual limitations	Relevant knowledge; learning ability; aptitude and interest; motivation
Conflicting knowledge due to inappropriate prior learning (negative transfer)	Presence of inappropriate values, attitudes, methods
Individual skill development inadequacy	Knowledge, skill, and ability achievement base; perceptual-motor skills and other relevant aptitudes; learning rate; commitment; self-discipline
Dysfunctional organization characterized by ineffective leadership, policy, or supervision	Power/control inadequacies; attitude of disrespect; capricious and arbitrary decision making; tolerance of peer pressure conducive to misconduct
Defective equipment or service provision; inadequate maintenance; material unreliability or failure	Adherence to performance standards; willingness to troubleshoot and to sustain or improve high performance standards

factors that relate to the criterion—reliable performance. Exactly which factors are relevant must be determined by an analysis of the required tasks that are to be accomplished. This establishes standards that are based on the actual requirements of the work to be done.

Establishing Employment Criteria. It would make little sense to select people for employment, training, or advancement unless the selection process effectively eliminated those who are not qualified to do the work and identified those who are best qualified to do the job. It is sometimes easy to forget that prior to the advent of litigation and legislation in the latter half of the 20th century, individuals often were appointed to both private and public sector positions on the basis of what today are considered inappropriate criteria. Nepotism, political expediency, and prejudice often took precedence over the ability to perform well. One of the legacies of those legal activities is the mandate to make employment decisions on the basis of bona fide occupational requirements (Equal Employment Opportunity Commission, 1978, 1979; Society for Industrial and Organizational Psychology, 1987). Consequently, no screening may be performed unless the criterion measures or estimates obtained through personal history or interviews, employment examinations, or other psychological or mental testing and assessments have been demonstrated to have a direct and significant relationship to acceptable job performance. Test measures that have been validated against construct or criterion validation measures are acceptable if those constructs and criteria themselves are valid with respect to the target position. Selection requirements and procedures should be determined by a formal job analysis and validated on a representative population. Job analyses typically describe the incumbent's job responsibilities; the physical, environmental, and organizational constraints under which the incumbent works; what the incumbent actually does to fulfill the job responsibilities; and indicators of successful performance. A distinction must be made between a position description and a job analysis. A position description is a statement made by management of what a job incumbent is expected to do. A job analysis is based on information collected from subject matter experts—usually a panel of job incumbents or first-line supervisors—that identify actual job performance. Job analyses often include elements of processes called *task analyses*, which describe how job elements are performed.

Job Analysis. A job analysis is some systematic procedure for describing a job in terms of duties performed and the knowledge, skills, and abilities required to successfully perform them. A properly conducted job analysis should identify those job elements, work environments, working conditions, and tasks that are essential and those that are less critical to job success. Means of measuring job candidates against the essential qualifications may then be established.

The most common way of conducting a job analysis is a combination of interview and questionnaire. Job analytic techniques most commonly employed include a review of existing job descriptions and other documents to identify the job's major elements and accountabilities. Next, discussions are held with several subject matter experts (SMEs), that is, job incumbents and supervisors: The latter are included because they often are aware of aspects of the job that are less obvious to the incumbent. Usually, the interview is unstructured, and the SME is asked to describe the most important and frequently occurring job duties. These two dimensions—importance and frequency—are at the heart of job analysis (Landy, 1989). Check lists and questionnaires have been used to supplement or substitute for the interviews. The information collected may be job- or worker-oriented in focus. Job-oriented approaches tend to emphasize the conditions of work, the results of work, or both. This approach concentrates on the accomplishments rather than the behaviors of the workers.

The worker-oriented approach focuses on the behaviors that comprise the job. Worker-oriented elements tend to be more generalized descriptions of behavior and less tied to the technical aspects of the job. Worker-oriented analyses produce data that are more useful in structuring training programs and in providing feedback to employees (Landy, 1989).

Observational techniques are important elements of job analysis. They often provide supplementary information when experienced workers are not fully aware of how they perform their jobs. Many jobs activities are so habitual that experienced workers often will forget to report them. Observations also are important because some individuals tend to report how a job should be done in theory or in accord with sometimes ignored "official procedures," when in fact they perform the work in quite a different way.

Sometimes a job analysis may be conducted only in terms of physical activities. Unless cognitive processes are also considered, the job analysis may not measure what it was indented to do. Interviews of SMEs should be designed to assist in identifying the underlying capacities required to perform the tasks. Here we are talking about personality traits and job-specific knowledge, skills, and abilities (KSAs), as well as other details that a survey instrument may not consider. Once defined, the KSAs are tied to the behavioral dimensions or job-relevant constructs.

After all job elements are identified, SMEs are requested to evalute the frequency, degree of importance, and physical effort required for their performance. Responses are averaged and weighted in relation to minimum and maximum performance levels. Results may then be used to develop both selection and performance appraisal criteria.

Validation of Selection Procedures. Validation of selection procedures may be categorized as content or predictive validity, the latter being subcategorized as concurrent validity or predictive validity. The type of validation procedures undertaken greatly depends on the selection requirements of the organization, the time frame in which the process must be completed, funding, existence of a litigious environment, and a variety of additional concerns. Regardless of which validation procedures are employed, content validity is desirable vis-à-vis behaviors seen on the job.

Content validity is concerned with whether or not a measurement procedure contains a fair sample of the possible performance situations encompassed by the job or its tasks. Content validity focuses on what is measured or estimates rather than on how it is measured, and it is a concept of growing importance in employment settings, particularly because criterion-related studies often are not technically feasible.

Criterion procedures validate test or evaluation scores to performance on some criterion measure such as score, rating, or job performance. In the case of content validity the criterion is expert judgment. If the criterion is available at the same time as scores on the predictor, then concurrent validity can be assessed. This often is the preferred approach when incumbent performance can be compared against that of new applicants. Most selection systems established for hiring or promotional bases employ either concurrent or predictive validation processes.

Concurrent validation is concerned with current capability rather than future performance. Concurrent validation procedures are administered to job applicants whose scores are compared with those of job incumbents. Their scores are then correlated with measures of their job performance to determine criterion performance levels. This approach is used to identify applicants who already possess a desired level of capability.

Predictive validity is future oriented. The choice of whether to consider predictive or concurrent validation depends on the using organization's needs. In a hiring situation this may be exemplified by asking "Can the applicant do the job *now?*" (concurrent validity) and "Is it likely that the applicant *will be able* to do the job?" (predictive validity). Predictive validity "is most important for work performance measures when they are used as predictors of future performance or as a part of any personnel decision procedure" (Landy & Farr, 1983, p. 17).

A limitation of the concurrent validation process is a restriction of range in test performance. Most of the incumbents used to establish the testing standards are capable of demonstrating acceptable or better performance levels. The applicant population would be expected to have a larger range of test scores because it would include individuals who would not achieve acceptable test scores. That restriction of range also will impact the precision with which the cutoff scores are established. Because the process uses only experienced individuals, it is not possible to get a true picture of the full range of test scores. Most incumbents can perform at least at a minimally acceptable level and consequently it is possible to get only a preliminary cutoff score. In predictive validation, individuals are administered tests prior to hiring and then are assessed over a specified period of time. This provides a broader range of test scores and a better estimate of cutoff scores to be used for hiring (Gebhardt, Crump, & Schemmer, 1985).

Measuring Required Qualities: Screening Elements

Each of the following screening elements is presented to describe the domains they address in the selection process. Note that there are overlapping qualities, which is desirable. Although not every program will have all of these elements, there must be a sufficient mix to assure that each criterion identified by the job task analysis is examined.

Assessment Centers and Other Job Simulations. A very reasonable way to consider applicants is to ask them to perform in situations that represent various elements of the job to be done. These analogs of the work setting provide for samples of behavior that demonstrate capabilities to perform the tasks that comprise the hiring criteria. Even though applicants typically have not been trained in the procedures or given the "school solution" to the circumstances, such simulations permit examination of native adaptivity. The presumption is that those whose untrained responses are closer to the desired outcome will have less training to do, so their success is better assured.

An assessment center is an evaluated process used by many police agencies as a component of their selection and promotional system. The assessment center consists of job-related (although not always job-specific) exercises that provide candidates the opportunity to demonstrate proficiency in several dimensions. Multiple individual and group exercises are conducted and observed by multiple raters. A given exercise may tap several dimensions. The dimensions are cognitive abilities and such competencies as perceptiveness and analytic ability, interpersonal and communication skills, and organizing and planning skills, to name just a few. The dimensions employed for assessment are determined through job analyses to be essential for effective police performance. The exercises commonly consist of role plays, group and individual exercises, and written exercises.

Selection Interviews. In some ways similar to job simulations, the selection interview is a sample of behavior, interaction, and style. Interviews can create impressions that may have a potent effect on the applicant's opportunity. To be certain that interviews address issues that are relevant to the job criteria, they should be structured or standardized. This is accomplished by addressing the same content areas with all applicants. Such standardization permits more uniform comparisons between applicants and give each the same, equal chance to present themselves. Selection interviews typically inquire about the same details that are a part of the application: education, employment, and other histories. Psychological screening also must be supplemented by an interview. Such an interview is ethically required as a critical element of psychological test interpretation. Such an interview involves developmental, medical, and psychological histories that are not a part of the departmental selection interview.

Criminal Background Checks. Through national registries, such as the National Agency Check Center (NACC) and the Defense Central Index of Information (DCII), computerized searches provide a ready index to recorded investigations in which applicants have been involved. Unfortunately, computers are no more accurate than the people who enter information into them. The result is that there is an error rate for these systems, and other checks may be helpful in confirming the absence of criminal information. Local agency checks (LAC) are the most frequently used. These are contacts with local police departments in the communities where applicants have lived, worked, or gone to school. In combination, the automated and local checks can identify egregious histories of criminal behavior, and also rumors or other potentially damaging information by clarifying past allegations that were disproved.

Credit Checks. The role of financial incentives for engaging in corrupt practices as well as in numerous forms of covert and overt criminal activity is widely recognized. Conventional wisdom postulates that a history of personal financial irresponsibility indicates vulnerability to engage in such activities. As a result, national intelligence community agencies consider financial responsibility as one of the matters that must be scrutinized during the process of granting clearance and access to security matters (Director of Central Intelligence, 1987). A research program area of The Defense Personnel Security Research and Education Center (PERSEREC) has been created to explore the relationship between financial responsibility and personal integrity variables (PERSEREC, personal communication, 1991). Police selection credit checks consist of additional queries of automated systems to determine if there is any history of financial irresponsibility. Certainly, any problem found must be discussed with the applicant to determine whether irresponsibility actually was demonstrated. Sometimes debts are unavoidable. Examples might be medical expenses or losses due to causes outside the control of the applicant. Clarifying the cause for the debt or bankruptcy is typically pursued by inquiry regarding the dunning of debts, repossession, or adverse legal actions.

Educational Requirements. Today there is less of a standard for what in the past were acknowledged levels of academic accomplishment. Accordingly, a high school degree, or even a college diploma, may not assure requisite academic skills or learning capabilities. Claims of educational achievement need to be confirmed, if only to attest to the veracity of the claim, and many agencies ask for additional data with which to demonstrate actual academic skill. The result is that there may be minimal criteria, such as high school education, as well as additional requirements, such as a writing sample (e.g., an autobiography) or a qualifying educational achievement or aptitude test. In some instances English is a second language, and such additional information combines with interview conversations to clarify applicants' ability to communicate. Such a "whole person" balance may be critical to assuring that the applicant is able to converse and write reports to departmental standard, while providing foreign language skills and multicultural knowledge necessary for the department to meet the needs of the community.

Biodata. The term *biodata* refers to a broad array of question types that refer to background information used in selection of job applicants. Biodata consists of answers to factual questions about life and work experiences, opinions, values, beliefs, and attitudes that reflect a historical perspective (Lautenschlager, 1994). These data are collected under the assumption that an applicant's past behavior is reasonably predictive of some future job-related behavior. Biodata questionnaires have been used for selection in a variety of occupations, including sensitive security ones and law enforcement occupations. See, for example, Azen, Snibbe, and Montgomery (1973), Casico (1975), Crawford and Wiskoff (1988), and Wiskoff, Parker, Zimmerman, and Sherman (1989).

Various types of biographic information have different predictive values, depending on the conditions and behaviors required by the job and its constituent tasks. Sharf (1994) assembled information from various sources and listed the following categories of personal history items found to be predictive of job success in some occupations:

Demographic classifiers	Personal attributes
Habits and attitudes	Home, spouse, and children
Health	Recreation, hobbies, interests
Human relations	Education and school activities
Money management	Self-impressions
Parental, home, childhood, teens information	Values, opinions, and preferences
Socioeconomic level, financial status	Work, employment
Social activities, memberships	Skills

He warned, however, of the need to exercise caution to avoid formulating questions that are prohibited by the Americans With Disabilities Act (ADA) and other federal civil rights legislation unless they are demonstrably job related. In addition, various state and local jurisdictions may prohibit other personal history inquiries (Sharf, 1994).

Employment History. Relevant work experiences can contribute meaningfully to preparing an applicant for law enforcement duty as many jobs provide training and skill development in areas directly adaptable to police work. Successful performance in those tasks also suggests some sense of how well the applicant applies himself or herself in the workplace. Such prior employment can be considered a window to understanding the applicant's work habits and commitment to perform effectively.

Employment Appraisal History. Separate from what applicants have done is how well they have done it. Performance appraisals can present records that reflect skill level, achievement, and professionalism. These are the on-the-job report cards that show how competitive and successful the applicant's prior work experience was. Some organizations, however, may have been advised by their legal counsel not to provide such histories to potential new employers lest they become involved in litigation by former employees who are not selected for subsequent positions.

References. An old adage among background investigators is that anyone dumb enough to list a character reference who would not recommend them is unfit for the job in consideration. Usually the most informative insights to character are provided by people not listed by an applicant. These may include former workplace colleagues (i.e., co-workers and supervisors), teachers, and neighbors. An increasingly helpful concept has been to seek the recommendations of the people with whom the applicant spends much of his or her time. Consideration of just who those people are also contributes to understanding the applicant's values and character.

Medical Clearance. This would seem an easy standard, but in actuality it has been in continuing transition. Two decades ago, minimal standards for physical attributes came under scrutiny, and have largely been replaced by performance requirements. Even health standards are being re-interpreted. The ADA has made the nexus of physical capabilities with job task requirements draw even closer. Under this act, employers have the obligation to modify work environments and practices to accommodate as full a range of individual variability as possible. The effect of this legislation is still being defined in law enforcement, but the goals of medical qualification are health and freedom from any condition that would interfere with or prohibit accomplishment of the tasks identified in the job task analysis.

Mental Health Screening. This element assesses the capacity to be reliable based on issues that stem from psychological health. Such screening typically is composed of psychological testing and a structured clinical interview. The testing can examine a wide range of features, but should be interpreted to standards for the law enforcement population. Clinical interviews, like employment interviews, should be structured, and with the applicant's consent, may be tape-recorded to preserve the responses should there be an appeal.

DEVELOPING A SCREENING PROGRAM

Screening cannot be accomplished as separate, unintegrated elements. The efficacy of the process relies on a design that builds credibility and fairness by consolidating each element to a criterion-related assessment program. This is a logical sequence of screening components that addresses the requirements of the job using a variety of selection procedures, many of which may overlap, providing the capacity for additional, confirming data. The elements presented in the previous section exemplify many of the contemporary methods. Some identify and measure features that would exclude the applicant (e.g., a history of criminal arrest, irresponsible credit practices, negative work evaluations, etc.). Others are distinctly application enhancing (e.g., academic achievements, similar work experience, special achievements, etc.). Not surprisingly, such factors have been grouped and organized in progressive selection concepts that combine in a two-step process that first addresses factors that would eliminate candidates, and then those that would specifically include them. These concepts are preceded by the legal framework that creates liability for improper hiring practices.

Liability Arising From Failing to Select the Right People (Unlawful Discrimination)

Selection is defined in the *Uniform Guidelines for Employee Selection Procedures* (Equal Employment Opportunity Commission, 1978, 1979) to include all personnel decisions pertaining to hiring, training, promotion, assignment, retention, and discipline. Generally speaking there are two sources of legal liability associated with the selection of police personnel: liability arising from failure to select the right people (unlawful discrimination), and liability arising from selecting the wrong person to be a police officer (negligent hiring).

Liability arising from employment discrimination may occur when a department unlawfully discriminates against a variety of parties, such as racial or ethnic groups or on the basis of gender of the applicant. An allegation of a disparate impact of an employment practice may occur when a complainant alleges that a facially neutral employment practice (e.g., a psychological test) falls more harshly on one group than another and cannot be justified by business necessity. Proof of discriminatory intent is not required because Congress was concerned with the consequences of the decision, not the motivation for it. Therefore, the complainant need only show that the challenged employment practice has a significantly disproportionate impact on the class of which they are a member. Thus if the complainant fails to show that the practice falls more harshly on one group there is no case. However, if the complainant does demonstrate disparate impact for any selection procedure, an employer may still justify that practice by evidence that it is a bona fide necessity.

A prima facie case of discrimination may be made under the so-called four-fifths rule. Under this rule the selection ratio of the protected class of applicants alleging discrimination must be at least 80% of the applicant ratio. Thus, if there were 500 applicants for a position, and 100 of them were in the protected class, the applicant ratio is .2. If 13 members of the protected class were selected among the 80 successful applications, the selection ratio is .1625 Because .1625 divided by .2 is greater than .8, there is insufficient evidence to sustain a claim of discrimination. However, if only 10 of the 80 successful candidates were in the protected class, the selection ratio would be .125. That ratio divided by the applicant ratio is less than .8 (.625), and a prima facie case of discrimination has been demonstrated.

Even though a prima facie case has been made, no discrimination will be held to exist if the selection process depended on a bona fide occupational requirement (BFOR). In such cases it must be shown that:

1. The selection decision has been validated; that is, the qualifying characteristic is indeed a BFOR. The definition of a BFOR has changed over the years as a result of several Supreme Court decisions and statutory changes. Nonetheless the basis for establishing whether a job requirement is or is not a bona fide one depends on the validity of the job element on which the selection test is based. The best means of establishing such validity is by means of a job analysis.

2. The selection instrument itself also must be validated; that is, it must be demonstrated that the selection instrument does indeed distinguish persons with the qualifying requirement from persons without it. Selection instruments include means such as educational requirements; licensing; written tests of aptitude, skills, personality characteristics, and integrity; job simulations (assessment centers); selection interviews; reference, criminal background, and credit checks, polygraph screening, and satisfactory completion of assignments held to be prerequisite to the target assignment.

Recommended Procedural Requirements.   Even though an organization feels that it has a bona fide requirement for personnel decisions that it does not recognize as having an adverse impact, the wise administrator will keep records and the rationale for all personnel decisions. However, rationales that are subjective are insufficient unless they have been validated. A major federal law enforcement agency was sued in a class action by Black special agents who, among other charges, alleged that in one of its division offices that Black agents were given a greater number of undercover assignments than were non-Black agents. The plaintiffs held that these assignments kept them from obtaining the broader based experience required for promotion.

The law enforcement agency defended its policy by alleging that the targets of most of its investigations in the city in question were criminal organizations made up exclusively of Blacks, and that non-Black undercover operatives were not likely to penetrate the target groups. This argument was rejected at trial, and the rejection ultimately was upheld by the Supreme Court, largely because the agency failed to provide sufficient validating data to substantiate the claim. Although the results of the litigation made clear what the law enforcement agency failed to do, no guidance was provided as what could have been done to substantiate the agency's case. One can only speculate what the courts will decide in any future case in which a protected group is given a disproportionate number of undercover assignments if a police department documents the policy in advance of litigation together with the reasons therefore and collects data substantiating the argument. Consideration might be given to:

- Providing an intelligence estimate of preponderance of ethnicly dominated target groups, and rationalizing that undercover assignments are proportional to target group ethnicity rather than to the proportions of officers who are members of that ethnic group.
- Conducting a survey of officers who have undercover experience to obtain their feelings of the likelihood of success and personal safety if given an undercover assignment to penetrate target gangs with similar or different demographic characteristics such as age or ethnicity.
- Operational data comparing the number of cases successfully completed when undercover operatives who are members of an ethnic group attempt penetration of criminal organizations dominated by their own or another ethnic group.

Liability Arising From Selecting the Wrong Person (Negligent Hiring)

The liability from negligently hiring arises from citizens or other officers who suffer because an officer in a position to execute police powers failed to do so in an acceptable fashion. Police departments are frequently called to account when they fail to protect individuals under constraint or custody (Wattendorf, 1993). They are also at risk of liability for failure to protect persons or property regardless of whether the injured party was under constraint or custody. In some cases, plaintiffs have alleged that employers should have been aware of characteristics of the employee that caused the harm. Although no court has specifically stated that psychological testing is necessary to discharge the employer's duty, we believe that such testing would have probative value in ascertaining whether an employer has indeed fulfilled his duty.

In law there is a principle called *agency* in which an employer is liable for the torts of an employee conducted on behalf of the employer. If the employer can demonstrate that the tort-feasor was not acting within the scope of his or her duties, no agency was held to exist, and the employer was not liable for the act.

However, there now is a trend requiring employers to defend suits filed by persons seeking redress for crimes committed by employees. Crimes such as thefts or assaults that victimize customers or co-workers are alleged to result from the negligence of the employer in hiring the alleged criminal.

Most states now recognize some form of negligent hiring as a common law tort. Negligent hiring suits are sustainable if a plaintiff can demonstrate that the police department had a duty to protect him or her from the harm sustained and that the officer was acting under color of his employment. The plaintiff also must show that the employing agency breached that duty—that the employee causing the damage was incompetent and that the department knew or should have known of this incompetence. The plaintiff must demonstrate that his or her injury was caused by the officer's incompetence, and that the incompetence was reasonably foreseeable by the employer. Finally, the plaintiff must show damage suffered as a result of the employee's incompetence.

It seems clear that law enforcement agencies would be negligent if they failed to identify and did employ applicants who can be demonstrated to be likely to behave in a manner that would invite such lawsuits. Because the attributes that are associated with such counterproductive behavior may develop after a person has been selected and trained, a police department may also have to periodically monitor all officers for changing behavior patterns that warn of increasing risk of such behaviors.

SCREENING IN AND SCREENING OUT

At this point it seems appropriate to discuss employee screening, a family of procedures that determine which candidates are not suited for a job (screening out) and which candidates are best suited for a job (screening in). Both of these procedures are used in the selection of police officers. Selection of an attribute used as a criterion for either screening in or screening out must be carefully selected. The administrator of a screening program should be satisfied that:

1. All criterion attributes are primary determinants of good police work and the criterion attributes cannot be changed as a result of academy and field training—or of institutional socialization. In many cases failure to meet criterion levels of attributes subject to modification due to training or socialization can be attributed to impediments, and the candidate may lawfully demand that a reasonable accommodation be made until he or she can be trained or socialized.

2. Is there an identifiable pattern of positive attrubutes that have been associated with good and poor police work? Do we know what these patterns are? Less than 2% of the California law enforcement agencies surveyed by Leake (1988) indicated that they have, or intend to, conduct validation studies for this purpose.

Establishing Screen-Out Criteria

Screening out is the elimination of applicants based on their failure to meet minimum criteria or evidencing factors that cannot be tolerated. The purpose is to reduce the applicant pool by eliminating those with incompatibilities. The basic element here is the obvious shortcoming of the factor in question, based on that factor's relatedness to the need for reliability. Screening out criteria for law enforcement have traditionally included minimums such as standards for educational requirements and the possession of a valid driver's license, as well as such incompatibilities as a history of righteous arrest or narcotic addiction. Whatever the screening out criteria, they must correspond with the criteria of reliability as defined by the tasks that comprise the law enforcement job.

Screening out evaluates for minimum qualifications, and it may be used to determine eligibility based on considerations such as age, physical fitness, and physical and mental health status, to the degree that they have been demonstrated to be disqualifying. Screening out must be justified in that employing screened-out applicants would result in failure to perform the job's essential activities, or to perform them in such a manner as to risk the safety or health of self or others. The focus of screen-outs is on an applicant's current status rather than on future job performance. Although a test score or evaluation rating may be arrived at, screening out must result in a dichotomous recommendation to the employment decision maker: Do not select versus consider for selection.

The more definitive the screen-out, the stronger or more direct should be the relationship to reliability. Absolute screen-outs are factors so clearly in violation of the goals of the criterion that any presence of the factor excludes the applicant. Whereas righteous criminal arrest is one such example, an arrest that was later followed by dismissal of charges could require additional consideration. For all screen-out criteria there should be a well-defined rationale that explains the reason for excluding applicants. A well-defined rationale is important when discriminating between features that cannot be tolerated and those that may receive case-by-case consideration, and in defining minimum standards for candidacy.

Choosing Procedures to Measure Screen-Out Criteria

Some "rule-out" features have face validity, such as the exclusion of persons who have egregiously broken the law. Others are derived based on the culture of the organization, for example, personnel must be residents of the community. Yet others are scientifically related directly to the performance criteria. Examples here may be drawn from actual critical incidents on the job (e.g., being able to run a distance that simulates a foot race and then climb a wall). Yet other examples are cutoff scores that derived from procedures that have been validated in compliance with documents such as the *Uniform Guidelines on Employee Selection Processes* and the *Principles for the Validation and Use of Personnel Selection,* published by the Society for Industrial and Organization Psychology, both of which have been given force of law in numerous cases in which allegation of employment discrimination is an important part.

Selection tests often measure knowledge, skills, aptitudes, and other attributes that have been demonstrated to be job relevant. The selection instrument usually has a built-in cutoff score to discriminate between those who have maximum potential to meet the needs of the department. Should the cutoff score be raised to require a higher or more stringent requirement, the number of positively appearing applicants (on the tested-for factor) who are actually not positive is reduced. This "accuracy" is achieved at the expense of a reduced field of candidates, and reduces the likelihood of incorrectly measuring the factor, but can only reduce—not eliminate—the presence of false positives (candidates who appear to be high in the factor, but are not). Reducing the cutoff score increases the likelihood of selecting more of the applicants with the desired factor, but at the same time increases the risk of false positives; assuming some applicants are better qualified than is the case (true negatives). This sort of logic is particularly important when considering the value the department places on specific factors, the validity of the method of measurement, and the extent to which the personnel pool can tolerate exclusions. This last point loops back to the liability of wrongful hiring. Many courts have entertained unlawful discrimination and negligent hiring cases due to insufficiently considered cutoff scores. Quite simply, the more specific the criteria, the stronger the need to evidence its relationship to job requirements.

Criterion Issues

We have some concern with what is perceived as a lack of meaningful discrimination of degree (or intensity) of the undesirable behaviors being predicted by most instruments, and with the relation of the intensity of behavior to test cutoff scores (Kurke, 1991).

It will be useful to envisage a matrix in which test scores representing a prediction of undesirable behavior (e.g., theft) are arrayed along the vertical axis (Fig. 4.1). High scores are those indicating that there is a high likelihood of undesirable behavior, and low scores indicate a low likelihood of undesirable behavior. A cutoff score can be established along the continuum as the employee selection decision-making threshold. As noted earlier, if the threshold is lowered, the correct identification of undesirable applicants will decrease.

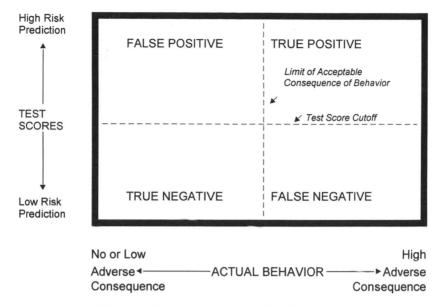

High Risk
Prediction

FALSE POSITIVE   TRUE POSITIVE

Limit of Acceptable
Consequence of Behavior

TEST
SCORES

Test Score Cutoff

TRUE NEGATIVE   FALSE NEGATIVE

Low Risk
Prediction

No or Low   High
Adverse ◄————————ACTUAL BEHAVIOR————►Adverse
Consequence   Consequence

FIG. 4.1. Cutoff scores versus predicted and actual behavior.

Returning to Fig. 4.1, let the horizontal axis of the matrix represent a continuum of intensity or undesirability of the class of behavior being tested. If the behavior we are talking about is theft, for example, there is a continuum of theft-free behavior from minor pilfering up through the most heinous theft-related crime. Often it is a test publisher who arbitrarily decides how bad the behavior must be and sets the threshold of acceptability (pass–fail) along the actual behavior continuum. At one extreme there could be a test in which a person who is likely to commit a transgression of a very minor nature that will cause little or no regret is treated as equal to a person very likely to commit a major transgression causing the department much regret through bad public relations or legal liability. At the other extreme could be a test that only discriminates the major potential transgressor. Few test publishers advise the test user where the cutoff along the consequence dimension has been set. Thus, one test may screen in for selection one type of behavior that another test deems cause for screening out. Here is an illustrative example. It may be that as far as sensitivity goes, a person whose test score indicates a risk that he or she might verbally abuse a traffic violator, and another person who might use undue or deadly force against a prisoner who talks back are at equal risk of not being hired.

A fixed cutoff score established for decision making is best used when there is a clear-cut demarcation between acceptable and unacceptable behavior. However, many of the criterion behaviors do not fall into clear-cut yes–no categories. A considerable amount of criterion behavior falls somewhere along a continuum ranging from exemplary to egregious, and the person responsible for selection decision making is required to establish a legally viable standard somewhere between these extremes. Selection of a cutoff score also requires validation. Leake (1988) reported that 30% of the California law enforcement agencies responding to a survey indicated that they screened out 21% to 80% of their candidates for psychopathology, a condition that appears in only about 15% of the state's population. A justification of the acceptance of the cutoff used in selection requires answers to questions such as: Does the police candidate pool have poorer mental health status than what can be found in the general population? If not, are the criteria used by the selection agencies valid in terms of appropriateness of the cutoffs used? If the cutoff criteria can be shown to be valid, were the testing procedures followed flawed in any way?

In addition to legal considerations, the police psychologist should consider the ethics of mislabeling a person as unsuitable when in fact the decision to label the applicant is based on a false positive finding. Quite apparently, the failure rate for a test can be lowered by altering either the threshold between acceptable and unacceptable behavior or altering the test cutoff threshold. However, if this is done, it is highly likely that the correct identification of poor performers will decrease. It seems clear that a large percentage of otherwise qualified job applicants may be rejected on the basis of suitabliity test results in order to identify an often small number of unsuitable employees.

Integrating Components to Identify Unsuitable Applicants

Departments need to make their hiring decision based on a variety of data inputs. A number of elements used to determine unsuitability were discussed earlier. How the results of these elements are combined in the overall decision is as important as the merit of any single factor. Absolute rule-outs, by definition, reject the applicant whenever they are present; it is a binomial equation: yes or no. Other factors may have differential weights, some being more important than others. These can be decided by a panel representing departmental interests, but the logic for each weighing should be defined in advance of consideration of any case, and spelled out so that the process is recoverable, accountable, and defendable. If a weighing system is used, of course, the same weights must be applied uniformly to all applicants.

Establishing Screen-In Criteria. Screening out attempts to eliminate unsuitable applicants. Screening in attempts to identify the most qualified applicants. Screening in is a complimentary, competitive process that qualifies applicants who have passed the screen out. Screening in should result in quantitative measures that allow qualified candidates to be compared with each other (i.e., predictions of degrees of job success). The screen-in process evaluates competitive rating factors and will identify the best qualified candidates so that the candidates who are most likely to be successful can be selected.

Criteria for screen ins are factors that reflect attributes, qualities, skill, and knowledge, and abilities that enhance candidacy. Whereas screening out requires, for example, applicants to be emotionally stable (or instability that does not exceed clearly defined limits), screening in values the job-related personality qualities and other job-related attributes that are specific to effective, reliable performance (e.g., the ability to deal with others, sound judgment, etc.).

The characteristics or factors that are suitable to screen in are more difficult to qualify due to the offsetting and compensating capabilities that exist among these features.

Choosing Procedures to Measure Criteria. Some screen-in criteria are measured by their mere presence; advanced or specialized training or professional experience are examples. Other factors are logical extensions of screen-out criteria. For instance, enhanced personal qualities such as higher intelligence, overall adjustment, and outstanding problem-solving skills are attributes that suggest potential that is in excess of minimum.

Other ways of choosing how to screen in depend on the same appraisal of test scores that is used in screening out. Here the higher scores determine the relative competitiveness of the applicant. No matter the method of determining which candidates are best qualified, any selection system used must be able to demonstrate that the applicants selected because of their enhanced potential, do in fact perform better on the job than those judged to be less qualified.

Integrating Components to Identify Most Qualified Applicants. As was the case with the selection rationale in screening out, screening in should combine the various criterion-related selection factors in a standardized fashion. Because screening in is more difficult to validate than screening out, the anchors between the screening criteria and reliable performance need to be quite clear. Preferably, the face validity, or obvious connection to the screening goal is well established. Certainly the way selection factors are combined in the ultimate hiring decision should capture the same appreciation for validity and equality as used in screening out.

One way of minimizing assessment errors has been suggested. The plan intends to reduce the consequences of any weaknesses of the elements used to screen by rating applicants by random groupings. Here is an example of how this proposal works. Applicants are evaluated using routinized screen outs and screen ins. Randomly selected groups of three applicants (who passed the screen out) are rated per their competitiveness with forced rankings of first, second, or third. Actual hiring begins with all applicants with first-place ratings. Once they are all on board, the next hiring round begins with the second-place applicants. Following this sequence, all the highest rated applicants are hired first. The value of this scheme is that the risks of selection error are randomized, reducing the risk of relying completely on specific criteria. Because so many factors can affect the accuracy of validation efforts, this is a procedure that can be a very reasonable precaution from being bound to questionable scores.

Three-Level Screening Procedure in Accord With ADA

It is self-evident that police applicants should not be encumbered by psychological or medical conditions that will interfere with the safe and effective performance of their duties. Prior to the passage of the ADA, in many jurisdictions applicants for police and other public safety positions received psychological and medical screening prior to receiving a job offer. Because the ADA prohibits discrimination against disabled individuals who are otherwise qualified for a position, the law requires that no inquiry concerning any disability may be made of any job candidate unless and until a provisional offer of employment has been made. As of this writing, many police departments are in the process of changing their selection procedures to comply with the law and at the same time, to ensure that all selected job applicants are screened for their ability to perform their jobs. A three-tier selection process is suggested that will combine screen-in and screen-out processes.

The first level of screening is to review all applications and screen out all applicants who do not qualify for nonimpairment related considerations such as age limits (criminal record, etc.), resulting in a list of qualified applicants.

The qualified applicants are then subjected to a screening-in process. Knowledge, skill, abilities, and other attributes, including relevant experience, are evaluated. Tests and other assessment procedures must validly measure characteristics that are bona fide job requirements. Upon completion of testing or other evaluation procedures, the applicants are ranked to create a list of best qualified candidates. A number of best qualified candidates, not to exceed the number of available or projected vacancies, are given conditional offers of employment, subject to medical and psychological screening out for disqualifying characteristics. Highly qualified applicants who have not received provisional offers of employment may be placed on a waiting list, pending vacancies that may be created as a result of the third level of screening.

The third level, a screen-out process, is a medical and psychological evaluation. This screening must clearly differentiate between those applicants who have a disqualifying impediment and those who do not. The screening device must not only identify a valid disqualifying condition, but it must also measure the degree of existence of the condition against a validated cutoff. This means that an existing condition must be present to the degree or extent that has been demonstrated to impede or prevent the applicant from performing the required activities of the job safely and effectively.

Candidates who have been screened out on the basis of a medical or psychological impediment have the right to seek reasonable accommodation to their disability. Such an accommodation may be reached if it can be determined that another factor, if present, can compensate for the impairment. The compensating factor may be attained through job redesign, training or rehabilitation, or by establishing the existence of a physiological or psychological condition that compensates for the impediment. Should the applicant be judged to be impaired, but otherwise qualified for the position to which he or she aspires (either with or without a reasonable accommodation), the applicant must be returned to the best qualified list and ranked as if there were no impairment.

Application to Special Duty Assignments

Screening for departmental personnel to assignments that are excursions from routine duty should require their own selection procedures. Each of the special duty opportunities should have its own job task analysis, and that should be used as the predictor criteria. Such separate, in-service considerations are necessary because these special duties can each have their own standards that define the personal qualities needed to assure reliability while doing that work.

Special duty assignments can be very varied. For example, undercover operatives need to be stable, but also particularly stress tolerant, self-reliant, and self-disciplined. More than this, the psychological features of each operative need to be understood to adequately make operational plans. Chapter 14 in this volume further specifies issues related to screening in for undercover work. In much the same way, detailed psychological data can be invaluable in selecting and in the training of hostage negotiators. Assessment data assists in ensuring that negotiators can effectively deal with others, but the information can also be used to fine tune negotiators, and identify who would be best to work how, in which circumstances.

Another example would be screening for Special Weapons and Tactics (SWAT) Team. Here there are some important differences in temperament between assault teams (including differentiating between best qualified for leader versus follower positions), and snipers (who have to be patient, low in impulsiveness, comfortable being alone for long periods of time, and of sufficient self-esteem to feel reasonably at ease with the concept of facing the use of deadly force). As with other specialists whose work is more likely to demand precision (e.g., explosive ordinance disposal), and because the assignments are more likely to increase the likelihood of involvement, greater care is needed in confirming that officers are continually ready for their assignments.

Routine periodic psychological re-evaluations are needed in most special duty work to assure reliablity. In some instances, such as undercover duty, this can be conducted before or after assignments. In other situations, such as SWAT, it may be more helpful to assess personnel annually, using some convenient schedule (e.g., their birth month) to re-evaluate, debrief, and support. Such attention not only sustains the visability of the reliability program, it permits routine interaction with the psychologist, a chance to become familiar with one another, and a chance to build a relationship that can be relied on if problems do occur.

ENSURING HUMAN RELIABILITY THROUGH TRAINING

A Continuing Selection Process

Training is one of the complementary processes that can influence reliability. As mentioned earlier, training's role can be varied, to include ensuring requisite skill fundamentals, compensate for other factors, and contribute to ensuring standards of performance. The following domains (see Table 4.2) exemplify the range and complexity of issues, and suggest ways that resources can apply training to assure reliable performance. The reader is also referred to chapter 10 in this volume on the role of the police psychologist in training elsewhere in this volume.

Knowledge Inadequacy. This domain addresses what needs to be known to accomplish job tasks. A distinction is made between what is *essential knowledge* (specific information relating to the work) and *essential skill* (ability to apply what is known). Essential knowledge includes a wide range of information that is relied on in order to perform. Examples might include language, math, or other basic informational prerequisites, to which specific information, such as knowledge of the law, would be added during police training. The factors that account for the shortfalls include the absence of essential knowledge, such as inadequate exposure to the subject matter. Educating with the needed information is the solution, but a closer look into the reasons for the shortfall may suggest particular training strategies to assure knowledge adequacy. For example, knowledge limitations might be contributed to by a lack of use of the information. It may have been learned but not dealt with sufficiently to sustain it. Accordingly, refresher training would be a recourse for essential information, if its refreshment is

TABLE 4.2
Ensuring Human Reliability Through Training Design

Domain: Reliability Degradation Factors to Be Addressed	Training Design Considerations
Knowledge inadequacy: Basic knowledge shortfalls; conflicting and/or irrelevant prior knowledge; lack of feedback	Education/curriculum development: Provide application exercises; provide feedback; ensure curriculum is relevant to teaching goals
Skill inadequacy: Individual potential limitations; inadequate prior proficiency; negative transfer from other tasks; prior underuse of skills; lack of skill feedback	Screening/selection for training: Provide proficiency training; training designed to develop positive transfer; ensure regular practice; provide feedback in training process and during operational situations
Dysfunctional organizational climate: Dysfunctional policies and leadership practices	Continuing management and leadership training; management to be held accountable for adequacy of training
Defective equipment and misuse of equipment resulting in system failure; inadequate manuals and other user or maintenance documentation; inadequate or inappropriate application of the equipment	System and equipment design and documentation: Adequate and appropriate training design can compensate to a limited extent for poor or inadequate attention to user characteristics in engineering design. Training and user manual design must consider training and document readability, comprehensibility, legibility, and durability.
Personal history impediments	Social, cultural, and legal history; integrity and ethics issues; relevant education and work experience
Educational/intellectual limitations	Relevant knowledge; learning ability; aptitude and interest; motivation

needed, as well as exercises or other proficiency methods to practice and retain accessibility.

A lack of feedback may also explain a knowledge shortfall, as there may not have been a suitable environment to assure correctness by repairing inaccuracies and learning how to keep current. Additionally, feedback helps to assure that information used is relevant for effective performance. Continually updating the content of instruction is necessary to assure that the essential information that is available addresses the changing conditions or trends in the workplace. This chapter began with a citation of how officers killed in the line of duty are now understood to have most frequently given the offender a break by dropping their guard. Knowing this could well keep unsuspecting officers from dropping their guard. As with any form of instruction, motivating the student to learn requires actively involving instructors with their classes, making the information learnable. This includes more than assuring that the information is necessary, it means making those learning it appreciate its importance. Active, involved instruction means to approach the information with instructional methods that engage students to capitalize on their abilities to understand, learn, retain, and use.

Skill Inadequacy. This domain addresses the "how to" of police work; being able to accomplish the tasks of the job. Individual potential is perhaps the most fundamental of the factors included in this domain. These elements are more difficult to deal with than the previous domain (knowledge inadequacy), in which the content was the issue. Here individual differences in dealing with that content, such as how students deal with their personal potentials, make the difference.

Among the factors of consequence are individual aptitudes and learning rates, perceptual and motor skills, motivation, and emotional factors. Perhaps the most formidable preventive or corrective action for these factors is the the selection process. Selection criteria should determine basic knowledge requirements for entry-level training, and training should confirm that the needed skills and attributes for successful performance are sufficiently available. Training here is a check on selection, and a confirmation that needed proficiencies are acquired. Failure to confirm evidences that what the selection criteria could not assure, instructional standards could.

Other factors influencing skill adequacy include previous requirements to properly use and demonstrate abilities, blockers (negative transfer), and lack of feedback. Proficiency training is recognized as the most commonly used means to counter negative effects of these factors. If previous proficiency standards are adequate, then training to such standards assures the development and maintenance of the skill. Likewise, conflicts that do not integrate skills learned for use in the field can result in negative transfer; blockers that interrupt effective application of skills. Training also needs to integrate the realities of the workplace (e.g., policies, standards, equipment). This should include regular practice and generous feedback.

Dysfunctional Organizational Climate. Just as individual attributes need to be well attuned to the work to be accomplished, the policies and leadership styles of the police organization also need to be tuned to the nature of the organization. This is the culture in which knowledge and skill are applied. These factors interact with all of the others, because organizational culture establishes the values in the workplace, influencing the climate and ultimately the productivity of every law enforcement organization.

Dysfunctional policies are those that are in conflict with each other, insensitive to the needs of the people within the organization, or unable to address changes in either. More specifically, guidance can fail because there can be workplace requirements for which there are no policies, or they may fall short and be inadequate by not going far enough. Conversely, policies can also be too rigid, detailed, and constraining because they go too far. Examples of policy factors that can contribute to successful, reliable performance include formal and informal corporate communications, supervisory practices, labor relations, adversity of work schedules, and the fairness of disciplinary actions, performance appraisals, and promotion opportunities. Effective policy development is a difficult process that requires continual re-evaluation and updating.

Dysfunctional leadership is another organizational failure on a personal level. Good leaders typically have personal characteristics that combine their understanding of others and situations with effective communication, decision making, and the ability to inspire. To some extent, leadership potential can be assessed, but even natural leaders can benefit from leadership training. Leadership preparation provides essential information, skill development, and an opportunity to practice and learn about how best to lead and to follow. The list of potential content that has been employed in leadership training is wide ranging. In addition to managerial skill development, it ensures uniform application of policy, which further reduces liability that might arise from misinterpretation of guidance, uneven application, or ignorance of required procedures.

Defective Equipment. Law enforcement professionals function amidst an evolving technology of crime-fighting equipment. Yet even when officers have the tools they need, they must know how and when to use them and there must be oversight to assure proper use.

Some failures of equipment or equipment systems lie in the inadequacy of the system's design to address the realities of the workplace. Systems that are so complex that they challenge cognitive or perceptual abilities may work well in the laboratory, but may not under fire. For instance, the demand characteristics for response time and precision may be very difficult to achieve during periods of intense workload or stress. Real field conditions can make complicated hardware too difficult to use. Redesigning such material to meet human factors requirements can often rework the technology to use it more reliably. It is necessary to train with the equipment under clearly specified procedures (keep it simple, stupid comes to mind). Skill acquisition and proficiency training can best enhance performance when conducted under actual field conditions (or their simulated analogs). Even well-maintained, state of the art equipment can contribute little to reliable performance if it is difficult to use and the "when" and "how" of its use are left to chance.

Levels of Training

Establishing effective training translates to a program that identifies at each level of organizational structure what is to be accomplished at that level. Training also prescribes instruction to assure knowledge and skill sufficient to the tasks required. The previous discussion presented selection as a means of initiating the acquisition of personnel who are likely to perform reliably, provided other factors are effectively sustained. Training has been presented as a logical and unavoidable check on the actual capability of personnel to learn and demonstrate basic police skill acquisition. The previous section emphasized how training needs to be a continual, career-long process that is inseparable from other reliability-enhancing components. The brief discussion of training levels that follows integrates training into the structure and function of a department.

Recruit Training. The most basic, recognized form of law enforcement orientation and preparation is the entry-level or recruit course. Typically conducted in a paramilitary fashion, this is a mutual introduction; students to police work and the organization (through trainers) to recruits. Beyond imparting knowledge, developing skill, and functioning as a selection follow-up, recruit training imparts organizational values, standards, and customs. Passing the course means the applicant has demonstrated achievement of basic knowledge and skills, and is ready to apply himself or herself under supervised field conditions.

Probationary Training and Supervision. The nurturing of the trainee as a professional continues during initial field duties. Field trainers need to be current regarding what has been instructed in basic training, and must have prescribed goals so that the probationary experience can complement and extend. Just like academy instructors, field trainers need to assure the relevancy of what they impart and actively interact with probationary officers in providing immediate, constructive feedback. Additionally, this is the first chance the developing officer has to do police work. How they feel about their work will develop from these experiences; field trainers have an unmistakable influence on generation of organizational values and culture.

In-Service Training. Update training assures proficiency and ability to meet changes in requirements and procedures. Course content can impart new information, such as intelligence or crime pattern data, or introduce new procedures or equipment for skill development. Other in-service work might include proficiency exercises and specialized training for specific skill development. Skills that require recertification include firearms proficiency, radar and breathalyzer use, hostage negotiation, or specialized weapons classes. In-service work can be programmed (e.g., conducting firearms requalifications) or it can be requirement driven (e.g., implementing policy changes or system modifications).

Career Training. This is the preparation of the department's people to deal with one another. Commonly referred to as *organizational development* or *human resource development*, this is a developing area that adds greatly to nurturing individuals as a part of the department, and builds managers and leaders. Career training prepares employees for their personal career development, supervisory responsibilities, and the shaping of what the department is to its people.

Training: The Nexus Between Selection and Job Performance

Validity Issues. The validity of a selection instrument or of any selection decision-making process is, in the long run, a measure of how well a candidate for a position would perform if selected for that position. To properly assess validity, one must have job performance criteria that are in themselves valid indicators of job success. Each criterion must be, in the terminology of civil rights regulations, a BFOR. The determination of which criteria are indeed BFORs requires considerable care. It must be recognized that there often is an intervening process between selection and on-the-job performance. Many, if not most, performance standards can be achieved only through the learning processes associated with training, on-the-job experience, and acculturation. Of particular importance to the police psychologist involved with the selection process is the role of training as a variable intervening between selection and job performance. There have been numerous instances in which success in training was the criterion against which the validity of the selection process was measured. Separate studies of the validity of a training program rest on subsequent job performance. When one thinks about it, selection can be viewed as a two-stage process: selection of job candidates for training and selection of trainees for employment as sworn officers. The implications of such an approach are clear: Efforts to assess the validity of the selection process must consider how screening impacts training, and how both screening and training influence measures of job success. The following is an example of how a federal law enforcement agency considered these relationships.

The screening procedure in use by that agency assessed applicants for primary agent training largely on predictions of their ability to successfully complete the primary agent training program. On its face, this selection screening appeared to be quite good: Once accepted, few candidates failed to complete their training successfully. In this validation, assessment depended on how well the agent cadets completed the academy's training program, which was divided into three elements: a physical training or development program, firearms instruction, and an academic portion that included instruction believed to be related to the agent's future assignments. However, there was little to indicate any relationship between the selection process results and subsequent on-the-job performance of academy graduates. There was a need to develop a means that would give the agency the ability to assess candidates prior to acceptance for primary agent training while still in the academy. There was also a need to evaluate during field trials prior to the completion of graduates' probationary period as special agents. A research program was designed to obtain a scientific and legally valid basis for identifying applicants and trainees who would fail to complete academy training succesfully, those who would perform less than satisfactorily after graduation from the academy, and those agents who would drop out of the agency early in their careers.

Early in the development of this research it was determined that there was no data by which the agency could defend its policy of allowing predicted training performance to dictate admission to the training program. Such a policy could be defended only if a nexus between training course content could be demonstrated with the job characteristics that were considered in subsequent agent performance evaluation. It was found that no scientifically or legally valid nexus existed. However, extensive job analyses and other studies had recently been completed. These actions were mandated by a prior court decision in which the agency had been the defendant in an employment discrimination lawsuit. These job analyses yielded information concerning job-related characteristics for the entire array of special agent assignments at the two lowest grade levels. The analyses became the basis for performance criteria.

The job analyses lent themselves well to developing job performance characteristics, which were incorporated into work plans (the statement of job performance standards and criteria against which the agents' annual performance ratings would be determined). These work plans met the court-ordered requirement for instruments that incorporated valid bases for personnel decision making by the agency. The analysis-based performance standards were identified as some of the data that could be used to validate elements of the primary agent training program and the program's graduation requirements. A research program was devised to assess the relationship between each element of the primary agent training program content to the special agent job analysis results and performance rating criteria. The program was designed to provide the agency's academy with information concerning the relationships between existing elements of the training program and, if results so indicated, to make recommendations for changes in relative emphasis of the various elements of the training program's course content. In addition, the program included a long-range follow-up of academy graduates (a longitudinal study) that would empirically determine the predictive value of training performance scores on subsequent performance evaluation ratings.

In detail, the study effort was designed to produce a special agent job requirements training document. The project started with the establishment of a job analysis for the cadets. This job analysis incorporated many of the job elements found in postacademy job assignments, together with job elements specific to persons in primary training status. This document was designed to provide performance criteria for periodic appraisals of cadet job performance, not unlike those that would be used annually during their career with the agency. The performance work plan, just like the one in use for all special agents, provided for evaluative ratings. As used, the ratings provided quantitative data for cadet review board determinations as to the cadet's suitability.

The project plan called for intensive data collection. For each cadet, demographic data were obtained. Such information included the geographic area (field division) from which the cadet was recruited, educational background (specifically academic major and degrees earned), prior law enforcement experience, age, gender, and ethnic information. Training was considered a variable, and data to be collected included the cadets' performance appraisal ratings, information as to if and why a review board was convened and the disposition thereof, class standing if the cadet graduated, or if the cadet did not graduate, the reason why. On-the-job (postgraduation) data to be collected included first duty station and assignment, performance appraisal ratings for the first 2 years, and awards or promotions. If the employee was no longer in the agency, the reasons for leaving were noted.

The plan for data analysis used the demographic variables as predictors of all other measures, and the training variables as predictors of on-the-job measures. Correlations between training performance appraisal measures, review-board-related variables, and class standing or reason for not graduating also would be obtained. It was anticipated that the analyzed data would point to needed course content or curriculum modification. In addition the validation data would be useful in justifying selection and training criteria as BFOR should such a need arise.

This concept appears to be a promising method of demonstrating validity of an integrated selection, training, and performance evaluation program. It is illustrative of the linkage between multiple validity determinants. All of the training program and curriculum requirements are validated against independently validated performance standards for working personnel. Such a framework allows, at the same time, for selection criteria to be validated against both valid training and valid actual job performance criteria.

The changing face of law enforcement makes it incumbent upon police agencies to ensure that its members are kept abreast of changing requirements of the job that directly affect who should do the job, and how it should be done. Additionally, increasing use of new technology can be particularly threatening to departments in danger of becoming obsolete in their ability to respond to changing social norms and increasing sophistication of criminals. The result is the need for a continually evolving organizational capacity to meet changing requirements. The comprehensive program just described is an amalgamation of recognized systems development elements, capable of enhancing the quality of recruits and ensuring their capability to perform.

Some Final Thoughts About the Meaning of Validity

Psychologists who develop tests have to be concerned with validity; psychologists who use tests in screening must also be concerned about it, even beyond the test parameters revealed in the instruments' manuals. When tests (or clinical judgment for that matter) are used to select individuals for entry or promotion within an organization there must be established criteria against which the decision-making process is validated. The primary and perhaps the only justifiable concern is whether the test actually measures or predicts what it has been designed to measure or predict, and whether decision making based on that test or any other means of personnel selection can be justified both scientifically and legally. The question that must be answered is whether an employment decision made on the basis of the test results can be justified by business necessity. There is widespread recognition that the business necessity of selection criteria can best be established by job and task analysis methods. Job analysis establishes what services or products are provided by job incumbents; what tasks must be performed to provide them; the knowledge, skills, and abilities needed to perform them; and organizational and environmental constraints that facilitate and inhibit performance of the task. Task analysis describes the way the tasks are performed by the incumbent alone or in combination with a work crew, and with or without tools or other equipment in the working environment.

Conceptually, the issue of validity becomes an intertwined process that can be thought of in terms of a flow chart. As depicted in Fig. 4.2, job and task analysis provide criteria for validating job and task performance appraisal systems. Job and task performance criteria in turn provide the basis for validating the process by which positions are filled from a pool of potential incumbents. As discussed earlier in this chapter, the screening process considers a variety of personal characteristics such as knowledge, skills, abilities, experience, prior job performance, psychological suitability, and other factors, all of which have been established to be justified by business necessity.

Although personnel decision making is properly based on assessment of the personal characteristics of potential job incumbents, the predictability of such a selection process is limited because the underlying analysis validating the processs fails to take explicit organizational variables into account. Figure 4.2 schematically incorporates a process parallel to that previously described for linking organizational performance to job and task performance, and for incorporating organizational character and culture into the validity matrix.

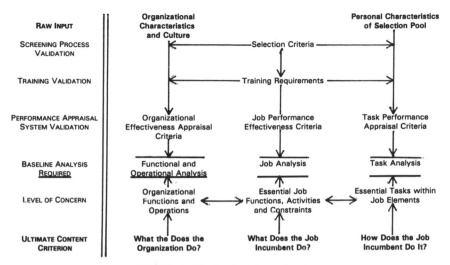

FIG. 4.2. Validation interdependencies.

Just as task analyses depend on determinations of significant tasks generated by job analysis, job analyses should depend on knowledge of the organization in which the job is embedded. An analysis of the organization's mission, function, and significant operations is needed to determine which job and task elements are essential. Essentiality of duties implicit in a job is a factor that may be used to determine whether an impairment interfering with performance of a duty may be used to disqualify a job applicant without violating the ADA. An analysis of the organization's functions and operations may also be used to assist in determination of whether an activity is essential to the job under investigation, or whether the duty can be assigned to another person holding a similar or different position. Therefore organizational, functional, and operational analyses may be instrumental in establishing measures of organizational effectiveness criteria, much as job analyses may be used to establish individual job performance criteria.

The ability to meet organizational performance criteria is further influenced by the organization's characteristics and its culture, factors that are particularly salient in police organizations. Indeed, the current trend from traditional policing methods to problem-oriented and other forms of community policing can be expected to induce changes in the way police agencies interact internally and with society at large. These changes can, and in some cases already have, influenced changes in departmental missions and operations. They have mandated the creation of new standards of performance and behavior of police personnel, and of selection and training criteria in at least one major city's police department. The question police managers and police psychologists must now face is whether existing selection and training criteria continue to have the same degree of validity in the face of changing concepts of policing and in the face of parallel changes in job performance criteria resulting from these new concepts.

CONCLUSIONS

Psychologists interested in working with law enforcement agencies and police counterparts alike must recognize that there are many influences on police behavior, and that reliable performance cannot be assured by any single factor. Effective policing requires a sophisticated understanding of the needs of the populations served, as well as the service providers. Psychologists may be able to contribute meaningfully to a number of factors that are involved in reliable performance on the job, but in isolation, the effort can easily be undone elsewhere. There must be an integrated concept of involvement that marries validation to each initiative that could have an adverse impact if not properly conducted. Because the environments (both community and police) are not static, there must be means with which to sustain awareness of effectiveness, as today's procedures may not work well in the future. Finally, there should be efforts to account for as many of the possible influences on reliable performance as possible. This chapter has addressed selection and training as ideally being very compatible, mutually enhancing elements. Just the same, either could be negated by other, potentially stronger factors; potentially, everything counts. Equating either selection alone or training alone to successful performance has yet to be demonstrated. The needs of communities served by the police in the 21st century are best understood in terms of a multifaceted personnel preparation capability in which selection, training, and caring for the force are well integrated and mutually complementary.

ACKNOWLEDGMENT

The authors gratefully acknowledge the invaluable assistance rendered by Cathie Murensky in reviewing a draft of this chapter, and for her invaluable recommendations for additions to the original draft.

REFERENCES

Azen, S. P., Snibbe, H. M., & Montgomery, H. R. (1973). A longitudinal predictive study of success and performance of law enforcement officers. *Journal of Applied Psychology, 57*(2), 190–192.

Casico, W. F. (1975). Accuracy of verifiable biographic information blank responses. *Journal of Applied Psychology, 66*, 664–670.

Crawford, K. S., & Wiskoff, M. F. (1988). *Screening enlisted accessions for sensitive military jobs* (PERS-TR-89-001). Monterey, CA: Defense Personnel Security Research and Education Center.

Director of Central Intelligence. (1987, November). *Minimum personal security standards and procedures governing eligibility for access to sensitive compartmentalized information* (DCI Directive No. 1/14). Washington, DC: Author.

Equal Employment Opportunity Commission. (1978). Adoption by four agencies of Uniform Guidelines on Employee Selection Procedures. *Federal Register, 43*, 38290–38315.

Equal Employment Opportunity Commission. (1979). Adoption of questions and answers to clarify and provide a common interpretation of the Uniform Guidelines on Employee Selection Procedures. *Federal Register, 44*, 11996–12009.

Gebhardt, D. L., Crump, C. E., & Schemmer, F. M. (1985). *Development and validation of physical performance tests, medical guidelines, and fitness programs for firefighters and police officers.* Bethesda, MD: Advanced Research Resources Organization.

Kurke, M. I. (1991). Dishonesty, corruption, and white-collar crime: Predicting dishonesty in the workplace. *Forensic Reports, 4*, 149–162.

Landy, F. J. (1989). *Psychology of work behavior.* Belmont, CA: Brooks/Cole.

Landy, F. J., & Farr, J. L. (1983). *The measurement of work performance.* London: Academic Press.

Lautenschlager, G. J. (1994). Accuracy and faking of background data. In G. S. Stokes, M. D. Mumford, & W. A. Owens (Eds.), *Biodata handbook: Theory, research and use of biographical information in selection and performance prediction* (pp. 391–419). Palo Alto, CA: CPP Books.

Leake, S. A. (1988, November). *Basic issues in the psychological screening of sensitive classes: Screening-in versus screening-out.* Paper presented at the Med-Tox Conference for Psychological Screening and Physical Disability Testing of Police, Firefighters and Correction, Santa Ana, CA.

Moray, N. (1994). Error reduction as a systems problem. In M. S. Bogner (Ed.), *Human error in medicine* (pp. 67–92). Hillsdale, NJ: Lawrence Erlbaum Associates.

Sharf, J. C. (1994). The impact of legal and equal employment opportunity issues on personal history inquiries. In G. S. Stokes, M. D. Mumford, & W. A. Owens (Eds.), *Biodata handbook: Theory, research and use of biographical information in selection and performance prediction* (pp. 351–390). Palo Alto, CA: CPP Books.

Society for Industrial and Organizational Psychology. (1987). *Principles for the validation and use of personnel selection procedures.* College Park, MD: Author.

Sokol, R. J., & Reiser, M. (1973, July). Training police sargeants in early warning signs of emotional upset. *Mental Hygiene*, pp. 303–307.

Uniform Crime Reports Section. (1992). *Killed in the line of duty: A study of selected felonious killings of law enforcement officers.* Washington, DC: Federal Bureau of Investigation.

Wattendorf, G. E. (1993). Avoiding liability for failure to protect. *The Police Chief, 60*(3), 49–50.

Wiskoff, M. F., Parker, J. P., Zimmerman, R. A., & Sherman, F. (1989). *Predicting school and job performance of marine security guards* (PERS-TRT-90-003). Monterey, CA: Defense Personnel Security Research and Education Center.

CHAPTER FIVE

Legal Issues Regarding Police Psychology

Catherine L. Flanagan
Forensic Psychological Services

This chapter presents the current status of the field of police and public safety psychology. Legal issues are explored and relevant legislation and case law are brought into the discussion as appropriate. An attempt is made to forecast where police psychology will be in the 21st century.

Despite the fact that the 1990s have been a challenging time—perhaps the most challenging time in the history of police psychology—the spirit of this chapter is one of optimism. In my opinion, the field of police psychology is alive and well. In fact, there exists a greater need than ever for the expertise of the psychologist who specializes in delivery of psychological services to high-risk occupations.

The decade of the 1990s appears to be a harbinger of great change in the field. Police and public safety psychology is growing at a tremendous rate, and practitioners are continuing to work toward developing and refining the tools of the profession. Setbacks have occurred and there has been a rather large amount of police psychologists leaving the field. At the same time, however, other psychologists are entering the field in large numbers. Despite these setbacks, police psychology has built a foundation that is sturdy enough to survive the challenges of the 1990s.

When the occurrences of the 1990s are placed into their proper perspective, one realizes how fortunate practitioners are to be working in police psychology at a time when so many new, exciting developments are taking place. There is the opportunity to make great strides in the field. The future of police psychology will be exciting and the pace of growth will be greater than it has ever been in the history of the field. What I envision is a broadening of the services police psychologists offer to law enforcement agencies. If nothing else is accomplished in this chapter, I would like to leave the reader with a sense of optimism regarding police psychology in the 1990s.

It is mainly from my perspective as former chair of the Police and Public Safety Psychology Section of Division 18, Psychology in Public Service, of the American Psychological Association (APA), that this chapter is written. As former chair, I am in the position of being in the center of what occurs in the field. It is in this light that opinions are offered regarding the direction of police psychology in the 21st century.

Rather than approach this chapter from a legal review perspective, I have chosen to discuss the most important issues that presently impact the practice of police and public safety psychology. In addition, an attempt is made to foresee which issues will do so in the future.

In looking back, I find it interesting that in an article entitled "Legal Issues between Psychology and Law Enforcement" in 1986, I spoke of the state of flux characterized by opinion and debate in the field.

In the introduction to that article, I wrote: "Law enforcement psychologists are experiencing a growing need to be conversant with legal issues and decisions that impinge upon them" (Flanagan, 1986, p. 1).

I wrote about the difficulty of the task for law enforcement psychologists and offered the opinion that this was due to both the newness of the field and the fact that a theoretical base was still being developed.

POLICE PSYCHOLOGY TODAY

Years later, the situation is similar to that in 1986. Many of the same problems still exist. Perhaps practitioners needed time to digest the situation they found themselves in. However, I sense a positive movement in the field. I see a change and growth in police psychology. This growth has already begun and, in my opinion, will continue into the next century.

The basis of our strength and professionalism lies in a combination of police psychology, forensic psychology, and industrial/organizational psychology. That is, the police psychologist must be able to combine what is needed from each specialty in order to function in the field. The police psychologist can no longer only rely on clinical knowledge about this specialty. This might appear to be an immense task, but it is one that is already under way.

I can remember back to the days when I worked as a staff psychologist at the New York City Police Department and the position of police psychologist began as predominantly clinical in nature. Today, one cannot function properly in the field as a clinician only. Other areas of expertise are needed.

Police managers will benefit from using the services of police psychologists who have a background that is sufficient to advise them of psycholegal issues with which they might have to contend. In addition to clinical knowledge, the police psychologist practicing today needs to have a knowledge of what legal issues impact his or her area of practice. The wise police psychologist functions with a view toward defending all services provided to an agency in a court of law or before federal commissions, such as the Equal Employment Opportunity Commission. This psycholegal knowledge must be on federal, state, and local levels.

Thus, it is desirable for the police psychologist to acquire sensitivity to such legal issues. In addition, a useful level of competence in the forensic areas related to the role of police psychologist also is essential.

Additionally, a knowledge of job analysis procedures, statistics, and data analysis is essential. See chapter 22 for a detailed discussion of job analysis procedures of which police managers should be aware and that police psychologists must understand and apply to their practice.

This discussion brings to mind one of the problems practitioners have experienced. This problem is a tendency for psychologists to work apart from others and to function in what might be termed "stiff competition" with colleagues. Along with this isolated functioning, there has been a tendency to closely guard one's data primarily due to what may be termed the *business* need for a competitive edge. However now an increased cooperation and sharing among colleagues is evident. Because of the rapid growth in the field, practitioners recognize the need to share data and to help build a greater theoretical base. There is at least one study under way that is attempting to accomplish this It is important that professionals continue to join together to work on the many critical issues that are before them. At the 1992 Police and Public Safety miniconvention in Washington, DC, the beginnings of a movement to unite had clearly begun.

The Police and Public Safety Psychology Section of the American Psychological Association (APA) functions as a Continuing Education Sponsor. We held formal Continuing Education Programs at both the 1993 APA Convention in Toronto, Canada, and the 1994 Convention in Los Angeles, California. The plan is to use the Continuing Education Program as a vehicle for sharing of information and data. This is the beginning of a more formalized training program for those of us in the field of police psychology.

In the 1990s, Police and Public Safety Psychology has been impacted by many fronts, experiencing difficulty from federal legislation, state legislation, and case law. We can either view this as a challenging and exciting time, or give up and leave the field. I suggest that the former is the better course of action to take.

LANDMARK CASES

Several landmark cases come to mind in looking back on police psychology. The important issues these cases dealt with are whether or not a police agency can order an incumbent officer to undergo a psychiatric/psychological evaluation, whether or not psychological evaluation of applicants abrogates their Constitutional rights, and the issue of vicarious liability. These issues will remain important issues into the 21st century. The landmark cases were: (a) *Conte v. Horcher* (1977), (b) *McKenna v. Fargo* (1978), and (c) *Bonsignore v. The City of New York* (1981).

These cases are discussed in this section. Additional cases are discussed after federal legislation has been presented.

Conte v. Horcher (1977)

Conte v. Horcher was heard in the State of Illinois in 1977. The basic issue of the case was whether or not the chief of police issued a "valid and proper" order for a police lieutenant to undergo a mandatory evaluation, also known as a fitness for duty evaluation.

In sum, an incident had occurred where the officer in question was alleged to have subdued, with force, a man who was in police custody. The court ruled that the chief was within his scope of authority to order such an examination in order to remain informed about the officers' ability to perform their duties. The case of *People ex rel. Ballinger v. O'Connor* (1957) was cited in support of the court's decision.

McKenna v. Fargo (1978)

This was a Jersey City, New Jersey, case in which questions arose regarding psychological testing for firefighters. Despite the fact that this case involved firefighters, the decision has been cited in court cases regarding other high-risk occupations including policing.

This civil rights action alleged that it was unconstitutional for Jersey City to require psychological screening for the position of firefighter. The District Court reasoned that the purpose of the testing was not to determine the orthodoxy of the firefighters' beliefs protected under the First and Fourteenth Amendments. Therefore, the court held that the testing did not infringe on these Constitutional rights.

Bonsignore v. The City of New York (1981)

At the time *Bonsignore v. The City of New York* was decided, I was employed as a staff psychologist at the New York City Police Department in the Psychological Services Unit. I recall the excitement that occurred when we heard the decision. This was an important case that had a great effect on psychological screening for police.

This case dealt with the issue of vicarious liability of employers. It was as a result of this landmark case that employers (e.g., police agencies) could be held responsible for the actions of their employees (e.g., police officers). In addition, employers would be held responsible to demonstrate that they used "reasonable precautions" to avoid hiring and retaining individuals psychologically unsuited for law enforcement positions.

These three cases, along with federal legislation and related cases, have formed the backbone of police psychology into the 1990s. The federal legislation referred to here includes The Civil Rights Act of 1964 and The Rehabilitation Act of 1973. A brief review of these laws is provided and I then proceed to more recent developments.

The Civil Rights Act of 1964

Title VII, Section 703h, of The Civil Rights Act of 1964 states that is it not unlawful for employers to use any professionally developed ability or psychological test, provided that such test, its administration, and action based on the results is not designed, intended, or used to discriminate because of race, color, religion, sex, or national origin. It also upholds that any test that has an adverse impact on employment opportunities of any race, sex, or ethnic group is illegal, unless justified by business necessity. Among the cases that deal with these issues are *Robinson v. Lorillard Corp.* (1971) and *United States v. Georgia Power Company* (1973).

Pursuant to Title VII, the Equal Employment Opportunity Commission issued *Uniform Guidelines on Employee Selection Procedures* in 1984. Under these guidelines, the use of any test that adversely affects hiring, promotion, or any other employment opportunity of classes protected by Title VII constitutes discrimination unless:

(a) the test has been validated and evidences a high degree of utility,
(b) persons acting upon the results of the test can demonstrate that alternative suitable hiring, transfer or promotion procedures are unavailable for use (*29 Code of Federal Regulations*, 1984, Section 1607.3).

At that time, the federal government had already taken a stand and advocated employment testing procedures that were job related. The government held that careful job analysis be conducted, that tests be selected on the basis of specific job-related criteria, that any screening and interviewing be job related, and validation of tests include norms that are representative of minority group members. *The New York State Correction Law* (Section 754) emphasizes the job relatedness of employment evaluation.

The Rehabilitation Act of 1973

The Rehabilitation Act of 1973 protects handicapped individuals' equal protection rights. Section 504 of the law (*29 USCS Sect. 794*) states:

> No otherwise qualified handicapped individual in the United States, as defined in section 7(7) [29 USCS Sect. 706(7)], shall, solely by reason of his handicap, be excluded from the participation in, be denied the benefits of, or be subjected to discrimination under any program or activity receiving Federal financial assistance or under any program or activity conducted by any Executive agency or by the United States Postal Service.

Cases related to this law have focused on the issue of whether an individual is "otherwise qualified" for a position despite any disability he or she might have. For example, in *Duran v. Tampa* (1978), it was ruled that rejection of a police officer candidate because of childhood epilepsy was in violation of the candidate's equal protection rights under the Rehabilitation Act.

In *Simon v. St. Louis County* (1981), a police officer paraplegic was found not "otherwise qualified." In fact, police officer position requirements were ruled to be "reasonable, legitimate, and necessary" requirements for all positions within the department.

Unforeseen legislation in the fields of psychology and police psychology came by surprise in the early 1990s. The legislation that has had great impact on the field of psychology is the Americans with Disabilities Act of 1990 and the Civil Rights Act of 1991.

Although I firmly believe that efforts are being made to overcome the problem, I think there still is a serious problem in the practice of psychology today, mainly in personnel screening. This exists especially for those psychologists conducting employment screening in the area of high-risk occupations. What has occurred is that the legislature, probably with good intentions, has passed into law acts that have a great impact on the practice of psychology in ways that the lawmaking body never understood or would have foreseen. The admirable intent of the legislature was to ensure that individual and group rights are not abrogated. However, in its attempts to avoid discrimination, the government has moved into an area where a vast amount of additional knowledge about psychology is required. In attempting to protect individual rights, the government has, in effect, added bias to some of the testing procedures and has almost rendered the tools of the psychologist less useful. Thus, although the goals were admirable, the route taken to attain these goals was uninformed. It has only been the great educative movement of all of psychology that has prevented this from occurring.

In my attempts to figure out what has occurred, I have reached the unpleasant conclusion that psychologists failed to educate legislators prior to their enactment of these laws. Psychologists did not foresee the wave of the future and did not see the need to unite, share data, build a stronger theoretical base for work, and take a proactive stand rather than a reactive stand. Practitioners need to be exposed to the media and to the public and not merely remain in offices working. With this in mind, the following major legislation is discussed: The Americans with Disabilities Act of 1990 and The Civil Rights Act of 1991.

The Americans With Disabilities Act of 1991

The Equal Employment Opportunity Commission (EEOC) is the agency responsible for enforcing the provisions of the Americans with Disabilities Act (ADA) as they relate to employment cases brought against any "entity" or employer, except for federal agencies. The ADA went into effect on July 26, 1992 for employers with 25 or more employees and on July 26, 1994 for employers with 15 to 25 employees.

Background. The Commission issued a proposed rule and sought comments regarding the Americans with Disabilities Act on February 28, 1991. When it became evident that a problem existed, a movement emerged in police psychology.

Two task forces or committees were formed to work on the ADA. One committee was formed from the Police and Public Safety Psychology Section of Division 18, Psychologists in Public Service, of APA. A second committee was formed from the Psychological Services Section of the International Association of Chiefs of Police (IACP). Both were chaired by the author.

The committees, still in existence, are broad based and consist of experts in the fields of police psychology, psychological testing, and forensic psychology. Committee membership is similar, but not identical, for the two committees. Members are Vesta Gettys, Robin Inwald, Michael Roberts, Ellen Scrivner, and James Shaw.

After months of work reviewing legislation and practices in the field, two documents were submitted to the Commission. These documents addressed the needs of police psychology. (See *Comments on the Equal Employment Opportunity Commission's Proposed Regulations to Implement Title I for the Americans with Disabilities Act of 1990,* dated April 19, 1991.)

The EEOC published its final regulations on July 26, 1991 and made few changes in the final rule. Because of ambiguity in the regulations, additional clarification is still being sought.

In December 1991, an article by the author entitled "The Americans with Disabilities Act and Police Psychology" appeared in *The Police Chief.* A consensus document prepared by the IACP's Psychological Services Section appeared beside the article.

The article was written to provide guidance on the effect of the ADA on police psychology. The following major points regarding the Committees' beliefs were made in the article:

1. Psychological tests could be conducted even if they screen out persons with mental disabilities.
2. Psychological screening could be conducted before a conditional offer of employment is made by an agency.
3. Questions relating to past alcohol use or abuse and drug use or abuse and criminal activity in the drug area should be permitted as long as they are an essential component of psychological screening for high-risk occupations.

These conclusions were based on a large amount of information. Overall, they were based on the purpose of psychological screening for high-risk occupations, the business necessity for comprehensive screening, and the job-relatedness of test instruments and evaluation procedures used.

The ADA extends the provisions of the Rehabilitation Act of 1973, under which most police agencies were already covered. It was concluded that the ADA requires clarification rather than substantial procedural changes in the work of police psychologists. It appeared that police and public safety psychologists serving high-risk occupations would be able to practice within the ADA with minimal, if any, changes in current practice.

The language in ADA is explicit in these areas in the following Sections in the Appendix: Section 1630.10, Section 1630.2r, Section 1630.2q, and Section 1630.15.

In Section 1630.10, "Qualification standards, tests, and other selection criteria," it is stated that:

> It is unlawful for a covered entity to use qualification standards, employment tests or other selection criteria that screen out or tend to screen out an individual with a disability . . . on the basis of disability, unless the standard, test or other selection criteria, as used by the covered entity, is shown to be job-related for the position in question and is consistent with business necessity.

In Section 1630.2r, "Direct Threat," it is stated that "Direct Threat means a significant risk of substantial harm to the health or safety of the individual or others that cannot be eliminated or reduced by reasonable accommodation."

In Section 1630.2q, the term *qualification standard* is defined as "the personal and professional attributes including the skill, experience, education, physical, medical, safety and other requirements established by a covered entity as requirements which an individual must meet in order to be eligible for the position held or desired."

In Section 1630.15, "Defenses," (b2), "Direct threat as a qualification standard," it is stated that "the term 'qualification standard' may include a requirement that an individual shall not pose a direct threat to the health or safety of the individual or others." This concept of direct threat as a qualification may be extended to psychological screening as a qualification standard. The psychological evaluation is a job-related qualification standard.

In accordance with the guidelines for pre-employment screening adopted by the Psychological Services Section of IACP, these evaluations are used in conjunction with other tests or requirements for job applicants. The psychological evaluation is one part of a very complicated application process and is not conducted as a pass or fail examination. In 1991, the Section adopted guidelines for psychological fitness for duty evaluations.

It was agreed that psychological testing is to be used to identify personality traits. It is very important to clarify that the EEOC regulations (Section 1630.2h) specifically omit from the definition of an impairment "common personality traits such as poor judgment or a quick temper."

The psychological examination is conducted for the purpose of identifying individuals who are unsuited for employment in high-risk positions on the basis of inappropriate personality traits or behavioral patterns.

Thus, psychological examinations are clearly job related, clearly a business necessity, and clearly are necessary to identify individuals likely to pose a direct threat to others because of behaviors and personality traits that are incompatible with the job of a police officer.

Questions related to past alcohol or drug use or mental illness history are used by a majority of police psychologists in specific standardized tests and in the psychological interview. The justification for this type of inquiry is that extensive research in the public safety field has demonstrated that admissions of behavior, focusing on alcohol or drug use and criminal activity, are significant predictors of poor performance in public safety positions (Inwald, Roberts, & Kaufman, 1991).

The ADA protects persons who have recovered from alcohol or drug addiction. Therefore, it is essential that any hiring decision must not use the admission of past drug or alcohol use as the sole criterion for exclusion, if that person is "recovered." The person's background and other factors (such as employment history) that might impact his or her suitability for the position in question must be thoroughly reviewed and an individual assessment made. Any hiring decision must not use the admission of past mental illness as the sole criterion for exclusion. Other factors that might impact the individual's suitability for the position must be evaluated.

In summary, the committees concluded that sufficient justification exists for placing the psychological examination and interview prior to a conditional offer of employment, for asking questions related to psychological and behavioral problems, and for using the most reliable and valid testing methods available for pre-employment and postemployment screening in high-risk occupations (Flanagan, 1991; Flanagan & Gettys, 1991).

On May 12, 1992, the IACP review committee sent a second document to the EEOC. This document was entitled, "Information Sheet on Definition of 'Medical Examinations or Inquiries' " and was addressed to Peggy Mastroianni, Counsel, Director of EEOC Policy Division. Because it was known that the Commission was in the process of compiling its definition of *medical examinations or inquiries* under ADA, the rationale for exclusion of certain psychological examinations from the definition was discussed.

The approach taken was to compile a list of factors in order to help clarify different types of psychological evaluations. We stated that the definition of medical examinations or inquiries should be based on:

- The intent of the psychological evaluation.
- The purpose of the psychological evaluation.
- The ways in which the psychological tests are used, rather than the tests themselves.
- The use of diagnostic categories, such as *DSM–IIIR*.
- The location of the evaluation (for example, whether the evaluation takes place in a personnel division versus a medical office).

A distinction was made between police psychological screening where diagnoses are not made and the classic medical model where diagnostic labeling of conditions according to the *DSM–III* model occurs.

It was stated that psychological evaluations are medical if the intent of the assessment is to diagnose or label according to the *DSM–III* model, the purpose of the evaluation is to find if a disability exists or to trace its etiology, the evaluation is conducted in a medical office, and the evaluation is tied to classic disabilities.

The position taken was that prehire psychological evaluations should not be classified as medical and should be permitted prior to a conditional offer of employment. It was explained that the purpose of these evaluations is to identify job-related traits and characteristics that would interfere with the performance of essential job functions and are based on business necessity. Such behavior patterns or behavioral traits and characteristics predict poor police and public safety officer performance. It was further pointed out that "common personality traits such as poor judgment or a quick temper where these are not symptoms of a mental or psychological disorder" are excluded from the definition of the term *impairment* in the ADA Interpretive Guidelines (at 35741).

Also cited was the case of *Daley v. Koch* (1989), discussed later.

During mid-January 1993, a letter arrived from the EEOC in response to the medical examinations paper. The letter was described as "an informal discussion" of the issues raised by the task force and not an official opinion of the EEOC. The letter stated that the Commission did not expect to state whether specific psychological tests are medical, but rather, similar to the task force's general approach, to provide factors that must be considered in determining whether a particular examination is medical. Whether psychological tests are medical may depend on the particular examination. A distinction was made between tests that discover disabilities and tests that explore job-related knowledge, skills, abilities, and other attributes.

It appeared from this letter that tests such as the Minnesota Multiphasic Personality Inventory (MMPI) could only be used after a conditional offer of employment has been made to an applicant, unless the Commission would accept the use of printouts without diagnostic labels. At that point, a two-stage process where the applicant's suitability would be assessed preoffer and stability would be assessed postoffer seemed feasible.

The EEOC's Enforcement Guidance Number 915.002 dated May 19, 1994 is conclusive. The Commission's instructions to its investigators appear to give them some latitude in their evaluations. They are instructed to evaluate inquiries on a case-by-case basis to determine whether they are disability-related. It states: "In many cases, a combination of factors will be relevant in the investigator's analysis of whether a procedure or test is a medical examination. In some cases, one factor may be enough for an investigator to determine that a procedure or test is medical" (p. 29). It also states that:

> The investigator should consider the following factors, among others, in making a recommendation concerning whether a particular test or procedure is a medical examination:
> - Whether the procedure or test is one that is administered by either a health care professional (doctors, nurses, psychologists and other mental health professionals, physical and occupational therapy professionals, and others in the health care field) or someone trained by a health care professional;
> - Whether the results of the procedure or test are interpreted by either a health care professional or someone trained by a health care professional;
> - Whether the procedure or test is designed to reveal the existence, nature, or severity of an impairment, or the subject's general physical or psychological health;
> - Whether the employer is administering the procedure or test for the purpose of revealing the existence, nature, or severity of an impairment, or the subject's general physical or psychological health;
> - Whether the procedure or test measures physiological or psychological responses of an individual, as opposed to the individual's performance of a task;
> - Whether the procedure or test would normally be administered in a medical setting (e.g., a health care professional's office, a hospital). (p. 28)

In *Daley v. Koch* (1989), the court ruled that character traits did not amount to a disabling mental condition within the meaning of the Rehabilitation Act of 1973. In this case, a New York City Police officer candidate was rejected because the applicant had shown "poor judgment, irresponsible behavior and poor impulse control." The court cited the landmark case of *Forrisi v. Bowne* (1986) and held that:

> (The) appellant's personality traits could be described as commonplace; they in no way rise to the level of an impairment. . . . The court rules that "poor judgment, irresponsible behavior and poor impulse control" do not amount to a mental condition that Congress intended to be considered an impairment which substantially limits a major life activity and therefore a person having those traits or perceived as having those traits cannot be considered a handicapped person within the meaning of the Act. If appellant had been perceived by the police department to be suffering from an impairment which substantially limits a major life activity, whether or not in reality he had no impairment, than he might qualify for relief under the Rehabilitation Act. However, it is clear from the facts that the police department never considered appellant to be suffering from an impairment which substantially limits a major life activity and did not diagnose appellant as having any disorder.

The court continued:

> Appellant was screened for the job of police officer and found to hold personality traits that made him unsuitable for the position. Appellant does not qualify as a handicapped person under the Act simply because he was rejected for employment by the police department.

Civil Rights Act of 1991

The EEOC is the administering body that interprets the Civil Rights Act of 1991. As with the ADA, there are again major questions regarding interpretation of this law.

The following appear to be the problematic paragraphs for police and public safety psychology:

> (l) It shall be an unlawful employment practice for a respondent, in connection with the selection or referral of applicants or candidates for employment or promotion, to adjust the scores of, use different cutoff scores for, or otherwise alter the results of, employment related tests on the basis of race, color, religion, sex, or national origin.

> (m) Except as otherwise provided in this title, an unlawful employment practice is established when the complaining party demonstrates that race, color, religion, sex, or national origin was a motivating factor for any employment practice, even though other factors also motivated the practice.

As a result of the Act, another task force has been formed through the Police and Public Safety Psychology Section of the APA, with Ellen Scrivner as Chair. There has been discussion that score adjustment may be permitted when the adjustments are part of the test and used for prediction accuracy and that what is not permitted would be adjusting the scores after the fact to affect race or sex—an unacceptable procedure. However, this is not to be considered as fact, and we must await further information from the EEOC on this matter.

Soroka v. Dayton-Hudson (1991)

The last case to be discussed here is that of *Soroka v. Dayton-Hudson.* Employers can expect a growing number of cases where the focus is whether or not employment testing and other screening procedures are an invasion of the applicant's right to privacy. Most of these cases regarding privacy have focused on drug testing. However, the *Soroka* case in California is a case in which test items relating to religion, bodily functions, and political beliefs were seen as invasive. High-risk occupations are excluded from the decision. The case has been settled out of court and thus leaves many unanswered questions.

CONCLUSION

In light of all of this, it is apparent that the field of police and public safety psychology is undergoing many changes. The field will not only survive, it will provide a better work product. Psychological tests and interviews must be job related and consistent with business necessity. The author suggests that psychological evaluations be placed postoffer. There exists serious concern that the mere fact that a psychologist is involved in the evaluation renders a particular test or procedure a medical examination. In this regard, Example 2 is of importance to the practitioner. The EEOC states:

> *Example 2*: A psychological test is designed to reveal mental illness, but R states that it does not give the test for the purpose of disclosing mental illness (e.g., R states that it uses the test to disclose merely tastes and habits). However, the test also is interpreted by a psychologist, and is routinely used in a clinical setting to provide evidence that can be used to diagnose mental health (e.g., whether an applicant has paranoid tendencies, or is depressed). Under these facts, this test would be considered a "medical examination." (p. 29)

It is recommended that agencies review their job requirements to ensure that they are directly related to the ability to perform the essential functions of the job in question. These essential functions should be identified in writing prior to implementing the hiring procedure.

It is imperative that police psychologists and employers have very clear statements of how personality characteristics are related to business necessity. Job analyses and job descriptions must be based on research that demonstrate job-relatedness and business necessity.

The 21st century will be a time when those police psychologists with the greatest knowledge in the area of psycholegal issues, clinical issues, and industrial/organizational issues will be in the greatest demand. The police manager would do best by using the services of these multidimensional, multitalented specialists.

REFERENCES

Bonsignore v. The City of New York, 521 F. Supp. 394 (1981).

Comments from the IACP Psychological Services Section Regarding the Americans with Disabilities Act (ADA). (1991, October 7). Psychological Services Section, International Association of Chiefs of Police.

Comments on the Equal Employment Opportunity Commission's Proposed Regulations to Implement Title I for the Americans with Disabilities Act of 1990. (1991, April 19). ADA Review Committee, Psychological Services Section, International Association of Chiefs of Police.

Comments on the Equal Employment Opportunity Commission's Proposed Regulations to Implement Title I for the Americans with Disabilities Act of 1990. (1991, April 19). ADA Review Committee, Police and Public Safety Psychology Section, Division 18, Psychologists in Public Service, of the American Psychological Association.

Conte v. Horcher, 50 Ill. App. 3d 151 (1977).

Daley v. Koch, 892 F.2d 212; 2nd Cir. (1989).

Duran v. Tampa, 451 F. Supp. 954 (1978).

EEOC Enforcement Guidance: Preemployment Disability-Related Inquiries and Medical Examinations Under the Americans with Disabilities Act of 1990. (1994, May 19). Number 915.002.

Fitness for duty evaluation guidelines. (1991). Psychological Services Section, International Association of Chiefs of Police.

Flanagan, C. L. (1986). Legal issues between psychology and law enforcement. *Behavioral Sciences & the Law, 4*(4), 371–384.

Flanagan, C. L. (1991, July). Employment screening and the Americans with Disabilities Act. *NYSPA Notebook, 3*(2).

Flanagan, C. L., & Gettys, V. (1991, Summer). Comments sent to the EEOC on proposed regulations for the Americans with Disabilities Act. *Public Service Psychology,* p. 5.

Forrissi v. Bowne, 794 F.2d 931; 45 Cir. (1986).

Guidelines for providers of pre-employment psychological evaluation services to law enforcement agencies. (1986). Psychological Services Section, International Association of Chiefs of Police.

Inwald, R. E., Roberts, M., & Kaufman, J. C. (1991, July/August). Research demonstrating the need for direct inquiries regarding alcohol use, drug use, and past psychiatric history for predicting public safety, security job performance. *Washington Crime News Service's Criminal Justice Digest, 10*(7).

McKenna v. Fargo, 451 F. Supp. 1355 (1978); U.S. District Court, NJ, May 25, 1978.

People ex rel. Ballinger v. O'Connor, 13 Ill. App. 2d 317 (1957); 142 N.E. 2d 144.
Robinson v. Lorillard Corp., 444 F. 2d 791 (1971).
Simon v. St. Louis County, 656 F. 2d 316 (1981).
Soroka v. Dayton-Hudson Corporation, 13 Cal. App. 4th 192 (1991).
United States v. Georgia Power Co., 474 F. 2d 906 (1973).

CHAPTER SIX

Law Enforcement Psychological Fitness for Duty: Clinical Issues

Anthony V. Stone

Occupational Health Group, Smyrna, GA

The law enforcement psychological fitness for duty (FFD) evaluation is a psychological evaluation of an incumbent law enforcement official to determine whether he or she is psychologically capable of exercising the police role. Usually the subject of the evaluation is a police officer, but it could be a dispatcher, nonsworn technician or jailer, animal control officer, or some other individual in a safety sensitive position within a law enforcement organization. The examination takes place in response to evidence that the employee may not be fit for duty and, therefore, is distinct from other kinds of psychological evaluations of incumbents (e.g., special assignment evaluations, postshooting assessments). The examination often goes further than addressing whether an officer is fit for duty. Under recent law, such evaluations must also address such issues as what interventions must take place before the officer becomes fit or what kinds of accommodations, if any, must be in place to permit the officer to work in spite of the difficulties.

The FFD evaluation lies somewhere at the intersection of risk management, mental health, labor law, and internal discipline. The parties in a police fitness for duty evaluation are characteristically the officer (or nonsworn employee), the department, and the community, all of which may have different concerns and needs. Departments are frequently concerned with such issues as (a) liability for the officer's actions (vicarious liability); (b) physical risk to the officer, other employees, and citizens; (c) the department's reputation; and (d) legal and human concern for the employee's rights regarding his employment.

Citizens' concerns include protection from law enforcement officials whose errors of commission might endanger them or whose errors of omission might leave them unprotected and vulnerable. The officer's concern (and herein reference to officers will refer also to civilian law enforcement officials) characteristically revolve around keeping a job, although this is not always the case. Occasionally officers are aware of a problem and regard the evaluation as an opportunity to get needed help, get transferred to a less stressful assignment, or leave law enforcement.

The FFD is a special kind of psychological evaluation—one that assesses the goodness of fit between individuals and roles. There are many instances in which psychologists are called on to do such evaluations, such as assessments of legal competence to stand trial, ability to have or maintain custody of a child, psychological disability, job-related abilities (pre-employment screening), and fitness for duty. Each one of these examinations asks the psychologist to look at different models against which the fit is to be addressed. In the competency examination, for example, there is is a well-defined competency model, elements of which might include the ability to cooperate with an attorney, understanding of charges and proceedings, and so on. In the custody evaluation, there is a less well-defined parental model. In the disability examination, there is a disability model in which disability is often quite well defined.

FITNESS FOR DUTY AS A DISABILITY EVALUATION

The FFD is a special case of a disability evaluation. As in the case of a disability evaluation, there is a model (i.e., a job description with knowledge, skills, and abilities requirements) against which a police officer is assessed. However, a typical disability examination (of the Social Security variety) asks essentially whether the individual can perform any job in the economy. That is, the issues addressed in the typical disability evaluation are whether the individual posesses the minimal skills to perform work—whether he or she can maintain attention, make basic decisions, meet minimal social demands, follow simple instructions, and so on.

In the law enforcement FFD examination the mental and emotional requirements are more narrowly defined and involve cognitive flexibility, emotional control, sensorimotor skills, lawful behavior, ability to command respect, judgment, interpersonal and communication skills, and a variety of other abilities associated with safety, security of the public, and risk to the department.

Because of its similarity to a FFD evaluation, the disability determination process used by Social Security is worth reviewing. The reason to look at this process is that whereas the Social Security process is well established and standardized, the FFD examination process is not. As a result, the integrity and indeed the legality of the process is often compromised. Thus, one of the purposes of this chapter is to create an argument that a standardized FFD process is desirable and an attainable goal.

In the Social Security process mental disability is well defined, and the method for assessing cases is standardized. Reviewers with defined credentials (licensed psychologists or certified psychiatrists) who have undergone a training program in disability determination review a standard set of forms and a series of medical-psychological records assembled for review. In addition, these reviewers may order additional evaluations from a panel of providers with defined credentials. These providers follow a protocol when assessing disability claimants and provide reports with histories, psychological testing, mental status examinations, and reports of daily activities. Based on a review of this material, the reviewers complete standardized forms that provide a diagnosis and rate functional limitations in work-related areas. A decision about disability follows directly from the ratings.

Unlike that process, law enforcement FFD evaluations are not uniform. Standards have only recently addressed some of the parameters of the evaluations, such as who should do the evaluations. There is no consensus on procedures, what reports should look like, how they should be done, what cutoffs should exist, and what the outcomes might be. To the extent that they are an unstructured activity with few if any rules, all involved with such evaluations are vulnerable, and municipalities for whom they are being conducted are in a catch-22 of being held to a standard under which they do not negligently retain officers but also under which they cannot eliminate officers for psychological dysfunction.

Clearly, the FFD evaluation can be understood as a special case of a disability determination process that lends itself to similar procedures. I would propose that the emphasis in a FFD evaluation be on functional limitations and that these limitations be addressed specifically and concretely by the psychologist. The only purpose for the diagnosis is (a) to provide a rationale for conducting the evaluation in the first place, and (b) to provide the basis for functional impairments.

In other words, the diagnosis provides the basis for exam and the focus for the inquiry regarding functional limitations. Once a diagnosis is made and reported, the focus of the examination should be on job-relevant functional limitations. Thus, an officer would not be considered unfit for duty because of depression. Rather, the officer would be considered unfit because of poor judgment, difficulty tolerating stress, problems with attendance, and so on.

Among other reasons for focusing on functional limitations in the FFD is that the Americans with Disabilities Act (ADA), which now affects all law enforcement agencies, requires that agencies attempt to accommodate persons with disabilities, including mental disabilities. Although much of the detail regarding this law will evolve in court, the concepts embedded within the Act are best addressed by describing functional rather than just diagnostic information. This is because functional information permits agencies to address the requirement in the law that employers make reasonable accommodation. For example, judging that someone could not be accommodated because of poor judgment under stress is different from determining that someone is unfit due to anxiety. Another issue germane to the disability examination and the FFD is the examinee's prognosis. Social Security policies somewhat arbitrarily provide that a person with less than 1 year of subthreshhold functioning does not meet the criteria for benefits. To extend this to the FFD, we would expect that to be considered unfit for duty there is an implied time dimension. How that time dimension is dealt with is discussed later, but it should be said that often, because of anticipated change in an officer's mental condition, the FFD process often goes beyond the disability determination process to include a process of contracting with officers and the agency to rectify problems.

OVERVIEW OF THE FITNESS FOR DUTY EVALUATION

Looking generally at the FFD examination, these are complex, difficult, and highly sensitive examinations. In these examinations psychologists often play the role of investigator, jury, and judge. Further, a law enforcement job is a career, and if found unfit for duty, an individual's ability to ever regain a law enforcement position is often compromised. At the same time, needs of the community and the department to have effective, competent, and psychologically stable officers is also an issue involving lives, reputation, and money, and this should also be regarded as of utmost importance. Therefore, a fitness for duty evaluation should not be undertaken lightly. The department should be willing to spend resources on the evaluation, and the psychologist should perform only a very thorough evaluation.

Thus, the stakes in a FFD are high for both the officer and the department. Errors creating false positives (i.e., a "fit" officer is judged to be unfit) almost invariably mean a ruined career. The opposite kind of error, however, where an unfit individual is allowed to remain in a sworn position, can be deadly or result in significant financial liability to a department. Therefore, the evaluation must be a thorough, detailed, and complete effort performed by psychologists who are familiar with the subtle issues involved in law enforcement. Looking at an extreme case, a brief mental status evaluation by a provider who, for example, is simply certifying someone to return to work after a hospitalization is not a fitness for duty evaluation.

I propose a multistage structure for considering the FFD process. Stage 1 under this structure is called *behaviors of concern* and involves the behaviors and events that gave rise to the evaluation. In Stage 2, *agency assessment*, the department becomes aware of the situation and defines it both as serious and having a psychological component. In Stage 3, the *evaluation phase*, the psychologist evaluates the officer and produces a report. If the officer is not fully fit and is retained with the agency, a Stage 4 exists; a *treatment plan phase* is implemented in which a contracted plan is provided and monitored.

Stage 1: Behaviors of Concern

In this stage a police officer engages in some behavior that calls into question his emotional stability, judgment, or self-control, and this, in turn, sends up a flag to supervisory personnel within the agency (the officer's chain of command, internal affairs, or other persons with agencywide responsibility). A number of behaviors might send up such a flag, including problems with alcohol, excessive force issues, admission to a psychiatric facility, emotional lability, spouse abuse, or bizarre, unusual, or seriously maladaptive behavior.

Clearly, there are a number of reasons for undertaking a FFD. I have sorted my own records from over the past 10 years into categories and have provided a statistical breakdown of my own FFD cases in Table 6.1. As the table shows, the most frequent circumstances giving rise to a FFD evaluation are concerns about excessive aggressiveness. This category of reasons for referral encompasses a broad spectrum of acts involving aggression, use of force, and domestic violence. Examples of this category would involve officers who threaten co-workers, officers whose spouses complain of domestic violence, and officers who seem to have frequent excessive force complaints.

Another broad category of events frequently leading to fitness for duty evaluations is substance abuse, almost invariably alcohol (as most departments are intolerant of illegal drug abuse). Alcohol abusers whose use of alcohol does not become associated with criminal activity are usually regarded as rehabilitation candidates. Officers who abuse other substances, including prescription medication, are typically terminated.

TABLE 6.1
Distribution of Fitness for Duty Referrals by Major Referral Issue

Domestic violence	9.43%
Substance abuse	15.09%
Suspected psychopathology	26.42%
Repeated poor judgment	13.21%
Sexual misconduct	3.77%
PTSD	3.77%
Excessive force issues	18.87%
Miscellaneous	9.43%
Total	100.00%

The third most common area requiring FFD examinations are general mental health problems that emerge on the job. These include threats of suicide, bizarre behavior, depression, and even discharge from mental health facilities where an officer may have admitted him or herself.

Which behaviors are likely to send up the red flag depends on the agency's relationship with the psychologist and their internal policies. Another variable is the existence of so-called *early warning systems* that some agencies have installed to identify at-risk employees. Under these systems, a referral for a psychological review can be relatively automatic when some events or series of events occur (e.g., a set number of excessive force complaints within a specified time frame). Furthermore, some agencies, for example, will send domestic violence cases to the psychologist, whereas others will send it to the Employee Assistance Program and others will maintain that it is a legal problem that should be handled through the courts. There is clearly no right answer on which behaviors should send up red flags, although training of supervisors in recognition of psychological problems is clearly essential.

One caveat at Stage 1 has been mentioned and bears repeating—that is that not all referrals for law enforcement FFD psychological evaluations are police officers. Civilian police employees, including emergency operators (dispatchers) and clerical personnel, are often referred for fitness for duty evaluations. In these cases, the criteria for fitness necessarily changes; however, in my experience severe impairment in operators, for example, can have serious consequences.

Stage 2: Agency Assessment

In this phase, someone within the agency becomes alerted to the officer's problem and the fact that the officer poses a threat to the agency. The behavior comes to the attention of someone in the department through a variety of channels. In some cases, the officer may report difficulties to a supervisor. In other cases, the seemingly problematic behavior comes to the attention of law enforcement personnel, either in one's own jurisdiction or others (e.g., as in the case where the officer is driving under the influence, engaging in domestic violence, and the like). In other instances, there is a formal or an informal early warning system within the agency that brings to the attention of supervisors the employee's behavior, often through direct observation by peers or supervisors.

How this works often differs from agency to agency and can depend on size and internal structure. Frequently, internal affairs is the final common pathway before the psychologist is involved, although it could be the chief's office, the head of personnel for the municipality, or even the head of training. However, in some agencies a supervisor may have direct access to a psychologist who might then, for example, be asked to informally assess the officer for possible referral for fitness for duty.

Typically the request for a FFD evaluation is a formal request, although some agencies simply like to rule something out and ask that a psychologist meet with an officer to make some preliminary determination regarding the need for the full FFD evaluation.

Some agencies have formal policies around FFDs, and others do not. Agencies that do not have formal policies governing FFD are vulnerable on challenges. A formal policy within the agency should provide some uniformity around what circumstances should give rise to an evaluation, who performs FFD evaluations, examiners' access to documents, officers' requirements to comply with the evaluation, and outcomes of evaluations (possible dispositions).

Stage 3: Evaluation Phase

In this stage an evaluator is enlisted to perform a FFD evaluation. Current International Association of Chiefs of Police (IACP) guidelines call for that person to be a licensed psychologist or certified psychiatrist with law enforcement experience. Guidelines do not specify how much experience, and there is not, as yet, credentialing for police psychologists. Thus, the level of experience of evaluators is likely to vary considerably.

Use of providers who lack experience with law enforcement can lead to unpredictable and damaging consequences, yet often such persons are used by unwitting agencies. In a common example, an agency will often let stand a doctor's return to work note even when the doctor has just released the officer from a psychiatric facility and the doctor has no relationship to law enforcement. Consider two other examples.[1] One such evaluation was performed by a physician who declared someone fit for duty based on a brief mental status evaluation. In this case, an officer threatened to deliberately crash his patrol car. He was briefly seen by a nonlaw enforcement psychiatrist who provided a two-paragraph note indicating that the officer had been agitated by an ongoing marital conflict but now had an unremarkable mental status and was therefore fully fit for duty. In a second example, basing his conclusion on a more thorough evaluation, a psychologist declared a sergeant fit for duty; however, the examiner concluded that he could work only in a less dangerous precinct.

Of course, the first example was an inadequate examination given the circumstances and did not at all address the possibility of relapse, any necessary interventions, or the long-term prognosis. The second example yielded a recommendation for an accommodation that would be quite in-

---

[1]Notice to readers: To clarify issues and methods relating to fitness for duty, this chapter contains a number of case examples. None of these employ the real names of individuals, and all examples represent either fictitious events or combinations of a number of different events. No example is, therefore, reflective of the behavior of specific individuals or agencies.

compatible with most law enforcement agencies' internal policies (i.e., substantial restrictions on assignment, having to monitor "dangerousness" of an assignment).

As with a disability examination, the FFD evaluation has two separate objectives: to determine whether a psychological impairment exists, and to determine whether, as a result of the impairment, an officer is unable to perform the requirements of the job (i.e., is functionally impaired vis à vis a police role).

Often in Stage 3 the psychologist is asked to give a reading on a situation, or to give a preliminary assessment. Indeed, it is often helpful to undertake a preliminary assessment. It may be that, based on the preliminary exam, a FFD process can be aborted, thereby saving both parties (the officer and the municipality) from the strain of a FFD evaluation.

The purpose of the preliminary examination (as well as the initial part of the full FFD) is to help address the question of whether an impairment seems to exist and whether it is properly addressed by psychological means. If either answer is negative, the results of the preliminary examination suggest that the mental FFD process be avoided. In other words, the preliminary examination is intended to be a kind of probable cause assessment for a full FFD examination.

Whether or not a preliminary examination is conducted, the first step of the full FFD examination itself is the preliminary review of records. It is frequently most efficient for the examiner to at least begin to review the documents surrounding the referral or to interview key individuals prior to the initial contact with the employee. Such documents could include internal affairs reports, hospital records (in the case where someone was recently discharged), arrest records (where the officer has been arrested), human service agency reports (where domestic violence or child abuse might be an issue), and similar kinds of documents. This preliminary review helps to structure the clinical interview. Additionally, it suggests the test materials that might be appropriate and may point to the need for external consultants where expertise other than the primary examiner's is required. Examples of this might include neuropsychological evaluations and medical consultations.

The second step of the evaluation process is to meet with the officer and immediately obtain releases and waivers so the officer gives informed consent to the evaluation. The parameters surrounding a FFD evaluation are that they are typically done under a direct order so that failure to cooperate would be seen as disobedience and subject to disciplinary action. The language of the informed consent form can make reference to the fact that the officer is ordered to take the examination and that the waiver is not given voluntarily but rather as a condition of employment. The waiver form should be basic and easy to understand. It should specify that the officer is being asked to undergo an evaluation at the request of the agency and that the evaluation is being conducted on behalf of the agency. It should further state that the results of the evaluation will be made available to the agency, to the director of the agency, or his representatives on a need to know basis. It must specifically state that there is no confidentiality during this contact. It is helpful to indicate on the waiver form that the examiner is not providing psychological services to the officer (Appendix A gives an example of a waiver form).

Officers occasionally resist these evaluations and either directly refuse or come equipped with tape-recording devices or wish to have an attorney present during the evaluation. Refusals can be minimized when there are formal internal policies regarding fitness for duty within the agency or when a written direct order is issued to the officer to appear. Some agencies even have officers sign informed consent documents when they are hired, giving the agency the right to perform any needed psychological or medical examination to determine subsequent fitness for duty.

Regarding recording devices or attorneys, I do not permit either such devices or any legal representatives (including union representatives) in my evaluation sessions; however, examiners should obtain their own legal counsel in this area.

Obviously, the content of the evaluation and the procedures used, should reflect the referral issues. It always make sense to conduct a mental status evaluation and to take a history. Beyond that, it is important to go over the officer's point of view in regards to the circumstances that led to the fitness for duty evaluation in the first place. In fact, I generally start my interview with the simple question, "Why are you here?"

Where questions of cognitive efficiency have been raised or where judgment seems impaired, it is appropriate to use tests of cognitive functioning such as the Wechsler or briefer IQ tests with the possibility that the Wechsler may be used if cognitive difficulties are suspected based on the preliminary testing. The Minnesota Multiphasic Personality Inventory (MMPI) is almost invariably appropriate. Of course, the examiner should expect that the officer will be somewhat defensive and even extreme defensiveness certainly does not indicate that serious psychopathology exists. It should go without saying that police officers experiencing fitness for duty evaluations are typically humiliated by the experience, scared of losing their career and strongly motivated to appear to be healthy.

Projective tests can get around some of the limitations of the response set deviance one encounters with the more objective tests; however, findings based on these tests may be harder to defend in court. What I do recommend is a multimethod approach to the assessment. Thus, a number of different ways of approaching the problem should be undertaken and convergence of findings should be reason for suspecting a diagnosis. In my opinion, projective testing alone should not be the basis on which an officer is found unfit for duty.

In addition to testing, IACP guidelines call for evaluators to obtain collateral information and interview sources whenever possible. I would underscore this requirement, as in most cases the issues to be addressed cannot be fully covered without such outside information. It is my experience that relatively few cases involve officers who willingly admit to problems or who exhibit an abnormal mental status. The more typical case is a personality disorder, the diagnosis of which requires collateral information.

It was mentioned earlier that occasionally outside personnel may need to be called in. For example, when the examiner does not have particular expertise in neuropsychology and findings begin to point to neuropsychological deficits, someone skilled in this area should be brought in. It should be assumed that the results of this evaluation can be brought before a court or a governmental commission and it should be remembered that someone's career may rest on the decisions. Hence, no less than the best available expertise should be brought to bear. I consult with the neuropsychologist and have the neuropsychologist prepare a report for me and then I take these findings and translate them into law-enforcement-related functional limitations.

In a perhaps less obvious example, in one occasion an officer was accused of sexual deviance and extortion of sex. In this case, an officer was suspected of having extorted sex from juveniles. For a variety of reasons, this was felt to be a psychological issue rather than a disciplinary issue and one of the ways this was approached was to enlist the help of a clinician skilled in evaluation of sexual deviance and pedophilia. Thus, in this instance, a multimethod approach to sexual deviance was employed including psychological testing, polygraph evidence, plethysmographic evidence, and clinical interview.

Approaches to the FFD sometimes have to be quite creative and on the spot. For example, an officer was said to have had significant acrophobia that would interfere with his ability to handle heights, but the officer denied this. Part of the evaluation of this man was an unannounced episode where he was asked to climb a ladder erected by the municipality's fire department under the direction of fire training personnel.

Once the evaluation is completed, a report is issued to the department. As was stated earlier, the purpose of the report is to address specific functional limitations that are intrinsic to the job of police officer. I have developed a form for this kind of assessment and submit this in addition to the more traditional psychological report to the department. The form, reproduced here as Appendix B, permits rating specific safety-sensitive aspects of the job and also requires a determination about fitness for duty and any accommodations. There is currently a debate regarding whether a more traditional psychological report should accompany the report that narrowly addresses functional issues.

As the law in this area seems to be evolving, the police psychologist should consider consulting an attorney in this matter. Even if a traditional psychological report is not issued to the department, one should be prepared and should be kept in the examiner's secured files. If one is issued to the department, it should be kept in a secure file separate from the personnel file, and access to the file should be restricted to persons with specific need to know.

It was argued earlier that a number of outcomes could evolve from a FFD evaluation. These include the following: (a) fully fit for duty, (b) fit for duty contingent upon some intervention, (c) unfit for duty pending the completion of some intervention, and (d) unfit for duty.

In addition to these outcomes, there have been occasions where fitness for specific duty kinds of questions have been asked. For example, occasionally an officer on a special unit (e.g. SWAT) was asked to be evaluated in regards to fitness for that particular assignment, in which case the determination may be that the officer is unfit for that assignment but fit for other law enforcement duty.

A final consideration here is what happens if an officer is found to be unfit for duty. Should the psychologist provide alternatives for the municipality to consider? The answer to this gets back to the question of policy and law. The ADA regards the employer as the municipality, not the police department. Thus, the municipality would be expected to attempt to accommodate the officer by looking at positions beyond the police department. Because the psychologist is familiar with the (now unfit) officer's abilities, it is reasonable for the municipality to use him or her as a consultant in the process of trying to accommodate the officer. Indeed, I am frequently asked about alternative positions for an unfit officer. Under those circumstances, it is appropriate to obtain the job descriptions and other documents relating to the position, and perhaps even consult with supervisors, before generating an opinion.

Stage 4: Treatment Plan Phase

In light of the Americans with Disabilities Act (ADA), the law enforcement FFD evaluation is no longer limited simply to yes or no questions about fitness for duty. Often the determination is that certain steps must be taken in order for this officer to be fit or to maintain fitness. For example, an officer who has a drinking problem, but otherwise has a good record, might be considered unfit pending completion of an alcohol treatment program, and thereafter fit contingent upon the officer's going into aftercare and taking Antabuse. Thus, it is often the case that some kind of condition be applied to the fitness for duty determination. This might be regarded as an accommodation that the agency can make with regard to the officer's impairment to conform to the requirements of the ADA. If the officer cannot comply with this accommodation (e.g., the officer drops out of treatment, relapses, etc.), then a finding of permanently unfit for duty is warranted and seemingly within the requirements of the ADA.

Where an officer is considered fit for duty contingent on completion of some program or some other kind of intervention, it is often the case that the evaluator develops a complex relationship between the officer, the department, and a treatment provider. The police psychologist should under almost all circumstances avoid entering a therapeutic relationship with someone they have evaluated for fitness for duty.

Once fitness for duty is determined and the officer is found in some way conditionally fit, another aspect of this process involves monitoring of this individual and determining when and if it is appropriate for the officer to return to different levels of status within the agency (e.g., light duty, patrol duty but not narcotics, etc.) Finally, where persons have residual problems or where their severity of their symptoms waxes and wanes, or where they have a chemical abuse problem and relapse, it may be appropriate to redo the fitness for duty evaluation with that in mind.

The period of time during which the department or the psychologist should monitor the officer would, in my opinion, vary with the condition. For example, one public safety worker suffered from diabetes that was in poor control due, in part, to his binging on food. He exhibited organic symptoms on occasion that seemed related to changes in blood sugar. The accommodation that was reached was that the officer would complete a log daily noting blood sugar level and the log was subject to audit by the chain of command and the departmental physician. Because the organic symptoms were disruptive and potentially dangerous, it was determined that such an accommodation would be required as long as the officer worked in a public safety position.

At the other extreme are individuals who go through discreet programs, such as a program of brief therapy. Once the officer has completed the program, monitoring might discontinue as well; however, a relapse of problematic symptoms might be regarded as a basis for another FFD exam or, if it is clear that the individual could not be accommodated further, grounds for termination.

Consider another example of a police officer who has 5 years of experience and goes out drinking one night with friends in a neighboring police jurisdiction. He becomes quite intoxicated and belligerent, and a bouncer asks him to leave, whereupon the officer flashes his badge, makes some vague threats, and displays his gun. This officer is then ejected from the club and becomes increasingly obnoxious to the point that club management calls law enforcement personnel to arrest him.

That is the situation. The department is concerned about the officer's judgment and restraint as well as its own reputation. They felt that they had enough data to dismiss this officer; however, they did refer this for a FFD.

The FFD evaluation consisted of a clinical interview, history, a substance abuse screening inventory, an MMPI, interviews with the officer's chain of command, as well as significant others in his life including his wife and a review of the documents surrounding the incident.

It was determined that this man was not fit for duty, but that he could be considered a good candidate for treatment. Thus, it is at this point that the treatment plan comes into play. It was recommended that, if he were to be retained by the agency, he undergo treatment while being placed on nonenforcement status. Upon completion of the program his fitness for duty could be re-evaluated.

The monitoring of police officers who are in a treatment program is in itself a complex topic. A major concern is to assure that the police psychologist does not have a dual relationship with the officer. In other words, it is inappropriate for the psychologist who will be evaluating the officer's fitness to return to work to simultaneously provide treatment. Such an arrangement will invariably undermine treatment and the return to work assessment. A rare exception might be made when the patient knows in advance what the recommendation will be and waives confidentiality with that in mind. This might be done if the patient were to want to avoid the stresses of a FFD evaluation.

The proper procedure is to refer the officer to an independent provider who will provide the police psychologist with information regarding attendance and participation in treatment and indications when treatment is completed.

The referral to a treatment provider should be done with a written formal treatment plan identifying interventions that may be required, the length of time that these interventions may be required or the conditions under which the requirement will be deemed to have been satisfied. A sample treatment plan is shown in Appendix C.

In addition, the arrangements for any treatment should be elucidated. Waivers and requirements for waivers should be defined in the treatment plan and details as to what will be reported to the department should be described.

Characteristically, the optimal arrangement is for the officer to be referred to a program with which the provider has some kind of a relationship or, if not, the provider should develop a relationship with the treating program. For example, when the issue is an officer's alcohol use, it may be appropriate to place the officer in a treatment program. Returning to work might be seen as contingent on his successfully completing the program and his continuing to work might be contingent on his maintaining sobriety and following aftercare requirements. In my opinion, contact with the treatment provider should be maintained. The provider should notify the police psychologist with information pertaining to dangerousness on the part of the officer. However, other information pertaining to treatment not directly affecting the officer's status should not be sought by the police psychologist.

It is essential to have an arrangement whereby the treatment provider notifies the psychologist if there is some deviation from the contract. When this occurs, the provider should confront the officer and determine whether in fact a formal deviation has taken place, and if so, this would be reported to the department. Otherwise, the contact with the department should be relatively minimal and when the officer has satisfied the requirements, this should be reported that at this point the officer would be considered fit for duty.

Let us now look at some problem cases. One frequently occurring example is the case where a person hovers around some hypothetical fitness for duty line, being fit sometimes but unfit at others. It would also be the case of someone who relapses on alcohol or in other ways. Both of these cases could be handled in one of two ways. First, in the original FFD evaluation, a note can be added to the report indicating that any further instances of this form of psychopathology would be considered sufficient evidence that the officer was nonresponsive to treatment and as such declare him unfit for duty. The other way that this can be handled is to simply indicate that what was seen as perhaps an adjustment disorder, or an acute problem with a good prognosis is now considered to be a more chronic problem and for this reason a second FFD might determine that the officer is unfit for duty.

Consider the situation where the officer is fine so long as he or she is taking psychiatric medications, but demonstrates an unwillingness to take medication, or the case in which the officer is simply noncompliant with treatment. In these instances, it is appropriate to indicate that the officer is simply unfit for duty.

CASE STUDY

To illustrate the fitness for duty process, consider the following fictionalized composite.

The officer in question (whom I will call Officer Jones) is a 29-year-old male, married with one child, who has been a patrolman in this agency of 50 sworn personnel for 5 years. By way of background, he has 1 year of college. His performance up until the events in question has been above average though not exceptional. He had one sustained complaint involving verbal abuse of a subject during an arrest several years prior to the event in question.

The FFD Stage 1 (in which the behavior is exhibited) began several months prior to the referral. The officer's chain of command reported having increasing concerns about this officer during this period. Concerns stemmed from a series of episodes in which the officer expressed a belief that his co-workers were abusing him, teasing him, and being generally disrespectful. Examples of this included his not being invited to a birthday party when other officers were invited. Other officers in this unit also reported privately to the supervisor that they felt extremely uncomfortable with Officer Jones providing backup for them. The supervisors reported that the quality of his arrests was poor, and his productivity was low.

An immediate precipitant occurred when a female whom Jones stopped for driving under the influence complained that the officer asked for her home address, wondered if he could contact her, and even when she said she was married he pressed the issue. When this was brought to his attention, he broke down at internal affairs and cried profusely.

It was at this point that Stage 1 evolved into Stage 2 in the FFD process. The supervisor began the process to initiate the fitness for duty evaluation. In particular, he addressed a memo describing these events to his major who, in turn, brought this to the attention of the administrative chief who determined that a fitness for duty exam would be appropriate. This was ordered consistent with the department regulations. The departmental psychologist was notified, and Jones was ordered to the appointment. He was placed on adminstrative (nonenforcement) status also at this time.

Prior to the conduct of the examination, the psychologist reviewed this memo and also reviewed internal affairs material on the officer as well as his personnel file. He also communicated with the lieutenant regarding some of the events and verified the completeness of the written documents.

Stage 3 of the process began when Officer Jones presented for the FFD evaluation. He was initially quite reticent to sign the waiver forms that were provided to him and was confused as to whether the evaluator was there for his benefit or for the benefit of the department. It took some time to clarify this and eventually the examiner was able to clearly identify that his role was to undertake a neutral examination of this man's ability to effectively perform in the police role.

It eventually came down to the fact this officer had no alternative, as he was ordered into this evaluation through departmental procedures. He thus signed the waiver form.

Officer Jones' history showed a good deal of family psychopathology. The officer was from a broken home, had virtually no contact with his father after about age 4. His mother grew up in extreme poverty and although she was not overtly abusive to him, was an alcoholic and intermittently quite neglectful. He was physically assaulted at one point by one of her boyfriends at age 12.

Officer Jones was something of an isolate in high school, but managed to do acceptably academically and then entered the military for 3 years, where he performed without incident. When he got out of the military, he had several brief jobs and then joined the police department. In that period of his life he married his wife, who at that time was 17, and who was herself an abused individual.

After joining the department, Jones' status as a police officer became the focus of his life. He had no close friends. In the year prior to my seeing him, Jones' marriage deteriorated, and his wife began spending more and more time with her parents. Thus began a period of decompensation for him. He became increasingly withdrawn at work, increasingly agitated and depressed, and incapable of thinking of about anything but his wife leaving him.

The FFD examination itself involved psychological testing and included a Slossen Intelligence Test (as judgment in this matter was an issue). Additional assessment devices included the MMPI, a formal mental status evaluation, a detailed history, and collateral contacts with the officer's wife.

Without going into a great deal of detail regarding results of the psychological, the MMPI yielded a valid profile, although the K scale was somewhat elevated (this is typical in the case of police fitness for duties). There were elevations on Scales 2, 4, 8, and 0, all with the exception of four slightly below 70 and four slightly above 70. Scale six was approximately 65. The Slossen IQ was 105.

Looking at this man's mental status, he presented as a depressed, emaciated, flat individual who was preoccupied, withdrawn, gaunt, and ruminative. His concentration was slightly impaired. Thinking was tangential. He reported problems sleeping and acknowledged that he was not able to concentrate well. He freely admitted his concerns about his wife. It was learned that he was not currently suicidal or homicidal, although he had vague thoughts of suicide but said that he would never hurt himself. He did realize that his behavior was maladaptive and he did feel some discomfort about performing police work, but felt that he remained marginally effective.

The officer's wife cooperated freely with this activity, as she was also aware that things were deteriorating for her husband. She was asked to sign waiver forms indicating her voluntary cooperation in this process and her awareness that the results would be reported to the department.

The wife confirmed that this man was desperate about their relationship. She maintained that she had considered divorce but was not prepared to act on her thoughts at that time. She seemed to genuinely want her husband to get help.

She said that he had not been physically abusive, but at one point he did threaten to hurt her and himself if the relationship could not be patched up. She said that her husband was frequently up at night, pacing the halls, and was preoccupied with their relationship and wrongs done to him at the police department. She also confirmed that a few developments began occurring 6 months prior to the evaluation, although she noted that he was always very dependent on her and became frantic at the thought that she might leave him. She said that he had threatened suicide on several occasions after fights. She also reported that they had been having frequent arguments largely about his extreme jealousy.

The FFD evaluation documented these findings and concluded that the appropriate diagnoses were dysthymia and dependent personality disorder. It was determined that the officer was not fit for duty due to poor concentration, poor judgment, and possible dangerousness toward his wife. Given his initially favorable adjustment to this department, it was also determined that he should be placed on light duty and provided a course of treatment. It was estimated that his prognosis with treatment would be fair and that he should be re-evaluated before being placed back to work.

Stage 4 of the process involved the referral of Officer Jones to a mental health provider and contracting with Jones in this regard. Specifically, a list of three providers was presented to the officer (with varying fee schedules), and he was to choose one within 1 week, and initiate treatment within 2 weeks of the date of signature. The contract specified that the officer was to be in treatment until he was formally released by the therapist. After 2 months he was to be re-evaluated to see if he was fit for duty and, if not, he faced permanent reassignment to a nonsworn position. Jones also agreed to assume financial responsibility for treatment and agreed to sign waiver forms permitting the provider to communicate freely with the FFD examiner.

Also during this phase, Officer Jones' compliance with treatment and progress was monitored. Because he complied with all treatment requirements, he was re-evaluated in 2 months. The re-evaluation involved recontacting key persons (the treating professional, light duty supervisor, wife), retesting with the MMPI, and a clinical interview.

In fact, this officer had not improved substantially in spite of treatment and was then found fully unfit for duty. He appealed the decision to a municipal commission, but the original decision was upheld.

CONCLUSION

A FFD evaluation is one of the most difficult evaluations a psychologist is called on to perform. The stakes are high for all participants and the supporting structures surrounding the evaluation are weak. With the implementation of the Americans with Disabilities Act (ADA) in July 1992, the stakes may be even higher and the issues more complex. However, the procedures outlined here and in the example are quite behavioral and should, therefore, facilitate compliance with the ADA. Additionally, these procedures address the issues of accommodation and rehabilitation, also important concepts under the Act.

To conclude this chapter, I state what seems obvious to me: that a job is one of the most important elements in a person's life. Further, a law enforcement job is a career, and once someone is found unfit for duty, often an individual's ability to ever regain a law enforcement position is compromised. Thus, finding someone unfit for duty should be taken extremely seriously and should be done using a multimethod approach so that consistency of results is attained. In my view, the balance is the safety of the public and the reputation of the department with the officer's career, and none of these should be taken lightly.

APPENDIX A

Provider Name
Provider Address

WAIVER OF PRIVILEGE OF
CONFIDENTIALITY

I, _____, understand that I am about to undergo/have undergone a psychological evaluation at the request of _____ (hereafter, department). I understand that the examiner is acting in the interest of the department in the conduct of the examination and may provide any and all results of the evaluation (tests, interviews, collateral contacts) to department and/or persons with a need to know within the department.

I hereby waive any privilege of confidentiality to which I might otherwise be entitled. I understand that the examiner is not in any way providing psychological services to me.

_____

Name   Date

_____

Witness   Date

APPENDIX B

Law Enforcement Fitness for Duty Questionnaire

Name of Employee: _____

Department and Division: _____

Date of Examination: _____ Date of Report: _____

Examiner: _____

I. Diagnosis:

Axis I. _____

_____

_____

Axis II. _____

_____

_____

II. Work-Related Limitations

Examiners: Please comment on the impact of the mental limitation(s) diagnosed above on work-related activities below using the following code:

1. *None* No impairment in work related function.

2. *Slight* (. . . or occasional) Adequate performance is slightly or occasionally compromised but not to such an extent that deviations automatically come to the attention of supervisors, create serious danger, or are life threatening.

3. *Moderate* Adequate performance is so compromised that deviations are likely to come to the attention of supervisors and close colleagues. The individual's deficits in this area may create a dangerous situation.

4. *Marked* Performance on this dimension is so compromised that it will be apparent to supervisors, peers, and citizens. Deficits in this area are such that, if the deficit is in a critical area, continuing to permit the employee to perform his job would be imminently dangerous to the employee, colleagues, and/or citizens.

N/A Not assessed on this dimension.

1. Ability to understand, remember, and execute complex instructions.

    _____

2. Ability to maintain attention and concentration for extended periods.

    _____

3. Ability to work at a steady pace and to complete work assignments within an appropriate schedule.

    _____

4. Ability to maintain regular attendance and be punctual within customary tolerances.

    _____

5. Ability to work without special supervision.

    _____

6. Ability to maintain a high level of alertness.

    _____

7. Ability to exercise flexibility in decision making.

    _____

8. Ability to exercise good judgment in unpressured situations.

    _____

9. Ability to exercise good judgment in pressured situations.   _____

10. Ability to interact effectively and appropriately with:
    the public.

    _____

    supervisors.

    _____

    work peers.

    _____

11. Ability to maintain socially appropriate behavior.

    _____

12. Ability to adhere to basic standards of neatness and cleanliness.

    _____

13. Ability to take charge, evoke an authoritative posture, and command respect.

    _____

14. Ability to be aware of hazards and take appropriate precautions.

    _____

15. Ability to set realistic goals.

    _____

16. Ability to drive a vehicle in a safe manner.   _____

RATING

17. Ability to drive an emergency vehicle in a safe manner. _____

18. Ability to appropriately supervise others. _____

19. Ability to make life and death decisions involving self and others. _____

20. (If alcohol or substance abuse) Ability to maintain abstinence from substances at work. _____

21. (If alcohol or substance abuse) Ability to maintain control over all use of substances. _____

22. Ability to effectively coordinate sensory experiences and motor activity. _____

23. Ability to tolerate verbal abuse from others. _____

24. Ability to use adequate judgment in the handling of firearms. _____

25. Ability to conform to the law in the handling of personal matters. _____

26. Ability to use restraint and otherwise avoid the use of force or threatened force in the handling of domestic matters. _____

III. Conclusion

A. Overall, I find that the above captioned individual is (check one):
  _____ fit for duty unconditionally.
  _____ unfit for duty.
  _____ fit for duty with the following contingencies:

_____

_____

_____

B. If the above captioned individual is unfit for duty, I find that it is (check one, if appropriate):
  _____ likely
  _____ unlikely
that he or she will regain full fitness for duty in the foreseeable future.

C. If the above individual is unfit for duty and is likely to regain fitness for duty in the foreseeable future, the following intervention(s) and/or conditions should be met:

_____

_____

_____

_____

D. Additional comments:

_____

_____

_____

_____

E. Signature

_____
Name of Licensed Professional   License Number

_____
Signature of Licensed Professional   Date

APPENDIX C

CITY
DEPARTMENT OF PUBLIC SAFETY

Treatment Plan

RE: John Q. Smith (hereafter employee)

1. Employee will enroll in and comply with all of the requirements of the program at Local Hospital including but not limited to the following:

   program attendance requirements (attendance to begin within 9 days of date of signature below)
   AA-CA meeting requirements (usually 90 visits in 90 days post discharge)

psychotherapy, family therapy, or chemotherapy

spouse abuse treatment

approval from attending physician when obtaining prescription for medication that may have intoxicating side effects

inpatient detoxification and/or treatment requirements abstinence from all intoxicating substances while in the program, testing (of bodily fluids or otherwise) for presence of substances

2. Employee agrees to maintain abstinence from all nonprescribed intoxicants (including alcohol in all forms) for a period of 2 years from the date of signature below. Thereafter, he agrees to not use any illegal intoxicant while in the employ of City. He also agrees to comply with any and all requests for random witnessed drug tests for 2 years from the date of signature below if he continues to be employed by City.

3. Employee agrees to initiate and maintain monthly (or more frequent at his or her election) contact with the psychologist until formally relieved of this requirement by the psychologist. This to be renegotiated at a later time, at which point an addendum to this plan will be made.

4. Employee will bear financial responsibility for all treatment.

5. Employee is aware that failure to fully comply with the terms of this plan in the absence of a reasonable and verifiable excuse, will result in employee's being declared unfit for duty. In addition, employee is aware that, for this reason, psychologist will contact the Office of Professional Standards (OPS), which may, in turn, initiate possible disciplinary action against him or her. In particular, the contact between OPS and psychologist:

will describe the employee's substance use history

will note the fact that the employee was granted confidentiality under City and Departmental policy

is noncompliant with treatment

is a danger to himself or others (if in a sworn position)

Under this provision, an attempt will be made to notify employee prior to communicating his fitness status to OPS.

6. Employee recognizes that Item 5 constitutes a contingent limited waiver of the privilege of confidentiality. So long as he or she is in compliance with treatment, confidentiality is offered within the limits specified under the City Ordinance.

_____   _____

Employee   Date

_____   _____

Witness   Date

Legal, Psychological, and Ethical Issues in Police-Related Forensic Psychology Evaluations

Eric Ostrov
Forensic Psychology Associates, Chicago

There are numerous legal, psychological, and ethical issues presented by police-related fitness for duty evaluations. This chapter addresses some of these issues and covers some of the relevant case law; ethics primarily concern those of the American Psychological Association both generally and for forensic psychology.

BACKGROUND

Legal issues include the chief's right to order a psychological evaluation of his officers in a fitness for duty context. A major legal and forensic psychological issue involves the degree of confidentiality the police officer-client can expect in the fitness for duty evaluation context. Issues of consent with respect to collateral interviews are presented because, to obtain such interviews, the collateral source must be told who the evaluator is, in effect informing the collateral source that questions about the psychological functioning of the officer-interviewee have been raised.

One forensic psychological issue concerns the necessity of gaining valid understanding of a person's functioning in what could be an antagonistic atmosphere: The chief has requested and ordered the officer to participate in this evaluation; the officer may regard the evaluation as an extension of the chief's ability to initiate discipline against him or even as part of a campaign of harassment; the officer may feel that the evaluation is an invasion of his privacy, not justified by what he may feel are the chief's unwarranted concerns. Conversely, the officer may feel that he does have significant psychological problems and has communicated that to the chief and that the evaluation represents distrust of his statements in the chief's eyes. In short, the officer may have an agenda that is separate from the objective of the evaluator, which is to determine as thoroughly, accurately, and objectively as possible what the officer's psychological state is: The officer's objective may be to be return or stay on active duty, or the opposite—to be placed on or remain on the medical roll.

Another forensic psychological issue concerns the use of psychological tests in this context. Psychological tests such as the Minnesota Multiphasic Personality Inventory (MMPI) often are normed on clinical populations whose motivation in taking the test is very different from that often found in a police fitness for duty context. The question arises as to the proper use of tests in such evaluations.

Other forensic psychological issues include: What are the elements of an acceptable report? Should a diagnosis be given? Is a diagnosis helpful to elucidate the department's understanding of the officer and for guiding any treatment recommendations? Is a diagnosis almost always stigmatizing to a certain degree?

Another issue concerns whether the psychologist should make specific recommendations concerning the officer's ability to work or whether the psychologist should provide the chief with as thorough and as accurate an understanding of the officer as possible and leave it up to the chief to extrapolate from that information whether, in the light of his knowledge of the nature of the work, the officer is fit for duty.

A relevant forensic psychological issue concerns how much credence should be given to sources of information stemming from sources outside the evaluator's office such as allegations made by citizens, neighbors, family members, or other police officers. Should the evaluator be confined to direct observations made in the interview and testing as well as the results of psychological tests administered by the evaluator?

An ethical issue concerns how much feedback to give to an officer-evaluatee, particularly if a recommendation adverse to the officer's apparent interest or desires is rendered. Should the officer be given the report if he or she asks for it? Should he or she be given any feedback at all or do the results of the evaluation "belong" to the department that ordered it?

RELEVANT CASE LAW AND PSYCHOLOGICAL RESEARCH

The chief's right to order a police officer to undergo a psychological evaluation has been addressed by *Conte v. Horcher* (1977). (In a subsequent case, *Baltz v. County of Will*, 1985, plaintiffs conceded from the outset the constitutionality of this requirement.) The Conte decision affirmed that in Illinois a police chief does have the right to order a "mental examination" for the purpose of determining "whether or not patrolmen are able to perform duties required of them." The decision stated, "an examination, either physical or mental, enables the Chief to ascertain the qualifications of a person to perform particular duties or to fill a particular position."

The importance of a chief's ordering such an evaluation when it is indicated was shown by a New York case, *Bonsignore v. The City of New York* (1981), which held the city liable for the off-duty harms caused by a police officer where the city failed to "adopt or implement a sufficiently effective program of psychological screening and monitoring of police officers." The jury found the defendant liable "because of defendant's failure to adequately consider the problem of identifying policemen psychologically unfit to carry guns." It was noted in that case that even though Bonsignore exhibited many of the characteristics that the department held should flag disturbed officers so that they could receive psychological help, in the 23 years that he was on the force he was never given a psychological evaluation. Expressed in that opinion was, "a police officer's perception of himself is such that he will not recognize his own problems" and in "about every case of suicide of a New York police officer or of the commission of a unnecessary act of violence on the part of a member, feedback trickles in after the fact on how fellow police officers and how level superiors noticed some demonstrative abnormal behavior which for some reason they chose to ignore." The opinion also cited evidence heard by the jury "that police officers are especially likely to suffer from emotional problems leading to marital difficulties and violent behavior." In this case the jury found that the City's efforts were so inadequate as to constitute gross negligence.

It is important to note that the harmful acts of a police officer will not automatically be imputed to his or her employer. The Supreme Court rejected automatic *respondeat superior* municipality liability for the acts of their employees (*Monell v. Department of Social Services*, 1978) absent a municipality's contributing to the untoward acts of its employees—for example by indifference or unreasonable failure to consider a police officer-employee's psychological state—the municipality will not be liable for the harm committed by the police officer-employee. One relevant case in this regard is *Aranciba v. Berry* (1985). In that case, the city of New York was held not liable for the actions of two of its police officers, "upon the absence of any facts regarding the specific officer(s) involved 'to suggest violent tendencies' . . . (and where there were) a number of formal review procedures that deal with such circumstances as civilian complaints and discharge of weapons." As a result, the opinion concluded, "plaintiff has failed to allege specific facts to support his theory of gross negligence or deliberate indifference, (therefore) this claim must be dismissed." Cases that buttress this position include *Chirieleison v. City of New York* (1975) and *Kieninger v. City of New York* (1975). In short, a municipality or department can protect itself against liability by taking reasonable steps to assure the psychological suitability of its members.

The confidentiality of the communications made in a fitness for duty evaluation have been addressed by a declaratory judgment obtained by the Chicago Police Department and Isaac Ray, Inc. in a case involving a Chicago police officer (*City of Chicago v. Fraternal Order of Police*, 1986). In this case, a police officer who had undergone a fitness for duty evaluation at Isaac Ray, Inc. claimed that the company acted illegally in communicating any information gathered during the evaluation process on the grounds that any such information was given in confidence under the Confidentiality Act of the State of Illinois (State of Illinois Mental Health and Developmental Disabilities Confidentiality Act). Isaac Ray, Inc.'s position was that the Act did not apply first, because it only applies to communications made "in connection with providing mental health or developmental disability services to a recipient" and second, because the fitness for duty evaluation was a service not to the recipient but to the agency requesting it. This view was upheld by the Illinois court and it was made clear that communications made in a fitness for duty evaluation are not confidential under the Act. It might be noted that in his opinion, the judge stated:

> The societal interests in the psychological fitness and well-being of its armed protectors should be apparent to all. . . . The officer's capacity to serve is, because of the very nature of his assignments, open to continuous monitoring by both those in and out of the Department. . . . Psychological evaluations conducted by the Isaac Ray Center are exclusively for the benefit of the Police Department. The Center does not serve as a therapist for the officer being evaluated. The non-confidentiality of these sessions was made known to the subject officer, and he signed a consent to the evaluation process. The psychologist is providing a service to the Department and is not providing a service to the individual officer. . . . There is, in my view, no therapist–recipient relationship created here and the (Confidentiality) Act does not apply.

The forensic psychological issues posed by trying in an optimal way to obtain a thorough, objective, and valid assessment of an officer-evaluatee in a fitness for duty context were addressed by Ostrov, Nowicki, and Beazley (1987). The primary thesis of this article was that the motivations of the officer and others must be taken into account when conducting a fitness for duty evaluation. In ordinary, treatment-related clinical evaluations there is a greater likelihood that the evaluatee is motivated to cooperate fully with the evaluation; that is because in those cases the evaluatee presumably is motivated to further the presumptive goal of that process, which is to facilitate receiving psychological help. In the fitness for duty context that presumption cannot be made because the evaluation is ordered by the chief or the police department not necessarily for the good (almost never solely for the good) of the police officer, but rather primarily for the good of the citizens of the municipality and the department itself. The motivation of the officer either not to cooperate fully or to promote a certain view of himself—whether as impaired or nonimpaired—this article held, increases the importance of using other sources of information in an attempt to achieve convergence of evidence pointing to appropriate psychological conclusions. The other evidence needed includes pertinent records when available, collateral source interviews, and objective psychological testing.

The appropriateness and validity of using clinical psychological tests in a forensic evaluation context has been addressed by several authors; the MMPI in particular has been the subject of relevant investigation (e.g., one issue was posed by Butcher & Harlow, 1987: "It is . . . not possible with confidence, to determine on the basis of a psychological test alone whether the patient is malingering" (p. 141). Another issue concerns the appropriateness of norms used in such evaluations. Recent research has shown that persons who at least in theory are motivated to present themselves as having psychopathology obtained higher obvious scale scores and lower subtle scale scores on the MMPI than do persons who presumably are not so motivated (for example, Dubinsky, Gamble, & Rogers, 1985). Grossman, Haywood, Ostrov, Wasyliw, and Cavanaugh (1990) showed that police officers who, according to interview ratings, are motivated not to return to duty differ with respect to several validity scales and in particular have higher obvious and lower subtle scale scores on the MMPI than do officers who are motivated to return to duty. Ostrov, Dawkins, Dawkins, Cavanaugh, and Holton (1990) helped validate use of the MMPI with police officers and provided the Chicago Police Department norms for the MMPI.

There is no discernible case law that pertains to proper use of collateral interviews. The issue could be framed, however, in terms of privacy, which is a Fourth Amendment Constitutional issue. It is applicable in this instance due to the fact that the evaluation is ordered and required by a governmental agency, namely the department or its associated municipality. That the department or municipality has the right to invade the officer's privacy to the extent of requiring a psychological evaluation has already been documented. Whether a further invasion of privacy extending to collateral sources, including making those sources aware that the officer is being psychologically evaluated, is at least arguably a different question. These issues are dealt with by assuming that collateral interviews with supervisors can be undertaken even without the officer's consent, provided the chief agrees to these interviews because the supervisors are in effect an extension of the agency that is ordering the evaluation in the first place. Moreover, because observation and evaluation of the officer and subsequent communication of those observations and evaluations to the agency is a part of the supervisor's job, the officer does not have a reasonable expectation of privacy with respect to those observations and evaluations. Nevertheless, the officer does have a right to expect supervisors not to unnecessarily make known the fact of the psychological evaluation to others not involved and should be informed of this fact by the chief. Collateral interviews with other sources such as relatives, friends, and co-workers are another matter and should only be undertaken with the officer's permission. A parallel issue—accessing any relevant or potentially relevant psychiatric or other psychotherapeutic records or communications—should be handled the same way. If the officer refuses, that source of information is not pursued. The officer, however, can be apprised with respect to both giving permission to contact collateral sources and giving permission to access records and communications, so that if he or she does not grant such permission both sources of information will not be available to counteract or militate against any adverse conclusions drawn from other sources of information.

There is no discernible case law pertinent to the desirability of providing a diagnosis in a report to the requesting agency. But several pertinent legal issues suggest themselves. A relevant legal consideration is the law of libel (malpractice arguably is not relevant because malpractice concerns a breech of duty between doctor or psychologist and patient or client and the officer in a fitness for duty context is neither the patient nor client of the psychologist). The primary defense to libel is the truth of the matter asserted and psychologists could argue that if they did a competent job and their conclusions were reasonable and warranted, they did not commit libel in attaching a possibly stigmatizing label to the officer. The truthfulness of a diagnosis, however, is always disputable and represents a source of legal risk for psychologists making such a diagnosis. On the damages side, officer-plaintiffs who asserted that a psychologist libeled them could assert that their professional reputation was harmed and ask for money damages.

One could envision a report leaving out a diagnosis; such a report could restrict itself to addressing pertinent questions such as whether the officer has the cognitive and emotional capacity required to adequately perform the duties of being a law enforcement official and in particular to carry a weapon and have arrest powers. On the other side of the coin, questions could be raised about a report that did not include a diagnosis. These questions could be framed in terms of standards of practice. It could be maintained that currently the standard nomenclature for both psychiatry and psychology is contained in the *DSM–III–R*. To thoroughly evaluate a person and not reach a *DSM–III–R* diagnosis, including, if appropriate, a diagnosis of no psychiatric illness (V71-09), could be viewed as a failure to frame one's thinking in standard ways. In the author's practice a diagnosis with respect to every officer evaluated is reached.

There appears to be no case or research that addresses the desirability of making specific recommendations to an agency regarding the officer's fitness for duty. The alternative is to just state psychological conclusions, leaving up to the department to determine whether the officer is fit. Again the matter could be argued in two ways. On the one hand, it could be argued that psychologists are expert only with respect to psychological functioning. Psychologists can state whether the officer is cognitively or emotionally impaired. It is unlikely that psychologists are expert with respect to the job descriptions of every officer position of every department they deal with. As a result, it could be contended, the psychologist should not extrapolate from psychological findings to a recommendation concerning the officer's ability to perform the duties associated with his or her position in the specific department being consulted to. The chief, for instance, in this view, knows the officer's duties and responsibilities better and is in a better position to make this extrapolation.

On the other hand, it could be maintained that police department administrators, although conversant with police work in their department, are not able except in the most extreme cases, due to a lack of familiarity with the implications of psychological disfunction, to make the necessary extrapolations. Thus, if the officer is found to have impaired judgment, police department administrators still may not understand exactly what impaired judgment is, with the result that they will not be able to extrapolate from that finding to a reasonable decision about the officer's fitness for duty, findings of impulsiveness, depression, and so forth. This view emphasizes the importance of the evaluating psychologist's being a police psychologist, who consequently is familiar with the demands and expectations associated with police work. To this end I, for instance, have gone along on many ride-alongs with patrol officers, primarily in the city of Chicago, but also in the suburbs and with the state police. The goal of these ride-alongs was to learn firsthand about police work. Almost all these ride-alongs have involved 8-hour shifts and participation in regular patrol officer duties. In any event, in my practice, specific recommendations concerning the officer's ability to be on duty as a police officer are made.

Another issue concerns the officer's ability to see the report written about him or her or obtain some feedback once the evaluation is completed. It may seem evident that the officer should have the right to see a report that is written about himself or herself. But there are countervailing considerations. One concern is that an officer may be in denial with respect to certain aspects of his or her psychopathology and that seeing the report might have an untoward effect on their mental state. For instance, one officer who was evaluated showed marked cognitive deficits as a result of an advanced case of AIDS and this officer was in denial with respect to even having AIDS. The report made clear that he did have AIDS and had resulting severe cognitive deficits. The officer wanted to see his report but it was feared that he was coping with a severe underlying depression with the result that it was not clear that it was in his best interest that he see it. Another consideration is that the report at times contains information gathered from collateral sources that could include persons who do not want the officer to know that they provided the information in question. Although it is likely that in any subsequent litigation the fact that these collateral sources provided the information in question would most likely be revealed, it is at times not evident that this information should be immediately be made available to the officer. Another consideration is that the officer as a layperson may not be able to understand language used in the report and may misunderstand it to the detriment of his or her mental state or psychological functioning. To illustrate, an officer who saw himself as an individual functioning within the normal range psychologically met *DSM–III* criteria for a schizotypal personality disorder. Reading that diagnosis in a report could be more distressing to that individual than if he were presented this information within the context of a helping treatment relationship.

Regarding the issue of making the report available to the evaluatee, one legal consideration involves the right of a recipient of mental health services to copy records. At least under Illinois law (Mental Health and Developmental Disabilities Confidentiality Act, Ch. 91 1/2, para. 804), if the recipient of such services is 12 years of age or older, he or she has that right. As noted earlier, however, the fitness for duty evaluation appears not to fall within the purview of that act. The contention is that because the department orders and pays for the evaluation, the ensuing report is their property. Thus, whatever the desirability of giving the officer a copy of the report, the evaluator arguably, absent the permission of the officer's department, has no right to give that report to him or her. It seems clear that with the permission of the department, a mental health professional designated by the officer should have access to the report if that mental health professional is willing to present and interpret the report to the officer.

If the department is not willing to allow its officer to obtain his or her report, an APA Ethical Principle, Principle 2.09, becomes relevant. Based on this Principle, the preferred position is to encourage the department as much as possible to allow feedback to be given to the officer. Specific data does not have to have to be shared, but a strong case can be made for feedback that enables the officer to obtain or facilitate effective remediation for any perceived dysfunction.

PERTINENT ETHICAL ISSUES

Ethical issues relevant to the fitness for duty evaluation began with the preamble and the American Psychological Association Ethics Code, which includes, "psychologists respect and protect human and civil rights." In a fitness for duty context, where the individual is ordered to participate, respect for dignity is particularly crucial. Unlike the usual clinical treatment setting, the individual is not seeking the evaluation and is not paying the bill. Although the psychologist is beholden to obtaining the facts and reaching valid conclusions in any event, superficially, he or she could be seen as an employee of the agency and not the individual; therefore, he or she could be viewed as more aligned with the interest of the agency than that of the individual. Ethically, despite the fact that the psychologist is consulting to and being paid by the agency, it is imperative that he or she respect the individual officer's dignity and worth and strive for the preservation and worth of his fundamental rights. To illustrate this consideration, an officer was evaluated and he revealed that he was having an affair. He gave the examiner permission to call his wife but asked that the affair not be mentioned. The affair was not directly relevant to the reasons for referral and perhaps needless to say, the examiner, when talking to the wife, should not have and did not make mention of it.

The preamble also states the psychologist will not knowingly allow his or her skills to be misused by others. Principle A states: "Psychologists strive to maintain high standards of competence in their work." Principle F states: "Psychologists are aware of their professional and scientific responsibilities to the community and the society in which they work and live. . . . Psychologists try to avoid misuse of their work. Psychologists comply with the law and encourage the development of law and social policy that serve the interests of their patients and clients and the public." That part of Principle 2.02(b)—"Psychologists . . . take reasonable steps to prevent others from misusing the information."—and Principle 8.03—"If the demands of an organization with which psychologists are affiliated conflict with the Ethics Code, psychologists clarify the nature of the conflict" and "seek to resolve the conflict in a way that permits the fullest adherence to the Ethics Code"— also apply. Psychologists must make clear to the officer that they are doing the evaluation on behalf of his or her department but not to the point that any violation of the rights or dignity of the officer will take place.

In the fitness for duty context these principles often translate into psychologists' not allowing themselves to become a tool of the agency to whom they are consulting. This issue may arise because the agency has an unspoken agenda with respect to the officer; for instance the agency may wish to deal with the officer punitively, dealing with his or her actions not his or her psychological state. For instance, an officer may have offended many of his or her superiors through his or her actions but not in a way that broke any laws or department rules. The administration may be hoping that the psychologist will find that the officer is psychologically impaired and thus not fit for duty, with the result that the officer will be unable to work and eventually may even be fired due to lack of capacity to meet basic expectations. Conversely, the officer may be well liked by the administration but the subject of numerous citizens' protests. The administration may be hoping that the psychologist will give him or her "a clean bill of health," thereby defusing any criticisms. In either case, psychologists must not allow themselves to be used; in all cases psychologists must render an opinion that is based on their best efforts to render opinions that are psychologically sound and accurate.

An aspect of Principle A—Psychologists "recognize the boundaries of their particular competencies and the limitations of their expertise. They provide only these services and use only these techniques for which they are qualified by education, training or experience"—is applicable in that clinical psychologists and police psychologists should be aware that they are not, for instance, competent in various kinds of industrial/organizational practice. Fitness for duty evaluations focus on psychopathology or psychological deficits that could interfere with being an effective, role-appropriate police officer. A police or clinical psychologist might not be able to decide, as an industrial/organizational psychologist might, who would be best qualified, for example, to be promoted or undertake a special assignment.

Another relevant aspect of Principle A is, "they maintain knowledge of relevant scientific and professional information related to the services they render." The Public Safety and Police Psychology Section of Division 18 of APA has been making every effort to develop and share standards for the profession and encourages research that could inform the practice of the profession. Noteworthy, too, in this context are professional meetings sponsored by organizations such as the APA, the FBI, and the Society for Police and Criminal Psychology, which allow police psychologists to keep abreast of developments in this field.

Principle 2D states, "Psychologists are aware of cultural, individual, and role differences including these due to age, gender, race, ethnicity, natural origin, religion, sexual orientation, disability, language, and socioeconomic status." Persons undergoing fitness for duty evaluations come from a wide variety of backgrounds. Ethically those backgrounds must be understood in order to conduct a competent evaluation. Relevant to this principle, Ostrov, Nowicki, and Beazley (1987) showed no racial bias in police candidate interviews, whereas Ostrov (1987) found significant differences by ethnic or racial group or by gender with respect to MMPI scale scores of on-duty police officers. Nevertheless cultural factors are always salient and effort must be made to appreciate the cultural background of the individual being evaluated.

A critical ethical principle with respect to fitness for duty evaluations concerns confidentiality (Principle 5). Zelig (1988) cited confidentiality as the most prevalent ethical dilemma facing police psychologists. Key statements are, "psychologists have a primary obligation and take reasonable precautions to respect the confidentiality rights of those with whom they work or consult, recognizing that confidentiality may be established by law, institutional rules, or professional or scientific relationships." Principle 5.03(a), which includes the statement "In order to minimize intrusions on privacy, psychologists include in written and oral reports, consultations, and the like, only information germane to the purpose for which the communication is made," is also relevant. The fact that legally state confidentiality acts may not apply to fitness for duty evaluations does not end all discussion of this subject. The client, for example, may not be aware that confidentiality is not part of the fitness for duty evaluation: Pursuing the evaluation in such a circumstance and then issuing a report to the referring agency in this case would be unethical. The psychologist must make every effort to inform the officer about the absence of confidentiality and the fact that anything he or she says could be included in a report to the police agency. If he or she signs a release of information form with respect to any current or former treatment then the fact that that information also could be included in a report to the agency should be made clear to the client as well. If the officer gives consent for collateral sources to be contacted, such as his or her spouse, then the lack of confidentiality with respect to statements made by the spouse should be made clear both to the officer and the spouse. Despite the psychologist's emphasis on lack of confidentiality in the interview, given the general principal of respect for confidentiality of information obtained, it appears ethically mandated that any information that the psychologist acquires about the officer that is potentially harmful to him or her and is not relevant to the fitness for duty evaluation should not be included in the report. This assertion seems particularly cogent in light of the fact that experience shows that in many departments strict confidentiality of the report within the department cannot be guaranteed (for example a clerk might see a report and then discuss that with a sergeant, and so forth).

Considerations associated with Principle 2.09, which includes the statement, "Psychologists take reasonable steps to ensure that appropriate explanations of results are given," have been discussed earlier. The officer has a right to know what the conclusions of the evaluation are and the bases of them. The specific report is the property of the department and the officer should either obtain the report from that department or from the psychologist with the department's permission. Sometimes there are reasons based on the officer's self-interest or for reasons of protection of others that the report is not made immediately available to the officer even with the department's permission. In those cases it is preferred that the report be presented to the officer through a treating psychiatrist or psychologist. In any event, the officer has a right to consult with the evaluator and learn in that way what the results, interpretations, and bases for conclusions and recommendations were.

RECENT DEVELOPMENTS

The Americans with Disabilities Act (ADA) covers all police departments. Under the Act, any marked impairment of a major life activity—or the perception of such impairment—is covered. It is likely that most officer psychological fitness for duty evaluations will be covered because arguably, at least a perception of possible impairment is always involved. The counterargument might be that the impairment in question is not one of a major life activity (such as talking or thinking). But there always will be at least arguable coverage. As a result, all such evaluations should address quite specifically in ADA terms whether the officer is qualified psychologically to perform the essential aspects of the job. If he or she is not, then the further question as to whether he or she would be qualified if reasonable accommodation were offered should be specifically addressed. Also addressed should be whether the officer reasonably could be expected to pose a direct threat in the workplace. In all instances, specific recommendations, when relevant and feasible, for treatment or rehabilitation should be made. Departments also must contend with potential negligent retention suits brought by injured citizens or others, as opposed to ADA failure-to-accommodate or discrimination-against-the-disabled suits. Another developing aspect of the law involves the interface between workman's compensation and ADA claims. At any rate, only careful, well-documented, well-reasoned evaluations by qualified experts can maximize the probability of correct, legally supportable decisions.

REFERENCES

Aranciba v. Berry, 603 F. Supp. 931 (1985).

Baltz v. County of Will, 605 F. Supp. 992, D. C. Ill. (1985).

Bonsignore v. the City of New York, 521 F. Supp. 394 (1981).

Butcher, J. M., & Harlow, T. C. (1987). Personality assessment and personal injury cases. In I. B. Weiner & A. K. Hess (Eds.), *Handbook of forensic psychology* (pp. 128–154). New York: Wiley.

Chirieleison v. City of New York, 49 App. Div., N.Y., 2d (1975).

City of Chicago v. Fraternal Order of Police, Circuit Court of Cook County, No. 85 CH 12695 (1986).

Conte v. Horcher, 50 Ill. App. 3d 151 (1977).

Dubinsky, S., Gamble, D. J., & Rogers, M. L. (1985). A literature review of subtle–obvious items on the MMPI. *Journal of Personality Assessment, 45,* 62–68.

Grossman, L., Haywood, T., Ostrov, E., Wasyliw, O., & Cavanaugh, J. (1990). Sensitivity of MMPI validity scales to motivational factors in psychological evaluations of police officers. *Journal of Personality Assessment, 55,* 599–561.

Kieninger v. City of New York, 53 App. Div., N.Y., 2d, 602 (1975).

Mental Health and Developmental Disabilities Confidentiality Act. (1979). Ch. 91 1/2, para. 801, 804.

Monell v. Department of Social Services, 436 U.S. 658 (1978).

Ostrov, E. (1987). *Chicago police department normative MMPI studies*. Unpublished manuscript.

Ostrov, E., Dawkins, M., Dawkins, M., Cavanaugh, J., & Holton, H. (1990). *A test of interviewer bias in police psychological screening interviews*. Unpublished manuscript.

Ostrov, E., Nowicki, D., & Beazley, J. (1987). Mandatory police evaluation: The Chicago model. *Police Chief, 54*, 30–35.

Zelig, M. (1988). Ethical dilemmas in police psychology. *Professional Psychology: Research and Practice, 19*, 336–338.

PART THREE

THE CORE TECHNOLOGY
OF POLICE PSYCHOLOGY:
COUNSELING

CHAPTER EIGHT

Employee Assistance Programs in Police Organizations

Nancy Gund
Woodburn Center for Community Mental Health

Ben Elliott
U.S. Department of Justice Employee Assistance Program

This chapter acknowledges the long tradition of Employee Assistance Programs (EAPs) in law enforcement. It focuses on the EAP model of professional service delivery as distinct from psychological service programs and peer programs and highlights some of the differences between EAP programs at the federal and local government levels.

Specifically, the chapter provides an overview of the EAPs in federal law enforcement. It then details the structure, operation, and service delivery characteristics of one EAP that operated effectively at the local level for at least 10 years. The chapter demonstrates how public law provided the driving force that established EAPs, and how different models emerged to meet the divergent needs of specific law enforcement agencies. Although all agencies embrace the common goal of providing law enforcement services, they differ in terms of unique law enforcement missions, size, and geographic distribution of employees. Hence, the delivery of services also differs.

FEDERAL LAW ENFORCEMENT ORGANIZATIONS

Employee Assistance Programs, formerly known as Occupational Alcoholism Programs (OAPs) are programs that help employees resolve personal problems that may affect their job performance and productivity. Designed to provide early detection of employee problems, EAPs generally focus on problem assessment, short-term counseling and referral to expert treatment resources, follow-up services, employee education, and management training on appropriate use of the EAP program.

Problems that EAPs respond to include, but are not limited to marital dysfunction; financial, legal, or relocation problems; substance abuse; job stress; traumatic incidents; and generic mental health problems. Generally, services are time limited and there is a strong emphasis on appropriate referral for long-term clinical interventions. Within this context, EAP programs differ from full-range psychological service units where employee assistance may be provided as one component of a broader array of psychological services.

Public Law and EAPs

The scope and priority of EAPs within the federal law enforcement community in many ways mirror the development of EAPs in federal, non-law-enforcement organizations. With the enactment of Public Law 91-616 in 1970, commonly referred to as the Hughes Bill after its sponsor, Senator Harold Hughes from Iowa, federal agencies were required to establish alcoholism programs for federal employees. A variety of additional public laws from Congress and issuance from the Office of Personnel Management (OPM) directed agencies to provide a progressively wider range of human resource services to federal employees. Most agency EAPs have adopted the "broad brush" approach to provide the full range of EAP services to their employees and family members, believing that any personal or family difficulty has an existing or potential impact on an employee's performance and conduct, and therefore is a legitimate concern to management. Over and above ensuring the personal well-being of employees, the rationale that drives the development of EAPs includes the need to maintain safety in the workplace and a productive work force.

EAPs and Law Enforcement

Prior to the development of EAPs, many law enforcement organizations were utilizing mental health professionals. These mental health professionals, typically psychologists, were assisting their organization in three major areas: (a) assessing potential risk in profiling past and future criminal behavior and providing assistance at hostage barricade situations, (b) assisting officers in dealing with occupational stress and coping with critical incidents, and (c) providing psychological screening for new hires and evaluating officers for psychologically based disabilities.

The emergence of EAPs provided an opportunity to expand mental health involvement in law enforcement organizations and to focus more directly on providing treatment services. This trend provided somewhat of a unique situation in that the services needed to be tailored to meet the needs of a unique culture that was not known for wide-ranging acceptance of mental health interventions. Hence, the range of approaches varied considerably. Some organizations kept the responsibilities separate, whereas other groups attempted some level of integration into existing psychological services. However, the roles were sometimes in conflict; therefore, many law enforcement groups developed policies to keep EAPs separate from other services such as those already mentioned.

It is widely accepted that law enforcement presents a variety of special considerations that typically represent a specialized work force. The mission of law enforcement fosters what is often referred to as a *closed community*; a community or bond between officers who are often under considerable stress, aware of their vulnerability, and on the defensive with the citizen groups they are sworn to protect. Thus, perhaps the single most significant development with EAPs in federal law enforcement is the peer counseling and peer support programs developed in most federal law enforcement agencies. Having officers or agents work with the EAP provides a significant level of credibility to the programs and helps to defuse the defensiveness. This concept has worked most effectively in areas of posttrauma debriefings, and during interventions with officers suffering from chemical dependency.

Federal Models

Programs in the federal sector are structured to provide EAP services in one of three primary ways: internal programs, contracted services, and service delivery systems that combine elements of other viable models in order to meet a specific service goal.

The *internal program model* staffs the EAP with full-time agency employees who provide traditional EAP services. Examples of this model include the programs in place in the Secret Service, the Federal Bureau of Investigation (FBI) and the Central Intelligence Agency (CIA).

The *external contracted model* uses outside providers to deliver clinical services but the program is coordinated inhouse by an agency program manager. Programs in the Drug Enforcement Administration (DEA), the U.S. Park Police, U.S. Marshals Service and the Alcohol, Tobacco, and Firearms Bureau conform to this model. The DEA, in particular, based their selection of this model on the results of an evaluation process that facilitated the determination of the EAP model that would be most effective to meet the needs of an agency whose employees are geographically dispersed across the nation and overseas. Subsequently, the program manager incorporated a trauma response protocol as another element of the EAP. This program component uses "Trauma Team" agents who receive extensive training to provide immediate support for agents who sustain traumatic incidents and to serve as a bridge between the incident and the program's area clinicians who represent the DEA/EAP program manager in the field.

The *combined services model* uses an outside contractor to operate the program within the organization to provide services to employee personnel and management. The program at the U.S. Customs Service is an example of this model and in my opinion this is currently one of the more cost effective and efficient program models in the federal law enforcement community. This model provides the full range of EAP services to employees nationwide. Program staff are located at Customs headquarters in Washington, DC, but have the ability to travel to various locations as needed. The majority of their work is telephone assessment and referral to local community resources.

Studies comparing external EAPs with internal programs have identified strengths and weaknesses for both. Generally, the external model receives a higher number of self-referrals and the internal model experiences a higher number of supervisory referrals. Consequently, internal programs are more effective in reaching the chemically dependent employees (more often supervisory referred), whereas the external programs are more effective in involving family members. This tendency is magnified in the law enforcement community, where the manager, in a quasi-military structure, is more likely to trust a support service that is part of the organization.

In summary, by establishing EAPs, federal law enforcement organizations have matched, and in some instances surpassed, efforts of other agencies. With organizations expressing an increased interest in progressive management and maximizing employee productivity, the future for EAPs in federal organizations, including law enforcement, is very strong.

A LOCAL POLICE DEPARTMENT

The Fairfax County Police Department is responsive to a 400-square-mile county located across the Potomac River from Washington, DC. The department was established with a chief of police, five sworn officers, and two clerks. It has grown into the largest local law enforcement agency in Virginia with 1,368 civilian and sworn personnel. Since its inception over 50 years ago, Fairfax County has developed from a rural community to a bustling technological center with a population of more than 840,000 people. With a median family income of $65,000, Fairfax is now one of the wealthiest communities in the United States (Fairfax County Office of Research and Statistics, 1991). Within those parameters, it also contains pockets of poverty, violence, drug and gang influences, everyday street crime, and an extraordinary split between the very wealthy and the poor.

The police department that responds to this large suburban community has a reputation for being one of the best in the United States, and it strives to maintain this standard as it grows and stretches to meet the needs of the community. Its police officers and civilian personnel, who comprise a small community in themselves, often give their entire careers to Fairfax County.

These dedicated men and women often put aside their own needs and their families' needs in order to provide for the safety of the community.

The Woodburn Center for Community Mental Health is also a county agency entrusted with a public service mission. One of three community mental health centers in Fairfax, it provides for the myriad of mental health needs of residents in the county.

The police department and Woodburn Center have worked together on many community projects over the years, and each has felt the rewards of these concerted efforts. They joined forces in the late 1970s to address the issues of police officer stress and forged ahead with a program designed to meet the specific mental health needs of police personnel in Fairfax County. What follows is a description of the Fairfax County Police EAP, its role as a mental health service provider, and some of its attempts to sort through the dilemmas that came with the task.

EAPs offer employees and management a unique opportunity to pursue the mutually beneficial goal of supporting and keeping a productive employee.

Part of the philosophy of EAP programs is that an organization's employees are among its most important assets and that if the problems in an employee's personal life interfere with job performance, it makes good business sense for that organization to provide assistance toward resolution of the problem. If the issue can be solved, losses to the organization and the individual are minimized. The organization, which may suffer because of decreased productivity through use of sick leave and increased health-care costs, reduces its concerns about the loss of investment in human resources through employee discipline and termination. The employee who may have experienced considerable distress get relief from the problem and returns to former levels of functioning.

The EAP model is an appropriate choice for the police organization interested in seeing its recruits and its significant financial investment in training through to retirement. (Fairfax spends about $60,000 training each recruit.) Contracting out EAP services also offers police departments an alternative to hiring its own psychological services professionals, which can create problems in areas discussed later in this chapter.

The Fairfax County Police Department (FCPD) EAP promotes its services to police personnel as a support mechanism for psychological well-being during their careers as police officers. Although it is unrealistic to assume that police personnel will ever fully embrace the cause of mental health, there is an organizational philosophy that establishes the EAP as a valuable resource to all employees. These ideas are present from the beginning when a person applies for a job as an officer with the Fairfax County Police Department. This complex process can take up to 6 months and from the beginning the message is clear that the department's hiring process is highly competitive, and that the candidates with the greatest strengths in each of the areas of competence will be selected. Applicants are tested rigorously in areas including a written entrance exam, a job-based physical agility test, an interview, a polygraph, and a background investigation. Comprehensive psychological and medical testing are done once the hiring process is complete. Applicants must agree to become nonsmokers and maintain strict standards for weight and health. In the end, a candidate's chances of being hired are 50 to 1. The message imparted from the beginning is that the applicant is hired for his or her strengths and potential to contribute to the department. Officers know they are expected to maintain their welfare and ability to perform all physical and psychological functions of the job.

History

The FCPD EAP began in 1977 as a component of the psychological assessment program that tested applicants for hiring. The psychologist in charge of the assessment program at the time began to receive informal requests for counseling from officers in the department. As the need to provide counseling services grew, the program began to take shape and the department agreed to contract with the Woodburn Center for the delivery of these services. At the same time, the department chose to establish a separate OAP for officers whose problems with alcohol affected them on the job. This program was administered by the personnel division commander, who in turn reported to the chief of police. Today such an arrangement would be unworkable, but it is important to recall that the early development of EAPs focused on alcoholism and job performance, and that the notion of assisting employees with a wider variety of problems was just developing. At the same time, many mental health professionals were ill informed about substance abuse issues and often felt less than competent to treat both psychological and substance abuse problems. Later, both personal and substance abuse problems came under the mandate of the FCPD EAP, which offered a broader approach to solving employee problems.

In retrospect, it was the need to define the role of the mental health clinician in the police organization that forged the path for what is today the FCPD EAP. The demands for competing mental health services within the department at the time included psychological assessment of recruits, general psychological counseling, alcoholism treatment, and a host of other requests, such as undercover psychological selection. The most current resolution came when the psychological assessment program became a separate entity and the counseling services program was incorporated into the EAP.

Professionals who provide psychological services to police departments have typically been confronted with conflicts over the multiplicity of roles and concerns about potential ethical problems. Psychological staff have often been called on to provide varied services such as the assessment of police officer candidates, fitness for duty evaluations, counseling for department personnel, hostage negotiation with street officers, and consultation and training to management. These various tasks have forced professionals to determine whether the client was the department, the officers in treatment, or the group. Whereas certain role conflicts were obvious, others were much more subtle and embedded in the diversity of requests for services. The clinician could acknowledge a clear conflict in counseling an officer and later conducting a fitness for duty evaluation. Less clear role conflicts happen as professionals provide treatment services to officers they may observe in other capacities, such as hostage negotiation.

Inhouse psychological staff have been vulnerable to such dilemmas, because their roles have often included more diverse tasks than outside contractors and pressure to perform these tasks came from police administration, not the mental health community. Consulting or contract mental health professionals have had somewhat more circumscribed roles with law enforcement agencies. In small communities where there are few professionals with expertise in police psychology, those professionals may be asked to provide services in conflicting situations. Mann (1980) pointed out the need to clarify the professional's role in working with police agencies and saw it as critical to the task.

An EAP administered by a community mental health center limits the opportunity for problems such as role conflict and divided loyalty, and is a particularly appropriate option in providing psychological services to police departments. Community mental health staff positions are secure, and if the department chose not to renew its contract, staff members would be deployed to other divisions in the agency. Because community mental health centers are not for profit, the conflict of private EAP consultants who use police contracts to sustain referral for profit businesses is eliminated. Inhouse psychological staff may be fired by the department that employs them, which can turn the job of providing psychological services into a political exercise or a process subject to the whims of the current administration. The community mental health EAP operates from a more neutral position and is freer to make decisions based on the needs of the population rather than on need to please the department, although even a program administered through a center is never entirely free of these pressures inherent in all EAPs.

The FCPD EAP set out in the early years of its evolution to establish clear and formal operating procedures, including a mission statement, program philosophy, formal lists of services rendered, and procedures for utilization. It also included the definition of confidentiality, maintenance of records, administrative operations, and the qualifications of staff.

Standard operating procedures are a minimum requirement to the functioning of any EAP. Gentz (1986) noted that it is especially important when offering psychological services to police organizations. Clear statements reduce the likelihood of professionals finding themselves in unresolvable dilemmas involving neutrality and ethics. The operational procedures negotiated with the police department and the Woodburn Center established the boundaries of the program and currently serve as a reference manual for all parties when issues arise.

There have been other specific advantages to the Fairfax County Police Department in contracting its EAP with Woodburn Center. A long-established positive relationship exists between the police and other Woodburn Center staff who have worked cooperatively to develop teams in hostage negotiation and mobile crisis response. Through this work, police personnel of all ranks have established a sense of trust, a collaborative relationship, and a less skeptical attitude toward mental health services. Although this appreciation for mental health does not always translate into an individual officer seeking assistance for himself or herself, it does contribute to the essential trust between the organizations.

The FCPD EAP also has the advantage of being able to tailor its services to better meet the needs of the department. Its staff time is allocated entirely to the FCPD EAP, not split between other mental health center populations or programs. (Woodburn also has county EAP contracts with the fire and rescue department and the sheriff's department.) This serves to promote and maintain staff members with police and mental health expertise. In contrast, outside consultants to police organizations are often viewed as having limited interest and understanding of police culture. If the contractor has several other EAPs, he or she may be seen as less useful by the department.

It is important to be aware of the unique characteristics of the law enforcement organization so personnel will see the EAP as responsive to their needs and feel comfortable taking advantage of them. Even though the Fairfax County Police Department has a credible and established EAP, a good working relationship with other mental health clinicians and a fairly sophisticated understanding of mental health issues, like other police populations, they are reluctant to seek assistance for themselves. The usual reserve most people have about contacting a therapist for professional help is magnified for the police officer who is characterologically disposed to manage life with high levels of autonomy.

It was also clear from the beginning that the traditional EAP model of assessment and referral could thwart the efforts of the officer who reluctantly seeks help. For just as the officer reservedly approached the EAP for services, he or she would probably be disinclined to take a referral to another clinician and start the process all over again.

Services

To make the program as accessible as possible, a short-term or time-limited treatment model that includes up to 3 months of service was established. The expectation for the 12-visit model was that it would attenuate the police officer's worry about having to start over, that many officers and their families could respond to a reasonably short-term intervention, and that a short wait list would make services available quickly to those in need. The FCPD EAP had to acknowledge that it could not respond to all the psychological needs of the department. Needs for long-term therapy outweigh the resources of the program, and all efforts are made to help people connect immediately with other resources when the employee requires long-term services. The EAP is available free of charge to all personnel, including civilians, sworn and retirees, and their families. Individual, marital, and family counseling is offered for personal and job-related issues.

The Woodburn Center's Emergency Services staff provides both telephone and walk-in crisis counseling, medication evaluation, and the ability to get in touch with off-duty EAP staff. It is staffed by clinicians and psychiatrists who specialize in crisis intervention. Aside from after-hours back up, Emergency Services staff is also available for second opinions concerning risk assessment and the need for hospitalization. In case of multiple urgent requests for services, such as critical incidents involving several officers, Emergency Services is able to provide triage and staff support. And because Emergency Services is also available to the two other public safety EAPs at Woodburn (fire and rescue and sheriff) the staff is experienced in areas of crisis management and intervention issues with public safety personnel. In a situation where the brief use of medication is appropriate, the psychiatrist would select a medication based on an understanding of the side effects of various medications and the specific shift work patterns so the officer's work performance would not be affected.

One of the most critical supports to EAP crisis intervention is 24-hour back-up emergency service through Woodburn Center. This service enables the FCPD EAP to respond to after-hours and weekend emergencies. The EAP must be able to provide timely crisis intervention and problem resolution because it is not unusual for police personnel to be in crisis as they contact the EAP. Some of the following scenarios are examples of the pressured conditions under which they come:

- An officer calls from his car phone as he sits in the parking lot of Woodburn Center. He is crying and barely able to get his words out. He states that he has been afraid to come in, so he just drove himself to the center hoping he would have to come in.
- An officer calls because his wife has threatened to tell his captain that he has been talking about suicide. He is not on very good terms with his supervisor, he feels trapped, and thinks counseling might be his only way out.
- An on-duty officer in full uniform arrives at the back door of Woodburn Center, hoping to talk to the EAP therapist. He is tearful, trembling, and thinks he is going crazy.

Support from Emergency Services staff allows the FCPD EAP to remain flexible in providing effective crisis intervention.

The majority of referrals to the FCPD EAP are related to marital, family, and job stress. Statistics from most recent years indicate that 25% of personnel come to the EAP for couples counseling, 20% come to address family conflict, and another 20% want to resolve job-related problems. These statistics seem to validate what we know about police families and their struggles to adjust and respond to the stresses of a police career. It is not new that police personnel have unique family problems that overlap with such stresses as shift work, the imminent dangers of patrol work, and the offensive chronicity of street crime. Whether or not they like it, police personnel and their families must accommodate the possibilities of death or serious injury in the line of duty, find ways to raise families with little time together, and maintain stability while being personally connected to grisly or violent events in their communities. Johnson (1991) emphasized the link between police stress and family distress and found that family life must be seen as affected by or contributing to the pressure of the job. Banks (1992) established a correlation between family conflict and job failure in the validation study of the psychological test battery for Fairfax County police officers. The variable family conflict (FC) from the Inwald Personality Inventory correlates significantly with job failure, suggesting that those officers who scored higher on FC were more likely than other officers to be unsuccessful on the job. Both of these studies and the FCPD EAP referral data point to the need to address the overlapping conflicts of police personnel and their families.

An important feature of the FCPD EAP is that all services are voluntary, meaning there are no mandatory referrals for services. Supervisors are trained to recognize common employee behavior that may indicate the need for counseling and they are encouraged to refer personnel to the EAP before problems begin to interfere seriously with job performance.

The EAP recognizes that there are occasions when the police administration must have a way of assessing the imminent psychological stability of active duty police officers. When a police officer's behavior is clearly outside the norm, is marked by unusual, bizarre, dangerous, or unprecedented actions, and raises serious liability questions, the department must have a mechanism for evaluating the officer. These assessments, commonly called fitness for duty evaluations, are not conducted by the EAP, as this would represent a serious role conflict. The FCPD EAP has assisted the department in finding outside consultants who have expertise in mandatory public safety evaluations. Such services are contracted out and paid for by the department on a case-by-case basis. If an officer is found fit after such an evaluation and there is a recommendation for counseling, the EAP can then assist the officer in seeking treatment.

As mentioned earlier, all referrals to the EAP, whether initiated by the employee, the family, or the supervisor are voluntary. Supervisors initiate 29% of referrals to the EAP, and 71% are initiated by the employee. Within that framework, there are several types and levels of voluntary referrals appropriate for various kinds of problems. Where job performance is the primary complaint, a supervisor may encourage the employee to utilize the services of the EAP by initiating a *job performance referral*, which specifies areas of noncompliance. The officer may accept or decline the performance referral. The employee is reminded that (according to operating procedures) no disciplinary action will be taken solely because he or she rejects the use of the EAP. The supervisor's main concern is correcting the employee's performance of duty, not whether the officer uses the EAP to assist in problem resolution.

Another type of supervisory intervention directed at encouraging use of the FCPD EAP is the *disciplinary diversion referral*. This type of referral is designed to provide the employee with a treatment alternative to serious disciplinary action such as suspension, demotion, or termination. The disciplinary diversion, which must be approved by the chief of police, gives the employee an option to address the problem through counseling or to take the prescribed discipline from the patrol bureau major. Again, the emphasis is on options, and the officer is assured by the major and other supervisors that there will be neither overt nor subtle retaliation if the diversion is declined. It is made clear to the officer that participation in the EAP is not the issue, the end result should be a return to satisfactory job performance. The most common disciplinary problems considered for the diversion program include an officer's use of alcohol that interferes with the job, personal or family problems that significantly impair work performance, or repeated citizen complaints and human relations violations.

The disciplinary diversion program addresses problems that produce dramatic changes in the employee's behavior, as opposed to long-standing complaints that represent an officer with severe character problems who is a poor fit for the job. The goal of the diversion is to salvage the previously effective officer for whom administrative discipline would not be useful.

If the employee is interested in considering the diversion, the EAP clinician will meet the officer to describe the program and determine if counseling or treatment services are appropriate. All attempts are made to establish a cooperative examination of the problem with the officer so an accurate assessment can be made and the officer can make an informed decision based on his or her best interest. If the EAP clinician does not advise counseling or if the officer does not want to participate in services, the major of patrol then proceeds with the disciplinary action. If the officer chooses to proceed with the diversion program recommendations, a referral will be made to a treatment provider in the community. The role of the EAP clinician then becomes that of case manager, monitoring and reviewing treatment along the way.

As part of the contract, the patrol bureau major agrees to make it possible for the officer to meet his treatment obligations by arranging a nonpunitive work schedule so the officer will not lose pay or be sent to an inappropriate work assignment.

Because the department agrees to withhold discipline and accommodate the needs of the officer, it must be informed as to whether the employee follows through with the obligations. As part of the diversion, the officer agrees to have some minimal information relayed to the patrol major through a signed release of information. The release of information enables the department to know if the officer is abiding by the agreement. Specifically, the release limits the FCPD EAP to reporting whether or not the employee accepts the referral, if he or she will need time away from work for treatment, if the employee is participating (as determined by the provider), and when the employee completes the treatment. No clinical information is shared and there is no contact between the treatment provider and the department, except in the case of a duty-to-warn situation.

If the officer does not abide by or withdraws from the diversion agreement, the department retains the right to proceed with the original discipline.

This program works particularly well with officers who have had a history of at least adequate job performance and who have developed a problem or series of problems that seriously impairs their performance on the job. It has also been effective in dealing with the problem of alcohol, because denial often prevents the problem drinker from seeking treatment until his or her job is at risk.

Peer Support Team

One other program the FCPD EAP assisted in organizing is the Peer Support Team. The purpose of the team is to prevent the development of posttraumatic stress disorder (PTSD) and the focus of interventions is on shootings, serious injuries to an officer or victim, and other extraordinarily gruesome events.

One of the early interventions to educate personnel about the need for a Peer Support Team happened in 1985 when the FCPD EAP studied the reactions of 23 police officers who had been involved in shootings, along with 3 officers who witnessed shootings. The EAP surveyed officers to determine evidence and level of PTSD symptomology on those who had been involved in shootings.

The results indicated that in the first week following the shootings 77% of the officers reported sleeplessness, 58% reported anxious feelings, 50% reported flashbacks, 35% reported nightmares, and 69% reported feeling "wound up." Even more remarkable were the PTSD symptoms that persisted 3 months after the incidents. Three months later, 38% reported continued flashbacks, 23% reported nervousness, 19% reported anger, and only 35% reported no symptoms. Officers also rated the degree of trauma they experienced as a result of the shooting; 25% described it as extremely traumatic, 36% said it was moderately traumatic, and 39% noted that it was minimally traumatic (Hays, 1985).

The information from the survey was most useful because it offered FCPD personnel internal data that reflected the psychological reactions of their own troops. Although clinicians could have quoted similar data concerning degree of trauma involved in other departments (Solomen & Horn, 1986) it is doubtful that it would have had the same educational impact.

The FCPD EAP made several attempts to establish a Peer Support Team but it was not until the department decided it wanted a team and took responsibility for organizing one that it became fully operational.

The Peer Support Team currently consists of 22 officers and 3 civilian personnel representing all substations, special units, and emergency communication. Team members have the role of providing support and information to their peers involved in critical incidents. Critical incidents are defined as those situations where an employee's action results in the death or serious injury of a person, situations where an officer is fired at or wounded in the line of duty, and situations judged by supervisors to be traumatic in nature.

When a critical incident occurs, emergency dispatch sends a team member and offers immediate support at the scene, such as contacting family members, arranging for transportation, and being with the employee. The team member will also provide information about department investigation procedure following such incidents so that the employee will not be left in anxious anticipation.

The team member will also offer some information about common psychological reaction to critical incidents and attempt to normalize the employee's emotional state. As part of that process, a Peer Support Team member will facilitate a referral to the EAP for a critical incident information session, which focuses on further educating the employee about traumatic stress reaction and gives the officer an opportunity to cathart the experience. This link to the EAP is particularly crucial, because referrals to the EAP are not mandatory after critical incidents, although this may change. It enables the EAP to recommend follow-up services if necessary and to extend services to the family.

The team is coordinated by the department, as opposed to the EAP, and is led by an officer responsible for the program's operation. The FCPD EAP works with the coordinator and the team members to provide ongoing training and psychological consultation. This cooperative arrangement offers the best of both police and mental health organizations in responding to the needs of the employee and in preventing PTSD sequelae.

This joint effort draws on the strengths of each organization and supports the differences in their respective professional roles. For instance, when the department began to reformulate the current Peer Support Team, the issue of confidentiality was raised. Unlike mental health professionals, peer support members cannot offer confidentiality to the officers during their time together. Sworn officers are obligated to respond to court subpoenas, grand jury investigations, and otherwise report the criminal behavior of fellow officers. In some instances, therefore, it would be untenable if the support member assisted the officer at the scene then had to testify against him or her in a court of law (i.e., after hearing that the officer had made a terrible mistake).

In order to resolve the concern about confidentiality, team members inform the officer from the beginning that they cannot offer confidentiality, and that they do not function in the role of a counselor. Team members do offer privacy and will not discuss the incident among the troops. Peer Support Team members also note that the department, including the internal affairs division, agrees not to interview team members as part of the investigation of an incident. Police officers who are involved in critical incidents are discouraged from talking to team members about the incident per se; instead team members help the officer focus on his or her current need for assistance and information during a stressful time. Team members then encourage officers to use the services of the FCPD EAP, where they can discuss the incident in a confidential setting.

A successful intervention in most cases involves services from both programs. A team that operates without access to mental health is in danger of mismanaging the at-risk officer and an EAP without access to a Peer Support Team is likely to connect with only a limited number of officers, except where referrals are mandatory.

As part of the redevelopment of the Peer Support Team, the department and the FCPD EAP made a clear decision not to train officers to be peer counselors. The peer counselor model is complicated by conflicting roles, maintaining professionalism, and assuring quality of training. Because of these issues, the peer counselor can prove to be a liability. Both the FCPD EAP and the department recognize the need to reach out to large numbers of personnel, particularly those who are reluctant to seek traditional mental health services. Officers, especially those in recovery from substance abuse problems, can offer a wealth of assistance to other officers in similar situations. Identifying and utilizing these officers as informal resources helps the department as a whole.

Training and Consultation

Training and consultation are other inroads to the provision of police-related mental health services. The EAP strives to train all personnel, from recruits to command staff, about the purpose and services of the program.

Prior to actual training from FCPD EAP staff, new police recruits are offered the opportunity to review their psychological test batteries with the department psychologist who administered the tests. The psychologist can answer questions, raise concerns, and apply the test data in a meaningful way to the job of patrol officer. Although the majority of recruits do not request the interpretive session, it is thought that offering the opportunity and otherwise providing information about the test battery demystifies psychological services to some extent. When recruits report to the Academy, they receive training from the FCPD EAP coordinator about police stress, the EAP program, and the Peer Support Team, which again reinforces the acceptability of seeking mental health services.

The FCPD EAP also offers training to all new first-line supervisors in areas such as identifying the officer who may be developing problems, documenting behavior, and encouraging officers to seek assistance using the various types of supervisory referrals. Particular emphasis is placed on teaching supervisors to make use of the EAP before the employee develops a serious discipline problem. Supervisors, like other police officers, are reluctant to consider the need for mental health counseling and should learn about the advantages of each intervention. The EAP also educates supervisors about areas of common complaints among police personnel such as alcoholism, posttraumatic stress, domestic violence, shift work, and family life. The purpose of addressing these content areas is not to train supervisors to diagnose problems, but to increase their awareness of issues and encourage their belief in the usefulness of mental health services.

The FCPD EAPs also offers roll call training on request in areas such as critical incident stress, alcoholism, conflict resolution, and stress management. Roll call training can be tailored to the special interests of the squad and are a good opportunity for personnel to see the EAP as responsive to their needs. Ride-alongs are another opportunity for the EAP to connect with personnel and market services. It is important that FCPD EAP staff have visibility and credibility with line staff in particular because they are the basis of most of the referrals.

The EAP is also directly involved in the ongoing training of Peer Support Team members, who meet every other month to increase their skills and address programmatic issues. Training is available as time permits to all other groups who request it. When time is not available or EAP does not have expertise in the area of interest, it enlists other resources to do the training.

Confidentiality

It is important for the EAP to establish from the outset the terms and limitations of confidentiality as it applies to its work with the police. Many misunderstandings can be prevented by communicating clearly with the police administrative staff and personnel about such matters.

Ethical dilemmas, including confidentiality, can often be "resolved through adequate forethought and planning" (Mann, 1980, p. 36). The police organization should be made aware of confidentiality as it applies to EAP interventions, especially those related to counseling services. Guidelines should be shared with the department and should include a description of the role of the clinician in cases of imminent risk, such as threats of serious injury to self and others. When a breach of confidentiality is necessary, the organization should be aware of how situations are likely to be handled, such as least intrusive processes first. The department should have some knowledge about how the EAP therapist assesses levels of risk, and how that applies to the type of intervention necessary. For instance, an acutely suicidal police officer who agrees to hospitalization is a very different kind of risk than an acutely paranoid psychotic officer who refuses family involvement and hospitalization. The first situation can be handled in a way that maximizes the officer's cooperation and protects much of his need for privacy. The second situation, which represents high levels of risk, would probably require breaching confidentiality to the department.

In situations of imminent risk, the department should have some understanding of the conditions that would require the EAP to inform or involve its representative and what types of clinical information might be shared. In my opinion, these are the situations that raise some of the deepest anxiety for the organization and should be clarified before issues arise.

Sharing ethical guidelines can help solidify trust with the police organization, which in turn promotes the appropriate utility of the program. As part of this communication, the department must understand that guidelines are not to be mistaken for doctrine. All ethical dilemmas cannot be predicted and matters of judgment cannot be scripted. Although it might relieve the anxiety of the department, and perhaps the clinician, if the EAP offered an exact description of how all imminent risks would be handled, all parties must acknowledge that circumstances vary, situations are mitigated by complex factors, and ethical considerations must be made on a case-by-case basis.

Clear and frank discussion with the department can prevent false assumptions about how confidentiality works, and clarify that ethical decisions are made by clinicians and not by the police department. Employees should also have a clear understanding of the limits of confidentiality prior to participating in counseling services.

Dilemmas

Issues related to risk assessment, risk management, and ethical responsibilities to protect victims from harm influence the mental health professional working with law enforcement agencies. Providing professional mental health services to police organizations always involves identifying risks, making decisions quickly, and intervening in some relatively uncharted territories of mental health work. Ethical considerations in general clinical practice are fairly well defined; it becomes far more complicated to determine appropriate courses of action when the client is an organization whose employees are charged with maintaining public safety.

Consider, for instance, some of the following scenarios as situations that present the EAP with questions of risk and management:

• An extremely anxious police officer is having trouble managing the stress of the job. He has made minor mistakes on the job, but has become seriously worried that he will not be able to use his gun if required.

• An officer experiences an acute reaction to having witnessed a motorcycle accident where a male victim's head was sheared from his body. The officer has not slept in 3 days, is quite agitated, and is insistent that he will report for the evening shift.

• A civilian emergency call taker reports with great shame that she has become addicted to cocaine. She denies any impairment on the job, but it slips that she has made some significant errors on calls that have not been discovered. She is also beginning to feel that her co-workers are conspiring against her.

• An officer reports that he is so angry he just intends to hurt somebody Anybody.

These situations raise fairly common concerns about managing risks and discharging responsibilities to protect victims from harm.

Although there are many more questions than answers to these situations, it is necessary for EAP clinicians to be well aware of the issues as they present themselves. EAP professionals must also be aware of the APA ethical guidelines and the *Tarasoff v. Regents of the University of California* (1976) case when considering necessary action. Courses of action in imminent risk situations can include warning the victim, contacting authorities, and hospitalizing the client either voluntarily or through commitment. Some of the most difficult questions that have not yet been adequately addressed by police psychology include: When does the duty to warn extend to the police administration and when or if the duty to warn or protect extends to the community at large if the client is a public safety officer?

Strengths and Weaknesses

After 15 years the FCPD EAP is grounded as an entity for the Fairfax County Police Department. It has established a level of trust that makes it accessible and workable. Perhaps as a result of credibility it has not evidenced itself well enough through program research and evaluation. Although the program documents utilization rates, intake categories, and statistics for various areas, it does not sufficiently study its successes and failures through ongoing investigation.

Other limitations of the EAP have to do with staff time. The FCPD EAP has only one full-time therapist, who also acts as the coordinator. Assistance is provided by two psychologists who are available on a very part-time basis. Whereas staffing requirements may be less of an issue for the private EAP consultant, it is often an issue for mental health centers that operate under serious budget constraints and require excessive justifications for staff positions. For that reason, the FCPD EAP is more reactive and less formative than is wise.

The FCPD EAP provides timely crisis intervention and short-term treatment services to department personnel. It appears to reach reasonable numbers of employees and rough estimates are that about 40% of the department's employees have used its services. It has focused most of its efforts on direct service because that is where the urgent demands are. In its attempts to respond to these needs it has less time to devote to the more traditional EAP functions of prevention, training, and consultation. Although the basic needs for training are covered, the FCPD EAP would undoubtedly be better served if it had more time and staff to provide services in the area of prevention. A variety of ongoing training workshops could stimulate personnel to use EAP services before they become crises or job performance is affected.

CONCLUSION

Providing psychological services to police organizations is a relatively new phenomenon. The American Psychological Association Division 18 for Psychologists in Public Service was formed in 1948 and Section 8, for Police and Public Safety, was formed in 1974 in response to the growing demands for mental health interventions from police departments across the country. How best to provide those services to police organizations is the challenge.

Professionals in the field have learned through their work some of what does and does not work in an evolving area of mental health work. As the base of experience grows, it becomes increasingly clear that no one psychological services program can provide for all of the diverse psychological needs of these organizations. The role of the EAP should ultimately be to provide services to those who seek counseling assistance and to provide training and consultation to encourage police personnel to seek assistance.

EAPs contracted with community mental health centers offer services free of role conflict and can work with department-employed or contracted mental health professionals to provide a range of services in areas such as hiring processes, fitness for duty evaluation, test validation, and forensic psychology. Whereas a wide range of services might be beyond the scope of any one of these mental health options, together they can serve the mental health needs of a diverse police community.

REFERENCES

Banks, C. W. (1992). *Validity of the Fairfax County police department psychological test battery.* Draft report.

Fairfax County Office of Research and Statistics. (1991). *Fairfax County profile.* Fairfax, VA: Author.

Gentz, D. (1986). A system for the delivery of psychological services for police personnel. In J. Reese & H. Goldstein (Eds.), *Psychological services for law enforcement* (pp. 257–282). Washington, DC: U.S. Government Printing Office.

Hays, V. (1985). *Post shooting psychological response.* Unpublished survey.

Johnson, L. B. (1991, May 29). *On the front lines: Police stress and well-being.* Prepared statement Hearing before the Select Committee on Children, Youth and Families. House of Representatives, 102nd Congress, First Session.

Mann, P. A. (1980). Ethical issues for psychologists in police agencies. In J. Monahan (Ed.), *Who is the client? The ethics of psychological intervention in the criminal justice system* (pp. 18–42). Washington, DC: American Psychological Association.

Solomen, R., & Horn, J. (1986). Post shooting traumatic reactions: A pilot study. In J. Reese & H. Goldstein (Eds.), *Psychological services for law enforcement* (pp. 383–393). Washington, DC: U.S. Government Printing Office.

Tarasoff vs. Regents of University of California, 131 Cal. Rptr. 14, 551 P 2d 334 (1976).

CHAPTER NINE

Professionally Administered Critical Incident Debriefing for Police Officers

Nancy Bohl

The Counseling Team, San Bernardino, CA

In ordinary citizens, the occurrence of severe stress reactions, in the form of nightmares, flashbacks, sleep disturbances, and anxiety, after involvement in major disasters is well known (Frederick, 1977; MacHovec, 1984; van der Kolk, 1984). That similar reactions could occur in police officers involved in shootings or other highly disturbing situations was not widely recognized until recently. What prevented any recognition of the degree to which police officers were at risk for the development of severe stress reactions was the fact that two assumptions were made. The first was that, because they are trained to deal with emergency situations and do so on a more frequent basis than ordinary citizens, police officers are not vulnerable to the development of the kinds of stress responses seen in civilians. The second assumption was that if stress symptoms occurred, they did so in a limited number of individuals, and no special attention needed to be paid. Police officers were tough and, as Reiser and Geiger (1984) put it, "time would heal" (p. 317).

During the 1980s, it became clear that these assumptions were not valid. A number of authors described the occurrence in police officers of the same kinds of symptoms seen in civilians (e.g., nightmares, flashbacks, and anxiety) after those officers had been involved in crisis situations in which their lives or the lives of others had been threatened (Ayoob, 1982; Blak, 1986; Carson, 1982; Loo, 1986; McMains, 1986; Nielsen, 1986; Reiser & Geiger, 1984; Stratton, 1984). Furthermore, it was recognized that, if left untreated, these symptoms could, and did, have long-lasting effects. Officers involved in shootings or other equally traumatic incidents developed posttraumatic stress disorder, displayed diminished work performance, left the force within a few years of a shooting, became involved in alcohol and other substance abuse, or even attempted suicide (Blak, 1986; Clements & Horn, 1986; Kroes, 1985; Perrier, 1984; Solomon & Horn, 1986).

Originally, attention was directed primarily to one particular situation as being sufficiently stressful to cause concern—an officer-involved shooting (Fishkin, 1988; McMains, 1986; Solomon & Horn, 1986)—but later it was recognized that a range of other situations also had the potential for being highly traumatic, and the concept of the critical incident was born (Gentz, 1991). By the end of the 1980s, the matter of critical incident stress responses in police officers was deemed of sufficient importance to merit a special conference on the topic, which was held at the FBI Academy (Reese, Horn, & Dunning, 1991). At the present time, far from being viewed as invincible, police are seen as individuals who, because of their repeated exposure to scenes of carnage and mayhem, may be especially at risk for the development of stress symptoms.

This chapter deals with professionally run critical incident debriefing for police. First some background material is presented. The critical incident is defined in detail, the nature of the reactions displayed by police officers is described, and the theoretical basis for professionally administered debriefing programs is explained. Second, a detailed account of the mandatory debriefing program used by the author with police in San Bernardino and Riverside Counties in California is presented, and the model is compared with the one developed by Mitchell for firefighters and other emergency personnel. Third, evidence is presented to show that the debriefing method achieves some measure of success. Fourth, some unresolved issues that merit further study are explored.

BACKGROUND MATERIAL

What Is a Critical Incident?

Various definitions have been offered of what constitutes a critical incident. According to Mitchell and Bray (1990), it is an event that has sufficient emotional power to overcome the usual coping abilities of the individual. According to Horn (1991), it is an event that is experienced on or off the job that is outside the realm of normal human experience and could be expected to produce significant emotional reactions in anyone. Nielsen (1986) stated that what characterizes the critical incident is that it is traumatic, unexpected, and a serious threat to the individual's well-being; contains an element of loss; and involves disruption of the individual's values or assumptions about the environment. Mitchell (1991) similarly, said that a critical incident is one in which the officer's expectations of perfect performance suddenly are tempered by crude reality; the officer sees her or his own imperfections and experiences a loss of self-confidence.

McMains (1991) and Gentz (1991) offered the most comprehensive descriptions. According to McMains (1991), a critical incident is a situation that reminds the officer of her or his own limits and overwhelms the individual's capacity to cope. One thing that makes the incident traumatic is that it brings home to the officer that he or she is not in total control of every situation but rather is vulnerable. The officer cannot maintain the myth of omnipotence and immortality. Gentz (1991) presented a similar argument. He said that the police officer experiences an event that cannot be assimilated into her or his current life perspective. The individual comes up against the reality of death. If the officer is sick and trembling, then the old self-concept of being perfectly controlled is challenged. Like McMains, Gentz said that the officer has a disturbing sense of his or her own vulnerability because the individual's usual defense mechanisms did not work. Gentz (1991) also agreed with Nielsen (1991) with respect to the element of loss. A critical incident involves loss because there may be death or serious injury, loss of a physical ability, or loss in terms of a major assault on the officer's values or assumptions about his or her environment. An important point made by Gentz (1991) was that a critical incident should be defined not in terms of the event but rather in terms of the impact it has on the individual. That is, a critical incident is one that, by definition, requires the individual to make extraordinary adjustments.

As noted earlier, the original concept of postshooting trauma has been broadened. The only danger at present is of going to the other extreme and listing virtually every situation that a police officer encounters as constituting a critical incident. Listed here are some of the specific examples cited by recent authors (Ayoob, 1984; Havassy, 1991; Mitchell, 1991; Mitchell & Bray, 1990; Nielsen & Eskridge, 1982; Stratton, 1984):

- Death (including suicide).
- Serious injury of another officer.
- Wounding or killing a suspect.
- Being wounded or in extreme danger.
- Witnessing serious multiple casualties.
- Traumatic deaths or injuries of children.
- Events that attract a great deal of media coverage.
- Situations in which the victims are known to the officer or remind him or her of a loved one.

- Traffic accidents or homicides that are particularly bizarre or gruesome.
- A failed rescue.
- An accidental death caused by the officer.
- A situation involving hostages.

Reactions to a Critical Incident

Immediate responses to a critical incident are physiological—muscular tremors, nausea, hyperventilation, faintness, sweating, and perceptual distortions (e.g., time being slowed down). All of these responses represent the body's attempt to mobilize for extreme stress. Subsequent reactions within minutes or hours of the episode include shock, fear, denial, anger, numbing, and a general feeling of unreality (Blak, 1986; Blum, 1987; Carson, 1982; Nielsen, 1986; Reiser & Geiger, 1984). These reactions have to do with the fact that the individual feels vulnerable; they represent an attempt to reestablish the control that was lacking during the incident (Horn, 1991).

Delayed reactions also can occur. Within several days or sometimes even weeks, the officer may experience grief, intrusive thoughts about the incident, flashbacks, nightmares, and other sleep disturbances. Although these reactions are especially troublesome to the individual (Ayoob, 1982; Blak, 1986; Carson, 1982; Hill, 1984; Mantell, 1986; Solomon & Horn, 1986; Stratton, 1984), they have some positive aspects. According to Gentz (1991), these symptoms are signs that the person is still attempting to adjust and to assimilate the experience, to find a new cognitive category into which it will fit. Additional delayed symptoms that may appear and that do not have such positive aspects are depression, emotional withdrawal, anxiety, guilt, paranoia about being watched, and sexual dysfunction (Carson, 1982; Fishkin, 1988; Hill, 1984; Loo, 1986; Mantell, 1986; Stratton, 1984). There may be delayed physiological symptoms as well, in the form of headaches and stomach aches. These represent anxiety in masked form. For the officer who is concerned about possible legal or other repercussions of the incident, it is easier to complain about headaches than about the worry itself.

Typically, the symptoms described in the preceding paragraphs are temporary. Within a few weeks or at most a few months of the critical incident, they gradually abate. However, in some cases—especially if no treatment was provided—the aftereffects of the critical incident are apparent many months later in the form of anger, hostility, irritability, problems about accepting authority, fatigue, inability to concentrate, loss of self-confidence, increased use of drugs and alcohol, and overindulgence in food (Ayoob, 1982; Blum, 1987; Carson, 1982; Fishkin, 1988; Loo, 1986; Mantell, 1986; Nielsen, 1986; Reiser & Geiger, 1984; Solomon & Horn, 1986; Stratton, 1984). Many of these long-term effects interfere with work performance and threaten the stability of close personal relationships. Ultimately, they may be responsible for early retirement, burnout, and suicide in police officers.

Not all of the aftereffects are negative. One positive aftereffect is that the officer may take some major step that had long been contemplated but about which he or she was hesitant. Examples are: an officer who was unhappily married before the incident decides afterward to get a divorce; an officer who was thinking about buying a house actually does so; an officer who has no children decides to become a parent. All of these responses constitute realistic attempts by the individual to come to terms with her or his own mortality.

Theoretical Basis for Treatment

During the 1980s, at the same time that attention was being called to the problem of critical incident stress in police officers, a number of authors described treatment programs administered by mental health professionals that either were in place or that the authors wished to see instituted (Alkus & Padesky, 1983; Blak, 1986; Fishkin, 1988; Garrison, 1986; Hannigan, 1985; Hill, 1984; Lippert & Ferrara, 1981; Mantell, 1986; McMains, 1986; Mitchell, 1983b; Somodevilla, 1986; Stillman, 1986; Trapasso, 1981; Wagner, 1986). Despite some minor differences in specifics, all of these programs were similar and were based on a set of assumptions that derived from crisis theory (Aguilera & Messick, 1986; Titchener & Kapp, 1981). My treatment program, which is described in the next section, rests on the same theoretical foundation.

Three very important assumptions are made. The first is that the individual being treated was functioning adequately and was free of serious psychological problems before the incident. The second, and related assumption, is that any symptoms displayed are not signs of serious disturbance; rather, the symptoms are those that would occur in anyone who had been exposed to a similar level of trauma. The third assumption is that any problems experienced are temporary. Because the intent is not to produce major alterations in personality or to deal with long-standing personal problems, treatment can be brief; often, it is confined to only a single debriefing. In such a setting, the mental health professional necessarily functions in a more directive way than would usually be the case. In addition to facilitating the expression of emotion about the incident, the professional provides support and reassurance. To the extent that specific information is provided about the normalcy of the officer's responses to the incident, the professional also functions as an educator. The goals of treatment are: (a) to alleviate the painful effects of the incident, (b) to prevent the subsequent development of a posttraumatic stress disorder, and (c) to restore the individual to the preincident level of functioning as quickly as possible (Mitchell & Everly,

1993). To accomplish the latter goal, it is important that treatment be administered relatively soon after the event, before the officer has time to see it in a maladaptive and self-critical way (McMains, 1991). Ideally, debriefing occurs within 24 hours of the incident.

THE BOHL LAW ENFORCEMENT MODEL

The debriefing technique I use with police officers derived originally from the pioneering work of Mitchell, a professional who, in a series of books and papers that date from 1982, has provided detailed accounts of how to carry out critical incident debriefings (Mitchell, 1982, 1983a, 1983b, 1984, 1986a, 1986b, 1986c, 1991; Mitchell & Bray, 1990; Mitchell & Everly, 1993). Although Mitchell's model provided a basis, I found, after continued work with police officers over the years, that his approach—which was developed to treat firefighters and other disaster workers—needed to be modified in a number of significant ways when the individuals being treated were police officers. In the description that follows, both similarities to, and differences from, Mitchell's technique are noted (all comparisons are based on Mitchell's most recent descriptions of his technique in Mitchell & Bray, 1990; Mitchell & Everly, 1993).

When Is a Debriefing Carried Out?

In my work with police in Riverside and San Bernardino Counties, California, the debriefing always is done as soon after the critical incident as possible. The facilitator interviews the officer or officers immediately after the incident and makes an assessment about what would be the most beneficial approach to follow. Frequently, the debriefing is conducted then. Sometimes, though, it is clear that an individual is too exhausted or hungry or that the individual simply feels unable to talk. Officers may say that they need to exercise, to see their families, or just get away from the scene. If that is the case, a debriefing is scheduled for some time within the next few days. If a group is involved, it is possible for different people to elect to do different things. Some may stay for an immediate debriefing, and others may elect to meet at a later time. The schedule, then, is flexible, with the paramount concern being how best to meet the needs of individual officers. The only limitation is that, if the debriefing is postponed, the delay period is not allowed to exceed 3 days. Also, it is made plain that the debriefing is mandatory.

My approach differs from the one described by Mitchell. Because he deals with disaster teams, Mitchell's assumption is that a fairly large group of individuals will be involved, and he outlines a whole hierarchy of interventions. These range from a large-scale *demobilization* of an entire disaster unit, to a smaller scale *defusing,* to a still smaller scale *debriefing.* In Mitchell's scheme, the debriefing is the most time consuming and intense of the three interventions. It is the only one that requires the presence of a mental health professional, but it is not used routinely. Rather, it is used when the other, shorter interventions have been tried and found to be ineffective. Consequently, it may be attempted as much as 3 weeks or more after the event, even though Mitchell acknowledges that a debriefing is best done between 24 and 72 hours after the critical event.

The Number of Participants at a Debriefing

In my work with police officers, it is not uncommon for the debriefing to involve only a single participant. That is because many situations—for example, an officer-involved shooting—involve only a single individual. Even if a group was involved in the incident, individual debriefings may be held first, within 24 hours of the incident; and then, within 1 week, the group will be brought together for another debriefing, the major purpose of which is to encourage bonding. The reason for this approach is that police officers who work on the street seem to do better in a one-on-one debriefing than in a group debriefing. Often, if several officers were involved in a single incident, they do not know each other and are reluctant to participate in a group debriefing. Special Weapons and Tactics (SWAT) teams, on the other hand, have a strong sense of group solidarity. They want to be seen in a group, and they are not embarrassed about talking about an emotional event before their peers. The situation that Mitchell described with emergency personnel is different. In his case, it is usual for a large group (20 or more) to be involved in a debriefing. These individuals, like police SWAT teams, probably functioned as a unit before and during the incident. Consequently, the maintenance of cohesiveness is a more important issue for them than for law enforcement personnel.

Who Conducts the Debriefing

The number of individuals on the debriefing team is variable. If peers or clergy are available, they are included, but it is possible for there to be only a single individual, the mental health professional. In Mitchell's system, where typically a large number of participants are involved, this approach is not feasible. A debriefing is led by a team of at least four individuals—a mental health professional, several peer support personnel, and perhaps a member of the clergy; and each member of the team has a designated role (e.g., leader, coleader, and doorkeeper) to play.

Duration of an Intervention

The duration of a debriefing varies according to the number of individuals involved. If only a single officer is seen, it may last for 45 minutes to 1 hour. If a small group is involved, the average time is 1½ to 2 hours. For larger groups, the time may extend to 3 or even 4 hours. The major determinant is that there be sufficient time for individuals in the group to ventilate feelings and to obtain support and reassurance. Mitchell's debriefings, which typically involve larger groups, necessarily last for longer, with 3 hours being an average duration.

Preparation for an Intervention

To prepare for the debriefing, I often walk through the scene of the incident. For example, if the debriefing involves an officer-related shooting, the shooting team that did the investigation will be interviewed to ascertain what happened. Useful background information is obtained. The commander may mention that he or she is worried about a particular individual who was involved in prior shootings or who is otherwise stressed (e.g., by being involved in a divorce).

In Mitchell's model, a more elaborate preparation is involved, but that is because, typically, his debriefings occur days or weeks after the event. He reported that members of the debriefing team meet first to review published reports of the incident and to engage in preliminary planning of the strategy to be followed at the debriefing. Afterward, there is a period of informal talk with the participants. Then, the team retires to a separate room to engage in more planning of strategy. Finally, they enter the debriefing room to conduct the debriefing.

Steps in the Debriefing

Phase 1. The first phase is the introduction, the purpose of which is to make clear to participants the nature of the process and who will be involved. The facilitator begins by telling the participants about herself and, if there is a peer counselor present, then he or she is introduced as well. Participants are told not only what the debriefing involves but also what it does not involve. Specifically, they are told that the purpose of the debriefing is to aid in recovery, and they are assured that information obtained during the debriefing will be confidential; also they are told that the debriefing is not a form of group therapy.

This phase is similar to the introduction phase employed by Mitchell. However, there is a one important difference. Mitchell makes clear to participants, at this time, that no one who does not wish to speak will be forced to do so; and he reports that, indeed, some unspecified proportion of firefighters and emergency personnel elect to remain silent during his debriefings. In my experience with police officers, that caution has been found to be unnecessary. Failure to take part in a debriefing is an extremely rare event and occurs in less than 5% of the cases. Generally, police officers are eager to say what happened, especially during the fact phase. There may be reluctance later to describe the feelings elicited by the incident; but, as discussed later, the experienced facilitator should be able to deal successfully with that reluctance.

The difference between Mitchell's experiences and mine may have to do with fact that, as already noted, the groups I see during a debriefing are considerably smaller than those seen by Mitchell. However, there is still a major theoretical difference between the two approaches. In my view, the explicit statement about not speaking may be counterproductive. If an officer is truly unwilling to speak, then the sensitive facilitator will respect that need. Nonetheless, every effort should be made by the facilitator to make individuals who take part in a debriefing feel sufficiently comfortable so that they are willing to participate fully in the debriefing process.

Phase 2. In my model, the second phase is a fact phase, during which participants tell what happened during the incident. The facilitator asks questions like the following: Where were you during the incident? Tell me about the experience. What was your role? Sometimes, it is helpful to ask a participant to go through the experience frame by frame, like a movie. When the facilitator listens to the accounts, she picks out issues to which she will return later during the feelings or reaction phase.

In Mitchell's system, the second phase also is one in which factual information is obtained about what happened during the incident. However, Mitchell discourages an early show of emotion at this time because he feels that such emotion makes participants feel anxious and like the debriefing is out of control. In my experience, the attempted distinction between phases of the debriefing that are cognitive and phases that are emotional is not meaningful. Consider a concrete example. Suppose that an officer is asked to state a fact but begins to express emotion. There is nothing to be gained by telling the participant to wait until later in the debriefing. The critical thing here is to be flexible. It is more important to respond empathically to the needs expressed by the individuals who attend the debriefing than to follow a rigid and arbitrary set of rules.

Phase 3. In my model, Phase 3, the thought phase, is one in which participants describe their thoughts during the stressful event. This phase is like the thought phase employed by Mitchell, except that participants are asked about all of their thoughts and not necessarily what occurred to them first, as in Mitchell's model. A further difference has to with the previously mentioned distinction that Mitchell attempts to make between cognitive and emotional domains. According to Mitchell, the thought phase is a transition from the earlier, more cognitive domain to an emotional domain. In my experience, the two domains are not so readily and neatly separated.

That even Mitchell finds the distinction difficult to maintain is shown by his statement that a debriefing can become intense during the thought phase. In their recent book, Mitchell and Everly (1993) reported that people sometimes walk out at this point and need to be brought back by a specially designated member of the debriefing team called a *doorkeeper*. In my experience with police officers, the problem of people walking out of a debriefing does not arise. On a few rare occasions, an officer who was in tears has left the room to compose herself or himself. In that case, the facilitator or some other member of the team went outside to make sure that the person was alright and told the officer to come back when he or she was feeling better. However, it is important to stress that, on these rare occasions, the officer came back voluntarily.

The difference between Mitchell's experiences with firefighters and emergency personnel and my experiences with police may be due to the fact that they are different populations. Police are more autonomous than firefighters and emergency personnel, and they are less used to working as part of a team. They would not tolerate a doorkeeper. However, again, there is a theoretical difference with respect to approach. In my view, it is intrusive to force people to attend a debriefing if they are too upset to be there. Also, if the debriefing is properly handled, people should not want to leave and there should then be no necessity to force them to return.

Phase 4. In my model, Phase 4 is the feelings or reaction phase, the purpose of which is to allow participants to express the emotions associated with the critical incident. At this time, the facilitator goes back to the factual statements made earlier by participants about their actions during the critical event. They are asked about what their feelings were while they were carrying out the actions they described earlier. For example, a participant might be asked: What did you feel when you realized that you had shot the suspect? What did you feel when you thought your partner had been shot?

What is helpful for participants is not the mere expression of emotions but rather the opportunity to validate feelings. Often, it is a revelation to discover that peers had similar feelings. Some emotions, it must be noted, are difficult to validate. For example, there is not much that even the facilitator can say to an individual who is experiencing strong guilt. In that particular situation, the guilt may be appropriate. Certainly, it is not helpful for the facilitator to say, "Well, you should not feel that way." In the debriefing situation, there are no "shoulds." An appropriate response by the facilitator is, "Okay, you feel guilty. What are you going to do with that guilt?"

Sometimes, police officers who were eager to speak during the fact phase do not want to describe their feelings at this point in the debriefing. An officer may say, "I felt just like he did" (indicating a neighbor who has just spoken). At that point, the facilitator may need to encourage the individual to speak by asking: What was the worst part of the experience for you? It is also possible for the reverse to occur. An officer may do little or no speaking during the fact phase and simply agree that the facts presented by his or her neighbors are correct. Yet, during the reaction phase, that same officer may voice emotions that are quite different from his or her neighbors.

In Mitchell's system, as in mine, the fourth phase is a feelings or reaction phase, during which the facilitator encourages participants to ventilate emotions. The major difference between the two approaches, however, is that I try to get at feelings by using information the participant already has provided. In contrast, Mitchell tries to get at feelings by asking: What was the worst thing about the event? What caused you the most pain? In my view, these are not the best questions to ask. For a police officer who was involved in a shooting, everything about the experience was bad. Consequently, questions of this type are not asked routinely. As noted earlier, they are used only if the individual is not otherwise responding.

Phase 5. In my model, Phase 5, the symptom phase, is one in which participants describe what they experienced at the time and are still experiencing. Most of the symptoms that participants talk about are immediate physiological responses like nausea and time slowing down. The facilitator tries to validate the participants' experiences. For example, if someone says, "I felt sick to my stomach," then the facilitator validates by saying that anyone would feel sick in that situation. However, it is important for others in the group to validate as well. The officer needs to know that her or his co-workers had the same reactions.

In Mitchell's model, symptoms are dealt with in two separate phases rather than one. First, participants are asked to describe what they experienced at the time, a few days later, and are still experiencing. The debriefing team may mention specific symptoms and ask if anyone has had those symptoms. During this phase, there is presumably a return to cognitions, as distinct from emotions. Then, there is a separate phase, the teaching phase, during which the facilitator tells participants that their stress responses are normal, and they are assured that the responses will subside. This phase, too, presumably is cognitive rather than emotional. Coping strategies, such as, diet, rest, exercise, and talking to the family are discussed.

In my experience with police officers, the separation into two phases was not found to be useful. Consequently, symptoms are dealt with in one phase that includes both the participants' statements about their symptoms and assurances by the facilitator that the symptoms are normal and they will subside. In contrast to Mitchell's experience, I have found that this part of the debriefing frequently has a strong emotional component. Participants are relieved when others share their symptoms. They no longer feel isolated. Most important, they know that they are not crazy.

Phase 6. Phase 6 of my model, the unfinished business phase, is one in which participants are asked: What in the present situation reminds you of a past experience? Do you want to talk about these other situations? There is no comparable phase in Mitchell's model. The unfinished business phase was added because experience showed that the incident for which the current debriefing was being conducted often acted as a catalyst. Participants were reminded of prior events, not all of which had involved a formal debriefing. When asked about these prior events, participants have a chance to talk about incidents about which they have strong and unresolved feelings. The debriefing ends with a greater sense of relief and closure than would otherwise be the case.

Phase 7. Phase 7 of my model is an educational or teaching phase. Participants are told about how to deal with their families and their children. For police, a special problem is the fact that a child may have heard that the officer killed someone. Another possibility is that family members may experience vicarious symptoms. Therefore, it is important to educate participants not only about what they have experienced so far but also about what they may experience after the debriefing. So, for example, participants are told: You may not be able to sleep tonight. You may find yourself arguing with your spouse a lot during the next few days. As in the symptoms phase, participants are reassured that their symptoms are normal and will go away. Feedback from police officers who have been debriefed makes it plain that they appreciate this attempt to prepare them, in a practical way, for the immediate future.

In Mitchell's system, there is also a teaching phase, as noted earlier, in which stress symptoms, both those already experienced and those that may be experienced later, are described, reassurance is provided about the normalcy of the responses, and coping strategies are discussed. Where the two models are different is that, at the end of Mitchell's teaching phase, participants are asked whether they can see anything positive or hopeful in the incident. The rationale is that the individual should try to see the incident as part of a growth experience. In my work with police officers, this approach has not proved to be useful. Officers who have seen their partners shot or killed or who have had to deal with cases of child abuse find it difficult to find anything hopeful or positive in the experience, no matter how well they handled the situation. If officers make spontaneous attempts to talk about positive aspects, they are not discouraged. However, this line of discussion is not followed routinely, as is done by Mitchell.

Phase 8. Phase 8 of my model, the wrap-up, is a time when questions are answered and participants are asked about whether there is any information they want passed on to their supervisors. In Mitchell's system, this phase is the final one; during it, the facilitator not only answers questions but also verbalizes feelings that were not openly expressed and sums up what has been said in the debriefing. This kind of verbalization of feelings is best done earlier. There is another difference from Mitchell's model. During this final phase, he has all team members make statements in which they indicate their support and offer encouragement. In my experience, such statements, however well intended, overpower participants. What works better for police is to have expressions of encouragement and support come from members of the peer group who were present at the debriefing.

Phase 9. Phase 9 of my model is a round robin. Each person is instructed to say anything that he or she wants to say. The remark can be addressed to anyone, but because others cannot respond directly, participants have a feeling of safety. The facilitator also contributes something at this time. This phase is not part of Mitchell's system. It was added because experience showed that it has a powerful effect on participants. Again, the theoretical difference between my approach and that of Mitchell needs to be noted. According to Mitchell, by the final phase, the debriefing should be back on solid cognitive rather than emotional ground. The round robin phase, on the other hand, constitutes an emotional ending. However, it is important to note that the emotions expressed are positive. The possibility exists for negative emotions to be expressed, but that never happens. For example, one police officer may say to another one, "I want you to know that I am glad you are my partner" or "I want you to know that Michael (a dead officer) loved you." A remark addressed to the facilitator might be "I am glad we did this." Thus, the debriefing ends on an upbeat note, with hugs, handshakes and a show of relief. Participants seem to experience a strong sense of bonding.

Afterward. Typically, participants do not leave but stay to talk informally with the facilitator, other members of the debriefing team, and each other. Before they leave, they receive handouts describing the initial symptoms experienced, symptoms they may experience later, ways to cope (e.g., exercise, meditation, talking to family members), and unsuccessful coping mechanisms to avoid (e.g., reliance on alcohol and drugs). For police officers in San Bernardino and Riverside Counties, the mandatory debriefing with a mental health professional is the first, but not necessarily the only, intervention after a critical incident. The officer has the option of requesting additional debriefings with a mental health professional, a peer support group, or a member of the clergy. Debriefings with nonprofessionals are extremely valuable because they provide a different kind of support than that provided by the professional.

DO THE TREATMENTS WORK?

It is unrealistic to think that a single debriefing will resolve all problems, so that the individual does not feel anything afterward or think about the incident. The major purpose of the debriefing is to prevent the occurrence of more serious problems weeks or months later. The question is: Does the debriefing accomplish that purpose?

According to McMains (1991) and Mitchell and Everly (1993), there are fewer resignations in departments that have critical incident stress debriefing programs than in departments that do not have such programs. There are several unpublished studies (cited in Mitchell, 1991; Mitchell & Everly, 1993) in which benefits were claimed, but because a treated group was not compared with an untreated control group, the findings of these studies are not conclusive. As noted by Mitchell and Everly (1993), the most convincing case would be made by a piece of research in which a true experimental design was involved, meaning that a comparison was made between individuals who had experienced critical incident debriefing and individuals who had not experienced critical incident debriefing.

To my knowledge, the only study of this type carried out to date was the one by Bohl (1991). Participants were male police officers drawn from the Inland Empire area of southern California, all of whom had been involved in a critical incident. The treated group ($N = 40$) came from departments that had mandatory debriefing programs, and the untreated group ($N = 31$) came from departments that did not have such programs. Members of the treated group received a 1½-hour group debriefing (with my technique) by a mental health professional within 24 hours after the critical incident. Three months later, each participant took three formal psychological tests, the State-Trait Anxiety Inventory, the Beck Depression Inventory, and the Novaco Provocation Inventory (a measure of anger). A fourth test, devised by Bohl, assessed the frequency of occurrence during the preceding week of six common stress symptoms—nightmares, flashbacks, difficulty falling asleep, difficulty staying asleep, loss of appetite, and excessive hunger. Although the two groups did not differ significantly on the measure of anxiety, they differed in the expected direction on the other three measures. By comparison with the untreated group, the treated group was significantly less angry and depressed; they also had fewer and less severe stress symptoms. Overall, then, the treatment seemed to be successful in reducing the distress caused by involvement in a critical incident.

A possible weakness in the study was that, due to the necessity to comply with regulations imposed by the participating departments, it was not possible to assign participants to the treated and untreated groups on a random basis. That lack meant that the results might have been due to pre-existing differences between the two groups. However, Bohl (1991) presented considerable evidence against such an interpretation. The treated and untreated groups did not differ with respect to the number of critical incidents in which they had been involved, age, marital status, or number of years on the job. The departments from which treated and untreated participants were drawn were essentially similar with respect to geographic location, size, philosophy, hiring practices, and socioeconomic level of the populace served. Further, the departments from which untreated participants were obtained had instituted mandatory debriefing programs by the time the study was over. Thus, even though the Bohl (1991) study did not meet all of the criteria for a true experimental design, it nevertheless presented the best evidence currently available that debriefing programs for police are beneficial.

UNRESOLVED ISSUES

There are two issues about which further research are needed: (a) Why do the treatments work? (b) Why do some people cope better with critical incidents than others? Current views on both of these topics are now considered.

Why Do the Treatments Work?

There are four commonly cited reasons for why the interventions work (Blak, 1991; Havassy, 1991; Mitchell & Everly, 1993). The first has to do with promptness. They are applied early, before the person becomes isolated and begins to utilize maladaptive coping mechanisms (such as withdrawal) that effectively isolate him or her from help. The second has to do with emotions. The debriefing interview offers an opportunity for emotional catharsis. The third has to do with cognitive factors. The individual has an opportunity to make sense out of what happened. The fourth has to do with the provision of peer support and group acceptance. Common themes emerge during the debriefing—anger, fear of repetition of the event, powerlessness, guilt, depression, distress about having behaved aggressively, questioning of the career choice, and reaffirmation of efficacy and competence.

Havassy (1991) suggested another reason that is worth considering in detail, which is that the debriefing works because it functions as a social ritual. She pointed out that rituals or prescribed ways of behaving have been used in all cultures as a way to deal with the emotions aroused by death and loss. Rituals are healing because they provide the participant with a sense of closure about the event. People outside of the police who have been involved in disasters can find support groups. Police need to find support groups within their own setting because they feel isolated from the public and also are committed to the maintenance of an image of control.

Debriefing is an ideal ritual because it is culturally sanctioned within the police culture; in many cases it is mandatory. The individual who is upset does not have to think about what to do. Also, the debriefing is shared by individuals from the same background. In the course of the debriefing, as in other rituals that involve loss, the individual's feelings are validated, and the result is that the person feels less isolated. He or she has participated in a shared social event within the community.

Why Do Some People Cope Better Than Others?

One factor in ability to cope may be the sheer number of incidents in which the individual has been involved. The effect of such involvement appears to be cumulative. There may be, finally, just one horrifying incident too many for a police officer who was functioning adequately before the incident (Blak, 1986; Clements & Horn, 1986; Perrier, 1984). On the other hand, prior experience need not be a negative factor. Nielsen (1991) pointed out that if the individual has been involved in prior episodes in which he or she coped successfully, then the sense of mastery is increased, and the likelihood of a favorable outcome is greater than if the individual was experiencing the first critical incident.

Previous training in how to cope also may be helpful. Ideally, what such training should do is to prepare the individual. If he or she feels adequate and possessed of the necessary skills to cope successfully, it is less likely that the critical incident will be perceived as threatening and potentially overwhelming (Mitchell, 1991).

Another factor to consider is the degree of concurrent stress. The critical incident needs to be seen in context as just one of many events in the officer's life (Nielsen, 1991). There is also the matter of the degree to which the officer was blamed for the event. As van der Kolk (1991) noted, the prognosis is better if the individual was not blamed for the incident.

Personality is yet another factor. Individuals with a strong sense of self should feel less threatened by failure to perform perfectly and so should do better than those with a weak sense of self (Nielsen, 1991; van der Kolk, 1991). Also, individuals who are able to ventilate their feelings and who try, afterward, to integrate the traumatic event into their total life experience (Horowitz, 1986) should cope more successfully than individuals who rationalize, deny, or ignore the experience.

SUMMARY AND CONCLUSIONS

The importance of dealing with critical incident stress in police officers now is widely recognized. Stress symptoms can occur after a variety of traumatic experiences, of which an officer-involved shooting is only one. Some reactions are immediate and represent mobilization for stress and attempts to re-establish cognitive control. Other reactions occur within days or sometimes even weeks of the incident and represent concealed anxiety, as well as continued attempts to assimilate the experience cognitively. Long-lasting responses may occur, especially if no treatment was provided.

The theoretical basis for treatment derives from crisis theory. It is assumed that the individual was free of serious psychological disturbance before the incident and that the symptoms are temporary. Treatment is brief, immediate, and directed toward alleviation of present symptoms, prevention of future symptoms, and restoration of an earlier level of functioning.

The treatment model developed by Bohl for police officers was described. Officers can be seen alone or in groups, immediately after an incident or within a few days; treatment can involve a team or only a single mental health professional; and, depending on the size and needs of the group, it can last anywhere from 45 minutes to 3 to 4 hours. There are nine phases. In the introduction, participants are told what the debriefing is about. In the fact phase, participants are asked to describe their roles during the incident. In the thought phase, participants are asked about their thoughts during the incident. In the feelings or reaction phase, participants are asked about what their feelings were while they carried out the actions described earlier during the fact phase. During the symptoms phase, participants describe what they experienced during the incident and afterward, and they are assured by the facilitator that their responses are normal and will subside. In the unfinished business phase, participants are asked about other prior situations that were similar. During the education or teaching phase, participants are told about symptoms that may be experienced later. In the wrap-up, questions are answered, and participants tell the facilitator anything they wish to have passed on to their supervisors. In the round robin phase, each person, including the facilitator, makes one statement that can be addressed to anyone and to which others cannot respond directly. Afterward, participants are told about how they can request additional help, and they are given useful handouts about how to cope.

The Bohl Law Enforcement model was developed specifically for police officers, and it differs, both in method and in philosophy, from the treatment model developed by Mitchell for firefighters and other emergency personnel. The many differences were pointed out in detail earlier and are only briefly mentioned here. The model for police is less structured and formal, and there is no sharp distinction between cognitive and emotional phases of the debriefing. Some procedures used by Mitchell have been found not to work with police (e.g., routinely asking what was the worst aspect of the experience and asking participants to see something positive in the experience). Some aspects of Mitchell's technique have been found to be unnecessary with police (e.g., forcibly returning unwilling participants to a debriefing).

Two of Mitchell's phases have been combined, and two new phases have been added (unfinished business and round robin).

Experimental evidence was reviewed to show that critical incident debriefing for police actually is beneficial. Finally, two unresolved issues were considered: Why do the treatments work? Why do some people cope better with critical incidents than others? Current views were described, but it is plain that more research is needed.

REFERENCES

Aguilera, D. C., & Messick, J. M. (1986). *Crisis intervention: Theory and methodology* (5th ed.). St. Louis: Mosby.

Alkus, S., & Padesky, C. (1983). Special problems of police officers: Stress-related issues and interventions. *The Counseling Psychologist, 11*, 55–64.

Ayoob, M. (1982, May–June). Post shooting trauma: Part one. *Police Marksman*, pp. 15–17.

Ayoob, M. (1984, October). Post-shooting trauma—The police association's role. *Police Product News*, pp. 13–15, 52.

Blak, R. A. (1986). A department psychologist responds to traumatic incidents. In J. T. Reese & H. A. Goldstein (Eds.), *Psychological services for law enforcement* (pp. 311–314). Washington, DC: U.S. Government Printing Office.

Blak, R. A. (1991). Critical incident debriefing for law enforcement personnel: A model. In J. T. Reese, J. M. Horn, & C. Dunning (Eds.), *Critical incidents in policing* (rev. ed.; pp. 23–30). Washington, DC: U.S. Government Printing Office.

Blum, L. N. (1987). Officer survival after trauma: The companion officer program. *Journal of California Law Enforcement, 21*, 28–32.

Bohl, N. K. (1991). The effectiveness of brief psychological interventions in police officers after critical incidents. In J. T. Reese, J. M. Horn, & C. Dunning (Eds.), *Critical incidents in policing* (rev. ed.; pp. 31–38). Washington, DC: U.S. Government Printing Office.

Carson, S. (1982, October). Post-shooting stress reaction. *The Police Chief*, pp. 66–68.

Clements, C. B., & Horn, W. G. (1986, October–November). Stress management in law enforcement. *The National Sheriff*, pp. 18–28.

Frederick, C. J. (1977). Current thinking about crisis or psychological intervention in United States disasters. *Mass Emergencies, 2*, 43–50.

Fishkin, G. L. (1988). *Police burnout: Signs, symptoms and solutions*. Gardena, CA: Harcourt Brace Jovanovich.

Garrison, W. E. (1986). Neuro-linguistic programing: An optional intervention to post traumatic incident counseling. In J. T. Reese & H. A. Goldstein (Eds.), *Psychological services for law enforcement* (pp. 351–356). Washington, DC: U.S. Government Printing Office.

Gentz, D. (1991). The psychological impact of critical incidents on police officers. In J. T. Reese, J. M. Horn, & C. Dunning (Eds.), *Critical incidents in policing* (rev. ed.; pp. 119–121). Washington, DC: U.S. Government Printing Office.

Hannigan, M. J. (1985, February). Counseling program for officers. *California Peace Officer Magazine*, pp. 49–51.

Havassy, V. J. (1991). Critical incident debriefing: Ritual for closure. In J. T. Reese, J. M. Horn, & C. Dunning (Eds.), *Critical incidents in policing* (rev. ed.; pp. 139–142). Washington, DC: U.S. Government Printing Office.

Hill, W. R. (1984, September). Police and post-killing trauma. *Police Product News/Buyers Guide*, pp. 57–59, 68–69.

Horn, J. M. (1991). Critical incidents for law enforcement officers. In J. T. Reese, J. M. Horn, & C. Dunning (Eds.), *Critical incidents in policing* (rev. ed.; pp. 143–148). Washington, DC: U.S. Government Printing Office.

Horowitz, M. J. (1986). *Disaster stress studies: New methods and findings.* Washington, DC: American Psychiatric Press.

Kroes, W. M. (1985). *Society's victims—The police.* Springfield, IL: Thomas.

Lippert, W., & Ferrara, E. R. (1981, December). The cost of coming out on top: Emotional responses to surviving the deadly battle. *FBI Law Enforcement Bulletin*, pp. 6–9.

Loo, R. (1986, February). Police psychology: The emergence of a new field. *The Police Chief*, pp. 26–30.

MacHovec, F. (1984). The use of brief hypnosis for post-traumatic stress disorders. *Emotional First Aid, 1*, 14–22.

Mantell, M. R. (1986). San Ysidro: When the badge turns blue. In J. T. Reese & H. A. Goldstein (Eds.), *Psychological services for law enforcement* (pp. 357–360). Washington, DC: U.S. Government Printing Office.

McMains, M. J. (1986). Post-shooting trauma: Principles from combat. In J. T. Reese & H. A. Goldstein (Eds.), *Psychological services for law enforcement* (pp. 365–368). Washington, DC: U.S. Government Printing Office.

McMains, M. J. (1991). The management and treatment of postshooting trauma. In J. T. Reese, J. M. Horn, & C. Dunning (Eds.), *Critical incidents in policing* (rev. ed.; pp. 191–197). Washington, DC: U.S. Government Printing Office.

Mitchell, J. T. (1982, Fall). Recovery from rescue. *Responses*, pp. 7–10.

Mitchell, J. T. (1983a, February). Emergency medical stress. *APCO Bulletin*, pp. 14–16.

Mitchell, J. T. (1983b, January). When disaster strikes. *Journal of Emergency Medical Services*, pp. 36–39.

Mitchell, J. T. (1984, January). The 600-run limit. *Journal of Emergency Medical Services*, pp. 52–54.

Mitchell, J. T. (1986a). Assessing and managing the psychologic impact of terrorism, civil disorder, disasters, and mass casualties. *Emergency Care Quarterly, 2*, 51–58.

Mitchell, J. T. (1986b, August). Living dangerously. *Firehouse*, pp. 50–52.

Mitchell, J. T. (1986c). Teaming up against critical incident stress. *Chief Fire Executive*, pp. 24–26, 84.

Mitchell, J. T. (1991). Law enforcement applications for critical incident stress teams. In J. T. Reese, J. M. Horn, & C. Dunning (Eds.), *Critical incidents in policing* (rev. ed.; pp. 201–211). Washington, DC: U.S. Government Printing Office.

Mitchell, J., & Bray, G. (1990). *Emergency services stress.* Englewood Cliffs, NJ: Prentice-Hall.

Mitchell, J., & Everly, G. S., Jr. (1993). *Critical incident stress debriefing: (CISD).* Ellicott City, MD: Chevron.

Nielsen, E. (1986). Understanding and assessing traumatic stress reactions. In J. T. Reese & H. A. Goldstein (Eds.), *Psychological services for law enforcement* (pp. 369–374). Washington, DC: U.S. Government Printing Office.

Nielsen, E. (1991). Factors influencing the nature of posttraumatic stress disorders. In J. T. Reese, J. M. Horn, & C. Dunning (Eds.), *Critical incidents in policing* (rev. ed.; pp. 213–219). Washington, DC: U.S. Department of Justice.

Nielsen, E., & Eskridge, D. L. (1982, July). Post shooting procedures: The forgotten officer. *Police Product News*, pp. 41–43.

Perrier, D. C. (1984). Police stress: The hidden foe. *Canadian Police College Journal, 8*, 15–26.

Reese, J. T., Horn, J. M., & Dunning, C. (Eds.). (1991). *Critical incidents in policing.* Washington, DC: U.S. Department of Justice.

Reiser, M., & Geiger, S. P. (1984). Police officer as victim. *Professional Psychology: Research and Practice, 15*, 315–323.

Solomon, R. M., & Horn, J. M. (1986). Post-shooting traumatic reactions: A pilot study. In J. T. Reese & H. A. Goldstein (Eds.), *Psychological services for law enforcement* (pp. 383–393). Washington, DC: U.S. Government Printing Office.

Somodevilla, S. A. (1986). Post-shooting trauma: Reactive and proactive treatment. In J. T. Reese & H. A. Goldstein (Eds.), *Psychological services for law enforcement* (pp. 395–398). Washington, DC: U.S. Government Printing Office.

Stillman, F. (1986). The invisible victims: Myths and realities. In J. T. Reese & H. A. Goldstein (Eds.), *Psychological services for enforcement* (pp. 143–146). Washington, DC: U.S. Government Printing Office.

Stratton, J. G. (1984). *Police passages.* Manhattan Beach, CA: Glennon.

Titchener, J. L., & Kapp, F. T. (1981). Family and character change at Buffalo Creek. In C. J. Frederick (Ed.), *Aircraft accidents: Emergency mental health problems* (pp. 23–32). Washington, DC: U.S. Department of Health and Human Services.

Trapasso, P. A. (1981). *High stress police intervention: Post-shooting trauma.* Massachusetts State Police, Psychological Services Unit, Boston, MA.

van der Kolk, B. A. (1984). Introduction. In B. A. van der Kolk (Ed.), *Post-traumatic stress disorder: Psychological and biological sequelae* (pp. 1–5). Washington, DC: American Psychiatric Press.

van der Kolk, B. A. (1991). The psychological processing of traumatic events: The personal experience of posttraumatic stress disorder. In J. T. Reese, J. M. Horn, & C. Dunning (Eds.), *Critical incidents in policing* (rev. ed.; pp. 359–364). Washington, DC: U.S. Government Printing Office.

Wagner, M. (1986). Trauma debriefing in the Chicago Police Department. In J. T. Reese & H. A. Goldstein (Eds.), *Psychological services for law enforcement* (pp. 399–404). Washington, DC: U.S. Government Printing Office.

CHAPTER TEN

Law Enforcement Families

Elizabeth K. White
Audrey L. Honig
Los Angeles Sheriff's Department,
Psychological Services Unit

Law enforcement employers since the early 1970s have begun to recognize a need to assist employees dealing with work-related stressors, both as an obligation to the employee and for self-preservation of the agency (absenteeism, stress retirements, etc.). Overall, this concept of stress and the workplace, however, is still a relatively new phenomena with a whole range of resources, or lack thereof, actually existing to address this reality. The idea that the work environment of law enforcement could have some impact on an employee including that employee's level of work productivity and general physical and emotional health, now seems generally accepted. There has even been some acceptance within the law enforcement community of the fact that this relationship is probably not unidirectional; the families may also impact and be impacted by the job. Indeed, some modicum of services to families has been in existence in some agencies for many years. The notion, however, that there exists a complex, cyclic relationship between the work life and home life of peace officers with each impacting and being impacted by the other has only recently moved to the forefront (Bibbens, 1986; Hartsough, 1991; Platt, 1975; Stratton, 1975).

Employers are now slowly beginning to recognize the need to provide more in-depth assistance to the families of law enforcement personnel. The Federal Bureau of Investigation (FBI) recently hosted a national seminar for police psychologists on the topic of law enforcement families. In addition, recent Congressional hearings have targeted law enforcement families as warranting further examination and possible assistance.

In order to understand the impact of the profession of law enforcement on the family, it is important to consider both direct and indirect factors. Job stressors obviously can impact law enforcement personnel directly. Peace officers then bring this impact home to their families (indirect impact), including the impact resulting from the fact that the career itself changes the officer. Many of the coping methods or adaptations that a peace officer may make in order to deal with the stress of a career in law enforcement are in themselves problematic to both the peace officer and his or her family. In addition, some job characteristics may have a direct impact on law enforcement family members.

This chapter discusses both the direct and indirect sources of stress on law enforcement families and examines the potential consequences and possible interventions.

DIRECT FACTORS: PEACE OFFICER

Once it is acknowledged that a peace officer may experience particular types of stress as a result of the job, it is an easy next step to conclude that he or she will bring that stress home to the family. Although we may like to believe that we can sufficiently compartmentalize our reactions to job-related problems, experience tells us that anything that stresses the peace officer stresses the officer's family system. Several authors have provided summaries of law enforcement stressors (Alkus & Padesky, 1983; Davidson & Veno, 1980; Eisenberg, 1975; Ellison & Genz, 1983; Farkas, 1986; Kroes, 1976; Kroes, Margolis, & Hurrell, 1974). The following characteristics are drawn from their research and includes stressors identified by law enforcement personnel themselves.

Job Characteristics

Fear and Danger. Although always a part of law enforcement, the ease with which suspects are able to obtain advanced weaponry, the influx of individuals from other cultures who have a different perception of law enforcement, and the increase in the willingness of suspects to assault a peace officer have greatly exacerbated the average peace officer's perception of danger, thus increasing his or her anxiety level. This increased anxiety level can show itself in a number of ways within the family system including increased irritability, lowered frustration tolerance, and health consequences, to name a few.

Financial or Administrative Danger. In addition to physical danger, peace officers are having to face civil litigation as well as internal scrutiny to a higher degree than ever before, which can significantly increase a peace officer's level of anxiety and uncertainty in the field (Reiser & Geiger, 1984;

Shealey, 1985). Every time peace officers take some action they must be cognizant of the fact that they are putting their job or even personal home on the line. The consequences of a perceived or actual error in judgment can be extreme.

Work Schedule. Shift work, rotating shifts, irregular or rotating days off, holiday work, unexpected overtime, court appearances on regular days off, on-call requirements, and involuntary overtime are all identified as problematic by peace officers. The negative impact of shift work, in particular, is well known and includes decreased sleep quantity and quality, inferior work quality, changes in mood, and so on (Hurrell, 1986; Kroes, 1976; O'Neil, 1986). An irregular or uncertain work schedule also obviously has a negative impact on social planning and recreational and relaxation activities.

Special Assignments. Although detective and special assignments are greatly prized, they often add additional stress to the system. Certain assignments (e.g., Narcotics, Vice, undercover, SWAT, etc.) involve long hours, additional training, on-call work, and an increased amount of time away from home. Many also involve a greater degree of risk or exposure to trauma (Farkas, 1986).

Trauma. Critical incidents (e.g., officer-involved shootings), exposure to trauma (e.g., mutilated bodies from a traffic accident), exposure to the pain and suffering of others, and exposure to man's adversity to man (assault, murder, etc.) all potentially impose a heavy toll on the average officer. The impact of critical incidents on peace officers is well documented (Reese, Horn, & Dunning, 1991; Reiser & Geiger, 1984). Over 86% of officers involved in a critical incident will show at least transitory posttraumatic stress symptoms. Lipson (1986) found that 50% of the peace officers exposed to the San Ysidro massacre were still exhibiting stress reactions as long as 6 months after the event. Ayoob (1981) reported that 95% of peace officers involved in a shooting leave the force within 5 years. Critical incidents may have an even more powerful effect on rural peace officers, who both live in and police a small community, because they are more likely to personalize the event or identify with the victims. Clearly these reactions and the resulting signs and symptoms do not manifest themselves solely on the job, but throughout the affected officer's life.

Role Confusion and Conflict. Many officers report difficulties related to the many different demands inherent in law enforcement (Alkus & Padesky, 1983). The peace officer must balance the need to apprehend a suspect with the need to protect the suspect's civil rights. Also, the peace officer must balance the role of peace keeper, public servant, and "crime buster." Again, resulting tensions and frustrations do not dissipate once outside the station door.

Stimulus Extremes. Peace officers must deal with an unusual combination of boredom and extreme arousal. A peace officer may spend a good portion of a shift doing routine tasks. This routine work is interspersed with moments of extreme arousal and occasionally life-threatening situations. Consequently, a peace officer must remain in a state of tension or readiness. The need to stay alert can result in a permanent state of arousal that is difficult to shut off at the end of the shift. Constant arousal can also result in emotional burnout and withdrawal.

Responsibility for Others. Peace officers must deal with the added stress of being responsible for the lives of other human beings (Bull, Bustin, Evan, & Gahagan, 1983; Maslach & Jackson, 1979; Reiser, 1982). On a regular basis, peace officers are asked to play the role of everything from social worker to priest. Often they are unable to effectively resolve the problems encountered in the field. In addition, much police work results in unfinished business. Peace officers may make suggestions or initiate interventions that they will never be able to follow up on. No closure is obtained. Peace officers do not know if they have had an impact.

External Stressors

Criminal Justice System. Peace officers report frustration and dissatisfaction with the judicial system, the correctional system, unfavorable court decisions (regarding criminals brought to justice as well as rulings that impact how peace officers do their job), inconsiderate court procedures (inconvenient scheduling, continuances, and the inability to schedule the peace officer's testimony), and lack of cooperation between different branches of law enforcement or even within a law enforcement agency. All of these system factors serve to increase the frustration of the average peace officer and can lead to a sense of futility.

Public Perception. Inaccurate or distorted press accounts and unfavorable public attitudes can have a great impact on peace officers. Officers report criticism from neighbors, friends, and sometimes even family members regarding actions taken by either a peace officer as an individual or actions taken by the department as a whole. Again, resentment and increased frustration are the consequence.

Scandal or Investigation. When the subject of an administrative, criminal, or civil investigation is a peace officer, the impact can be felt agencywide. Investigations of this nature, whether founded or unfounded, can impact officer morale and decrease self-esteem. In addition, they may further exacerbate the negative public opinion problem already identified, resulting in increased hostility, decreased respect, and further alienation. Many peace officers feel the need to defend the department or the individual being investigated. This problem is further exacerbated if peace officers work in a rural area or live in the same community where they patrol.

Organizational Stressors

Training. Many officers feel they are inadequately trained to handle the various job demands. Feelings of inadequacy and vulnerability on the job can lead to overcontrol and increased authoritarianism off the job.

Poor Supervision. Many peace officers report inadequate or nonexistent supervision. In some agencies, it is not unusual for training officers to themselves have as little as 2 to 3 years experience in the field. Supervisor attitude can greatly alleviate or aggravate stress in the work environment.

Workload and Equipment. One of the most frequent complaints reported by law enforcement personnel references being asked to do too much with too little. With the current governmental budgetary crises, cutbacks often leave peace officers with insufficient or inadequate equipment, insufficient backup, and not enough time to do quality work. The peace officer may be left feeling sabotaged and overwhelmed. Basic officer safety issues are raised with increased anxiety in the field as the result.

Pay, Promotion, and Recognition. Many peace officers complain of inadequate pay. Promotional practices are seen as either unfair or just unavailable (Alkus & Padesky, 1983). Many peace officers have concerns regarding the parity of promotional systems in regard to women and minorities. Lastly, many peace officers complain of inadequate rewards or recognition. Whereas criticism for mistakes is common, recognition for a job well done is felt to be rare. Sad but true, we tend to then turn around and treat others the way we have been treated, using the same punitive system that ignores positive accomplishments and pounces on every error.

Support. Many peace officers report concerns regarding lack of support from middle and upper management. They perceive that the higher echelon is more concerned with politics than police work. Department policies may be seen as arbitrary, ineffectual, or punitive. Peace officers cite the lack of input into important decisions as a further stressor.

Rank. Although promotion is often a source of self-esteem and results in improved benefits and pay, it can also be a source of increased stress (Kroes, Margolis, & Hurrell, 1974). Middle managers (sergeants, lieutenants, etc.) report they often feel the added stress of being caught in the middle between line staff and upper management, unable to satisfy the demands from one side without compromising the needs of the other (Alkus & Padesky, 1983; Reiser, 1982). In addition to the familiar frustrations with overwork, excessive paperwork, and so on, middle managers report additional concerns regarding the fact that they are held accountable for the behavior of their subordinates regardless of whether or not it is feasible to exercise realistic control over them.

Family-Friendly Policies. The process of shift selection, regular days off, time off, work location, and so on, very rarely takes family needs into consideration. Maternity leaves are just now becoming acceptable; paternity leaves are usually not an option. Although many agencies have off-duty social events, few are family oriented (picnics, children's sporting events, etc.). If anything, organizational policies and procedures often create a sense of competition between the department and the family, with the peace officer caught in the middle (Hartsough, 1991; Silbert, 1982; Stratton, 1975). A peace officer who does not want to work a particular assignment or shift because of family reasons is often seen as disloyal and as having skewed priorities. Asking for a day off for family reasons is translated into family problems; that is, the peace officer is unable to keep his home life at home. The sense of competition may be felt even more strongly if the peace officer has a special assignment. During large-scale emergencies, peace officers are often expected to attend to the needs of the community without first being allowed to verify the well-being of their own family members, much less take care of family needs for support or assistance. This policy forces peace officers to choose between their roles as a parent and spouse and the demands of the job, and can result in dangerously distracted and resentful employees.

DIRECT FACTORS: PEACE OFFICER SPOUSE AND FAMILY

Many of the stressors identified by peace officers as particularly problematic have a direct and immediate impact on spouses and family members, too. In addition, spouses and children face unique stressors as a result of their loved one's chosen profession.

Job Characteristics

Fear and Danger. Each time a husband or wife sends a peace officer spouse off to work, the issue of danger surges to the foreground either consciously or unconsciously. This fear is enhanced by the fact that the media often announces an officer-involved incident long before the officer or the department has had the opportunity to assure the spouse that the peace officer is uninjured. Each incident involving a peace officer, even a near miss, increases the fear level for all spouses (Reese, 1982). Spouses also have access to newspapers and are not unaware of the increased lethality and weaponry of those their loved ones are paid to confront.

Financial and Administrative Danger. Spouses are also aware of the increased risk for financial or administrative consequences of the job. These consequences will have a direct impact on the spouse and family as well as the officer. Spouses may feel that their financial security rests squarely on the peace officer's judgment and to a certain extent his or her luck.

Work Schedule. Although a spouse may or may not have to deal with the actual sleep disruption of shift work, all of the other potentially negative aspects of shift work definitely can affect spouses (Reiser, 1982). Work scheduling issues are one of the top complaints of spouses (Brunner, 1976; Engler, 1980). The peace officer is often unable to provide reliable transportation for or even attend children's academic, social, or sporting events. Holidays and birthdays are equally problematic and require some creativity on the part of all family members. Often last-minute changes in plan are required due to a late arrest or unexpected court date. If a nondepartment spouse also works, he or she may not see the department member spouse for several days if their shifts and regular days off do not coincide. Lastly, many female spouses express concern regarding their peace officer husband working the graveyard shift, because it results in their sleeping alone and feeling vulnerable during the night.

Special Assignments. Although having a spouse secure a special assignment can be a source of pride for spouses as well as peace officers, the unique needs of special assignment positions (e.g., longer hours, on-call work, an increase of time away from home, and greater degree of risk) can negatively impact spouses (Farkas, 1986; Reiser, 1982). Although a slight pay differential may be seen as an advantage, because spouses do not directly experience the perks of the assignment, they may see it as inadequate compensation for the debt incurred in terms of decreased family time and increased risk.

Trauma. Although spouses and family members are not directly exposed to the trauma of police work, many peace officers do discuss work incidents with their spouses. This very effective means of reducing the officer's trauma can on occasion result in a certain amount of secondary trauma to the spouse (Hartsough, 1991).

Role Conflict. Spouses may experience a different form of role conflict than their peace officer husband or wife. On the one hand, most spouses feel the need to stand behind their peace officer. Female spouses often discuss their identity as the woman behind the badge who is the listener and the nurturer. On the other hand, spouses are normal human beings with problems and needs of their own. The conflict comes about if the spouse feels they can no longer be human. Many spouses report they feel they cannot bring problems to their law enforcement spouse because they are concerned about further burdening an already overwhelmed peace officer.

Opposite Sex Partners. Many spouses report concerns regarding their peace officer spending long hours working closely with a person of the opposite sex (Coughlin, Hern, & Ard, 1978; Reiser, 1982). The need for solidarity and close-knit support among peace officers is well known. When the partner is of the opposite sex, however, this bond can feel uncomfortable or even threatening to a spouse. Partners share a special relationship that can generate jealousy or envy in a spouse. A peace officer may share more with a partner concerning fears, hopes, and frustrations, than with a non-department spouse.

"Uniform Junkies." Wherever there are men and women in uniform, there will be "uniform junkies," those individuals who are attracted to the authority or the aura of danger and excitement that surrounds the field of law enforcement. Peace officers often receive a higher than average amount of unsolicited "passes" from the citizens they come in contact with, on duty or off, once their profession has been identified. This kind of attention may make spouses uncomfortable (Coughlin, Hern, & Ard, 1978; Reiser, 1982).

Firearms. Whereas the peace officer has made a commitment to becoming proficient and comfortable with firearms, spouses, who often have had little exposure to weapons, may be uncomfortable both on their own behalf and on behalf of children in the house (Bibbens, 1986; Stratton, 1975). For some, the peace officer's weapon can also become a constant reminder of the dangerousness of the job.

External Stressors

Public Perception. Negative public perception can have just as much, if not more, impact on peace officer spouses as on the officers themselves (Gilmartin, 1986). Spouses are often the member of the couple who represents the couple to the outside world. The spouse attends nondepartment social events, transports to and is involved in children's activities, and often is responsible for the day-to-day requirements of banking, shopping, and so on. Many spouses feel the need to defend their peace officer spouse or the department when they hear negative opinions expressed. Again these negative opinions can come from the media, friends, or family members. Even the children of a peace officer can be impacted. Especially during adolescence, peace officer children are often ostracized by peers or dared to act to prove they are not controlled by their peace officer parent.

Scandal or Investigation. Spouses share the embarrassment and decreased self-esteem that their peace officer spouse may experience due to departmental scandal or personal investigation. The public and the department hold peace officers to a higher moral code both on and off duty. Normal human failings are not tolerated. All law enforcement can be tainted by the actions of a few. This situation may be further exacerbated for spouses when peace officers work in a rural area or live in the same community where they patrol. There is no possibility of anonymity for the spouse or for peace officer children.

Organizational Stressors

Budget Constraints. Spouses share their peace officer spouse's concerns regarding workload, insufficient equipment, and decreased manpower, because it again raises the issue of officer safety. Although they do not deal with the frustration of trying to do too much with too little, they are aware that decreased manpower and insufficient equipment translates to less backup, longer backup response time, and officer safety issues related to not having the right equipment when it is crucially needed. A second issue is the curtailment of psychological benefits that may accompany budget cutbacks. Spousal access to psychological services is often the first to be cut (if it exists at all).

Pay and Promotion. Many peace officer relationships are more traditional in that the nondepartment spouse either is a full-time parent or works only part time. The financial status of the family unit, therefore, relies more heavily on the pay and promotability of the peace officer. Quality of life for the spouse and children will be tied to the peace officer's status.

Rank. Although rank can also be a source of self-esteem for the peace officer's spouse, many spouses report feeling the additional pressure of being in a politically more sensitive environment. Whether at a department function or out in public, spouses of higher ranking department employees recognize that their behavior will reflect back on their department spouse.

"Family-Friendly" Policies. The lack of family-friendly policies described earlier also have a great impact on the family. Family members receive a clear communication from many agencies that they are second

priority. This can be particularly offensive because many family members feel they already have compromised above and beyond the call of duty for their law enforcement member. In the case of a major disaster or critical incident, family members may feel abandoned, fearful, and resentful that their peace officer is not there for them. They may blame the department; they may also blame the peace officer.

INDIRECT FACTORS: PEACE OFFICER ADAPTIONS

When peace officers walk in the door, they bring home the stress that accumulated on the job. This stress impacts the family through the officer. There is also the impact on the family that occurs as a result of the adaptions peace officers may make to the job stress they experience.

Emotional Overcontrol or Suppression. Many peace officers deal with the stress of law enforcement by shutting down emotionally. Numerous authors have documented the tendency of peace officers to demonstrate emotional detachment, emotional blunting, or emotional repression in response to the environment in which they work (Bibbens, 1986; Hill, 1981; Maslach & Jackson, 1979). Eventually, a peace officer may become uncomfortable with any experience or display of affect (Stratton, 1975). Although this emotional control or suppression has benefits on the job in terms of control and may protect the officer from some of the emotional consequences of being a peace officer, it extracts a heavy cost. Many officers are unable to turn the emotions back on when they go home each night. The result is often emotional detachment and withdrawal from family members, decreased communication, inhibited expression of affection and intimacy, and subsequent marital distancing. Peace officers may have difficulty with experiencing empathy for family members and their needs and problems. They may also become cut off from potential emotional support, further exacerbating stress symptoms.

Machismo. A related issue is the tendency of peace officers to buy into the macho image (Garner, 1979; Hogan, 1971; Snibbe, Fabricatore, & Azen, 1975; Trompetter, 1986). This macho image includes an emphasis on the traditional masculine role, suppression of affective expression, overreliance on physical prowess, and an inability to admit weakness or ask for assistance. A macho style can impact law enforcement relationships through lack of communication of affect and needs, expectation of a traditional female role from the spouse (for males), and refusal to address relationship concerns or obtain counseling (Fell, Richard, & Wallace, 1980).

Rigidity and Authoritarianism. Law enforcement agencies typically are described as paramilitary organizations. One potential risk of being immersed in such an organization is an overidentification with the concept of *chain of command.* Because most law enforcement personnel have a more traditional view of family hierarchy, it may seem like a natural extension to give orders at home and to expect them to be obeyed (Stratton & Stratton, 1982). It is not intentional and may not be a conscious expectation; however, for some peace officers the boundary between work and home can become blurred regarding the chain of command, resulting in orders given to both spouse and children. Once orders are given, compliance is expected. Peace officers are trained that a noncompliant suspect can constitute a threat to officer safety. Sometimes a peace officer's insistence on compliance can become a rigid, knee-jerk reaction. This reaction can then be brought home and inappropriately applied in the handling of a spouse or child. A challenging teenager becomes not only a threat to a peace officer's parental authority, but can on some level be confused with a threat to physical safety.

Us–Them Philosophy. Many peace officers develop an us–them philosophy as a means of dealing with a hostile environment (Stratton, 1975). Peace officers expect to be lied to and become cynical and suspicious of individuals they meet in performing their job (Davidson & Veno, 1980). This philosophy can easily cross over the boundary into family life (Potter, 1978). A peace officer may end up cross-examining a child about recent activities or become preoccupied with the idea that a spouse is cheating (Southworth, 1990).

Overprotectiveness. As peace officers are exposed to more and more deception, victimization, and violence, they tend to become more fearful on behalf of their family. Peace officers may decide to protect their spouses from the horrors of the job by not talking about work incidents (Madamba, 1986; Stratton, 1975) or by becoming extremely restrictive when it comes to the activities of a spouse or child. However, lack of sharing leads to decreased intimacy and rigid curtailment can lead to rebellion.

CONSEQUENCES

Documentation for the notion that the identified stressors are, in fact, taken home is easy to locate (Blackmore, 1978; Davidson, 1979; Davidson & Veno, 1980; Niederhoffer & Niederhoffer, 1978; Southworth, 1990). For example, several authors have noted that law enforcement personnel often appear to take home anger or frustration related to work stressors, displacing it into their relationships (Bibbens, 1986; Means, 1986; Stratton, 1975). It is important, however, to summarize how that impact may be manifested in law enforcement families.

Relationship Impact and Divorce. Both peace officers and their spouses recognize the negative impact of a peace officer's job on the family (Coughlin, Hern, & Ard, 1978; Davidson & Veno, 1980; Engler, 1980; Kroes, 1976). In a study by Blackmore (1978), 37% of the peace officers reported serious marital difficulties. Kroes, Margolis, and Hurrell (1974) reported that 79 of 81 peace officers surveyed said that their job had a negative effect on their family. Niederhoffer and Niederhoffer (1978) believed that the profession of law enforcement undermines fundamental family relations. Examining actual data on divorce, however, produces a somewhat mixed picture. Researchers report levels ranging from normal (review by Terry, 1981) to 2 to 4 times the national average (Kroes, 1976). A 1989 study by Came et al. (cited in *On the front lines: Police stress and family well-being,* 1991) indicated that 75% of police marriages in large metropolitan areas are likely to end in divorce. Lastly, marital discord, in itself a problem, is also the most commonly reported factor involved in police suicides (Danto, 1978).

Domestic Violence. The same factors that lead to marital distress can also lead to domestic violence. Displacement of anger, decreased communication and conflict management skills, alienation and withdrawal, and decreased trust, all serve to create an environment that can place a law enforcement relationship at greater risk for domestic violence. In addition, certain job characteristics such as habituation to force, seeing force as a viable solution, rigid chain of command, expectation of compliance, and the absence of outside input due to police solidarity enhance the risk even more (Honig & White, in press; Stratton, 1975). Neidig, Russell, and Seng (*On the front lines,* 1991) found that 41% of male officers and 34% of female officers reported violent assaults in their marital relationships. Dr. Leanor Johnson (*On the front lines,* 1991) reported that 10% of the spouses participating in a recent study on police stress indicated that they had been physically abused by their mates at least once during the 6 months preceding the study. Forty percent of the peace officers interviewed admitted they had been violent with their spouse or children during the same 6-month period.

Parent–Child Impact. In a study by Kroes (1976), 20% of the children of peace officers were described as having emotional problems. Lack of availability of peace officer parents (due to shift work, on-call work, scheduling, etc.) can result in resentment and withdrawal on the part of the children. Overwhelmed peace officers may resent the demands of their children, becoming irritable when interaction finally occurs. Decreased trust, overprotectiveness, and an authoritarian "give orders" style can result in tension and conflict between peace officers and their children (Alkus & Padesky, 1983; Coughlin, Hern, & Ard, 1978; Reese, 1982). Rigid, authoritarian peace officer parents are not seen as approachable or "huggable" (Southworth, 1990). In adolescents, such a restrictive and rigid style can breed rebellion.

Alcohol and Substance Abuse. Peace officers have long been identified as being at high risk for alcoholism (Bibbens, 1986; Blackmore, 1978; Kroes, 1976). A 1987 study by Hepp (*On the front lines*, 1991) suggested that as many as 30% of all peace officers abuse alcohol. The rationale behind this high rate of substance abuse varies from escapist drinking (Kroes, Margolis, & Hurrell, 1974) to unofficial department acceptance and peer pressure. Whatever the source, the impact of alcohol on the family has been well documented over the last 20 years.

Health Consequences. Several good studies have summarized the health consequences of being a peace officer (Kroes, 1976; Terry, 1981). Blackmore (1978) reported that 36% of his sample of peace officers had serious health problems. The most common consequences include high blood pressure, coronary heart disease, gastrointestinal disorders, and so on. Once health consequences appear, they constitute an additional emotional and financial drain on an already overstressed family system.

Emotional Consequences. Depression, anxiety, and problems with anger management, are all a part of the picture and can be the response to cumulative law enforcement stress. As described under the section on trauma, posttraumatic stress symptoms in response to shootings and other critical incidents are also fairly common (Cooper & Marshall, 1976; Reiser & Geiger, 1984). Researchers are examining the concept of police burnout as a way of summarizing the general impact of law enforcement job stress (Chamberlin, 1978; Daviss, 1982).

Suicide. Although the evidence is somewhat mixed, a review of the research indicates that peace officers do seem to commit suicide at a higher rate than the rest of the populace (Allen, 1986; Fell, Richard, & Wallace, 1980; Heiman, 1977; Terry, 1981). The frightening statistic exists that a peace officer is more likely to take his or her own life than to be killed in the line of duty (Kroes, 1976). This trend is even more alarming given the fact that peace officers are selected for their above-average levels of emotional stability and intelligence (Hooke & Krauss, 1971; Lefkowitz, 1975; Reiser, 1973). In addition, police suicides are likely to be underreported. Law enforcement agencies are often hesitant to discuss suicide among peace officers. Often a peace officer suicide is misidentified as an accident. If a peace officer fails to draw a weapon knowing he or she is going into a potentially lethal situation, it is difficult to know whether it was in fact a mistake.

INTERVENTIONS

Organizational Interventions

Management Consultation and Education. The first and most important intervention must be at the management level. In order to implement many of the interventions described here, management must first be educated. Stress factors and stress consequences, as well as potential solutions, must be detailed. Stress consequences must be defined in terms of cost factors including increased absenteeism, increased accident rates, decreased productivity, and health- and stress-related retirements. Family-friendly policies that allow for flexibility must become the norm.

Selection. Selection procedures and background checks should include contact with spouses to access specifically their awareness of potential relationship stressors involved in law enforcement and ways to mitigate their impact. Selection procedures for special assignments can also include spousal input.

Orientation. Spousal orientation is also invaluable. Orientation includes ride-alongs and tours of facilities to familiarize spouses with the job requirements of their peace officers' positions. Firearm safety and handling plus a visit to the firing range can decrease anxiety regarding a weapon in the house. Presentations on law enforcement stress, stress management, and the potential relationship impact of a job in law enforcement can help increase awareness and allow for planning to mitigate any potential negative effects. Guest speakers from among the ranks of successful law enforcement couples can assist new couples in developing healthy coping methods.

Seminars and Workshops. Families in general tend to go through stages of development. In addition, peace officers also change and may go though stages as well. Consequently, it is important that ongoing seminars and workshops or support groups be available both as "booster shots" regarding issues presented at orientation and as opportunities to exchange information about new problems that surface as the peace officer's career progresses or as family situations change (e.g., birth of a child, etc.). In addition, peace officers often report that seminars or workshops on topics such as parenting and communication with adolescents, are particularly helpful.

Critical Incident Debriefings. Whereas most departments now offer critical incident debriefings for peace officers, the impact on spouses is often ignored. A second debriefing offered either to the spouse individually or in conjunction with the peace officer can significantly decrease spousal anxiety and prevent future difficulties. Such a debriefing may be critical to the spouse's providing ongoing emotional and job support to the peace officer.

Department Trainings. In addition to off-duty seminars and workshops, many departments offer courses on stress management, alcohol education, sensitivity and communication training, surviving a critical incident, and so on. Any training that assists the peace officer in developing a better wellness plan and stress management skills, or that improves his or her communication skills, will have an impact on the family.

Psychological Services. The majority of law enforcement agencies are now offering some form of individual, short-term counseling to peace officer employees. Some also offer marital or family therapy. A few offer assistance directly to spouses for individual treatment. The availability of psychological services will encourage peace officers and their families to obtain assistance should a problem arise. What happens to one commonly affects all.

Supervisor Trainings. By training supervisors in the early detection and appropriate referral of employee problems (both individual and family related), departments can catch potential problems before they escalate.

Research. It is in the best interest of each department to take responsibility for exploring the impact of job stress on peace officers and their families and for designing means of mitigating the impact wherever possible.

SUMMARY

For some peace officers, pursuing a career in law enforcement can have a potentially negative impact on the individual officer as well as his or her family. Job factors may negatively impact the peace officer directly, resulting in stress that may then be brought home to the family. These same job factors may also have a second, indirect influence in that they may encourage the peace officer to develop various coping mechanisms and adaptions to the job that have the potential to negatively impact family relationships. In addition, job stressors can also negatively impact law enforcement spouses and children directly. In such a case, the entire family begins to pay a toll in terms of marital discord, divorce, and strained or distant parent–child relationships. The cycle can then run full circle, with home problems potentially causing emotional and physical distress in the peace officer, which in turn may result in poor work performance, increased absenteeism, and even increased risk for incidents of excessive force.

Each law enforcement agency has a responsibility to recognize the negative impact a career in law enforcement may bring to bear on family members and an obligation to provide assistance. The agency can significantly impact the law enforcement family by creating family-friendly policies and by offering psychological assistance such as critical incident debriefings that take spouses into consideration, spousal orientations, workshops and seminars on couples issues, and ongoing psychological counseling. By providing this assistance, the department not only discharges an obligation to the law enforcement family members, but the department can also have a real and measurable impact on peace officer work performance. Because the peace officer cannot help but be negatively impacted by home stress, any intervention that improves the functioning of the family will in turn improve the overall functioning of the peace officer both at home and in the workplace. By making a commitment to assisting law enforcement families, law enforcement agencies are actually acting in the best interest of the agency as a whole as well as the community that the agency serves.

REFERENCES

Ayoob, M. (1981). The killing experience. *Police Product News.*

Alkus, S., & Padesky, C. (1983). Special problems of police officers: Stress related issues and interventions. *Clinical Psychology, 11*(2), 55–64.

Allen, S. (1986). Suicide and indirect self-destructive behavior among police. In J. T. Reese & H. A. Goldstein (Eds.), *Psychological services for law enforcement* (pp. 413–417). Washington, DC: U.S. Government Printing Office.

Bibbens, V. E. (1986). Quality of family and marital life of police personnel. In J. T. Reese & H. A. Goldstein (Eds.), *Psychological services for law enforcement* (pp. 423–427). Washington, DC: U.S. Government Printing Office.

Blackmore, J. (1978). Are police allowed to have problems of their own? *Police Magazine, 1*(3), 47–55.

Brunner, G. (1976). Law enforcement officer's work schedule reactions. *Police Chief, 43*(1), 31–31.

Bull, R., Bustin, B., Evan, P., & Gahagan, D. (1983). *Psychology for police officers.* Chichester, UK: Wiley.

Chamberlin, C. (1978, March). Anomie, burnout & the Wyatt Earp Syndrome. *Law & Order, 78,* pp. 20–21.

Cooper, C., & Marshall, J. (1976). Occupational sources of stress: Symptoms in police officers. (Doctoral dissertation, California School of Professional Psychology, 1986). *Dissertation Abstracts International, 47,* 01B.

Coughlin, A., Hern, S., & Ard, J. (1978). *You know you're a peace officer's wife when. . . .* San Francisco: Davis.

Danto, B. (1978). Police suicide. *Police Stress, 1*(1), 32, 36, 40.

Davidson, M. (1979). *Stress in the police services: A multifaceted model, research proposition & pilot study.* Unpublished dissertation, University of Queensland, Australia.

Davidson, M., & Veno, A. (1980). Stress and the policeman. In C. Cooper & J. Marshall (Eds.), *White collar and professional stress* (pp. 136–166). New York: Wiley.

Daviss, B. (1982). Burn out. *Police Magazine, 5*(3), 9–11, 14–18.

Eisenberg, T. (1975). Job stress and the police officer: Identifying stress reduction techniques. In W. H. Kroes & J. J. Hurrell (Eds.), *Job stress and the police officer: Identifying stress reduction techniques* (HEW Publication NIOSH 76-187). Washington, DC: U.S. Government Printing Office.

Ellison, K., & Genz, J. (1983). *Stress and the police officer.* Springfield, IL: Thomas.

Engler, L. J. (1980). *Rotating vs. permanent shift schedules.* Unpublished master's thesis, Rutgers University, Newark, NJ.

Farkas, G. (1986). Stress in undercover policing. In J. T. Reese & H. A. Goldstein (Eds.), *Psychological services for law enforcement* (pp. 431–438). Washington, DC: U.S. Government Printing Office.

Fell, R., Richard, W., & Wallace, W. (1980). Psychological job stress and the police officer. *Journal of Police Science and Administration, 8*(2), 139–149.

Garner, G. (1979). *Police role in alcohol related crises.* Springfield, IL: Thomas.

Gilmartin, K. (1986). A learned perceptual set and its consequences on police stress. In J. T. Reese & H. A. Goldstein (Eds.), *Psychological services for law enforcement* (pp. 445–448). Washington, DC: U.S. Government Printing Office.

Hartsough, D. (1991). Stress, spouses and law enforcement: A step beyond. In J. Reese, J. Horn, & C. Dunning (Eds.), *Critical incidents in policing* (pp. 131–137). Washington, DC: U.S. Government Printing Office.

Heiman, M. F. (1977). Suicide among police. *American Journal of Psychiatry, 134,* 1289–1290.

Hill, W. (1981). Stress, police officers and survival. *Police Stress, 4,* 35–36.

Hogan, R. (1971). Personality characteristics of highly rated policemen. *Personnel Psychology, 24,* 679–686.

Honig, A., & White, E. (in press). Violence and the law enforcement family. In *Law enforcement and the family* (National Symposium on Law Enforcement and the Family). Washington, DC: U.S. Government Printing Office.

Hooke, J., & Krauss, H. (1971). Personality characteristics of successful police sergeant candidates. *Journal of Criminal Law, Criminology & Political Science, 62,* 104–106.

Hurrell, J. (1986). Some organizational stressors in police work and means for their amelioration. In J. T. Reese & H. A. Goldstein (Eds.), *Psychological services for law enforcement* (pp. 447–450). Washington, DC: U.S. Government Printing Office.

Kroes, W. (1976). *Society's victim—The police: An analysis of job related stress in policing.* Springfield, IL: Thomas.

Kroes, W., Margolis, B., & Hurrell, J. (1974). Job stress in policemen. *Journal of Police Science and Administration, 2*(2), 145–155.

Lefkowitz, J. (1975). Psychological attributes of policemen: A review of research and opinion. *Journal of Social Issues, 31*(1), 3–26.

Lipson, G. (1986). San Ysidro massacre: Post traumatic stress among the police as related to life stress and coping style. (Doctoral dissertation, California School of Professional Psychology, 1986). *Dissertation Abstracts International, 47,* 05B.

Madamba, H. J. (1986). The relationship between stress and marital relationships in police officers. In J. T. Reese & H. A. Goldstein (Eds.), *Psychological services for law enforcement* (pp. 463–469). Washington, DC: U.S. Government Printing Office.

Maslach, C., & Jackson, S. (1979). Burned out cops & their families. *Psychology Today, 12*(12), 59–62.

Means, M. S. (1986). Family therapy issues in law enforcement families. In J. T. Reese & H. A. Goldstein (Eds.), *Psychological services for law enforcement* (pp. 140–142). Washington, DC: U.S. Government Printing Office.

Niederhoffer, A., & Niederhoffer, E. (1978). *The police family from the station house to the ranch house*. Lexington, MA: Lexington Books.

On the front lines: Police stress and family well-being. (1991, May 20). [Hearing before the Select Committee on Children, Youth, and Families, House of Representatives]. Washington, DC: U.S. Government Printing Office.

O'Neil, P. (1986). Shift work. In J. T. Reese & H. A. Goldstein (Eds.), *Psychological services for law enforcement* (pp. 469–476). Washington, DC: U.S. Government Printing Office.

Platt, R. (1975, September). The policeman & his family: A unique social entity. *Texas Police Journal, 23*(8).

Potter, J. (1978). The liberation of the police wife. *Police Magazine, 1*(3), 39–42.

Reese, J. (1982, September). Family therapy in law enforcement: A new approach to an old problem. *Federal Bureau of Investigation Law Enforcement Bulletin*, 43–47.

Reese, J., Horn, J., & Dunning, C. (Eds.). (1991). *Critical incidents in policing*. Washington, DC: U.S. Government Printing Office.

Reiser, M. (1973). *Practical psychology for the police officer*. Springfield, IL: Thomas.

Reiser, M. (1982). *Police psychology: Collected papers*. Los Angeles: LEHI.

Reiser, M., & Geiger, S. (1984). The police officer as a victim. *Professional Psychology: Research and Practice, 15*(3), 315–323.

Shealey, T. (1985, December). Putting the cuffs on stress. *Prevention*, pp. 61–65.

Silbert, M. (1982). Job stress & burnout of new police officers. *Police Chief, 49*(6), 46–48.

Snibbe, H. M., Fabricatore, J., & Azen, S. P. (1975). Personality characteristics of white, black and Mexican-American policemen as measured by the 16PFQ. *American Journal of Community Psychology, 3*(3), 221–227.

Stratton, J. (1975, November). Pressures in law enforcement marriages: Some considerations. *Police Chief*, pp. 44–47.

Stratton, J., & Stratton, B. (1982, May). Law enforcement marital relationships: A positive approach. *Federal Bureau of Investigation Law Enforcement Bulletin*, pp. 8–11.

Southworth, R. (1990, November). Taking the job home. *Federal Bureau of Investigation Law Enforcement Bulletin*, pp. 19–23.

Terry, W. (1981). Police stress: The empirical evidence. *Journal of Police Science and Administration, 9*(1), 61–75.

Trompetter, P. S. (1986). The paradox of the squad room—Solitary solidarity. In J. T. Reese & H. A. Goldstein (Eds.), *Psychological services for law enforcement* (pp. 533–535). Washington, DC: U.S. Government Printing Office.

CHAPTER ELEVEN

Counseling Issues and Police Diversity

June Werdlow Jones
Drug Enforcement Administration

Today law enforcement officers are individuals diverse in culture, gender, and sexual orientation. Police work is stressful; being an ethnic minority, female, or homosexual in any workplace including police departments is also stressful. Common police stressors may be intragroup, organizational, interpersonal, or individual in nature (Violanti, 1988). With so many types of pressures involved in police work, the causes present an infinite number of possibilities requiring exploration by helping professionals. However, peer counselors, managers, psychologists, or counselors charged with counseling minorities, women, and homosexuals should expect that in addition to the traditional rationale supplied by clients regarding their perceptions of stress-related complaints unique to police work, such as inferior assignments or nonempathetic supervisors, when counseling minorities, counselors and managers will frequently encounter complaints unique to minorities as well as the perception of the origin of those complaints.

This chapter identifies ethnic minority, women-related, and gay and lesbian issues that a police counselor or manager may expect to encounter, and offers practical approaches to assessing the ability to assist individual clients (police officers). Because individual police officers frequently are referred to counseling by their departments, this chapter also provides practical advice for assisting the agency client as a whole.

ETHNIC MINORITY CONCERNS

Cultural Diversity

Cultural diversity is a term used to refer to ethnic differences and to refer to the assortment of cultures in the workplace. More than one half of the U.S. work force consists of minorities, immigrants, and women, which means the so-called mainstream is now almost as diverse as the society at large (Thomas, 1990). Thus, today the overall work force is culturally diverse. It has been predicted by many experts that in the near·future the workplace will be even more diverse.

By the year 2000, the work force will look very different than it does today. Women will be the majority, and there will be an increase in the minority population (Hosansky, 1991). Because cultural diversity is an eventuality in the future, and to a great extent already here today, it is essential for police administrators, managers, and counselors to understand the impact of cultural diversity in order to maximize positive effects for police departments and minimize negative effects to minority police officers. Failure to fully tap the potential of everyone in a given police department will undoubtedly hamper that department's ability to meet performance standards. A study conducted by Cox, Lobel, and McLeod (1991) regarding diversity confirms this assumption. Groups composed of homogenous cultures and heterogenous cultures were examined. The results indicated that groups composed of people from collectivist cultural traditions displayed more cooperative behavior than groups composed of people with individualistic cultural traditions (Cox et al., 1991). With the outcome of police enforcement operations being so dependent on effective teamwork, the implications for composing and managing a culturally diverse department are clear.

There is also something to be said for police departments being representative of the communities that they serve. An understanding of the residents served by a given police department can be useful in delivering services. Police departments such as those in Los Angeles and Miami that serve large Hispanic populations may even find it necessary for officers to speak some Spanish. Nonetheless, in many urban cities, tensions are building and have indeed erupted between the police and the communities. Experts suggest that training is necessary to sensitize officers to ethnic groups residing in communities they police.

Police Culture

It has long been theorized that the police have a culture unique to themselves. According to Dunham and Alpert (1989), the culture of a police department reflects what that department believes in as an organization.

These beliefs are reflected in the department's recruiting and selection practices, policies and procedures, and training.

Characteristics or attributes associated with the police culture must be identified to assist counseling agents with understanding collective and individual police behavior. Identification of these characteristics may also assist counselors in assessing the origins of minority concerns.

Burke (1992) identified at least six attributes unique to the police culture: conservatism, machismo, pragmatism, mission orientation, prejudice, and suspiciousness.

Conservatism is an attribute associated with the police culture. Generally police tend to be more conservative than the general population. Being conservative has some positive effects; however, it can also translate into closed-mindedness and traditionalistic views regarding recruitment, hiring, and promotion of minorities and women.

Machismo is seen as a trait characteristic to many male police officers. In a profession where mental and frequently physical assertiveness is so vital, it is not surprising that masculinity is highly valued. One can easily speculate how this element may affect male officers' tolerance of female police officers.

The *mission* of police is also viewed as part of their culture. According to Burke (1992), there appears to exist a collective police mentality in which officers come to see themselves as guardians of morality whose duty is to protect "civilized" society from "the scum on the streets." With this strong mission-oriented mentality, there may be a propensity for projecting; any entity police view negatively, including minorities in general who frequently are stereotyped as being criminals, offer a justification for alienation.

Pragmatism on the part of the police is viewed as having come from the concerns of police officers about safety. Consequently, they generally tend to be very practical and functional, and have a response-oriented mentality versus consideration of innovation, experimentation, or research. The positive impact of this trait may translate into a willingness to work with minority males to obtain desired results in an enforcement situation. However, it may also mean that male officers are less likely to work with a female partner because they expect that their safety will be jeopardized.

Prejudice unfortunately is seen as characteristic of the police. In policing, it is necessary to be discerning in the performance of duties to be effective and safe. Nevertheless, police customarily reflect the predominant attitudes of the majority toward minorities. Because police generally are more conservative than the general public, it probably follows that they are slightly more racially prejudiced, which can have adverse effects for ethnic minorities in the police work force.

Suspiciousness is viewed as a hallmark of police officers that means that just about any new program implemented by management to improve ethnic or gender interaction will be met with some skepticism.

Furthermore, police culture is to some degree predicated on the presence of danger and the potential for violence, which leads to a generalized suspiciousness, isolation from the community, and a cohesive, informal occupational group with its own stratification systems and norms (Martin, 1989).

Managing Diversity

Most experts agree that a diverse work force is better than a homogenous work force. One psychologist has demonstrated through practical training exercises that diversity can improve group performance. In Cohen's workshop scenarios, he has found that over 90% of time the group scores better than the best individual, and that heterogenous groups score better than homogeneous ones (Hosansky, 1991). There are several arguments favoring effectively managing a diverse work force and numerous consequences are faced if a stand is taken against proper management.

There are many negative consequences of not effectively managing a diverse police department, ranging from not using personnel efficiently to costly lawsuits. Faced with the repercussions associated with mismanagement of a diverse work force and the benefits to be gained when diverse work forces are effectively managed, most police administrators will direct efforts toward productive management.

Managing a diverse work force means understanding that the concerns of women, minorities, and disabled employees often differ from those of White male workers. Employers need to create environments that are conducive to the growth and development of all employees. They need to address and alleviate concerns about racial, sexual, and other types of harassment. The commitment and sentiment must be expressed in recruitment, selection, and retention of minority police officers to ensure that police departments remain culturally and gender diverse.

Police Recruitment

The benefits of a culturally diverse police department were discussed earlier in this chapter. To realize the advantages of cultural diversity, police departments must recruit considering minorities as an asset. Similarly, the police recruiter must share the ideology that cultural and gender diversity is good for the police department.

Affirmative action and other means of increasing the representation of ethnic minorities and women are valid issues to be addressed by police recruitment officials. Because most police departments are public institutions, they have already entered into the formal and legal debate on affirmative action. Consequently, many police departments today have either voluntarily complied or have been compelled by the courts to hire minority men and women officers. The debate over the fairness and legality of affirmative action programs has gone on for some time and probably will continue in the future; the debate is beyond the scope of this chapter. However, police departments committed to increasing their representation of women and minorities should keep the following points in mind:

- Minority and women's professional organizations are a good source for recruiting minority male and female candidates.
- Minority and women's colleges provide a source for recruiting men and women minority candidates.
- Assignment of unbiased recruitment officers and interviewers are essential in ensuring that minority men and women candidates will be recruited and selected.
- Recruitment presentations and interviews should be fair in order to attract minority men and women candidates and to avoid accusations of discrimination.
- Potential officers are more encouraged to seek employment in departments where others like themselves have been hired, so recruiters should expect and be prepared to address minority men and women candidates' interest in the department's current minority and female ratio.

The Police Recruiter

Because the racial and gender composition of a given police department is so dependent on those recruited, it is essential that the recruiter not be prejudiced or work so independently that selection is permitted to occur in a capricious manner. Thus, careful thought and consideration should precede the appointment of police recruiters.

One authority on reducing sexual harassment in police departments advocates establishing hiring and promotional processes that specifically test candidates' attitudes toward women and minorities; it is further suggested that the results of these processes be used to weed out potential harassers (Spann, 1990). Similarly, police recruiters should be scrutinized minimally, the same as entry-level officers, with emphasis on detecting prejudices and biases.

Police Selection and Interviewing

Generally, police work is highly coveted, resulting in large numbers of people applying for a relatively small number of positions. In some police departments the ratio is about 20 applicants for each available position. Many police recruiters will agree that with the large percentage of police applicants for limited positions, like it or not, the stages of selection from the interview on become a weeding out process. Police selection is a critical aspect of maintaining a diverse work force in policing. Results will not be obtained even if funding and time are committed to recruiting minorities when unfair selection criteria are applied.

The police interview is typically a point where minority candidates feel different. The racial composition of an interview panel, the types of questions asked, the manner in which questions are posed, and the interpretation of answers supplied by minorities are potential issues.

The composition of the interview panel is essential for promoting an atmosphere where the minority candidate is likely to be at ease. An opportunity to identify with others like himself or herself is useful to the candidate as well as to the interview panel. The minority interviewer may be able to assist during deliberations in clearing up any cultural misconceptions.

It is essential that the interview be conducted in a fair and equitable manner. Because screening interviews may result in lawsuits if something inappropriate is said, interviewers should receive specific training. To reduce risk of being perceived as unfair, police managers should document what is and what is not said at interviews. It is suggested that employers develop a standard interview form for applicants to sign at the end of the interview, listing the topics covered (Milano, 1989). Additionally, when background interviews are conducted the disproportionate number of minorities involved in crime must not be taken out of context.

Essentially, the point to be made here is that minorities applying for positions in the police department may come from disadvantaged homes. Today, nationally 61% of all African American children are born out of wedlock and the number approaches 80% in many cities. For African American children, the likelihood of living with both parents until age 17 dropped from 52% in the 1950s to 6% in the 1980s. Their communities are saturated with crime and drugs. Schools, if the children attend at all, are dysfunctional (Rainie, 1991).

It is not uncommon for people from disadvantaged homes to have family members who have been involved in criminal activities. However, it does not necessarily follow that the police candidate is involved in crime. Background investigations should be aimed at clearing up damaging information obtained from other sources. Undesirable associations should always be examined closely and thoroughly as opposed to being taken at face value. Discerning background investigations are the key to weeding out the undesirable as well as selecting suitable candidates.

Any psychological screening of minority candidates for police positions should take into consideration ethnocentric factors.

The Police Academy

The police academy presents another challenge to many male and female minority police candidates. Recruits are probably scrutinized more at this point than at any other stage in the selection process. As a result, the potential for management and counseling consultations regarding adverse personnel actions is more likely.

Most police academies expect that the training staff will be tougher on candidates in training than in the field. Consequently, the police academy presents a challenge for management and staff because the setting provides fertile territory to act out repressed or expressed bias or discrimination. It is quite easy for a staff member who harbors resentment or prejudice against minorities to single out a minority recruit and harass him or her in such a way that the recruit resigns or looks so bad that he or she is fired. Even staff members and management personnel who may, on occasion be generally impartial, may display biased behavior toward minorities. For example, many minority police officers can recall admonishments during their training days to some degree for congregating or socializing too much with other minorities. Because police departments expect their recruits to conform, a minority recruit who does not heed the warning may expect repercussions.

In the example cited about a bias toward minority cohesiveness, experts on cultural diversity have challenged the notion that minorities assembling is somehow negative because Whites are not chastised for congregating (Smith, 1988). Nevertheless, when a recruit is forbidden contact with others like himself, it may create even more problems, such as loss of an important support system coupled with a bewilderment that may lead to an interpretation and internalization that there is something wrong with associating with others like himself.

How situations such as minorities being cohesive are handled is crucial in managing culturally diverse police departments. Traditionally, individuals have been expected to conform and to minimize or ignore their differentness. However, this perspective overlooks the benefits of diversity. A new trend in management of a culturally diverse work force involves shifting the focus from changing the individual to capitalizing on the positive influences of the differences. Often minority recruits in the police academy also feel different in other ways.

The police academy may present the first occurrence of a minority feeling as if he or she stands out or as if he or she is being examined as if under a microscope. Minorities may often feel that nothing they do goes unnoticed. Although generally one goal of the police academy is to convince the recruit that the staff is omniscient and that the recruit is continuously under observation, if a minority recruit is unduly singled out, it may result in complaints of discrimination. Often the sensation of being scrutinized more than other recruits is not valid. However, because ethnic minorities and women are more conspicuous, training staff members may simply notice their shortcomings earlier than those in other recruits who are not as noticeable.

Police academies also present opportunities for feelings of isolation to develop and perpetuate in the life of a minority recruit. Often, although regarded as a minority with respect to the overall national population, many minority police recruits arrive from large metropolitan areas where the minority is literally the majority. The latest census data reveal that about 30% of the total African-American population still live in almost complete racial isolation (Rainie, 1991). Yet, on arrival at the academy there may only be a few, if any, other recruits from the same cultural background. This indeed can lead to culture shock, and with all of the competing priorities, the range of responses may run from trying to ignore concern to allowing it to be all-consuming. One predicable response is for minority recruits to seek comfort from those most like them—other minorities.

Feelings of inferiority in police recruits may also abound in the police academy. With the advent of affirmative action programs, other students and staff may make comments about the recruits having received preferential consideration for selection. Even if there exists an affirmative action program within a police department, minorities should not receive negative feedback from the police staff about special consideration given during the selection process.

It is essential that police academy staffs be educated with respect to sensitivity and be provided with the facts as they relate to any initiative to recruit ethnic minorities and women to minimize misunderstanding and rumors.

Once a police academy staff member, believing that he was doing a minority staff member a favor, warned her that the next recruit class consisted of a large percentage of minorities whose interview scores where considerably lower than the norm. Further, it was advised that they as staff members should brace themselves to deal with the inevitable onslaught of incompetents. The staff member cited a friend in personnel as his source for the information.[1] One can speculate about the reception the minorities in this class would receive if the staff had already prejudged them to be inferior and incapable of learning. Further, the recipient of the information was an ethnic minority, which brings up the issue of special considerations or responsibilities of minority staff members.

Minority staff members often experience ambivalence in the training academy setting with respect to their roles in assisting minority students. Sometimes minority students, believing they need someone to talk to who can identify with their concerns, may be inclined to seek out minority staff members. When these encounters are overt, often the student is reprimanded for breaking the chain of command and the staff member is chastised for having minority students nearby. Conversely, when meetings of this sort are covert, students and staff run the risk of being misinterpreted and often the behavior is labeled as fraternization. Nonetheless, no matter how the situ-

---

[1]This experience is related as it was told to the author.

ation is interpreted, generally what usually is involved in minority staff–student interaction is a form of mentoring or counseling. What constitutes crossing the line must be considered carefully.

Sensations of being overly examined, isolation, and inferiority by minority recruits, whether real or imagined, can impact performance. Hence, police academy managers should formulate a minority affairs program or appoint a counselor available to counsel minorities and women when a need arises. In addition to the advocate's position to help the students, he or she could also provide the staff with collective reactions from minority men and women to the training program.

Police Retention

To reap the benefits of having a culturally diverse police department, of course, minorities must be retained. For this to occur, race relations must improve, affirmative action or comparable programs must be implemented and properly defended, diversity valued, and an overall attitude of sensitivity toward ethnic and female minorities must be promoted by police management.

Race Relations

The commission examining the beating of Rodney King by Los Angeles Police reported that racism in the department is as harsh as this message from one White officer to another: "Sounds like monkey-slapping time" (Rainie, 1991). The mere discussion of the Rodney King incident among an ethnically diverse group of police officers is enough to incite polarization.

Race relations within police departments can be considered mediocre at best. When minorities were first allowed to become police officers, their assignments were restricted and often inferior. For example, police departments placed limitations on occupational mobility (Blacks could not arrest White suspects), lower job performance evaluations were frequently given to Blacks by their White supervisors, and exclusion from leadership and supervisory roles was common (Charles, 1991). Then after several decades, in the 1960s and 1970s, police departments slowly began to permit minority officers to work in the mainstream. Unfortunately, the rate of progress varied, resulting in numerous lawsuits being filed alleging civil rights violations in the 1970s. Although the general tendency of the courts to favor minorities in the lawsuits could be construed as benefiting the careers of minorities (and this is somewhat questionable when one considers resistance received by minorities from the opposition), it did little to improve race relations.

Minority officers often see majority officers as oppressors, and majority officers often harbor feelings of resentment when they see minorities promoted, convinced that affirmative action or comparable programs were designed to personally put them at a disadvantage.

Microinequities, subtle discrimination, and *gender bias* are all terms used to describe instances of ambiguous discrimination in which unjust actions taken against a minority can be attributed to stereotyped perceptions versus work performance (Edwards, 1991). Examples include a minority officer's good idea being attributed to a White officer, a female being mistaken for a secretary, and an African-American officer being mistaken as the criminal in an enforcement scenario.

Initiatives designed to improve race relations should incorporate an underlying theme that diversity is positive. Even in business, the term *melting pot* is the wrong metaphor to use today, for at least three reasons. First, if it was possible to melt down Scotsmen and Dutchmen and Frenchmen into an indistinguishable broth, the same is not possible with African Americans, Asians, and women. Their differences do not melt so easily. Second, most people are no longer willing to be melted for even 8 hours a day. Third, the thrust of today's flexible, collaborative management requires a ten- or twentyfold increase in tolerance for individuality (Thomas, 1990).

Affirmative Action and Other Initiatives

Is affirmative action a dirty phrase? If the written debate or the silent verbal debate is any indication, then affirmative action is certainly a concept that evokes strong emotional responses. Rarely are minority and majority police officers observed discussing affirmative action, and when they do, regardless of rank, tension is a significant component of the discussion. As Carter (cited in Lane, 1991) remarked "It's hard to hold an honest conversation about affirmative action; it may be harder still to hold an honest conversation about the reasons why it's hard to hold an honest conversation about affirmative action" (p. 56).

However emotional the controversy about programs designed to select and retain minority male and female police officers become, managers and counselors should remember that the objectives of such initiatives are to maintain a culturally diverse police department, the benefits of which have been discussed.

The means for retaining minorities are essentially the same as those required to retain all officers. Promoting a sense of purpose, providing opportunity for advancement, and fair treatment are needed. Unfortunately, unfair practices of some police departments demonstrate that minorities are not always afforded the same opportunities as other officers in the aforementioned areas. Consequently, affirmative action programs have been developed either on a voluntary or court-ordered basis in police departments throughout the United States.

Sensitivity training is an essential component to the success of affirmative action and similar initiatives. Often, majority officers focus on the preferential treatment given minorities rather than on the discrimination that compels police departments to provide equal opportunity to minorities. Ironically, many minorities also experience ambivalence about affirmative action because majority members and sometimes other minorities question their selection or recruitment.

The bottom line on affirmative action is that if a police department has voluntarily developed or been compelled to develop and implement a program, it will be a more effective initiative if all members of the department are at least familiar with its objectives and are committed to its success. However, managers and counselors must be prepared to deal proactively (training) and reactively (counseling minorities) to any consequences of these programs.

Promotions

Promotion of minority officers may be influenced by the police department and the officers themselves. Unfortunately, obstacles may exist from the department or individual officers that may hamper a minority officer's chances of being promoted.

Individual officers are generally influenced by their cultures, and sometimes culture can play a significant role in not being promoted. The notion of organizational culture as it pertains to women is discussed later in this chapter; however, sometimes an individual's culture may conflict with the organization's culture. Some cultures frown on promoting oneself, and instead individuals are expected to humble themselves. In an organization such as the police department that expects its members to be self-confident and aggressive, a humble attitude generally will not aid in getting promoted. It is necessary for police departments to be aware of any cultural peculiarities that should be considered during promotional deliberations.

The Bureau of National Affairs' (BNA) Challenge of Diversity Report indicates that an obvious way of increasing the sensitivity of managers to the needs of women, minorities, and people with disabilities is to promote members of these groups to management positions. One company broke through the glass ceiling that keeps minority employees out of executive jobs by creating a pool of lower level minority managers who were doing an excellent job but seemed stalled in their positions. Police departments can also assist in minority promotions by initiating and monitoring programs designed to assist in this endeavor.

Generally within police departments, when the economic situation is favorable, more officers are hired and when the financial conditions are not promising, less hiring is accomplished. This tendency for police departments to hire in waves has caused large periods of time to occur between junior and intermediate ranks of officers. These intervals become significant when the circumstance of minority officers is considered. In the 1980s, the results of several lawsuits led police departments to hire and promote more minorities, especially African Americans. Consequently in the mid- to late 1980s, many African Americans were promoted in police departments based on affirmative action goals. Today many departments' promotional objectives have been met and many officers junior to the most recent wave of officers promoted complain that the window of opportunity is closing; that the opportunities for advancement have not been readily made available to them.

R. Roosevelt Thomas (1990), Executive Director of the American Institute for Managing Diversity, Inc. described a cycle where management has great expectations after recruitment of large numbers of minority men and women this way: The stage now seems set for the natural progression of minorities and women up through the pipeline. Management leans back to enjoy the fruits of its labor. Then frustration occurs when the anticipated natural progression of promotions fails to occur. Minority men and women see themselves plateuing prematurely. Management is then upset (and embarrassed) by the failure of its affirmative action initiative and begins to resent the impatience of the new recruits and their unwillingness to give the company credit for doing the right thing. Depending on how high in the hierarchy they have plateaued, alienated minorities, male and female, either leave the business or stagnate (Thomas, 1990). Closely related to the myth that unmonitored affirmative action programs will lead to promotions is the myth that if minority officers (or any other officer for that matter) work hard enough they will eventually be promoted.

A widespread U. S. myth is that cream will rise to the top. According to Thomas (1990), in most companies what passes for cream rising to the top is actually cream being pulled or pushed to the top by an informal system of mentoring and sponsorship. The importance of career guidance by key senior officials in minority promotions cannot be overlooked.

Lack of access to an informal political network in the police department is another barrier to minority promotions (Sullivan, 1989). The fact that not enough minority officers have been promoted to form a political base hinders the ability to help more minority officers to be promoted. Nevertheless, mentoring is one way to improve an officer's probability of being promoted. For this reason, police departments should re-examine their official positions on minority police organization affiliations because often such associations can have positive affects. For the aforementioned reasons, and in the interests of mentoring, it is recommended that police executives not consider minority associations as threatening, but rather as a means for minority police officers and managers to identify with and help each other deal with special concerns. It should also be noted that most, if not all, of these associations have open memberships that do not restrict participation to any particular ethnic group.

The Minority Police Manager

Promotion in the ranks of police departments generally is considered a confidence-boosting, positive experience. However, for the newly promoted minority police manager, the confidence-boosting ideology may not necessarily apply. Within a short time frame (if not during the newsbreaking itself), newly promoted minority police managers hear comments about the desert of their promotion, and although there may be mental justification of the promotion, the negative comments also elicit self-doubt.

Additionally, there frequently are other minorities to deal with who were passed over. Newly promoted minority managers may feel ambivalence: They are proud that they were promoted, yet sorrowful that many of their minority peers were not promoted. The fact that the glass ceiling does really exist in some police departments makes it difficult for newly promoted minority managers to, in good conscience, be reassured that their minority peers will eventually be promoted. Further, there usually are other problems awaiting newly promoted minority managers after they assume their new positions.

After minority police managers assume their new role, they are faced with a unique situation. When something does not go well with subordinates or supervisors, in addition to considering the array of possibilities, the issue of discrimination must also be considered. Minority police managers have said that they have almost gone insane trying to isolate a particular cause of conflict with subordinates or supervisors. Although conflict or interaction problems cannot always be blamed on discrimination, unfortunately all too often they can be. Also unfortunate is that the discrimination is so subtle that it is difficult if not impossible to prove. In short, minority managers often feel isolated.

It is also not uncommon for minority managers to feel as if they are being micromanaged. Many believe that superiors do not trust their ability to lead or manage. Consequently, they may feel powerless knowing that their decisions may be overturned simply if subordinates complain to upper management. Minority (as well as all) police managers need a support base when operating with their subordinates and peers.

Minority managers may also experience ambivalence about their relationship with lower ranked officers, whether they supervise them or not. As in the example presented about minority relationships at the police academy, senior field officers sometimes mentor junior officers. Provided this type of mentoring does not interfere with objectivity, it could be beneficial.

Conversely, other minority police managers interact negatively with minority subordinates by being more harsh toward them apparently in an effort to minimize speculation that there are relational improprieties. This type of minority manager may alienate minority officers and be insensitive to their concerns. Obviously there must be a balance maintained between favoritism and indifference and police executives and counselors must be aware of this spectrum and provide an atmosphere where minority police managers do not feel that they have to treat minority subordinates any differently and certainly not more harshly than other subordinates. Counselors should also be aware that subtle biases and discrimination do occur, and they should be prepared to listen to minority managers so that they can be helped to develop appropriate coping skills.

ASSISTANCE

The previous section identified concerns of ethnic minority police officers. Obviously, some stress is inherent to police work; however, other stressors unique to minority officers can be attributed to their ethnicity alone and can be minimized through organizational changes. This section provides practical suggestions for police department administrators, managers, and counselors to assist minority police officers.

Counseling

First and foremost, all police officers should have access to a confidential comprehensive counseling program. Although police officers are notoriously distrustful of mental health services, at least one study has indicated that between 37% and 80% of police respondents were somewhat willing to utilize psychological services provided they could do so without becoming known to the department (Ebert, 1986).

Most large metropolitan police departments have counseling available for use by their personnel. Watson (1986) suggested an ongoing counseling program throughout the career of the police officer at stages covering selection, probation, early career, midcareer, late career, and retirement. As with any other officer, objectives change in each of these stages for the minority officer as well. Because minority officers may have been disadvantaged prior to their police service, during the selection and probationary period they may require special counseling to deal with their concerns. As minority officers progress through their careers they are able to cope with certain external behaviors (Watson, 1986). A preventive counseling approach certainly would present advantages to include identification of serious problems sooner.

A Multiculturalistic Approach

Multiculturalism is an approach that recognizes that it is neither necessary nor desirable for different ethnic groups to shed their cultural identities to participate in the larger community. The trend in the United States is moving away from assimilation into the so-called melting pot, and toward the goal of a cooperative pluralism that enables each ethnic group to preserve its cultural identity (Cesarz & Madrid-Bustos, 1991).

Derald Wing Sue (1991), a renowned scholar of multiculturalism, presented forthright insight into minority problems, and he stressed the importance of using a multiculturalistic approach when counseling ethnic people. Sue (1991) acknowledged that those culturally different from their peers may feel that their differences are unacceptable, which often leads to feelings of inferiority.

As has been emphasized throughout this chapter, traditional approaches to counseling and dealing with minority concerns may not be effective. Although many of our conventional theories of counseling and psychotherapy were derived from White definitions of normality and abnormality, psychologists today recognize the importance of allowing people to be different for their own sake, and for the benefit of companies and organizations that realize the advantages of cultural diversity by improving their competitive edge. To implement a multiculturalistic strategy, training is essential for change to occur in officers, managers, and those counseling minority officers (Sue, 1991).

To embark on a multiculturalistic counseling approach, counselors must become more culturally aware of their values, biases, stereotypes, and assumptions about human behavior. There is potential for traditional counseling to be ineffective or counterproductive when counselors minimize or deny the existence of racism. Minority perspectives may be influenced by experiences of racism and discrimination that may cause many minority clients to enter counseling with an uncertainty of the counselor, the counseling process, and the institutions from which the process is embedded. Counselors must begin to use culturally appropriate intervention strategies based on the premise that no one style of counseling is appropriate for all populations and situations (Sue, 1991). Further, those counseling minority officers should expect complaints of discrimination, and subtle ethnic or gender biases.

Counselors and other police helpers must be familiar with the police culture as it may have an impact on minority complaints as well as the minority perspective, because minorities too are influenced by the police culture. Counselors should be cognizant that police generally are stubbornly independent, preferring to handle their problems alone. Further, because police officers are also a cohesive group, they like to try to help each other. Obviously, this mentality makes it less likely they will willingly seek professional counseling even when they really need it. Minority officers are probably as reluctant to seek counseling as the police populace in general. We have already seen in police culture that police tend to be more prejudiced and conservative than the general population, which has negative implications for minority officers.

What does all of this mean for police counselors? Things may or may not be as they initially seem. Minority officers may use their ethnic status as a crutch or minority officers who legitimately are victims of discrimination may refuse to consider the issues and blame themselves for their problems. In any event, awareness of the problem is essential in assisting distressed minority officers.

Whether a police psychologist or a psychological consultant, police departments may call on those offering psychological services to their personnel for a host of reasons relating to personal counseling and development of programs to assist minorities in the areas of concern identified in this chapter.

Equal Employment Opportunity Concerns

Probably the most sensitive circumstance that police psychologists, clinicians, and managers must deal with is assisting minority officers to discern if they have been victims of discrimination and, if so, advising those officers what to do about it. To be able to competently assist minorities regarding issues of discrimination, counselors and managers should be familiar with the Equal Employment Opportunity (EEO) Act of 1972, as amended and the Civil Reform Act of 1978. Counselors should also be familiar with the police department's policies for handling EEO complaints and what additional resources may be available. Although counselors and managers have an obligation to the police department, there is also an obligation to individual police clients. Should a counselor or manager determine that a session with a minority officer concerning an EEO issue presents a conflict of interest, it is probably better to terminate the session and make a referral rather than attempting to counsel concerned that the client may be directly or indirectly influenced in one direction or the other based on the counselor or manager's own interests.

When initially hearing a complaint from a minority officer about discrimination, counselors should be careful not to use condescending remarks that would give an impression that the officer is imagining the problem. Consider that many police officers filing EEO complaints and lawsuits have indicated that when they were encountering discrimination, they often felt as if they were losing their minds. For example, Mat Perez, a Hispanic supervisory FBI agent who filed an EEO complaint and subsequently a lawsuit against the Bureau, believed he was going insane until he consulted others (Sanchez, 1990).

When counseling minorities about EEO concerns, it is essential that the counselor or manager be exceptionally careful not to unduly influence them about what action to take. It may be just as detrimental mentally and occupationally to file an EEO complaint as it would be not to file a complaint. Because so much is at stake, the minority officer must feel as if the decision is his own. Probably for as many officers who will seek counseling as the first step in filing a formal complaint, just as many also seek counseling only as a means of venting their frustration without the intent of filing a complaint.

In any event, to afford police departments an opportunity to improve race relations, it is incumbent on minority police helpers to identify common problems expressed by minority officers, and to bring them to the attention of police administrators without violating confidentiality by describing situations in such a way as to identify the officers presenting the complaints.

Peer Counseling

Some advocates suggest that given the police culture and the tendency to call on each other for assistance anyway, the tendency can be exploited beneficially in the form of peer counseling. Peer counseling programs are based on the premise that with proper guidance, police officers are in many cases more appropriate helpers for the majority of the problems faced by police officers, at least for initial contact. Peer counseling is also based on the premise that often the best person to intervene with a police officer is another officer (Linden, 1988). The BNA report suggests that employees develop self-help procedures and counseling for minority employees. This concept certainly encompasses minority associations and underscores the need for special counseling to address the special concerns of minorities.

In the federal government, EEO officers[2] are nonmanagement personnel and thus may be viewed as peer counselors. The federal government has found having EEO officers as peers versus managers reduces the chances of a conflict of interest and facilitates conflict resolution at an informal stage. The private sector appears to have extended the EEO peer counselor role.

Companies have developed what are referred to as *consulting pairs.* These companies allow their workplace disputes to be handled by people whose backgrounds and experiences mirror those of the workers. Their objective pairs examine all of the possibilities, miscommunications, and prejudices. They also learn to apply the company's own culture to the issues at hand (Deutsch, 1991). Police departments could implement similar programs by working with another police department analogous to how personnel from other departments currently are used to comprise promotional interview panels.

Sensitivity Training

Police administrators need to ensure that their personnel receive training aimed at confronting prejudicial assumptions that create misconceptions and barriers during interaction within police departments. The BNA report asserted

---

[2]The federal government offers several courses to state, local, and federal agencies regarding EEO guidelines and the development of EEO programs. Two relevant courses are: "Introduction to the Federal EEO Program" and "Personnel Management for EEO Staffs." Additional information may be obtained by writing to the U. S. Office of Personnel Management, Federal Building, Room 3406, 600 Arch Street, Philadelphia, PA 19106.

that stereotypes continue to create obstacles for ethnic and female minorities. Workplace research finds that African Americans continue to face being characterized as lazy, arrogant, and intimidating. Generally, stereotypes, biases, and prejudices that convey a message of nonacceptance or exclusiveness are often acted out because of fear. Training is one way to reduce these fears.

Seminars designed to sensitize officers to the plight of oppressed minorities are becoming increasingly popular. Charles King, the head of the Atlanta-based Urban Crisis Center conducts workshops fashioned to improve race relations within corporations, organizations, and government agencies. Negative perceptions of African Americans' behaviors by Whites are exposed. For example, King confronts Whites by asking them why they always sit together, to get them to understand how African Americans feel when the same question is posed to them (Smith, 1988). Essentially one goal of any sensitivity training is to improve race relations through providing a new perspective with the expectation that perceptions will change and stereotyping and bias will be eliminated. It should be noted that the success of sensitivity programs may be dependent on the length of the training.

A study conducted by Smith and Lubin (1980), which examined the correlation between emotional arousal and the length of sensitivity training, detected a rise and fall pattern in anxiety, depression, and hostility. Smith and Lubin concluded that the rise and fall pattern in emotional arousal was dependent on adequate time for the elicitation of negative affects and on contact with other groups involved in similar training. Therefore it is recommended that sensitivity training be conducted for an appropriate period of time and with appropriate isolation.

An objective of sensitivity training for police officers should also include improving the relationship between the police and ethnic groups in the communities policed. In many cities, tensions are building and have indeed erupted between the police and the communities. Experts suggest that training officers about what to expect culturally from the communities they serve can alleviate some of the tension. For example, Deputy Sheriff Douglas Hinkle (1991) trains officers in the mores of Hispanic cultures. Hinkle exposes customs relating to Hispanic machismo and the practice of bribery (expected by police in some Hispanic countries). These revelations provide a different viewpoint that may influence officers' interpretations of any scenario they may encounter. Education designed to sensitize can help reduce the likelihood that an officer inadvertently causes a situation with a minority citizen to escalate based on misinterpretations (Hinkle, 1991).

Those police departments that have offered sensitivity training generally have found them to be effective. Specialized training courses created and offered by the Royal Canadian Mounted Police on policing in a multicultural society have made such a difference that they have been adopted and adapted by other police forces (Himelfrab, 1991).

Management Setting the Tone

Experts agree that one way of ensuring that racism is decreased is by management setting the tone. Studies are showing that people in authority can play a crucial role in heading off expressions of ethnic and racial hatred simply by making it clear that they will not be tolerated (Blanchard, 1991).

Intense training should be directed to those managers responsible for implementing cultural diversity programs because nothing changes until management's behavior changes.

Publications

Another way for police departments to educate their employees, to demonstrate a commitment to battling discrimination, and to encourage diversity and promote an overall sense of sensitivity to minority officers is to produce publications on appropriate topics. For example the FBI's (1987) *Intercultural Communication: Tips for the Investigator* is an example of a publication that promotes sensitivity.

WOMEN'S ISSUES

Today, women are represented in most police departments across the United States and their numbers are increasing. Between 1979 and 1986, the proportion of women in policing increased from 4.2% to 8.8% of all municipal officers (Martin, 1989). As in the case of cultural diversity, gender diversity is also viewed as having a positive effect in the workplace. Thus, women's increased representation can be considered beneficial to police departments.

Women bring a unique perspective to police work. A survey indicated that certain police departments conducting studies found fewer public complaints made against female officers than against male officers, and that the former were also more effective in defusing potentially violent situations. Women are more likely to be independent, energetic individuals with wide-ranging interests and relatively few somatic complaints (Hargrave, 1986).

Women in law enforcement experience many of the same special problems encountered by ethnic minorities. One argument for increasing the representation of women in law enforcement may be that there is safety in numbers. As one expert puts it, in large male-dominated departments where only one or two women are left to fend for themselves, even the best managerial intentions are not likely to bring about success (Spann, 1990).

In recruitment, selection, and retention areas with respect to ethnic and women minorities, concerns overlap. As with recruiting ethnic minorities, care should also be taken when selecting recruitment officers for recruitment of women. The BNA report suggested that officials conducting interviews should be selected for their reputation for treating men and women equally and the interview process should be scrutinized so that selection criteria are explicit and gender neutral.

Based on the findings of a recent study, researchers suggest that departments must increase their female applicant pools to increase women's representation in policing. Affirmative action has been identified as one means of widening the applicant pool (Martin, 1989). In fact, Warner (Warner & Steel, 1989) concluded that utilization rates for women police was partially dependent on the maintenance of affirmative action programs.

Interview

As in the case of all minorities, care should be given when constructing the composition of the interview panel. If possible, a female officer should be on the panel. Martin (1989) acknowledged that the potential for bias is great during selection unless interviewers are carefully screened, trained, and provided with structured interview formats. Questions addressed to women about pregnancy and child care should probably be avoided.

Academy

Women's biggest concern in the academy is that they stand out and are noticed quickly. Most police trainers will admit that the women are generally known by name, background, and reputation before they even arrive at the academy. Staff members more often than not take an approach to be sensitive toward female candidates or "ride" them harder than the men if it is their belief that women officers should behave just like male officers. In a study cited previously, academy instructors rated male recruits as more emotionally suited than females for law enforcement work (Hargrave, 1986).

This may explain why women are more often likely to be accused of not being as aggressive as male recruits. And when women are accused of not being sufficiently aggressive, they often feel self-conscious and pressured to behave in a manner contrary to their disposition. Granted, police culture as well as the nature of police work dictate that officers be self-assured and confident when performing their duties. However, women candidates often accused of not being assertive attempt to compensate by only acting more aggressive. Has a police academy staff truly accomplished its goal if the recruit only acts more aggressive (which is aggressiveness not grounded in self-confidence) and after graduation the recruit reverts to the more comfortable posture of being unsure of herself?

The point to be made is that more careful evaluation or assessment should be made about whether a recruit is indeed too timid, and if this is the case, determining to what extent it will impact adversely on her duties. Many female recruits feel as if they have to undergo a personality change to successfully complete the academy.

Because most departments take women's physical stature into account when physical fitness assessments are being made, physical agility is not as much of an issue as it used to be; however, physical size may also be a problem for women as it relates to those staff members who believe women should not be officers. Scenarios may always be constructed that will predispose the female trainee to failure, if that is indeed the desired outcome.

Firearms are another area where many female recruits have traditionally experienced difficulty. Often the problem has been one of strength (trouble with the trigger pull). However, with the recent widespread utilization of semiautomatic weapons (which have a lighter trigger pull) by police departments, strength is becoming less of a problem.

Male peers can also pose a problem for women police recruits at any time during their academy stay. Studies examining academy performance have found that a woman's ability to adapt to her new role and men's willingness to accept her as a patrol officer is of equal importance to the woman's job performance (Hargrave, 1986). It follows then that the lack of cooperation or bias from male officers toward female officers can have negative effects on their work performance.

Women police officers are especially prone to gender bias, a subtle form of discrimination where outward manifestations are based on internalized bias or stereotypes directed toward members of the opposite gender. In a study by Geis and Butler, on unconscious sexism and racism on the job, the investigators found that gender bias is real and is an unconscious reaction based on largely submerged beliefs. The researchers say that because females are expected to be less competent and they are not expected to take the initiative, when and if they do, they are violating social expectations and are disapproved of (Bass, 1990).

"There is strong evidence of hostility toward the idea of female police officers" (Warner & Steel, 1989, p. 298). Because law enforcement is considered a nontraditional profession for women, probably most female police officers have already encountered or will confront at some point in their career instances of gender bias.

Gender bias does not necessarily have to occur between supervisor and subordinates; it can occur between subordinates and it can occur between subordinates and female supervisors. A common example of gender bias during the police academy experience would include a situation whereby a shy female recruit is confronted with not being sufficiently aggressive by staff members, but a male recruit of similar disposition is never confronted by the staff.Recognizing that officers are dependent on each other for successful police operations, law enforcement is essentially a team occupation.

Consequently, if the team decides to cause or allow one individual to fail due to shunning and so on, it is very likely that the individual will indeed fail.

The kind of gender bias where an individual female officer conducts herself contrary to even one male officer's preconceived notion of how females should behave is sometimes enough to catapult a female's reputation into a downward spiral that literally never ends. If, for example, academy instructors have concerns about a female recruit and the rest the training team feels as though as a whole it is adversely affected, often they many leave the female member out to hang. Female officers are also presented with many double standards by their superiors.

Another manifestation of gender bias may be the kind of evaluation a female officer receives from her supervisor. Some studies have found gender differences in performance noting that male officers and supervisors tended to hold negative attitudes toward women officers. The studies also found that the public was equally satisfied with male and female officers, but that male supervisors rated the women as less effective in comparison to men when handling violent situations (Martin, 1989). Even informal situations present an opportunity for misunderstanding of female officers.

Women may receive undue attention if they become too friendly with male class members. Appearances of fraternization are discouraged; however, if the female recruit keeps to herself she is just as likely to experience condemnation. This syndrome of microscrutinizing female interaction with male officers may also pose a problem for women in formulating mentoring relationships with men.

Sexual harassment can also be a component of the academy experience for female recruits. Women encountering harassment during this time frame are probably less likely to report instances for fear of reprisal or misunderstanding by the training staff, which may not consider her to be a team player or, worse yet, perceive her to be one incapable of keeping the well-preserved code of silence when she leaves the academy.

The police academy presents an opportunity for police departments to start new officers off on the right track with respect to equality. All new recruits should receive some type of EEO briefing in the beginning of their training so that candidates are exposed to departmental policies from the beginning. The facets of discrimination and sexual harassment should be included as subjects in the EEO presentation. Because females generally have a much higher academy attrition rate than males (Hargrave, 1986), counseling should be made available to women while they are in the police academy. It should be noted, though, that management's support of EEO programs is essential in gaining support from the rank and file.

Role modeling is the best way to ensure that new officers understand that a department is serious about its sexual harassment policy. Middle and upper managers must provide examples of nonharassment as well as intervening in situations where sexual harassment has occurred. Implementation of policies by management against harassment in police work is essential to obtaining a desired outcome. Research on affirmative action shows a strong correlation between the desired outcome and management's clear commitment to implement policies (Martin, 1989).

Retention

Although women are entering the field of law enforcement in record numbers, unfortunately many are also leaving. Some women discover that policing is not a job for which they are suited. Some find that the environment is hostile or unpleasant for women, but not men. Still others experience difficulties in meshing policing with family life, and inadequate light duty and pregnancy leave policies make having a family and continuing to work difficult or impossible (Martin, 1989). The BNA report indicated that assertive women are seen as too aggressive and women who exhibit stereotypical female behavior are viewed as too weak. Additionally, women are denied promotions because of family responsibilities.

"Lack of satisfaction" is a catch-all category and a rationale for many women leaving police work. Lack of satisfaction may stem from problems with peers (gender bias), lack of promotional opportunities (glass ceiling), or a lack of desirable assignments. There is a general feeling among women police officers that they must prove themselves to male officers and superiors, especially in the area of violent encounters with criminals.

Much of the police culture is to some degree predicated on the presence of danger and the potential for violence that leads to a generalized suspiciousness, isolation from the community, and a cohesive, informal occupational group with its own stratification system and norms. Consequently, this culture permits majority officers to justify their objections to certain minority officers, especially women. Most of men's objections to women officers focus on their physical differences, and are expressed in terms of concern for physical safety and women's alleged inability to deal with physical violence (Martin, 1989).

Acquiring a mentor has been identified in extensive management literature as an essential component for workers to progress professionally. Previous research has found that mentorship is related to career progress, organizational influence, and advancement (Ragins, 1991). Consequently, women may face the glass ceiling because of the lack of sponsorship. Men do not appear to face the same obstacles women face in obtaining effective mentors.

In a study conducted on gender differences regarding barriers to gaining a mentor, Ragins (1991) sought to examine the obstacles and to provide insight into what inhibits the development of mentoring relationships. A key conclusion made by the researchers was that women seemed to perceive the presence of more barriers than men in obtaining a mentor, although in actuality there were no significant gender differences in protege experience (Ragins, 1991). The researchers acknowledged that a limitation of their study was that the research was perceptual and not necessarily functional. However, some of the respondents were self-conscious about seeking a male mentor for fear that people would think that there was a sexual relationship going on. Naturally, women police officers are especially susceptible to this kind of thinking because their work environment is dominated by men.

Women leaving police work because of family–work conflicts generally take their children and spouse into their decision making. Children and spousal concerns can affect officers. Scheduling and lack of appropriate day care may affect the female officer. Many former female law enforcement officers indicate that they felt compelled to quit because of problems with obtaining adequate child care. Single parents are especially prone to feelings of guilt when work and home schedules conflict.

Pregnancy on the job and maternity leave policies also affect women. Even an adverse policy is preferable and may be less stressful for female officers than working for departments that do not have clear policies at all. In those departments without a clear policy, female officers are more likely to be under more stress during pregnancy and maternity leave, because they do not know what to expect and are literally at the mercy of their immediate supervisor. Under these circumstances, female officers are sometimes prematurely placed on light duty, which often means loss of desirable assignments, loss of use of departmental vehicles, surrender of weapons, and even loss of monetary compensation if overtime is no longer authorized. These deprivations can certainly be stressful for the female officer. Although some women officers are prematurely removed from enforcement operations, other officers are forced to perform enforcement duties beyond when they should.

One rectifiable criticism commonly expressed by women police officers about pregnancy and their work is that often they are not "heard" during the decision-making process when their fates are being determined.[3] Women also believe that they are treated differently by their supervisors after children are born. Specifically, females are often viewed and treated differently with respect to assignments. Superiors often decide who will work late based on which subordinates are single parents. Often single parents are excluded from certain assignments without ever being consulted. Supervisors should discuss late assignments with all subordinates. It could be that allowances

---

[3]Perceptions of female officers and supervisors of female officers discussed in this portion of the chapter were common sentiments expressed to the author at conferences, workshops, and in informal conversations.

may need to be made for single parents in cases of emergency, as with all officers who happen to be parents.

Supervisors should not assume that single parents cannot deal with scheduling. Many women say that they are never consulted when late assignments arise. Some supervisors say that after failed initial attempts to assign mothers late work, they merely stop asking. Unfortunately, this begins a self-fulfilling prophecy. The supervisor does not ask the female officer to work late because he or she thinks the officer will not be prepared to work late. Although frustrated, the female officer is now conditioned to expect differential treatment. She may be automatically overlooked by the supervisor. Problems such as these can obviously be resolved if the officer is encouraged to volunteer more, the supervisor communicates more, and policies are written with enough flexibility for supervisors to deal with individual situations as they arise.

Female Ethnic Minorities

Because minority ethnic women make up a large percentage of all women in law enforcement, it is surprising that more has not been written about them. In a study, minority ethnic women made up 45% of the female applicants and 44% of females who completed academy training (Martin, 1989). Regardless of their numbers, it follows from evidence presented earlier in this chapter that they probably receive a double helping of discrimination and bias, resulting in special concerns.

A recently published article that discussed interviews conducted with "women of color" about their experiences at work effectively demonstrated that minority women frequently receive an extra helping of discrimination and bias. Often they receive the force of stereotyping directed at both at minority men and women. They are also often the target of hostile jokes. As the women indicated, stereotypical remarks or jokes are enough to throw everything off balance and generate feelings of inferiority (Southgate, 1992). It is also logical to assume that minority women have special issues with respect to promotions.

As in the case of the newly promoted minority male manager, minority women if promoted are also likely to be faced with speculation from their peers as to the desert of her promotion. However, this speculation does not end with just majority officers. Newly promoted minority females may experience some resentment from other females and other ethnic minorities who may speculate that they have simply been promoted by management to satisfy two quotas. After assuming their new roles as supervisors, minority women are also likely to experience intense scrutiny from subordinates and superiors; usually they feel as if they have to prove themselves. Often when majority male officers eventually adjust and acquiesce to minority male superiors, the identification of maleness helps, and when majority males adjust to White female supervisors, the identification of race helps, but there is no such baseline relationship available to support ethnic minority female supervisors. Research is necessary to understand the special considerations of minority ethnic women officers, especially because it is estimated that they constitute almost half of all women officers.

ASSISTANCE

Counselors and managers of women police officers can assuage women's concerns in several ways. Policy development and implementation regarding sexual harassment, pregnancy on the job, and maternity leave can help women officers. Policies concerning pregnancy and maternity leave should be as clear as possible with enough flexibility to permit the supervisor and female officer to reach a consensus.

Sexual Harassment

Women in law enforcement are likely to encounter some form of sexual harassment during their career. Women in nontraditional careers, such as police work, are particularly prone to sexual harassment. In a paper that offers practical suggestions to reduce the incidence of sexual harassment, the typical victims were found to be younger women in nontraditional jobs (Spann, 1990). Often female officers try to deal with situations of sexual harassment without any assistance.

Many independent females choose law enforcement as a career. In one study of female officers, they were found to score more in the direction of independence, self-determination, and spontaneity (Hargrave, 1986). Therefore, it is not surprising that many of them would probably first try to deal with sexual harassment on their own before bringing complaints to management or counselors. Many female victims of sexual harassment try confronting the offending officer first. Sometimes this approach may work because part of the police culture dictates a strong sense of doing the right thing. However, counselors and trainers should keep in mind that what the "right thing" to do in cases of sexual harassment varies with the situation and the female officer.

Because filing sexual harassment complaints can have an even more adverse effect on their careers (i.e., other officers turning on them), women officers should be encouraged to make their own decisions with respect to a particular course of action in sexual harassment counseling. Women should be presented with the wide variety of options available to them so that they can make informed decisions and calculate the outcomes of those decisions. One point that should be emphasized on examination of the recent Anita Hill versus Clarence Thomas controversy is the importance of identifying the need for women to be aware of the time constraints with respect to formal sexual harassment complaints. During training, female officers should be made aware of their rights regarding statutes of limitations.

Superiors and counselors must be sensitive to the fact that if an officer brings a complaint of gender bias, sexual harassment, or other concerns, in most instances she has already tried to deal with the problem alone first and that the situation probably has escalated. Therefore, condescending remarks should be avoided. However, the counselor or manager should try to determine what efforts the female officer has made to attempt to resolve the problem and advance from there. The counselor's or supervisor's roles are to assist female officers in identification of the problem and solutions or coping skills.

Sexual harassment policies should be widely publicized and strictly adhered to by upper and lower management as an example to all. Training regarding the components and enforcement of sexual harassment policies is a logical solution to decreasing the incidence of sexual harassment. It is difficult to actually measure the incidence of sexual harassment, because as with rape, female officers frequently fail to report sexual harassment. Counselors should be aware that women police officers are also influenced by the code of silence unique to the police culture, which may mean that officers can be in a state of denial when they do seek counseling.

Counseling

Probably the best contribution law enforcement executives can make to the mental well-being of their female officers—and all of their officers—is to provide them with a confidential, appropriate, and adequate means for seeking counseling and a means for preventing some of the issues discussed here from ever occurring. Sexual harassment counseling may take the form of individual or group counseling.

To retain women officers, the Madison (WI) Police Department and the City Affirmation Action Office formulated a special psychotherapeutic support group for women officers designed to help them confront gender and sexual harassers more effectively (Spann, 1990).

Integration Training for Women

Prevention of sexual harassment and gender bias and the improvement of women police officers' work environment can be accomplished through sensitivity training for all officers and managers and through awareness education for women officers. Training geared toward helping women understand socialization concepts unique to men can also be beneficial to female police officers. The purpose of this type of training is not necessarily to change women but to give them tools so that they have a fair chance at knowing how the "game" is played; it is a form of empowerment. Most experts agree that women and men are socialized differently. A consequence of different socialization is that in predominately male institutions or organizations, such as police departments, there is already an established standard operating procedure (an organizational culture) in place based on male socialization criteria.

Sociologists have theorized that all cultural systems have a set of core ideas that form the basis of communication in that culture (Thornberry, 1990). If this concept is true, then identification of the basis of communication in the police culture is essential for assisting women and ethnic minorities who may enter the profession at a deficit, not having been socialized according to the dominant culture. As E. D. Hirsch (cited in Thornberry, 1990) said "to be culturally literate is to possess the basic information needed to thrive in the modern world" (p. 33). Further, Hirsch argued that whether we like it or not, rules for success are indeed set by the relatively powerful, and that in order to succeed everyone, regardless of origin, needs to be culturally literate with respect to the same basic information. Existence of male cultural literacy is probably the best argument for providing training to female workers in nontraditional occupations.

The politics of male-dominated organizations such as police departments have been structured by men, and thus it is more realistic to train women to understand and function effectively than to expect the organization to change rapidly enough to support women officers. This is not intended to mean that women should change and become men; just as in the situation with ethnic minorities, the objective should be to create a work environment that values diversity. However, while the United States aspires to reach this goal, women can be helped through education.

Correctional officials appear to be progressive in the area of training women. Many agencies have been offering training for women employees that addresses issues such as sexual harassment, management strategies, and supervising men in prison. In a recent survey conducted, all responding law enforcement agencies had formalized training programs with almost half offering training to address the specific needs of women employees (Bergsmann, 1991). Thus training such as Women On the Team (WOTT) helps female officers to adapt and understand the general politics of interaction with men within the organization.[4]

---

[4]DEA's Federal Women's Program offers a course to its female special agents, intelligence analysts, and diversion investigators designed to provide them with additional skills to permit them to do their job well in a demanding environment. Some of the course objectives include how to explore and expand productive means of communication with superiors, peers, and subordinates; how to assess personal and professional needs for networks, support systems, and vertical connections and how to perceive; and how to formulate organizational needs and goals more effectively and utilize them to achieve career enhancement.

Upward mobility issues for women officers may be influenced positively in a number of ways. Affirmative action programs have been noted as one means for ensuring that women are promoted. In a survey cited earlier, in departments with court-ordered affirmative action, women made up 3.5% of all supervisors. In those with voluntary affirmative action programs and those without affirmative action plans, they accounted respectively for 2.4% and 2.2% of all supervisors (Martin, 1989). Aside from affirmative action, gaining mentors and education[5] on leadership can assist women officers in breaking through the glass ceiling.

Sensitivity Training

Because women in nontraditional occupations such as police work are especially susceptible to gender bias and sexual harassment, male officers should be offered training aimed at reducing the incidence of discrimination against women.[6]

Female police officers work in an extraordinarily complex male dominated subculture where loyalty to the crew often takes precedence over all else and is seen as a prerequisite for survival on the job. Moreover, the majority of police officers' work is spent considerably removed from management view and immediate control. Consequently, the odds of managers confronting retaliation toward sexual harassment victims in a direct and timely way are clearly quite low. For these reasons, other approaches to addressing the prevention of harassment and intervention are necessary (Spann, 1990), such as sensitivity training.

I was fortunate enough to spend a week in such training. Initially, I was reluctant because I thought it would just be one of those "gripe sessions" where women talked negatively about their male counterparts (I did not feel as if I needed to go away for a week to attend yet another one of those sessions). However, I was pleasantly surprised and felt I walked away with skills that I could and have since used. Politically speaking, I have a better understanding of how men think, how certain women's behavior can be misunderstood, how to negotiate and finalize agreements, what "owing" really means, and so on. In other words, I was empowered. Many of the women who completed the training with me told me that they also felt this same sense of empowerment, having acquired the understanding and developed the skills necessary to survive.

DEA makes available the WOTT training on a contract basis. For more information contact DEA's Federal Women's Program Manager, U.S. Department of Justice, Drug Enforcement Administration, Washington, DC 20537.

[5]The federal government offers a leadership and women's course to federal, state, and local government employees. Additional information may be obtained by writing to the U. S. Office of Personnel Management, Federal Building, Room 3406, 600 Arch Street, Philadelphia, PA 19106.

[6]A course entitled "Preventing Sexual Harassment, A Workshop for Employees" is offered to federal, state, and local government workers through the U. S. Office of Personnel Management's Regional Training Center, Federal Building, Room 3406, 600 Arch Street, Philadelphia, PA 19106.

Many law enforcement agencies already appear to be engaging in some form of sensitivity training. In a recent survey, 76% of the responding law enforcement departments require all staff to take courses on sexual harassment awareness to satisfy in-service requirements. Fifty-nine percent offered training to decrease gender and racial bias and stereotyping and to increase awareness and understanding of gender differences (Bergsmann, 1991).

In training of this nature, trainees need to hear that they are not being singled out for some kind of punishment, but rather, are exploring and addressing a cultural problem in which everyone has had a role, and which everyone must now help solve. Punitive or polarizing training techniques should be avoided (Spann, 1990).

Sensitivity Training for Managers

Training for police managers responsible for supervising women is necessary to ensure that all other efforts aimed at improving women's work environment are not thwarted. Often even when women obtain positive results in policing, their methods are criticized by biased supervisors. For example, in studies where a difference was found in male and female behavior, the possibility was not considered that the women's style in resolving conflicts and disputes might have had a beneficial effect rather than a negative effect. Women's lower arrest rates may mean that they are not taking enough initiative (as was indicated) or it could indicate that women handled the situations better than male officers, if the latter caused incidents to escalate into confrontations that resulted in unnecessary arrests (Martin, 1989).

Thomas (1990) sympathized with the middle managers who are often breaking new ground. He acknowledged that these managers need help, sympathy, to be told that they are pioneers, and to be judged accordingly.

Any training of managers should address affirmative action or other hiring and promotional initiatives to assist ethnic minorities and women. Affirmative action policies have been shown to have a positive effect on women being promoted. Case study data from five police agencies showed that affirmative action policies have widened women's opportunities to receive specialized assignments (Martin, 1989). The BNA report also indicated that committees making promotion decisions should avoid gender-biased criteria in the evaluation of women candidates. Police managers must also receive training designed to detect and reduce the incidence of sexual harassment.[7]

---

[7]The federal government offers several courses to state, local, and federal agencies for supervisors and managers regarding EEO guidelines and prevention of sexual harassment. Two relevant courses are: "Role of Supervisors and Managers in EEO" and "Preventing Sexual Harassment: A Workshop for Supervisors and Managers". Additional information may be obtained by writing to the U. S. Office of Personnel Management, Federal Building, Room 3406, 600 Arch Street, Philadelphia, PA 19106.

For more information regarding women's issues, see Appendix A, which reports the results of a survey conducted by the author (Stansbury, 1993) of female law enforcement officers.

GAY AND LESBIAN ISSUES

Homosexuals are one of the largest minorities in the law enforcement workforce. It is estimated by gay rights groups that gays represent about 10% of city police departments. However, because many homosexuals fear reprisal, it is difficult to determine an exact figure (Remesch, 1990). It has been demonstrated thus far in this chapter that minority officers, regardless of their ethnicity or gender, are assets by promoting diversity. Furthermore, all strive to be treated fairly by other members of their respective police departments. Such is also the case with gay and lesbian officers.

More police departments have begun to actively recruit gay and lesbian officers.[8] For those departments recruiting gay and lesbian officers, one of the most cited reasons has been to enhance diversity and realize the advantages. For example, the New York Police Department assigned a lesbian officer to a beat patrol in a homosexual community after requests from district leaders. Although it is difficult to assess all of the benefits of her assignment, both the community and the police believe it improved their overall relationship (Lorch, 1992). Hiring of openly gay and lesbian officers may also reduce fear and suspiciousness of the homosexual community of police. Although the recruitment of gay and lesbian officers may have a practical effect, for many departments, hiring openly homosexual individuals is not as simple as police administrators opting to launch a campaign.

Penal statutes are by far the greatest barriers to hiring openly homosexual officers. Many states still have laws that prohibit sodomy. Dependent on the position of police administrators on the hiring and recruitment of gay and lesbian officers, the law has been used as a rationale, ignored, or reformed. Administrators opting to ignore or promote legislation to reform sanctions against homosexuality or to protect gay rights have come under attack by the public. For example, Police Chief Tom Potter of Portland, Oregon recently became a target in an anti-gay battle after he marched in a gay pride parade in part to support his daughter who is a lesbian police officer. Due to these controversies, those counseling gay and lesbian officers must realize that state laws may affect an officer's willingness to reveal his or her homosexuality to co-workers or even to a counselor.

Counselors and police managers working for some departments may experience a conflict of interest when counseling gay and lesbian officers. Often police administrators charge their management staff with an obligation

---

[8]The New York Police Department and the Los Angeles Police Departments have at one time or another actively recruited gay and lesbian officers.

to bring to the attention of other department entities any known violations of the law by officers. If this is true for your department, consider verbal and written disclaimers indicating that there is an absence of confidentiality for certain behaviors such as homosexuality, drug use, and so on. This situation is problematic and clearly underscores the need for a clear policy, especially because the very officers in need of counseling may be denied counseling through departmental channels due to the nature of their problems.

In addition to the problems gay and lesbian officers face with respect to the law, they are fighting for equal rights in the larger world. The point in the political developmental progression that gays find themselves today is probably the most critical and stressful. With many gays now openly professing their homosexuality, opponents are better able to focus opposition that leads to a more fervent confrontation. There are groups opposing gays in and outside of police departments. The aggregate stress of everyday life for the homosexual officer is likely to be staggering. Deciding whether to be openly gay and the consequences of that decision may be made after countless hours of pondering whether the counseling is from self, friends, or professionals. The support or lack of support a given officer receives from management and counseling staff will most certainly affect the ultimate decision to reveal one's sexual orientation.

In the police department, preconceived homophobic attitudes are likely to permeate. Gay and lesbian officers are probably discriminated against in an open manner more than any other minority group today. It has been widely demonstrated in relevant literature that there exists a police culture that fosters attitudes of conservatism, machismo, and suspiciousness. Although lesbian officers who conform to a stereotype of exhibiting masculine characteristics are more likely be accepted by colleagues than male homosexual officers, generally the very existence of homosexuality is viewed as so extreme from the police culture that little, if any, common ground is left for openly gay officers to assimilate. For example, the general conservative ideology of the police with respect to issues such as family values stands opposite that of a more openminded homosexual community. Burke (1992) suggested that the general police culture prohibits officers from tolerating homosexual colleagues, let alone condoning their recruitment.

When one considers the opposition that gay and lesbian officers face in hiring, it is not surprising that openly gay officers are sometimes harassed. One survey revealed that 23% of gay men and 13% of lesbians experienced some type of abuse from colleagues because of their sexual orientation (Berrill, 1986). Although harassment frequently takes the form of stereotypical gags, some gay and lesbian officers have been the victims of more severe harassment such as being left alone to handle dangerous suspects or situations. Regardless of the type of harassment, gay and lesbian officers may be more likely to handle incidents of harassment informally.

It has been demonstrated that the police culture is one that discourages tattling,[9] so gay and lesbian officers may be reluctant to complain to superiors about differential treatment or harassment. Instead, a minority officer may feel his or her only recourse is to handle harassment situations alone, which leads to anxiety. Because gay and lesbian officers may be reluctant to choose the formal complaint process to handle those situations, counseling may present an effective means for them to discuss frustrating situations.

Gay and lesbian officers, like other minorities, often feel isolated. However, unlike ethnic minorities who often are able to identify with members of their own ethnic group, some gay and lesbian officers find it difficult to identify with the homosexual community. One lesbian officer recently told a reporter that she rarely socializes with the gay community and is unsure of what is expected of her as a lesbian officer working in a homosexual community (Lorch, 1992). Therefore, counselors and managers working with gay and lesbian officers can expect to hear complaints about feelings of isolation.

Gays and lesbians strive for the same acceptance as others and seek understanding. To this end, a few professional associations[10] have been formed and designed to enhance understanding between the lesbian and gay community and personnel of the agencies of the criminal justice system represented by its members. Obviously, police managers and counselors may use these types of organizations as resources to improve relations and learn more about the gay community.

ASSISTANCE

Because fear is often the source of conflict between majority officers and gay and lesbian officers, police department personnel should be trained to learn more about gay and lesbian issues. Sensitizing officers to gay and lesbian concerns can enhance a department's overall effectiveness by re-ducing citizens' complaints and fostering a sense of support among gay and lesbian officers. Counselors and managers called on to coordinate such training should keep in mind that gays are sensitive to homophobic attitudes and stereotyping and thus should use care when selecting instructors.

There is potential for individual values to be more evident when it comes to viewing gays and lesbians primarily due to the relatively slow assimilation process and the stage of the civil rights fight that gays currently are engaged in. Recall that we have seen that the police culture tends to be slightly more

---

[9]Police studies have identified what has been referred to as a code of silence involving a conspiracy of silence of police with respect to misconduct observed (Delattre, 1989).

[10]New York's Gay Officers Action League (GOAL) and in California, The Golden State Peace Officers Association are examples of professional associations seeking to improve police/gay community relations (Remesch, 1990).

conservative than the public. One way to minimize the likelihood that gays will be misrepresented is to consider gays and lesbians as potential instructors or assisting in other ways with training. The Rehoboth Beach Police Department in Delaware recently invited the group Gay Men and Lesbians Opposed to Violence (GLOV) to provide instructors for a police training course on the gay community. In addition to instructor consideration, course content and methods of instruction must also be considered.

Because the purpose of gay sensitizing classes is to conform the behavior of officers, instruction methods that incorporate behavioral techniques will most likely be more effective. The New York Police Department's Recruit Training Program on gay and lesbian issues, heralded as a model training program, incorporates hypothetical situations as a means to train officers. It is also recommended that role playing be involved in the training to provide participants with interaction experiences for future recall. Although not designed as a training experience, departments where police officers pose as gays in undercover operations have learned firsthand what gay bashing feels like. Law enforcement training specialists regard sensitivity training to be most effective when it is practical rather than theoretical and when it addresses real situations (Berrill, 1986).

Another essential element in the success of training designed to sensitize officers to working with gays is course content. Although AIDS education may be appropriately included in drug training, it may also be fitting to include it in gay sensitivity training in an effort to dispel myths about contracting the disease and to dismiss stereotypes that most gays are HIV positive. Legal matters and encouraging tolerance for diversity should be broached in training. Further the department's policy with respect to courteous interaction with citizens, appropriate ways to deal with gay and lesbian victims, and inclusion of how certain remarks or physical gestures may be interpreted by gays should also be discussed in training.

Training to sensitize police officers to gay and lesbian concerns should occur during the police academy experience as well as on the job. Training may also serve to protect police departments when officers must be reprimanded for discriminatory behavior.

As pointed out elsewhere in this chapter, the overall climate in a given department is most likely to be affected by the policies made by management and the enforcement of such policies. Gay and lesbian officers working for those departments with a consistently enforced written policy forbidding discrimination of officers and citizens based on sexual orientation are more likely to feel supported. Police departments across the nation recently appear to understand the need for such directives. For example, in 1993 the Maryland State Police established a policy stating that the department would not discriminate on the basis of sexual orientation in hiring employees. This policy is being implemented in spite of the fact that there exist laws in Maryland against sodomy. A thorough policy will also declare that employees and citizens will not be discriminated against based on sexual orientation and the consequences for such misconduct by personnel.

Gay rights activists suggest that police departments should respond vigorously to police abuse complaints. Twenty percent of the complaints received by one national hotline for victims of anti-gay harassment and violence were of police abuse, including verbal epithets, physical assault, entrapment, unequal enforcement of the law, and deliberate mishandling of cases (Berrill, 1986).

Former Chief Issac Fullwood of the Washington, DC Metropolitan Police recently had to defend against complaints from the gay community that members of the department responded inappropriately to a social gathering held in the District. During a lengthy news interview, Fullwood condemned the actions of two of his senior level commanding officers and asserted that they would be disciplined accordingly (Keen & Chibbaro, 1992). The point to be made here is that police administrators should incorporate standards of conduct for their personnel regarding interactions with gay officers and enforce whatever policy has been established.

Some police departments have discovered that appointing an official liaison may help relations with the gay community. Official liaisons have been used in Boston, Chicago, Los Angeles, San Francisco, Washington, DC and elsewhere in an advisory capacity to the chief of police. Liaison personnel generally respond to complaints and requests for assistance from minority communities and help local gay people feel the police are more accessible to them (Berrill, 1986). Counselors and managers may be ideal for the position due to their experiences in receiving complaints relating to gay issues.

Making counseling available to gay and lesbian officers is essential for ensuring productive workers. Gay and lesbian officers are in a high-risk category for stress-related psychological symptoms. Furthermore, homosexuals are also in a high-risk category for certain medical illness, such as AIDS. Because those with AIDS currently bear such a sociological stigma, it is essential that police administrators provide homosexual officers with a means of receiving counseling. Some gay and lesbian officers who have contracted AIDS in the past have felt compelled to exhaust personal funds for medical treatment to avoid using their medical plans and risking detection as HIV positive. In addition to providing counseling to officers with AIDS, counselors can also provide confidential liaison with other medical professionals to coordinate the best possible care for infected officers.

Summary

The impact the public and colleagues have on gay and lesbian officers is far reaching. Although a few police departments are openly recruiting gay officers, most are not. Some departments have implemented policies that recruiters and interviewers are not to pose questions or make decisions regarding sexual orientation. Nevertheless, a perception many gay and lesbian officers have is that even if they are comfortable disclosing their sexual orientation, others would prefer that they conceal their homosexuality. Consequently, many gay and lesbian officers feel compelled to hide their homosexuality from their departments to avoid discrimination. Although homosexuals may be the only minority group able to conceal their status due to a general absence of tell-tale signs, being "in the closet" is not without psychological consequences. The stress of being compelled to suppress one's sexual orientation may be overwhelming for some gay and lesbian officers.

Recognizing that the overall premise of Employment Assistance Programs is that employees experiencing a healthy personal life are more likely to be more productive workers, it would behoove police administrators with counseling programs to utilize them effectively to maximize productivity.

Although gay and lesbian officers' problems may appear to be the same as other minority groups, many of their concerns are unique to them. For example, unlike the protections afforded other minority groups, many gay and lesbian officers are not a protected class under the law. Therefore, counselors must be sensitive to gay and lesbian officers' situations as they relate to departmental policies and the statutes governing particular locales, because the reality of how frustrating a situation may be is related to many factors.

The debate about gays in the military is most likely to have an effect on how gays will be accepted on many police departments. The current political climate seems to suggest that it is not correct to ask about sexual orientation on hiring. However, once on board gay individuals should keep their sexual orientation secret. If this posture continues, counselors and hotlines should expect more gay and lesbian officers to seek counseling because of being compelled to suppress one's sexual orientation. In effect many gay individuals' worst fears are being realized because many believe that revealing their homosexuality may have a detrimental effect on their occupations.

Although this was written for the benefit of all gay and lesbian officers, one of the most important facts the reader must conceptualize is that gay and lesbian officers are not a homogenous group; they are individuals just as heterosexuals are individuals.

History has taught us from the struggles of other minority groups that the point in time where the fighting for rights occurs is possibly the most emotionally demanding. With gay and lesbian citizens being at such an unsettled stage in their struggle, they are very likely to be anxiety ridden and seeking counseling.

CONCLUSION

Minority police officers have special concerns that need to be addressed to maximize their potential. Police departments that are sensitive to minimizing discrimination are more likely to capitalize on the employment of a diverse work force.

All initiatives directed at improving race relations and addressing cultural diversity should take into account the notion that minority men and women are not comfortable conforming to the dominant culture.

Police administrators must realize that progressive change will probably be met with some opposition. Recall from the section on the police culture that police generally tend to be more conservative than the general populace. When the fact that every culture, including corporate culture, is generally resistant to change, it is conceivable that women, ethnic minorities, and homosexuals have been met with opposition. However, because discrimination on the basis of race, ethnicity, gender, or sexual orientation can be detrimental to the mental well-being of officers, resistance should not dictate attempts to make changes for the better.

APPENDIX A

One way to ensure a cross-representative sample in a study of issues affecting women in law enforcement was to administer a questionnaire during conferences designed specifically for this population. The National Organization of Black Women in Law Enforcement (NOBWLE), Inc. and the Interagency Committee on Women in Federal Law Enforcement (ICWIFLE) conferences were selected due to timing considerations and their proximity to the author's town of residence.

Approximately 100 participants attended the NOBWLE conference held in August 1992 in Philadelphia, PA. The author administered the questionnaire at the closing session of the conference and received about 40 completed surveys. Over 750 participants attended the ICWIFLE conference held in November 1992 in Washington, DC. The survey was made available to conference attendees during registration and in the exhibit hall. Efforts to collect completed surveys were made through announcements by the conference chairwomen, and at various drop-off points. Spirited urgings by the author resulted in submission of over 200 completed surveys. A few surveys from each conference were excluded from the sample due to respondents not appearing to be sworn law enforcement personnel. The final sample size of this study was 192. Although a specific breakdown of the conference participants is not available, both conferences were national in scope, resulting in attendees arriving from all parts of the United States.

Women In Law Enforcement Issues Questionnaire

1. Check the space which best describes your position rank:

11.5% / $n = 22$ a) Sworn police officer or agent/uniform.
64.4% / $n = 124$ b) Sworn police officer or agent/nonuniform.
 6.2% / $n = 12$ c) Sergeant, Corporal (or supervises under 10).

8.3% / $n = 16$ d) Lieutenant, Supervisory Agent (or supervises over 10).
2.1% / $n = 4$ e) Captain, ASAC (or commands a division).
1.0% / $n = 2$ f) Commander, Colonel, SAC or above (commands an office).
3.1% / $n = 6$ g) Other, please specify: _____
3.1% / $n = 6$ Did not answer

2. Check the space which best describes your ethnicity:

59.4% / $n = 114$ a) White American
31.2% / $n = 60$ b) African American
 1.6% / $n = 3$ c) South American descent (other than Mexican)
 2.1% / $n = 4$ d) Mexican descent
 0.0% / $n = 0$ e) African descent (non-American)
 0.5% / $n = 1$ f) Jamaican descent & other Caribbean
 1.0% / $n = 2$ g) Asian descent
 0.0% / $n = 0$ h) Middle Eastern descent
 0.5% / $n = 1$ i) Native American
 0.0% / $n = 0$ j) Central American
 2.1% / $n = 4$ k) Other _____ (please specify)
 1.6% / $n = 3$ Did not answer

3. How long have you been an officer in your department?

 3.6% / $n = 6$ a) Under 1 year
12.5% / $n = 24$ b) 1–2 years
18.2% / $n = 35$ c) 3–5 years
30.7% / $n = 59$ d) 6–9 years
17.7% / $n = 34$ e) 10–15 years
15.6% / $n = 30$ f) Over 15 years
 2.1% / $n = 4$ Did not answer

4. How many *total* years have you worked in law enforcement (including previous jobs)?

 1.6% / $n = 6$ a) Under 1 year
 4.7% / $n = 9$ b) 1–2 years
12.5% / $n = 24$ c) 3–5 years
29.7% / $n = 57$ d) 6–9 years
27.1% / $n = 52$ e) 10–15 years
23.4% / $n = 45$ f) Over 15 years
 1.0% / $n = 2$ Did not answer

5. Check the space which best describes the authority upon which your department has been granted to police:

8.9% / $n = 17$ a) Municipal
0.5% / $n = 1$ b) County
3.6% / $n = 7$ c) State
82.3% / $n = 158$ d) Federal
0.5% / $n = 1$ e) Private, please specify: _____
1.0% / $n = 0$ f) Other, please specify: _____
3.1% / $n = 6$ Did not answer

6. Check the space which best describes the size of your department or agency:

12.0% / $n = 23$ a) Less than 100 sworn officers
23.4% / $n = 45$ b) 101 to 1,000 sworn officers
36.5% / $n = 70$ c) 1,001 to 5,000 sworn officers
 9.9% / $n = 19$ d) 5,001 to 10,000 sworn officers
16.7% / $n = 32$ e) 10,001 and over sworn officers
 1.6% / $n = 3$ Did not answer

7. What percentage of the total officers in your department are female?

25.5% / $n = 49$ a) 5% or less
36.5% / $n = 70$ b) 5%–10%
26.0% / $n = 59$ c) 10%–20%
 8.3% / $n = 16$ d) Over 20%
 3.6% / $n = 7$ Did not answer

8. Check the space which best describes the educational requirements for your position:

14.6% / $n = 28$ a) High school diploma or equivalent
 5.2% / $n = 10$ b) Some college
 3.1% / $n = 6$ c) A 2-year college degree
75.0% / $n = 144$ d) A 4-year college degree
 1.0% / $n = 2$ e) Post-Bachelor's degree
 0.0% / $n = 0$ f) No educational requirement
 1.0% / $n = 2$ Did not answer

9. During your initial interview for your position, were there any females on the interview panel?

23.4% / $n = 45$ a) Yes
65.1% / $n = 125$ b) No
11.5% / $n = 22$ c) N/A (No interview) or No Answer

10. The following phrase best sums up my police academy experience:

54.2% / $n = 104$ a) I feel I was *definitely* treated fairly and equitably by staff and other students.

33.9% / $n = 65$ b) I feel I was *somewhat* treated fairly and equitably by staff and other students.

7.3% / $n = 14$ c) I feel I was *not* treated fairly and equitably by staff and other students.

2.6% / $n = 5$ d) No academy required for my position.

2.1% / $n = 4$ Did not answer

11. During your police academy experience did you feel your department provided you with an appropriate and adequate means of seeking counseling or advice if you choose to do so?

38.5% / $n = 74$ a) Yes

50.0% / $n = 96$ b) No

0.0% / $n = 0$ c) N/A

11.5% / $n = 22$ Did not answer

12. Gender bias is a subtle form of discrimination wherein female officers are treated differently (generally negatively) than their male counterparts. Do you believe that you have encountered gender bias during your tenure?

82.3% / $n = 158$ a) Yes

16.7% / $n = 32$ b) No

1.0% / $n = 2$ Did not answer

13. If you answered yes to Question 12, what was the type of bias? Check all answers that apply.

51.0% / $n = 98$ a) Being ignored

16.1% / $n = 31$ b) Hostile actions (please specify):

42.7% / $n = 82$ c) Indifferent actions

19.3% / $n = 37$ d) Work sabotaged

13.5% / $n = 26$ e) Left to handle dangerous situations alone

23.4% / $n = 45$ f) Made to "look bad" intentionally

14.6% / $n = 28$ g) Not "covering" for you when everyone else is being covered for

18.6% / $n = 36$ h) Reluctance of subordinates to follow your orders

30.2% / $n = 58$ i) Sighs or comments when *you* make suggestions

25.0% / $n = 48$ j) Other, please describe:

14. My immediate supervisor is:

91.1% / $n = 175$ a) Male

7.8% / $n = 15$ b) Female
1.0% / $n = 2$ Did not answer

15. The following phrase best describes my supervisor:

71.9% / $n = 138$ a) From my perspective as a female, he or she treats me
                      the same as the male officers.
6.8% / $n = 13$ b) From my perspective as a female, he or she treats me
                      more leniently than the male officers.
16.1% / $n = 31$ c) From my perspective as a female, he or she treats me
                      more harshly than the male officers.
5.2% / $n = 10$ Did not answer

16. Below you will examine four sexual harassment scenarios. For each scenario, please prioritize your responses by speculating what you believe would be your course of action if facing a similar predicament from most likely (1) to least likely (5) (Results presented are only reported for respondents' most likely answer):

a) Lately one of the male officers assigned to your team corners you every time you're alone and goes into graphic detail about what he would like to do to you sexually; you are not interested in him. You:

65.6% / $n = 126$ 1) Try to handle the situation completely alone.
7.8% / $n = 15$ 2) Seek advice from other officers.
12.5% / $n = 24$ 3) Seek advice from your supervisor.
2.1% / $n = 4$ 4) Seek counseling from a professional.
8.3% / $n = 16$ 5) File a sexual harassment complaint.
3.1% / $n = 7$ Did not answer

b) Officer X has just driven you back to the office after he made a "detour." During the unexpected stop, he parked the car in a desolate area and began to kiss and fondle you. Since you're not interested in Officer X and he has never tried anything like this before, you were completely caught off guard. On the way back, Officer X makes it clear that he intends to behave in a similar manner when he gets you alone again. You:

37.0% / $n = 71$ 1) Try to handle the situation completely alone.
7.8% / $n = 15$ 2) Seek advice from other officers.
30.2% / $n = 58$ 3) Seek advice from your supervisor.
1.0% / $n = 2$ 4) Seek counseling from a professional.
20.8% / $n = 40$ 5) File a sexual harassment complaint.
3.1% / $n = 6$ Did not answer

c) With the officers on your unit, almost anything goes. They talk freely and graphically about sex in your presence; and there are nude posters of women displayed in your work space. Your male supervisor seems to go along with them. One evening a celebration takes place and as everyone else starts to get intoxicated, you decide its time to leave. However, as you get closer to the door, you're stopped by a couple of officers and pulled back in. Suddenly almost all of the officers surround you and in a frenzy began to touch you all over. You know that if you're not able to escape, you will be raped. Finally, one of the officers (you have no idea who) comes to your rescue, pulls several of the officers away, and you're able to escape. Your supervisor was also present. Now it's the following week and the officers on your unit are behaving indifferently or hostile toward you. You suspect that they are afraid of what you will do next. What will you do?

10.4% / $n = 18$	1) Try to handle the situation completely alone.
3.6% / $n = 7$	2) Seek advice from other officers.
5.2% / $n = 10$	3) Seek advice from your supervisor.
31.2% / $n = 60$	4) Seek advise from your supervisor's superior.
10.4% / $n = 20$	5) Seek counseling from a professional.
34.9% / $n = 67$	6) File a sexual harassment complaint.
4.2% / $n = 8$	Did not answer

d) Old Officer X is at it again. Although you were able to avoid being alone with him when he was the same rank as you, now he is your supervisor. True to his word, almost every time you're alone, he attempts the kissing and fondling routine. You've tried to reason with him until you're blue in the face to no avail. Worse yet, he has started to criticize unfairly your performance and indicates that he will stop if you just "give in" to his advances. You:

9.4% / $n = 18$	1) Try to handle the situation completely alone.
3.6% / $n = 7$	2) Seek advice from other officers.
31.2% / $n = 60$	3) Seek advice from your supervisor's superior.
6.2% / $n = 12$	4) Seek counseling from a professional.
43.2% / $n = 83$	5) File a sexual harassment complaint.
2.1% / $n = 4$	6) Other
4.2% / $n = 8$	Did not answer

17. In the examples in Question 16 would you respond in the same manner if your supervisor was a female versus a male?

56.8% / $n = 109$	a) Yes
19.8% / $n = 38$	b) No
23.4% / $n = 45$	Did not answer

18. Do you believe you have personally encountered sexual harassment on the job?

63.0% / $n = 121$ a) Yes
32.8% / $n = 63$ b) No
 4.2% / $n = 8$ Did not answer

19. If you answered yes, which scenarios presented in Question 16 relate to your experience? Check as many spaces as apply:

50.5% / $n = 97$ A. (Verbal only)
17.2% / $n = 33$ B. (Lone officer, physical)
15.6% / $n = 30$ C1. (Group harassment, verbal and visual)
 2.1% / $n = 4$ C2. (Group harassment, physical)
26.6% / $n = 51$ D1. (Supervisor, verbal)
 8.9% / $n = 17$ D2. (Supervisor, physical)
 6.8% / $n = 13$ E. Other, please specify: _____
33.9% / $n = 65$ Did not answer

20. Is your department's sexual harassment policy (check all spaces that apply):

52.6% / $n = 101$ a) Adequately publicized?
43.2% / $n = 83$ b) In your opinion, fair?
26.0% / $n = 50$ c) Enforced?
14.6% / $n = 28$ d) Consistently applied?
37.5% / $n = 72$ e) Supported by management?
26.0% / $n = 50$ Did not answer

21. Women within my department are:

33.3% / $n = 64$ a) Just as likely as men to be promoted.
63.5% / $n = 122$ b) Less likely than men to be promoted.
 3.1% / $n = 6$ Did not answer

22. If you answered "less likely" in Question 21, what do you think is the reason? Check as many spaces as apply.

27.1% / $n = 52$ a) Women have less seniority than the men.
53.5% / $n = 103$ b) Women don't have sponsors/mentors as readily as men.
34.9% / $n = 67$ c) Women receive less career development.
41.1% / $n = 79$ d) Women don't get assignments which lead to promotion.
 4.7% / $n = 9$ e) Women aren't interested in being promoted.
 8.3% / $n = 16$ f) Women aren't taking tests/applying for promotions.
10.9% / $n = 21$ g) Lack of an affirmative action program.

8.3% / $n = 16$ h) Other, please specify: Most common answer cited in-
            volved utilization of the "good ole boy" network.
34.9% / $n = 67$ Did not answer

23. Does your department have a clear policy related to pregnancy and
performance of police duties?

26.6% / $n = 51$ a) Yes
64.6% / $n = 124$ b) No
 8.9% / $n = 17$ Did not answer

24. If you answered "yes" to Question 23, do you believe the policy is
adequate?

20.8% / $n = 40$ a) Yes
10.9% / $n = 21$ b) No; Please explain what the policy lacks: _____
68.2% / $n = 131$ Did not answer

25. Does your department have a clear policy related to maternity leave?

49.0% / $n = 94$ a) Yes
39.6% / $n = 76$ b) No
11.5% / $n = 22$ Did not answer

26. If you answered "yes" to Question 25, do you believe the policy is
adequate?

28.1% / $n = 54$ a) Yes
20.8% / $n = 40$ b) No; Please explain what the policy lacks: _____
51.0% / $n = 98$ Did not answer

27. If you answered "yes" to Question 23 (pregnancy) and Question 25
(maternity leave), are your departmental policies flexible enough to permit
you and your supervisor some discretion?

26.6% / $n = 51$ a) Yes
14.6% / $n = 28$ b) No; Please give examples:
58.9% / $n = 113$ Did not answer

28. Does your department offer any training designed to assist women working in a predominately male organization?

11.5% / $n = 22$ a) Yes; briefly describe:
85.9% / $n = 165$ b) No.
 2.6% / $n = 5$ Did not answer

29. I believe training such as that described in Question 28 is:

77.1% / $n = 148$ a) Necessary
15.1% / $n = 29$ b) Not necessary
 7.8% / $n = 15$ Did not answer

30. Are members of your department offered any sensitivity training to increase their effectiveness in understanding women and minorities?

42.7% / $n = 82$ a) Yes, it's geared to increase effectiveness with
                          3.6% / $n = 7$ Women
                          7.8% / $n = 15$ Other minorities
                          24.5% / $n = 47$ Both
48.4% / $n = 93$ b) No
 8.9% / $n = 17$ Did not answer

31. I believe training such as that described in Question 30 is:

84.4% / $n = 162$ a) Necessary
 9.4% / $n = 18$ b) Not necessary
 6.2% / $n = 12$ Did not answer

32. Has your department provided you with a confidential, appropriate, and adequate means of seeking counseling/advice regarding women's issues if you choose to do so?

33.9% / $n = 65$ a) Yes
58.9% / $n = 113$ b) No
 7.3% / $n = 14$ Did not answer

33. Although record numbers of women are entering the field of law enforcement, unfortunately scores of women are also leaving the profession. This irony has resulted in only small overall increases of women in policing. If you were to leave the field of law enforcement, what would be the *most* likely reasons? Please rank (1 [most] to 3 [least]) likely reasons (Top three answers included in results and not ranked):

19.3% / $n = 37$ a) Salary
38.0% / $n = 73$ b) Want to pursue another line of work
24.5% / $n = 47$ c) Start your own business
28.6% / $n = 55$ d) Work environment; specify:
23.4% / $n = 45$ e) Lack of promotional opportunities
12.5% / $n = 24$ f) Returning to school
 9.4% / $n = 18$ g) Job wasn't what you expected
14.6% / $n = 28$ h) Spouse

29.7% / $n = 57$ i) Children
 9.4% / $n = 18$ j) Sexual harassment
19.9% / $n = 25$ k) Other; Please specify: Stress and long hours that inter-
                     fered with family life were cited the most in this area.

34. Please identify the single most difficult thing you face as a female police officer/agent in your department:

_____

_____

35. Please identify any women's issues you believe should additionally be addressed in this questionnaire:

_____

_____

_____

36. If you are in a racial minority, please identify any special concerns you believe are unique to you:

_____

_____

_____

37. If you are a supervisory law enforcement officer, please identify any special concerns you believe are unique to you:

_____

_____

ACKNOWLEDGMENTS

The author is indebted to Special Agent Sandy Barfield, United States Customs Service for her granting permission as the president of NOWBLE to administer the questionnaire. Actually, I owe her more than can be adequately expressed, as this request was received on short notice and she really encouraged the participants to complete the questionnaires.

The author is also grateful for the permission granted and assistance of Special Agent Debra K. Mack, FBI and Special Agent Mary Ann Gordon, FBI, Co-Chairwomen of the 1992 ICWIFLE Conference.

REFERENCES

Bass, A. (1990, March 20). The bias below the surface. *Boston Globe*, 20, F5.

Bergsmann, I. R. (1991, December). ACA women in corrections committee examines female staff training needs. *Corrections Today*, pp. 106–108.

Berrill, K. (1986). *Police/gay community relations: Old problems, new hope.* Unpublished manuscript.

Blanchard, F. (1991, July 16). New way to battle bias: Fight acts, not feeling. *The New York Times*, p. C1.

Burke, M. (1992, January). Cop culture and homosexuality. *The Police Journal*, pp. 30–39.

Cesarz, G., & Madrid-Bustos, J. (1991, December). Taking a multicultural world view in today's corrections facilities. *Corrections Today*, pp. 68–71.

The challenge of diversity: Equal employment opportunity and managing differences in the 1990's. (1990). Rockville, MD: Bureau of National Affairs (BNA) Communications.

Charles, M. T. (1991). Resolving discrimination in the promotion of Fort Wayne police officers. *American Journal of Police, 10*, 67–87.

Cox, T. H., Lobel, S. A., & McLeod, P. L. (1991). Effects of ethnic group cultural differences on cooperative and competitive behavior on a group task. *Academy of Management Journal, 34*, 827–847.

Delattre, E. J. (1989). *Character and cops, Ethics in policing.* Lanham, MD: University Press of America.

Deutsch, C. H. (1991, September 9). Workers pair up to end disputes. *New York Times.*

Dunham, R., & Alpert, G. (1989). Principles of good policing: Avoiding violence between police and citizens. *Critical issues in policing: Contemporary readings* (p. 164). Prospect Heights, IL: Waveland Press.

Ebert, M. K. (1986). Issues in providing psychological services to law enforcement personnel. In *Psychological Services for Law Enforcement*. Washington, DC: U.S. Government Printing Office.

Edwards, A. (1991, January). The enlightened manager: How to treat all your employees fairly. *Working Woman*, pp. 45–55.

Hargrave, G. E. (1986). Differences in entry level test and criterion data for male and female peace officers. In *Psychological services for law enforcement.* Washington, DC: U.S. Government Printing Office.

Himelfrab, F. (1991, November). A training strategy for policing in a multicultural society. *The Police Chief*, pp. 53–55.

Hinkle, D. P. (1991, September). The police & the Hispanic community: Creating mutual understanding. *Law Enforcement Technology*, pp. 52–55.

Hosansky, T. (1991, May). Corporate referee. *Successful Meetings*, pp. 54–61.

Intercultural communication: Tips for the investigator. (1987). Washington, DC: U.S. Government Printing Office.

Keen, L., & Chibbaro, L. (1992). Chief Isaac Fulwood: "Give us a chance to do a better job." *The Washington Blade, 23*, 1–17.

Lane, C. (1991, September 30). A victim of preference: The bitter ironies of affirmative action. *Newsweek*, p. 56.

Linden, J. (1988). Police peer counseling—An expanded perspective. In *Police psychology: Operational assistance*. Washington, DC: U.S. Government Printing Office.

Lorch, D. (1992, July 13). Openly gay in blue: Officers tread warily. *New York Times*, p. B9.

Martin, S. E. (1989). Women on the move?: A report on the status of women in policing. *Women & Criminal Justice, 1*, 21–39.

Milano, C. (1989, August). Re-evaluating recruitment to better target top minority talent. *Management Review*, pp. 29–32.

Ragins, B. R. (1991). Easier said than done: Gender differences in perceived barriers to gaining a mentor. *Academy of Management Journal, 34*, 939–951.

Rainie, H. (1991, July 22). Black and white in America. *U.S. News & World Report*, pp. 18–21.

Remesch, K. (1990, December). Several cities begin recruiting gay cops. *Police*, pp. 46–75.

Sanchez, C. (1990, November 11). FBI story. *The Washington Post Magazine*, p. 21.

Smith, P. B., & Lubin, B. (1980, March 5). Emotional arousal during sensitivity training as a function of length of the experience. *Group and Organization Studies*, pp. 97–104.

Smith, V. E. (1988, March 7). Black and white in America. *Newsweek*, pp. 26–29.

Southgate, M. (1992, March). Women of color: On the front lines of a changing workplace. *Glamour*, p. 224.

Spann, J. (1990). Dealing effectively with sexual harassment: Some practical lessons from one city's experience. *Public Personnel Management, 19*, 53–69.

Stansbury, J. (1993). *How women law enforcement officers handle sexual harassment*. Unpublished manuscript.

Sue, D. W. (1991, Winter). Multiculturalism. *American Counselor*, pp. 6–14.

Sullivan, P. S. (1989). Minority officers. In R. Dunham & G. Alpert (Eds.), *Critical issues in policing: Contemporary readings* (pp. 331–345). Prospect Heights, IL: Waveland Press.

Thomas, R. R., Jr. (1990, March–April). From affirmative action to affirming diversity. *Harvard Business Review*, pp. 107–117.

Thornberry, T. P. (1990). Cultural literacy in criminology. *Journal of Criminal Justice Education, 1*, 33–49.

Violanti, J. M. (1988). Operationalizing police stress management: A model. In *Police psychology: Operational assistance*. Washington, DC: U.S. Government Printing Office.

Warner, R. L., & Steel, B. S. (1989). Affirmative action in times of fiscal stress and changing value priorities: The case of women in policing. *Public Personnel Management, 18*, 291–309.

Watson, G. (1986). Thoughts on preventive counseling for police officers. *Psychological services for law enforcement*. Washington, DC: U.S. Government Printing Office.

PART FOUR

THE CORE TECHNOLOGY OF POLICE PSYCHOLOGY: TRAINING

CHAPTER TWELVE

The Role of the
Police Psychologist in Training

Elizabeth K. White
Audrey L. Honig
Los Angeles Sheriff's Department,
Psychological Services Unit

In order to understand the diversity possible within the field of police psychology training, it is necessary to first describe the evolution and diversity of training as a concept. *Webster's New World Dictionary* (Neufeldt & Guralnik, 1988) describes training as "to instruct so as to make proficient." The original concept of training historically implied a trainer or teacher who imparted new knowledge to trainees or students. This concept of training, however, was inadequate and over time was enlarged to include concepts such as training in graduated steps where each piece of learning became a building block for future learning. Soon, it was discovered that a single exposure to training did not guarantee learning, which gave birth to ongoing training, refresher courses, and so on. It was recognized that some types of skills and knowledge could not be acquired through a classroom format, which gave rise to simulators, role-play training, on-the-job training, experiential training, and mastery training. The concept of training also needed to expand to include both preventative training, which developed skills to avoid a difficulty, and reactive, situation, or problem-specific training, which responded to an existing problem and attempted to correct or repair the damage. Finally, it was recognized that training individuals reached only one layer of the training pool, whereas training managers or supervisors enabled the trainers to reach not only the target individuals but resulted in a "trickle down" effect, influencing a larger percentage of the training population. The further up the organizational chain the training targets, the more widespread and effective the training can be. At these upper levels, however,

257

the original concept of the classroom and teacher becomes even more restrictive and ineffective. When the target of change is an organization, the face of training changes even more dramatically. The teacher–student relationship becomes instead that of consultant and consultee. The means of influence becomes participation in such activities as planning committees, management consultations, recommendations, impact studies, and so on. Although the original goal of training—imparting knowledge and assisting others to become proficient—remains the same, the ways and means of training now must evolve to become extremely flexible in order to meet the changing needs of both the organizations and the individuals requiring that training.

When examining the role of police psychologists in training, it is important to take into consideration the evolution and expansion of training already described. Targets for training must include not only individual peace officers but middle and upper management. Often, for training to be effective, it is these upper levels of management that must first be brought on board. The means of training must be responsive to the population as well as to the material being presented. Training must be preventive, recurrent, and reactive. Within the field of law enforcement, there are several professional organizations at the state level such as the California Peace Officer's Association, the California State Training Institute, and Peace Officer's Standards and Training, as well as international organizations such as the International Association of Chiefs of Police that attempt to regulate or define training for law enforcement personnel. Training has become an elaborate and diversified field. This diversity is a mixed blessing for the police psychologist. Although it offers unlimited possibilities in terms of how to train, who to train, and what to train, it also creates a great deal of complexity. Designing a training program that addresses the multilevel needs of an organization such as law enforcement can be extremely challenging. This challenge is further complicated by the history that exists between professionals in the fields of law enforcement and psychology.

Traditionally, members within the two fields have been wary, if not actively antagonistic, toward each other. In the past, law enforcement came into contact with the field of mental health through one of four ways: (a) watching "do good" psychologists testify on behalf of criminals, (b) dealing with psychologist "failures" who have been released by a mental health practitioner after a peace officer brought them in for involuntary hospitalization (because they were a threat to themselves, to others or because they were gravely disabled), (c) watching as psychologists appear to protect and encourage "malingering" peace officers who are claiming psychological trauma but who are perceived as just weak or abusing the system, and (d) seeing psychologists as the enemy who has the power to keep an officer or potential officer off the force (pre-employment screenings or fitness for duty evaluations). Consequently, it is not surprising that many peace officers have had little respect or liking for psychologists in the past. Psychologists' view of law enforcement personnel, traditionally, tended to be just as biased. Many psychologists saw the average peace officer as unfeeling (and therefore unhealthy), rigid, and authoritarian, with an inappropriate sense of humor.

Over the last 10 years, both psychologists and law enforcement personnel have had opportunities to alter stereotypical views. But one of the aftereffects of the mutual distrust that has existed in the past has been lack of familiarity and knowledge about the opposite field. Most psychologists do not have a clear conception of what a peace officer does or what it is like to be a peace officer. On the other hand, many peace officers (from line staff through management) do not have a clear conception of what psychologists do. Some do have a basic understanding of the process and rules of counseling (e.g., confidentiality), but very few have any idea of the services a police psychologist can offer law enforcement personnel above and beyond psychological counseling.

Consequently, the first task for a police psychologist who wishes to become a proficient trainer is to become a learner. It is unlikely that the field of law enforcement will ever fully embrace the field of psychology. However, law enforcement personnel can be convinced to accept a specific psychologist who has taken the time to indoctrinate himself or herself into the culture of law enforcement. In essence, a police psychologist separates himself or herself from the field of psychology, or more specifically the mental health field, and identifies himself or herself as an individual who has an understanding of the culture and needs of a law enforcement organization. The police psychologist absorbs as much as possible of the law enforcement culture through reading, research, observational learning, and in vivo exposure (ride-alongs, visiting law enforcement facilities, contact with law enforcement personnel). This learning is targeted at understanding the world of law enforcement rather than gathering ammunition to change it. It is the responsibility of the police psychologist to gain a thorough understanding of the law enforcement culture in order to assess where a psychologist's skills and resources might be of greatest assistance.

The onus of responsibility falls on the police psychologist to learn about the world of law enforcement; to identify when, where, and what kind of training is called for based on the input obtained; and to present this information to management so that they can clearly see the value of the training. A logical presentation with a rationale based on the psychologist's own professional or cultural bias will not necessarily be sufficient. The organization will need to be sold on the situation's relative cost and benefits. Although it is very rare for an organization to successfully diagnose a problem and recognize what remediation is necessary, most law enforcement agencies can recognize symptoms of distress and are very receptive to a concrete, realistic proposal that includes problem definition and possible solutions. Law enforcement managers are very much pragmatists. Their primary concern must be liability potential and cost savings. All potential trainings must be examined from that perspective.

In this chapter, an attempt is made to identify basic issues specific to offering trainings to law enforcement agencies and to describe three major training categories. It is not meant to be an exhaustive list of all possible trainings in the area of police psychology. What is possible is truly only limited by the applications that can be envisioned by the police psychologist combined with his or her ability to market or sell these ideas to others.

Trainings can be divided into three general categories: (a) trainings that enhance the individual employee as a person (i.e., wellness trainings), (b) trainings that address the individual employee as a professional (i.e., informational or skill trainings), and (c) trainings that address the individual within the structure of the organization (i.e., organizational trainings). Each of these training categories has specific pitfalls and issues to be taken into consideration during program development.

WELLNESS TRAININGS

Definition and Rationale

Wellness training includes any training that focuses on the peace officer as a person. The goal of this kind of training is assisting the peace officer toward improving his or her lifestyle through learning new, health-enhancing behaviors and ideas. Wellness training is based on the concept that how an individual manages his or her life, and the accompanying inherent stressors, will have a significant impact on job performance.

Large corporations have already recognized the connection between lifestyle, coping, and job performance. Evidence of this connection can be seen in statistics documenting decreased performance, increased sick leave, job burnout, and so on. Much of the current literature focuses on the organizational costs of specific problems such as drug and alcohol addiction (Hollingsworth, 1989; Westbrook, 1987). The areas targeted by wellness trainings, however, have been expanded to include smoking cessation, dietary habits, exercise habits, and more (Templin, 1990).

Included in this area of wellness training has also been a large category of interventions that go under the general label of stress management. The sources of stress are varied and include psychological, interpersonal, and organizational stressors. Whatever the origin, how an employee deals with stressors in his or her life will impact job performance, both directly and indirectly (illness, depression, etc.). It is extremely difficult, however, to identify specific causal relationships when it comes to wellness issues. The most accurate conception of the problem would have to include some acknowledgment of reciprocal influences involving job, home, and person factors. Stress management and wellness programs, however, are an essential component of an overall effort to curtail excessive force, promote employee health, and reduce workers' compensation and disability retirement claims (Kolts, 1992).

Special Considerations in Conducting Wellness Trainings

Departmental Support. There are several special issues that must be taken into consideration when developing any kind of training for law enforcement personnel. As discussed earlier, the first consideration in planning wellness trainings is being able to justify such trainings to the management of the agency involved. Trainings that are voluntary and involve personnel during off-duty time are obviously the easiest to justify. In essence, the department need only sanction the use of the psychologist's time, provide compensation or allow for the charging of fees, give permission for promotion of the training through department means (i.e., teletype, inhouse newspaper or magazine, flyers, etc.), and possibly provide the physical setting and materials needed for the training. A presentation that provides a rationale for the training, documents costs and benefits of offering the training, and delineates practical applications will be most likely to secure departmental approval and support. When the training becomes on duty or required, a separate set of considerations surfaces. Because wellness trainings are usually voluntary, special considerations regarding required trainings are dealt with in the next section.

Participant Support. Once departmental support is obtained, the next crucial step is obtaining interest, support, and cooperation from the potential participants. Whether the training is voluntary or departmentally regulated, an attempt must be made to justify the training to the participating peace officers.

One of the primary considerations in planning trainings for law enforcement personnel is how the training is marketed or packaged. Law enforcement personnel's view of psychologists is still influenced by earlier perceptions of psychologists as "touchy-feely" or "do gooders" who sometimes are potentially dangerous to a law enforcement officer's career because of the role they may play in pre-employment screenings and fitness for duty evaluations. Consequently, peace officers are often hesitant to voluntarily participate in any form of psychological training. Marketing must be high profile, utilizing various media such as videotapes played at briefings, professional-looking flyers, and teletype announcements. The marketing must adequately explain the purpose, techniques, and utility of the training. The issue of packaging becomes paramount during the marketing stage. It is obvious that a training entitled "Coping with the emotional aftermath of traumatic incidents" would be received quite differently than one entitled "Surviving an officer-involved shooting," or even "Wellness strategies to enhance performance." This packaging must begin in the very first flyer and go beyond the titling and advertising of the training. The credibility of the trainer is as important as the presentation. A trainer can begin to establish credibility by carrying this packaging into his or her presentation style and materials and by keeping it in mind as he or she selects the skills and strategies to be taught.

Law enforcement personnel are generally less comfortable with solutions that may appear contrary to the stereotypical picture of a good officer (strong, controlled, macho, etc.). Consequently, the recommended techniques and skills must be acceptable methods for obtaining the identified goal. Law enforcement personnel are legendary for their suppression of affect, their emphasis on mental and physical toughness, and their tendency to minimize or deny vulnerability (Hogan, 1971; Reiser, 1974). Trainings are more effective with law enforcement personnel if they take into consideration the existing cognitive set of the average peace officer.

For example, many peace officers operate under an illusion of invulnerability, an "it will never happen to me" orientation. Or there is the belief that if something does happen, there will be little or no emotional or mental impact. If the training topic is surviving a critical incident, this orientation will have to be taken into consideration in planning the training. An illusion of invulnerability may interfere with law enforcement personnel even seeing the relevancy of a training on emotional survival. One solution to this type of problem is to enlist the aid of peace officers who have been involved in critical incidents and who are willing to speak openly about their experience. Another tactic would be using analogies that parallel cognitive rehearsal and coping strategy planning with accepted law enforcement activities such as tactical planning with a partner, physical training, or firearm qualifying. A third method would be to emphasize learning about critical incident stress in order to be supportive of a fellow officer. The world of law enforcement is a close-knit family. A peace officer may not be able to recognize a need for critical incident coping skills for himself or herself, but every officer has had a friend or colleague who has been negatively impacted by involvement in a shooting or other critical incident. In summary, when working with law enforcement personnel, a psychologist must be flexible and tailor the training to both the needs and the mind-set of the population being served.

A related consideration in obtaining participant buy-in is the issue of the credibility of the training. Most law enforcement personnel tend to be very pragmatic and concrete. Alongside the issue of acceptability of the training material will be convincing the officers that these new methods or techniques will actually be effective in resolving the identified problem. They will look for the practical application of the material being presented.

The fourth major consideration in planning law enforcement trainings is that of presenter credibility. In order to have credibility in the law enforcement community, a psychologist must have met all the normal requirements in reference to expertise in the topic being presented. In addition, however, the psychologist must have a working knowledge of the world of law enforcement, including command structure, organizational jargon, department policy and procedures, and so on (Ebert, 1986; Stratton, 1985). It is mandatory that the psychologist has some idea of what it is like to be a peace officer. If the psychologist cannot speak the language or provide examples and suggestions that demonstrate an understanding of the world of law enforcement, he or she will be dismissed as an outsider, no matter how knowledgeable the psychologist is on the topic being taught.

Another important consideration relates to how the training is conducted. Law enforcement personnel, like everyone else, will usually revert to using coping skills and strategies that are most familiar. In addition, like most people, law enforcement personnel show similar learning curves in response to various teaching techniques. They will retain about 20% of what they hear, 50% of what they see and hear, and about 90% of what they say and do (Fisher, 1989). It is essential that trainings emphasize experiential learning, including techniques such as mental rehearsal, role playing, feedback, and so on (Garrison, 1990; Rodriguez & Franklin, 1986; Zenike & Zenike, 1988).

Experiential learning is a powerful tool. One demonstration performed during an academy stress management lecture involved describing to the class an experiment in physiological reactions to stressful events. A book was dropped on the floor, resulting in a loud noise. The class was asked to describe their reaction to this predicted event. Despite the preparation, the majority of the class experienced the normal parasympathetic response to a loud noise. The demonstration was repeated later in the class, but the book was caught before it hit the ground. When the class was asked to describe their reaction to this nonevent, many noted that they had reacted despite the fact that nothing had actually occurred. These types of experiential demonstrations greatly assist law enforcement personnel in understanding concepts such as stress and help to motivate them to attend to and see the relevancy of stress management trainings.

A significant problem to take into consideration in providing wellness trainings to law enforcement personnel involves general logistics problems. Scheduling is complicated by shift work, unusual days off, rotating days off, and absence due to court appearances. Trainings, especially voluntary ones, have to be scheduled with unusual flexibility. A second issue involves selecting a centrally located facility that is both comfortable and private.

A final key issue is confidentiality. Participative or interactive trainings involve a certain amount of self-disclosure and risk taking. Although solidarity within the field of law enforcement is well known, it does not usually extend to feeling comfortable showing vulnerability in front of peers. Unfortunately, gossip within the field of law enforcement is rampant. Concern regarding confidentiality and loss of face in front of colleagues has made group therapy a somewhat unpopular form of intervention for law enforcement personnel.

An additional issue regarding confidentiality is, of course, confidentiality with the respective agency. Law enforcement personnel need the reassurance that the psychologist will not use information obtained in the training against a participant, nor will this information be passed along to command staff. A summary of the issues related to obtaining support for wellness trainings from both line staff and management is presented in Table 12.1.

Proposed Wellness Training Topics

In examining the possible trainings applicable for the law enforcement community, many of the trainings can be presented much as they would be to any other population with little or no modifications. Some of the trainings

TABLE 12.1
Summary of Key Points in Obtaining Support and Cooperation
for Wellness Trainings

Line Staff	Middle and Upper Management
1. High visibility promotion of training necessary to overcome line staff mistrust and lack of knowledge of psychological staff and expertise.	Voluntary wellness trainings are usually done on personnel's own time. Management need only approve advertisement, psychologist's time, and so on.
2. Packaging de-emphasizes psychological and "feeling" language and highlights practical applications.	
3. Method of training is acceptable to a nonpsychologically minded population.	
4. Trainer has credibility with law enforcement population.	
5. Training has credibility that it will solve the identified problem.	
6. Training uses participatory or experiential learning.	
7. Confidentiality of participants is guaranteed.	
8. Scheduling of training is flexible and takes into consideration shift work, unusual days off, and the need for a central location.	

have to be tailored in order to be of maximum assistance to law enforcement personnel. Lastly, several trainings are pertinent only to law enforcement personnel or emergency services personnel. The following is a list of potential wellness training topics plus a summary of any special issues related to presenting that topic to law enforcement personnel:

1. Smoking cessation.

2. Coping with bereavement.

3. Eldercare: assistance with understanding the financial, medical, legal and emotional issues involved in caring for an elderly individual (parent, grandparent, etc.).

4. Assertiveness training.

5. Weight management and eating disorders.

6. Parenting skills. Law enforcement personnel often have difficulty with parenting in three areas. Law enforcement parents tend to be overprotective of children because they know what is out there and are afraid on behalf of their children. They also often have difficulties because they expect their children to be in their chain of command and to obey without question any rule or regulation. Finally, there is a tendency for law enforcement personnel to become adept at shutting down their affect as an adaptation to police work. This can cause a general distancing and alienation from loved ones that is especially difficult on children.

7. Alcohol and drug abuse. Law enforcement personnel often must deal with the additional issue of tremendous peer pressure. Drinking with fellow officers after a shift, often known as "choir practice," has become a law enforcement tradition. Choir practice is a method for socializing and cementing solidarity among officers and is used as a general stress management technique.

8. Spousal orientation. Literature on law enforcement relationships suggests that law enforcement personnel have great difficulties with marital discord (Blackmore, 1978; Kroes, Margolis, & Hurrell, 1974; Singleton & Teahan, 1978). Consequently, many agencies currently offer spousal training or orientation that includes ride-alongs, tours of jail and station facilities, instruction in firearm safety, question and answer sessions with established law enforcement couples, presentations on typical stressors in law enforcement relationships, and discussions regarding the counseling resources available to law enforcement couples and spouses.

9. Retirement. Many law enforcement personnel experience some difficulty adjusting to life without the fast pace, adrenaline rush, and high drama of being a peace officer. An additional problem arises out of a common defense mechanism employed by law enforcement personnel, that of denial. The officer may never have realistically pictured himself or herself as getting old or as retiring.

10. Surviving critical incidents. The long-term emotional, cognitive, and behavioral consequences of having been involved in a critical incident have been well documented (Lipson, 1986; Stratton, Parker, & Snibbe, 1984). An estimated 60% to 70% of law enforcement personnel leave the force within 5 years after being involved in a lethal critical incident (Horn & Solomon, 1989; Simpson, Jensen, & Owen, 1988). Approximately 50% divorce within 2 years (Simpson, Jensen, & Owen, 1988) or experience marital discord (Sheehan, 1990). Wellness trainings that focus on education regarding normal critical incident response patterns, agency policy and procedures after a critical incident, and proper mind-set, and that encourage personal involvement and strategy planning can significantly impact recovery after a critical incident (Garrison, 1990; Hoff, 1978; Solomon, 1990). A wellness training on surviving critical incidents is a preventive, educational measure and should not be confused with critical incident defusings or debriefings, which are conducted after an incident has occurred and whose goal it is to minimize the impact of the incident.

11. Stress management. Law enforcement has been described as one of the most stressful occupations around (Selye, 1976). A review of the literature on police stress reveals a high incidence of health consequences (Fell, Richard, & Wallace, 1980; Hurrell, 1977; Lester, 1981; Terry, 1981), alcoholism (Blackmore, 1978; Kroes, 1976), and suicide (Kroes, 1976; Terry, 1981). Police stress also has been connected to subsequent job performance problems (Moore & Donohue, 1978; Singleton & Teahan, 1978). Obviously, some wellness training targeting stress management is indicated. However, in designing stress management training for law enforcement personnel, it is important to identify and address the factors law enforcement personnel find most stressful. Although peace officers do identify the rather obvious stress factors involved in police work (e.g., taking a life in the line of duty, duty-related violent injury to self or partner, injury to a small child, etc.) as problematic (Sewell, 1981), these incidents are few and far between. Peace officers identify as most stressful on a day-to-day basis factors such as court rulings and procedures, administrative policies and decision making, and inadequate or faulty equipment (Sewell, 1981).

INFORMATIONAL AND SKILL TRAININGS

Definition and Rationale

Informational and skill trainings are those that focus on the peace officer as a professional and assist the peace officer to better perform his or her job requirements. Many of these trainings are mandated by the respective department and reflect recommendations and requirements set forth by the various different agencies that govern law enforcement trainings. Many of the considerations discussed in the section on wellness trainings also apply to informational and skill trainings and consequently are not repeated here unless additional information or elaboration is necessary.

As peace officers perform their duty, they are required to demonstrate a variety of different skills. An officer must have above-average communication skills, must be versed in issues of cultural awareness and sensitivity and must be able to de-escalate and appropriately manage potentially explosive conflict situations. A peace officer must have at least a basic understanding of mental illness, crisis management, and victimology. Some officers go on to develop special expertise in hostage negotiations, peer counseling, and so on.

All of these areas represent issues of human behavior and thus fall under the auspices of the field of psychology. Some represent subspecialties within the field (i.e., cross-cultural psychology, trauma psychology, etc.). At the beginning of the chapter, an emphasis was placed on the psychologist identifying what the needs of law enforcement personnel are and then providing the necessary training to meet those needs. A psychologist is identified as an expert in human behavior. It may be, however, that the psychologist will have to undergo some additional training or supervision in order to properly provide for all of the needs of his or her contract agency or employer. It was suggested that potential trainings were only limited by the creativity of the psychologist and his or her ability to justify the training to management. That statement may need to be modified to "training possibilities are only limited by the imagination, marketing skills, and expertise of the psychologist involved."

Special Considerations in Conducting Informational and Skill Trainings

Identification of Topics. One potentially problematic issue in dealing with informational and skill trainings has to do with identification of appropriate topics. Several topic areas are self-evident. Law enforcement work necessitates that a peace officer come into contact with persons of all races, religions, and sexual preference. Other obvious topics include training in handling the mentally ill and a training that addresses handling individuals who are victims or who are in extreme crisis.

A number of additional trainings are suggested by current events or problems. After the 1992 incident involving motorist Rodney King, many southern California law enforcement agencies re-examined their policies and procedures regarding the use of force. Research was generated regarding what factors influence use of force and trainings were initiated to assist law enforcement personnel in their decision-making process regarding use of force versus possible alternatives to force.

More often, however, the type of training needed may be unclear because the problem has not been accurately identified, or the problem has been correctly identified but it is not a true skill deficit issue. As a hypothetical situation, management requests a training on communication skills for a particular station that has shown a high rate of citizen complaints. After speaking with several sergeants and officers at the unit, it becomes apparent that the problem relates more to a set of memos issued over the last few months by a new operations lieutenant dictating several unpopular procedural changes. The line staff is frustrated and upset and feel they have no say in what happens to them. They then go out into the field irritated and with slightly lower frustration tolerance than normal. The appropriate training in response to this problem may be a team building between management staff and line staff or even just a consultation with the lieutenant.

Part of the police psychologist's training function may be to identify what kind of assistance is needed and then respond to that need. The need may be one identified by an outside force such as one of the state regulatory agencies, management, or the psychologist. The psychologist may need to do some research, informal data gathering, or even a full-fledged needs assessment in order to correctly identify what training, if any, is called for.

Management and Line Staff Support. Once again, the psychologist must deal with the issue of support. For mandatory trainings, cooperation and support must be sought from both upper management (those that order the training) and middle management (those that are seen as role models or who have the ability to "make or break" a training). For those trainings that are required by some outside regulatory agency, the presentation to upper management need only document the requirements and present course syllabus that demonstrates point-by-point coverage of required material to be sufficient.

For internally generated trainings, however, a more comprehensive presentation will be required. The outlay on the part of the department for required trainings will be considerably larger than for voluntary trainings. Estimated costs must include salary expenditures for the personnel involved, coverage for duty positions, and so on. Consequently, management will scrutinize the rationale for such trainings more thoroughly.

For internally generated trainings, upper management will be most interested in how this training translates into behaviors that are important to management. For example, peace officers who have better communication skills will be more comfortable and confident in the field, less likely to generate complaints, and less likely to be involved in an altercation that may result in the injury or death of a citizen or a peace officer. The presentation to management should emphasize issues of liability and cost savings.

Gaining the support of middle management is also crucial. A highly respected sergeant can significantly undermine a training with a well-placed sarcastic comment. Although a captain may approve a training, it is often a scheduling sergeant who actually makes the necessary arrangements of who, when, where, and so on. In many cases, line officers look up to and revere sergeants and seniors (line staff with considerable time in the field) and will follow the lead of these individuals when it comes to anything new.

The investment of middle management in trainings will be related more to their role as a supervisor. Middle managers will want to know how this training will make their life as a supervisor easier. Middle managers think in terms of problem employees, employee performance, and disciplinary action. Middle managers will support a training if they can see that it will result in personnel who experience fewer problems and consequently perform better and are easier to manage. Middle managers must also believe that the training will actually result in line personnel obtaining the identified course objectives.

The issues regarding gaining support from line staff will be the same as those identified in wellness training (e.g., credibility of teaching staff, practical application of materials presented, etc.). There are two additional points, however, that are relevant when the training is mandatory. The first of these is owning the problem. When a peace officer attends a voluntary training, the officer has already self-selected himself or herself as needing assistance. For a mandatory training, however, the participant may not even label the target of the training as a problem. Consequently, the first goal of the training will be to assist the participants in identifying the problem and owning it as a problem for them personally. Only then can the trainer move on to establishing the training as a viable and practical method of dealing with the problem. Often it is helpful to start a training by describing the problem being addressed and soliciting actual field examples that demonstrate the problem in action. After the training, the instructor may decide to readdress those original problems and have the class attempt to identify how the situation would be handled given the new information and skills.

A second potential area of difficulty may involve the fact that the training is mandatory. The issue of forced attendance can be a mixed blessing. Mandatory trainings often evoke grumbling and passive aggressive behavior. They can exacerbate whatever conflicts are currently ongoing between line staff and management. On the other hand, a mandatory training gives law enforcement personnel permission to receive assistance that they would be unable to request on their own for fear of being stigmatized. For example, most peace officers complain when required to attend a mandatory debriefing after a shooting incident. Yet the vast majority of officers participate willingly and report having benefited from attending a debriefing. A summary of the issues related to obtaining support for informational and skill trainings from both line staff and management is presented in Table 12.2.

TABLE 12.2

Summary of Key Points in Obtaining Support and Cooperation for
Informational and Skill Trainings

Line Staff	Upper Management	Middle Management
In addition to those mentioned under wellness trainings, add the following key points:	1. Identify cost of proposed training in terms of materials, psychologist's time, participants' time, and so on.	1. High visibility promotion of training to middle management with explanations of course purpose and goals.
1. Assist line staff in identifying the problem as a problem for them personally in order to establish personal investment.	2. Identify benefits of proposed training in terms of fiscal and organizational relevance (i.e., decrease in absenteeism, citizen complaints, stress worker compensation claims, etc.).	2. Packaging de-emphasizes psychological and "feeling" language and highlights practical applications. Crucial because middle management staff are likely to be older, more seasoned employees, suspicious of psychological assistance.
2. If the training is mandatory, address the ambivalence or resistance regarding mandatory trainings.	3. Identify potential costs of not conducting training in terms of fiscal and organizational relevance (i.e., liability issues, increased sick time, etc.).	3. Assist middle management in identifying the problem as a problem for them personally. Identify how training will make middle management's job easier (fewer problem employees, less absenteeism, etc.).
		4. Methods of training acceptable to a nonpsychologically minded population.
		5. Training has credibility to resolve the identified problem.
		6. Trainer has credibility with middle management. It is particularly helpful if middle management has had previous experience with a psychologist in the role of consultant (i.e., of direct benefit to middle management).
		7. If the training is mandatory, address ambivalence regarding mandatory trainings.

Training Retention and Follow Through. An additional area of concern is that of training retention and follow through. It is important that the psychologist build into the training the opportunity for program evaluation and ongoing supervision and feedback. The police psychologist cannot afford to simply initiate the training and hope that the new skills and techniques taught will adequately address the targeted area. Training must be an ongoing intervention. It is essential that the psychologist monitor the progress of the trainees, obtain feedback, make necessary adjustments, and provide consultation. Each training is a foot in the door with law enforcement personnel and consequently must be a success experience for the law enforcement personnel involved. As an added benefit, close monitoring and thorough follow through yields additional information about the law enforcement culture, the particular organization, and the morale of the employees, as well as identifying other potential problem areas for subsequent interventions and trainings.

Proposed Informational and Skill Training Topics

1. Handling the mentally ill. This training is designed to assist law enforcement personnel in understanding the various types of mental and emotional problems they are likely to be exposed to. This will enable peace officers to better predict the behavior of mentally ill individuals and to develop strategies to safely manage them.

2. Crisis management. This training assists law enforcement personnel in understanding how individuals feel, think, and behave when in crisis. Law enforcement personnel develop methods for dealing with individuals in crisis that take into consideration officer safety, the need to obtain necessary report information, referral resources, and so on. This enables the peace officer to be more sensitive to individuals in crisis when performing necessary police functions.

3. Cross-cultural training. This training provides personnel with a basic understanding of the mores and customs of various different cultural groups with which they will interact. This added information assists the peace officer in choosing strategies that will respect an individual's culture and enhance the probability of a cooperative and satisfactory citizen contact.

4. Cross-cultural awareness. This training encourages law enforcement personnel to identify their own cultural beliefs, recognize any bias that may be present, and learn strategies to prevent these biases from interfering with job performance, a goal consistent with department policy and philosophy. The training is designed to be participatory and experiential.

5. Peer counseling basic training. This training assists personnel in developing basic crisis management techniques including active listening, sui-

cide assessment, identification of appropriate referrals, and so on as part of a peer support program.

6. Communication training (e.g., tactical communications, verbal judo, etc.). Most law enforcement agencies have some training that addresses how personnel communicate with citizens and suspects. A major goal of these types of trainings is to recognize law enforcement personnel's contribution in escalating or de-escalating interactions with the public and to develop verbal skills that will maximize the likelihood of obtaining voluntary compliance while enabling the peace officer to remain calm and disengaged.

7. Psychological indicators of behavior. This training targets background investigators and interviewers and assists them with reading nonverbal behavior, developing listening skills, and understanding dynamics of behavior as a function of the person and the environment.

8. Hostage negotiations. This training assists law enforcement personnel in understanding mental illness and the dynamics of hostage situations.

9. Domestic violence. This training assists law enforcement personnel in developing an understanding of domestic violence dynamics and a working knowledge of possible referrals and resources. Because law enforcement personnel often have a strict, problem-solving approach to situations, this training also addresses the frustration personnel may feel when they are unable to fix the problem or when the principles involved are unable to accept the assistance.

10. Gay community. This training assists law enforcement personnel in understanding the gay community, recognizing any bias they may have regarding homosexuality and developing strategies to prevent these biases from interfering with job performance.

11. Sexual assault. This training assists law enforcement personnel in understanding the dynamics and impact of sexual assault. This will enable the peace officer to handle the victims of sexual assault with greater sensitivity and will facilitate the initial contact and information-gathering procedures.

12. Use of force. This training assists law enforcement personnel in developing a continuum for the use of force that includes nonphysical alternatives for gaining compliance. Provides information regarding the psychological situational factors affecting the use of force and identifies possible influences, both internal and external, that impact use of force (expectations, fear, anger management, etc.).

13. Critical incident performance. Although critical incident survival is listed under the category of wellness trainings, training can also target performance during a critical incident. Stress inoculation training, developing a survival mind-set, mental rehearsal, role play, and so on, can actually improve performance during a critical incident.

ORGANIZATIONAL TRAININGS

Definition and Rationale

Organizational trainings address the systemic needs of the agency. The goal of these trainings is to improve the functioning of the organization as a whole. After leaving the level of rank and file, most peace officers are involved less with traditional police work and more with issues related to supervision and management. Examples of organizational trainings would be training supervisors to enhance productivity, give feedback appropriately, spot troubled employees, handle discipline constructively, and so on. A second area would be assisting managers with time management or management style. A third area might be training management in the impact of the environmental setting on employees (i.e., the relationship between overcrowding and performance) or explaining about the dynamics of change (e.g., how changes in policy impact line staff, how change should be implemented). These types of trainings can be group trainings with several middle and upper managers attending or individual consults or tutorials.

Special Considerations
in Conducting Organizational Trainings

Once again these trainings still reflect issues of human behavior. In this case they address the interaction between human behavior and organizational policy and procedures. Again several of the special considerations relevant for wellness and informational and skill trainings will be applicable. Support must be obtained at both the upper and middle management levels. Trainings must take into consideration the mind-set and culture of law enforcement. Packaging and marketing will be key issues. The same learning issues will apply. However, there are a few additional concerns relevant when conducting organizational trainings.

Upper and Middle Management Populations. As mentioned earlier, it is crucial that the psychologist assist participants in recognizing the identified problem area as relevant to them personally (i.e., owning the problem). When conducting organizational trainings, however, this issue may pose additional problems because the participants will usually be middle and upper level management. This participant pool is likely to be slightly older, more rigid, and more distrustful of psychological trainings than new recruits who have had more exposure to and acceptance of psychological interventions. It is usually easier to convince upper and middle management to authorize a psychological training for line staff than for themselves.

Follow Through. Follow-up will also be more crucial for this population. Most trainings are asking for a change in behavior that may generate some resistance—"But we have always done it this way." Until the new methods become comfortable and natural, additional availability for consultation is essential.

Consistency. A third important organizational issue will be that of consistency across all levels of the organization. In the world of law enforcement, as in most paramilitary organizations, change occurs from the top down. A training on sexual harassment will be significantly undermined if training officers, sergeants, or lieutenants repeatedly make sexist comments or are perceived to discriminate against female officers. Planning organizational trainings cannot proceed without the visible verbal and behavioral support of all levels of management.

Proposed Organizational Training and Consultation Topics

1. Introduction to psychological services. This training provides an orientation to all employees regarding psychological assistance available to individuals and to supervisors.

2. Psychological aspects of supervision. This training provides basic training in supervisory skills.

3. Teaching the trainee. This training provides basic instruction for field training officers in learning theory, teaching style, and so on, in order to enhance their skills as trainers.

4. Early warning intervention and referral. This training targets supervisors and assists in identifying employees in distress and designing and implementing supportive interventions.

5. Problem employee identification. This training targets supervisors and assists them in developing better skills for handling employees with performance behavioral problems by designing and implementing supportive interventions.

6. Substance abuse awareness. This training targets supervisors and assists them in understanding the dynamics of substance abuse and trains supervisors in early identification and referral of individuals with possible substance abuse problems.

7. Supervising use of force. This training targets managers and helps them to recognize the soft signs of individuals who are at risk for a force-related incident, to identify patterns of excessive force, and to implement a plan of action in response to force concerns. Also discusses the dynamics

that can lead to force (situational as well as personality factors) and discusses supervisor procedures that can decrease the likelihood of force incidents.

8. Sexual harassment awareness. This training assists supervisors in the recognition of and appropriate response to incidents of sexual harassment. Assists line personnel in identifying what constitutes sexual harassment, particularly the more subtle forms, and in understanding the dynamics and impact of sexual harassment.

9. Critical incident triage. Critical incident triage technically falls in the gray area between training and therapeutic first aid. Triage includes defusings and de-escalations (which usually occur on site and during or immediately after the incident) and formal debriefings (24–48 hours after the incident concludes). Triage usually combines educational materials and training with emotional ventilation and problem solving and serves as an organizational first aid. Debriefings (and to a smaller extent, defusings and de-escalations) benefit the individual as well as the department by decreasing the likelihood and the intensity of both short-term reactions and long-term trauma related to critical incidents such as line of duty death of an officer, officer suicide, plane crash, and so on. Critical incident triage involves trainings or first aid sessions that are designed to prevent or minimize widespread damage to the organization (e.g., stress retirements, lost time, decreased productivity, etc.) that can occur in response to critical incidents.

Critical incident triage is often offered by a department's Employee Assistance Program or Psychological Services Unit. However, for an organization that might not have available counseling resources, a properly prepared training psychologist can provide gray area trainings such as these that impact all levels of the department. In conducting critical incident triage, it is important to include all impacted individuals regardless of rank or job function (sworn and civilian), although it is best to keep each group homogenous in order to increase comfort and participation.

10. Grief management. Grief management consultation constitutes a gray area between training and first aid. Grief defusings or de-escalations assist law enforcement personnel in dealing with death. Due to the high degree of solidarity experienced by most law organizations, the death of a colleague often has widespread impact. Defusings, which include educational materials regarding grief reactions, can be provided on a unit level with consultations provided on a management level to help mitigate the impact of loss-related incidents.

11. Team building. Team building enhances the cohesiveness and communication skills within a particular unit through experiential exercises and didactic training on topics such as management style, communication style, personality, and so on.

12. Dealing with change. This type of consultation can be initiated whenever a major policy change is implemented. It is designed to assist supervisors

and employees in adjusting to change and accommodating to the new system (e.g., closing of a station, change in force policy, civilianization of sworn positions, etc.).

13. Committee participation and consultation. It is essential that the police psychologist provide consultation and recommendations to key policymaking and training curriculum committees.

SUMMARY

Although it is useful to divide the various trainings into three different areas, the police psychologist should be aware that actual programs may cross all three training categories. The role of the police psychologist in training is a lesson in perseverance, flexibility, and versatility. It requires the psychologist to draw in equal parts from the fields of social, industrial/organizational, clinical, educational, and police psychology. The police psychologist is often in the uncomfortable position of marketing a product to a somewhat distrustful consumer who recognizes the need for the product but knows little about it and has even less liking for it. Consequently, the majority of the responsibility falls squarely on the shoulders of the police psychologist, who must: (a) become familiar with the culture and needs of law enforcement, (b) recognize where psychological intervention is beneficial, (c) design a training program that takes into consideration law enforcement culture, and then (d) market that program effectively to management and training participants. Lastly the police psychologist must go beyond the traditional definition of classroom training and utilize any and all means (one-on-one consultations, participation on committees, "water cooler" therapy, etc.) to assist law enforcement organizations to achieve their identified goals.

REFERENCES

Blackmore, J. (1978). Are police allowed to have problems of their own? *Police Magazine, 1*(3), 47–55.

Ebert, M. K. (1986). Issues in providing psychological services to law enforcement personnel. In J. T. Reese & H. A. Goldstein (Eds.), *Psychological services for law enforcement* (pp. 249–252). Washington, DC: U.S. Government Printing Office.

Fell, R., Richard, W., & Wallace, W. (1980). Psychological job stress and police officers. *Journal of Police Science and Administration, 8*(2), 139–149.

Fisher, S. (1989). *Adult learning principles workshop.* Pelham, MA: HRD Press.

Garrison, W. E. (1990). Modeling inoculation training for traumatic incident exposure. In J. T. Reese, J. M. Horn, & C. Dunning (Eds.), *Critical incidents in policing* (pp. 107–118). Washington, DC: U.S. Government Printing Office.

Hoff, L. A. (1978). *People in crisis.* Menlo Park, CA: Addison-Wesley.

Hogan, R. (1971). Personality characteristics of highly rated policemen. *Personnel Psychology, 24,* 679–686.

Hollingsworth, J. (1989). Putting a dollar sign on human life. *EAP Digest, 19,* 61–62.

Horn, J. M., & Solomon, R. M. (1989). Peer support: A key element for coping with trauma. *Police Stress*, 25–27.

Hurrell, J. (1977). *Job stress among police officers—A preliminary analysis* (United States Department of Health, Education and Welfare NIOSH7604228). Washington, DC: U.S. Government Printing Office.

Kolts, J. G. (1992). *The Los Angeles County Sheriff's Department: A report by special counsel James G. Kolts and staff*. Unpublished report.

Kroes, W. (1976). *Society's victim—The police: An analysis of job related stress in policing*. Springfield, IL: Thomas.

Kroes, W., Margolis, B., & Hurrell, J. (1974). Job stress in policemen. *Journal of Police Science and Administration, 2*(2), 145–155.

Lester, D. (1981, October). Occupational injuries, illnesses and fatalities in police officers. *Police Chief, 43*, 63.

Lipson, G. (1986). San Ysidro massacre: Post traumatic stress among the police as related to life stress and coping style. (Doctoral dissertation, California School of Professional Psychology, 1986) *Dissertation Abstracts International, 47*, 05B.

Moore, L., & Donohue, T. (1978, November). The patrol officer: Special problems/special cures. *Police Chief, 45*, 42.

Neufeldt, V., & Guralnik, D. (Eds.). (1988). *Webster's new world dictionary of American english*. New York: Simon & Schuster.

Reiser, M. (1974). Some organizational stressors on policemen. *Journal of Police Science and Administration, 2*, 156–159.

Rodriguez, G. J., & Franklin, D. (1986). Training hostage negotiators with psychiatric patients: A "hands-on" approach. In J. T. Reese & H. A. Goldstein (Eds.), *Psychological services for law enforcement* (pp. 497–499). Washington, DC: U.S. Government Printing Office.

Selye, H. (1976). *The stress of life* (rev. ed.). New York: McGraw-Hill.

Sewell, J. (1981) Police stress. *Federal Bureau of Investigation Law Enforcement Bulletin, 50*(4), 7–11.

Sheehan, P. L. (1990). Critical incident trauma and intimacy. In J. T. Reese, J. M. Horn, & C. Dunning (Eds.), *Critical incidents in policing* (pp. 331-334). Washington, DC: U.S. Government Printing Office.

Simpson, B., Jensen, E., & Owen, J. (1988, October). Police employees assistance program. *Police Chief, 83*–85.

Singleton, G. W., & Teahan, J. (1978). Effects of job related stress on the physical and psychological adjustment of police officers. *Journal of Police Science and Administration, 6*, 355–361.

Solomon, R. (1990). The dynamics of fear in critical incidents: Implication for training and treatment. In J. T. Reese, J. M. Horn, & C. Dunning (Eds.), *Critical incidents in policing* (pp. 347–357). Washington, DC: U.S. Government Printing Office.

Stratton, J. G. (1985, February). EAP: A profitable approach for employees and organizations. *Police Chief, 31*–33.

Stratton, J. G., Parker, D. A., & Snibbe, J. R. (1984). Post traumatic stress: Study of police officers involved in shootings. *Psychological Reports, 55*(1), 127–131.

Templin, N. (1990, May 21). Johnson and Johnson wellness program for workers shows healthy bottom line. *Wall Street Journal.*

Terry, C. (1981). Police stress: The empirical evidence. *Journal of Police Science and Administration, 9*(1), 61–75.

Westbrook, L. (1987, October). EAP spells help for troubled employees. *Security Management*, 51–55.

Zenike, R., & Zenike, S. (1988, July). Thirty things we know for sure about adult learning. *Training*, 57–61.

CHAPTER THIRTEEN

Hostage Negotiations Team Training for Small Police Departments

James L. Greenstone
Fort Worth, TX
Police Department

THE NEED FOR HOSTAGE TEAM TRAINING

The training of hostage negotiators can be the determining factor in the successful resolution of the hostage and barricade situations confronting most municipal police departments today. This chapter describes one successful method of accomplishing such training within a relatively small department and suggests how this training can be effectively implemented. Additionally, it may serve as the basis for a training manual on this highly specialized subject. Although the training program described is designed as a total program, it is anticipated that the content of specific programs will vary and be supplemented according to need. This program has been developed over a 3-year period and has been evaluated externally through command post simulations. The material contained in this chapter was developed and tested with and on police officer negotiators from several departments around the country, but with special emphasis on the members of the author's hostage negotiations team. Some of the information given to the team is based on specific team and departmental needs and some is more generic. All material should be applicable to almost any department and especially to those with relatively limited training budgets. A global attempt is made to cover all areas considered relevant to the task of negotiating, interacting with command staff, dealing with the public both before and after the situation, and preparing for dealing with the stressful situation of actually responding to and enduring a hostage or barricade incident. All training is done as a team and the concept of *teamness* is considered most relevant. Team members come to rely on each other and to respect each other's opinions and relevant suggestions. Such interaction is vital to the overall process of negotiations as well as to the necessary working relationships between all members. Members often become the trainers of the other members and at other times become the trainees. All training, however, is conducted under the direct supervision of the designated team trainer.

RATIONALE FOR HOSTAGE NEGOTIATIONS TEAM TRAINING AND SELECTION PROCEDURE FOR TEAM MEMBERS

The underlying concept of hostage negotiations team training is the development of feelings of teamness among the team members. This is further enhanced by the unanimity required in the selection of new team members. From the inception of the team and the designation of the officer responsible for the team's training program, the establishment of rapport and collegiality between the members is of significant importance. No ranks are used, although certainly all are aware of those who are designated to take charge of the team on a day-to-day basis and those who have command authority during an actual incident. Team members are urged, both directly and through exercises, to be open with each other, support each other, and constructively criticize each other. Discussions and critiques done within the team are not dealt with outside the confines of the team unless it is agreed to by team members or required by departmental policy. The strengths of each member of the team are tapped as necessary and all procedures are open to re-examination by the team as it sees fit, again within the confines of the established policy on such matters. As explained, even this policy is, can be, and should be developed by the hostage team and submitted through departmental channels for necessary approvals. This gives the team a vital role in an area that affects them directly.

Team Selection

Selection of the members of the hostage negotiations team is a multilevel process. Even so, the choosing of team members should begin with the team itself. Requiring that all candidates submit a letter of intent, not be under any adverse administrative action, have the approval of their immediate supervisor, and ultimately be approved by the chief of police is a good way to begin.

The process begins with a letter of intent from a prospective candidate for team membership. The letter sets out his or her desire to be on the team as well as qualifications and pertinent background for utilization by the team. If the team members feel that the letter is sufficient to indicate relevant and substantial qualifications, the prospective member is invited to a personal interview with the team at its next meeting. Questions concerning qualifications, reasons for desiring team membership, commitment to the team training requirements, willingness to complete outside readings, availability for formalized training as necessary at a regional police academy, and willingness to conform to team policies regarding equipment and the like are discussed. Generally, because of philosophical considerations, members of the tactical team are not considered for dual membership on the negotiations team. Although not a hard and fast rule, this practice is pervasive within the department and seems to be most effective for members of both teams. Subsequently, the candidate is excused and the team members vote. Unanimity is required for acceptance. If obtained, the name and qualifications of the candidate are presented to the chief of police by the chief negotiator. Approval being obtained at this level, the candidate is notified and invited to the next training session, which usually occurs within 2 weeks. Orientation and team indoctrination begins at that time. Should a candidate not receive a unanimous vote from the team subsequent to the team interview, he or she is notified of same, and his or her letter is kept in the team file with the negative vote notation. If desired, the reasons for nonselection are explained to the applicant, and suggestions for reapplying are made where applicable.

The rationale for a unanimous vote of the team to include a new applicant is important. Because team members must be willing to work very closely with all other team members, and to be open with them, each member must be accepting of a new member. If not, problems may occur later, in close situations in which stress is imposed and individual personality traits may become evident. Under such circumstances, the entire success of an operation may be jeopardized when individuals cannot or will not work closely with each other or because of a lack of personal respect or rapport. If each member has had the actual and legitimate right to reject an applicant, his or her acceptance of the applicant is seen as a willingness to work closely with that person and to give to and receive from him or her in the course of the team's interaction with each other. Less is hidden that might create difficult problems later beyond those already present due to the hostage incident in which they are involved.

The team oriented approach to member selection seems to be effective and often precludes the selection or appointment of team members from other departmental sources. If the team procedure is in place and seems to work in selecting the best possible members from those available, and if the presentation to the chief is done properly and specifically, a well-qualified team can be assembled by the team itself. This seems desirable because it is the team that must work within itself and therefore should be able to discern with whom it can work best.

TRAINING METHODS

Modules (80 Hours)

The basic training modules are arranged into 12 separate areas of concern. Eleven of the 12 modules are currently accounted for, and the last module is left open for future use and expansion of the training program. The use of 11 areas of training was based on the areas felt to be necessary to develop a fully trained team rather than being arbitrarily determined. Initially, input was sought from other negotiators and team members concerning those areas necessary to successful hostage team performance. Eleven areas for the initial training program were selected with the additional module being reserved for future use, perhaps for specialized or advanced training, without necessitating a complete rewriting of the instructional program. Additionally, the use of modules enhanced the tracking system utilized to be sure that adequate time is spent on each area relative to the needs of the hostage negotiator. Each module is assigned a training hour requirement. All lesson plans for each training session were keyed to a specific module or modules and those attending that session were recorded. At any time, it is possible to know exactly how many hours of training in each module each member of the team has completed. Once the entire 80-hour basic training has been completed by a team member, he or she is given a comprehensive final examination. If successful, the candidate is awarded a specially designed certificate of team affiliation.

Basic Hostage Negotiations (30 Hours). The Basic Hostage Negotiations module is based on the training given to negotiators by the Federal Bureau of Investigation (FBI) Training Academy at Quantico, Virginia, and from other relevant sources. It includes all relevant basic issues concerning preparing for and actually negotiating in hostage and barricade situations. Although 30 hours of negotiations training in and of itself is insufficient to properly train a novice negotiator, included here are only those elements dealing with recognition of hostage situations, diagnosis of hostage takers, handling of demands, dealing with deadlines, face-to-face negotiations, and similar areas. Other areas normally included in the overall basic training in formalized academy courses are dealt with in separate modules.

Equipment (2 Hours). Equipment is an area often overlooked or reserved for highly technical training. Many times, when equipment is discussed, the only equipment dealt with in any detail is related to telephone communications, by public service or hostage phone, with the hostage taker. In this module, consideration is given both to team equipment and to equipment of the individual hostage negotiator. Team equipment includes such items, in addition to the hostage phone, as flip charts, markers, bullhorn, batteries, first aid kit, toilet paper, plastic bags, notebooks, check lists, pens, and masking tape to mention only a few. Personal equipment refers to that for which each negotiator is responsible and may need at the scene of an actual incident. Such items include check lists, pens, pencils, personal notebooks and notes, personal communications equipment, procedural references, personal hygiene articles, snack food, extra clothing, seasonal clothing, team jacket and cap issued to each member, personal first aid kit, flashlight, and other personal comfort and individual negotiator items. Periodically, "show downs" of all negotiator equipment are held during regular training sessions. Not only is this an opportunity to check each member's gear, but it is also used as a way of exchanging ideas between team members regarding equipment to be included or excluded from the items carried. Each team member is required by team policy to have all of their personal equipment available to them at all times for deployment. Team equipment is maintained in the armory of the department and one team member is assigned to check the operational level of this equipment and to report to the team members. All team members have responsibility for team equipment even though one member is assigned to make periodic checks. Additionally, all team equipment is distinctively marked so that, as needed, the tactical team will know to transport team equipment to the scene of an incident.

Policy (4 Hours). Knowledge of policy concerning negotiating, team organization, and function are important for all team members. The initial formulation of policy can best be done by the negotiators who must work under the policy adopted. Policy can be developed by the team based on perceived team needs and operational constraints. Once this is done, meeting with those who will have to approve such policy and implement it are crucial. Certainly, the chief of police, his designate, the on-scene commanders, the tactical commanders, and any others directly affected should be included in these policy work sessions. Once all are in agreement about policy and procedures, the team policy can be drafted and adopted. Periodic review of policy concerning hostage negotiations should be done during team training and changes suggested as necessary. Among team members, there should be no ambiguity about team and departmental policies. As questions arise, they should be resolved rather than allowed to present during an actual incident. Difficult areas in policy development might be, but are not limited to:

1. Circumstances for negotiating.
2. Mobilization of negotiating team.

3. How long to negotiate.

4. When to make face-to-face contact with the hostage taker.

5. Relationship with tactical team.

6. Negotiable items.

7. Role of commanders.

8. Chain of command.

9. Discontinuance of utilities.

10. Safety of all concerned.

11. "Green light" considerations.

12. Police officers as hostages.

13. Perimeter establishment.

Team Duties (3 Hours). The individual responsibilities of each team member form the backbone of the hostage negotiations procedure. Although certain members of the team may find themselves used in certain positions more than others, all team members are trained and expected to be able to function in all areas of responsibility on the team. Regardless of the situation or the availability of team manpower, the team must be able to function effectively. Training and cross-training is one way of accomplishing this. Exercises are designed with this need in mind and each negotiator is evaluated in all areas.

For our purposes, there are five major positions on the hostage negotiations team. Additional positions are also mentioned, along with method used to provide for them. The major positions include: (a) primary negotiator, (b) secondary negotiator, (c) coach, (d) intelligence coordinator, and (e) negotiations coordinator or liaison.

Additional positions that can be filled by unassigned negotiators, negotiators from other departments with similar training, reserve officers, off-duty personnel or extra officers include: (a) messengers, (b) intelligence interviewers, (c) assistants to the intelligence coordinator, (d) members of the "think tank," and (e) guards.

In addition, there may be a need for help in installing and repairing the hostage phone system or other electronic equipment used at the scene. Officers familiar with electronics or reserve officers who may have related civilian jobs can be effectively utilized. Each of the major and additional positions are defined clearly by job descriptions published and issued to each team member. This information is maintained in individual negotiator notebooks for ready reference at any time. In this way, it is not necessary to require memorization of this material, and yet it is always available for use simply by referral.

Penal Code (1 Hour). Knowledge of the provisions of the penal code relative to hostage situations enables the negotiator to relate in a knowledgeable way to the often raised concerns of hostage takers about what they can expect legally if they surrender. A negotiator must be credible at all times, and this information increases credibility. In addition, case law relating to hostage situations is also reviewed periodically. Although only limited case law exists in this particular area, knowing how the courts view the negotiator function and the process of negotiations with regard to departmental policy adherence adds a measure of seriousness to the overall training process. Rather than being viewed as a mere additional duty of the department, a member of the negotiating team comes to realize how important his or her job and the training to accomplish the job really is.

City/Community Interface (2 Hours). The time to get to know who represents the resources in a particular community is prior to an actual hostage or barricade incident. Not only the department, but also the negotiating team in particular, will probably have to interact with various civilian supervisors and workers within city departments and county agencies. Meeting with these individuals and exchanging procedural information, phone numbers, and emergency information in advance of the need for such information will ease the tension of an actual incident later on. Voices heard only over the phone will be associated with specific faces and such associations will prove valuable. Both the team members and the city personnel will be able to learn from each other and be better able to understand the constraints under which each works or may have to work under unusual conditions.

Those who might be asked to participate in the interface with the department's hostage negotiations team include, but are not limited to, city mayor; city manager; councilpersons (as deemed necessary); telephone company security supervisor; electric, gas, and water companies; news media; local radio and television stations, as necessary; school superintendent; president of the local school board; airport and seaport authorities; military base commander; and others as deemed necessary in particular communities or special circumstances.

Such a meeting can take place en masse or in smaller groupings as the schedules of those invited permit. Such meetings should be interactive and convey information about the function and purpose of the negotiating team as well as receiving information concerning emergency procedures.

Practical Exercises and Command Post Practical Problems (8 Hours). Central to any meaningful training program is the practical application of material learned within a relatively safe environment. In this environment, situations can take on an air of realism while being a safe place to make mistakes and to learn from them. Command post simulations are designed to provide a variety of experiences and problems and allow each negotiator to experience each position on the team and adapt to it. Simulations can concentrate on dealing with particular types of hostage takers, or be used only to allow rotation of team members through each of the team positions. As with all practical and live situations, a thorough critique follows as soon as possible after completion of the training or live incident.

This portion of the training program differs from a subsequent section that brings together with the command post function of the team the tactical team of the department and their interface with the negotiators. The negotiations team command post function must be intact before a joint training exercise can be attempted and success anticipated. Several command post simulations are held during the course of a training year, whereas it is generally practical to hold only a few joint training programs. Obviously, the way that this is done can be modified to fit particular departmental needs. The important aspect of this is that such training should be held in order to solidify the effects of classroom training and exercises. Additionally, realism should be attempted whenever possible. Role playing and simulations can approach reality if proper planning is done, those in charge understand the procedures for such simulations, and proper safety is allowed for and ground rules rigidly adhered to. If this concern is felt and communicated at all departmental levels, the result will be a team of negotiators ready for real-world incidents should they occur.

Negotiator Stress Survival (2 Hours). This module provides the negotiators with specific suggestions and procedures for dealing with their own stress encountered before, during, and after a hostage incident. These suggestions and procedures are set in place by an understanding of how stress operates on the body and the mind and what happens when normal stress becomes distress. Relaxation exercises are practiced and an examination is made of those stress-producing behaviors that may be encountered when attempting to negotiate with a hostage taker or barricaded subject.

Nutrition is also discussed. Food and snack items to be carried by each negotiator as part of his or her personal gear is of prime concern. Food items that may contribute to the overall experience of stress on the part of the negotiator are discouraged and more healthful items are recommended. Negotiators are encouraged to consider their own food and vitamin needs carefully as part of their preplanning for a hostage incident. Attempting to bypass these needs while under stressful conditions may jeopardize an entire operation. Relying on other sources to provide food and drink may also increase the negotiator's already stressed condition. Knowledge of how stress affects the body and mind, coupled with specific instruction, provides each officer with usable and practical information.

The importance of the debriefing process in negotiator survival is also emphasized. The policy of the team is consistent with the departmental policy concerning debriefing postincident. Meetings are held, usually by the chief or his designate, with both the tactical and negotiations teams attending. The purpose of these meetings is to discuss both the positives and negatives of the incident, and to make suggestions for improvement of procedures. Additionally, the general meeting and the separate team meetings allow for ventilation among and between the members of the respective teams, as well as a time for discussing specific team concerns.

The place of negotiator stress survival in all phases of hostage negotiations cannot be overemphasized. The assumption is often made that a police officer, and to an even greater extent the trained negotiator, is not as vulnerable to the alleged effects of stress as are other persons, not so trained. It must be understood that stress is real and poses a significant potential negative factor that must be examined and dealt with.

Review of Previous Nondepartmental Hostage Situations (8 Hours). This section of the training program involves the review of hostage situations handled by other departments or agencies both in this country and in others as appropriate. In some cases, verbatim narratives are reviewed as available. At other training sessions, tapes are studied as a way of examining and improving negotiating techniques. All cases are provided to team members in as much detail as possible for maximum effect. Maps of incident areas, actual voice recordings of negotiations, descriptions of witnesses, and a "stop-action" approach are all provided to allow in-depth assessment of what happened, what should have taken place, what mistakes were made, and what might have been done differently. From this, suggestions for improving team procedure and for avoiding similar problems are developed. Positive aspects of these incidents are also scrutinized, developed, and added to the team operating procedures as appropriate.

Review of Departmental Hostage Situations (8 Hours). Although departmental hostage situations are reviewed during debriefing of the incident, additional scrutiny can be of much benefit to the team members. Discussion of procedures, review of taped material when available, and examination of charts and other records kept can allow for early recognition of problems and course corrections if necessary prior to the next incident. Members have a chance, within the safe environment of the team meeting, to talk about their own behavior and the behavior of other team members. In so doing, they can see both the strengths and weaknesses in what was done and examine their personal feelings about their behavior. The need for defensiveness and justification is low under these conditions and necessary understanding and change is possible to a greater degree than under less safe circumstances. Whenever possible, tapes are obtained of the actual incident. These may come from the news media coverage or from tape made at the scene by members of the department. Few have the opportunity to actually see themselves under actual conditions. To the extent that this is possible, members of the negotiating team may gain greater self-confidence and be able to change nonproductive behaviors. Such viewing may also help to examine team procedures and tactical and negotiating team interaction to a greater and more beneficial extent than can be done during simulations and role plays.

Simulations With Tactical Team Interface (12 Hours). To a great extent, the culmination of the training process is the joint training exercises with both the hostage negotiations team and the tactical team. Such training brings together the entire departmental response to a hostage or barricade incident and allows for the exercise of all related functions. From the role of the chief of police, to the on-scene commanders, to the tactical team and negotiations commanders, to the functions of the reserve components and dispatch, all can be examined in relationship to each other. The key is realism.

Realism must be established and pursued at all levels and over a sufficient period of time to allow for adequate functioning and training of all units involved. Commanders are allowed to command and negotiators are allowed to negotiate against a hostage taker who is portrayed by an actor or a well-trained role player. Such role players are not previously known to the team if at all possible. Departmental procedures are practiced at all important and relevant junctures and adequate records are kept of both the positive points and the mistakes made. A person assigned as a process observer and another as a cameraperson are very helpful to the training experience. The process observer can be a nonpolice officer, nonnegotiator who is familiar with procedure and can make notes unfettered by other responsibilities. A local mental health professional may be a good person for this job. The cameraperson can be either a nonpolice officer or an unassigned officer who can operate a video camera. Both should be tagged as invisible and encouraged to roam throughout the entire hostage incident scenario. Such freedom can give added vantage points from which to review the training later. Tapes and notes can be made from the hostage taker's and hostage's point of view and from the police vantage points. Comparisons can be useful during regular training sessions. Knowing what was done and the apparent effect of a particular approach is often enlightening. Knowing about how procedures were viewed by those not involved in the actual training simulation is a valuable source of critical material.

These simulations can be altered as needed to give all major teams involved the chance to exercise their procedures. For example, two endings can be scripted for a hostage scenario. One can provide for a negotiated ending whereas the other will require tactical intervention. Good communication between those coordinating the simulation is necessary for this to have the desired effect.

The length of simulations should be long enough to accomplish the training mission. This may mean a 5- or 6-hour scenario or one lasting 1 to 2 days as time and manpower permit. The more varied the conditions occurring during the simulation, the better in terms of allowing all concerned to train under changed and changing conditions and to test the team members' ability to adapt to the changes. The way in which team members handle such personal matters as food and water, clothing, and hygiene are other practical training concerns that could pose problems during an actual incident. Logistical capabilities can also be tested in this way. Interaction with local utilities and the like can also be accomplished as practical and be evaluated.

Planning for such a major training event is important. Although team members should not be privy to the details of a scenario prior to its beginning, detailed planning must be undertaken and each element of the role playing scripted for maximum benefit. Departmental training officers can be responsible for this planning without allowing the details to be divulged. Outside training resources provide another approach, while providing an external evaluation of the teams involved. One department's negotiations team and tactical unit can provide the necessary manpower and coordination for a sister department in exchange for similar training at another time. In addition to maintaining the security of the scenario, such an interchange can add to the realism of the training and allow a department's negotiators to experience a situation as close as possible to the actual incident. Undeniably, such realism at all levels is the key to the successful use of this type of training procedure.

Communication Exercises

As an adjunct to the training process, structured communications exercises are utilized to demonstrate and evaluate the specific components of effective verbal and nonverbal interaction. These exercises stress such elements as:

1. The importance of two-way interaction between negotiator and taker to the success of a hostage incident.
2. The results of not listening.
3. How hidden agendas can interrupt and paralyze interaction and problem solving.
4. The importance of listening for and responding to feelings as well as content material.

5. How active listening improves communication.
6. How to interpret and respond to nonverbal cues.
7. The importance of rapport building.
8. How understanding your own communications skills affects negotiations.
9. What factors influence communications breakdown.
10. How to recover from a communications error.

Experiential Exercises

In addition to the communications exercises central to the negotiator function, additional experiential material is introduced to accomplish (although not limited to) the following:

1. The development of trust between hostage negotiations team members.
2. The identification of individual personal characteristics of the team member that could help or hinder effective interaction with a hostage taker, barricaded subject, or other team member.
3. The proper use and function of the secondary negotiator and coach.
4. The specific role functions of each team member.
5. The handling of unusual situations.

Formal Courses

Even with the structured and regular training provided to the team members within the department, all are encouraged to take related formal courses at local and regional police training academies. These courses are necessary to assure continued certification by the Commission on Law Enforcement Officer Standards and Education as a member of a hostage negotiations team with the authority to intercept wire and oral communications during a hostage incident. Local laws and requirements should be consulted. Additionally, such courses in both basic and advanced hostage negotiations techniques help to bring up to speed the newer members of the team in a very efficient manner, and serve to complement the team training of the more experienced negotiators. Other courses encouraged for enrollment by members of the negotiations team include, but are not limited to, the following:

1. Critical incident response.
2. Penal code.
3. Cults, sects, and deviant movements.

4. Current police practices.
5. Terrorism.
6. Crisis intervention.
7. Media relations.
8. Serial murder.
9. Tactical response.
10. Interviewing.

Concurrent Training

Although training for negotiators is the central focus, related training in hostage negotiations procedures is essential for those who must command such situations and for those who may find themselves as the first responder to a hostage or barricade incident. These first responders include such personnel as patrol officers, patrol supervisors, firefighters, and emergency medical service providers. What the chief of police understands about his or her team and will trust them to do, and what the first response officer, regardless of function, does or does not do on arrival, can affect overall outcome and the safety for all concerned.

First Responders. This category includes police officers, firefighters, emergency medical service personnel, and anyone else who may be expected to arrive on the scene of a hostage or barricade incident prior to the advent of the hostage negotiators and the tactical team. Courses for this group focus on what is the appropriate response when initially responding to a potential or actual situation. The importance of communications between responders is stressed and practical considerations are examined. Knowledge of what to expect under such circumstances and how to respond successfully can be the major determiner of actual hostage negotiations once begun. If the initial contact is handled correctly, this can set the stage for the advent of the negotiators and support their ability to resolve the situation in a safe and reasonable manner. The converse is also a reality and for that reason, such courses are necessary.

Chiefs of Police. Knowledge of hostage situations, implementation of departmental policy, and trust of his or her negotiators and their training are some of the concerns of a chief of police facing a hostage or barricade scene. Yet, often there is not enough interaction between these functional components of a department prior to an actual situation. The negotiations team trains and the chief runs the department. One may not understand or appreciate the capabilities and responsibilities of the other. Short courses for chiefs of police specific to the issues of policy, team training, hostage situations generally, and hostage takers specifically, can help to bridge this gap. The more that the chief knows about the quality and quantity of training received by the negotiators, and the more that is known about how his or her team will function under actual conditions, the greater the degree of trust between these two elements that can be developed. In an actual incident, the chief can then trust that all that can be done will be done and further that the negotiators who directly represent him or her and the department will do well in such a capacity.

RETRAINING

Review of Basic Modules (50 Hours)

Constant review of basic material is essential for the maintenance of team proficiency and readiness. Some of the initial 80 hours of training may not be necessary in their entirety and therefore a retraining schedule will be helpful. Retraining can be limited to the modules presented or expanded as individual team needs dictate. The same is true for the maintenance training schedule described later.

The Retraining Schedule includes, but does not have to be limited to, the following:

- Basic negotiations (12 hours)
- Equipment (2 hours)
- Policy review (1 hour)
- Team duties (1 hour)
- Penal code and Supreme Court decisions (1 hour)
- City and community interface (1 hour)
- Practical exercises and command post simulations (8 hours)
- Negotiator stress survival (2 hours)
- Review of previous nondepartmental incidents (7 hours)
- Review of departmental hostage situations (8 hours)
- Simulations with tactical interface (8 hours)

Additional Exercises

Part of ongoing performance proficiency concerns can be met by utilization of exercises within the team training environment that can assist the negotiators in understanding and appreciating the personalities and the unique needs of each other member of the team. These can range from communications exercises that focus on more difficult areas of the process to interpersonal simulations that reinforce, address, or seek to modify personal areas between negotiators. Creativity and the freedom to seek out new approaches to team concerns and to team needs is an important component if this type of interaction is to be utilized effectively in police negotiator training.

Maintenance Training (20 Hours)

Once the basic training and retraining cycle have been completed, maintaining the negotiators' skills at peak levels over an extended period of time often becomes a real problem for trainer and department. In small departments, where hostage incidents occur infrequently, morale as well as efficiency can be an ongoing concern. The maintenance schedule will keep training current but must be altered and tailored as the needs arise and as the team seeks more advanced skills.

The maintenance schedule includes:

- Basic hostage negotiations (5 hours)
- Practical exercises and command post simulation (4 hours)
- Negotiator stress survival (1 hour)
- Review of previous, nondepartmental incidents (2 hours)
- Review of departmental hostage situations (2 hours)
- Simulations with tactical team interface (6 hours)

ADVANCED TRAINING

Specialized Negotiating Techniques

Once negotiators have received, and are comfortable with, the basic techniques of negotiations and are thoroughly familiar with their responsibilities within their team, it may be possible to introduce more sophisticated information and procedures. Any viable information that increases the ability of the negotiator to do the job better and more effectively should be considered. Most material that is available will not be directly related to police negotiations and will have to be carefully adapted to ensure acceptance and proper utilization.

An example of this type of advanced training is the material and procedures provided by such groups as the Harvard University Negotiations Project. Although not specifically designed to be used in the usual police hostage situations, the material is valuable and adaptable. Utilizing such information within a police negotiations system is somewhat complicated and requires some rethinking of previously learned concepts and adding to others in order to do the job more efficiently. Making such material acceptable and usable may require the deep involvement of already well-trained team members. Such material is introduced, and is helpful, only if all team members are already well grounded in basic and standard techniques. More information is available to those interested from the author.

Related Areas

Negotiators are encouraged to attend any training course that might be related to the negotiations process even though not specifically intended for them. Such courses might include Cults and Deviant Movements and Stress Management and Nutrition. Although not specifically aimed at police negotiators, such courses touch on areas of real and significant importance in terms of job performance. Knowledge of particular cultures, sects, and peculiarities of specific subgroups with whom the negotiator may come into contact during an incident is certainly beneficial. Knowledge of stress management techniques and of nutritional requirements when under stress can better prepare the officer for his specialized task.

PRACTICAL PROBLEMS

Attendant to any training that includes practical problems are certain areas that must be considered and planned for if such training is to be maximally useful. Most would probably agree that the hands-on part of training is most important to skill development in any area when such skills will be utilized in the field. This is certainly true in this area. Considerations for practical problems should include concerns about equipment, command post functions, and tactical and negotiating team interface.

Equipment

Practical problems are excellent opportunities to exercise both team and personal equipment. Doing so allows flaws to be discovered and to be corrected under safe conditions so that the same problem does not arise during more vital incidents. Teams should be encouraged to respond to practice sessions as though they were responding to the real thing. Problems should be noted and addressed at the debriefing and during subsequent training sessions of the team. Failures in equipment or lack thereof should be corrected on the scene if possible and remedied afterward if necessary. Equipment should also be checked to be sure that it will perform under conditions likely to be encountered during an actual situation.

Command Post

Sometimes, procedures in which one is trained are not exactly like those to be utilized under actual conditions. Negotiators should receive training in command post functions and also be familiar with any modifications of standard command post activities that may occur or be expected by those in command. The practical exercise provides an opportunity not only to make mistakes within a safe environment, but also to test procedures under closely monitored conditions. The use of a process observer who is not attached to any unit or assigned to any duty is a good way to understand what is effective and what is not. Even a nonpolice process observer is valuable for this purpose. The function of the command post in support of the overall negotiations objectives should not be underestimated. If the command post is effective in executing its responsibilities, the negotiator can do the job with greater precision.

Tactical and Negotiating Team Interface

Tactical team and negotiating team members should train together as frequently as possible. Even though it would be assumed that because both are members of the same department, that each would understand, respect, and support the functions of the other, this may not be so. The answer may be frequent, combined training that allows each to see the other in action and to understand how each performs. Joint and separate debriefing after training is also important to accomplish this purpose. When misunderstandings arise, they are dealt with in a sensitive and realistic manner in order to resolve the issue without further problems.

During training exercises, realism on the part of the tactical team and the negotiations team during their interactions is vital. In this way, procedures common to both and to the overall process can be examined and developed as necessary. Additionally, team members on both sides can begin to examine the functions of each and better understand how each is related to the other.

A FINAL NOTE

An external evaluation of the department's negotiations team is an excellent method, not only to assure all concerned that the team measures up to real-world standards, but also to maintain the morale of team members. A recognized expert in the field of hostage negotiations can be used if available and cost effective. More experienced teams from other departments can be called on to perform such evaluations and these can be scheduled at the end of a major training segment completed by the department's team members. The evaluation is then discussed with the team during the debriefing session and key points, both pro and con, are thoroughly analyzed. The evaluator then submits a written statement to the chief of police. In this way, the evaluation results can be utilized and disseminated to other key members of the command staff as deemed necessary. Posting of this evaluation statement, especially if it is a positive one, can have obvious effects. Teams that handle only occasional barricade or hostage incidents gain an additional benefit from an external evaluation. By testing their skills against an experienced negotiator-evaluator, such teams can determine if their training has adequately prepared them for the real thing. If not, training can be modified immediately. If they have been properly prepared, they can continue their training knowing that, should they be called on to function, they are ready to do so. Command level personnel will also be encouraged by this information.

PART FIVE

SUPPORTING
POLICE OPERATIONS

CHAPTER FOURTEEN

The Care and Feeding of Undercover Agents

Neil S. Hibler
Levinson, Ltd., Alexandria, VA

An undercover law enforcement officer is summoned to speak with superiors because they believe he is exploiting his status and reveling in the freedom of the "other side of the street." This undermines mutual trust and leads to suspicions that jeopardize the continuing progress of the operation. In another case, undercover personnel request transfer from the program after an operation is administratively closed out after months of activity without promise of success. The operational officers are convinced that their careers are forever tainted. In yet another case, supervisors pressured an undercover (UC) to accelerate progress despite the absence of promising leads. The UC hangs out at an underworld den, becomes intoxicated, and tries to recruit a cocktail waitress as an informant. Unbeknownst to him, she is an informant for another law enforcement agency, reports what she believes is the impersonation of a law enforcement officer, and the UC is arrested. Even "successful" cases can bring surprises. Days before the trial of a major criminal indicted with evidence collected by an undercover, the operative says he feels badly about setting the subject up because he has come to know him and is sympathetic to the plight of the subject's family; he asks if he can be a character witness for the defense. In another example, after completing a sensitive 2-year undercover assignment, the operative returns to his squad room to find his peers have been promoted to other duties and the stranger who is well settled at (what used to be) his desk is irritated by the operative's questions about all the changes. Worse yet, new office requirements and procedures leave the operative ill prepared to competitively produce in the routine duties that are used to judge his performance. The consequence is that the officer is unpromotable, effectively penalized for being undercover.

These are only a few of the real-life circumstances that can occur in undercover work. Farkas (1986) reported that one federal agency has found the chief sources of stress in these endeavors to be supervisor–subordinate relationships, the role requirements on the UC, and the strain on marital and social relationships. The consequences included changes in the operatives' sense of comfort, attitudes toward some laws, sympathy for criminals, and erosion of the agent's value system. In another sample, Farkas found about half of the operatives labeled themselves as having psychological problems after 5 months of assignment; one third felt contact with a psychologist would have been desirable. Even in leaving this special duty problems were encountered. Forty-two percent found difficulty making the transition to other assignments. The facts of life in the undercover lane are that the personal and organizational risks are so pervasive that clandestine duty should be a place to visit, but not to stay.

Law enforcement agencies that employ undercover work in their crime-fighting capabilities find the experience to be very different than that depicted by Hollywood. Unfortunately, it has little of the glitter and none of the glory. To be successful on all counts, undercover operations require considerable preparation, teamwork, and care. This chapter addresses the risks from the perspective of an agent who is also a psychologist, providing a program that has been successful in a number of federal agencies. The reader may be a mental health professional, agency leader, supervisor, case agent, or operative. All need to know the expectations of the other; all have a role and need to be involved.

PSYCHOLOGICAL SUPPORT
TO UNDERCOVER OPERATIONS

The goal of undercover operations is to develop prosecutable evidence by accessing subjects and their activities from the inside. The benefit of such operations is in their ability to exploit criminal activities fully, with credible evidence and testimony by a trusted reporter: a law enforcement officer who witnessed the wrongdoing firsthand. The goal of psychological support is to ensure that all of the people involved are understood, and their needs and risks are addressed to assure the success of the mission. There is an unmistakably clear requirement for an honest broker between all parties involved. To accomplish this there must be some definitions that are agreed on. These include recognizing that success or failure is the consequence of many factors, some of which are beyond the control of the agency. Accordingly, the team needs to carefully consider many facets of the case, but cannot hold the undercover officer accountable for the final outcome; it is a team effort. For this same reason, the operation is under the control of the team chief or case agent, and not the UC. Any operation must begin with a plan that is based on credible intelligence that defines the nature of the targeted activity and therefore the operational requirements and risks. The plan needs to have a beginning, middle, and end. Goals need to be clear and specific, and the proposed course must blend available resources with the need. The dynamics of a single operative and the target can be complex, particularly if the target figures are unknown entities; yet the complexity is multiplied when multiple undercovers are used or involved with informants. To ensure that these dynamics are understood and effectively incorporated into covers and the design of the operation there can be no privacy; the client is the undercover program. Consequently, there is no professional confidentiality, although there must be a healthy respect for discretion. These are challenging roles, because everything counts.

This chapter separates the preparation of and care for undercover agents into phases. Each section addresses how psychological support is involved in the "cradle to grave" sense of seeing personnel through from selection to their return to routine duties. Ultimately, all undercovers must make such a return. Allowing them to remain outside the normal career path for too long renders them useless. The preventable long-term consequences of UC work are burnout, feeling unappreciated and disrespected, and being uninterested in routine duty, if even able to do it.

Six phases of involvement comprise an integrated model with which to implement behavioral science into undercover work. Figure 14.1 depicts a time line that demonstrates the sequence of support phases. Each segment is integrated with that which preceded and that which follows. Throughout there is emphasis on the professional requirement that operatives let others know how they are doing, to include how they perceive others as well as how they personally feel.

In each of these phases there are necessary tasks for agency leaders, supervisors, the case agent, operative, and consulting mental health professional. In addition to these considerations, options are presented that provide a variety of ways to be sure needs are recognized and met.

SELECTION

The purpose of selection is to identify those best qualified for undercover assignments. Although a wide range of personality features can be used to do this work, there are some contraindications that would potentially raise risks for the individual, the operation, or both.

Screening out is a concept that directs the elimination of applicants who have features incompatible with the job to be done. The absolute psycho-

Start   End
 | |
SELECTION → TRAINING → OPERATIONAL PLANNING → DEPLOYMENT → DECOMPRESSION → REINTEGRATION

FIG. 14.1. A phased support model for providing psychological support.

logical screen outs for undercover work are essentially the same for police
work in general. This is an important consideration because some agencies
do not use psychological entrance screening, but even those that do cannot
guarantee that previously screened officers have not changed. Even initially
fit personnel can face personal challenges that overwhelm. Accordingly,
screening for undercover selection requires a fresh assessment that uses
both measures of normal personality dynamics and, if present, psychopathology. Nominees for undercover work should be performing competently
in their present assignment, have effective interpersonal skills, and have
sufficient career experience to have crystallized their basic law enforcement
skills. New trainees who have not learned how to do their agency's routine
duties will have no job to return to when their tour in UC work is over.

Screening in is a concept in which selection looks for qualities that suggest
an applicant has skills, knowledge, or abilities that would make him or her
particularly well qualified for the specific work requirements. Included in
screening in is the prerequisite of passing the screening-out process. Therefore applicants who meet screening-in requirements do not have contrain-
dicated features, but do have special qualifications that would enhance their
ability to perform. Such qualifications are broadly described here, but have
at least two levels of consideration. The first demonstrates general abilities
that include a proven record of being able to work both with others and
alone, being able to work reliably without a great deal of direct supervision,
demonstrated good judgment (particularly under stress), and being able to
handle boredom due to stagnation in progress. The second screen-in level
addresses readiness and suitability for a specific operation. Qualifications
here include the absence of current conflicts at work or home (personal
life) that would interfere with commitment to the impending assignment;
categorical attributes as defined by age, race, ethnic origin, or gender; geographic, cultural, or experiential knowledge, as seen in being streetwise to
the inner city or experienced in the subculture in an industry; and specialized
abilities, including speaking foreign languages or knowing how to perform
specific skills, such as bank accounting or flying an airplane. The first level
of screening in is needed for entry into the program, the second for participation in a specific operation.

Formal psychological testing and a structured clinical interview are recommended components of the screening process. Both methods are needed
to determine the indications and contraindications that may exist. The test

instruments the author uses are the FIRO-B, Minnesota Multiphasic Personality Inventory (MMPI), the Sixteen Personality Factor Test (16 PF) and a home-grown sentence completion test that serves as a modest projective technique. Projective tests are designed to sample thoughts without providing cues or structure. The result is the revelation of information that might otherwise not have been possible. The other instruments have demonstrated a capability to recognize personality traits, dynamics, and difficulties. Together, the battery measures both characteristics that are relatively stable over time and do not change (personality traits) as well as states, or how things are going right now. Current readiness is an important distinction because it transcends all phases of the operation.

State–trait distinctions apply to initial screening as well as readiness testing for those entered into the program but not examined for over 6 months. People's status can change quickly, but barring obvious, dramatic shifts in challenges faced or performance contributed, testing should not be considered valid for more than 6 months, or 1 year at best. The personality traits do not change a great deal, but the emotional states do vary and it is possible for an operative to have been ready for assignment when initially screened, but not at a later time. Therefore additional testing is a consideration prior to deployment or during the course of prolonged operations. Entry-level test results can provide an effective baseline for comparisons, a personal standard with which to assess changes for better or for worse. This issue is revisited in later phases.

Interestingly, those who volunteer to be undercover operatives seem to come from three major groups. The largest of these consists of investigators or special agents who are concerned about their ability to be competitive. They correctly conceive the UC role as an opportunity to do something that will allow them to be more visible than their peers. The correctness of this vision is that they are actually the only ones able to report what they have accomplished. UCs have little direct, eyes-on supervision; the office has to rely on what the operative says to stay informed. Accordingly, the UC role provides a unique opportunity to do whatever is necessary, but to portray those efforts from the operative's own lips; no one else actually knows what happens day to day. For these same reasons, a second group of volunteers seeks to be included in UC activities.

Some investigators hate to be supervised. The whole idea of having to be overseen is uncomfortable. It is no surprise then that for these investigators the chance to go undercover is a chance to elude supervision and do their own thing. This is the second largest group.

The third and last group consists of essentially normal investigators who are in a jam in their current assignments, unhappy with the location, people, or pressure. They will do anything to get out of the situation, even go undercover.

What these descriptions suggest is that undercover volunteers are to a large degree fringe elements, dissatisfied with their circumstances and hoping to improve their situations by going undercover. Surely those who are complacent, self-satisfied, and self-satisfying would see undercover work for what it is: long, sometimes hard, often dangerous, and nearly always unappreciated. Most special agents who are satisfied with their circumstances and their futures are hesitant to consider undercover work. They see it for what it is: long, thankless efforts for which there is little chance to improve their circumstances and plenty of opportunity to stagnate. Altogether normal (self-satisfied, complacent, or happy) personnel will most often have nothing to do with it.

One of the reasons for selection precautions is based on the reality that those who seek involvement in an undercover program are not always those who are best qualified. Volunteerism is important to ensure motivation to be successful, but more needs to be done. Training is intended to round out capabilities by building skills and confidence.

TRAINING

Training is the second phase in preparing undercover personnel. The selection process identifies competent investigators who have sufficient field experience to assure they would be able both have identity with the mainstay of routine investigative work and to demonstrate that they have the abilities to be effective in undercover assignments. The skills used in undercover operations are in large measure extensions of these basics, emphasizing the importance of first being able to convincingly deal with others, employ self-discipline, and demonstrate initiative, effective judgment, and tolerance under stress. Selection also continues during training: It is the initial shakedown that checks the features and motivations that are screened. The role of training is to enhance operational skill by providing knowledge about specific procedures and operational applications within the undercover arena.

This training phase includes focus on the behavioral or psychological issues that are important to enhancing skill development and building personal and program resources that support operational goals. It begins with personally sharing the results of entry screening and extends to looking at how personality dynamics interact under a variety of UC scenarios. This includes effects among members of the operational team and interactive issues arising from the personal traits and styles of the subjects targeted. Training is intended to instill personal and interpersonal insights, reinforced and integrated throughout the life cycle of the operation.

The training model employed here uses the Psychological Phased Support Model in the UC classroom. Each element of the model is explained, and within each, expectations are shaped. These include establishing the legitimacy of openly involving personal issues in the operational agenda. The concept is that the patient is the operation, and all who deal with it have feelings, beliefs, and ideas that need to be communicated. In other words, undercover work requires knowing where the players are emotionally. What counts? Anything that could influence undercover team members. The payoff is knowledge; those who direct the operation can make necessary alterations only if they know what is going on. To ensure reporting by operatives, responses to the information that is shared should be supportive. Even bad news is good, because corrections can be made only when problems are known. This concept—that the personal status of operatives is the business of the team—is further enhanced by providing whatever resources or changes may be necessary to ensure the well-being and safety of those involved. This is a two-way street. The players need to recognize that they are worthy of unusually involving commitment, provided they are determined to contribute to problem solving. They have to keep others informed about how they are doing. The Early Warning Model (Reiser & Sokol, 1971) is used to follow, monitor, and benevolently intervene as needed.

The concept behind the Early Warning Model is to recognize and correct difficulties before they become a risk to the individual's ability to effectively deal with the operation. Even well-screened and trained personnel, due to circumstances with which they are forced to deal, may not be ready to go undercover, or if undercover, to face specific activities or to continue with their role at all. Psychological readiness indicates that even the best officers can be diluted by potent, recent troubles, or less obvious circumstances that are cumulative over time. Knowing how the officer is doing will allow effective sequencing, modifying, and redirecting of efforts to ensure the operational plan. When readiness is in question, it is important to evaluate, and if indicated, prescriptively support those involved. Consultation may suggest changing the pace or scope of the operation, providing additional expertise or support to assist activities, directly intervening to psychologically aid team members, or a combination of these options. The consultation process starts with knowing how each person is doing, personally, with teammates or their significant others (who are not in the operation, but can surely influence those who are), and then assuring that needs are addressed.

Failure to work out difficulties as they occur is most frequently seen in signs of posttraumatic stress disorder (PTSD). This condition consists of stress indicators (anxiety, depression, ruminative thoughts, flashbacks, sleep disturbance, etc.). Onset of features could be simultaneous to an unusually stressful event, or as late as 6 months or more later. Addressing the problem at the time it happens is the surest way of reducing the impact, particularly in the long term. Because UCs can experience their stresses in isolation, close monitoring is essential, as is a reminder that it is important to let others know how they are feeling, what they think about, and how they are doing. This concept is first introduced when the psychologist meets the prospective undercover agent as they prepare for their new duties.

In training, investigators are given a structured clinical interview and provided with test feedback in a private session with the consulting psychologist. This permits clarification of information gathered during selection screening by using past experiences, test results, and motivations to fine tune expectations. Personal strengths and weaknesses are discussed in terms of developing best suited operational scenarios, cover identities, and coping strategies. Sources of emotional support are also identified. All of this helps to recognize how to revive the UC, so that operational planning can include opportunities for replenishment. An understanding is also sought of the accustomed reliance that is made of the operative by their significant others, and the extent to which their personal and emotional obligations affect their readiness. This interview with the psychologist is also a chance to meet the psychologist who would intervene should that be helpful during or after operational deployment. It is a personal opportunity to exchange information, emphasize program goals, correct misperceptions, and bond.

In the classroom, lecture material addresses psychological issues in each of the operational phases to include stress management, the Early Warning Model, and behavior-science-generated operational modifications—the concepts that underlie the psychologist's role. Team and self-monitoring of stress levels is conducted using an instructional guide that exemplifies changes in coping. These changes could be in feelings (emotions), behaviors, and physical symptoms that are more intense, frequent, or persistent. Figure 19.1 of chapter 19 on organizational management of stress (this volume) on the early warning signs of difficulty in coping (Hibler, 1978) shows the features used to demonstrate the kinds of things that could otherwise go unheeded. This list is not all inclusive; it is intended to legitimize the common sense of team members. For example, suicidal threats are not listed. You do not have to be a rocket scientist to figure out that when people talk about taking their life, they are not happy.

Critical incidents (e.g., shootings, woundings, deaths, etc.) are presented as specific examples of the need for intervention, but it should be emphasized that the more frequently encountered consultations arise from internal communication difficulties. Considering all of the possible combinations of players (undercovers, informants, case agents, and supervisors) all kinds of frustrations occur. Not the least of these are struggles in dealing with targeted subjects. That topic is addressed next.

OPERATIONAL PREPARATIONS AND PLANNING

Getting ready for an operation can involve a number of psychologically driven actions that assure readiness, define roles, and ensure compatibilities. This requires coordination among all members of the operational team.

Considerations include setting goals, arriving at shared expectations, establishing intelligence requirements, and anticipating dynamics between operatives, their supervisors, and the target. Finally, there is preparation for the inevitable midcourse corrections.

Every operation should have clearly defined goals, as well as a well-planned course with which to achieve them. The need for such specifics arises from the fact that it is all too easy to hold the undercover agent accountable for progress, when other factors are more likely to be responsible. One experienced federal law enforcement agency reports that about one third of all its undercover operations are closed out without arrests. The point is that even carefully conducted operations hold no guarantee of success. Such is the nature of this work, a point not popularized by Hollywood, nor well understood by highly motivated undercovers who can easily feel they failed. Well-defined operational goals and a course that requires periodic checks on progress are reasonable ways to realistically shape expectations. Failing to do so may result in misperceptions that artificially pressure the team during the operation and bring recriminations afterward.

Operational goals are formidably shaped by intelligence information about the target (i.e., persons, activities). Such information provides vital data to make judgments about the circumstances that will be faced. These circumstances include who is doing what and how. Simple "trolling" for activity by placing an undercover in a setting to see what pops up is very different; trolling is to operate without a plan. The risk of operating without careful planning is to leave the burden of success on the undercover, rather than relying on a network of people and information with which to understand what is happening. An intelligence network also permits an array of flexible options. Intelligence sources, of course, include an analysis of recorded complaints, witness and informant data, exploitation of subjects (co-conspirators) during interrogation, electronic eavesdrops, and other resources. There is never enough intelligence, but some basics should be addressed in order to prepare the undercover operative.

Although short-term operations, particularly within well-understood circumstances, may not require preparation as extensive as long-term, deep cover operations, it is always reasonable to ponder whether or not the operative is right for the case, and whether he or she is ready. Factors that contribute to the goodness of fit of the UC for the operation include the demands that will be made on the UC based on the nature of the transaction to be made, the sophistication of target, the past performance of the target regarding similar circumstances (to aid in predicting the target's reactions), the amount of control demanded by the target, and the likelihood of risk to the UC. These factors aid in planning the operation by dictating the amount of backstopping (bona fides and history) needed for the UC, the street knowledge that would be expected of the UC to sustain the cover, and a sense of what precautions to take to control the operation and protect the safety of the operative. Other issues to address in advance include an understanding of the compatibility of the UC to the target and other operational team members.

Compatibility is not necessarily a requirement, but where it does not occur easily, strategies should be available to ensure that things can be worked out. The term *compatibility* is intended to address the relative interpersonal harmony between people. The more effective the interpersonal chemistry, the greater the likelihood of trust, disclosure, and effectiveness. To conceptualize the potential for compatibility, a simple continuum is proposed. It is based on the work of William James. On one end of the continuum is the quality of *tender-mindedness*, and *tough-mindedness* on the other. As these terms imply, this concept captures a full range of personal power. People are normally distributed along this continuum, with most near the middle range. The need to be more careful in considering assignments and preparation comes with those at the extremes. Tender-minded types tend to be less assertive, easily influenced by their circumstances, and welcome offerings of advice and support from their case agent and supervisors. In comparison, tough-minded types are far more assertive, not easily influenced by their environment, and independently tell others to be reasonable and do it their way. Consider how this influences members of the operational team, for example, the UC and the handler—the case agent. The following combinations illustrate some of what has been experienced in the field

Example 1
Undercover operative   Case agent
Tender-minded   ×   Tender-minded

This is a circumstance in which there is frequently the complaint that no one is in charge. The reason is that there is a great deal of communication between the UC and the handler, but they are considered by supervisors to be "in bed together." The UC does many unnecessary things that are approved and appreciated by the handler in mutual admiration: lots of excuses, little action.

Example 2
Undercover operative   Case agent
Tender-minded   ×   Tough-minded

This is a situation in which the operative soon complains that he or she is not understood, appreciated, or treated with respect. The operative's need to be heard is a mismatch with the case agent, who is seen as being cold, insensitive, unappreciative, and overbearing. It may not be a problem of consequence in short operations, but in the long term it is a formula for UC stress.

Example 3

Undercover operative		Case agent
Tough-minded	×	Tender-minded

Here the operative is in control, the formula for an operation to be out of control. The operative is contemptuous of the handler, challenges directions, takes liberties, and struggles to be in charge. The case agent is powerless, embarrassed, and struggles to defend himself or herself.

Example 4

Undercover operative		Case agent
Tough-minded	×	Tough-minded

Actually, this has been found to be the smoothest running of the pairings. There is a natural, unspoken understanding of the need for each to give a great deal of distance to the other, and no hesitation to make clear what is important.

To summarize the compatibility issue within the operational team, there are several issues of importance for personnel at the extremes of the continuum. Tender-minded operatives can often work best with other UCs in multiple UC assignments. The presence of compatible others shares responsibility and provides opportunity for immediate feedback and support. They want to be understood, liked, and able to access their handlers at any time. Meetings should be frequent, social, and deal with personal as well as operational business. In contrast, tough-minded operatives prefer to meet only when necessary. In meetings, the handler should have an agenda (focusing on the operation rather than personal issues). The meeting is over when the agenda is done. Meetings will be businesslike and the UC will have a strong preference to make decisions whenever possible. This penchant to make the decisions by the tough-minded UC arises because they feel that being allowed to decide is a sign of confidence. This logic continues to predictably demonstrate that extensive oversight (micromanagement) by a supervisor of the tough-minded UC inevitably results in rebellion by the undercover. To avoid such problems, handlers and superiors should decide what should be done, and the tough-minded operative should be depended on (whenever possible) to determine how to do it.

The same dynamics apply to the interactions with targets. Where there is to be a long-term operation or where the objective of the operation is to obtain disclosures from the subjects, compatibility is very important. Screening of the operative easily identifies his or her attributes, including whether or not they could be described at one extreme or the other of the tender–tough-minded continuum. Targets are a little more difficult to evaluate, but indirect assessment can often be conducted with great accuracy and credibility.

Determining the personality features and dynamics of target subjects is typically not necessary in casual scenarios, such as a store front, street buys, or where subjects are unknown. Yet knowledge of these characteristics can be very helpful in scenarios that target specific subjects, or attempt to recruit a "weak link" (as an informant) in a criminal ring. Specifically, such information provides insights as to who should access, how, and under what circumstances. Additionally, preparation of an access UC is assisted by knowing beforehand about the same sorts of interactive dynamics with the subject (or between subjects) that have been planned with his or her own handling (case) agent. The consequence is that it is possible to anticipate issues regarding the subjects' need to struggle for control, power, or safety. Knowing the subjects' needs allows developing credibility and empowers disclosure. How such assessments are accomplished is actually straightforward. All that is needed is someone who is familiar with the subject(s) and a psychololologist who can administer and score standardized testing.

Mental health professionals are well practiced in understanding the features of persons who are described by their patients. Perhaps the most common example is of a marital partner, who is seen in isolation, and details many descriptions and features of their mate. As this example suggests, the descriptions are provided through the perceptions of the reporter. Accordingly, rather than a purely accurate picture, the descriptions are shaped by the reporter (as if distorted by a lens), which needs to be understood so that any distortions that occur can be recognized. As an example, consider a very wimpish informant who is angry at a targeted subject, feels abused by him or her, and is in part satisfying vengeful needs by cooperating with authorities. Surely descriptions by such a source would likely exaggerate the target's potency and be critical of the unfairness they have suffered. Of course, people who feel they have been abused or exploited justify their own innocence, excuse their failures, or try to please authorities. The adjustment made is to modify these descriptions, see the subject as having clay feet, and otherwise recognize the likelihood of distortions. An even more objective way to collect descriptions is for the psychologist to use a psychological test instrument, the NEOPI. This test (NEOPI/NEOPI–R)[1] has an observer form, which is completed by someone knowledgeable about the subject. This instrument has proven to have an unusually high interrater

---

[1]NEOPI/NEOPI–R is authored by Paul T. Costa, Jr. and Robert R. McCrae and published by Psychological Assessment Resources, Inc. The test measures five domains and 30 facet scores, to include neuroticism, narcissism, and openness. Scoring is facilitated by available on-site computer software.

reliability. This means that ratings by one observer are very much like those of another, even though the two reporters may not know each other, or when the nature or the relationships with the subject are very different (e.g., one being a girlfriend, another a co-conspirator). The psychologist will be able to use this test information on its own, or can also use its self-administered form of the test on the observer to better understand the dynamics shared between the observer and the target. Overall, such assessments have proven valuable in getting operations started. Assessments build confidence with access agents and provide additional information that supervisors respect as a contribution to controlling the case (confirming that specific UCs have promise against specific targets) and reducing risks due to mismatches.

Preparing undercovers for their roles can also include building cover identities. This is probably the area where supervisors will first see strivings or struggles. For the undercover who is trying to prove himself or herself there is often a pull for a role and accompanying accoutrements they feel necessary to be credible. Hollywood has also been of influence here; the thought of "Miami Vice" suggests the image. Requests for exotic trappings may be appropriate to the operation, but most often it is a reflection of the UC's personal needs. A rule of thumb often used in the intelligence business is handy here; covers should be as much like the actual, real, genuine UC as possible. People are more credible being themselves than something they are not; it is easier, too. Surely "bad guys" have all kinds of personality features, so rather than trying to work around some characteristic, incorporate it. There really are, of course, subjects out there who have some personal problems, including fear of flying, difficulty getting along with others, and the like. Whatever the real UC shortcomings are, it is simpler to blend them into the cover and role portrayed than to try to deny their presence.

The last pre-operational topic deals with being sure that the plan includes features that ensure opportunities to aid communications within the team and for catching breath and making operational adjustments. These issues become more important in longer or more intense operations. The first is to appoint a senior supervisor who is not in the chain of command for that operation as a safety valve. The concept is to have a person for the UC or the handler to go to without using their position as a hammer to jam up the other. The safety valve is a mediator, a marriage counselor, and a problem solver who can be asked to listen without creating a fuss. In other words, the safety valve concept is intended to provide an outlet with which to resolve difficulties without having to escalate problems to solve them. Additionally, the presence of a safety valve sends the message that some arguing is expected and planning has prepared the team to deal with it.

The next feature is the preplanning of refocus points. These reviews are necessary to confirm that things are on track, or to recognize the need for and to make needed changes. All involved need to participate, to ventilate without attribution. This can most effectively be conducted away from the operational arena. Real "subjects" take vacations and business trips; so can UCs in their "subject" role (just work the travel into the cover). These refocus points are a time to re-evaluate the original goals, reshape them as necessary, reassure all involved when progress is slow, and personally replenish. When the UC has been away from family, this can also be a time for reunion, and to reward (if accommodations are well selected) those who serve by waiting. This is an important issue. Such reunions provide the opportunity to check on the UC's personal needs, including the needs of those with whom they share closest support. Remember, if UCs have a problem, the operation has a problem. Finally, these refocus points are needed in planning from the outset because they are an effective forum for the unforseen issues that can never be anticipated. Refocus points need to be in the operational plan because undercovers are loathe to ask for a break. When things have been going disturbingly slowly, UCs feel they do not deserve a rest. When things are very busy, UCs do not want the operation to stop, even for a day.

DEPLOYMENT

Doing it. This phase is the test of selection, training, and operational planning. The results are responsive to critical questions, to include: Is it safe? Is it productive? What will it cost? Interestingly, costs are more than the financial and manpower expenses of the activity. They include the toll in demotivating deployed personnel and ruining careers; the consequences can be traumatizing.

All that has preceded should make this phase of the operation come together. For that reason, emphasis is placed on some of the issues that can easily be overlooked. These are factors that can be the glue that holds the elements together. These issues involve setting ground rules between contact or handling agent and operative or UC, caring for families left behind, tinkering and fiddling with communications and compatibilities, and stress management techniques.

Prior to initiating operational activity it can be helpful to have all of the participants get together to share plans, shore up details, and orient to one another. This pre-operational meet (PROM) is a dress rehearsal that is intended to unite the plan with the players. This is a time to establish mutual expectations as to who owns what, how things might be done, and what to do in emergencies. Examples include establishing how operatives and handlers are to communicate, how and where they are to meet, how often that is to occur, and under what circumstances additional contacts or meetings should be requested. Emergency procedures are particularly important, to include what to do if significant others in the life of the operatives require the attention of their loved one.

To facilitate the security and well-being of families left behind, operatives who are deployed away from their home base should have an office friend function as a go-between. In advance of the operation, that friend should know about any special needs of the family, and when the investigator is deployed, should be prepared to cut through red tape for the spouse should any agency business need to be transacted on their behalf. Additionally, consideration should be given to any special events that may be affected by the absence. Such events might include birthdays, anniversaries, and the like. This stay-behind liaison person also works out reunions, such as pre-planned focus point meetings (away from the operational setting). If it is at all possible for visits with the family at that time, they should be arranged. Emphasis on the folks at home is important for a number of reasons; the most frequently encountered regards the unintentional stress that is created for loved ones. The majority of undercover volunteers do so because they want to demonstrate their abilities, so they work for recognition. A very simple way to attempt success is to work long hours, even if much of the time spent is seen by others as not critical to the role. UCs often feel the need to live in cover long hours to "feel" the role. Families are often neglected when the UC is in role, because the family is not part of the cover. The trouble is that families in these circumstances often feel neglected, resulting in anger. When the return home finally does occur, it is not a pretty situation. Spouses call this a "glory boy" syndrome; it can be very destructive. The cure is obvious, UCs must get their priorities straight. Their family must come first, and everything else follows.

Fine tuning of the roles within the operational team inevitably occurs during deployment. Relationships are formed, tested, and fussed with. Failures in communication between team members are the chief reason for psychological intervention. It really is "marriage" counseling. If a safety valve was not assigned and a problem has arisen, it may be helpful to have an outlet on scene and see that a safety valve is appointed. If there are differences in opinion as to where things are, or what should be done, have a refocus meeting to assess status of the operation and the continuing suitability of the plan. If the players seem to be wavering, it may be time for a psychological dipstick, a chance to assure psychological readiness. Stress management is an important part of operatives' routine, and like the intensity of the role, can be modified to meet the changing challenge.

Stress management with undercover operatives is both a personal responsibility and an agency obligation. Yet the streetwise UCs know only they themselves can ensure their happiness. A conceptual frame that has been effective is one that says "You are the only one who will really know how hard it was and no one will really care." It is a sort of maudlin reality, but it has more credibility than any promises that could be made. Ultimately, UCs will leave this work, and must have something to return to. Planning for that future is an important stress management commitment that should be made at the beginning of the UC experience. That will better assure that priorities are not confused or lost. This is the start of a practical stress management model that focuses on stress inoculation by lifestyle.

Figure 14.2 serves to portray the sort of information that has been valuable to many operatives in training. Although they would ideally involve such personal commitment throughout their experiences, this sort of strategy has been considered to be reasonable for many deployed UCs. It legitimizes personal goal setting, organizationally supports taking company time to deal with stress, and puts the undercover on notice that there is an expectation that he or she will be committed to sharing the responsibility for working things out, but recognizing that some things are, quite simply, theirs.

DECOMPRESSION

This is the phase in which the operation is closed out, and the undercover shifts from being undercover to documenting what they did while undercover and preparing for trial. The operational plan should have addressed roles and activities, and ongoing refocus meetings should have developed a prosecutive strategy. Now the undercover role is ended, the cover is lost, and there must be a return to the role of law enforcement professional. It can be a change of great magnitude, especially if the operation is administratively shut down because it was not productive. As mentioned earlier, these can be real letdowns. Perhaps one way to additionally reassure disappointed personnel

Caring for my mind
- Goals (professional/personal)
- Time management (priorities)
- Dipstick check (on course?)

Caring for my body
- Exercise
- Diet
- Sleep
- Smoking and drinking

Caring for my soul
- Supportive relationships
- Quality time with others
- Quality time for self

Meeting my needs by facing them
- What's mine and what's reasonable to expect from others

FIG. 14.2. Practical stress management.

is to remind them that firemen get paid for each shift, whether there is a fire or not; they do their job by being able and ready. Cases that end with subjects to prosecute can have problems with undercovers, too.

For operatives who enjoyed the freedom of their cover and the break from routine and supervision, returning to their routine law enforcement role can be hard. Frequently they complain that they are unappreciated, that they feel micromanaged, and that is not helped by office staff who see the UC as a prima donna who thinks he or she is better than they are. In other instances the undercover who had close access to the target may feel that they betrayed the subject's trust, that they victimized the subject's family, or they empathize with the subject's circumstances that promoted the crimes. This is the Stockholm syndrome, plain and simple. It can be prevented if refocus sessions and debriefings during deployment include focus on how the operative feels about the subject, the subject's circumstances, and what will happen to the subject (and his or her family) when convicted. It is harder to reorient such feelings just before trial, but it can be accomplished most easily by understanding that this happens when basically "good" people are asked to do a hard job that requires deceit (something good people do not easily do) and betrayal of a relationship (which is also a bad thing in every other setting). It can be hard to see the awful consequences that fall on innocents, such as subject's family, knowing that you were involved in the crisis. The need however, is to redirect the responsibility to the subject, and to "reblue" the officer, who has nearly completed a very difficult job. It is also this kind of a message that says undercover duty is a place to visit but not to stay.

REINTEGRATION

In training it was emphasized that undercover life is not real. Living in cover is not being who someone really is. Undercover assignments are just another part of law enforcement, only a piece of the cloth of police work. It might be worthy of being a career-long specialty if it was personally or professionally enhancing, but that rarely happens. Personally it too easily puts the operative's life on hold, allowing a reversal of priorities. Professionally things are on hold, too. While the UC is out doing things his or her colleagues would not do, they are doing the things that must be done to be competitive and successful by organizational norms. Undercovers often cannot recapture the ground lost to their contemporaries. Organizations can nibble on their young; law enforcement agencies are carnivores that can devour their operatives. Returning undercover volunteers back to routine law enforcement duties is a managerial obligation.

During this phase operatives are often tense because they lose the status they believe they had in role. The men may have to again wear a necktie

and shave and everyone has to again look like a law enforcement professional. They have to go back to regular hours, regular work, and regular
people. It can all feel very irregular.

Reintegration is the "exit" phase of undercover duty. It is hardest for those
with the most unrealistic expectations. It is more likely to be satisfying if
personal goals are not subverted, because it is unlikely that the tour will
accelerate a career or enhance personal relationships. Reintegration allows
the replenishment of the operative in all their roles. Reintegration returns
the investigator to routine duties. That is good for the UC and the agency.

Psychological support during this "re-bluing" process includes ironing out
communications difficulties between co-workers and supervisors. Occasionally the UCs struggle with what they perceive to be rejection, criticism, and
underappreciation. They may expect the new supervisor to owe them for
all of their undercover work, but in reality the new line supervisor may have
little understanding of or appreciation for the contribution made by the UC.
An often heard complaint is that the supervisor is saying, "What have you
done for me lately?" Actually, this next supervisor may not be aware, at all,
of the effort spent while undercover; they can easily be indifferent about it.
The result is that there can be struggles for control. The line supervisor may
be seen by the agent as being all too nosy and invasive. No wonder undercover programs can have checkered reputations, and their progeny can be
resistant and challenging to manage. Likewise, managers can be perceived
by UCs returning to office work as cold, complaining, and confrontational.
Enhanced communication seems to make everything work better.

DISCUSSION

All of the six phases of psychological support have now been addressed. In
each examples of interventive or consultative activities have been presented
to explain how psychological perspectives could be applied across a variety
of undercover experiences. There are many ways for psychologists to work
closely with undercover programs, operations, and personnel. The model
proposed here requires the psychologist consultant to be an honest broker
who considers the mission to be the client. Functionally, the effort focuses on
entrance screening, readiness checks, and intervening in crises. Unlike the
expectation that Hollywood creates, problems most often involve communications difficulties between members of the undercover unit or management.

Mental health professionals can make significant contributions to undercover law enforcement activities, provided they know enough about the
needs generated by such work to offer relevant, practical help. The credibility
of the consultant will in great measure rest on his or her ability to earn the
trust of all involved.

REFERENCES

Farkas, G. M. (1986). Stress in undercover policing. In J. T. Reese & H. A. Goldstein (Eds.), *Psychological services for law enforcement* (pp. 443–440).

Hibler, N. S. (1978). The psychological autopsy. *Forensic Science Digest, 5,* 41–46.

Reiser, M., & Sokol, R. (1971). Training police sergeants in early warning signs of emotional upset. *Mental Hygiene, 55*(3), 303–307.

CHAPTER FIFTEEN

Using Hypnosis for Investigative Purposes

Neil S. Hibler

Levinson, Ltd., Alexandria, VA

Few investigative techniques have stirred as much controversy as the use of hypnosis to enhance the memories of those involved in criminal events. The critical importance of using hypnosis forensically lies in the potential to create false memories, information that is inaccurate but has the full confidence of the interviewee. The consequence is that there is no way for anyone to tell, on the basis of hypnotic recall alone, if the memory is enhanced or forever tainted. The process by which such contamination occurs is confabulation, complex psychological processes that supplant emotionally satisfying fantasy for weak, absent, or psychologically unacceptable recollections.

Police departments and courts across the country have been wrestling with how best to use the technique in the investigative process. Although the method has been documented in America for over 100 years (Gravitz, 1983), it did not come into vogue until the early 1970s. What has followed has been a lively swing and return of the legal pendulum.

What follows is a selective tracing of the controversy to the present. Departmental personnel need to be aware of the policy and guidelines that have been effective. Likewise, mental health professionals who would assist law enforcement agencies need to know how to contribute. Without a co ordinated approach, criminal investigations that could well be served by enhanced memory might fail to develop important information or, in the course, create legal difficulties that would eventually be to detrimental to prosecution. Following a brief discussion of the issues, the design of hypnosis programs used in the federal government are provided. Included are procedures that have been found effective in pursuing recollections hypnotically, both for investigative purposes, and in the courtroom. This presentation details the Federal Model for forensic hypnosis; today it is the most widely used guidance in the country (Hibler, 1984).

THE COURSE OF THE CONTROVERSY

Modern uses of hypnosis as a memory aid for law enforcement are developments of the pioneering work of Dr. Marty Reiser, founder of the Los Angeles Police Psychological Services Unit (Reiser, 1976; Reiser & Nielson, 1979). Initially, the technique seemed to be so promising that veteran police officers were trained in hypnosis and deployed to use the technique with witnesses and victims. At the same time, this ground swell of enthusiasm ran into escalating resistance from the scientific and professional communities.

Despite some dramatic case resolutions[1] there were also cases in which the hypnotically recalled information was clearly incorrect, despite vows of confidence from those who had been hypnotized. Scientifically, the complexity of hypnosis, memory, and individual psychology became readily apparent. The forensic effects of this complexity raised a great cause for precaution (American Medical Association, 1985).

Loftus (1979) made a further precautionary argument, emphasizing the natural malleability of memory and the potential of hypnosis to deform recollections even further. Orne (1979) also assessed the status of hypnotic recall, identifying potentially influential factors such as expectation and suggestion. There are in fact, many ways memory, much less hypnotically accessed memory, can be affected to result in inaccuracy (Hibler, 1987a).

Perhaps one way to delineate the influences on recall is to consider those that are internal (within the psyche of the interviewee) or external (environmental or interpersonal processes that affect those that are internal). Among the factors that comprise the internal sources of contamination are the mechanisms by which information is intrapsychically handled. These include dissonant effects of confabulation. There are also ego defense mechanisms that the witness self-imposes to understand the event in a manner that maintains self-esteem. External factors are the grist for this mill, which include all that which is perceived. External factors may directly or indirectly satisfy internal needs. Accordingly, the effects of suggestion, the need to

---

[1]One particularly noteworthy case was the kidnapping at Chowchilla, California. The recollections of a school bus driver, who had been abducted along with his bus full of young children, allowed the description of a vehicle used by the abductors, and a license plate, that resulted in identifying and convicting the guilty parties.

please, and other influences are complex and occur with or without hypnosis. There can be no guarantee that contaminants can be controlled simply by carefully managing the hypnotic interview. These are influences that can occur independently of hypnosis, and can be in place before the carefully conducted forensic hypnosis interview.

The natural interaction of these internal and external factors theoretically presents a high potential for distortion. Well-recognized examples include information that is incidentally exposed to a witness that may feed the need for closure. For instance one well-recognized eyewitness contamination would be to expose a suspect in isolation, as opposed to being in a lineup, and asking the witness if that suspect was the person who committed the crime. The press of such an exposure is to suggest that the suspect has been identified with confidence; it is entirely possible that the witness could be prone to endorse the identification. Another factor that is potentially suggested by this example is investigative zeal, which may evoke witnesses' desire to please. With this explanation, the endorsement could be a natural, unintentional act that satisfies the police, the implied suggestion being, "We (the police) did our best, and here's who we feel did it." The potential influence of implications such as these is that in virtually every case there are potent factors that could affect outcome, no matter what techniques are used.

In police work there are innumerable interactions that can alter the confidence and content of what witnesses and victims disclose. Some arise from interactions with police, whereas others may occur within the interactions shared with family, friends, or other witnesses. All of these influences operate without hypnosis (Hibler, 1984). That is why, for example, proper police procedure requires presentation of suspects in a lineup. Just the same, these potentially distorting factors have failed to be considered by a number of forensic hypnosis authors, who attribute forensic risks to hypnosis without consideration of other naturally occurring phenomena that affect the same, often incorrect outcome (e.g., Geiselman, Fisher, Cohen, Holland, & Surtes, 1985; Orne, 1979; Orne, Soskis, Dinges, Carota, Orne, & Tonry, 1985).

The consequence of the controversy over the suitability of hypnosis as a forensic tool has been to polarize the literature. The extremes are defined at one end by academic researchers, who are unable to evidence any scientific merit to the procedure when using laboratory studies, and at the other end, anecdotal evidence from actual applications, in which unquestionably accurate information was obtained with hypnosis (Hibler, 1992). Differences between mock crimes experienced under laboratory conditions, and the realities of being a crime witness appear to account for much of the failure for memory to be hypnotically enhanced in research studies. Watkins (1989) cogently examined shortcomings in studies that had been used to support prohibition of the forensic use of hypnosis. He concluded that there have been several sources of bias in such research, and that efforts to bar hypnosis from the forensic arena would be an injustice. Watkins proposed the careful use of the technique, emphasizing the indisputable importance that hypnosis has played when used with appropriate procedural safeguards.

Udolf (1983) further advocated the use of procedures that would guide a conservative use of the method. Reviewing a number of precautions suggested in the literature, he concluded that the independent corroboration of hypnotically derived information is the most certain way to ensure that recollections are accurate. Although this is a very conservative approach, the value of such confirmation is that it provides incontrovertible confirmation that the information derived was accurately recalled. For example, when a witness describes a subject of a robbery, and that subject is later identified and found to match evidence (e.g., fingerprints, DNA, etc.) found at the crime scene, or to be in possession of the booty (fruits of the crime) there is confirmation that the identification is accurate. Courts understand such evidence. If hypnosis was involved in obtaining information that resulted in the subject's identification, then it appears reasonable to declare that the hypnotic effort was accurate. Such incontestable results avoid conflict with the issues central to the forensic hypnosis controversy. These issues include evidencing the validity of trance or trance depth or other research-driven controversies, which could otherwise lose sight of the fact that memory may have been accurately recalled (as proven by independent corroboration).

The requirement for independent corroboration was first employed by agencies of the federal government (Ault, 1979) and remains the procedural hallmark for all nationally based law enforcement agencies in the United States (Hibler, 1987b). These agencies employ a number of other precautions to control as many of the potential memory contaminants as possible. Law enforcement authorities well know what the realities are; investigators need accurate information or they cannot resolve and prosecute their cases.

PROGRAM DEVELOPMENT AND MANAGEMENT

Establishing the capacity to conduct hypnotic interviews requires careful coordination between the law enforcement agency and a consulting (hypnotically trained) mental health professional. In the federal government liaison officers are appointed and trained, so that each agency has *hypnotic coordinators.*[2] These coordinators ensure that not just the interview is ar-

---

[2]This term was coined within the FBI, which trained a special agent to work within each major field office. Other federal investigative agencies have used smaller cadres, regionally positioning experienced investigators across the nation or the globe to assure ready coverage. The Federal Forensic Hypnosis Seminar trains federal investigators in a "team approach" (Ault, 1979) in which investigators work with mental health professionals in coordinating, conducting, and investigatively pursuing the results of hypnotic interviews.

ranged, but that the case is appropriate, the interviewee is available and prepared, records the session, and afterward, follows all relevant revelations with investigative leads. These leads are the goal of the interview; to identify a suspect, or otherwise continue the investigation with corroborated information. This law enforcement professional's role is, within the federal government, also of assistance during the hypnotic session.

Special agents are familiar with crime-fighting aids and procedures that are rarely known to mental health professionals. The consequence is that the assistance of these specially prepared investigators during hypnotic inquiry can well aid in recognizing case data that can be further developed via crime analysis or laboratory methods. There are also expectations of the mental health professional that can exceed traditional clinical training and experience.

Note that the federal government has adopted a model that requires interviews to be conducted by a mental health professional, licensed at the independent level of practice, certified in the use of hypnosis and appropriately experienced in forensic applications. Liability drives the mandate for professionals. The fact that the liable issues are psychological in nature enables only mental health professionals to reduce the risk of difficulties that can occur with interviewees who can be, and often are, emotionally traumatized. Lay hypnotists, to include law enforcement officers trained as lay hypnotists, cannot provide the professional and legal protection required.

Mental health professionals who have not had supervised experience with investigative uses of hypnosis need to seek supervision from a colleague recognized in the field. A recommended resource if supervision is needed, is the American Society of Clinical Hypnosis (ASCH).[3] ASCH is the largest professional hypnosis organization in the country and now the source for certifying hypnosis training for health professionals. This group has also developed an informed consent format, which is useful in nonfederal law enforcement cases. Federal cases have their own format, although both can be used (see Appendices A and B). Because practitioners interested in this work require training and supervision, departments who would use their services need to assure the requirement is fulfilled.

CASE REVIEW

All involved in the consideration and execution of a forensic hypnosis interview should consider not just how to conduct the session, but whether or not the circumstances are appropriate for the method (Hibler, 1984). Case review should be conducted within the agency to examine features that could define the promise of an attempt with hypnosis.

---

[3]The American Society of Clinical Hypnosis, 2200 East Devon Avenue, Suite 291, Des Plaines, IL 60018-4534, (708) 297-3317.

To start the consideration of a case, put hypnosis aside for a moment. Consider the potential value of testimony based solely on witness perceptions at the time of the crime. For example, is it logical to expect the witness or victim to have been able to see (or hear) anything of investigative importance under the conditions in which the exposure occurred? To use an actual example, hypnosis was declined in a multimillion dollar arson case because it was unrealistic to expect the witness to sufficiently enhance an image of a person running away, in the dark, over 100 yards away.

Further, there must be some incontrovertible way that any hypnotic recollection could be independently corroborated. Usually this requirement is addressed by physical evidence, such as fingerprints, hairs and fibers, ballistics, or serological evidence suitable for DNA assay. Without such confirmatory information, hypnosis is a fishing expedition that cannot be defended in the courtroom.

The need for evidence with which to confirm the identity of a suspect and other crime analysis dictates that it is premature to use hypnosis unless all traditional investigative methods are exhausted. The traditional methods will have to be employed even if hypnosis is used, so using them first may obviate the need for hypnotic efforts. Not surprisingly, about one third of the cases that seek permission for hypnosis early in the investigative process are solved simply by holding hypnosis in abeyance until routine actions are completed. Occasionally there are cases in which hypnosis might be used as the case initially breaks open, but these instances are rare. These are circumstances in which, for example, there is a kidnapping, and prosecutive risks can be sacrificed in order to save a life.

There are also contraindications for using hypnosis. As explained earlier, the memory of a witness or victim can be tainted by a number of processes. Many of these contaminants are naturally occurring, but others may be unintentional consequences of investigative activity or the good intentions of supportive relationships. Accordingly it is important to assure that in the case review process questions are asked to the potential interviewee as to who they have spoken with, and how their sense of the events may have changed. Departments that have an appreciation for the many issues of eyewitness testimony and hypnotic recall take care to isolate witnesses, avoid exposing them to case facts, and allow indecision without pressure to please investigators. It can be helpful to inquire about how else the interviewee has come to know about the case. Newspaper, television, radio, and conversations with friends and loved ones can have potent effects. Perhaps the worst case example of (potential) contamination has already been mentioned: the presentation of a suspect's photograph by police, accompanied by the suggestion that there is cause to consider that the individual is connected with the crime.

Another potential difficulty that can present when considering hypnosis, is that of a witness whose motivation to participate is suspect. There are cases on record in which reward notices have brought forth persons claiming to have critical knowledge, "if only" they could recall the details. Federal agencies have found polygraph examination a most helpful aid in determining the motivation of such persons. Alternately, the author is familiar with one case in which there was a witness who all too willingly lead authorities on a wild goose chase with the information he provided. He was eventually found to be the murderer.

No matter how important the case may appear, there is an overriding need to use hypnosis only when the indications are right. Pressure to solve the case should not be allowed to overcome logic; imprudently jumping the gun to use hypnosis is likely to bring even greater (political) attention when the method's misapplication detracts from the case's prosecution. Ideally, the decision to approve hypnosis is made by a senior representative of the agency, based on case facts, legal counsel, and counsel with a hypnosis consultant who would not be conducting interviews in the case.

Additional coordination is necessary to assure that legal considerations are addressed. Nonfederal cases may have state law precedents that suggest the importance of particular considerations or guidelines that would affect how hypnosis is conducted. Be certain that prosecutive counsel is obtained in this regard.

The mental health professional asked to directly aid investigators should not adjudicate issues that would affect the suitability of his or her services. For example, the mental health professional should not decide whether or not to approve the use of hypnosis. A priori knowledge of the case could later be claimed to have altered the hypnotic approach, such as coaching or persuading the interviewee to agree with preconceived conclusions. The department also needs to consider legal and investigative factors in order to assure the consultant that conditions for using the technique are appropriate.

PREPARING FOR THE HYPNOTIC INTERVIEW

A number of considerations are helpful in coordinating the actual interview. Persons anticipating the session may have many questions about what to expect from hypnosis, how the process will be conducted, and what will happen to any information they might provide. Each of these areas are important to the management of the interview and its potential to assist.

Ideally, anyone who would be considered for interview would be precautioned not to discuss the matter under investigation, and in every way possible, be kept from exposure to information regarding the investigation (e.g., media data). This should be routine for any witness (victim), and is an important precaution in all cases.

In addition to confirming precautions against unwitting contamination, the contact to arrange an approved interview should also shape the interviewee's expectations. For example, it is important to know that hypnosis will be conducted by a licensed mental health professional. Further, they should know that the session is videotaped to provide a detailed record of what is said and what occurs (to include nonverbal communication and possibly a number of hypnotic techniques that use finger movement or writing to respond). It may also be helpful for the interviewee to know that the method can take several hours, but that time passes quickly. Finally, there should be an opportunity to answer any questions that may arise regarding the procedures to be used or hypnosis itself. Investigators who handle arrangements should be able to pass along any questions raised by the interviewee, but ideally, would be sufficiently knowledgeable to answer the most commonly made inquiries. These include questions such as these:

Is hypnosis dangerous? What are the risks? There are no risks inherent to hypnosis itself. If someone is concerned that they are too troubled by the experience, or that it may be too great a challenge to face, the mental health professional will decide on the appropriateness of an interview.

What does it feel like to be in hypnosis? A variety of descriptions could be used to describe the experience, ranging from not feeling much different, to feeling very heavy, or light, or (alternately) both. As a natural state it is quite comfortable, even calm. What happens is that the capacity to focus or attend to detail is concentrated. Attention is usually intense enough that awareness of things other than the issue of interest is diluted. Just the same, even in deepest trance the interviewee is in control of their actions. For example, interviewees can decide not to answer a question, can ask for a break, or even terminate the trance on their own.

If the experience (the crime) was very difficult to endure, how does the mental health professional deal with an interviewee's reluctance to again face their ordeal? This is one reason why mental health professionals are involved in the process. They are experts in dealing with anxious persons, and should be prepared to work comfortably with an interviewee who has been traumatized. Hypnosis is a treatment modality of choice for dealing with anxiety-related disorders. Its use in the investigative interview capitalizes on its tranquilizing qualities. Even though these interviews are not used as psychotherapy, they nonetheless have a therapeutic effect.

Will the interviewee remember everything, and will it be accurate? Expectations should be very modest; consider the interview an experiment. Maybe it will be helpful, maybe it will not. The likelihood is that in hypnosis recollections will include some information previously described, as well as some that is different (in conflict with earlier statements), or some may be entirely new. The interview is not intended to be a test of the veracity of the interviewee because any recollection could be inaccurate, with or without hypnosis.

What will be done with the information the interviewee might provide?
Any recollections that have investigative interest will be turned over to
authorities to pursue. The product of the interview is data with which to
conduct further investigation. It is of unknown accuracy or value, and
has to be corroborated before it can have probative merit.

Arrangements for the location of the interview should include a quiet
space that is large enough for the participants to be videotaped. The equipment to be used should be able to record at least 2 hours, without interruption, and ideally it would have a character-generated digital clock within
the recorded image. The clock is necessary to evidence the completeness
of the recording and is helpful as an index to locate segments for review.
If the camera does not have its own time-keeping device, a clock can be
placed in camera view so that the recorded image includes the elapsed time.
As important as the video recording is the quality of the audio component
of the record. What really is needed is a microphone that is separate from
the camera; built-in microphones do not have the capacity to assure a clear,
distinct record. The best circumstance is for each person in the interview to
have a lavaliere microphone that inputs sound through a mixer. Such a
set-up allows all involved to be on the record, and for adjustments to be
made, through the mixer, so that recording levels have a balanced quality.
If multiple microphones are not available, a lavaliere microphone for the
interviewee may be sufficient to assure that their remarks are saved.
Incidently, it is often helpful to drive multiple VHS recorders by connecting
them in series, so that multiple, original quality tapes are available. Designate
one set of the tapes produced as a master, protected by being entered into
evidence. Other copies can be used for review, and shared with other
jurisdictive agencies if multiple jurisdictions are involved.
The arrangements for an interview conclude by bringing the interviewee,
the mental health professional, and investigators together in a quiet, comfortable setting that is set up with a camera and microphones.

CONDUCTING THE INTERVIEW

Federal investigators use a planned script, a format that sequences the interview using logical, legal, and memory-enhancing elements that facilitate
information processing and protect the integrity of the procedure. Also important in this structure is a progressive development of information that
permits rapport to build. Because federal investigators employ a team model
(using multidisciplinary specialists), their outline is detailed to integrate the
interactions of the participants.

Nonfederal agencies, or private practitioners, can modify the federal outline that follows, as local courts may present the need to be responsive to
court precedents that employ Hurd Rules.[4] The major differences in the
Federal Model and suggestions in Hurd, is the Federal Model's requirement
for case review, the use of multidisciplinary interviewers, and the requirement for independent corroboration of information developed with hypnosis. One aspect of the Hurd provisions is for only the interviewee and the
mental health professional to be involved.

In both models, all aspects of the interview are tape recorded. However
there are times when the trauma experienced by an interviewee has been
significant, and a brief, private meeting is warranted to ascertain his or her
emotional status (and the appropriateness of an interview). Just prior to the
interview the mental health professional may be introduced to the interviewee, and can privately discuss the interviewee's adjustment and condition.
Emotional contraindications are not usually present but need to be considered to ensure the welfare of the interviewee. Indications of particular concern would include prepsychotic levels of distress, disordered thinking or
reality contact, or inappropriate expectations (e.g., well-engrained misperceptions about hypnosis, the purpose of the interview, or indications to
doubt their voluntariness).

Clinicians should recognize that for many traumatized interviewees hypnotic recall may get in touch with feelings as well as memory. The result is
often for abreactions to occur. These are dramatic emotional displays that
can suddenly erupt, releasing repressed feelings that had been bottled up
until accessed during trance. Although not essentially dangerous, these displays can be quite unsettling if not expected, particularly if the mental health
professional is not prepared to work through the outburst with the interviewee. Not only must the hypnotically qualified mental health professional
be experienced in dealing with trauma, he or she should be certain that
others present have an understanding of what hypnotic behavior might
occur. The hypnotherapist is in charge of the interview and must be able
to perform whatever intervention may be needed to ensure the comfort and
well-being of the interviewee.

The following outline summarizes the content, flow, and interaction
among participants during interviews conducted by our government's agencies.

---

[4]Hurd Rules were devised by Dr. Martin Orne in *State v. Hurd* (1981) 86 N.J. 525. A. 2d
86. These guidelines attribute a risk to the presence of anyone other than the hypnotherapist
being present during interview. Although there has been significant evidence since that time
that this (and other precautions suggested) may be less important than assumed, many
jurisdictions have nonetheless adopted these safeguards, establishing precedence for forensic
uses of hypnosis for memory enhancement.

STRUCTURED INTERVIEW OUTLINE (FEDERAL MODEL)

Participants include the hypnotically qualified mental health professional, a specially trained investigator, the interviewee, and as appropriate, others who would operate the camera, do police artist drawings, or review case facts to aid the hypnotic team in knowing if further inquiry about any specific area could be important.

If the case investigator is present during the interview, any communications offered should be in writing; a note passed to the special agent participating in the interview (on receipt, the interviewing agent considers whether or not to ask a question based on the note, phrasing and sequencing the question to flow with the inquiry; the agent also saves the note, after having written down the time the note was received and initialing it, all such communications are retained with agents' notes).

Everything that happens is video recorded.

Opening the Interview

Special Agent (Hypnosis Coordinator):

- Announces the location of the interview, the date, the current time, and identifies self and all others present.
- Asks permission from the interviewee to tape record the interview.
- States the purpose of the interview (matches the issue to be discussed that is stated on the consent form).
- Turns attention to the mental health professional.

Mental Health Professional:

- Explains hypnosis, which may include: asking the interviewee if he or she has previously been in hypnosis and what he or she knows about hypnosis, defining hypnosis, explaining misconceptions, and describing trance characteristics and what it feels like.
- Explains procedures to be used, which may include: trance induction, trance deepening, time distortion as used in regressing to the event, and inquiry techniques (e.g., television effects, ideomotor signaling, automatic writing, posthypnotic suggestion, etc.)
- Explains potential risks (e.g., re-experiencing of unpleasant feelings if the event was an uncomfortable experience, adding that if the interviewee at any time would like assistance, he or she is to ask for help).
- Mentions that the special agent (hypnosis coordinator) will also ask questions and attend to administrative requirements.
- Attention is then turned to the special agent (hypnosis coordinator).

Inquiring Without Hypnosis

Hypnosis Coordinator:

- Obtains informed consent by asking the interviewee to read, and if he or she concurs, to sign the consent form. The coordinator then asks the mental health professional to also sign, acknowledging that prior to granting consent the interviewee was advised about the procedures to be used and any risks that could occur.

- Conducts (nonhypnotic) debriefing and tells the interviewee that now (as well as later, in hypnosis) he or she will be asked to (chronologically) describe what happened, and that there will be many opportunities to repeat the sequence of events, as it will be reviewed over and over again. Next, the hypnosis coordinator asks the interviewee to explain the event as it appears now, regardless of whether that is how he or she described it before, and asks the interviewee to describe the event in question and "to begin at the beginning." Questions are kept to a minimum and all inquiry is open ended (e.g., "How else might you describe that? What else might be said about that? What makes it appear that way?"). The coordinator uses silence comfortably, not rushing, pushing, or reinforcing any statements, and prompts or acknowledgments are used only as necessary to move descriptions along (e.g., "Uh-huh . . . I understand . . . I hear you . . . Okay . . . , etc.). The interviewee is asked to go over the event again; questions are asked in the context of the interviewee's descriptions (the event is described until interviewers are satisfied that they have a good understanding of it).

- Attention is then turned to mental health professional (to involve hypnosis).

Mental Health Professional:

- As an option, to prepare the interviewee, may induce trance as an introduction to hypnosis, and demonstrate trance phenomena to develop familiarity and build comfort with the procedure, and rapport with the hypnotherapist, and validate trance by actively demonstrating trance phenomenon, or by passive observation of natural trance phenomenon.

- Induces the trance.

- Enacts age and time regression to re-experience the event. Note: Trance management is the responsibility of the mental health professional. During hypnosis he or she is present to deal with any of the interviewee's needs; interrupting to assist in regaining comfort if the interviewee becomes distraught, responding to the interviewee when asked, and managing abreactions if they occur.

- Turns attention to the hypnotic coordinator to conduct an inquiry.

Inquiring With Hypnosis

Hypnotic Coordinator:

- Conducts hypnotic debriefing useing the same chronological format as in earlier nonhypnotic inquiry and incorporating (open-ended) questions passed along from the case investigator, asking them at the point in the interviewee's narrative where the issue is in context. The hypnosis coordinator works with mental health professional as well. Once simple recall is exhausted, the doctor explores areas with techniques such as ideomotor signaling and automatic writing, and posthypnotic suggestions for working with a police artist, or later, for spontaneous recall. The doctor also terminates the trance in order to change videotapes, or to allow for meals, rests, or other breaks. The coordinator announces prior to a break (a period in which the interviewee is off camera) that no one speak about the case and states the time that the interruption is occurring, then announces the time the taping picks up, and asks the interviewee if he or she discussed the case while off camera (which should not have happened, but if so, detail what was said).

If the interviewee incriminates himself or herself, the hypnotic coordinator has the mental health professional terminate hypnosis and the interview. The hypnotic coordinator should advise the interviewee of his or her rights and seek legal counsel from prosecutive authorities before continuing.

Mental Health Professional:

- Terminates trance.
- Asks if the interviewee is okay (should assure that the interviewee feels alright before concluding the association).

As this outline indicates, the interview is used as fully as possible to understand what happened. Keeping in mind that the purpose of the interview is to explore memory to the maximum, this multidisciplinary approach capitalizes on such expertise as best serves the need. It permits detectives to use their skills, and professional hypnosis experts to use theirs. After the interview the hypnotic coordinator reviews notes and recordings and assures that investigative leads are sent out in the attempt to corroborate important information that was developed.

USE OF HYPNOTICALLY DEVELOPED INFORMATION
IN COURT

The prosecutive strategy must incorporate how to frame the hypnosis issue. The strategy for using information that was hypnotically derived and independently corroborated is to present the independent corroboration as evidence, not the hypnotic process.

During discovery, the defense will most likely seek copies of tape recordings, which is to be expected. The defense will likely have their own expert examine this material, and that expert may render opinions as to the evidence of trance, depth, and the course of the interview. The bottom line however, is whether or not the hypnotically recalled information did in fact correctly identify facts and circumstances that can be proven to relate to a specific suspect or other issues in the case.

The departmental hypnosis expert can have opinions regarding any number of issues relative to the interview he or she conducted, but the only way of knowing if efforts were valid is the independent corroboration. Accordingly, other issues, such as proving the presence of hypnosis and so on can be avoided, as the proof of memory enhancement is evident in the confirmation.

CONCLUSIONS

The use of hypnosis for investigative purposes is modestly holding up to the test of time. The initial zeal with which it was applied gave way to theoretically based controls that have been adopted by some courts, in spite of any evidence that guidelines alone really safeguard memory. Cases in the federal arena have developed a growing set of precedents in which the Federal Model was helpful to the investigation and was supportable in the courtroom.

Federal agencies have enjoyed about a 12% rate of success, with hypnosis. This means that about one case in eight is materially enhanced, as demonstrated by corroborated results. In these cases the investigation was able to proceed, sometimes to only conclude with later, nonhypnotic barriers. However, that 12% is a measure of hope, and a serious consideration for cases that are stalemated and unable to continue. Certainly hypnosis is not appropriate in many cases, and even when it is, there is only a very modest possibility that it will help. Just the same, hypnosis is well demonstrated as a potentially valuable tool for law enforcement. Whether it aids or confuses an investigation will depend on whether it is used in a fashion that respects the limits of hypnosis, investigative capability, and the reality of the court.

APPENDIX A: FEDERAL MODEL

Consent for Hypnosis

I *(print name)*_____ hereby agree, voluntarily and freely, to undergo hypnosis, and be interviewed under hypnosis to assist the (NAME OF LAW ENFORCEMENT AGENCY) with an investigation in progress. I understand that, unless I request otherwise, a Special Agent of the (NAME OF LAW ENFORCEMENT AGENCY) may be present during the interview. I also understand that a transcript or other method of preservation may be made of the interview and that the transcript or other method of preservation may be used for any lawful purpose connected with the investigation or action based thereon. Dr. (NAME OF HYPNOTICALLY QUALIFIED MENTAL HEALTH PROFESSIONAL), a mental health professional, has explained the procedure(s) to be used and that, while recalling details of unpleasant events, I may experience some discomfort; but that apart from such discomfort there are no known risks or expected complications from the procedure to be used. The purpose of the interview under hypnosis is to assist my memory in recalling the following:

_____

X_____   _____
SIGNATURE OF INTERVIEWEE   DATE

I have personally counseled the interviewee on the purpose of the interview and on the procedure to be performed.

_____   _____
SIGNATURE OF MENTAL HEALTH PROFESSIONAL   *DATE*

APPENDIX B: SAMPLE INFORMED CONSENT
FOR FORENSIC HYPNOSIS INTERVIEWS

Consent for Hypnosis

DATE: _____

TIME: _____

I, _____, hereby agree voluntarily and freely, to undergo hypnosis and be interviewed under hypnosis in order to assist with an investigation. I understand that videotape and audiotape recordings will be made of the entire interview and that these methods of preservation of the interview may be used, as to be determined by my attorneys, for any lawful purpose connected with this investigation. In many jurisdictions, courts have held that a person who has been hypnotized cannot testify in court about anything remembered during or after the hypnosis, except in their own behalf. Consequently, in consenting to hypnosis, I understand there is a possibility that anything remembered, once the hypnosis begins, may not be admissible in a court of law. The only way to fully protect my potential right to testify is to forego the use of hypnosis. I understand that the procedural guidelines courts require in hypnosis situations will be followed. But, I have had the opportunity to consult with legal counsel concerning my rights, and in consenting to hypnosis, I hereby agree that I do not have a cause of action against [*mental health professional's name*].

It has been explained to me that memory is imperfect, whether or not hypnosis is used. Memory is not like a tape recorder, and rarely will all the details of any recollection be fully accurate. People have been shown to be capable of filling in gaps in memory, of distorting information, and of being influenced in what is "remembered" by leading questions or suggestions. Our memories may sometimes be influenced through reading, movies, TV, or conversations. Thus, research has shown that there is no guarantee that information remembered through hypnosis (or through ordinary recall) is factually accurate. On the other hand, information that is so remembered through hypnosis may in fact be accurate. But, the only way one may know definitively whether something recalled under hypnosis is accurate is to obtain independent corroboration. Thus, if I should remember something under hypnosis, I should regard this information as simply one more source of data that cannot be relied on as more accurate or necessarily superior to material already in conscious awareness, without corroboration.

_____, a mental health professional, has explained the procedures to be used during the course of this hypnosis session and any questions I had concerning this procedure have been answered to my satisfaction. The purpose of this interview under hypnosis is to assist my memory in recalling _____

_____
_____
_____
_____
_____.

                                     _____
                                            Interviewee
Witnesses:

_____
Mental Health Professional

_____
Witness

ACKNOWLEDGMENTS

This chapter is an update and expansion of *Managing a Forensic Hypnosis Program*, a paper presented at the Federal Bureau of Investigation's World Conference on Police Psychology, Quantico, VA, December 1985. The views of the author do not necessarily represent those of the United States Government.

REFERENCES

American Medical Association. (1985). Scientific status of refreshing recollection by the use of hypnosis. *Journal of the American Medical Association, 253*, 1918–1923.

Ault, R. L. (1979). FBI guidelines for use of hypnosis. *International Journal of Clinical and Experimental Hypnosis, 27*, 449–451.

Geiselman, R., Fisher, R., Cohen, G., Holland, H., & Surtes, L. (1985). Eyewitness memory enhancement in the police interview. *Journal of Applied Psychology, 27*, 358–418.

Gravitz, M. (1983). An early case of investigative hypnosis: A brief communication. *International Journal of Clinical and Experimental Hypnosis, 31*, 224–226.

Hibler, N. (1984). Forensic hypnosis: To hypnotize or not to hypnotize, that is the question! *American Journal of Clinical Hypnosis, 27*, 52–57.

Hibler, N. (1987a). *The role of suggestion in police interviews*. Paper presented at the 29th Annual Scientific Meeting of the American Society of Clinical Hypnosis, Las Vegas, NV.

Hibler, N. (1987b). *The use of hypnosis by investigative agencies of the United States*. Paper presented at the I-Denta International Congress on Terrorism, Stuttgart, Germany.

Hibler, N. (1992). *"Real-life" experiences with forensic hypnosis*. Paper presented at the 1992 Annual Scientific Meeting of the Society for Clinical and Experimental Hypnosis, Alexandria, VA.

Loftus, E. (1979). *Eye-witness testimony*. Cambridge, MA: Harvard University Press.

Orne, M. (1979). The use and misuse of hypnosis in court. *The International Journal of Clinical and Experimental Hypnosis, 27,* 311–341.

Orne, M. T., Soskis, D. A., Dinges, D. F., Carota Orne, E., & Tonry, M. H. (1985). Hypnotically refreshed testimony: Enhanced memory or tampering with evidence? In *National Institute of Justice: Issues and practices in criminal justice.* (pp.). Washington, DC: U.S. Government Printing Office.

Reiser, M. (1976, November). Hypnosis as a tool in criminal investigation. *The Police Chief,* pp. 36–40.

Reiser, M., & Nielson, M. (1979, November). *Investigative hypnosis—A developing specialty.* Paper presented at the Annual Conference of the American Society of Clinical Hypnosis, San Francisco, CA.

State v. Hurd, 86 NJ 525 A. 2d 86 (1981).

Udolf, R. (1983). *Forensic hypnosis.* Lexington, MA: Lexington Books.

Watkins, J. G. (1989). Hypnotic hypernesia and forensic hypnosis: A cross-examination. *American Journal of Clinical Hypnosis, 32,* 71–83.

CHAPTER SIXTEEN

Psychological Autopsy:
An Investigative Aid

Michael G. Gelles
Naval Criminal Investigative Service

The psychological autopsy is a postmortem investigative tool that helps to ascertain the decedent's role in his own demise. It is an investigative tool that helps to reconstruct the decedent's background, personal relationships, habits, character, and coping patterns. Its purpose is to contribute to the understanding of the relationship between the decedent's lifestyle and his death. The purpose of this chapter is to provide some guidelines, definitions, and applications of this procedure in law enforcement and forensic investigations. The most frequent question asked in an investigation of a medically unattended death is whether the individual who was alone committed suicide or died accidentally. On occasion the question is asked whether another person was present and whether it was intended or not. These questions involve complex issues of fact, behavior, and intent, and are at times unanswerable. Opinions should not be rendered without detailed information about the death scene and victim's history (Hazelwood, Dietz, & Burgess, 1981).

By definition a psychological autopsy is a clinical-investigative tool that assists in clarifying the manner of death in a suicide, homicide, or accidental death by focusing on the psychological aspects of the death. Its primary purpose is to understand the circumstances and state of mind of the victim at the time of death. The procedure involves the reconstruction of the lifestyle and circumstances of the victim together with the details of behaviors and events that led to the death of the individual. The psychological autopsy is a postdictive analysis. It is speculative and probabilistic. However, it is the best conclusion giving a logical understanding of the relationship between the deceased and the events and behaviors that preceded the death (Berman & Litman, 1993). The accuracy of a psychological autopsy is contingent on available records and interviewees. The technique utilizes interviews and the review of records to form the foundation of the opinion. Several adjunctive scales can be utilized in conjunction with a psychological autopsy. These scales provide support to a subjective opinion. These empirically referenced scales can improve the overall reliability and validity of the psychological autopsy. It is often because of an absence of information that the psychological autopsy is utilized; therefore, the collection and analysis of data in the most professional and empirical fashion is critical. Its specific purpose is to form a logical understanding of death from tangible physical evidence, documented life events, and intangible and often elusive emotional features.

There have been a variety of adaptations to the psychological autopsy since its inception in 1958, by Robert Litman. The original procedure was requested by the Los Angeles County Medical Examiner to clarify the manner of death through the understanding of behavior and personality factors. The psychological autopsy serves as an adjunctive aid to the pathologist or medical examiner-coroner in determining the manner of death of a decedent. It can provide the medical examiner with an additional dimension in assessing the circumstances, behaviors, and motivations of the decedent prior to his or her demise. It can also serve the forensic pathologist in a way that is similar to the way in which the psychological evaluation serves the internist by clarifying the relationship of psychological factors to physical illness. It provides assistance to the medical examiner who attempts to evaluate all dimensions of a death, from the physiological to the behavioral. The psychological autopsy can also function as a consultative aid to lawyers and litigants in regard to the disposition of civil suits and insurance claims. Finally, the psychological autopsy can contribute in clarifying those behavioral factors that may differentiate an accidental death from a suicide. The accurate representation of manner of death on death certificates impacts on the subsequent collection of statistics. This procedure can have enormous ramifications in studying and preventing suicide and promoting safety (Shneidman, 1993).

This chapter focuses on the psychological autopsy as it pertains to police psychology and its use as an investigative aid in law enforcement. In addition to its use in helping to differentiate a suicide from an accidental death, the psychological autopsy can function as a profile. Similar to a psychological profile, it can provide valuable insight into the deceased in a variety of criminal investigations. In many cases, the manner of death of an individual is very clear (e.g., homicide or suicide); however, at other times the circumstances of the death may be vague. The lack of clarity at times may lead to some doubt for an investigator as to whether the death was self-inflicted or accidental. In the case of homicide, the character style, behaviors, and motivations of the decedent prior to death may prove to be helpful in developing leads or suspects in the case. More specifically, the reconstruction of a murder victim's personality may provide the investigator with insight into the types of activities engaged in or individuals the deceased affiliated with prior to death.

Given that psychological profiles are generated from crime scene and investigative interviews, the use of the victim profiles may also provide an additional perspective. The term *equivocal death analysis* is often used synonymously with psychological autopsy. It is frequently conducted by criminal investigators. The procedure, which is very similar if not identical, puts emphasis on the crime scene. Because criminal investigators specialize in crime scene study, they avail themselves of data derived from forensic science. Psychologists who have expertise in behavioral science derive information from character study and the understanding of behavior. Therefore, the term *psychological autopsy* best fits the work of mental health professionals. It is important for any clinician to recognize the implications and ramifications of this procedure. The technique can be met with resistance from a variety of sources. Psychological opinion remains highly controversial due to its subjectivity and at times mystical influence. Therefore, the opinion offered in a psychological report must be sensitive to the potential reactivity and possible overinvestment in the psychologist's opinion. Due to unfamiliarity in the forensic setting, law enforcement personnel may rely on the psychological opinion to resolve vague and uncertain cases. Some may suggest that the psychological autopsy is as good as the investigation. It is important for both law enforcement personnel and professionals to recognize that the psychological autopsy is a clinical investigative tool that relies on the investigation for basic facts and circumstances. However, it goes beyond investigative data with the use of personality theory and behavioral data to render opinions and formulations regarding the deceased. Finally, it is important to re-emphasize that the result is an opinion and just that.

There are few guidelines and standards for conducting a psychological autopsy. A recent American Psychological Association (APA) panel that reviewed the Iowa disaster has made several valuable procedural recommendations to include a statement regarding its speculative nature and the need for psychologists to conduct several interviews themselves in the reconstruction of the personality (Poythress et al., 1993). The report should always emphasize that the results are a speculative review of events and conclusions regarding the personality of the deceased. Therefore, the report is subject to considerable variability and should be viewed only as an investigative aid. Although it has been recommended that clinicians collect their own data in a psychological reconstruction, this process is often impractical.

In an attempt to validate the subjective, several empirically based criterion-referenced scales have been developed to more accurately evaluate the behavior that is attributed to the development of a decision regarding manner of death (Jobes, Casey, Berman, & Wright, 1991; Rosenberg et. al., 1988). The analysis utilizes information about the deceased and aids in reconstructing the deceased's contributions to his or her own demise (Jobes et al. 1991). These criterion-referenced scales offer specific research support regarding the differentiation between suicide and accidental death.

Psychological autopsies on the average take from 12 to 20 hours to complete. Although there are no specific agreed-upon outlines to follow, there is some agreement as to the type of data that should be collected, and the individuals who should be interviewed (Ebert, 1987). This chapter provides some suggested outlines that may assist in the interview and collection of data from individuals who have relevant information to provide to an investigation. This chapter also offers some suggested training experiences for psychologists and investigators who will conduct and participate in the review.

The necessity for accuracy and a thorough review of available data is unquestionable in any clinical assessment. However, much of the data is contingent on the investigation and investigative agents. Although some interviews can be conducted by the psychologist (and several interviews should, especially family and close peers), the bulk of the procedure is completed by the investigator.

The validity of the technique is contingent on the accuracy of the investigation. The investigatory data that is compiled is critical to the psychologist conducting the review. It is the only representative data he or she has regarding the lifestyle of the deceased.

TRAINING

Although any psychologist can conduct a psychological autopsy it is strongly suggested that the psychologist become as familiar as possible with the process of criminal investigation and forensic pathology. It is suggested that the clinician become familiar with the proceedings of police investigations, crime scene analysis, and interviewing techniques. Several crime scene seminars are given throughout the country in accordance with law enforcement continued education. Additionally, the psychologist should attempt to attend a basic forensic pathology seminar to become familiar with a variety of death scenarios, wounds, pathology, environmental conditions, and physical autopsy findings. Investigative interviewing seminars are also available to provide insight into the manner in which the investigators conduct the interview during the investigations. Finally, the psychologist should become well versed in the suicidology literature, personality theory, and high-risk behavior.

The psychologist's role is not to critique the investigation but to become familiar with and critical of the type and manner in which evidence was collected. The rule of thumb should be not to accept what is present, but to request what is missing to ensure that all the necessary information is available for a thorough and comprehensive review.

Because it is important for the psychologist to become familiar with the law enforcement procedures it is also important for the investigators to receive some training in the manner in which psychological autopsies are conducted. It should be considered important to provide training to criminal investigators regarding the types of information and data necessary to conduct a psychological autopsy. This should be considered a first-line control in regard to the variability of investigations and collection of data used in psychological reviews. This form of training can be easily achieved during any in-service or basic investigations course. There is always potential for the loss of evidence at a crime scene and during an investigation. Often the investigator is not thinking about an investigation with the same concerns as a psychologist conducting a psychological autopsy. Earlier in this chapter several recommendations were offered regarding the type of adjunctive training a psychologist should have to understand and be conversant with in the world of forensic investigations. Investigators would benefit from training in the areas of suicidology, autoeroticism, self-deliverance (Humphrey, 1991), high-risk behavior, and substance abuse. The investigator would further benefit from training in the type of evidence that is of interest and importance to a psychological autopsy: personal effects, books, videos, and correspondence. Providing investigators with outlines regarding interview strategies and specific types of information is invaluable on later review of secondhand data. This chapter should serve as a guideline for both investigator and psychologist.

CONDUCTING THE PSYCHOLOGICAL AUTOPSY

There are several questions that are to be answered when conducting this procedure. The primary questions include: How did the individual die and when? Why at that particular time? What is the most probable mode of death? Why might the individual commit suicide (Shneidman, 1993)? Secondary questions would include: What was the deceased like? What occurred in his or her life that could have been stressful? What were his or her reactions to those stressors? Therefore, the psychological autopsy attempts to understand the deceased's personality characteristics. From this the individual's influence on a situation is clarified, as are the effects of those events on the individual's capacity to endure stressful circumstances and difficult situations.

The first step in a case review is to examine all that is available: Crime scene photographs, descriptions, drawings, conditions, witnesses, environmental conditions, and location are of particular interest in regard to motivation, and what a person may have been doing at a particular place during a particular time under certain environmental conditions. This is followed by record reviews and interviews. The clinician should prepare questions for the investigator or provide the investigator with a prepared outline of additional material that will help to clarify issues regarding behavior and motivation.

After the completion of record reviews and any additional collection of interview data, the clinician should provide an analysis and opinion regarding the case. An attempt should be made to reconstruct the static features of the personality, coping style, reaction to stress, temperament, attachment, and interpersonal relationships. Trauma in life should be explained in regard to its impact on personality development and coping. Also any medical or mental disease process, if present, should be factored into the style in which the individual lived, as well as substance use and abuse. Family history in regard to ages and causes of death of deceased family members should be noted. Finally, a time line should be constructed executing as closely as possible the last hour to days to weeks of the individual's life, for up to 12 months. Close attention should be paid to circumstances and communications prior to death that may explain how the individual died. Particular focus on self-inflicted wounds and intent in differentiating accidental death or suicide is critical. The results of the analysis should be communicated in a clearly written report documenting the sources of information, and a statement regarding the speculative nature of the findings.

Procedure

Begin with the necessary crime scene information taken from police reports. Identify information that will also include important data describing status of relationships and support systems as well as occupational status. The combination of occupation and education gives insight into socioeconomic status of the deceased.

Include name, age and date of birth, gender, race, marital status (single, married, divorced, widowed, separated), occupation, level of education, and home address (where victim was living at the time of death). Provide date and time of death and indicate whether it was a suicide act or other. Give location (address and scene description; e.g., friend's house, parents' home, victims; include photographs). Describe details of discovery, provisions for rescue, written communications (note, diary, etc.), and communication of suicidal intent, written or oral (communication to whom). Detail acts of violence that accompanied the suicidal act, and any other details obtained from the scene.

After obtaining necessary details from the crime scene, proceed to record and evidence review. Record reviews and interviews should be considered some of the most valuable sources of information. Crime scene analysis (photographs and descriptions) also provides valuable data. It is a valuable source in determining whether the suspected mortal wound was self-inflicted. These data are critical and can be determined by a forensic pathologist in corroboration with the investigator. Additionally, the crime scene is the final act in life. It often can provide valuable insight into the deceased and the relationship between life and death. The where, what, and how can often be personal statements about life and death. In suicide there are often logical connections; in the event of accidental death the circumstances may present in a more vague fashion.

Additionally, the physical autopsy and toxicology results provide the necessary information to begin the psychological autopsy because these results clarify manner of death. Include cause of death as determined by a pathologist or physician and blood alcohol and other toxicology results.

Medical records and any other records, including work records, school records, or pastoral counseling records are helpful. Additionally, mental health clinics often keep separate clinic files on patients that may include information that has not been filed in a medical record. Finally, if the victim has spent any time in military or civilian prison, records of contact and initial evaluations can be helpful.

The collection of personal effects including diaries, notebooks, correspondence, photographs, or other personal effects and possessions, provides invaluable data to the profile of the deceased. Titles of books read or videotapes collected are also important data. Style of clothing in the closet, presence of opposite-sex clothing, or other sexual paraphernalia are critical. These items are often found in the victim's residence if the residence is not the crime scene. (An autoerotic death is considered accidental and often repeated or compulsive behavior. Evidence of prior activity can be detected on doors and other anchors for ligature suspension.) Attention should be paid to assisted suicide (Humphrey, 1992). After all the available physical evidence is collected, the major component of interview data should be collected and analyzed.

The interview data collected can easily be skewed and distorted, specifically following the death of a friend or loved one. Often relatives and friends do not like to describe negative things about the deceased. Also, the relatives and friends may overcompensate in their responses as a means to defend against guilt and anger directed toward the deceased. For example, in possible suicides there can be guilt reactions that distort the nature of the relationship with the deceased. There can be anger in accidental deaths toward the deceased for acting either impulsively or without regard for the consequences on others, specifically loved ones who depend on their livelihood. There is a natural defensiveness to accepting death of a loved one, especially a child. The denial is often powerful and a primary component in the distortion of information.

The necessity for accurate and comprehensive interviews is critical. The psychologist will often need to either train or provide outlines to investigations that highlight the type of information needed.

As noted earlier, the APA following their review of the Iowa Case (Poythress et. al., 1993) recommended that the psychologist conduct several of the interviews, particularly those pertinent to reconstruction (e.g., family and peers). Depending on logistics, geography, and lapse of time between death and case review, this may be only the ideal. If the psychologist is on staff with a local police department the geography should be less of a hindrance; however, if the psychologist is conducting the autopsy from a distant location telephonic interviews will have to suffice. This is all dependent on whether the family or peers will talk with the psychologist. Unfortunately, due to much media attention in a case, many people will perceive the request for an interview for purposes of a psychological autopsy as proof positive that a suicide has been concluded. Therefore, it is critical that when a psychologist contacts a survivor, he or she should emphasize that a psychological autopsy is part of the case review process. Its purpose is to provide insight into the personality and motivations of the deceased prior to death. It should be emphasized that although the psychological autopsy offers a professional opinion regarding the manner of death, it is not the determining factor in the manner or cause of death. As mentioned earlier, manner and cause of death is determined only by a pathologist.

There are two types of interviews that need to be conducted. The first is the interview of witnesses to the death event and related incidents. These individuals are interviewed like any other witness to a crime with an emphasis on their observations. The second type of interview is completed with those individuals who had personal knowledge of the deceased. This includes friends, relatives, work colleagues, and acquaintances. Individuals who have knowledge of the deceased receive a more structured interview.

The purpose of this interview is to gain objective information about the deceased that is not part of a routine criminal investigation.

Individuals who would receive a structured interview include those who have had personal knowledge or contact with the deceased. This type of interview requires a high degree of rapport between the interviewer and interviewee. A direct appeal for the interviewee's help often assists in clarifying the purpose of the interview and the value of their contributions. Careful attention needs to be paid to both overt and covert communications that might illuminate the decedent's role in his or her demise. The following are several general guidelines for structured interviews.

The credibility of the reference is in part based on the frequency, duration, and quality of the relationship with the deceased: How long did you know the deceased? When did you first meet? How often did you associate with the deceased? How close was your relationship? What was the nature of your relationship (friend, relative, peer, co-worker)? When was the last time you saw the deceased?

Asking an interviewee to respond to questions such as "What was (name of the deceased) like?" may further validate the nature of their association and provide opinions about the deceased. Utilize this part of the interview to facilitate rapport, being sensitive to the interviewee's sense of loss. Emphasize the value of the interviewee's contributions.

Initial reviews of interview data should focus on the identification of the following: What was the decedent's familiarity with the weapon or method? Was the death scene visited prior to the death? Did the decedent rehearse the method? Did the lethal method correlate with the decedent's lifestyle (e.g., guns and hunting, drowning and boating, swimming, fishing)?

Inquiries into changes in the deceased's emotions and behavior are helpful in deeming the deceased's reactions to experiences. Patterns of adjustments to stress and observations of progressive deterioration of coping skills may be identified. Questions include: Did you observe any noticeable behavioral or emotional changes in the deceased? How did he or she cope with problems in his or her life? What changes did you notice in the deceased's mood? When did these changes occur? What was going on in his or her life at that time? Intent is a critical factor in evaluating the likelihood of suicide.

It is important to determine the perspective of the deceased at the time of death, and factors that may have been influential. Despite the investigator's reaction to a particular event, the deceased may have considered the event or the action to have been provocative of a lethal act. Questions include: What problems, difficulties and concerns did the deceased have? When did they start? How much of a problem was that for him or her? It is also important to ask the interviewee about whether he or she was aware of any direct or indirect suicidal preoccupations. For example, "I'll kill myself. I can't cope anymore. The world would bebetter without me. The voices are telling me to kill myself. I can't stand it anymore." More subtle clues include giving possessions away, saying goodbye, talking about prolonged sleep and escape, and planning for survivors.

It is important to ask about the frequency, intensity, and duration of any of the following symptoms. Questions include: How severe was that? How often did it occur? How long did it last? When did it first occur, and were there any changes in this pattern?

- Sleep difficulties: Trouble falling asleep, recurrent awakenings early morning rising, abrupt awakening in the morning accompanied by anxiety or restlessness.
- Physical complaints: Low back pain, muscular tension, abdominal pain, diarrhea, constipation, vomiting, jaw pain. Were they treated, when, and by whom? List any medications that were used over the counter or prescribed.
- Headache: Persistent or recurring.
- Appetite: Decreases, lack of pleasure for favorite foods, weight loss in absence of dieting. Changes in eating patterns, overeating.
- Indigestion: Continual heartburn, gas, cramps, nausea.

- Libido: Deceased sex drive. Were there changes in level of sex drive (e.g., decrease or increase; lack of pleasure or ability to perform). Evidence of any autoerotic activity. Articles of pornography or sex aids.

Suggested interview guidelines for family members and long-term peers are outlined in the following. The purpose of the interview is to assess character style and long-term enduring patterns of behavior.

It is important to be sensitive to family members doing interviews. Family members need to be supported emotionally. It is recommended that the interviewer call ahead and schedule a time to speak with the family either in person or on the telephone depending on geographic locations. It would be insensitive to cold call a parent, relative, or spouse and ask them pertinent and in-depth questions about the deceased. On occasion, the interviewee may be hostile or resentful of the interview because it may interpreted as verifying or affirming a suicide when the family believes the manner of death to be homicide. Finally, in the course of development, children naturally strive to be separate and individual from their family of origin. It is a natural and adaptive progression of events. As a result, children often keep separate many aspects of their lives from their family of origin.

Personality characteristics ascribed to the deceased include: What was his or her general approach to life? What was he or she like? The use of indirect psychological assessment instruments is appropriate to flush out specific adjectives that described the deceased and particular habits. These scales include the NEO (Neuroticism, Extraversim, Openness) Personality Inventory–Revised (Costa & McCrae, 1989) and the Adjective Checklist. Both of these scales are observer rating scales that are intercorrelated across several personality factors. This form of data enables the clinician to compare the observer's readings against empirically derived normative groups. It fortifies the observed personality traits with a research database one step beyond pure subjectivity.

- Personal interests and hobbies: What types of activities were enjoyed during recreational and free time? How did he or she relax? What were his or her most enjoyable activities?

- Coping style: How did he or she react to stress, change, transition, loss, frustration, rejection, and criticism? Did he or she express his or her feelings openly? How did he or she deal with anger?

- Interpersonal relationships: Did the decedent have many relationships or few? Were his or her relationships acquaintances or more close relationships? Was the decedent a socially inclusive or reclusive individual? Would he or she have a focused group of friends or wide variety of friends with different interests and affiliations? Inquire across the developmental spectrum; childhood, school years, adolescence, adult.

- Communication style: Did the decedent communicate openly or was he or she more inhibited? Did the decedent tend to verbalize thoughts and feelings or act them out behaviorally? Were his or her communications spontaneous or more reflective?

- Marital/dyadic relationship history: Describe marital status. Describe any mental conflict or trouble in the relationship. Explain number and length of marriages; current living arrangements; number, age, and sex of children; where the children live; changes in relationship with spouse and children; and threats or actual divorce or separation. Were there any recent deaths in the family? Was there a history of abusive behavior? What was the overall quality of the current relationship. Give a dating history.

- Family of origin history: Describe parental marital history, family medical history, history of family member psychiatric hospitalizations and treatment, and family suicide history. Provide number, ages, and sex of siblings. Was there a family history of sexual abuse or other forms of child abuse or family violence? Was there a family history of alcoholism or substance abuse? Was there a history of family separations due to deployment, incarceration, or other circumstances? Describe separation from whom at what age and for how long. Give the death history of the victim's family (suicides, cancer, other fatal illnesses, accidents, ages of relatives at death, and other details).

- Past problems: Describe any troubles, pressures, tensions, or anticipated problems during the past year. List and describe any observed or expressed symptoms of depression. List any immediate danger signals that had been communicated (Rosenberg, 1988).

- Work history: State the victim's occupation and length of time in current position. Identify any recent demotions, promotions, or difficulties with colleagues or supervisors. State perceived level of work satisfaction (poor to excellent). State the victim's employment history (jobs lost, retirement, promotion) and the frequency of job changes and reasons for change or termination.

- Military history: Identify periods and time in military service. Indicate if the decedent was involved in any combat or exposed to any traumatic incidents. Describe type of discharge. Identify any awards or medals received, or any known disciplinary action while in the military.

- Medical history: Describe any significant illness and treatment. Describe any recent change or loss in health status. Describe any injuries, accidents, or hospitalizations. List current medications and history of compliance. Indicate if the decedent was HIV positive.

- Psychiatric history: Identify any past psychiatric history including diagnosis, hospitalization, and forms of psychotherapy. Indicate the length and dates of treatment. Identify any prescribed medication or other treatment (e.g., electric shock treatment). State evidence of personality disorder or significant problems with anger, impulsive, emotional modulation, self-destructive or self-defeating behavior, or self-mutilation.

• Alcohol history/drug abuse history: Describe the role of alcohol or drugs in the victim's overall lifestyle. Identify victim's behavior changes during periods of alcohol or drug abuse (e.g., hostile, altercations, loss of consciousness). State victim's usual alcohol consumption and evidence of addiction to alcohol, number of detoxifications, DUI, blackouts, frequency of intoxication, and work-related alcohol abuse. State whether the victim was enrolled in alcohol and drug abuse programs (inpatient or outpatient treatment). Identify drugs victim used, if any. State if the victim was addicted to drugs.

• Financial status: Describe the victim's financial situation (recent losses, success or failures). Often a credit check will be helpful in accessing necessary financial information.

• Legal status: Describe any current or past legal or criminal actions against the victim. State the victim's criminal record (number and length of jail or prison terms, nature of the offenses). State if the victim had been accused of any sexual misconduct or spousal abuse.

• History of prior suicide attempts: Provide dates and descriptions of prior attempts and threats. Was there provision of rescue in any past attempts or gestures? Give the circumstances surrounding attempts; were there precipitants or catalysts? Include type of medical or psychological intervention received after suicide attempt (dates and length of treatment, type of treatment, hospitalization on an inpatient psychiatric unit).

• Interviewee's explanation of the death: Ask interviewees how they explain what happened. It often will help to crystallize their perception of the deceased and why he or she may have taken his or her life.

If the interviewee had proximal contact with the decedent, the following outline is offered to collect more recent data. This data may be helpful in the construction of a time line documenting and accounting for as much time and as many events as possible just prior to death. The time line is discussed later in this chapter.

• Personality and lifestyle prior to death (2-week period before death): Describe the basic personality (relaxed, intense, jovial, gregarious, withdrawn, outgoing, morose, bitter, suspicious, angry, hostile, combative). Describe any noted recent changes in victim's mood or symptoms of mental illness. Describe the victim's recent changes in behavior such as eating, sleeping, sexual patterns, drinking, driving, taking medications, social relationships, or hobbies. Describe victim's reaction to stress and typical stress reactions (impulsive, withdrawn, overly assertive, hostile).

- Interpersonal relationships: Describe intensity and frequency (many vs. few, casual or intense). Describe any recent uncharacteristic behavior including gambling, promiscuity, fighting, and withdrawal from friends. Describe victim's friendship group. Describe manner in which time was spent.
- Recent agency contacts: Document any contacts with mental health professionals, chaplain, physician, legal assistance, Relief and Family Advocacy Program, and so on.

Ask the interviewee to provide a detailed description of the deceased when he or she last saw the deceased alive; include behavior, appearance, and activity. Ask for references to provide confirmation of other interviewees who may have had association with the deceased or saw them prior to death. Additionally, other individuals can provide information not previously developed. Finally, ask interviewees if they have any additional comments.

There are two key concepts agreed on in the literature that help in differentiating a death as a suicide. These concepts are self-infliction and intention (Jobes et al., 1991; Rosenberg et al., 1988; Shneidman, 1993). Physical and medical evidence including crime scene, autopsy and toxicology reports, can be used to determine self-inflicted death. The Empirical Criteria Checklist (Jobes et al., 1991) provides a good example of the indicators that differentiate suicide from accidental death. Jobes et al. (1991) attempted to logically and empirically identify behaviors that differentiate intention and self-infliction. Based on his research, behavior can be a determining factor in clarifying the manner of death as either accidental or suicide. The Empirical Criteria Checklist assists the clinician in organizing the available data in such a way as to compare findings to previously judged cases with similar data. Although self-infliction is often easier than intention to determine, the scale ensures that multiple factors are present before a judgment is rendered. Rosenberg et al. (1988) also attempted to differentiate intention and provide guidelines to collect appropriate data.

Despite what may be obvious at a crime scene, all the data need to be assembled to most accurately assess intent. Crime scene photography and physical autopsy are very significant inputs for the determination of self-inflicted wounds. It is necessary to have both self-infliction and intent in determining a death or a suicide. Intention may be explicitly communicated by the decedent in both verbal and nonverbal forms. Examples of verbal expressions include: I'm going to kill myself; I wish I were dead; People would be better off without me. Nonverbal examples include artistic drawings, doodles, and other methods.

In attempting to differentiate a suicide from an accidental death, a comparison of lifestyle to lethal act can be helpful. For example, if the victim appeared to have a history of either high-risk behavior (e.g., rock climbing or sky diving), or engaging inactivities without consideration of potential hazard, there may be a relationship between life and death. If the decedent had a history of impulsive, reckless, and treacherous behavior without consideration of safety or consequence of action, the death may be accidental. Finally, if the decedent attempted to survive, there may be evidence to suggest that the death was accidental, even if the lethal injury was self-inflicted. Many victims of suicide gestures that result in death do not initially have the intention of dying. Often they are just seeking attention. The following guidelines provide a structured approach to gathering information regarding intent.

Special Phrases and Criteria (Rosenberg et al., 1988)

The types of evidence of intent that follow are not listed in order of significance or importance. Examples of verbal expressions include written diary notes, audiotape recordings, and videotape messages. Nonverbal expressions might include drawings or a very recent, potentially lethal attempt where a timely discovery led to rescue. This list is not meant to be exhaustive. Recent behaviors and feelings are deemed more important, but historical data also bear on the decision. Serious depression, for example, is usually a recurrent problem, and a person who has experienced a serious depression in the past is at higher risk of another depressive episode years later.

1. Preparations for death inappropriate to or unexpected in the context of the decedent's life. Examples include unexplained giving away of possessions and making provisions for the future care of children or pets.

2. Expression of farewell or the desire to die or an acknowledgment of impending death. Examples: I won't be here to be kicked around anymore. You were real important to me. Have a good life. You'll be sorry when I'm gone. I can't stay around to face the future.

3. Expression of hopelessness. Examples: It just doesn't matter anymore. It wouldn't make any difference if I. . . . What's the use of . . . ? Actions signaling hopelessness include giving up activities or medical treatments that are clearly necessary to sustain life.

4. Expressions of great emotional or physical pain or distress. Examples: This pain is killing me. I can't stand it anymore. I cannot live like this. It is too much for me to take. Indirect manifestations of extreme pain may be seen in failures to obtain relief from standard medical treatments.

5. Effort to procure or learn about means of death or rehearse fatal behavior. Examples include recently purchasing firearms or ammunition, stockpiling potentially lethal drugs, purchasing rope, and obtaining access to high places.

6. Precautions to avoid rescue. Examples include locking doors; going to a prearranged, secluded place; telling lies about one's whereabouts; and arranging to be alone.

7. Evidence that decedent recognized high potential lethality of means of death. Examples include a pharmacist or physician taking an overdose of a highly lethal drug or the decedent's researching different drugs to determine their degree of lethality.

8. Previous suicide attempt. Previous attempts include self-destructive acts carried out with the goal of killing oneself or with an awareness that the consequences could be lethal. The more recent attempts and those with a high potential lethality may be more significant indicators of intent. Previous attempts, however, need not be recent or potentially highly lethal. Furthermore, the methods used in the previous attempts may differ.

9. Previous suicide threat. A threat need not be a coercive statement made to force another person to do something—it can be a statement of intent. Examples of threats include playing with a gun and saying "I'm going to shoot myself." Thoughts or fantasies about suicide (such as an imagined reunion with a dead relative) should be differentiated from threats, although questions about such thoughts or fantasies should be asked.

10. Stressful events or significant losses (actual or threatened). Examples include loss of relationship (with a boyfriend, girlfriend, child, or spouse), intangible losses (not being elected to a desired office or being passed over for a promotion), loss of self-esteem, or financial losses. Anticipating difficult changes may constitute severe stress, even when those changes represent "desired" transitions such as leaving for college or getting promoted at work.

11. Serious depression or mental disorders. Depression is not used here to refer to a brief period of sadness. It is a mental disorder characterized by a serious and pervasive loss of pleasure and loss of interest in one's unusual activities that lasts at least 2 weeks. Additional signs of depression are excessive guilt ruminations, loss of energy, loss of appetite, or a marked change in weight. Because depression is usually a recurrent disorder, a past history of depression may indicate a persistent problem. A person may commit suicide when he or she appears to be recovering or getting more energy. Depression or another mental disorder need not have been diagnosed by a mental health professional. Signs of impairment by a mental disorder might include inability to care for oneself, inability to maintain relationships, or previous psychiatric hospitalization. Other mental disorders include manic state or manic-depressive illness, difficulty controlling impulses, psychoses, substance abuse disorders, and organic mental disorders. A person with a mental disorder may commit suicide in response to a perceived command that was part of a hallucination (for example: My mother is calling me to join her in heaven. The space creatures told me that if I did not kill myself they would torture me).

In his most recent textbook *Suicide as Psychache*, Shneidman (1993) summarized several of his views on suicide. Shneidman defined *psychache* as the "hurt anguish, soreness, aching, psychological pain in the mind" (p.). He continued that it is "intrinsically psychological the pain of excessively felt shame, guilt, humiliation, loneliness, fear, angst, dread of growing old, or dying badly" (p. 51). Suicide occurs when psychache is unbearable. Therefore he concluded that suicide also has to do with different thresholds for enduring psychological pain (Shneidman, 1985, 1993). To correlate suicide with any specific demographic factor may miss the motivation for suicide of intolerable pain. Referring to Murray's theory of psychological needs, Shneidman concluded that suicide is not necessary adaptive but adjustive. Suicide relates to psychological needs in that it stops the unbearable pain caused by frustrated psychological needs felt by the individual to be vital to life. Shneidman (1985) referred to the following 10 commonalities of suicide:

1. The common purpose of suicide is to seek a solution.
2. The common goal of suicide is cessation of consciousness.
3. The common stimulus of suicide is intolerable psychological pain.
4. The common stressor in suicide is frustrated psychological needs.
5. The common emotion in suicide is hopelessness-helplessness.
6. The common cognitive state in suicide is ambivalence.
7. The common perceptual state in suicide is constriction.
8. The common action in suicide is aggression.
9. The common interpersonal act in suicide is communication of intention.
10. The common consistency in suicide is with lifelong coping patterns.

Finally, Shneidman emphasized the role of the unconscious in contributing to suicides. What is referred to here are those deaths that appear to be subintended. These suicides fall into the category of accidental death where the use of poor judgment, high-risk behavior, substance abuse, neglect, or self-destructive lifestyle incurs the possibility and probability of death. Therefore in the execution of restitution the clinician must be sensitive to the level and degree of lethality in the final act. High lethality obviously has significant implications for intent and communicates that the decedent definitely wanted to die. Medical lethality suggests that death was a result of some act by the deceased but one that may have had a more covert role. Low lethality would more likely suggest a small but perhaps insignificant role, whereas absence of lethality would suggest no lethality (e.g., natural causes).

Special Considerations

There are several special considerations that should be attended to in specific circumstances. These considerations are outlined here.

- Gun shot: Victim's knowledge and experience with firearms, victim's experience handling weapons (reckless or cautious), prior firearm accidents, recent purchase of firearm.

- Overdose: Victim's knowledge of drugs and potential dangers; prescription or street drugs, or premature refill requests. Was victim under the influence of drugs, or was there a history of prior overdoses and how were they treated? Was there carelessness in the use of medications, how did victim track pill intake? What was the source of medication or drugs?

- Hangings or asphyxia: Explore sexual involvement. Was the victim clothed, and did he or she have pornographic or sexual apparatus nearby? Describe known sexual activity, perversions, deviance, interest in asphyxia techniques, and experience with rope (Hazelwood et al., 1981).

- Jumping, drowning, vehicular death: State the reason for the victim to be at the place of death. Often these deaths are the most difficult in which to differentiate the manner of death (e.g., suicide vs. accident) due to the variability of intent and self-inflicted behavior (Berman, 1993).

Finally, standardized indirect assessment instruments can be utilized to further assess the deceased personality. The NEO–R and Adjective Checklist are two well-established psychological tests that are adapted for secondhand observation of behavior. The indirect assessment instrument can be completed by family members and peers who had a well-established relationship with the deceased. The results provide a standardized personality profile empirically validated in a normative sample of the population.

Report Writing

The written report is a presentation of the data and an analysis that presents the opinion of the clinician. Psychological autopsy reports have no standardized guidelines. The following outline is a suggested framework in keeping with a comprehensive clinical assessment.

- Introduction: The introduction should introduce the technique and the method used to evaluate the data. It should indicate who has requested the psychological autopsy, the data that was reviewed, and who the psychologist interviewed. For example, the introduction should mention the use of crime scene data, investigative interview, available records reviewed, and who was personally interviewed by the psychologist. The introduction should note if any adjunctive psychological tests were used for purposes of indirect assessment. Finally, the introduction should reflect the speculative nature of the findings and the degree of validity and reliability.

- Identifying information: Include name, age, address, marital status, religious practices, occupation, and any other details.

- Presenting problem: The presenting problem should reflect in sequence the details of the death and pertain to facts: the crime scene, investigative summary, events known to precede the death, and a time line of events 4 hours to 12 months prior to the death. This can be derived from interviews with peers, colleagues, and significant others who had the last formal contact with the decedent. Note any significant upsets, preserves, tensions, or anticipation of trouble; changes in the victim before death (habits, hobbies, eating, routines, and sexual patterns); and reaction of informants to the victim's death.

- Past history: This section should reflect as comprehensively as possible the decedents past psychosocial history, including development, past medical illness and psychiatric history (psychotherapy and suicide attempts), family constellation and history, and educational and occupational history. Death history of the family should be included in this section: (cancer, accident, illness, suicide, and ages at death).

- Victimology: This section should describe the personality factors, typical patterns of reaction to stress, periods of maladjustment to interpersonal relationships, coping style, hobbies, interests, perversions, substance use and abuse, and fantasies or thoughts (dreams) or fear of death or suicide.

- Opinion/formulation: This section should reflect there construction of the factors and events that contributed to the death. It is the section in which the clinician offers a hypothesis regarding the death. This section integrates the recent events as they related to the past history and personality formulation of the deceased. In this section hypothesis for and against suicide or accidental death can be expressed. Assessment of intention and a rating of lethality is offered.

The purpose of this chapter has been to provide some investigative guidance and direction to a technique that can have significant contributions to the determination of the manner of death. It generalizes beyond the forensic investigative arena into the arena of epidemiology, contributing to a better understanding of the factors that lead to particular types of death. Additionally, it can offer insights to educators who train in the areas of safety and suicide awareness. In the more pure criminal setting, insight into the victim can often help narrow the scope of suspects in a homicide.

CONCLUSION

It is hoped that this chapter and others like it offer some guidelines that improve the consistency and uniformity with which these procedures are conducted. It provides guidance for the later development of quality assurance and professional guidelines in conducting psychological autopsies.

Although a highly controversial, speculative technique, there is a place for psychological autopsy. The author does not recommend the use of this technique in every law enforcement case because it is an adjunctive tool to an investigation and not a component of an investigation. Perhaps epidemiologists and academic studies of suicide may consider this technique as a part of their experimental design.

This chapter offered some guidelines and outlines to conduct psychological autopsy. There remain loose guidelines and standards in conducting this procedure. It would be helpful in the future to design not only standards and guidelines through perhaps an APA task force but guidelines that go beyond the initial findings from the 1993 Iowa review that would also include training criteria. As mentioned earlier, it is very difficult to review a case without the knowledge of police investigative procedures and forensic science. These matters and others should become the focus of psychologists who conduct psychological autopsies to ensure that this valuable and helpful technique is not amateurishly lost to criticism of those who are against the technique and also have little experience in its value to police psychology.

REFERENCES

Berman, A. L. (1993). Forensic suicidology and the psychological autopsy in suicidology: Essays in Honor of Edwin S. Schneidman. In A. A. Leenaars (Ed.), *Forensic suicidology and the psychological autopsy* (pp. 248–267). Northvale, NJ: Aronson.

Berman, A. L., & Litman, R. E. (1993). *Psychological autopsy.* Unpublished manuscript.

Costa, P., & McCrae, R. (1989). *Reused NEO Personality Inventory.* Odessa, FL: Psychological Assessment Resources.

Ebert, B. W. (1987). Guide to conducting a psychological autopsy. *Professional Psychology Research and Practice, 18,* 52–56.

Hazelwood, R. R., Dietz, P. E., & Burgess, A. W. (1981). The investigation of autoerotic fatalities. *Journal of Police Science and Administration, 9,* 404–411.

Humphrey, D. (1991). *Final exit.* New York: Bantam Doubleday.

Jobes, D. A., Casey, J. O., Berman, A. L., & Wright, D. G. (1991). Empirical criteria for the determination of suicide manner of death. *Journal of Forensic Sciences, 36,* 244–256.

Poythress, N., Otto, R., Darkes, J., & Staw, L. (1993). APA's expert panel in the congressional review of the USS Iowa incident. *American Psychologist, 48,* 8–15.

Rosenberg, M. L., Davidson, L. E., & Smith, J. C. (1988). Operational criteria for the determination of suicide. *Journal of Forensic Sciences, 33,* 1445–1456.

Schneidman, E. (1985). *The definition of suicide.* New York: Wiley.

Schneidman, E. (1993). *Suicide as psychache: A clinical approach to self destructive behavior.* Northvale, NJ: Aronson.

CHAPTER SEVENTEEN

Tactics and Negotiating Techniques (TNT): The Way of the Past and the Way of the Future

James L. Greenstone
Fort Worth, TX
Police Department

The divergence of tactical and negotiating teams from a common attitude toward, and a common body of knowledge for effectively dealing with, hostage, barricade, and suicide incidents raises the spectre of serious problems in such circumstances. This chapter discusses the problem of team divergence, includes some of the common body of knowledge needed, and suggests some of the possible solutions to this dilemma. The focus of this chapter is not new. It comes to us from the past and perhaps it represents a better way for the future.

Somewhere along the line, a good idea may have become sidetracked. What started out to be a comprehensive approach to hostage and barricade situations has developed into two separate camps, both designed to accomplish the same thing in separate ways. Early concepts stressed the importance of training in both tactical and negotiating techniques for all of those involved in such incidents. Perhaps this note from the past is a lesson for the future. In the pursuit of highly specialized tactical units and equally proficient negotiating units, the potential synergism of cross-trained personnel has been lost or at least dissipated. There is that pervasive tendency for tactical officers to feel that their job, by its nature, does not require them to develop the skills of communications and psychological sensitivity. Negotiators may share similarly parochial feelings from their particular advantage. *Veritas est in media*: The truth is in the middle; a phrase for us all to remember in this context. Although the development of specialized tactical and negotiations units has a certain value above and beyond the combining of such units, that value may be lost or at least diluted by lack of interaction and meaningful joint training experiences. To the degree that each understands and appreciates the other, the potential for successful resolution of these critical incidents will be increased. This requires more than a cursory acknowledgment that each team exists, and a commitment to become involved in the learning of the knowledge base from which each operates. Formal schools and in-service training are a start. Joint training exercises will help to resolve misconceptions and increase mutual appreciation. Attitude is the key issue, and attitudes are difficult to change. However, the beginning of attitude change is a change in behavior. Commanders and special teams members can aid this process by being open to joint involvement and to the learning that can take place as a result. No one has the corner on knowledge in general, or on the specific knowledge necessary to resolve volatile and highly sensitive situations such as hostage takings, barricades, or suicides. Mutual respect, knowledge, and training, however, can boost the information base for both and foster better overall procedures.

HISTORY AND BACKGROUND INFORMATION

Proper and accepted current thinking about the handling of hostage, barricade, and suicidal incidents indicates that those police personnel who are best trained in hostage negotiations procedures have the best chance of bringing about a successful resolution to a given incident (Culley, 1974; Fowler & Greenstone, 1983, 1987; Greenstone & Leviton, 1982). Success in these situations is usually defined as a resolution in which there is no loss of life to any of those involved in the incident including police, hostage taker, and hostages. Tactical team involvement is a must so that proper containment of the situation can be accomplished. With this containment, negotiations techniques are maximally effective. In hostage situations, when properly trained negotiators are allowed to do the job for which they were trained, given the required amount of time necessary, and given the support that they need, the incidence of death to hostages, hostage taker, or anyone else involved is minimal. (FBI, 1985)

Sample success rates from various cities in the United States are revealing. In Houston, Texas, in 450 incidents from 1978 to 1990 only two deaths have occurred. In Forth Worth, Texas, of 40 hostage incidents, 100% have been resolved without loss of life. In the New York Police Department, from 1976 to the present averaging approximately 240 incidents per year, there has been a 99% success rate. Research in the San Antonio, Texas, Police Department indicates that assaulting a hostage taker results in a 78% chance of injury or death; with chemical weapons, a 50% chance of injury or death; and with controlled fire, a 100% chance of injury or death. With the use of the "contain and negotiate" method, there is a less than 1% chance of injury or death to those involved. In Chattanooga, Tennessee, over a 15-year period in which literally hundreds of hostage, barricade, and suicidal situations have been handled, only three persons have been lost to suicide. When hostages have been held, the success rate over this 15-year period is 100% utilizing the accepted procedures and trained police negotiators.

A partial review of the literature available in the area of hostage and barricade situations indicates:

> Since its inception, the contain and negotiate method has been eminently successful in safely resolving the majority of steadily escalating hostage situations in the United States. (W. R. Fowler, personal communication, January 1991)

> Trained negotiators must be had and used to be successful. (Greenstone, 1992, p. 2)

> We have learned, in numerous hostage, barricade, and suicide situations over the past 9 years (1980–1989), that techniques of Crisis Intervention and Hostage Negotiations have allowed us to resolve every situation without loss of life (Fowler & Greenstone, 1989, p. 100)

> In a comparative study of negotiating with mentally disturbed hostage takers, it was found that "trained negotiators are significantly better able to respond to mentally disturbed hostage takers." (Borum, 1987, p. 3)

COMMON PROBLEMS FOR TACTICAL OFFICERS AND NEGOTIATORS

1. Lack of coordination between tactical and negotiators in terms of communication and procedures.
2. Lack of mutual trust because of lack of mutual understanding.
3. Inadequate intelligence gathering and dissemination to and from both tactical and negotiations.
4. Allowing negotiator to handle face-to-face negotiations without adequate tactical backup. Hostage negotiations is not an individual event, it is a team effort.
5. Overreliance on mental health professionals rather than giving adequate support to the negotiator.
6. Failure to protect the negotiating team from unnecessary intrusions.
7. Negotiations coordinator and tactical commander not allowed to perform in their respective jobs due to frequent interruptions and additional assignments.

8. Failure to do adequate shift change briefings for everyone who is involved on both tactical and negotiations units.

9. Reluctance of primary negotiator to be honest with the tactical or on-scene commander about being replaced.

10. Feelings of failure if the subject commits suicide.

11. Inadequate selection criteria for team members.

12. Inadequate membership on tactical and negotiations teams and failure to provide for adequate mutual assistance agreements.

13. Failure to cross-train tactical members and negotiators on procedures and equipment.

14. Failure to engage in sufficient combined training events.

15. Failure to have both teams exercise together with neighboring departments.

16. Failure to provide continuous and updated training.

17. Lack of involvement of commanders in the training exercises of both tactical units and negotiating teams.

18. Lack of weapons safety.

19. Lack of clear understanding by all involved of what a particular training event is supposed to accomplish.

20. Lack of crisis management training for the on-scene commander.

21. Fear, by the on-scene commander, of loss of control to the tactical team or negotiations unit.

22. Overinvolvement of the on-scene commander or the boss in either negotiations or in the tactical response.

23. Inappropriate restraints placed on special teams because of lack of understanding of what each does.

24. Lack of trust between tactical teams and negotiations teams due to a lack of understanding of the function of each.

25. Inappropriate people being allowed to interact with negotiators or tactical officers during an incident. (FBI, 1991)

SPECIFIC INFORMATION FOR BOTH TACTICAL OFFICERS AND NEGOTIATORS

Some of the information that may be important for all involved to understand is mentioned in the following lists. This information is usually not presented together. It may be seen as team specific and therefore not for dissemination to other teams. However, as should be apparent, understanding of this information for tactical teams members as well as for negotiators is vital to overall success.

Steps to Management of a Hostage Situation

- Establish communications.
- Check for drug or alcohol use on the part of the hostage taker.
- Debrief any hostages who are released.
- Interview those who may have made initial contact and the first response officers.
- Gather intelligence on the hostage taker.
- Develop intelligence information on the building or site of the hostage taking.
- Activate tactical unit and negotiators.
- Identify demands and what is and is not negotiable.
- Establish a command post.
- Call out reserve force as soon as possible, if needed.
- Adjust for daylight or night operations.
- Secure medical and fire services at the scene.
- Maintain invisible deployment of all personnel.
- Control news media and establish a media center.
- Determine the mental state of the hostage taker.
- Stall for time.
- Establish an insulated area for negotiators.
- Direct telephone communications.
- Control all perimeters.
- Maintain control of negotiators.
- Remain flexible.
- Establish effective inner perimeter with tactical officers.
- Set the outer perimeter with unassigned officers, reserve forces, city workers, or other reliable personnel.
- Assure that all technical aids are available for both tactical unit and negotiations team.
- Secure adequate facilities and space for use as a general command post with necessary facilities for negotiators.

Immediate Demands of a Hostage Situation

- Attend to police needs.
- Consider media needs and respond as soon as possible.
- Reroute or cut off utilities as needed, depending on specific nature of situation.

- Notify fire department to stand by at scene and specify location.
- Have emergency medical services respond to the command post and stand by at specific location.
- Keep EMS and firefighters informed of developments.
- Attend to crowd control and traffic issues.
- Seek out and interview relatives of the subject as possible.
- Have a plan to deal with politicians and municipal officials who may arrive on the scene.
- Be considerate of the needs of business owners and merchants in the area and how the situation may be impacting on them.

Initial Patrol Duties at a Hostage Situation

- Set command response in motion.
- Set initial perimeters.
- Initiate crowd control.
- Notify supervisor.
- Notify tactical unit and negotiators.
- Establish initial command post.
- Take charge of scene.
- Maintain control of scene until relieved by supervisor or until tactical officers and negotiators arrive.
- Keep episode from escalating.

Command Response

- Establish contingency plans.
- Assure the smooth flow of information both up and down the chain of command.
- Coordinate all officers on the scene and define specific areas of responsibility.
- Designate field commander.

Benefit, Purpose, and Function of Tactical Units at a Hostage Situation

- To operate in teams of four or more, sometimes in multiples of two with four as a minimum.
- To be cross-trained with other members of the team.

- To exhibit high personal discipline.
- To bring to bear skill and proficiency with special weapons.
- To be able to respond more effectively because of intensive physical conditioning.
- To have knowledge of explosives, booby traps, and hostage negotiations techniques.
- To be responsible for implementation of appropriate tactics and utilization of needed equipment in high-risk situations.
- To provide motivation to hostage takers to negotiate with authorities.
- To support efforts of hostage negotiators.
- To provide intelligence about and surveillance of the hostage or barricade scene.
- To perform fire control missions by securing a commanding position and keeping desired areas clear.
- To maintain strict fire discipline.
- To maintain invisible deployment.
- To perform rescue missions as required.
- To assist police and fire units regularly engaged with mobs, looters, arsonists, and insurgents as requested by on scene commander or in response to preplanned strategies.

The Eight Elements Necessary to Evaluate a Potential Hostage Situation

1. A need to live on the part of the hostage taker.
2. A threat of force by the authorities.
3. Communications between the hostage taker and the authorities.
4. A leader among the hostage takers.
5. Substantive demands.
6. Containment by the tactical unit.
7. Time.
8. A negotiator for the police who is capable of helping or hurting the hostage taker, but who always expresses a willingness to help.

Successfully Dealing With Hostage Taker Demands

- Start off by giving yourself a lot of room to negotiate.
- Make the hostage taker work for everything he gets.
- Get something in return for each concession made.

- Use time to your advantage.
- Keep a log of all demands and of all concessions made.
- Do not give in to the hostage taker too much or too fast.
- Do not ask for demands.
- Do not bring up old demands.
- Do not dismiss any demand as being trivial.

Evaluation of Deadlines

- Remember, very few deaths have occurred as a result of deadlines.
- Deaths that occur prior to the start of negotiations do not count for "green light" consideration.
- If the only demand is to die and the suicide potential of the hostage taker cannot be evaluated, tactical intervention may be necessary.
- Generally, ignore deadlines by talking around them. Change the subject, if necessary, or blame the bureaucracy or the brass for the delays.
- If you are not on the phone with the hostage taker prior to the deadline, call a few minutes prior to the deadline and stay on the phone as the time passes.

How to Measure Progress in a Hostage Situation

- No one has died.
- Hostage taker is talking more.
- Content of conversation is less violent.
- Speech patterns change.
- An increased willingness on the part of the hostage taker to talk about his or her personal life.
- Greater resistance by the hostage taker to the negotiator getting off of the phone.

Handling the Surrender of the Hostage Taker

1. The details of the surrender should be considered carefully and together by tactical and negotiating team members. Everyone must be "on the same sheet of music."
2. Talk about the details of the surrender with the hostage taker.
3. Do not take the surrender, or the ritual that may surround it, lightly.

4. Do not show your own anxiety by talking too much about the surrender.

5. If hostage taker is reluctant to come out, ask about the reluctance and attempt to reassure.

6. Maintain a positive attitude about the surrender and speak about "when" the hostage taker comes out rather than "if" he or she comes out.

7. Take enough time to plan the surrender well, but not too much time or detail to scare the taker.

Communications Techniques to Be Employed During Hostage Takings, and With Barricaded Subjects

1. Start with an opening statement that tells the hostage taker or subject who you are, what you are or who you represent, and why you are there.
2. Use broad opening statements to encourage talking.
3. Focus on the hostage taker and not on the hostages.
4. Reflect the feelings of the taker in order to help establish rapport.
5. Acknowledge the hostage taker's feelings without agreeing or disagreeing.
6. Remember, "understanding" does not imply "agreement."
7. Do not be afraid of silence. Use it as necessary as a tool.
8. Clarify comments or demands.
9. Do not use clichés, especially if they are unfamiliar to the subject or inappropriate in context.
10. Attempt to keep a positive focus.
11. Compliment the taker if appropriate.
12. Do not express disapproval unless this is calculated carefully.
13. Request clarification if needed and utilize open-ended questions.
14. Do not impose your values on the hostage taker or on the hostage.
15. Avoid becoming defensive.
16. Remain accepting of what the hostage taker says.
17. Allow the hostage taker to vent feelings.
18. Attempt to maintain a problem-solving mode to the conversation.
19. Do not trivialize anything the hostage taker says.
20. Do not become angry unless you have planned such a response.

Nonjudgmental Words and Phrases That Can Help
When Talking With the Hostage Taker and Which Can
Help Avoid Dead Spaces in Your Conversation

- First, I'd like to get to know you better.
- Could you tell me more about it.
- I would like to hear your side.
- Could you share that with me?
- I guess that's pretty important to you.
- Tell me about it.
- That's interesting.
- I see.
- Is that so?
- Oh!
- Uh huh.

What the Negotiator Can Provide to the Tactical Unit
and to Command

1. Information on the level of threat and the emotions of the hostage taker.
2. Intelligence information gleaned from the conversations with the hostage taker and hostages.
3. A profile of the hostage taker and of the hostages.
4. Location of the subject and of others involved.
5. A diversion or surprise factor when needed.
6. Time.
7. Assistance in formulation of the tactical plan as needed.

Gathering, Understanding, and Utilization
of Intelligence Information During a Hostage Taking
Barricade or Suicide Situation

1. Gathering, understanding, and utilization of intelligence information is the joint responsibility of the tactical unit and the negotiating team.
2. No team has exclusive rights to intelligence material.
3. Intelligence must flow down from the top and up from the bottom to be most effective.
4. Ultimate success in a hostage situation depends on the efficient collection, processing, and dissemination of information.

5. If the outcome of a critical situation is to be the result of a calculated response rather than chance, decisions at all levels must be made on an informed basis.

6. Information gathering must be selective. Too much is as bad as too little.

7. Good intelligence gathering depends primarily on knowing the right questions to ask and of whom to ask them.

8. Effective intelligence gathering is the result of preplanning and on-scene skillfulness.

9. Tactical intelligence must be obtained rapidly at the scene and effectively analyzed. Specific information must then be passed to the decision makers.

10. The operational value of all raw intelligence gathered must be evaluated quickly and effectively.

11. A site must be established for the evaluation of raw intelligence that is secure and all information must pass through this area.

12. All information should be reduced to writing as soon as possible.

13. Intelligence information must be constantly evaluated for relevance and reliability.

14. All people are involved in some relationships that are revealing of who and how they are. Hostage takers are also so involved.

15. Pay particular attention to modus operandi, utilization of unfamiliar weapons, unusual demands, and specific behavioral patterns.

16. What can you discover about the hostage taker's personal relationships and those of the hostage?

17. Attempt to determine if the hostage taker is working alone or in concert with others.

18. If working with others, what is the hostage taker's relationship with the others in the group?

19. Find out if the hostage taker is known in the community or if a stranger.

20. Attempt to ascertain information about the hostage taker's politics, ideology, and social background.

21. Try not to guess at information or at its meaning. To assume anything adds variables that could thwart the overall operation.

FUNCTIONS OF TACTICAL TEAM MEMBERS

The team leader is responsible for completion of the team mission; plans, organizes, and implements specific tactics used for each assignment; controls, directs, and leads the team. The leader communicates all intelligence to on-scene commander.

The marksman provides long-range and intermediate-range defense, antisniper control, and accurate base support fire at all ranges.

The observer serves as the spotter for the marksman, provides close-range and intermediate-range defense, and serves as radioman.

The scout leads the team to objectives and returns by scouting routes of ingress and egress, provides security for team, and provides close-range defense.

The rear guard provides security, close-range defense, and close-range firepower against a barricaded suspect in a fortified position.

TACTICAL USE OF THE NEGOTIATOR

The old line in this regard was, "Don't tell the negotiator anything about the likelihood of a tactical intervention. He might give it away to the hostage taker."

The reality is that not a single case of "giving it away" has been reported or documented by the FBI. (1991) On the other hand, the negotiator has often been vital in facilitating a tactical resolution. Many cases have been documented in this regard.

The negotiator should know what is going to happen tactically. Negotiators are part of the overall team and overall team operation. Negotiations do not fail because it is necessary to utilize the tactical unit. Because tactical officers and negotiators work together, negotiations become part of the overall resolution of a particular incident.

HIGH-RISK FACTORS

The high-risk factors (Fuselier, Van Zandt, & Lanceley, 1991) are critical to be understood by both tactical officers and negotiators. If these factors begin to appear or are already present within an incident, the likelihood of death to the subject or to the hostages increases dramatically. Intelligence becomes a vital issue. If negotiators become aware of these factors, in any number, the tactical role of the negotiator is enlarged. The tactical commander should be notified that a tactical solution may be necessary. Although negotiations still may be possible, all involved must know the risks when these factors are present. As the number of high-risk factors increases, the risk of homicide followed by suicide increases. The factors include:

1. The subject deliberately commits an action that he or she knows will cause a response from, as well as a confrontation with, the police.

2. The victim is known and specifically selected by the subject, especially if the subject has had a romantic involvement with the victim, or if the victim is a family member.

3. Past history of problems between the subject and victim severe enough to warrant police intervention, especially if the problems involve allegations of wife or child abuse or the victim filed a complaint.

4. Direct threats against the victim combined with no substantive demand.

5. History of previous similar incidents.

6. The hostage taker has experienced multiple recent life stressors.

7. Cultural background of subject emphasizes significance of "loss of face," or importance of male dominance in relationships.

8. Lack of familial or support systems.

9. Verbalization of intent to commit suicide.

10. Subject has given a verbal will or has "set his affairs in order."

11. History of impulsive acts.

12. Feelings of hopelessness and helplessness.

13. Negotiation team's gut feelings about the incident.

14. Test firing weapons.

SUMMARY

The author has often heard officers say, "I can't attend the negotiations school because I am now a tactical officer, not a negotiator," or "The department won't let me attend because I have been transferred to the tactical team." A tactical commander responded indignantly, after it was remarked that he had a trained negotiator on his team, "But he is not a negotiator today, he's a tactical officer."

The important point is one of a common attitude toward hostage and barricade situations. Whether or not tactical officers and negotiators are members of the same team or members of separate teams, a common body of knowledge, reflecting a common attitude, may make these operations more effective. A common attitude, a common body of knowledge, and separate teams may be the key to success. All must be "on the same sheet of music" and approach with a common goal.

Current attitudes may reflect:

1. Negotiations is not "real" police work.

2. The real work to be done is to be done by tactical units and not negotiators. In various departmental meetings, when requesting vol-

unteers for tactical and negotiations teams, many hands are raised for tactical membership; few, if any, for negotiators.

3. The purpose of negotiations is to "humor" the taker until it is time to use the tactical team to resolve the situation.
4. We have to try negotiations, but when it does not work, the tactical team will "take care of it."
5. Some departments establish a tactical team without also establishing a negotiations unit.
6. Some departments will have negotiators without a tactical unit to back them up.
7. If a smaller department gets into trouble and does not have a tactical or negotiations unit, they think that they can call the larger metropolitan tactical unit and that they will always be available to do what the smaller department has neglected to do.

A recent local situation reflects some of the difficulties. The situation ended with the death of the subject by a sniper. Although the subject finally provoked his own death, more emphasis could have been placed on gathering the limited amount of intelligence available and using it to develop some meaningful negotiations strategy. Much emphasis was placed on the tactical solution, equipment, and additional officers. Negotiations tried without success to make contact with the subject. Tactical units were then employed. The attitude was not to see if more could be done from the standpoint of negotiations. The attitude reflected what needed to be done from a tactical perspective.

Tactical and negotiations teams should be separate for greater effectiveness. Even though separate, both should share a common body of knowledge and common attitude toward the resolution of these incidents. Each should train with the other, understand the other, and treat each other as part of the same operation with similar goals even though their specific jobs are different.

Solutions to problems are not accomplished by having negotiators and tactical officers on the same team or having two separate teams that are uninvolved with each other.

Solutions are accomplished by common orientation, common approaches, common training, and common attitudes.

As shown in Fig. 17.1, this chapter has focused on the ways in which tactical units and negotiating teams have diverged in their approach to common critical incidents. The suggestion was advanced that the earlier format of training involving all in both tactical and negotiating techniques (TNT) might be the way of the future for special teams in these areas. Specific information and suggestions about the material needed in common is also

TACTICAL TEAM------------> *COMMON TASKS* <------------NEGOTIATIONS TEAM

------------------------> *COMMON ATTITUDES* <------------------------

------------------------> *COMMON PURPOSE* <-------------------------

JOB-SPECIFIC   JOB-SPECIFIC
TASKS--------------------> *COMMON TRAINING* <----------------------- TASKS

FIG. 17.1. Common bonds that must be developed between tactical and negotiating teams.

given and explained. Although this chapter is not to be construed as comprehensive in scope, it suggests what may be a more efficient and cost-effective way to train Special Weapons and Tactics units within police departments and sheriff's departments of almost all sizes. More importantly, this chapter suggests that there is a direct relationship between the degree to which tactical and negotiating teams understand and work together, and the probability of successful resolution to the critical incidents mentioned.

REFERENCES

Borum, R. (1987). *Developing effective negotiation strategies for dealing with mentally disturbed hostage takers.* Unpublished research manuscript.

Culley, J. A. (1974, October). Defusing human bombs-hostage negotiations. *FBI Law Enforcement Bulletin,* pp. 1–5.

FBI (1991, June). *Advanced Special Topics Seminar,* Johnson County Community College, Overland Park, KS.

FBI (1985). *Hostage Negotiations Seminar,* FBI Academy, Quantico, VA.

Fowler, W. R., & Greenstone, J. L. (1983). Hostage negotiations. In R. Corsini (Ed.), *Wiley encyclopedia of psychology.* New York: Wiley.

Fowler, W. R., & Greenstone, J. L. (1987). Hostage negotiations. In *Concise encyclopedia of psychology.* New York: Wiley.

Fowler, W. R., & Greenstone, J. L. (1989). *Crisis intervention compendium.* Littleton, MA: Copley.

Fuselier, G. D., Van Zandt, C. R., & Lanceley, F. J. (1991, January). High risk factors and the action criteria in hostage/barricade situations. *FBI Law Enforcement Bulletin,* pp. 2–3.

Greenstone, J. L. (1989). *A hostage negotiations team training manual for small and medium size police departments.* Dallas, TX: Leviton & Greenstone.

Greenstone, J. L. (1992, January). The key to success for hostage negotiations teams: Training, training and more training. *Police Forum.*

Greenstone, J. L., & Leviton, S. C. (1982). *Crisis intervention: Handbook for interveners.* Dubuque, IA: Kendall-Hunt.

PART SIX

ORGANIZATIONAL DEVELOPMENT AND SUPPORT

CHAPTER EIGHTEEN

Organization Consultation to Law Enforcement: An Essay From the Field

Ellen Freeman Kirschman
Ellen Kirschman & Associates
Oakland, CA

Sometimes when I am consulting I imagine myself to be a floating figure in one of Russian painter Marc Chagall's fanciful paintings. On a good day I hover high in the air, wafted along on currents of energy and excitement, feeling smart, strong, and safe in the company of competent, good-humored, action-oriented people. On other days I fall rudely to the ground, literally shot down by a relentless angry hammering at the way things are in the world and at me personally for being the outsider who cannot fix it.

Police organizations are like Chagall's dream landscapes, filled with symbolic images. Powerful emotional and cultural forces threaten to polarize employees and undermine the work effort. It is my job as organizational consultant and clinician to link those emotional and cultural forces to individual experience in order to better assist the organization in its task (Walima & Kirschman, 1988).

Never has my role been more demanding or complicated. We live in times of rapid and tumultuous social change. Our institutions are in flux. We feel disconnected from government and from each other. Bewildered and anxious, we polarize around strong, familiar images in search of simple solutions to problems that seem hopelessly complex. Police, like the rest of us, struggle to function in their multiple roles as family members, citizens, and workers—a task made more complex by the variety of new roles they are required to adopt in their changing social institutions (Shapiro & Carr, 1991, p. 4).

Police can be no better than the society they serve. The mandates they are expected to fill are burdened by unresolved historical tensions between individual rights and majority rule. They are the holding environment for society's aggression, containers of impulse in an increasingly violent and fragmented culture. They are both transmitter and scapegoat for values held by the majority. They are paid to bear the unbearable. Society expects them to resolve problems they did not create and enforce laws they did not make, laws that are often 15 years behind current social mores. This is an impossible goal and they are doomed to fail more than they succeed. How individuals and organizations respond to this futility is often the field in which organizational consultants labor the hardest.

CHAPTER OVERVIEW

This chapter starts first with a brief history of organizational services to law enforcement and then goes on to describe process consultation, a psychodynamic model of organizational consulting that focuses primarily on group activity and the relationship between the individual, the group, and the task. Specific concepts crucial to process consultation will be addressed: leadership and authority; the clarification of roles, functions, and tasks; group relations; group dynamics; the holding environment; and organizational culture.

Process consultation differs from more traditional forms of organizational intervention in which the expert consultant arrives to solve an already-defined problem. For the process consultant, problem definition and organizational diagnosis are developed in tandem with the agency so that the locus of expertise is ultimately seeded in the agency and does not leave with the consultant. In fact the process consultant's real expertise is in assisting agency staff to understand their own group dynamics, rather than in solving problems. What distinguishes process consultation from group therapy is that the work is done in the service of the organizational task rather than individual development, although individual development can be an unanticipated benefit. The values and hazards of this particular model and how it contrasts with other types of organizational interventions are discussed throughout.

A BRIEF HISTORY OF ORGANIZATIONAL SERVICES
TO LAW ENFORCEMENT

It has been three decades since law enforcement and psychology teamed up to apply behavioral science principles to policing. These applications included direct services to individuals, pre-employment selection, fitness for duty evaluations, career guidance and placement, training, management consultation, community relations work, and crime-specific interventions such as hostage negotiation and criminal profiling (Kirschman, Scrivner, Ellison, & Marcy, 1992). In general, the focus of the first decade of police psychology was on the individual.

Two decades ago the focus changed. Researchers developed data that implicated organizations in the health and well-being of individual officers. Kroes, Margolis, and Hurrell (1974a, 1974b; see also Kroes & Gould, 1979) found that lack of administrative support and rigid authoritarian practices were a particularly pernicious source of stress for officers, exceeding the expected stress of line of duty danger. Officers, like other workers, were prepared to work in a professional, not a bureaucratic system (Kramer, 1974). Researchers investigating the causes of police stress and burnout (Aldag & Brief, 1978; Broderick, 1977; Danto, 1978, 1979; Ellison & Genz, 1978; Johnson, 1972; Munro, 1974; Reiser, 1974; Toch, 1978) turned from identifying bad people toward uncovering bad situations (Kirschman, 1987). Police psychologists began to apply organizational theory to law enforcement in an effort to flatten hierarchies, raise supervisorial consciousness, and mediate between subcultures. Police administrators studied organizational theory and looked to the private sector and to academic psychology for new models of management that would improve labor relations, leadership, productivity, organizational communication, and decision making (Swanson & Territo, 1983).

This was a startling development on two fronts. First, it brought into question the wisdom of the traditional we–they boundary that isolated police professionals from nonpolice professionals. What had been a closed system was now importing ideas, information, and expertise from business and industry. Second, private sector models appeared to challenge the paramilitary structure of policing in favor of a more collegial form of governance. Concepts like participative management and team building were frequently cited and many police agencies began to develop mission statements and talk about values.

There was, and still is, skepticism about these new ideas and their benefits. Organization consultants had to work hard to overcome suspicion that these trends were merely new ways for management to get rank and file to cooperate while continuing to dominate them and deny them participation in important decisions (Gustafson et al., 1981). Consultants had to prove that they were not merely management shills whose agendas supported the administrators who paid their fees. At the same time, consultants had to reassure managers who feared they were losing authority and power to line level officers. Organization consultants had to wend their way carefully through this minefield of mutual projections. To align with one faction or interest group was to abandon another and risk losing credibility and trust as a consultant (Gustafson et al., 1981).

Among the skeptics were those who thought that organizational theories based on research conducted in business and industry had limited generalizability to human service organizations (HSOs) such as hospitals, social services agencies, schools, and police departments. Kouzes and Mico (1979), for instance, criticized organization development technology because it was industry specific. They believed industry operated from a simple structural paradigm with profit being a clear quantifiable goal and measure of success. The goals of HSOs, on the contrary, were ambiguous, problematic, unclear, intangible, and qualitative. They described HSOs as associations of spheres of influence and control they called *domains*. The three primary domains—policymaking, management, and service delivery—each operated by contrasting principles, had different views of reality, employed different success measures, and used various modes of work. They believed organization consultation was best utilized to "create opportunities for people to confront the tensions caused by the interactions of these disjunctive domains" (p. 462).

The more complex the organizational task, the more subgroups are inclined to substitute their own group task as the defining goal of the organization. This is a familiar scenario in police organizations where the city council, administrators, and line-level personnel seem perpetually at odds over such issues as the definition of their primary mission, the apportionment of scarce resources, and norms of behavior. These same conflicts extend even to the service providers who argue about the relative importance of the many mandated and optional police services; a far cry from the relative simplicity of profit and loss.

The 1980s and 1990s saw a move toward purposefully enlarging the domain of collaboration in law enforcement with the creation of community-oriented policing, which can be described as an effort to widen the collaborative domain between police and citizens by maximizing contact with the community, and increasing communication, exposure, and accountability. Problem definition and problem solving are done conjointly with the consumer or customer of police services. Access to city services is restructured and authority redistributed between municipal departments so that the line-level officer can solve a social or community problem by going directly to another city department for assistance. The experience and expertise of private industry is indelibly stamped on community policing through strategies and concepts of customer service, research and development, and a variety of marketing and service delivery techniques.

Such collaborative efforts are not always welcome because the existence of an impermeable boundary between police and community can be reassuring to both sides. Police are concerned that a coalition with the community will result in a civilian review board and the unwelcome intrusion of uninformed, hostile citizen groups into police management. While most communities welcome community policing, some believe the presence of substations and beat officers in their neighborhood is tantamount to living in occupied territory.

Public servants still have many more masters to serve than their counterparts in private industry. As organizational consultants assist police in these troubled times, they will have to move beyond simplified industrial models in order to deepen and expand their understanding of the gordian relationship between individuals, groups, institutions, and culture. The consultation model described in the next section presents neither formulas nor recipes for how to go about this; rather it suggests certain stances, values, and areas of inquiry that organizational consultants could employ to optimize the impact of consultation work with law enforcement. These concepts are drawn from several theorists but primarily from systems theory, the work of group relations theorist Wilfred Bion and the Tavistock Institute for Human Relations in London.

ROLE AND TASK OF THE PROCESS-ORIENTED CONSULTANT

The work of the organizational consultant is psychodynamic; phenomenological; systemic in scope; sensitive to issues of race, gender, and authority; and focused more on process than content and more on group relations than individual personality. The consultant's role is that of participant/observer, not expert. The consultant is a mutual learner along with clients, and not a trainer, although occasional training may be necessary. The consultant is not a meeting facilitator, an encounter group leader, a strategist, a planner, or a therapist, although he or she is much interested in the data of individual experience, particularly anxiety, and he or she uses interpretation as an intervention tool.

The work of psychodynamic, process-oriented consultation contrasts significantly with interventions that rely predominantly (and optimistically) on conscious, rational thinking for data about the organization. Such interventions (Ayres & Flanagan, 1990; Reese & Goldstein, 1986) tend to focus on well-defined measurable problems (e.g., productivity) or teach specific skills. They are popular with law enforcement because they resonate with aspects of the police culture that emphasize a nonemotional, nonthreatening, control-based, goal-oriented approach to problem solving.

Entering the System

Each time participant/observer consultants contract with a client they must study the new culture they are entering. I learned the value of being a participant/observer when I was a drama student observing people at work. My professor had warned me that bad acting resulted from false and romantic assumptions about the character one played. Great actors, he said, understood that Macbeth roamed the halls of his drafty, ill-lit castle wrapped in a stinking bearskin cape for warmth. His life was both corporeal and cerebral. It was not enough to portray only his tortured emotions. For a drama project I took a job in a Times Square dance hall. I observed firsthand that the work was tedious and that business was conducted according to a stringent unwritten etiquette, violation of which brought censure and social expulsion from the dozen or so female dance partners who represented most of the erotic archetypes from ancient and modern history. This was a big surprise, as I was expecting to find only licentiousness and anarchy in such a wanton enterprise. It was also an enduring first lesson in the benefits of immersing myself in the occupational subculture of the workplace.

Years of consulting experience have supported the soundness of that unexpected lesson, especially when the occupational culture is distorted by projections and contains values vastly different from one's own (Kirschman et al., 1992). There is no textbook treatment or classroom lecture that can approximate the information, perspective, and credibility one gains from firsthand observation and participation at the worksite. Officers care more about how many hours consultants have spent riding in a patrol car in the middle of the night than where they earned their doctorates.

Leadership and Group Dynamics

Human beings live and work in groups. Our memberships in groups are reassuring when they address our needs and frightening when they threaten to overwhelm our sense of individuality. We hold memberships in many groups at once—work, family, community, and so on—and those groups may be related, sometimes cooperatively, sometimes competitively. It is axiomatic that one cannot take the individual out of the group or the group out of the individual (Shapiro & Carr, 1991).

Organizations are structured, intentional associations of groups with an agreed-on task. Process consultants spend much of their time working with groups and considering the relationship between individuals, groups, leadership, authority, and task. These relationships are uniquely strained in the police culture because individual personality is so often squashed by the standardization of labor, projections from society, and the pressure to conform and bond together against a seemingly hostile public.

Understanding how leadership and authority is connected to group behavior is crucial to organizational diagnosis. Often the police chief or manager who has first contacted the consultant is both the source and bearer of the problems the consultant will address. When working with individual leaders, I look at how group and organizational behavior promotes or impedes individuals from exercising personal or vested authority. I ask myself a number of questions: Is leadership related to the whole organization or to certain segments only? Is authority delegated on the basis of competence or other factors like gender, race, or politics? How clear are leaders about the role and task of the agency and its subunits. How knowledgeable is the chief about these dynamic factors in the agency? What is the relationship between overt and covert, formal and informal leadership? Can new leaders emerge? Are current leaders cut off and isolated? What projections do leaders attract and why? How can such projections be returned to the rest of the organization?

The way in which group dynamics influences individuals and impacts the exercise of leadership and authority was described by Bion (1975; Rioch, 1975; Shapiro & Carr, 1991). Bion hypothesized the existence of two levels of group functioning: conscious, rational, task-oriented activity known as *work*, and unconscious, irrational activity known as *basic assumption* life. Bion described three basic assumptions seen in group activity: *dependence* (the shared assumption that groups come together to meet their dependency needs rather than to work); *fight or flight* (the assumption that groups assemble not to work but to fight or flee from the leader or to get the leader to collude with the group in fight or flight activity); and *pairing* (the assumption that the group is organized to produce a pair who will save the day rather than require the group to collaborate in the solution to a problem). Turquet (1985, p. 71) added a fourth assumption, *basic oneness*, in which a group operated as if it were all of one mind, and was all the individual members needed to survive in the world. All of these "as if" states of group activity exist along a continuum ranging from universal and normal to exaggerated and pathological and each has its light and dark sides. Dependency on the leader, for instance, can be seen in team spirit and group loyalty as well as in the tragic consequences of following a Jim Jones or a David Koresh.

During a consultation I ask myself: What is the basic assumption life of this group at this time? Sometimes I will formulate an "as if" question using a description of the group activity based on one of the four assumptions. For example, why is this group acting as if there is only one competent person in the room and no one else can do any work (an assumption of dependency)? The answer usually provides enough insight into the group dynamics to allow me to present an interpretation for the group's consideration.

Dependency is the predominant assumption in the police culture. This contradicts stereotypical views of police as fighters. Although police do fight, of course, they have pressing needs for job security and their predilection for variety and action is best satisfied within a contained holding environment in which they are well cared for. *Holding environment* is a term borrowed from family therapy to describe the way in which families manage and contain the emotional aspects of family life (Shapiro & Carr, 1991, p. 7). The power of holding environments to contain aggression and minister to dependent needs is best seen in the breech. Even small rents in the holding environment generate major shifts into a fight or flight reaction. Shoring up the integrity of the holding environment, normalizing dependency, balancing individual and organizational responsibility, and linking all to effective police work is a critical task for the organization consultant.

THE ROLE OF THE POLICE INSTITUTION AS A HOLDING ENVIRONMENT

Police are a holding environment for society. Society depends on police for basic safety needs and to help manage anxiety about the aggressive impulses of others. Reaction to the Rodney King verdict strongly demonstrated the degree to which some members of society regard police as the source of the aggression they are seeking to stop. The perception that they cannot depend on the very social institution created for their protection constitutes a serious deprivation because institutions are social systems that "function as a collective defense against anxiety" (Menzies, 1975, p. 281). Police institutions serve police employees in the same way by providing a collective defense against the anxiety generated by the job itself.

Adults are ambivalent about dependency because dependence threatens deeply held values of autonomy, independence, and free will and is reminiscent of a primitive, childlike aspect of ourselves. This is especially difficult for law enforcers because of cultural projections about police and masculinity that imprison officers as much as they imprison those who create the projections (C. Hampden-Turner, personal communication, 1980).

When individual officers feel disconnected from their institutions, or the institutions themselves disconnect from society, we see disorder within police departments and the increase of basic assumption activity—particularly fight or flight activity—as manifested by vigilantism, brutality, burnout, labor unrest, and the perversion of authority. Although society has every right to expect police to hold to a higher standard, it is also obligated to provide the support necessary to maintain that higher standard. Neither the dependent needs of society nor the dependent needs of officers can be ignored because of their intrinsic relatedness.

The process consultant models the holding environment by providing employees a container in which to learn to understand and manage the social and intrapsychic experiences that are attached to police work:

despair (Bonifacio, 1991), ambivalence, fear, dependence, impulsivity, cynicism (Niederhoffer, 1967), anxiety, frustration, and the ongoing dilemma between the humiliation of passivity and remorse for aggression (Charlton, 1982). I work with leadership at all levels of the organization to apply the authority of their role to secure the work environment so that it becomes a safe base from which to take risks. Law enforcement takes risks in order to make things secure. Conversely, things must be secure in order to take those risks.

Although police officers are by no means children, the metaphor of childhood is illuminating. A child who cannot depend on the accessibility and stability of a parent has no freedom to risk or explore. Echoes of this persist into adulthood. Although chiefs may have little or no direct relationship to many of their employees, they are related in the employee's mind. When the chief arrives at the scene of a critical incident it almost always carries a symbolic measure of concern and reassurance that far exceeds the chief's ability to influence the situation at hand. Conversely, weak leadership or constantly changing leadership raises organizational anxiety and interferes with the accomplishment of real work. I witnessed near revolution in an agency in which the officers felt abandoned by their chief. Whereas the line level sought a vote of no confidence, managers talked about ignoring the chief because it was their agency and they could run it despite him or without him. In another agency, line-level staff sought to bring their concerns directly to the city council and to the media because they felt their leadership no longer understood or cared about their welfare. They perceived their leader to be kind and well meaning, but ineffective and politically powerless in a city structure in which other department heads had the strategic acumen needed to lobby for their own. This nice but ineffective chief left his employees feeling as though they were running their own ship without the authority to do so. His staff spent an enormous amount of time worrying and complaining about their uncertain future, feeling like they were riding a rudderless ship through the turbulent macroenvironment of city hall.

The technology of critical incident debriefing exemplifies how dependence can be normalized in the service of the task by honoring the universal human need to depend on something larger than oneself in times of stress. These advances were preceded by a cultural reframing of dependence, a normalizing of the range of psychological reactions to stressful aspects of the job, and permission to both offer and accept a container for the exploration of the individual human experience of traumatic stress (Kirschman, 1992). One of the most impressive and moving aspects of a critical incident group debriefing, for example, is the affirmation of team members' feelings for each other. The depth of this intense connection is not openly or directly addressed in daily work because of cultural prohibitions (including homophobia) against the open expression of dependency and affection. Discussing this attachment is reassuring in that the group together acknowledges and reinforces how crucial interdependence and collaboration are to their tasks. Although the drama experienced by field personnel is rarely mirrored in the conference room, the ability to collaborate productively around any task is related to the experience individuals have as members of a group.

CONSULTANT STRATEGIES

As a dependent culture, police agencies frequently rely on experts to tell them what is wrong and what to do about it. What the process consultant prefers is to create an atmosphere that facilitates the consultees' discovery that they possess both the data and the means of interpreting this data themselves. This is often frustrating to the client who may wonder why they are spending money on a consultant who refuses to tell them what to do! Instead, the consultant adopts what Shapiro and Carr (1991) called an interpretative stance, inviting the consultees to make sense of their own reality by capitalizing on the uniquely human enterprise of making meaning. The group, with the consultant's guidance, shares each members' unique experience and together negotiates how these divergent experiences connect to the larger organizational context (Shapiro & Carr, 1991).

The consultant challenges the group to remain open to individual experience, rejecting a fervent closemindedness that Shapiro and Carr (1991) called *pathological certainty*. Pathological certainty is a cognitive distortion that prevents groups from absorbing information that contradicts the certainty of present ideas. It also shores up anxiety and reduces the appearance of chaos by creating simple polarities that become anchors in a turbulent environment—the familiar we–they dichotomy: They are brutal, we are brave; they are cowards, we are cautious; they are tyrannical, we are assertive. High levels of certainty are endemic to police training and closely correlated to control issues that are paramount to the police task. The consultant avoids colluding with these distortions and models a sort of professional astonishment and Socratic questioning of pathological certainty as well as other negative cognitive habits common to law enforcement such as catastrophizing, overgeneralizing, selective attention, perfectionism, and the rush to solutions.

Negotiated interpretations and self-observation are process skills that belong to those who learn them and will rest with the organization after the consultation is complete. Owning these skills minimizes the paradoxical habit agencies have of resisting the information they demand from the expert. For example, I was working in a management retreat with a group in which relations were extremely strained between managers and the chief. The managers felt the chief was aloof, hid in his office, and caused trouble when he came out. What they did not see was how they as a group isolated him from information and offered him little in the way of support, consolation, or companionship. His managers repeatedly acted as though he were the only person in the group authorized to make a decision and when he did, they criticized the decision, withdrew in angry silence, or threatened to ignore it completely. As luck would have it, this dynamic repeated itself at the retreat over a relatively minor matter. When the consultant pointed this out, there was no disputing the immediate behavioral data: The group was "caught in the act" as it were. Although this alone did not stop the behavior, when it happened again the group now owned a negotiated interpretation on which to hang their organizational hats and possessed words to describe a dynamic concept they had previously only been able to feel. "Are we again isolating the chief? Why are we not making decisions for ourselves?" These questions came from the group, not the consultant.

A negotiated interpretation may begin with the consultant prompting the group to ask itself the question: "Given that we agree that we are engaged in a particular task, how can we attempt to make sense of the behavior we are observing and experiencing in relation to it?" (Shapiro & Carr, 1991, p. 6). Because role is the framework in which person and context link, process consultants also ask individuals to discuss what is happening to them in their roles and why, and then collaboratively link those responses to the organizational task. Very often these responses are lyrical and metaphorical as people describe feeling like they are choking, or lost, or about to explode. For example, the experience of a child sexual assault investigator revealed subtle confusion over the investigator's task, conflicting values concerning the rights of victims versus the rights of suspects, polarized perceptions held by male and female personnel about these rights, systemwide issues concerning the degree of support the investigator should need, and boundary issues regarding how political pressures and the reformation of child sexual abuse laws influenced the investigation. Each domain had different views about these issues that they subconsciously put into the investigator. Because the investigator carried many of these conflicts for the organization, he was constantly under exceptional levels of stress. The consultant worked with the affected individual to interpret and link these broad issues in the service of conducting an effective investigation.

Linking individual experience to the mutual work endeavor is what distinguishes this strategy from group therapy or the encounter group movement of the 1960s, in which organizational consultants frequently overemphasized interpersonal relationships and underemphasized the work task (Dyer, 1987). Failure to link individual experience to task, role, and organization leaves the agency vulnerable to a compelling focus on personality. Although personality is relevant to group functioning it is often a distraction from systemic issues in which the actors may change but problems stay the same.

It is just as important to ask why a group needs an individual to behave a certain way at this time as it is to coach the individual on behavior or ask why this individual chooses to jump into the organizational breech. Chronic complainers frequently express the unhappiness experienced by many employees in much the same way organizational consultants are the ones who ask the hard questions that are on everyone's mind. The presence of individual idiosyncrasy or pathology needs to be recognized, managed, and acknowledged, but not at the expense of failing to interpret or question the underlying systemic issues. Unfortunately, individual pathology is easier to identify and remedy than are large, systemwide organizational problems. Measures that focus on the individual—pre-employment screening, fitness for duty evaluations, and the prediction of violence—have been invaluable in assembling a hardy, competent work force, but they do not and cannot address the crucial, ongoing relationship between task, role, person, and group.

Consultants must utilize their own individual experience with agencies as a source of data about the agency itself, particularly because agency personnel often project on the consultant that which is needed or missing. For example, when I am feeling particularly stupid or incompetent while working with a group, I will often ask if others are feeling the same. I might probe for hidden norms that stifle creativity by making it unsafe to make mistakes, ask questions, or say "I don't know." Because I often work at the behest of the chief, I frequently assume that people are projecting attributes onto me that are similar to those they project on the chief. In the retreat described earlier, I was first set up with a question to which there existed no satisfactory response. This ultimately allowed me to recognize that dynamic when it happened to the chief.

A FINAL WORD AND CAVEAT

Process consultants are not all-purpose consultants. We are best used to consult to issues of leadership, power, and authority. We can also be very helpful in optimizing the work of other more content-oriented consultants. For instance, managers in an agency were projecting many of the agency's problems onto the supervisors. Fix the supervisors and we fix our problems, they thought. An expert consultant presented an excellent class in discipline and training to supervisors, but it was clear to him that his work could not be applied until other systemwide issues were addressed and projections were withdrawn so that the managers could work on their own problems. The presence of a process consultant to work on these systemwide issues ultimately optimized the work of the expert in discipline and training.

Because process consultation attends to systemic, often subconscious group dynamics, it cannot be packaged. It takes time to diagnose the needs and idiosyncrasies of each client agency. When is the right time to call for a process consultant? This varies, although in my experience it frequently occurs when the chief executive officer is feeling a great deal of stress, frustration, and conflict. The presenting problem may only be a ticket in the door and the real issues may be waiting in the wings. The consultant first measures the possibility for effective interventions by how open the chief and executive officers are to negotiating the organizational diagnosis, especially if it is expanded beyond the presenting complaint. In one instance, I was asked to consult to an agency that was unable to retain female officers despite mammoth efforts on the part of the chief, who was profoundly frustrated by this. I uncovered so much anger toward the chief and accusations of unfairness to all employees that I had to reframe the diagnosis to suggest dealing with long-standing issues of authoritarian management practices. When the chief refused to renegotiate the diagnosis or the desired outcomes to include those larger issues of authoritarian management practices, the consulting work was doomed to failure.

The current financial crisis affecting government forces managers and consultants to work quickly toward solutions that realistically require a 12- to 18-month commitment before agreed-on results are visible. It is the nature of change that it is seen mainly in retrospect: People remember how it used to be and realize it is not that way anymore. It is also in the nature of change that there will be a period of resistance and "change back" messages from the environment (Lerner, 1985). The consultation process must be long enough to absorb both. Process consultation has many ups and downs: Personnel are frequently angry and discouraged with the consultant and tempted to find another. The basic assumption here is one of pairing and finding a magical combination that will solve all the problems. This often results in consultant "shopping," in which a series of consultants pass through a revolving door, leaving the agency despairing of making any changes for the good. Without resources to support a 12- to 18-month consultation, it may be better to not begin.

However, here may be where the established domain of collaboration between law enforcement and psychology (Kirschman et al., 1992) can result in each being able to creatively negotiate an arrangement that fairly accommodates the others' financial considerations without diminishing the depth or quality of the consultation work.

REFERENCES

Aldag, R. J., & Brief, A. (1978). Supervisory style and police role stress. *Journal of Police Science and Administration, 6,* 362–367.

Ayres, R., & Flanagan, G. (1990). *Preventing law enforcement stress: The organization's role.* Washington, DC: U.S. Government Printing Office.

Bion, W. (1975). Selections from: Experiences in groups. In A. Colman & W. Bexton (Eds.), *Group relations reader* (pp. 11–20). Sausalito, CA: GREX.

Bonifacio, P. (1991). *The psychological effects of police work.* New York: Plenum.

Broderick, J. (1977). *Police in a time of change.* Morristown, PA: General Learning Press.

Charlton, R. (1982, April). *Some vocational hazards of policework and their psychological treatment.* Paper presented at Psychotherapy and Law Enforcement: Issues and Techniques, University of California at San Francisco.

Danto, B. L. (1978). Police suicide. *Police Stress, 1*(1), 95–99.

Danto, B. L. (1979). Police stress—Its causes and types. *Police Product News, 3*(10), 56–60.

Dyer, W. (1987). *Team building: Issues and alternatives* (2nd ed.). Menlo Park, CA: Addison-Wesley.

Ellison, K., & Genz, J. (1978). The police officer as burned-out samaritan. *FBI Law Enforcement Bulletin, 47*(3), 1–7.

Gustafson, J. P., Cooper, L., Lathrop, N. C., Ringler, K., Seldin, F. A., & Wright, M. K. (1981). Cooperative and clashing interests in small groups, Part I. Theory. *Human Relations, 34*(4), 315–339.

Johnson, T. (1972). Police resistance to police community relations: The emergence of the patrol subculture. *Journal of Forensic Sciences, 17*(3), 485–486.

Kirschman, E. (1983). Wounded heroes: A case study and systems analysis of job related stress and emotional dysfunction in three police officers. *Dissertation Abstracts International, 44,* 1279B. (University Microfilms No. 83-19, 921).

Kirschman, E. (1987). Organizational development: Buddha in search of the barrel. In H. More & P. Unsinger (Eds.), *Police managerial use of psychology and psychologists* (pp. 85–106). Springfield, IL: Thomas.

Kirschman, E. (1992, March). Critical incident stress: Cracks in the occupational persona. *Law Enforcement Technology,* pp. 22–27.

Kirschman, E., Scrivner, E., Ellison, K., & Marcy, C. (1992). Work and well-being: Lessons from law enforcement. In J. Quick, L. Murphy, & J. Hurrell (Eds.), *Stress and well being at work* (pp. 178–192). Washington, DC: American Psychological Association.

Kouzes, J., & Mico, P. (1979). Domain theory: An introduction to organizational behavior in human service organizations. *Journal of Applied Behavioral Science, 15*(4), 449–469.

Kramer, M. (1974). *Reality shock.* St. Louis: Mosby.

Kroes, W., & Gould, S. (1979). Job stress in policemen: An empirical study. *Police Stress, 1*(2), 9–10, 44–46.

Kroes, W., Margolis, B., & Hurrell, J. (1974a). Job stress in police administrators. *Journal of Police Science and Administration, 2*(4), 381–387.

Kroes, W., Margolis, B., & Hurrell, J. (1974b). Job stress in policemen. *Journal of Police Science and Administration, 2*(2), 145–155.

Lerner, H. G. (1985). *The dance of anger.* New York: Harper & Row.

Menzies, I. (1975). A case-study in the functioning of social systems as a defense against anxiety. In A. Colman & W. Bexton (Eds.), *Group relations reader* (pp. 11–20). Sausalito, CA: GREX.

Munro, J. L. (1974). *Administrative behavior and police organization.* Cincinnati, OH: Anderson.

Niederhoffer, A. (1967). *Behind the blue shield.* Garden City, NY: Doubleday.

Reese, J., & Goldstein, H. (1986). *Psychological service for law enforcement.* Washington, DC: U.S. Government Printing Office.

Reiser, M. (1974). Some organizational stressors on policemen. *Journal of Police Science and Administration, 2*(2), 156–159.

Rioch, M. (1975). The work of Wilfred Bion on groups. In A. Colman & W. Bexton (Eds.), *Group relations reader* (pp. 11–20). Sausalito, CA: GREX.

Shapiro, E. R., & Carr, A. W. (1991). *Lost in familiar places.* New Haven, CT: Yale University Press.

Swanson, C., & Territo, L. (1983). *Police administration: Structures, processes, and behavior.* New York: Macmillan.

Toch, H. (1978). Police morale: Living with discontent. *Journal of Police Science and Administration, 6*(3), 249–252.

Turquet, P. (1985). Leadership, the individual and the group. In G. Gibbard, D. Colman, & M. Geller (Eds.), *Group relations reader, 2* (pp. 71–88). Washington, DC: A.K. Rice Institute.

Walima, S., & Kirschman, E. (1988, October). Health resource coordinators: Organizational consultation services. *Police Chief,* pp. 78–81.

CHAPTER NINETEEN

Organizational Management of Stress and Human Reliability

Martin I. Kurke

Drug Enforcement Adminstration (Retired)
and George Mason University

This chapter treats stress as it affects human performance within the context of police organizational needs. Stress is generated from a number of different categories of sources and is manifested in terms of changes in human reliability, which in turn impact the effectiveness of the organization. A dynamic model of stress generation as a mediator of both individual and organizational value systems is presented. Various sources of human reliability are considered together with means of preventing or correcting lowered human reliability. The model is then elaborated on and extended to include various forms of management interventions directed to reduction of harmful stress, thereby enhancing individual and group work performance and, in turn, improving organizational effectiveness.

THE NEED TO OPTIMIZE STRESS
IN POLICE ORGANIZATIONS

It is no secret that police officers are being subjected to an inordinate amount of stress, and that stress is a two-edged sword. It has long been recognized that the quality of performance will increase in response to certain stressors up to some point, after which there occur degradations of performance (Yerkes & Dodson, 1908). It follows then, that to survive and grow, any organization must ensure the existence of an optimal amount of stress on its staff. Stress, if properly managed, can motivate activities that result in survival and growth. But stress, like costs, must be contained if the organization's objectives are to be achieved. Stress is a useful management tool, but like fire, it can be either a good servant or a bad master. Attempts to cope with stress as a bad master will yield emotional, behavioral, or physical warning signs, and if not controlled, can affect the agency's bottom line as well as its personnel's health and career plans. Maladaptive stress can lead to lowered morale, ineffective performance, an increased likelihood of maladaptive behavior, and accidents, as well as increased employee turnover.

STRESS IN THE POLICE WORKING ENVIRONMENT

Stress may be viewed as the embodiment of conflict resulting from demands for performance of bodily and social (including occupational) functions imposed by any constellation of environmental and psychological, factors that either stimulate or inhibit one's ability to satisfactorily perform physiological, psychological, or social (again including occupational) functions. Berkhout (1970) categorized the intervening factors into enviromental and psychological stressors. A third category of intervening factors, relating to one's physical condition, must also be considered. Some of the stress factors that may impact on a police officer's ability to function well, if at all, include the following:

- Environmental stress factors
    Vibration and acoustic noise
        Chronic noise and vibration levels
        Intense (destructive) vibration and noise
    Perceptual deficits
    Thermal stress
    Atmospheric variations (air pressure, composition, circulation)
    Chemical stress, including those induced by foods and drugs
    Physical work overload
- Physical condition stress factors
    Health deficits
    Physical fitness deficits
    Age-induced performance degradation
    Pregnancy
- Psychological stress factors
    Monotony and boredom
    Job and task anomalies
        Job- and or management-induced anxiety, frustration, fear
        Equipment or operational procedural demands incompatible with
        physical and mental capabilities
    Disruption of circadian periodicity (e.g., shift work)
    Genuine danger

Learning and training state
Social and family interaction degradation

The psychological literature is replete with studies, theories, and discussions of psychological stress in the working environment. Much of this literature has been reviewed elsewhere. See, for example, Beehr and Franz (1987), Fletcher (1988), Kahn and Byosiere (1992), Keita and Jones (1990), and Levi (1990). Ostrov (1986) observed that stress related to police work breaks down into organizational, operational, and situational components. Organizational stressors center on work-related conditions such as shift work and lack of supervisory support. Operational stressors include the life-threatening nature of police work, boredom, tension between the police and the community, threats of civil liability, and lack of support at home. Being shot or shooting a citizen, working in a disaster situation, and other critical incidents are examples of stress-generating situations. A study of stress in an English provincial police force identified the relative impact of stressors across the ranks and found that constables were more likely to feel stressed by time pressures and deadlines, long working hours, working with civilians, and police politics; sergeants by having to manage or supervise, working in isolation and lack of consultation; and high-level managers by criticism by the media. The authors concluded that stressors most often affecting police officers derive more from organization and management considerations than from front-line duties (Brown & Campbell, 1990). Based on academic research and his experience on the street Violanti (1988) presented a model of stress peculiar to the police environment. The model categorized police work stressors into four categories.

1. Intragroup stressors, which include (a) the discrepancy between the police conception of justice and the workings of the criminal court system, (b) conflicts between the officer's role of social controller and community helper, and (c) strains on family relations resulting from a perceived need to depersonalize interactions with the family to shield them from police work.

2. Organizational stressors, which include (a) administratively required paperwork and red tape; (b) conflicting demands imposed by different supervisors; (c) lack of feedback and lack of support from organizational superiors; (d) dead-end positions; (e) feelings that supervisors do not trust them, and a punishment-centered management philosophy; and (f) poor communications within the organization.

3. Interpersonal stressors characterized by breakdowns of relations with peers or supervisors.

4. Individual stressors such as shift work, boredom, and lowered self-esteem, which in combination with the other stressors lead to burnout (Violanti, 1988).

Another scheme for the classification of stress in the police and other working environments categorizes stress as arising from three sources: the ambient environment, the organizational environment, and extraorganizational stressors such as dysfunctional family relationships, economic conditions, and legal issues. Ambient environment stressors include both physical and physiological conditions that have the potential for affecting human performance. Examples of this category include acceleration, chemical stressors, fatigues, glare, heat, noise, and vibration (Boff, Kaufman, & Thomas, 1986; Boff & Lincoln, 1988).

Organizational stressors include the organization's human resource system, intrinsic job factors, the design and operability of equipment and tools used, the design of the work facility in which the work is performed, and organizational culture, leadership, structure, and control systems. Ivancevich and Matteson (1987) proposed a framework for organizational stress relating the consequences of organizational stress to the individuals who make up the organization (Fig. 19.1). They consider two types of differences (a) biologic and demographic, including factors such as age, gender, occupation, health status, and education; and (b) cognitive and affective differences, including need levels, locus of control, personality type (A and B), hardiness, self-esteem, and social support available to the individual. These factors

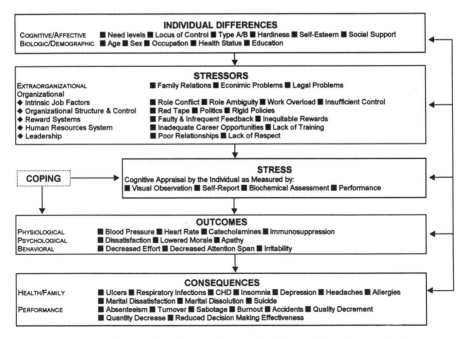

FIG. 19.1. Organizational stress framework (adapted from Ivancevich & Matteson, 1987).

impinge on each of the remaining portions of the framework: stressors, stress, outcomes, and consequences.

Organizational and extraorganizational stressors are mutually interactive and induce the psychological and physiological condition we call stress. The individual's ability to cope with stress is influential in determining its physiological, psychological, and behavioral outcomes and consequences of those outcomes. They categorize the outcomes as those that impact on the individual's health and family, and those that impact on the individual's performance. The full set of consequences feed back to modify the stressors. Hibler (1978) considered stress in terms of the ability of an individual to cope with the world, categorizing the adverse responses into three types: emotional, behavioral, and physical, and provided the examples of each type of indicator shown in Table 19.1.

Hibler pointed out that it is the degree of change from a person's own baseline emotional, behavioral, and physical conditions and the duration, frequency, and intensity of those changes that signal difficulty in coping with stressors.

STRESS AS A MEDIATOR OF VALUE SYSTEMS AND ORGANIZATIONAL EFFECTIVENESS

The author is convinced that to understand and successfully cope with stressors in the workplace, one must start by knowing the police agency's management needs for survival and growth. One also needs to know what the individuals who make up management and staff need for their personal survival and growth. Some of these needs are:

Management Needs	*Employees' Needs*
Responsiveness to operational needs	Self-esteem
	Performance record
Responsiveness to administrative needs	Remuneration
	Job security and advancement
Reputation for performance	Personal time and space for family
Cost containment	and significant others
Responsiveness to political pressures	Intangible benefits of membership in a police organization.
Interagency cooperation	

In some cases, the management's needs and officer and other employee needs coincide in that satisfying the needs of management also goes a long way toward satisfying the personal needs of the organization's component

TABLE 19.1
Categories of Adverse Responses to Stress

Emotional	Behavioral	Physical
Apathy	**Withdrawal (avoidance)**	**Preoccupation with illness**
• The "Blahs"	• Social isolation	(intolerant of/dwelling on
• Recreation no longer	• Work-related with-	minor ailments)
pleasurable	drawal	
• Sad	—Reluctance to accept	**Frequent illness** (actually
	responsibilities	sick)
Anxiety	—Neglecting responsibilities	
• Restless		**Physical exhaustion**
• Agitated		
• Insecure	**Acting out**	**Use of self-medication**
• Feelings of worthlessness	• Alcohol abuse	(inordinate)
	• Gambling	
	• Spending sprees	**Somatic indicators**
Irritability	• Promiscuity	• Headache
• Overly sensitive		• Insomnia
• Defensive	**Desperate acting out**	—Initial insomnia
• Arrogant and	**(getting attention; cry**	—Recurrent awakening
argumentative	**for help)**	—Early morning rising
• Insubordinate, hostile	• Administrative infractions	• Change in appetite
	—Tardy for work	—Weight gain
Mental fatigue	—Poor appearance	—Weight loss (more
• Preoccupied	—Poor personal hygiene	serious)
• Difficulty in concentrating	—Accident prone	• Indigestion
• Inflexible	• Legal infractions	• Nausea
	—Indebtedness	• Vomiting
Overcompensation (Denial)	—Shoplifting	• Diarrhea
• Exaggerate/grandiose	—Traffic violations	• Constipation
• Overworks to exhaustion	• Fights	• Sexual difficulties
• Denies problems and	—Child/spouse abuse	
symptoms		
• Suspicious, paranoid		

people, and vice versa. In other cases, management's value systems and needs and the personal value systems needs of its people conflict, contributing to both organizational and individual stress. Figure 19.2 models the dynamic flow of this process. The depiction of dynamics of the work environment, including the organizational culture and management's value systems, illustrates how the needs of management influence its operational style, expressed in the way it generates and applies the rules and procedures for the organization. At the same time, each individual in the organization has his or her own unique personal acculturation and value system. That system is driven by the structure and dynamics of the individual's needs and the coping mechanisms for dealing with stress. The personal system allows the individual to select from a repertoire of coping mechanisms. At

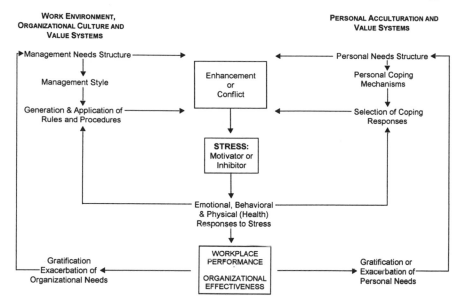

FIG. 19.2. Stress as a mediator of value systems and organizational effectiveness.

any given time the individual's and management's system may induce stress derived from the conflict itself. In addition, stressors of different types arising from the situation will act in one of a number of different ways. The individual stressor effects may have an effect on each other; an additive effect summating the effects of the component stressor effects, a synergistic effect greater than the sum of the individual effects, or a subtractive effect in which one effect cancels in whole or in part the effect of the other stressors.

When conflicts arise people bring into play a repertoire of coping mechanisms that may include increased or decreased motivation to perform, psychological responses such as defense mechanisms, change in attitudes and motivation, changes in physiological response and resistance to disease, and changes in behavior, including alcoholism and substance abuse, child and spouse abuse, increased absences and tardiness from work, or sloppy performance. Management's response to these manifestations of employees' stresses may be to protect itself by promulgating and enforcing new policies, procedures, and changes in working conditions that may ameliorate or exacerbate the stress on the employees.

A very considerable concern to management is the impact of the consequences of stress on the work performance of individual officers. If the individual's work performance is enhanced, the officer's needs are to some extent gratified. If, on the other hand, the quality or quantity of performance is inhibited, the officer's personal need structure may be modified and new or modified coping mechanisms may be established. The change in performance may result from informal self-assessments, peer comments, or formal job performance appraisals.

Management may recognize qualitative or quantitative change in individuals' work performances, and they may become aware of work group (e.g., squad, shift, etc.) or overall departmental effectiveness. As with individuals, the shift may be positive or negative. If the former, the department's management may be gratified: if the latter, the needs may be exacerbated. In either case management may modify its administrative or operational rules and procedures accordingly.

Workplace performance and organizational effectiveness measures feed back into personal system dynamics and the workplace environment. Personal and organizational responses in conjunction with changing extraorganizational conditions will feed back and recycle into the system in a dynamic manner, resulting in a new constellation of stress, outcomes, and consequences.

CONVENTIONAL EMPLOYEE-FOCUSED APPROACH TO STRESS MANAGEMENT

Once stress has been established to be counterproductive, management typically adopts and sponsors self-help programs of counseling, therapy, physical fitness, and team building, all of which place the onus on the employee to manage their own stress. Some organizations go further. They recognize management's role in creating the stress and look for ways to reduce the source of stress. They may make available to all their employees physical fitness, health maintenance, and Employee Assistance Programs (EAPs) to help employees deal with the personal consequences of stress. Such approaches, although indeed useful, have limited utility because personal stress reduction requires employees to develop and allocate their own resources to manage responses to conditions imposed by management. To achieve maximum usefulness, management must consider the working conditions that inhibit individuals' ability to manage the excessive stress that reduces the ability to perform safely and effectively.

TECHNOLOGY OPERATIONAL APPROACHES TO STRESS OPTIMIZATION

There are at least two other approaches in addition to sponsoring EAPs, where management, recognizing their contribution to stress, seeks to establish active programs to control the source of stress on both employees and management. Two such stress source reduction approaches can be developed. One such approach may be categorized as an organizational evaluation and management approach. This approach includes management interventions such as:

- Altering work force size to meet management's needs for productivity. Obviously, budgetary and other considerations limit the size of the overall work force. However, consideration should be given to reallocating the existing overall work force so that elements are not under excessive stress, largely because they are undermanned.
- Rescheduling work assignments, shift schedules, and travel consistent with optimal human performance and psychological capabilities and limitations.
- Modification of management attitudes and practices that induce destructive stress; instituting improved reward and punishment consistent with performance.

The second approach is based on the utilization of psychology's technology base. It requires management to consider job performance requirements within the context of the established procedures imposed by the working environment. Its three basic requirements call for:

- Providing job performance skill acquisition training and skill retention programs. However, encouragement by management is not sufficient. Rank and file and sergeants or other first-level supervisors must be made to recognize the need to obtain those skills.
- Ergonomic review of ambient working environment, equipment, and systems, followed by replacement or modification of stress- and accident-inducing conditions. (Sometimes rather simple and inexpensive human engineering design changes have demonstrably reduced accident incidence and product liability losses.)
- Reviewing and revising operational procedures that cause stress.

The objective of stress reduction programs focusing on technology and organizational factors is to optimize those ergonomic factors that tend to increase human capabilities and to reduce those ergonomic factors that will reduce human resistance to stress. Both of these approaches look to the organization, the working equipment, and other aspects of the man-in-the-workplace conditions. They examine the interactions between personnel and these work environment conditions, and then consider the desirability of changes designed to reduce inefficiency, ineffectiveness, the likelihood of burnout, errors, and accidents. When combined with the more conventional approaches, it becomes possible to manage stress by identifying and countering those factors that are destructive to performance reliability.

STRESS AND HUMAN PERFORMANCE RELIABILITY

Early attempts to mitigate the impact of stressful factors that combine to be destructive to performance reliability focused on the selection process. During World War II it became necessary to recruit undercover agents for the Office of Strategic Services (OSS), the precursor to today's Central Intelligence Agency. An assessment procedure was developed and applied during training of such agents, and during the course of training the candidates were assessed on the following job-related factors that were held to be basic to the needs of OSS and required of all recruits:

Motivation for Assignment: war morale and interest in proposed job.

Energy and Initiative: activity level, zest, effort, initiative.

Effective Intelligence: ability to select strategic goals and the most efficient means of obtaining them; quick practical thought—resourcefulness, originality, good judgement—in dealing with things, people or ideas.

Emotional Stability: ability to govern disturbing emotions, steadiness and endurance under pressure, snafu[1] tolerance, freedom from neurotic tendencies.

Social Relations: ability to get along well with other people, good will, team play, tact, freedom from disturbing prejudices, freedom from annoying traits.

Leadership: social initiative, ability to evoke cooperation, organizing and administrative ability, acceptability of responsibility.

Security: ability to keep secrets, caution, discretion, ability to bluff and mislead. (OSS Assessment Staff, 1948, pp. 30–31).

Those recruits whose contemplated assignments would take them behind enemy lines were also assessed as to their physical, observation, and reporting abilities, and propaganda skills. It is asserted that deficiencies in any or several of these factors taken collectively will reduce the ability of employees to resist job-related stressors to the detriment of performance of the job. All of these factors were assessed during the course of training by multiple evaluators, a technique that evolved into today's assessment center methodology.

Another by-product of the OSS procedure is the *human reliability* concept that, inter alia, approaches stress management in a performance-focused way. Originally concerned with the reliability of employees engaged in national security or in hazardous working environments, clinical psycholo-

---

[1]*Snafu* was popular slang during World War II. The more polite version stood for situation normal, all fouled up.

gists working in such sensitive organizations focused on the personal characteristics of actual or potential employees. Events such as that exemplified by nuclear power plant accidents and near accidents, several aircraft disasters, and other critical incidents brought more attention to the user–equipment–organization triad (Swain & Guttmann, 1980). Human factors and other industrial/organizational psychologists were instrumental in introducing the notion that the working environment, work culture, and ergonomic characteristics of the job are as important to the reliability of the work system as are the personal characteristics of the people manning the system (Office of Emergency Operations, 1992; Swain & Guttman, 1980).

The Department of Defense has for many years been concerned with the need to improve human performance in military organizations using complex equipment systems. Initially concerned with improving weapon system effectiveness by including human engineers in system design, it was learned that other human factors considerations such as training, the constraints of operational procedural requirements, and tailoring of organizational function and structure all influenced the ability of military personnel to do their jobs. Failure to adequately take these concerns into account degrades the performance of the people who constitute the system and thereby generates personnel stress. A means for integrating the various personnel-related concerns for the development and acquisition of equipment and systems designated as MANPRINT (Booher, 1990) was developed. Although the orientation of MANPRINT is not stress reduction per se, the concept may be co-opted for that purpose. It may be expanded to encompass the development and operation of law enforcement systems whether or not they are technology based. A *law enforcement system* may be defined as any integrated combination of people, equipment, and working environments assembled to reach a law enforcement operational or administrative goal. They are created to accomplish specific law enforcement activities within operational, administrative, and management guidelines. Management often has the ability to optimize the strength of its employees by considering the MANPRINT rules of thumb:

- People performance affects system performance.
- Skill is a function of aptitude and training.
- Measure operational performance by time and accuracy.
- Operational task procedures are determined by a mixture of working environment, equipment design, organizational culture, and administrative decision making.
- Creators of operational tasks should take these factors into consideration and bear significant responsibility and accountability for the effectiveness of operational performance. (Barber, Ching, Jones, & Miles, 1990)

If we accept that stress levels of individuals affect the reliability of the system, then a look at the component domains of human reliability appears to be in order. The Professional Performance Checklist developed by Besco (1990) identified six human reliability domains to be investigated by workers concerned with improving the performance of airplane pilots. This check list has been modified by the author for more general use. As modified, it becomes possible to identify those sources of reliability degradation, determine which of the sources induces counterproductive stress, and establish programs to reduce the stress, thereby preventing or correcting lowered human reliability. Four domains of human reliability may be considered: obstructions to human performance; knowledge and skill inadequacies; dysfunctional organizations, climates, and attitudes; and deficient equipment or service delivery systems and procedures.

Human Performance Obstructions

The first domain to be considered are physiological and psychological obstructions, many of which generate stress, or exist as a result of stress. Correction or prevention measures including screening employees, providing treatment or counseling, and modification of the organizational and working environment. The option of screening, once a prevention panacea for creating a work force free of medically and psychologically disabled persons is now restricted by provisions of the Americans With Disabilities Act. Many disabled persons will be protected from screening, and in such cases the employing organization will have an obligation to provide reasonable accommodations, including changes in the working environment (Perritt, 1991). Such changes could involve improving accessibility within a facility or changes to working equipment, job redesign, or modificaton of performance standards. A list of representative human performance obstructions, together with means for preventing or correcting lowered reliability are illustrated in Table 19.2.

Knowledge and Skill Inadequacies

Individuals whose job requirements exceed the knowledge or skills of the incumbents are likely to become stressed and may exhibit the emotional, physiological, and behavioral consequences. Examples of such threats to acceptable job performance and organizational effectiveness are found in Tables 19.3 and 19.4. Prevention of knowledge- and skill-related inadequacies include provision for acquisition of new or continuing educational programs, screening and selecting job or promotion applicants to identify those who are most likely to take advantage of and benefit from such provisions, and organizational development and team building to influence management encouragement of employees to take advantage of the availability of those provisions.

TABLE 19.2
Domain: Human Performance Obstructions

Source of Reliability Degradation	Influencing Factors	Prevention/Correction of Lowered Reliability
Health deficits	Incapacitation, illness, physical condition, nutrition, injury, disease, substance abuse, emotional health	Screening; provide medical treatment, wellness programs, etc.
Irregular rest/sleep	Sleep cycle, poor facilities, irregular schedules, shift work cycle	Refine work schedules; ergonomic facilities design
Fatigue	Exertion, exhaustion, mental fatigue, physical workload, mental workload	Refine scheduling practices and workload assignments
Inadequate environment	Light, air quality, humidity, air flow, acceleration, vibration, seat comfort, rotation, visibility, sound level, temperature	Improve environmental conditions; ergonomic/human factors design of working environment
Interpersonal conflicts	Sources of conflict: Organizational, attitudinal, management practices, lifestyles, experience level	Personal counseling; organizational development/team building
Personal stress	Family illness and strife, career threats, deaths, labor disputes, romance, personal tragedy, money	Personal counseling; organizational development
Personal history impediments	Social, cultural, clinical, and legal history; relevant work experience	Screening

Note. Adapted from Besco (1990) by permission.

Dysfunctional Organizational Climate and Attitudes

In general, the sources of degradation of human reliability cited in Table 19.5 are, unlike the preceding ones, more under the control of management than of individual workers. Consequently the likelihood of prevention of unwanted stress in this domain is management's responsibility. Corrective and preventive measures open to management include screening potential and actual managers and other employees to identify and select applicants who are less likely to induce or perpetuate dysfunctional organizational environment, counseling and training staff to maintain a well-functioning work environment, and imposition of quality control, feedback, and accountability for such maintenance. Organizational development and team-building programs to encourage fair treatment on the job and in performance appraisal may be critical for the establishment and maintenance of a well-functioning workplace.

TABLE 19.3
Domain: Knowledge Inadequacy

Source of Reliability Degradation	Influencing Factors	Prevention/Correction of Lowered Reliability
Individual's capacity to be educated	Learning ability, emotional health, motivation	Screening of individual
Inadequacy of requisite acquired knowledge	When was knowledge acquired? How was it acquired? Self-taught, observational, formal, intuitive	Screening; provide education
Prior use of knowledge	Frequency, range, depth, interference	Develop application exercises
Feedback on knowledge level	Source of feedback, accuracy, regularity	Provide feedback
Meaningfulness/relevancy of education	Facilitates, utilization of knowledge, effectiveness of education, currency of knowledge	Curriculum with relevant content
Degree of personal interaction with learning	Objectives, needs, quality of instructors, course content, method of teaching	Use of active learning methods
Degree of compatibility with the organization	Organizational policies and practices, role models, organizational image, ethics, payoffs to organization and individual	Organizational development; organizational consistency

Note. Adapted from Besco (1990) by permission.

TABLE 19.4
Domain: Skill Inadequacy

Source of Reliability Degradation	Influencing Factors	Prevention/Correction of Lowered Reliability
Individual potential	Learning rate, perceptual motor skills, motivation, emotional factors	Selection; training/retraining; reassignment or release
Prior proficiency	Where, when, proficiency level	Provide training
Compatibility of prior habits	Conflicts, generalizations, sequences, locations	Training to develop positive transfer
Frequently used skills	How often, degree, depth, precision	Provide regular practice
Awareness of skill deficiencies	Requires skills, personal acceptance of deficiencies, influence of leaders and peers	Arrange for feedback; motivational counseling

Note. Adapted from Besco (1990) by permission.

TABLE 19.5
Domain: Dysfunctional Organizational Climate/Attitudes

Source of Reliability Degradation	Influencing Factors	Prevention/Correction of Lowered Reliability
Dysfunctional management policies and procedures	Internal communication systems, supervisory practices, labor relations, adequacy/comfort of work environment, adverse work schedules, unfair discipline, performance appraisal, and promotion opportunities, degree of tolerance for misconduct and counterproductive behaviors	Management retraining; revise management procedures and policies; management accountability
Ignored performance	Performance monitoring system inadequate or nonexistent, subtle messages concerning management disinvolvement with employee behavior, low earnings	Arrange for performance monitoring and employee accountability
Excellence discouraged or penalized	Excellence/innovation "rewarded" by more work or difficult job assignments, criticism, double standards, designated as "troublemaker" or "whistleblower"	Identify and remove punishing factors
Poor performance encouraged	Peer acceptance, management disinvolvement, labor relations, sick leave	Provide positive incentives and consequences
Dysfunctional leadership	Issues of self-esteem, power, yea saying, disrespect, subjectivity in relationship with subordinates, capricious and arbitrary decision making, tolerance of peer pressures conducive to misconduct and counterproductive behavior	• Establish leadership standards & accountability • Leadership screening • Leadership training • Team building

Note. Adapted from Besco (1990) by permission.

Defective Equipment or Service Delivery Systems and Procedures

This domain is concerned with the adequacy of the equipment police officers must use and the procedures they must follow on the job. As illustrated in Table 19.6, sources of reduced reliability may include stress induced by psychological, physiological, and environmental demands imposed on offi-

TABLE 19.6
Domain: Defective Equipment, Service Delivery System/Procedures

Source of Reliability Degradation	Influencing Factors	Prevention/Correction of Lowered Reliability
Equipment failures	Structural, electrical, software, system failure modes: redundancy, quality control standards and procedures	Remove causes of failure through engineering and/or human factors system design; improved inspection and quality control
System beyond or at limits of human capabilities	Frequency threshold, response time requirements, precision requirements, saturation, workload demands	Human factors design/redesign; training
Narrow performance margins	Cognitive and perceptual motor requirements, multitask requirements, conflicting performance requirements	Select or train; restructure system or tasks
Error-prone system or equipment design	System logic, stereotypes, input processing, output procedures, unforgiving designs, safety engineering considerations	Redesign the system or operational procedures
Awkward input alternatives	Locations, sensitivity, incompatibilities, ergonomic considerations	Redesign input devices and procedures
Inadequate feedback	Sources of feedback, reliability of feedbacks	Improve feedback procedures and devices
Ineffective safety instructions or warnings	Design and location of warnings, signs, labels, and instructions, personal attitudes, awareness/vigilance levels, and level of reinforcement concerning compliance with safety procedures	Human engineering-based design of warning devices, labels, signs; training; management enforcement of safety rules

Note. Adapted from Besco (1990) by permission.

cers who are required to conduct operations or perform other duties that have been imposed by administrative procedures or equipment and work facilities that are not compatible with the capabilities and limitations of the employees. Reduction of stress related to this domain includes ensuring that equipment and facilities are designed or redesigned to conform to human capabilities by imposition and reliance on human factors (ergonomics) standards, selecting and screening individuals who will be required to operate or maintain the system, identifying and training qualified individuals on system operations and system safety, and job design and work schedules to ensure optimization of the human–system interfaces.

MANAGEMENT STRATEGIES FOR DEVELOPING AND MAINTAINING HUMAN RELIABILITY

Each source of human reliability degradation for the various domains may be considered to be stressors that may impact psychologically or physiologically on the individuals. When the locus of impact is at the emotional, behavioral, or physical level, prevention or treatment of adverse effect must at the individual level. Stressors also impact on the organization, and when their impact is felt on workplace performance and organizational effectiveness, prevention and correction of adverse impact may have to rely on modifications of the organization's administrative and operational systems, the organizational culture, and environments. Figure 19.3 illustrates how various intervention techniques may be applied. It shows three intervention strategies, each concerned with different loci of interest.

Conflict Resolution Interventions

Given that conflicts produce stress, one approach to stress reduction lies in resolution of conflicts. In recent years both the mental health and the legal professions have sought means to resolve conflicts between individuals, families, and organizations by means other than litigation, which provides its own sources of personal and financial stress. A variety of alternative dispute resolution methods have received widespread support among professionals and government agencies tasked with resolution of disputes (Administrative Conference of the United States, 1987). The methods most well known to behavioral scientists are counseling, arbitration, and mediation. Folberg and Taylor (1984) distinguished among the three. Of the three, arbitration is the technique in which the conflict is resolved by a third party who listens to both sides' presentations, and makes a binding (and court-enforceable) decision based on a pre-established criterion such as existing legislation, legal precedent, or fairness. Information on the arbitration process may be found in Coulson (1973) and Elkouri and Elkouri (1985).

In counseling, the intervenor may be a counselor, psychotherapist, or manager who must gain rapport with the parties, assess the real problem, and apply the intervention strategy dictated by the intervenor's professional expertise.

In mediation, the intervenor is a selected third party facilitator who often follows a six-part sequence of (a) structuring the problem and gaining rapport with the parties, (b) finding the relevant facts and isolating the issues, (c) helping the disputants create alternatives, (d) guiding negotiation and decision making, (e) clarifying and writing an agreement or plan of action,

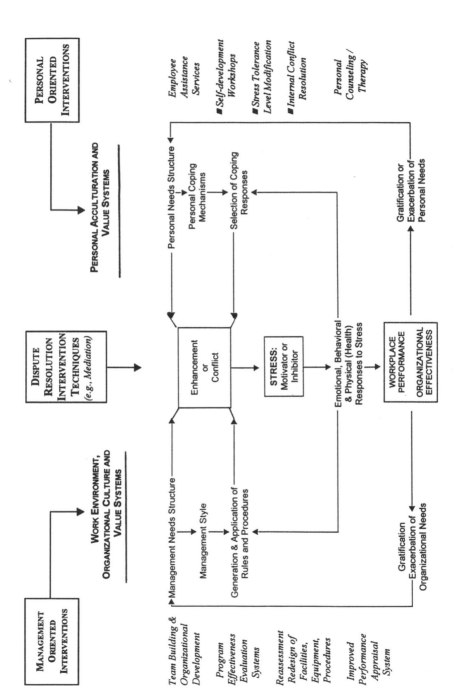

FIG. 19.3. Organizational stress intervention strategies.

and (f) providing for legal review and processing. Most frequently used by attorneys, psychologists, and other mental health professionals in resolving family and child custody disputes (Bienenfeld, 1983; Coogler, 1978; Haynes, 1981), mediation has gained wide acceptance in resolving labor–management, and community disputes (Duffy, Grosch, & Olczak, 1991; Folberg & Taylor, 1984; Kagel & Kelly, 1989; Moore, 1986).

Personal-Oriented Interventions

As noted earlier, employee-focused approaches to stress management place the onus on stressed employees to manage their own stress. Management often provides employees the opportunity and the resources to ameliorate stress or resolve the organizational and extraorganizational conflicts that cause the stress that reduce the employee's effectiveness. Techniques such as counseling, psychotherapy, workshops, and other training may be provided to help resolve the employee's internal conflicts or modify the employee's stress tolerance level. The objective of such personal-oriented interventions is to modify the employee's personal needs structure to be more in consonance with the organization's culture and value systems. Interventions also may result in development or modification of the employee's coping responses and the likelihood of selecting coping responses that are less destructive to the individual and the organization.

Police agencies, like other government agencies and businesses, often structure personal-oriented interventions through EAPs that may provide assistance programs related to mental health, financial, or legal problems. EAPs provide a mechanism for management and employees to cooperate in supporting and keeping employees with problems as productive members of the organization. The EAP concept is based on the axiom that an organization's employees are among its most important assets. If their problems interfere with job performance, losses due to the poorer performance can be minimized or eliminated if the organization provides some means by which the employee can resolve the problem.

The goal of EAPs is threefold: (a) resumption of adequate job performance by distressed employees, (b) improved clinical status (i.e., recovery or rehabilitation) of distressed employees resulting from interventions, and (c) improved ability of organizational environments to function in a preventive manner, thereby reducing the occurrence of the kinds of disorders toward which the EAP interventions are directed (Roman, 1992).

Management-Oriented Interventions

The intervention model depicted in Fig. 19.3 includes some of the management-oriented interventions that can impact on the work environment, organizational culture, and value systems by modifying the management needs structure, management style, and consequent rules and procedures established by management for attaining its goals and objectives. Cole (1988) proposed a strategy by which management may avoid problems that occur when employees, especially those who are high achievers, recognize that management practices do not tolerate their attempts to improve personal and organizational efficiency. In their frustration, such people tend to become counterproductive or dead weights at best. The strategy includes:

1. Employment of organizational development (OD) professionals to review the way people work together and are being managed. Such professionals should be external to the organization because inhouse OD staffers are more likely than external ones to make recommendations that will perpetuate the organization's values, policies, procedures, and problems.

2. Create and implement a management development or training program to improve interpersonal competence, and collaborative and cooperation skills.

3. Adopt and make good use of a performance appraisal system that will allow employees to learn how they stand. In addition to conventional performance appraisal of employees, the employees should be given an opportunity to anonymously appraise their own supervisor's management and communication skills; such appraisals being reviewed by the supervisor's own second- or third-level supervisors. The higher level management will then be able to obtain a bottom up view of all supervisory personnel in addition to the top down view afforded by conventional appraisal systems.

Interventions such as team building and organizational development; reassessment of procedures; new or modified equipment facilities and procedures to remove the consequences of dysfunctional equipment, facilities, or system procedures; and the development of better performance standards might be appropriate to the occasion.[2]

Ayres and Flanagan (1990) identified 11 management practices and organizational characteristics that are major sources of stress in many law enforcement organizations.

1. Autocratic quasi-paramilitaristic management model.
2. Hierarchial structure of police organizations.

---

[2]Work environments, organizational structures, and value systems with their accompanying needs structure, management style, rules, and operating procedures are also characteristics of labor unions. Therefore, a potential exists for applying this model to relations between individuals and their unions, and to conflicts between police management and collective bargaining units. In such cases, an appropriate set of union management-oriented interventions will need to be identified.

3. Poor supervision.
4. Lack of employee input into policy and decision making.
5. Excessive paperwork.
6. Lack of administrative support.
7. Role conflict and ambiguity (i.e., lack of or conflicting organizational missions, values goals, and objectives).
8. Inadequate pay and resources.
9. Adverse work schedules.
10. Boredom.
11. Unfair discipline, performance evaluations, and promotion practices.

They also averred that the increasing educational level and professionalization of police work can be expected to lead to increasing frustration with stress-inducing factors. They therefore suggested that enlightened law enforcement managers will commit to developing a healthier work environment, and they provided a number of strategies to be followed by police organization managers for doing so. The first strategy is to examine the workplace to identify workplace stressors and commit to reducing those stressors and their effects. Among the other recommendations for reduction of organizationally generated stress include encouragement of upward communications, pushing autonomy downward, ensuring fairness in dealing with all employees of the department, and caring about those employees. Such a management philosophy must be accompanied by changes in the organizational culture.

Programs designed to change the police organizational culture are likely to be ineffective unless the agency has a deep committment to change, and there exist the leadership skills needed to implement cultural changes such as, for example, a shift from the traditional authoritarian management and to the acceptance of officers' personal traits that best support the practices of many forms of community policing. Culturally generated and maintained organizational changes and their impacts on morale and motivation can be ameliorated or exacerbated by management, and most particularly by the leadership exhibited by first-line supervisors. After a literature review and study of this aspect of organizational climate, Delaney (1990) concluded police first-line supervisors are rarely trained in leadership philosophy or techniques because of training course unavailability and internal bureaucratic intertia mitigating against making such learning and skill training available.

That a law enforcement agency's management can beneficially generate, commit to, and maintain such organizational culture changes has been demonstrated by the Bureau of Alcohol, Tobacco, and Firearms (ATF). In 1981, ATF, an agency of the U.S. Treasury Department, was threatened by Reagan administration plans to break it up and have its functions distributed to other

Treasury Department agencies. Under a new agency director, a strong effort was made to make the agency more viable through a major two-track organizational change. The first track involved a number of administrative structural and functional changes. The second track was designed to produce (a) a revised ATF mission statement, (b) a management values statement, (c) a list of 30 qualities a manager should possess, (d) a set of expectations outlining the management practices expected in ATF, (e) a compendium of competencies managers and supervisors should possess, and (f) manager and supervisor training to reinforce them. The agency executives committed themselves to support and pass on the new ATF values, to model them through their own behavior, and reinforce them at every available opportunity. This continuously reinforced approach altered ATF's management culture from a relatively autocratic, fragmented organization to one that induced considerably less harmful stress and resulted in increased production. In 1983, with only a 6% increase in enforcement staff, ATF investigated 47% more cases involving 51% more defendants, and seized 254% more firearms and 1561% more explosives than it did in 1983. Such dramatic changes in productivity have been recognized as hard work by ATF occurring as a result of management's willingness and ability to change the organization's culture (Coffee, 1988).

STRESS IS AN ELEPHANT AND WE DARE NOT BE BLIND

Folklore tells of six blind men who tried to describe an elephant based only on what part of the elephant they touched and felt. One of them felt the animal's side and described a wall. Another grabbed the tail and identified elephants with rope, and the one who grasped the trunk insisted that an elephant was a species of snake. Another held the leg and insisted that an elephant was a tree. One felt the ears in motion and identified the animal as a fan, and the remaining blind man, who happened to have been a soldier before his blindness, grasped the tusk and described a spear. Each blind "expert" described the elephant on the basis of his own limited exposure and within the constraints of earlier experience with some analogue to the part of the elephant he touched and felt. In like a manner, stress means different things to mechanical engineers, musicians, mathematicians, physicians, clinical psychologists and other mental health professionals, industrial/organizational psychologists and other human resource and organizational behavior professionals, and engineering psychologists and human factors engineers. Unlike the blind men of folklore, these professionals are not content with describing their elephant: They are also trying to manage or control it. Such diversity between approaches to the control and management of stress within the context of each of the expert's professional interests cannot be faulted, except when disciples of different professions attempt to deal with a problem common to each of them. At that point, some unifying principle other than the name of the phenomenon is called for.

So it is with stress in the workplace. In this chapter, stress has been quite properly discussed in terms of its impact at various level within the police organization. The concept and meaning of stress at these various levels are important and appropriate to those police psychologists whose competence is commensurate with their approach to stress management. The bounds of their competence very often limit their ability to resolve stress-related issues in a holistic fashion. This chapter introduces the concept of human performance reliability as an indicator of stress at various functional levels within police organizations. Listed here are four different sources of stress expressed in terms of reliability degradation. In a parallel column are listed foci of stress management appropriate to the potential degradation domain.

Type of Reliability Degradation	*Focus for Police Stress Management*
Change in psychological and physiological responses	Prevention and treatment focus on the individual
Change in operational effective-ness	Prevention and correction focus on law enforcement systems and operations
Change in organizational performance	Prevention and correction focus on organizational culture and environment
Change in workplace-related efficiency	Prevention and treatment focus on management style

Stress within an organization impacts on directly affected individuals and on the organization in which they serve. Prevention or treatment of the condition, to be effective, must reach the individuals' at risk, the individual's organization, its operations, and its management. Fig. 19.3 illustrates three classes of intervention that are available for the management of stress: personal-oriented interventions, management-oriented interventions, and dispute resolution interventions. They are targeted, respectively, to personal acculturation and value systems; work environment organizational culture and value systems; and conflict resolution. The thesis of this chapter is that reduction and containment of harmful stress calls for the concurrent application of the professional competencies of psychologists who have expertise in mental health, organizational behavior, human–system environment interaction, and interpersonal and interorganizational conflict resolution. It is safe to say that at this time the availability of competence in all these areas does not exist in many, if any, of today's police psychologists. Indeed, today's police psychologists are unlikely to be competent—or even conversant—in more than one of these fields. Unless or until the availability of police psychologists with multispecialty competence changes, any professional seeking to solve stress-related problems would be well advised to supplement his or her expertise with those of professionals who can provide the needed expertise. Training of future psychologists and future police psychology certification programs should ensure sufficient training in enough different psychological specialty areas to ensure that all relevant aspects of stress management are recognized and considered. Trying to deal with an elephant identified only as a rope, a wall, a snake, a tree, a fan, or a spear can lead to mismanagement resulting from suboptimal resolution of the problem at best, or at worst to disaster.

REFERENCES

Administrative Conference of the United States. (1987, June). *Sourcebook: Federal agency use of alternative means of dispute resolution.* Washington, DC: Author.

Ayres, R. M. & Flanagan, G. S. (1990). *Preventing law enforcement stress: The organization's role.* Washington, DC: National Sheriffs' Association.

Barber, J. L., Ching, H. L. F., Jones, R. E., & Miles, J. L. (1990). *MANPRINT Handbook for RFP development.* Washington, DC: U.S. Army Research Institute.

Beehr, T. A., & Franz, T. M. (1987). The current debate about the meaning of job stress. In J. M. Inancevich & D. C. Ganster (Eds.), *Job stress: From theory to suggestion* (pp. 5–18). New York: Haworth Press.

Berkhout, J. (1970). Psychophysiological stress: Environmental factors leading to degraded performance. In K. B. De Greene (Ed.), *Systems psychology* (pp. 407–450). New York: McGraw-Hill.

Besco, R. O. (1990). *Making leaders more effective with the professional performance analysis checklist.* Lakewood, CA: Professional Performance Improvement.

Bienenfeld, F. (1983). *Child custody mediation: Techniques for counselors, attorneys and parents.* Santa Monica, CA: Science & Behavior Books.

Boff, K. R., Kaufman, L., & Thomas, J. P. (Eds.). (1986). *Handbook of perception and human performance.* New York: Wiley.

Boff, K. R., & Lincoln, J. E. (Eds.). (1988). *Engineering data compendium: Human perception and performance* (Vol. III). Wright-Patterson Air Force Base, OH: Harry G. Armstrong Aerospace Medical Research Laboratory.

Booher, H. R. (Ed.). (1990). *MANPRINT: An approach to systems integration.* New York: Van Nostrand.

Brown, J. M., & Campbell, E. A. (1990). Sources of occupational stress in the police. *Work & Stress, 4,* 305–318.

Coffee, J. N. (1988, Fall). Tenacity: Changing the management culture of the Bureau of Alcohol, Tobacco and Firearms. *Federal Management Institute Journal,* pp. 31–37.

Cole, D. W. (1988). Evaluating organizations through an employee assistance program using an organizational development model. In M. J. Holosko & M. D. Feit (Eds.), *Evaluation of employee assistance programs* (pp. 107–118). New York: Haworth Press.

Coogler, O. G. (1978). *Structured mediation in divorce settlements: A handbook for marital mediators.* Lexington, MA: Lexington Books.

Coulson, R. (1973). *Labor arbitration: What you need to know.* New York: American Arbitration Association.

Delaney, W. P. (1990). *The role of leadership in police organizational stress.* Unpublished masters thesis, California State University, Sacramento.

Duffy, K. G., Grosch, J. W., & Olczak. P. V. (1991). *Community mediation: A handbook for practitioners and researchers.* New York: Guilford.

Elkouri, F., & Elkouri, E. A. (1985). *How arbitration works.* Washington, DC: Bureau of National Affairs.

Fletcher, B. (1988). The epidemiology of occupational stress. In C. L. Cooper & R. Payne (Eds.), *Causes, coping, and consequences of stress at work* (pp. 3–50). New York: Wiley.

Folberg, J., & Taylor, A. (1984). *Mediation: A comprehensive guide to resolving conflicts without litigation.* San Francisco: Jossey-Bass.

Haynes, J. M. (1981). *Divorce mediation: A practical guide for therapists and counselors.* New York: Springer.

Hibler, N. S. (1978). The psychological autopsy. *Forensic Science Digest, 5,* 41–46.

Ivancevich, J. M., & Matteson, M. T. (1987). Organizational level stress management interventions: A review and recommendations. In J. M. Ivancevich & D. C. Ganster (Eds.), *Job stress: From theory to suggestion* (pp. 229–248). New York: Haworth Press.

Kahn, R. F., & Byosiere, P. (1992). Stress in organizations. In M. D. Dunnette & L. M. Hough (Eds.), *Handbook of industrial and organizational psychology* (Vol. 3, pp. 571–650). Palo Alto, CA: Consulting Psychologists Press.

Kagel, S., & Kelly, K. (1989). *The anatomy of mediation: What makes it work.* Washington, DC: Bureau of National Affairs.

Keita, G. P., & Jones, J. W. (1990). Reducing adverse reaction to stress in the workplace: Psychology's expanding role. *American Psychologist, 45,* 1137–1141.

Levi, L. (1990). Occupational stress: Spice of life or kiss of death? *American Psychologist, 45,* 1142–1145.

Moore, C. W. (1986). *The mediation process: Practical strategies for resolving conflict.* San Francisco: Jossey-Bass.

Office of Emergency Operations. (1992, May). *Toward advanced human reliability programs: Structural development considerations for extreme risk environments.* Washington, DC: White House Military Office.

OSS Assessment Staff. (1948). *Assessment of men: Selection of personnel for the Office of Strategic Services.* New York: Rinehart.

Ostrov, E. (1986). Police/law enforcement and psychology. *Behavioral Sciences & The Law, 4,* 353–370.

Perritt, H. H. (1991). *Americans With Disabilities Act handbook* (with 1992 supplement). New York: Wiley.

Roman, P. M. (1992). Another core element. *Employee Assistance, 5*(5), 5–6.

Swain, A. D., & Guttmann, H. E. (1980). *Handbook of human reliability analysis with emphasis on nuclear power plant applications.* Albuquerque, NM: Sandia Corporation.

Violanti, J. M. (1988). Operationalizing police stress management. In J. T. Reese & J. M. Horn (Eds.), *Police psychology: Operational assistance* (pp. 423–435). Washington, DC: Federal Bureau of Investigation.

Yerkes, R. M., & Dodson, J. D. (1908). The relation of strength of stimulus to rapidity of habit formation. *Journal of Comparative & Neurological Psychology, 18,* 459–482.

PART SEVEN

NEW DIRECTIONS

CHAPTER TWENTY

Community Policing: New Roles for Police Psychology

Ellen M. Scrivner
Visiting Fellow, National Institute of Justice

An era in policing is ending. As we approach the turn of the 20th century, police departments are embracing concepts of community policing and de-emphasizing the incident-driven police response. This approach to policing will bring fundamental change to how police officers do their jobs and will alter tradition-clad practices that have formed the cornerstone of police services in this century. Moreover, it will create a certain amount of turmoil as police departments struggle to incorporate change. Police psychologists stand to play a key role in affecting and managing these changes because of what they bring to the process: substantial knowledge about police officers and police organization behavior. Consequently, new roles for police psychologists will emerge and current practices may be challenged by what promises to be an innovative and exciting time in the evolution of modern policing.

Ironically, it was at the turn of the 19th century when another major change in policing occurred. Police wrested control of their departments from the influences of powerful politicians and put an end to the era of scandal and corruption that had undermined confidence in the police and tainted their reputation. As police forged new efforts to become more professional, they established centralized administration of police departments, paramilitary organizational structures, and a commitment to reactive patrol. This new era of policing also brought the command and control management philosophy that dominated law enforcement for the rest of the century and saw the emergence of the reactive and incident-driven policing model (Sparrow, Moore, & Kennedy, 1990).

Community policing addresses some of the failures of the incident-driven police response. It is the product of reform-minded and more highly educated law enforcement managers who realize that they have been less than successful in maintaining order and controlling crime. These managers seek new solutions to how police departments think and work, use strategic management concepts, and support the notion of research to answer questions and inform policy. They represent the new breed of law enforcement leaders; the "supercops" (Tharp & Friedman, 1993). Like their counterparts at the turn of the last century, they seek to make bold changes to improve the quality of police services. Their commitment to community policing is one way to achieve this change.

In many respects, the same police leaders who champion community policing were instrumental in the growth of police psychology. Police psychology was born of the social turbulence of the late 1960s and early 1970s (Reese, 1987). Over the past two decades, however, police management support has helped to strengthen police psychology as a discipline. Seeking new technologies to improve the delivery of police services, these managers encouraged the use of psychologists and the new sets of skills that they brought to police organizations. Currently, these skills are fairly well entrenched in police agencies and have become institutionalized in some of the nation's police departments (Kirschman, Scrivner, Ellison, & Marcy, 1992).

The development of community policing challenges police psychology to reach beyond traditional roles and to meet the opportunities presented by a changing law enforcement. This challenge requires some understanding of the evolution of community policing in order to frame how it may influence police psychology.

DEVELOPMENT OF COMMUNITY POLICING

Community policing has been evolving over the past 15 years. However, the proliferation of drugs and guns in the nation's communities, skyrocketing homicide rates involving community youth, and highly publicized incidents of police brutality forced the concept of community policing to the forefront. There it has been represented as a more recent panacea for urban problems and embraced as a central element of the criminal justice agenda of the current presidential administration. Community policing did not develop in response to just these concerns, but its designation as an "era" of policing does appear to be more recent.

Kelling and Moore (1988) described three eras of policing: the political era, the reform or "professional" era, and the community policing era. Each represents a different way of thinking about policing and a different strategy for managing the police function. The community policing era presents a striking contrast to the "respond, control, and back in service" dimensions that characterized the reactive, or professional, police response but that were less successful in controlling crime. Moreover, it is a phenomenon born of research that attempted to evaluate past practices and studied new initiatives that could assist in the management of police departments.

In the 1970s, landmark studies, such as the Kansas City Preventive Patrol Experiment (Kelling, 1974), questioned how police practices affected crime and forced an examination of the foundations of reactive patrol. Sparrow et al. (1990) reported that experienced law enforcement managers who examined the bedrock traditions of modern policing concluded that traditional police practices had a limited effect on crime and also produced community dissatisfaction with police performance.

Spelman and Eck (1987) discussed the research lines that established a foundation for problem-oriented policing. They grouped 20 years of studies into five categories: police discretion, problem studies, police management, community relations, and police effectiveness.

- Police discretion: Research on this subjective and controversial practice identified the need for guidelines and policies to prevent abuse of discretion.

- Problem studies: Problems that were not exclusive to law enforcement and that involved police interface with other community agencies, such as drunk driving or responding to the mentally ill, were the focus of research to develop a better understanding of the nature of crime.

- Management initiatives: Contemporary management practices and strategies comparable to those used in private industry, such as management by objectives (MBO), began to be tested in police departments.

- Community relations: Strained relationships with minority communities promoted research on community relations efforts and products were gradually expanded to include greater involvement with citizens in preventing crime and reducing community fears.

- Effectiveness: Research on patrol deployment, emergency procedures, and managing criminal investigations showed that police operations could be flexible without sacrificing effectiveness. This research led to the implementation of crime analysis to determine criminal trends, thereby permitting more efficient use of patrol officers and detectives.

This growing emphasis on police research, much of it federally funded, created a national forum for discussing police performance. Gradually, a more sophisticated literature developed and the emphasis for carrying out the police mission began to shift. Police practitioners questioned the reliance on the police emergency response system to dispatch officers to crime scenes and began to focus greater attention on crime control and crime prevention strategies. The practitioners joined researchers in questioning the efficacy of the police crime control mission and saw a need for the police to become more involved in proactive problem solving. Subsequently, new models of policing began to emerge.

Models of Community Policing

Mastrowski, Worden, and Snipes (1993) identified three models of community policing. The most long-standing is the problem-oriented policing model, which differs from the aggressive, order maintenance, and the community building models.

Problem-Oriented Policing Model. Community policing has been described as an outgrowth of problem-oriented policing and frequently the two terms are used interchangeably. Goldstein developed the concept of problem-solving policing in 1979. Goldstein (1979) argued that police could be more effective if they addressed the underlying conditions and problems that caused crime instead of responding only when a crime had occurred. In an attempt to develop guidelines to better define and measure police effectiveness, Goldstein developed the notion of solving crime problems by using diverse resources and involving people outside of the criminal justice system. Although appearing to incorporate the elements of community policing, Goldstein's basic rationale for problem-oriented policing was more specific. It centered on programmatic problem analysis, collaborative initiatives to design and implement problem solutions, and then monitoring the results. These efforts clearly opened the door to cooperative problem solving and to public participation in the process. It was this level of public participation that Skolnick and Bayley (1988) eventually defined as the key to community policing.

Order Maintenance Model. The second model identified by Mastrowski et al. is the aggressive, order maintenance model that developed from the critical *broken windows* article by Wilson and Kelling (1982). The authors encouraged police to anticipate problems and to attend to early signs of community deterioration rather than waiting to respond only after serious crimes had occurred. In their view, the symptoms of neighborhood decline, among other things the broken windows, represented signposts of the pending incursion of more serious crime. These data could be used by crime analysts to forecast developing trends and to determine areas where police needed to provide proactive responses that stopped short of arrests or citations. The aggressive order maintenance of the broken windows model did not preclude arrests but it did emphasize the use of other interventions to identify those who brought trouble to the community. Hence, street stops, warnings, or mobilizing informal social control in neighborhoods were encouraged as a means to maintain order.

Community Building Model. This model focused police attention more on victims and potential victims of crime in the community. Drawing heavily on crime prevention techniques and service provider roles of the police and other public sector agencies, this model emphasized providing human services. Frequently it requires the police officer to act as an ombudsman to effect changes that will deter crime. For example, the officer might be instrumental in getting other agencies to clean up a vacant lot to reduce the level of drug dealing at that location.

In the evolution of community policing, problem-oriented policing has been more clearly defined and is the more structured model. As of this writing, however, none of the models have provided a generally accepted definition of community policing. Trojanowicz and Bucquerous (1990) addressed community policing as a "philosophy of policing" that is based on the concept of police and citizens working together in creative ways to solve problems related to crime, disorder, and neighborhood decay. Prothrow-Stitz and Weissman (1991) called it the "public health of police work" and equated it to community violence prevention programs as a means to curb youth violence. Brown (1992) defined it as a "working partnership" between police and the law-abiding public to prevent crime, arrest offenders, find solutions to problems, and influence the quality of life. A conference on community policing, sponsored by the U.S. Department of Justice in August 1993, also stressed the partnership concept.

Lacking a standard definition, community policing also takes different forms. In some departments it is primarily a philosophy of policing; in others, it is a specific community-based program, a unique patrol experiment, a special Community Oriented Police (COP) unit, implementation of foot patrol, or the model precinct adopted by the New York City Police Department. Hence, community policing may mean different things to different departments and to different communities. However, the partnership concept seems to be a relatively consistent element. It represents a dramatic change from repressive styles of policing and the "we–they" element of the police culture, and a landmark change in how police work gets done. Yet, requirements for fundamental change in police behavior also shape the obstacles to implementation. Some obstacles defined by Rush (1992) include: hardline police managers who rule by fear, union distrust of management, traditional values of police organizations, community political leadership, and communities enriched by diversity that lack a central core. These obstacles highlight the behavioral elements associated with the transition to community policing and suggest varied roles for police psychologists.

ROLES FOR POLICE PSYCHOLOGY

Community policing represents more than a simple policy change. In addition to working the street differently, community policing will change the nature of the police institution and will involve a rethinking of basic management strategies. The strategies of particular significance to police psychologists are those that involve the key elements of the organization, the management of its human resources. From this perspective, the ways that police select, train, supervise, and evaluate officers are all subject to change.

Police Selection

The most likely changes for police psychologists will involve expanding current screening activities in order to select police candidates who are appropriate for the community police role. A recent examination of police psychology practice in the nation's largest police departments showed that 71% of the sample of psychologists were engaged in pre-employment screening and that they used a traditional clinical battery to assess police candidates (Scrivner, 1994). Hence, a relatively substantial knowledge base exists on how police officers respond on pre-employment psychological tests and there is a fair amount of agreement on the clinical interview information that raises concern about police job candidates. Unfortunately, these data come from screening out models and from related validity studies that focused on screening requirements for reactive patrol. It is uncertain if requirements for a different and more proactive form of patrol behavior can be assessed from current normative data because characteristics needed for community policing are virtually unexplored. The timing is favorable, however, because psychologists are now incorporating procedural changes that are anticipated to come from the Americans With Disabilities Act (ADA) requirements. Thus, including the needs of community policing in job analyses and updated validation efforts in these revisions would be appropriate.

Beyond expanding current selection activity and the requisite validation studies, community policing presents opportunities to build on the existing knowledge base and to create other ways to evaluate police candidates. Legal issues and fair employment practices have linked police psychology to a narrow range of screening instruments but the advent of community policing provides an opportunity and a challenge to develop innovative screening technologies and to incorporate new instruments into current batteries. Data analysis may also change and the high performance technologies of engineering or expert systems may be examined for their abilities to improve the profiling of viable candidates.

These changes are particularly timely because the two groups convened to study police use of excessive force specifically questioned practices of psychology relative to pre-employment screening and the prediction of police use of violence. The Independent Commission To Study The Los Angeles Police Department (1991) and the Los Angeles County Sheriff's Department Report by Special Counsel James G. Kolts (1992) supported the use of psychologists in police departments but their reviews were not favorable on the current status of pre-employment screening to address excessive force. Arguably, the methodology and analysis of a specific problem, the mission of such study groups, is unable to capture peripheral but closely intertwined issues that are related to the central problem. For example, these reports devoted very little attention to the pre-employment issues of reliability of measurement, legal issues surrounding public employment, or affirmative action concerns. What was significant in both reports, however, was the minimal attention from police psychology to a prevalent police concern, the issue of excessive force. The question logically follows if police psychology is sufficiently responsive to other significant concerns of modern law enforcement such as community policing because the voice of police psychology, in contrast to the other disciplines, has been strangely silent about this significant law enforcement development.

Training and Organizational Development

As of this writing, there is no national assessment of training targets for community policing, but both recruit training and certainly training for veteran officers will be affected. In many respects, identifying the community policing skills and developing new recruit training packages may be less complex than meeting the needs of veteran officers committed to the incident-driven philosophy. Changing attitudes will be central to developing skills for building community partnerships and simple revisions of training seminars will not accomplish this goal. Rather, a sustained organizational development focus will be required for police agencies with a strong commitment to community policing. The organization efforts to change attitudes will need to address the fundamental changes in the police role and the transition to a more independent level of functioning required by community policing.

Fundamental Role Changes. Consolidating organization change will require linking training efforts at the officer level with top-down interventions to facilitate fundamental role changes across the organization. Incumbent officers with a "by the book" patrol style are likely to have the more difficult adaptation. For this group, the new requirements may border on trauma because community policing can remove them from the isolation and anonymity of the police cruiser and substitute foot patrol and storefront offices for the traditional police station. For those who are resistant to these changes, a developmental emphasis will need to be considered to help officers adjust to the increased familiarity between the police and the public, more face-to-face contact with citizens, less social distance, and greater involvement in building community ties. Though calls for emergency services and making arrests will remain a major task of the police, the narrow focus of performing only these functions will be replaced by promoting cooperation with a broad spectrum of residents in order to enhance the quality of community life. Rather than relying on a threatening police presence to support a goal of arresting offenders, officers will be encouraged to see community members within a broader context. Conversely, the community perceptions of the police are subject to change.

Resistance to this fundamental role change may extend beyond the patrol officer to include supervisors and commanders who are uncertain and anxious about shifting priorities and new requirements for performance. Thus, as police organizations undergo the uncertainty attendant to comprehensive organizational change, police psychologists may find a stronger emphasis on use of organizational development skills to assist the agency in striking a balance of implementing new roles and missions while maintaining the capacity to provide emergency police response.

From Command and Control to Independent Functioning. The author's experience in training community police officers suggests a linkage between the organizational development emphasis and encouraging a more independent level of functioning in police officers. For many officers, the authoritarian organization structure and the paramilitary focus have fostered a certain dependence through the controls imposed on officers that tell them where to go, what to do when they get there, and what will happen if they do not do it right. Recruits are hired and officers are promoted based on their capacity to conform to these criteria. In addition to greater levels of independent functioning, not to be confused with ability to take physical risks, this reorganization of how police work is done will bring other changes to the roles and missions of the cops on the beat, their supervisors, and the commanders.

- Responsibilities of line officers will shift to broadening their interactions with local residents and expanding their role in securing the safety of the community.
- Increased collaboration between the police and the public to maintain order and prevent crime implies contractual relationships with citizens and encourages coalitions with community activists.
- Expanded patrol activities will include initiating home visits to citizens, police-sponsored youth activities, and special attention to problems of vulnerable populations such as children and the elderly.

- The problem-solving orientation that demands a more sustained contact with community residents will change the extent of peer contact.
- Officers will be on their own more frequently. They will be tested out in assignments previously reserved for commanders, such as organizing or speaking at public meetings.
- Officers will need preparation to face challenges to integrity because independent functioning can also bring increased opportunities for police misconduct.
- Personal organization skills will become more important. For example, learning to set limits to avoid being overwhelmed by community demands and activities will need to be incorporated as a police skill.
- The need for time management skills will be critical and is a further manifestation of how community policing changes police work. Patrol officer time on shift essentially has been managed by others, ranging from supervisors to police dispatchers. One community police supervisor indicated to the author that this was one of the larger problems his department faced when implementing community policing.
- Officers will need to be trained in other specific skills that bolster independent functioning, included, but not limited to, skills that involve prioritizing problems and tracking the progress of solutions, decision making, interpersonal communication skills, conflict resolution, and negotiation tactics.
- Current training trends in police academies will need to be reconsidered, including an evaluation of whether the police academy is the best place to teach community policing.
- Training methodologies may be modified to strengthen officer development through competency-based skill training and through use of instructional techniques such as case study methods, role taking, and direct observation of community processes.
- First-line supervisors will also be affected. Those entrenched in chain of command supervisory styles will need to learn how to function more like team leaders and become comfortable in decentralized systems.
- New staffing patterns will require changes in evaluating subordinate performance. Training that strengthens this level of functioning and that facilitates team building clearly will be needed.
- Many midlevel and senior police managers will need help in shifting from the traditional command and control style to an interpersonal orientation that is more effective to get things done in a decentralized system.
- While a new balance is evolving between independent functioning and command and control in decentralized systems, there will be a need for ongoing organizational development as a forum to address the problem issues that surface during this transition.

- Executive staffs implementing change in a system mired in tradition will need support through ongoing executive development to help them develop a comprehensive community policing plan with appropriate goals and objectives for communitywide programs that need to be coordinated with other agencies.

- One of the most significant undertakings will be for police supervisors and commanders to learn to trust the decision-making capacity and judgment of patrol officers. It is quite possible that this particular change may become the major stumbling block in the whole process of implementing community policing.

IMPLEMENTING CHANGE: FORM VERSUS SUBSTANCE

Goldstein (1993) recently addressed the need to confront the complexities of the community policing task aggressively in order to make changes of substance. In contrast to tinkering at the margins or oversimplifying the process, he called for fundamental change in the traditional ways that police agencies are managed. To this end, he cited five interdependent dimensions of change that in his view are necessary to the survival of community policing. In many respects, they touch on the organizational needs cited earlier. They include refining the police function and public expectations, analyzing and responding to specific problems that citizens bring to police attention, facing up to the limited-capacity criminal justice system and broadening police interests beyond arrest powers in order to get the police job done, seeking alternatives to arrests through problem solving and diversifying how police work is done, and changing the working environment of police agencies by reframing the atmosphere and expectations inherent to paramilitary, superior–subordinate relationships. These dimensions address complex training and organization development needs and challenge police psychologists to explore new ways to respond to a changing organization.

Crafting the Partnership

External to the organization but equally important in terms of training and development are the community advisors, citizen groups, and other community service providers that constitute the community policing partnership. In many communities the cooperative relationships needed to accomplish mutual goals may be soured by a prior history of adversarial relationships. Because of cynicism on both sides, mutual distrust, turf issues, and the "we–they" syndrome, these partnerships can be difficult to initiate, and it is doubtful if a brief orientation program can sustain a viable working relationship. Rather, a focus on building a cohesive working group within a process framework may be the more viable alternative for police, community advisors, and the other city and county departments involved in service delivery.

Briefly, community policing will involve police psychologists in new roles, some of which expand traditional functions, whereas others open new doors for the application of psychological knowledge and principles of behavior change. These roles are likely to craft new partnerships between psychologists and police leadership. As such, they will present new opportunities for the practice of police psychology to influence social concerns and public policy.

A BROADER VIEW OF COMMUNITY POLICING

From the perspective of professional psychology, community policing may have the potential to introduce broader social changes to the nation's communities. For police practitioners and policymakers it clearly represents a new way of thinking about the police role in society. However, the dimensions of this role may have even greater impact than community policing advocates envisioned. For psychologists, it opens a door to examine how a new approach to policing can influence social conditions that underlie criminal behavior.

Within this context, an area that is unexplored is the effect, if any, that community police officers will have on the youth of the communities they serve. The community police officer as a role model, or as a mentor to high-risk youth, offers a new perspective on how police may influence the adolescent experience and one that is diametrically opposed to police–adolescent traditions. Prothrow-Stith and Weissman (1991) came closer to exploring this notion by including community policing along with gun control, high school violence prevention programs, and comprehensive family policies as interventions to reduce teenage violence. Their comments addressed the prevention aspect of community policing, but a more specific outcome may be the potential for daily positive interactions between community police officers and at-risk youth.

Because community police initiatives frequently are implemented in disadvantaged communities, the community police officer may become a counter to destructive role modeling of other community influences, notably the drug dealer or gang leader. Whether it is because of fear or peer pressure, the expression of adolescent developmental needs to feel strong, invincible, and invulnerable through the use of deadly weapons represents a departure from traditional adolescent rebellion and rites of passage. Conceivably, the police officer in the community may represent another departure and a different type of success story with greater staying power than the short-lived success story of the community drug dealer. Hence, intervention in the unprecedented levels of adolescent violence may become a by-product of community policing.

Police mentoring or modeling influences can be examined from the perspective of social learning theory (Bandura, 1977). Through this lens community policing could be viewed as presenting a different set of life expectations to the urban adolescent. Despite other viable role models in diverse and complex communities, the continuous visibility attendant to the 24-hour police presence, the observation of power and prestige symbols associated with the police role, and an enhanced awareness of rewards that differ from drug dealer reinforcements all suggest that the community police officer could become a model for observational learning and a vehicle to influence adolescent behavior.

Another application of psychology pertains to the community building model of community policing. This model seems to embrace the principles of community psychology by encouraging social change through strengthening the efficacy of disadvantaged communities and improving the quality of community life. Within this context, the disenfranchised would have a larger stake in community life. However, the long-standing resentments and suspicions of police, a not inconsequential problem, would have to be overcome.

These generalizations of community policing are nowhere near to being tested out, and it is only the test of time that will determine if this form of policing has the capacity to play a broader role in solving nonpolice problems related to crime. For that matter, enthusiasm about community policing generally needs to be tempered with caution because so much remains to be known about its effectiveness.

To date, community policing has not been evaluated sufficiently and the evaluations currently in process seem to be producing mixed results. For example, Sadd and Grinc (1993) reported on an evaluation of the federally funded Innovative Neighborhood-Oriented Policing (INOP) programs and on the problems that were common across evaluation sites. The issues essentially involved officer resistance and minimal support related to lack of knowledge about community policing activities. Their study showed that officers viewed community police units as elite, "empty suit" attachments that lacked legitimacy because they did not run 911 calls, the management reorganization of the week, or "Officer Friendly" community relations efforts. Moreover, only a few of the sites evaluated were actually engaged in problem solving. One of the biggest problems was an insufficient level of training in that police departments typically exposed officers to the new community policing concepts in a 2- to 3-hour in-service module. Other evaluation concerns suggested that although fear of crime may have been reduced, the incidence of crime did not change but was simply displaced. Hence, it may be difficult to sustain the initial optimism of communities, particularly when there has been a long-standing distrust of the police.

These evaluations represent qualitative efforts to study diverse programs with different structures and they are among the first attempts to study the effectiveness of community policing. However, they present important information that needs to be incorporated into ongoing community policing strategies. Equally important to these efforts are contributions from psychological knowledge that may help to strengthen community policing from a theoretical standpoint. When psychological theory is combined with this progressive law enforcement development, collaborative applications may result in novel interventions in disturbing community problems such as adolescent violence.

These notions may seem far afield from the goals of traditional police psychology but they bear some similarity to the philosophy underlying federal initiatives, such as "Operation Weed and Seed" (U.S. Department of Justice, 1992). Designed to provide a comprehensive, multiagency approach, this macrointervention seeks to change the social context of community violence by coordinating law enforcement and social services resources. It involves four basic elements: prevention, intervention, treatment, and neighborhood restoration. The "weed" component proposes to combat violent crime, drug use, and gang activity in high-crime neighborhoods; the "seed" component infuses resources into the community that are directed to recreation, job and life skills development, mentoring, health resources, and education programs. This initiative focuses on services for high-risk youth and provides a framework to address the interaction of violent crime and social deprivation in targeted high-crime areas. It is relevant to police psychology because community policing is proposed as the bridge between these activities, and many of the other health–justice partnerships.

Broader social interventions and the development of public policy generally are not considered in discussions of the work of police psychologists. The literature tends to focus on functional activities, technical assistance, or research studies usually related to validating pre-employment screening. Psychologists, however, do bring a different perspective to police organizations and have been an influence for change. This influence may have larger implications for society as a whole. Clearly, the mission of police psychology could be framed as improving the effectiveness of the delivery of police services to the community. But that mission could incorporate police psychology as a force for change in responding to national crises such as the current spiral of community violence. Police psychology's involvement in working to strengthen community policing represents such an opportunity.

As law enforcement engages in unprecedented innovations, police psychology can be an active participant in one of the more exciting eras of modern policing. It is clearly a time for growth and expansion, but opportunities will be lost if practice issues are not addressed, and other disciplines will step in to fill the vacuum. Issues such as fragmentation of police psychology services, lack of technical innovation, and failure to apply psychological theory to understand contemporary police problems need to take precedence over guild issues or police psychology will lose ground. Although the police psychologist brings many resources to a changing law enforcement, it is not at all certain that these resources are being fully exploited. The movement to community policing presents new channels to expand the level of services provided to police departments, including both research and practice. Finally, it represents a threshold that needs to be crossed if we are to advance police psychology into the 21st century.

REFERENCES

Bandura, A. (1977). *Social learning theory.* Englewood Cliffs, NJ: Prentice-Hall.

Brown, L. P. (1992, October). Community policing: A partnership with promise. *The Police Chief,* pp. 45–48.

Goldstein, H. (1979). Improving policing: A problem-oriented approach. *Crime & Delinquency, 25,* 236–258.

Goldstein, H. (1993, August).*The new policing: Confronting complexity.* Paper presented at the Community Policing for Safe Neighborhoods: Partnerships for the 21st Century, National Institute of Justice, U.S. Department of Justice, Washington, DC.

Independent Commission of the Los Angeles Police Department. (1991). *The report of the Independent Commission of the Los Angeles Police Department.* Los Angeles: Author.

Kelling, G. L. (1974). *The Kansas City preventive patrol experiment: A summary report.* Washington, DC: Police Foundation.

Kelling, G. L., & Moore, M. H. (1988). The evolving strategy of police. In *Perspectives on policing.* Washington, DC: National Institute of Justice.

Kirschman, E., Scrivner, E., Ellison, K., & Marcy, C. (1992). Work and well being: Lessons from law enforcement. In J. C. Quick, L. R. Murphy, & J. J. Hurrell (Eds.), *Stress and well-being at work: Assessments and interventions for occupational mental health.* Washington, DC: American Psychological Association.

Kolts, J. G. (1992) *The Los Angeles Sheriff's Department: A report by Special Counsel James G. Kolts & staff.* Los Angeles: Author.

Mastrowski, S. D., Worden, R. E., & Snipes, J. B. (1993, October). *Law enforcement in a time of community policing.* Paper presented at the annual convention of the American Society of Criminology, Phoenix, AZ.

Prothrow-Stitz, D., & Weissman, M. (1991). *Deadly consequences.* New York: HarperCollins.

Reese, J. T. (1987). *A history of police psychological services.* Washington DC: U.S. Government Printing Office.

Rush, G. E. (1992, October). Community policing: Overcoming the obstacles. *The Police Chief,* pp. 50–55.

Sadd, S., & Grinc, R. M. (1993, June). *Evaluation of the INOP program.* Paper presented at the Fourth Annual Conference on Evaluating Crime and Drug Control Initiatives, U.S. Department of Justice, Washington, DC.

Scrivner, E. (1994). *The role of police psychology in controlling excessive force.* Washington, DC: National Institute of Justice.

Skolnick, J. H., & Bayley, D. H. (1988). Theme and variation in community policing. In M. Tonry & N. Morris (Eds.), *Crime and justice: A review of research* (Vol. 10, pp. 1–37). Chicago: University of Chicago Press.

Sparrow, M. K., Moore, M. H., & Kennedy, D. M. (1990). *Beyond 911: A new era for policing.* New York: Basic Books.

Spelman, W., & Eck, J. E. (1987). *Problem-oriented policing: Research in brief.* Washington, DC: National Institute of Justice.

Tharp, M., & Friedman, D. (1993, August 2). New cops on the block. *U.S. News & World Report,* pp. 22–25.

Trojanowicz, R., & Bucquerous, B. (1990). *Community policing: A contemporary perspective.* Cincinnati, OH: Anderson.

U.S. Department of Justice. (1992). *Operation Weed and Seed implementation manual.* Washington, DC: U.S. Department of Justice.

Wilson, J. Q., & Kelling, G. L. (1982, March). Police and neighborhood safety: Broken windows. *Atlantic Monthly,* pp. 29–38.

CHAPTER TWENTY-ONE

Human Resources Management

Lance W. Seberhagen
Seberhagen & Associates, Vienna, VA

Human resources (HR) are the people who do the work of the organization—not just the top executives but all of the people from top to bottom. The value of these resources to the organization depends on how well the organization manages its "portfolio." This chapter provides an overview of some of the best ways to maximize the value of HR for the good of the organization and the employee. The chapter addresses some of the special concerns of police departments and other law enforcement agencies, but the basic principles apply to any organization.

As a starting point, let us look briefly at a "typical" large police department. The department has 920 employees, including 770 sworn officers and 150 nonsworn or civilian employees, as shown in Table 21.1. The department has its own training academy but all other HR functions (e.g., recruitment, selection, position classification, compensation, personnel rules, labor relations) are provided by the central personnel department of the city or county government.

Poor HR management in a law enforcement agency like the one shown can lead to a variety of serious problems, such as:

1. *Mission.* The HR system does not support the goals and objectives of the law enforcement agency. The central personnel department provides a low level of service and has little understanding of law enforcement operations. HR functions are haphazard, uncoordinated, costly, and ineffective.

2. *Position classification.* Job descriptions (i.e., class specs) are based on military-style ranks, giving a misleading description of the work that sworn

TABLE 21.1
A Typical Large Police Department

| Job Classification | Salary Grade | Sworn Personnel | | Function |
		Number	Percent	
Sworn Employees				
Chief of Police	36	1	0.1%	Manager
Deputy Chief of Police	32	1	0.1%	Manager
Major	30	4	0.5%	Manager
Captain	26	14	1.8%	Manager
1st Lieutenant	24	15	1.9%	Supervisor
2nd Lieutenant	23	25	3.2%	Supervisor
Sergeant	20	65	8.4%	Supervisor
Corporal	18	130	16.9%	Asst. Supervisor
Private First Class	17	132	17.1%	General Officer
Private	16	383	49.7%	General Officer
Subtotal, Sworn		770	100.0%	
Nonsworn Employees				
Forensic Lab Supervisor	25	1	0.7%	Crime Lab
Research Analyst III	25	1	0.7%	Research & Planning
Admin. Assistant III	23	1	0.7%	Secy to Chief
Research Analyst I	21	1	0.7%	Research & Planning
Radio Dispatcher III	18	4	2.7%	Communications
Research Assistant	17	3	2.0%	Research & Planning
Police Dispatcher II	16	9	6.0%	Communications
Admin. Aide V	14	1	0.7%	Records
Office Supervisor	14	1	0.7%	Clerical
Radio Dispatcher I	14	40	26.7%	Communications
Police Services Aide	13	37	24.7%	Station Clerk
Admin. Aide IV	12	1	0.7%	Records
Office Assistant IV	12	1	0.7%	Clerical
Admin. Aide III	11	7	4.7%	Records
Stock Clerk II	11	1	0.7%	Clerical
Admin. Aide II	10	14	9.3%	Records
Office Assistant II	10	3	2.0%	Clerical
Admin. Aide I	9	3	2.0%	Records
Office Assistant I	9	7	4.7%	Clerical
Clerk Typist II	8	14	9.3%	Clerical
Subtotal, Nonsworn		150	100.0%	
Total, All Employees		920		

officers actually perform. Managers and employees lack information about the full of range of assignments performed in the agency. Career tracks often have major gaps or dead-end assignments.

3. *Employee selection.* Entry-level and promotional selection procedures do not identify the best qualified candidates. Cheating occurs on exams. Candidates file discrimination complaints.

4. *Compensation.* Salary grades have little relationship to the difficulty and responsibility of the work performed, causing pay inequities. The only way to advance to a higher salary grade is to become a supervisor. Overtime pay is out of control.

5. *Training and development.* Patrol is used as the developing ground for all other units, with no return to patrol. Employees seldom transfer between units, except to move out of patrol. Performance appraisals provide little constructive feedback. Supervisors provide no long-range career counseling. Career planning is difficult because assignments and training opportunities are unpredictable. Employees are unprepared for new assignments and must learn everything on the job. Managers have tunnel vision due to their narrow range of agency experience.

6. *Deployment.* The agency has too many supervisors, too many desk jobs, and not enough officers on the street. Managers have little information about the talent available in the agency. Sworn officers are working in positions that should be filled by nonsworn employees.

7. *Stress.* Morale is low. More officer stress is caused by the internal administration of the agency than by law enforcement activities.

A law enforcement agency may not have all of these problems at the same time, but these problems often go together as the result of poor HR management. Although many law enforcement agencies have improved their HR management since the 1970s, budget cutbacks and downsizing in recent years have often caused major setbacks in the HR area. A good HR system costs something in the short run to develop, but that investment normally yields a profit in the long run. However, when money is tight, it is hard to make the initial investment. Therefore, this chapter focuses on the most practical, cost-effective approaches for HR management.

LEGAL STANDARDS

One reality of contemporary HR management is that everything has gotten very legal. Lawyers are everywhere. Every decision and action by an employer may be subject to litigation by applicants or employees who believe they have been wronged. Thus, HR professionals need to be familiar with the law because legal compliance (as well as legal defense) needs to be designed into everything. A complete review of all legal requirements in the HR area is beyond the scope of this chapter, but some of the major laws affecting law enforcement agencies are:

1. *U.S. Code, Section 1981 (Civil Rights Act of 1866).* Enforced by the federal courts, the Code prohibits employment discrimination on the basis

of race, color, and national origin and has no limit on the damages that an employer might have to pay for intentional discrimination.

2. *Fair Labor Standards Act (FLSA) of 1938, as amended.* Enforced by the U.S. Department of Labor (DOL), the Act regulates minimum wages, overtime pay, compensatory pay, and other related matters. Originally the FLSA did not apply to state and local governments, but amendments in 1966 and 1974 extended coverage to all public sector employees, except elected officials and their immediate staffs. State and local governments challenged the constitutionality of these amendments, but in 1985 the Supreme Court eventually upheld the law after much litigation. Congress passed additional FLSA amendments in 1985 to respond to some of the concerns of state and local governments, but the law is still evolving in this area, particularly with regard to law enforcement officers.

3. *Equal Pay Act of 1963.* Enforced by the U.S. Equal Employment Opportunity Commission (EEOC), the Act prohibits sex discrimination in wages for performing essentially the same work, unless wage differences are based on a seniority system, a merit system, a system based on quality or quantity of production, or any other factor other than sex.

4. *Title VII, Civil Rights Act of 1964, as amended.* Enforced by EEOC, the Act prohibits employment discrimination on the basis of race, color, sex, religion, and national origin. Title VII is the primary antidiscrimination law but has limits on the damages that an employer might have to pay for discrimination. EEOC has issued various guidelines for Title VII, but none is more important than the *Uniform Guidelines on Employee Selection Procedures*, which were issued jointly in 1978 by EEOC, Civil Service Commission (CSC—now Office of Personnel Management, OPM), DOL, Department of Justice (DOJ), and Department of Treasury (DOT), as the primary statement of federal policy on employment testing.

5. *Age Discrimination in Employment Act (ADEA) of 1967, as amended.* Enforced by EEOC, the Act generally prohibits employment discrimination on the basis of age for persons who are age 40 and older. From 1986 to 1993, the ADEA temporarily permitted age-based hiring and retirement policies for certain public safety jobs, including law enforcement officers, to give EEOC time to study the issue. Although EEOC concluded that age-based policies for public safety jobs were not justified, at the time of this writing Congress was considering ADEA amendments that would have permitted the use of age-based policies for hiring and retirement in public safety jobs.

6. *Rehabilitation Act of 1973.* Enforced by DOL, the Act prohibits employment discrimination on the basis of handicap by federal contractors (Section 503) and federal grantees (Section 504). DOL and EEOC have agreed to coordinate the Rehabilitation Act and the Americans with Disabilities Act (ADA).

7. *Title I, Americans with Disabilities Act (ADA) of 1990.* Enforced by EEOC, the Act prohibits employment discrimination on the basis of disability. The ADA is intended to be coordinated with the Rehabilitation Act of 1973. The central requirement of the ADA is that employers must give "reasonable accommodation" to persons with disabilities, but there are many practical questions about what this means. EEOC (1992, 1994) has published some guidance, but its policies in this area are still evolving.

Since about 1970, employment discrimination has been the major source of litigation in HR management, especially in law enforcement agencies. This trend will probably continue because the Civil Rights Act of 1991 gave new life to Title VII by removing litigation barriers that had evolved through various court decisions and, for the first time, by allowing compensatory and punitive damages for intentional discrimination under Title VII. Employers can do a better job of avoiding discrimination lawsuits if they have a better understanding of the various forms that discrimination can take. Some of the major forms of discrimination are:

1. *Overt discrimination.* This is intentional discrimination in which there is an open expression of hostility or hatred against applicants or employees of a particular group (e.g., "No Irish need apply"). Harassment is probably the most common type of overt discrimination found today (e.g., a supervisor makes sexual behavior a condition of employment or allows employees to create a hostile work environment for a particular group).

2. *Disparate treatment.* This is intentional discrimination in which an employer applies different standards to applicants or employees based on their group identity (e.g., different selection procedures, segregated facilities).

3. *Disparate effect.* This is unintentional discrimination in which the employer uses the same policy or procedure for all applicants or employees, but the policy or procedure has an unintended negative effect (or "adverse impact") on one or more groups, compared to the group that fared the best, and the policy or procedure cannot be justified as a business necessity. Title VII limits this form of discrimination to employee selection procedures, but other laws may be interpreted more broadly.

4. *Reasonable accommodation.* This is intentional discrimination in which the employer fails or refuses to provide reasonable accommodation to the special needs of a group, when the employer's policy or procedure cannot be justified as a business necessity. This form of discrimination is likely to occur, for example, when employers require employees to work on their sabbath day, prohibit ethnic dress, or refuse to adjust test administration procedures for disabled persons.

5. *Retaliation.* This is intentional discrimination in which the employer takes adverse action (e.g., reject application, give punitive transfer, supervise

more closely, deny pay increase) against an applicant or employee because the person opposed a discriminatory practice, filed a discrimination complaint, or cooperated in an investigation or hearing of a discrimination complaint, regardless of the merits of the original discrimination complaint, unless the employer can justify the action by showing improper conduct by the persons affected.

Affirmative action is generally defined as the process of self-evaluation and remedial action by an employer to eliminate discrimination within its own organization. There must be a clear finding of discrimination, and the corrective action must be designed only to eliminate the old discrimination, without creating new discrimination. This is a fine line to walk, with many pitfalls. Therefore, most employers limit themselves to establishing a clear EEO policy, conducting outreach recruitment (to supplement but not replace regular recruitment), developing job-related selection procedures for hiring and promotion, eliminating artificial barriers to employment, providing EEO training to employees and supervisors, and installing an internal EEO complaint system. More extreme remedial action, such as quota-based hiring or promotion, generally must be approved by a court.

PROFESSIONAL STANDARDS

The legal standards already described above are normally based on generally accepted professional standards, which are defined by common practice, research findings, professional textbooks and journals, and actual published standards. Published standards can be very helpful in summarizing and highlighting the consensus of opinion on important professional issues but should be viewed with some caution. Published standards may not address all important issues (particularly if there is no clear consensus of opinion among professionals) and may be obsolete on some topics if the standards are not updated regularly. More ominously, special interest groups have found that they can obtain more favorable legal treatment if they manipulate professional standards to their advantage. Some professional standards also seem more designed to market the services of the profession than to provide meaningful technical guidance.

There are a variety of professional standards that are applicable to the HR function in law enforcement agencies, but some of the major professional standards are:

1. American Educational Research Association (AERA), American Psychological Association (APA), and National Council on Measurement in Education (NCME). *Standards for Educational and Psychological Testing* (1985). Provides guidance on employee selection and assessment.

2. American Psychological Association. *Ethical Principles of Psychologists and Code of Conduct* (1992). Provides guidance on the assessment and treatment of applicants and employees, particularly when psychologists are involved.

3. Commission on Accreditation for Law Enforcement Agencies. *Standards for Law Enforcement Agencies* (1983). Provides guidance on a wide range of law enforcement functions, with several chapters on HR topics.

4. Society for Industrial and Organizational Psychology (SIOP). *Principles for the Validation and Use of Personnel Selection Procedures*, 3rd edition (1987). Provides detailed guidance on employee selection and assessment to supplement the more general AERA/APA/NCME *Standards*.

5. Task Force on Assessment Center Guidelines. *Guidelines and Ethical Considerations for Assessment Center Operations* (1989). Provides guidance specifically for assessment centers to supplement the AERA/APA/NCME *Standards* and SIOP *Principles*.

JOB ANALYSIS

Job analysis is a general term that refers to the study of positions or job classes to provide descriptive information about duties, responsibilities, necessary qualifications, working conditions, and other aspects of the work. Key terms related to job analysis are:

1. *Job task.* A discrete work activity performed by one person to achieve job-related objectives (e.g., drives car, makes arrests, writes reports). About 50 to 200 job tasks are needed to provide an accurate description of most jobs, depending on the complexity of each job.

2. *Job duty.* A group of related job tasks (e.g., supervision, patrol, criminal apprehension, traffic, court services, training, equipment maintenance). About 5 to 20 job duties are needed to provide an accurate description of most jobs, depending on the complexity of each job.

3. *Worker characteristics.* The knowledges, skills, and abilities (KSAs) that a job incumbent must have to ensure at least acceptable work performance.

4. *Position.* The smallest organizational unit. A set of duties (behavior) and responsibilities (desired results) assigned or delegated by competent authority that is normally performed by one employee. A position may be vacant or filled by an employee. For budgeting purposes, one full-time position may be divided into two or more part-time positions and designated as either temporary or permanent.

5. *Job classification* (or *job class* for short). A group of positions that are similar enough in job duties, responsibilities, and necessary qualifications that an organization could properly place them under the same job title and treat them alike for purposes of HR management.

6. *Job incumbent.* The employee who fills a particular position.

7. *Position description.* A written statement of the official duties, responsibilities, necessary qualifications, and other information used to define a position.

8. *Job classification specification* (or *class spec* for short). A written statement of the official duties, responsibilities, necessary qualifications, and other information used to define a job class. Also known as a *job description.*

9. *Job series.* Two or more job classes that perform the same kind of work within an organization but that differ in their level of difficulty and responsibility (e.g., Clerk I, Clerk II, Clerk III).[1]

10. *Occupation.* A generalized job class as defined by the most common and important job duties and responsibilities found in essentially the same job class across many different organizations or establishments.

11. *Job group.* A general term that refers to two or more jobs or occupations that have at least one thing in common (e.g., the accounting group vs. the engineering group, managers vs. professionals, skilled trades vs. unskilled trades, sworn vs. nonsworn).

Job analysis identifies and defines the work performed by each position and job class in the organization. This descriptive information provides the necessary foundation for the organization's HR system. A clear understanding of the work is needed before one can make informed decisions about organizing work efficiently, establishing equitable compensation plans, developing valid employee selection procedures, designing job-related training programs, or meeting other important HR needs.

There many possible job analysis methods. Whatever method is used should (a) be designed to meet the objectives of the job analysis and (b) provide results that are accurate, complete, up to date, reliable, and unbiased. No one method is perfect. Therefore, a multimethod approach usually gives the best results because one method can fill in the gaps of another method. Independent verification of job analysis results by different methods is also an effective way to ensure valid results. If different methods produce contradictory or inconsistent results, no conclusions should be made about the job until further investigation is done to resolve the inconsistencies. A good multimethod approach often includes the following job analysis methods:

---

[1]Following common practice in the field of job analysis, this chapter capitalizes specific job titles that might be found within an organization, leaving generic occupational titles in lower case.

1. *Literature review.* Review of external publications (e.g., articles, books, reports, studies, and papers) about general occupations and specific job classes (particularly within the same industry) can provide an introduction to the general nature of the work and provide other useful background information. The *Dictionary of Occupational Titles* (DOL, 1991) and detailed occupational data from the U.S Bureau of the Census are two popular sources for this type of job analysis.

2. *Document review.* Review of internal documents (e.g., job descriptions, job analysis reports, organization charts, compensation plan, employee selection procedures, training programs, operational manuals, policies and procedures, general orders, training bulletins, safety and health data, activity reports, videotapes of work activity, and union contracts) from the target organization can provide useful information about the specific jobs being studied, even though the information is likely to be incomplete and out of date, to familiarize the job analyst with the organization and the jobs to be studied before beginning any extensive field work.

3. *Direct observation.* Firsthand observation of the work (e.g., guided tours, ride-alongs, viewing key events), often done with interviews, allows the job analyst to see the whole job at one time, with all of its complexities and working conditions. Observation also gives better understanding to the review of job-related documents, as well as an opportunity to examine records, reports, and other work products at various stages of production.

Of course, observation has its limitations. For some jobs, one can observe all important job duties in 30 minutes; for other jobs, one would need at least 1 year to see everything. Jobs that are more physical in nature are also more observable than jobs that are more mental in nature. The job analyst must also take care not to create any safety hazards or to interfere with normal work productivity. As a general practice, observation should be part of every job analysis but should never be used as the only source of job information.

4. *Interviews.* Interviews with people who are knowledgeable about the job can provide much useful information. Job incumbents are in the best position to describe actual job duties, the frequency of actual job duties, and the actual working conditions. On the other hand, supervisors and managers are in the best position to say what job incumbents are supposed to do and which duties and responsibilities are most important to the organization. Job incumbents, supervisors, and managers can all give insights about what qualities job incumbents need to perform the job, but this type of interview data is often less accurate and complete than data regarding job duties. Regardless of who is interviewed, interviews should generally follow a standard set of questions to facilitate data collection and analysis.

5. *Questionnaire surveys.* All of the job analysis methods described here are good for developing reasonably exhaustive lists of job tasks, KSAs, working conditions, and other aspects of jobs but are not so good for evaluation.

The questionnaire survey is best used at this point in the job analysis to present a consolidated list of items to a sample of "experts" (usually job incumbents, supervisors, or managers) for rating purposes. Items may be rated on importance, frequency, and other measures as appropriate. The survey results provide a statistically based consensus of expert opinion about the job (e.g., what job tasks are most important or time consuming, what KSAs are most important, what positions are most similar).

Standardized or customized questionnaires may be used. Off-the-shelf, standardized questionnaires are inexpensive and provide comparability to outside databases but contain only general data and are not available for every occupation or job group. Customized questionnaires provide exactly what data are needed for each job analysis but are more expensive to develop and lack comparability to other studies. The best approach is to use both types of questionnaires, if resources permit, when appropriate standardized questionnaires are available.

6. *Top management review.* It is always a good idea to have top management (e.g., chief executive, deputy chiefs, division heads) review the preliminary results of the job analysis to see if the overall findings and conclusions are consistent with the organization's philosophy, policy, and objectives. If a job is not properly defined, top management may want to initiate some formal changes to the job, which should be documented in the final report of the job analysis.

Some of the most common mistakes in job analysis are to (a) study an unrepresentative sample of positions; (b) rely too heavily on one source of information, without independent verification; (c) fail to collect all of the data needed for a given purpose; and (d) rely on obsolete data. For more information on job analysis and related topics, see Gael (1983, 1988), Ghorpade (1988), and McCormick (1979).

POSITION CLASSIFICATION

Position classification is the sorting of positions into homogeneous groups (i.e., job classifications) based on the kind and level of work performed. The main goal of position classification is to simplify HR administration by reducing all of the positions in the organization to a smaller number of job classifications without losing any meaningful information. For example, an organization with 1,000 positions may find that only 100 different kinds and levels of work are actually being performed. If so, the organization can save much time and money by sorting its positions into 100 job classes and then designing its HR system (e.g., recruitment, selection, training, compensation) to serve the 100 job classes, rather than 1,000 individual positions. Another benefit of job classes is that the HR system will be more equitable because similar positions will be treated alike regarding work rules, training, compensation, promotion, layoffs, and other HR matters.

In huge organizations (e.g., federal government) the most practical approach for position classification is to create a general set of theoretical class specs and then assign positions to the theoretical class spec that most closely describes the position in question. This type of system inevitably contains a lot of error in the description and classification of positions, but sometimes that is the best that one can do in a given situation. However, for most organizations it is practical, and certainly more effective, to describe all positions first and then develop system of job classifications specifically tailored to the work performed in the organization, as described in the following.

Before positions can be classified, the organization must first conduct a job analysis to provide a detailed description (e.g., primary function, duties, responsibilities, worker characteristics, working conditions) of each position in the organization. HR staff should then sort all positions by work unit and draw a complete organization chart from the position data to make sure that all positions are covered and that each position has one—and only one—supervisor.

Using these data, one can sort positions into homogeneous groups, based on the kind and level of work performed. Within reasonable limits, the definition of each group is a judgment call for each organization. Some organizations prefer narrow job classes; others prefer broad job classes. Broad job classes minimize HR administration and facilitate employee mobility but can hamper the development job-related programs and cause inequities if dissimilar positions are treated alike. Narrow job classes facilitate the development of job-related programs but require more HR administration and impede employee mobility. Narrow job classes can also cause inequities if similar positions are treated differently. The trick is to reach a balance between broad and narrow job class definitions according to the best interests of the organization and its employees.

The process of sorting positions into reasonably homogeneous job classes requires two phases. The first phase is to sort positions according to the *kind* of work performed (e.g., plumber vs. accountant) and requires several rounds of sorting until the various kinds of work are identified precisely enough to meet the needs of the organization. There is more than one right way to do this. In a law enforcement agency, the process would generally flow from these key questions:

1. Is the position sworn or nonsworn? (This topic is explored in more detail later.)

2. Is the position a manager (i.e., has full administrative and functional responsibility for supervising one or more supervisors), a supervisor (i.e.,

has full administrative and functional responsibility for supervising at least one subordinate), or a nonsupervisor (including both lead workers and regular workers for now)?

3. What general function does the position perform: patrol, traffic, investigation, special operations, field station, security, crime prevention, records, communications, crime lab, property, research and planning, computer services, human resources, accounting, vehicle maintenance, building maintenance, general administration? (Add or revise general categories as needed.)

4. Within each general function, what homogeneous groups can be identified? For example, within the investigation function, one might find the following types of investigators: criminal, fraud, fugitive, internal, juvenile, major case, organized crime, traffic, and undercover. (Some of these groups might be combined or divided further, depending on the size and philosophy of the organization.)

The second phase of sorting positions into homogeneous job classes is to sort positions according to the *level* of work performed (e.g., Clerk I, Clerk II, Clerk III), based on varying degrees of difficulty, complexity, responsibility, and necessary qualifications within each kind of work. There is more than one right way to sort positions by level. Here are some common methods:

1. *Position evaluation.* The classifier applies the organization's quantitative job evaluation procedure (see following) to each position. Positions are then assigned to levels according to the salary grades determined by the job evaluation points. This method is rigorous but overly empirical and time consuming, resulting in varying levels from one job series to another that often have little or no logical basis.

2. *Specific criteria.* The classifier meets with subject matter experts (e.g., senior job incumbents, supervisors, managers) to identify and define objective, job-related criteria that indicate where natural breaks occur between levels in each job series, according to traditional practice and organizational needs. These criteria tend to be very technical and individualized to each job series, resulting in varying levels from one job series to another. This approach is good in theory but hard to do in practice. Job experts often disagree on what the criteria should be, the criteria tend to become obsolete as jobs respond to the changing needs of the organization, and much work is needed to develop specific criteria for each job series.

3. *General criteria.* The classifier meets with top management to decide how many levels to have in each job series (usually one to four levels) and to develop general criteria for each level, based on management philosophy and the needs of the organization. There may be occasional exceptions to the rule, but each job series normally has the same number of levels and the same criteria for defining levels, at least for nonsupervisory jobs. Super-

visory job levels are normally based on other criteria (e.g., number of employees supervised, budget). This approach to defining levels is the easiest to understand, develop, and administer, although still meaningful and job related. For nonsupervisory jobs, most organizations recognize three or four distinct levels, using criteria such as the following:

a. *Level I.* Entry or trainee level. Performs a limited range of assignments that are low in difficulty. May require some education or training but little or no direct experience. Works under close supervision.

b. *Level II.* Full performance level. Performs a wide range of assignments that are low-to-medium in difficulty. Requires 1 to 3 years of experience equivalent to Level I. Works under general supervision.

c. *Level III.* Expert performance level. Performs a wide range of assignments that are medium-to-high in difficulty. Serves as a lead worker to train subordinates and provide functional supervision. Requires 3 to 5 years of experience equivalent to Level II. Works under general supervision.

d. *Level IV.* Super expert performance level. Performs wide range of assignments that are high in difficulty. Serves as lead worker to train subordinates and provide functional supervision. Requires 3 to 5 years of experience equivalent to Level III. Works under administrative supervision.

After sorting positions into homogeneous job classes, one must assign a job title to each job class to provide a job identifier for HR administration, budgeting, contracts, and other official purposes. As a general guide, job titles should be descriptive, concise, consistent, nondiscriminatory, respectful, and pronounceable. *Chief* and *Director* should be reserved for the highest level managers. *Manager* should be reserved for second- or third-level supervisors and should not be used for nonsupervisory jobs. A supervisory job is one that has both administrative and functional authority and is more than just a lead worker. Titles should not imply the age or sex of the job incumbent (e.g., Junior Accountant, Office Girl, Policeman).

Many law enforcement agencies have traditionally used military ranks (e.g., Corporal, Sergeant) as job titles. This is an undesirable HR practice because military ranks do not describe the kind or level of work performed and create a situation in which job assignments may be assigned in a haphazard fashion. A better approach is to (a) use functional job titles (e.g., Patrol Officer, Patrol Supervisor) only, or (b) link functional job titles to military ranks (e.g., Patrol Supervisor, Traffic Supervisor, and other first-level supervisors are formally listed as job assignments under the rank of Sergeant). Table 21.2 shows examples of the kinds of functional job titles that are often found in a police department.

TABLE 21.2
Common Police Job Assignments

No.	Job Title	No.	Job Title
Top Management		39	Juvenile Investigation Supervisor
1	Director of Police	40	Juvenile Investigator
2	Deputy Director of Police	41	Major Case Investigator
		42	Undercover Investigation Supervisor
Patrol		43	Undercover Investigator
3	Chief of Patrol		
4	District Commander	**Special Operations**	
5	Deputy District Commander	44	Chief of Special Operations
6	Field Commander	45	Special Operations Supervisor
7	Patrol Supervisor	46	SWAT Officer
8	Airport Patrol Supervisor	47	SWAT Supervisor
9	Airport Patrol Officer	48	Tactical Operations Supervisor
10	Station Supervisor	49	Tactical Officer
11	Building Security Officer	50	Police Helicopter Pilot
12	Canine Handler		
13	Executive Security Officer	**Crime Prevention**	
14	Master Patrol Officer	51	School Liaison Supervisor
15	Patrol Officer	52	School Liaison Officer
16	Patrol Officer Candidate	53	Crime Prevention Supervisor
		54	Crime Prevention Officer
Traffic		55	Community Relations Supervisor
17	Selective Traffic Enforcement Supervisor	56	Community Relations Officer
18	Selective Traffic Enforcement Officer		
19	Traffic Investigation Supervisor	**Technical Services**	
20	Traffic Investigator	57	Chief of Technical Services
21	Traffic Supervisor	58	Inspections Supervisor
22	Traffic Officer	59	Inspections Officer
23	Alcohol Testing Officer	60	Communications Supervisor
24	DUI Enforcement Officer	61	Police Dispatcher
25	Traffic Accident Specialist	62	Media Services Officer
		63	Forensic Lab Supervisor
Investigation		64	Evidence Technician
26	Chief of Investigation	65	Evidence Custodian
27	Case Coordinator	66	Crime Analyst
28	Court Liaison	67	Fingerprint Analyst
29	State's Attorney Liaison	68	Forensic Hypnotist
30	Civil Investigation Supervisor	69	Police Artist
31	Civil Investigator	70	Police Records Supervisor
32	Criminal Investigation Supervisor	71	Police Training Supervisor
33	Criminal Investigator	72	Police Training Officer
34	Fugitive Investigator	73	Range Master
35	Intelligence Investigation Supervisor	74	Research and Planning Supervisor
36	Intelligence Investigator	75	Research and Planning Analyst
37	Internal Investigation Supervisor	76	Supply Officer
38	Internal Investigator	77	Vehical Maintenance Coordinator

The last step in the position classification process is to write a class spec (or job description) to provide an official definition of each job class. Class specs are not intended to be all-inclusive, restrictive, or precise descriptions of any one position but provide a convenient summary of the findings and conclusions drawn from all of the raw position data. Class specs provide the primary basis for establishing salary grades and administering the HR system, but the raw position data should also be retained for reference purposes. Class specs should meet the following standards:

1. *Accurate.* The content should be factually correct and complete. Jobs are constantly evolving. Therefore, individual class specs should be updated whenever major changes in the job are known to occur. A good practice is to review all class specs annually, update individual class specs as needed, and update all class specs at least every 5 to 10 years, whether they need it or not.

2. *Objective.* Class specs should describe each job as it is actually performed, without giving a false impression. If there are differences between what job incumbents are doing and what managers want them to do, management should take appropriate action to correct these differences. Class specs should also describe the job in the abstract, without being influenced by characteristics of job incumbents (e.g., work performance, friendship, race, sex, age).

3. *Consistent.* Class specs are often used to compare two or more different jobs. Therefore, the content, format, and style of class specs should be consistent to facilitate comparisons between jobs.

4. *Concise.* Ideally, class specs should be no more than two pages in length so that all information can be printed on one sheet of paper, front and back. Unnecessary words and excessive detail should be avoided.

5. *Understandable.* The average person should be able to get a fairly clear picture of the job from reading the class spec. Thus, class specs should be written in plain English, with no obscure jargon or abbreviations.

6. *Documented.* The name of the organization, job title, job code number, and salary grade should appear at the top of each page of the class spec. The class spec should also contain the date that the class spec was developed or last revised. Page numbers are helpful, too.

Within the framework of these standards, the content, format, and style of class specs should be adapted to meet the needs of each organization. Appendix A shows a class spec for Patrol Officer to illustrate one approach.

JOB EVALUATION

Job evaluation is often confused with job analysis. Whereas job analysis is a procedure used to describe jobs, job evaluation is a procedure used to assess the value of jobs to the organization, with the ultimate purpose of providing internal equity in salary grades. The focus is on the job itself, not the job incumbent (e.g., work performance, friendship, race, sex, age). Job evaluation is essentially a two-stage process. The first stage rank orders all jobs; the second stage assigns jobs to salary grades. Job evaluation is normally conducted by a management committee but may also be conducted by others (e.g., outside consultants, cross-section of employees). The most common methods of job evaluation are:

1. *Whole job ranking.* The first step is for the raters to define the organization's concept of job value (e.g., contribution to the success of the organization, labor market value), including what factors to consider (e.g., skill, effort, responsibility, and working conditions) and not to consider (e.g., characteristics of job incumbents). After the definition has been reviewed and approved by top management, the raters can rank all jobs by assessing the overall (or whole job) value of each job compared to the overall value of every other job.

The next step is for the raters to assign each job to a salary grade. When there is very high agreement among the raters that a certain job should be assigned to a particular salary grade, that job becomes a benchmark job. After all of the benchmark jobs have been identified, the raters assign the remaining jobs to salary grades based on their rank order in comparison to the benchmark jobs and a group decision among the raters on where to set the dividing lines from one grade to the next.

As the last step, top management should review and approve the final ratings and grades to ensure that the results reflect the policy of the organization. Job evaluation is a useful tool for assisting managers to make consistent policy decisions but cannot substitute for management judgment.

The whole job ranking method is practical and effective when there are relatively few jobs to be evaluated (i.e., 50 or less) and the raters have good knowledge of all jobs. As the number of jobs increases, the whole job ranking method becomes difficult and unreliable.

2. *Quantitative ratings.* The first step is to identify a common set of rating factors that reflect each job's value to the organization. The most widely accepted rating factors are skill, effort, responsibility, and working conditions because these traditional rating factors were written into the Equal Pay Act of 1963. However, most organizations divide these four general factors into 5 to 15 more specific factors (e.g., necessary education and experience, mental effort, physical effort, supervision received, supervision exercised, impact, hazards, work environment).

Each rating factor is assigned a total number of points (or percentage weight), and point levels are further identified and defined within each factor, according to the needs and interests of each organization. Each job is rated on every factor, and a job's value is the sum of the points from all rating factors. The validity of the rating procedure is then checked by rating a sample of benchmark jobs whose relative value is already well established in the organization. If any of the benchmark jobs are out of line, the rating factors are adjusted as needed to reflect the proper value of the benchmark jobs.

Points can be translated into salary grades by using an equation developed from a regression analysis of the points and grades of the benchmark jobs. Judgment can also be used to set the point values for each salary grade, based on a review of the points for each job compared to the points and grades of a broad range of benchmark jobs. As always, top management should review and approve the final results to ensure that the ratings and grades reflect management policy.

Quantitative ratings are most practical for medium- and large-sized organizations that have many job classes. Each job can be evaluated in a consistent fashion, using abstract rating scales and a few benchmark jobs, without requiring the raters to know all jobs in the organization.

3. *Market rates.* Salary surveys define job worth in terms of the prevailing market wage rate for each job in the applicable labor market. If reliable salary survey data are not available for a job, the organization equates the job to similar jobs for which salary survey data are available or falls back on a whole job evaluation approach to fit the job into an appropriate salary range.

Market rate systems can be used by any sized organization and appear to be highly objective and scientific. However, the survey results are probably neither objective or scientific. Many subjective policy decisions must be made in developing the survey sample (e.g., geographical area, size and type of organizations, number of organizations) and analyzing the data (e.g., actual salaries vs. salary ranges, salary only vs. total compensation, reliability of data, level of comparability). Survey-based salary ranges are overly empirical, resulting in oddities due to survey error rather than to market forces or organizational needs. Extensive surveys are needed to cover as many jobs as possible, but other organizations may not be willing or able to provide the compensation data requested.

A better approach is to rely primarily on rational job evaluation methods (i.e., whole job ranking or quantitative ratings) and conduct salary surveys on a small number of benchmark jobs in the target area only to assess the general competitiveness of the organization's salary levels. Across-the-board adjustments can then be made in salary grades or salary schedules, as needed.

A good job evaluation procedure must be reliable, valid, and fair. The procedure is reliable to the extent that it provides consistent results from rater to rater and from time to time, assuming no changes in the jobs being rated. The procedure is valid to the extent that salary grades reflect the relative contribution of the job to the success of the organization. (Many organizations have suboptimum job evaluation because they simply adopted rating scales developed elsewhere without tailoring them to the needs and interests of their own organization.) The procedure is fair to the extent that salary grades are not biased for or against any job incumbent, regardless of the true value of the job to the organization.

Job evaluation is not an exact science but merely a systematic guide for making salary grade decisions. There is no substitution for good judgment. If strict application of the job evaluation procedure gives an odd or inconsistent result, particularly for jobs that are on the borderline between two grades, judgment should be used to place the job in the salary grade that makes the most sense for the good of the organization.

Job evaluation can be used in various ways in a law enforcement agency. Here are the major alternatives:

1. *Ranks only.* There is no job evaluation. The rank of the officer is not necessarily related to the value of his or her job assignment. This approach maintains the traditional military model, gives the maximum flexibility in assigning officers to jobs, and is easy to administer. However, this approach can also result in extreme pay inequities, favoritism, low morale, and waste of resources.

2. *Job classes linked to ranks.* Job evaluation is used to determine the salary grade of each job class (or job assignment). Jobs are then assigned to ranks according to the salary grade of each rank, with temporary salary differentials used whenever an officer is assigned to a job that is rated at a higher grade than his or her rank. This approach maintains the traditional military model, gives pay equity, and provides reasonable flexibility in job assignments. However, this approach requires considerable development and maintenance for proper administration. Therefore, some agencies use a less formal approach in which jobs are evaluated but not officially tied to ranks. The value of each job is then used as a guide for assigning officers (e.g., any job rated within plus or minus one grade of the officer's rank grade), but the agency retains the option to assign the officer to any job, if needed. This less formal approach has greater flexibility and ease of administration, and retains a fairly good linkage between rank and job value, as long as there are not too many exceptions to the rule.

3. *Job classes with no ranks.* The military rank structure is completely replaced by functional job classes whose grades are determined by job evaluation. This is the same approach that government jurisdictions normally use for nonsworn jobs. The result is a high level of pay equity but little flexibility in assigning officers to jobs. Officers can transfer only to those

positions within the same job class, and formal recruitment and selection procedures are needed to move officers from one job to another. Law enforcement agencies have so many jobs within the rank structure that such a pure job class system is usually impractical and counterproductive.

POSITION MANAGEMENT

Rather than allowing jobs to evolve haphazardly in response to random events or the personal interests of job incumbents, organizations should have an active program of position management. Job classes should be created, revised, or abolished, as appropriate, on a continuing basis to set priorities, fix responsibilities, and meet other organizational needs. At the same time, organizations should attempt to integrate the interests of job incumbents and the organization to make jobs more interesting, challenging, and motivating. Organizations should not only look at individual jobs but also the flow of employees through the organization (e.g., entry points, vertical tracks, lateral paths) to see if there are sufficient opportunities for employee development and advancement. This type of analysis is especially important for law enforcement agencies because they generally operate as closed systems. All sworn employees are hired into one low-level sworn job, and then all other sworn jobs are filled by internal promotion or transfer of sworn employees.

Table 21.3 shows an example of how one police department used position management to redesign its sworn ranks. Military job titles were replaced by functional job titles. Supervisory ranks were clearly indicated by the titles Supervisor, Manager, or Chief. Each new rank was linked to specific job assignments (not shown) that were appropriate for each salary grade. The Corporal rank was converted from an assistant supervisor to a high-level, technical police officer. The levels of nonsupervisory officers were expanded from two to six to provide more opportunities for advancement below the first-level supervisor. The supervisory ranks were spread more evenly across Grades 21 through 36 to reflect the various levels of difficulty and responsibility in these jobs. Employee selection was conducted on a competitive basis for Police Officer Candidate, Master Police Officer I, and all supervisory ranks. All other advancement was based on noncompetitive advancement criteria. The patrol job series was redesigned as follows:

1. *Police Officer Candidate.* All sworn employees enter the department through this job. Police Officer Candidates (POCs) receive 13 weeks of classroom training at the Police Academy, 2 to 3 weeks of working one shift in every work unit in the department, and an additional 13 weeks of field training in patrol from a Field Training Officer. For the rest of the 1-year

TABLE 21.3
Position Management in a Police Department

| | Old Sworn Ranks | | | New Sworn Ranks | | |
Job Classification	Salary Grade	Function	Job Classification	Salary Grade	Function
Chief of Police	36	Executive	Chief of Police	36	Executive
	35			35	
	34			34	
	33		Deputy Chief	33	Executive
Deputy Chief	32	Executive		32	
	31		Police Manager III	31	Manager
Major	30	Manager		30	
	29		Police Manager II	29	Manager
	28			28	
	27		Police Manager I	27	Manager
Captain	26	Manager		26	
	25		Police Supervisor III	25	Supervisor
1st Lieutenant	24	Supervisor		24	
2nd Lieutenant	23	Supervisor	Police Supervisor II	23	Supervisor
	22			22	
	21		Police Supervisor I	21	Supervisor
Sergeant	20	Supervisor	Master Police Officer II	20	General Officer
	19		Master Police Officer I	19	General Officer
Corporal	18	Asst. Supv.	Police Officer III	18	General Officer
Private First Class	17	General Officer	Police Officer II	17	General Officer
Private	16	General Officer	Police Officer I	16	General Officer
	15		Police Officer Candidate	15	Trainee

probation period, POCs work as a Patrol Officer under very close supervision from a Patrol Supervisor.

2. *Patrol Officer I.* All sworn employees who pass the 1-year probation period for Police Officer Candidate advance to the rank of Police Officer I, where they work at least 2 years as a Patrol Officer I, under close supervision, to perform regular patrol of assigned areas that generally have lower crime rates. After 2 years of acceptable performance as a Patrol Officer I, they advance to Police Officer II. At that level, they may work as a Patrol Officer II or transfer to a specialized assignment (e.g., Canine Handler I, Criminal Investigator I, SWAT Officer I, Traffic Officer I).

3. *Patrol Officer II.* Sworn employees in this assignment perform regular patrol of assigned areas that generally have higher crime rates.

4. *Patrol Officer III.* Sworn employees in this assignment identify areas with the most serious crime problems in their district. Then, in coordination with their supervisor, they develop and implement special plans to patrol the target areas, using any patrol method (e.g., foot, bicycle, marked car),

as appropriate, possibly involving a team of Patrol Officers. They may also serve as Field Training Officers.

5. *Master Patrol Officer I.* Sworn employees in this assignment patrol the entire district, normally focusing on hot spots of criminal activity, using a variety of patrol methods. They also conduct follow-up investigations of crimes best handled at the district level, generally investigating less difficult and complex cases than those handled by Master Patrol Officer II.

6. *Master Patrol Officer II.* Sworn employees in this assignment patrol the entire district, normally focusing on hot spots of criminal activity, using a variety of patrol methods. They also conduct follow-up investigations of crimes best handled at the district level, generally investigating more difficult and complex cases than those handled by Master Patrol Officer I.

The police department used here recognized that a strong patrol function was important to the success of the department but found that officers were transferring out of patrol and not coming back due to limited opportunities for growth and advancement in patrol. Thus, one of the objectives of their new rank system was to develop experienced police generalists who could apply broad technical knowledge in the patrol function. Accordingly, the new sworn ranks included five levels of increasingly difficult and complex patrol assignments to provide a meaningful technical career track in patrol. The department also established a general policy that nonsupervisory officers at the rank of Police Officer II and above, with a few exceptions (e.g., Canine Handler, Major Case Investigator, light duty officers), should rotate to a new job assignment every 2 years, with a tour of duty in patrol on every other job assignment. The development of police generalists not only prepared officers for patrol but also prepared them for supervisory and managerial assignments, where it is also important to see the big picture and understand the interrelationships among all of the various work units in the police department.

CIVILIANIZATION

Law enforcement agencies are staffed by sworn officers who have law enforcement powers and nonsworn or civilian employees who do not. Citizens and elected officials often complain that there are not enough law enforcement officers on the street to fight crime. Many explanations are possible for this situation (e.g., low-profile patrol methods, heavy deployment of officers on night shift, high ratio of supervisors to officers, general lack of sworn officers), but one of the most important (and overlooked or ignored) reasons is that sworn officers are being assigned to jobs that do not require sworn status (e.g., Garage Mechanic, Tow Truck Operator, Pilot, Security Guard, Supply Clerk, Records Clerk, Secretary, Radio Dispatcher, Evidence

Technician, Research Analyst, Budget Manager, Personnel Manager). Thus, adding more sworn officers to the budget will not necessarily increase the numbers of officers on the street unless there are controls on how these officers are used.

Another consideration is cost. Sworn officers generally cost more than nonsworn employees. The kind of nonsworn assignments that sworn officers usually perform would be rated at a lower salary grade than the officer's sworn rank if the position were filled by a nonsworn employee. However, even if a sworn officer were assigned to a nonsworn position that was worth the same salary grade, the sworn officer would still cost more because sworn officers receive much greater benefits than nonsworn employees. For example, sworn officers normally receive better health, life, and disability insurance coverage; 20-year retirement; clothing allowance; and take-home cars, as well as special rights and privileges (e.g., lunch on the clock, disciplinary protections). These extra benefits are designed to meet the needs of officers who perform true sworn duties but are provided to all sworn officers, regardless of job assignment. The cost of selecting, training, and equipping a sworn officer is also more than that for a nonsworn employee. Thus, the total employment cost is much greater for a sworn officer than for a nonsworn employee. If money is wasted by placing sworn employees in nonsworn assignments, there will be less money available to hire sworn officers for true sworn assignments.

The *Standards for Law Enforcement Agencies* (Commission on Accreditation of Law Enforcement Agencies, 1983) contains two standards on civilianization. Standard 16.3.1 states that law enforcement agencies should not assign sworn officers to civilian positions, except for temporary assignments to meet an urgent agency need or to broaden an officer's experience. Standard 16.3.2 says that law enforcement agencies should conduct an annual review of all positions to see which positions should be designated as civilian.

Exactly what is a *sworn* position? The *Standards for Law Enforcement Agencies* defines a sworn position as one that requires "law enforcement authority," but it does not provide any more detailed criteria to guide the implementation of the standards. The author has not found any other generally accepted criteria for defining a sworn position but has used the following criteria successfully in a number of law enforcement agencies:

1. The position makes arrests (e.g., Patrol Officer, Criminal Investigator).
2. The position supervises employees who make arrests (e.g., Patrol Supervisor, Criminal Investigation Supervisor, and the chain of command up to Police Chief).
3. The position is in a natural career track with positions that make arrests or supervise arrests (e.g., Court Liaison in same track as Criminal Investigators).

4. The position is specifically required by law to be a sworn position.

If a position does not meet any one of these criteria, the position should be designated as a nonsworn position and be given a different job classification from those used for sworn positions. Left to their own devices, law enforcement agencies have often used counterproductive, wasteful, and self-serving reasons to justify sworn status for a position, such as:

1. *The position supervises sworn officers.* Law enforcement officers have a strong belief that a nonsworn employee should never supervise a sworn officer because the civilian would then have the authority to order the sworn officer to make an arrest, use his or her weapon, and so on. However, if a sworn officer were assigned to a position that did not make arrests (e.g., records clerk, radio dispatcher, research analyst), there is no real need for a sworn supervisor. For those rare occasions when a sworn supervisor would be needed (e.g., to evaluate weapons proficiency or review an off-duty arrest), the sworn officer could report to a designated sworn manager for that limited purpose, reporting to a nonsworn supervisor for everything else.

2. *The position works on a professional level with other sworn officers.* Some sworn officers feel that they cannot develop a good working relationship with civilians because they do not share the same background and experience. But both sworn and nonsworn employees in a law enforcement agency are working toward the same goals and objectives for the organization. If each employee is doing his or her job properly, sworn status should be irrelevant. Sworn officers must also work on a professional level with civilians outside of their agency (e.g., judges, attorneys, government officials). Therefore, if a sworn officer cannot work effectively with civilians inside of his or her agency, it is unlikely that he or she can work effectively as a sworn officer at all.

3. *The position must maintain credibility with other law enforcement agencies and the general public.* Credibility is best established by good work performance, not sworn status. If the employee is properly trained, acts in a professional manner, and does his or her job well, the employee will be credible. At the same time, sworn officers should not assume that their sworn status will make up for poor work performance. Other law enforcement agencies are civilianizing their positions, too, so future contacts with these agencies are more likely to be with civilian employees.

4. *The position has access to sensitive or confidential information.* Millions of civilian employees in government and private industry have access to sensitive or confidential information every day with no adverse consequences. Thus, civilian versus sworn status is not a significant predictor of security problems. Proper selection and training of confidential employees, as well as other routine security practices, provide more cost-effective se-

curity than requiring those employees (e.g., Secretary to the Police Chief) to be sworn employees.

5. *The position testifies in court.* An employee (e.g., fingerprint examiner, crime lab analyst) does not necessarily have to have sworn status to testify as an expert witness on behalf of a law enforcement agency. The courts evaluate each expert on an individual basis, according to education, experience, and other qualifications relevant to each case.

6. *The position stores or otherwise handles evidence.* An employee can learn about the rules of evidence and other related matters by attending a few relevant training courses without having to meet all of the other requirements for sworn status.

7. *The position is required to work nights, weekends, holidays, and other odd times.* Many other jobs in government and private industry require long hours, odd shifts, and on-call status without the requirement of sworn status. When positions of this type are filled, the agency should use appropriate selection procedures to hire reliable employees who are willing to work under these conditions.

8. *Qualified civilian employees cannot be attracted due to low pay.* The placement of a $40,000 sworn officer in a $20,000 position is not the proper solution to this problem, except on an emergency basis. Low pay is only one of many possible reasons why qualified employees cannot be attracted to fill a position. A complete investigation is needed to see what should be done. The source of the problem may be faulty recruitment, poorly designed selection procedures, inadequate training, hostile co-workers, bad supervision, lack of necessary supplies or equipment, misclassified position, or inequitable salary grade. If low pay is the problem, the agency should work with the personnel department to raise the salary grade, not waste a sworn officer in a nonsworn position.

9. *Politics will permit the agency to add sworn positions to its budget but not civilian positions, forcing the agency to use sworn officers to fill critical positions that would normally be filled by civilians.* The law enforcement agency has to do a better job of justifying its civilian positions to government officials and the general public. If the civilian positions are still not approved, the agency should explore other solutions (e.g., transfer civilians from less critical positions, develop more efficient methods, use part-time employees, contract-out), rather than using sworn officers.

10. *The position increases the promotional opportunities for sworn officers.* The agency should provide satisfying careers for sworn officers, but this is not the way to do it. Higher level, nonsworn positions (e.g., Data Processing Manager, Budget Manager, Personnel Manager) require specialized education and experience that is not usually found in the sworn ranks. The agency will not prosper if it fills key nonsworn positions with sworn officers who must learn everything from scratch.

11. *The position provides a break from the stress of regular law enforcement work.* Many sworn officers seek nonsworn positions because it provides a 9-to-5 desk job, Monday through Friday, free from the stresses and strains of true sworn assignments. When agencies allow this to occur, they abuse the military rank concept that gives wide latitude in the assignment of sworn officers. Employee stress is a legitimate problem, but it should be generally handled in other ways (e.g., counseling, training, job rotation, better supervision, time off), without wasting sworn officers in nonsworn positions. If sworn officers are allowed to fill nonsworn assignments for stress reduction, career development, or special agency needs, these assignments should be limited to a maximum of 2 years, followed by a return to regular sworn duties for at least 2 more years before the officer may be given another nonsworn assignment.

12. *The position provides an alternative to dismissing officers who cannot perform sworn duties satisfactorily.* If a sworn officer cannot perform sworn duties due to a temporary disability, it would be appropriate to transfer the officer to a light duty assignment, on a temporary basis (i.e, up to 2 years), even if it were a nonsworn position. However, if the officer had a long-term disability, the officer should resign from the sworn service and take disability retirement or transfer to a nonsworn position as a nonsworn employee. If the officer were simply incompetent to perform sworn duties, the officer should be dismissed if all else fails, rather than be assigned to an out-of-the-way nonsworn position.

The ADA is going to challenge many traditional staffing practices in future years. Under the ADA, law enforcement agencies cannot discriminate against disabled officers by denying them light duty assignments and allowing non-disabled officers to have light duty assignments, including positions that could be performed by nonsworn employees. Thus, if agencies do not limit sworn officers to sworn assignments, they will be obligated to hire and promote disabled persons to any rank, as shown by at least one court case (*Kuntz v. City of New Haven*, 1993).

EMPLOYEE SELECTION

When an organization needs to hire or promote employees, managers have three basic options: (a) select the most qualified candidates, (b) select friends and relatives, or (c) select candidates at random. The textbook answer is, of course, to select the most qualified employees, but surprisingly few organizations make this choice or do it very well. The basic principles of good employee selection are described here.

1. *Definition.* Under well-accepted legal and professional standards, an *employee selection procedure* is any assessment device (or test) that is used as the basis for an employment decision, such as hiring, promotion, transfer, layoff, or dismissal. This broad definition includes minimum qualifications (e.g., education and experience requirements), training and experience ratings, seniority, written tests (e.g., math and reading ability, job knowledge, personality), job sample tests (e.g., typing, physically demanding tasks), simulation exercises, assessment centers, interviews and oral exams, performance appraisals, reference checks, background investigations, polygraph tests, drug tests, medical exams, and probation periods.

2. *Legal concerns.* It is not illegal to test job applicants, but employee selection is heavily regulated (e.g., nondiscrimination, immigration, privacy), so it is easy to violate the law if one is not careful. For example, employers are required to monitor their employee selection procedures for adverse impact (by race, sex, age, etc.). Tests that screen out one group significantly more than another are subject to challenge but can be defended if they predict work performance or serve other legitimate business purposes.

Employers are also required to make reasonable accommodation to disabled persons in test administration and job design to avoid artificial limits on employment. Each disabled applicant and job assignment should be studied on an individual basis to see what accommodations are reasonable and necessary. After these accommodations have been made, the employer may assess the relative qualifications of the disabled applicant, along with other applicants, and select the most qualified applicant for the job.

During the 1970s, many lawyers advised organizations to avoid lawsuits by replacing written tests and other objectively scored measures with subjective interviews and ratings on the theory that subjective selection procedures were not covered by the law. This was bad advice because subjective selection procedures generally have limited value in predicting work performance and because the Supreme Court eventually ruled in *Watson v. Fort Worth Bank and Trust* (1988) that subjective selection procedures were covered by the law and had to meet the same standards as objective selection procedures.

3. *Cost/benefits.* The cost of developing good employee selection procedures has been grossly exaggerated by lawyers and others who oppose government regulation and professional standards in this area. The truth is that the average cost per job can be quite reasonable (i.e., $5,000 to $25,000 in 1994 prices, although law enforcement tests often cost more due to the complexity of the projects and the high probability of litigation), particularly if the organization employs an inhouse Testing Specialist, has an ongoing test research and development program, maintains reasonably homogeneous job classifications, develops selection procedures that are relevant to more than one job, participates in cooperative studies with other organizations,

and seeks competitive bids when hiring consultants. However, the cost of good selection procedures is usually more than offset by the resulting gains in productivity and efficiency, as well as reduced employee turnover, from selecting better employees. Thus, managers should view employee selection as an investment, not just as another business expense, because good selection procedures can actually return a net profit for the organization.

Employee selection procedures are most useful when (a) a wide range of job performance is possible; (b) good performance is worth much more than bad performance; (c) many employees are selected for one job group, or a few employees are selected for critical jobs; (d) employees tend to work in the same job group for a long time; (e) the applicant pool contains a mixture of candidates from bad to good; (f) the most predictive selection procedures are used; (g) proper test administration procedures are followed; (h) applicants are selected in top-down rank order; and (i) many applicants are tested but only the best are selected. Good selection procedures can improve productivity and efficiency, and also provide the best defense in the event of litigation regarding sensitive or controversial selection decisions. Managers should consider all of these factors when planning for employee selection.

4. *Organizing the testing function.* The "testing team" has four key roles that must be played to ensure good employee selection. If qualified, one person can play more than one role, but it is often more efficient to have different people in each role. The first role is the *Testing Executive*, a high-ranking official who establishes policy, controls resources, and evaluates the effectiveness of the employee selection program. Second is the *Testing Specialist*, a professional employee or outside consultant who is available as needed to develop selection procedures and provide expert advice on all technical, legal, and ethical matters related to employee selection. Third is the *Testing Coordinator*, a professional employee who supervises the day-to-day operation of the testing program. Fourth is the *Test Administrator*, a professional or clerical employee who administers tests to job applicants and performs test scoring and record keeping.

Every organization that hires large numbers of employees or makes critical selection decisions (e.g., executives, superstars) should be guided by a Testing Specialist. This assignment requires a strong background in job analysis, psychological testing, employee selection, and statistical analysis. Testing Specialists normally have at least a master's degree in industrial/organizational psychology, or a related field, plus 2 years of experience in the development and use of employee selection procedures. The other roles on the testing team are less technical and require only one course on employment testing.

5. *Test development.* The process of developing good employee selection procedures typically requires (a) a job analysis to define important job tasks and necessary worker characteristics, (b) development of a selection plan,

(c) construction of job-related tests, and (d) review of the tests by subject matter experts to verify test content. Investigation of statistical relationships between test scores and measures of work performance is desirable but not always necessary or feasible. Selection procedures should measure all qualities needed for successful job performance (e.g., knowledge, skill, ability, personality, interests). The final selection process should be fully documented, including a technical report that explains how each procedure was developed and validated, and a manual that explains how to administer and score each procedure. After development, selection procedures should be reviewed periodically, or whenever job duties are revised, to ensure that the selection procedures are still effective predictors of job performance.

6. *Test administration.* The value of a well-developed employee selection procedure can be destroyed if it is not administered properly. Proper test administration generally requires (a) sufficient staff, facilities, and equipment, (b) identification of examinees, (c) standard conditions that permit examinees to give their best performance, (d) compliance with test administration manuals (e.g., directions to examinees, time limits), (e) accurate scoring, (f) prevention of cheating, and (g) test security (e.g., limited access to test materials). As an example of what can go wrong, one jurisdiction recently had to develop and administer a whole new Firefighter promotional exam because the Test Administrator did not collect, or somehow lost, some of the test answer sheets completed by examinees.

7. *Standards.* Good employee selection procedures should (a) provide consistent measurement, (b) predict work performance or other business objectives, (c) predict equally well for all applicants, (d) avoid safety or health hazards, and (e) be practical to administer. The major professional standards for employee selection are the *Standards for Educational and Psychological Testing* (AERA, APA, & NCME, 1985) and the *Principles for the Validation and Use of Personnel Selection Procedures* (SIOP, 1987). The major legal standards are the *Uniform Guidelines on Employee Selection Procedures* (EEOC, CSC, DOL, DOJ, & DOT, 1978), and the EEOC's (1992, 1994) emerging guidelines under the ADA.

8. *Recruitment.* Many organizations attempt to reduce selection costs by using restrictive recruitment methods (e.g., word of mouth, referral agencies, short application deadlines) to limit the number of job applicants. This approach is self-defeating because it reduces the quality of the applicant pool, which eventually reduces the quality of the employees selected. For good employee selection, there should be open recruitment (e.g., newspaper ads, wide publicity, reasonable deadlines) to attract a large applicant pool that is representative of the relevant labor force. If necessary, selection costs can be controlled by using a minimum qualifications questionnaire to screen out obviously unfit applicants and then using random selection to invite the desired number of applicants for further testing.

9. *Training versus selection.* Some managers believe that they can hire anyone and then train them to perform any job well. This approach is doomed because a combination of selection and training is needed for most jobs. Employee selection is needed to identify applicants who already have certain job-related qualities that are difficult or impractical to develop through employee training programs (e.g., intelligence, personality, physical ability, basic education, lengthy specialized education). Employee training is best used to develop those job-related qualities that would be difficult or impractical to develop outside of the organization (e.g., knowledge of internal policies and procedures, skill in operating specialized equipment used on the job).

APPENDIX A

Good City Police Department

TITLE: Patrol Officer I

GROUP: Sworn, Nonsupervisor

CODE: 049-16

DATE: 3/7/95

Class Definition

Under close supervision, patrols assigned area in police cruiser to enforce criminal and traffic laws, maintain peace and safety, and provide general assistance to public. Performs other related duties as assigned.

Major Duties

1. *Patrol.* Patrols assigned area of city by foot and police cruiser. Maintains radio contact with police communications center. Reports unusual or suspicious behavior or events that may require police response. Checks buildings for suspicious open windows and doors. Responds to calls or initiates action, as appropriate.

2. *Criminal apprehension.* Responds to criminal violations. Restores peace. Secures scene to protect evidence. Calls for assistance, if needed. Interviews victims and witnesses. Identifies, collects, and preserves evidence. Pursues and apprehends suspects. Makes arrests. Advises suspects of their rights. Searches suspects for weapons and evidence. Seizes contraband and stolen property. Interrogates suspects. Transports suspects to jail. Writes police reports. Testifies in court.

3. *Traffic enforcement.* Responds to traffic violations. Pursues and apprehends traffic violators. Issues traffic summonses, warnings, and vehicle repair notices. Writes police reports. Testifies in court.

4. *Safety emergencies.* Responds to traffic accidents, fires, floods, earthquakes, or other disasters. Secures scene to protect victims and property. Gives first aid. Calls for medical assistance and other emergency services, if needed.

5. *General assistance.* Provides general assistance to improve public safety and security. Assists lost or stranded persons. Searches for lost or missing persons. Removes stalled vehicles and other hazards from roadway. Directs traffic at busy intersections if traffic signals malfunction. Advises residents and businesses on crime prevention and security.

6. *Entry training.* During first year on job, receives 13 weeks of classroom training at Police Academy and 13 weeks of field training from Field Training Officer. Works rest of 1-year probation period as Patrol Officer under very close supervision.

NOTE. City provides reasonable accommodation in employment to persons with disabilities.

464

Important Worker Characteristics

A. *Knowledge of* (1) arrest;* (2) city geography;* (3) city government structure and functions;* (4) court policy and procedures;* (5) crime prevention;* (6) crime scene analysis;* (7) department structure and functions;* (8) department written directives;* (9) emergency commitment procedures;* (10) emergency medical treatment;* (11) family crisis intervention;* (12) law enforcement;* (13) law enforcement information systems;* (14) news media relations;* (15) other law enforcement agencies;* (16) patrol;* (17) search and seizure;* (18) self-defense;* (19) state and city criminal laws;* (20) state and city traffic laws;* (21) traffic enforcement.*

B. *Skill in operation of* (1) auto; (2) camera;* (3) standard police weapons;* (4) two-way radio.*

C. *Ability to* (1) apply principles to solve practical problems; (2) define problems, establish facts, and draw valid conclusions; (3) analyze problems quickly and take appropriate action under stress; (4) observe and remember events accurately and completely; (5) read legal and other technical materials; (6) write legibly; (7) write routine reports and correspondence; (8) calculate fractions, decimals, and percentages; (9) speak clearly and audibly; (10) handle stressful or sensitive public contacts; (11) work cooperatively; (12) provide courteous service; (13) work long hours.

D. *Other:* (1) emotional stability; (2) integrity; (3) physical fitness.

* Developed primarily *after* employment in this job class.

Minimum Qualifications

1. High school graduation or GED.
2. Minimum age of 21.
3. No tobacco use.
4. Valid driver's license.
5. Must pass all tests and other selection procedures used for this job.

Probation Period

Officers must pass a 12-month probation period to achieve regular status in this job.

Working Conditions

Works on street. Works rotating shifts, weekends, and holidays. On call 24 hours, 7 days per week. Exposed to armed and dangerous persons. Exposed to safety and health hazards.

REFERENCES

American Educational Research Association, American Psychological Association, and National Council on Measurement in Education. (1985). *Standards for educational and psychological testing.* Washington, DC: American Psychological Association.

American Psychological Association. (1992). Ethical principles of psychologists and code of conduct. *American Psychologist, 47,* 1597–1611.

Commission on Accreditation for Law Enforcement Agencies. (1983). *Standards for Law Enforcement Agencies.* Fairfax, VA: Author.

Gael, S. (1983). *Job analysis: A guide to assessing work activities.* San Francisco, CA: Jossey-Bass.

Gael, S. (Ed.). (1988). *The job analysis handbook for business, industry, and government.* New York: Wiley.

Ghorpade, J. V. (1988). *Job analysis: A handbook for the human resource director.* Englewood Cliffs, NJ: Prentice Hall.

Kuntz v. City of New Haven, 2AD Case 905 (U.S. District Court, Conn. 1993).

McCormick, E. J. (1979). *Job analysis: Methods and applications.* New York: AMACOM.

Society for Industrial and Organizational Psychology. (1987). *Principles for the validation and use of personnel selection procedures.* (3rd ed.). College Park, MD: Author.

Task Force on Assessment Center Guidelines. (1989). *Guidelines and ethical considerations for assessment center operations.* Pittsburgh, PA: Development Dimensions International.

U.S. Department of Labor, Employment and Training Administration. (1991). *Dictionary of occupational titles* (4th ed.). Washington, DC: U.S. Government Printing Office.

U.S. Equal Employment Opportunity Commission, Civil Service Commission, Department of Labor, Department of Justice, Department of the Treasury. (1978). Uniform guidelines on employee selection procedures. *Federal Register, 43,* 38290–38315.

U.S. Equal Employment Opportunity Commission. (1992). *A technical assistance manual on the employment provisions (Title I) of the Americans with Disabilities Act.* Washington, DC: U.S. Government Printing Office.

U.S. Equal Employment Opportunity Commission. (May 19, 1994). *Enforcement guidance on preemployment disability-related inquiries and medical examinations under the Americans with Disabilities Act of 1990.* EEOC Order 915.002, Volume II of Compliance Manual. Washington, DC: U.S. Government Printing Office.

Watson v. Fort Worth Bank and Trust, 108 S.Ct. 2777 (1988).

CHAPTER TWENTY-TWO

Human Factors Psychology for Law Enforcement Agencies

Martin I. Kurke
*Drug Enforcement Administration (Retired)
and George Mason University*

Vesta S. Gettys
*Industrial & Law Enforcement Psychological Services, Inc.,
Oklahoma City, OK*

The terms *human factors, ergonomics, human factors engineering*, and *human engineering* are often used interchangeably to describe a multidisciplinary endeavor that is concerned with designing man-made objects so that people can use them effectively and safely, and creating environments suitable for living and work. If equipment and workstations are not designed and arranged to meet the requirements and capabilities of humans, the people who use that equipment will not be able to perform required tasks, or will make errors in their attempts to do so. Such errors may degrade system performance, and compromise both the safety and the success of the mission for which the equipment was designed (Huchingson, 1981). This chapter describes ways that attention to human factors research projects can contribute to improved reliability of law enforcement personnel. It then introduces human factors as an essential element of MANPRINT, a system for incorporating manpower, personnel, human engineering, and other domains into the development and acquisition of equipment to increase the efficiency and reliability of performance by law enforcement personnel. The chapter continues with a new role for human factors in establishing reasonable accommodations for impaired law enforcement personnel, as required by the Americans with Disabilities Act.

HUMAN FACTORS IN SYSTEM DEVELOPMENT
AND ACQUISITION

In an article in *The Police Chief,* a senior police range officer identified four characteristics that should be considered when selecting a handgun for police use: (a) the officers' physical and mental abilities to competently manipulate and employ any weapon systems they are issued; (b) the caliber and the weapon's ability to eliminate an offender's ability to attack the officers; (c) the reliability and effectiveness of weapon's design as it affects officers' ability to aim, shoot, and reload; and (d) simplicity of handling—particularly while under operational stress (Riddell, 1991). Clearly, at least three of these characteristics are related to the human factor component in the design, acquisition, and use of the weapon. Failure to adequately pay attention to the strengths and limitations of the humans who have to use equipment can increase the risk of a wide range of gun-related mishaps, and subsequent investigations of gun-related accidents or charges of improper use of firearms may result in findings adverse to the officer or imposition of liability on the department. Often, when a weapon is purchased by an agency, most attention is given to the weapon's operating specifications, design, and engineering specifications. Much less attention is given to the characteristics and limitations of the user. Arguably, the proximate cause of some gun-related accidents is a decision by the department to procure a weapon system with built-in hazards.

In many instances investigators of casualty or property damage inducing events find that the incident can be attributed to operator error or human error. A long list of incidents could be generated, including incidents involving police weapons, nuclear power plant accidents (the Three Mile Island incident), the shooting down of an Iranian airliner by the U.S.S. Vincennes, the Arthur Kill oil spill, the malfunctioning Hubbel space telescope, and numerous aircraft accidents. Investigative reports on these incidents often infer that some operator or maintainer was inattentive, had poor training, or was indifferent to or incapable of performing properly. But, as Ferguson (1992) pointed out, terms such as *operator error* are grossly insulting to the operator: The human errors that caused the incident were more likely errors made by the designer of the equipment who failed to take into account the inherent limitations of the one component the designer could not control, the people who operate or maintain it. Because equipment used by police agencies is rarely designed by the using organization, the person who procured equipment designed by or for the vendors should bear or share the responsibility for the incident.

Officials responsible for putting equipment into the hands of users rarely, if ever, conduct an analysis of the precursors to the casualty-inducing incident. However, product liability and tort negligence lawyers will do so. In an attempt to assign liability for the incident, they have the ability to investigate the accident backward from the incident to the situation in which it occurred. The lawyers focus on the design of warnings and training, the design of the equipment as it was influenced by the standards and specifications; on the personal characteristics of the involved parties, and the adequacy of the selection processes when the individuals operators were hired (Kurke, 1986, 1988).

Figure 22.1 diagrams the process that leads to human error (e.g., an accident) occurring within a work environment. The error itself often may be traced back to the way human characteristics were marshaled to meet requirements for the performance of a system that may or may not include equipment. Translation of those requirements and characteristics into equipment or service delivery design, acquisition of equipment, training of personnel selected to perform the task lead to momentary states we may refer to as incident-inducing milieux. The large box depicting a milieu shows it as consisting of an interaction of the involved parties' knowledge, skill, aptitude and ability state; their functional level, and the capabilities and limitations of the equipment or system as they existed at the time of the accident, and as they are influenced by the ambient and operating environment and the constraints or facilitations provided by the culture in which the organization operates.

HUMAN RELIABILITY ISSUES

The need to consider the wide variety of psychological factors influencing human performance in operational systems and environments gave rise to the human reliability approach to the prediction of behavior in operational

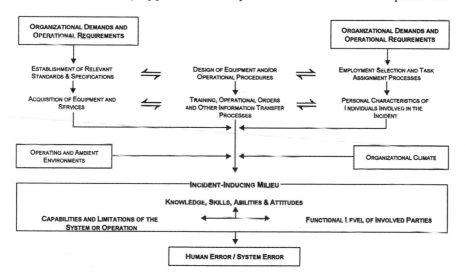

FIG. 22.1. Etiology of human error in a system or organizational context.

systems and environments. Some research attention was focused on the determination of factors that could affect the risk of security violations or other inappropriate behavior in sensitive or hazardous working environments, and other research attention was devoted to the identification of personal characteristics of actual or potential employees that might be indicators of risk. The occurrence of highly visible and well-publicized accidents like the Three Mile Island incident, several aircraft disasters, and other critical incidents focused more attention on the user–equipment–organization triad (Swain & Guttmann, 1983). Human factors and other industrial/organizational psychologists were instrumental in introducing the notion that the working environment, work culture, and ergonomic characteristics of the job are as important to the reliability of the work system as the personal characteristics of the people manning the system (Miller & Swain, 1987; Swain & Guttman, 1983). A White House study on improving human reliability in extreme risk environments noted that ergonomics (i.e., human factors) is an area that is often ignored to a substantial degree and that this "lack of attention to ergonomics will have a profound effect on stress tolerance, causing emergence of interpersonal conflict, lowered production, and incorrect decisions and recommendations in an operational extreme risk environment" (Office of Emergency Operations, 1992) and it was recommended that the issue of ergonomics receive more attention.

Chapter 19 on organizational management of stress and human reliability (Kurke, this volume) discoursed on the five human reliability domains derived from the work of Besco (1990). A condensed list of sources and the means of prevention or correction of human reliability degradation with human factors implication appearing in that chapter is shown in Table 22.1.

The next section of the chapter describes two situations in which human factors and ergonomic design specifications can be applied to increasing human reliability in irregular rest or sleep conditions, and dealing with situations beyond the limits of human capabilities. A third example illustrates the application of changing a training design to reduce information overload and increase proficiency.

THREE EXAMPLES OF THE INFLUENCE
OF HUMAN FACTORS ON HUMAN RELIABILITY

Law enforcement agencies spend a great deal of time and energy selecting the best equipment for their employees: the latest in cars, radios, armor, guns, and patrol cars. No one would argue that tools and equipment play a major part in the success of police operations. However, of equal importance is the individual officer who uses these machines. In this section, three examples that illustrate the interaction between people and the machines

TABLE 22.1
Human Factors Influence on Human Reliability

Human Factors Means of Prevention/Control of Human Reliability Degradation	Source of Human Reliability Degradation	Factors Influencing Human Reliability
Human factors/ergonomics design specifications	Equipment failures	Structural, electrical, software, system failure modes, quality control standards and procedures
	Health deficits	Incapacitation, illness, physical condition, nutrition, injury, disease, substance abuse, emotional health
	Irregular rest or sleep	Sleep cycle, poor facilities, irregular schedules, shift work cycle
	System beyond limits of human capabilities	Frequency thresholds, response time requirements, saturation, workload demands
	Ineffective safety instructions or warnings	Design and location of warnings, signs, labels, and instructions; personal attitudes, awareness, vigilance levels, and level or reinforcement concerning compliance with safety procedures
Restructuring or improving the environment	Inadequate or hazardous environment	Light, air quality, air flow, acceleration, vibration, seat comfort, temperature, visibility
Redesign of feedback or input/output devices and procedures	Awkward input alternatives	Location, sensitivity, incompatibilities, ergonomic considerations
	Inadequate feedback	Sources and reliability of feedback
	Prior proficiency	Where, when, proficiency level maintenance
Training design, practice schedule	Infrequently used skills	Required skills, personal acceptance of deficiencies, influence of leaders and peers

they use and people and working conditions are cited. The three examples include shift work and circadian rhythms, the cumulative effects of stress, and reducing information overload in vehicle training.

Shift Work: Working With Circadian Rhythms

Shift work is a fact of life in law enforcement agencies that are on duty 24 hours a day. In order to provide law enforcement services day and night, administrators are required to assign individuals to various work shifts, and to periodically change work schedules for their employees. There is a large body of research on shift work and performance, and some of this research is applicable to police operations.

Humans have built within them cycles that approximate a 24-hour clock called *circadian rhythms*. There are times within any 24-hour period when a person is most alert (measured by blood pressure, heart rate, ability to do cognitive tasks, etc.), and periods when all biological functions are at a low ebb. Knowledge of how sleep and wake changes affect performance goes back several decades (Kleitman, 1933, 1939). Much research on work schedules and efficiency was published in the 1960s. Aschoff (1965, 1969) and Kleitman (1963) described setting and resetting circadian rhythms. Some early work on the effect of changes in efficiency of workers under various shift conditions can be found in studies by Alluisi and Chiles (1967), and Ray, Martin, and Alluisi (1961). More recent studies and books that summarize research in this area include Colquhoun (1972) and Alluisi and Fleishman (1982). A recent study also looks at 12-hour shift schedules specifically in a police context (Cunningham, 1990).

It is hard to draw specific conclusions from the extensive research on circadian rhythms, because motivation to change can interact very strongly with the physiological effects of change. For example, most studies that measured job performance of individuals changing from an 8-hour 5-day week to a 10-hour 4-day week indicated no loss of performance, or an increase in productivity. Several researchers (Bloom, 1961; Johnson, Naitoh, Lubin, & Moses, 1972; Mott, 1976; Mott, Mann, McLaughlin, & Warwick, 1965; Rentos & Shepard, 1976) conclude that general satisfaction resulting from factors like cutting down on commuting time, having more days off together, and so on can help counteract the cumulative effects of fatigue over a longer working day.

One consistent finding is that response to changes in schedules varies with individuals. Some are more adaptable, and some are less. As people get older, their ability to adapt quickly to schedule changes seems to diminish. It takes about 30 days for the biological clock to completely reset to a new sleep and wake pattern, and there is an initial period of disturbance that peaks at about 7 days. Studies reported in Colquhoun's (1972) text, and in Ashoff (1965) indicate that people adjust more quickly to shift changes if the individual is asked to stay up later (day to swing, or swing to night shifts) rather than get up earlier.

Police administrators might be well advised to advocate permanent shifts whenever possible, and if rotations are necessary, rotate shifts with the clock rather than backward to minimize the effects of time changes on the job performance of their officers.

Performance Reserve and the Ability to Keep on Responding

Many factors affect an officer's ability to do his or her job. Stress, training, equipment, mood, and temperament, and even what was eaten for lunch can enter the equation. On one occasion, with the same training and equipment, an officer responds appropriately; on another occasion, that same officer can be brutal, insulting, or ineffective in dealing with a problem. Sometimes, teaching officers about the human side of the performance equation and how circumstances can limit their ability to respond may help them avoid situations where they respond inappropriately.

Understanding the Effects of Stress on Performance. An easily understood bank account model seems to provide a framework for understanding the effects of stress on performance. In the bank account model, there are two components, a checking account and a savings account. The checking account is readily available energy, built on hours of sleep, good nutrition, interest in our job, training, and experience. This is the energy the officer draws on to handle day-to-day activities. However, when something extraordinary occurs, the officer may have to dip into his or her emotional reserves, and the ability to respond in high-stress situations may be a function of the officer's emotional savings account.

Stress and the Ability to Keep on Responding. The savings account is the reserve you can draw on if you have to, and this energy is available for only a short time. Stress tends to decrease the savings account, or performance reserve. Holmes and Rahe (1967) provided a Life Stress Chart that outlines the risk of major health changes based on the number of changes that have occurred in a person's life during the past year. Major expenses, such as the death of a spouse, divorce, or separation, make a big drain on an individual's emotions. However, many small things occurring together can add up to a high level of stress. If individuals are stressed out, their ability to handle job stress and even routine problems is decreased. Other factors that put a drain on an officer's ability to respond are poor nutrition, physical disability, sleep loss, and so on.

The Importance of Stress Recognition and Reduction. It is important to train supervisors to recognize radical changes in performance of
officers under their command. When officers who have performed efficiently
over a long period of time begin to change their behavior, the supervisors
need to find out why. Symptoms of temporary stress conditions might include
an increase in absenteeism or an avoidance of people. Officers under stress
are slower to make decisions and more likely to make mistakes when they
have to respond to stressful situations. Supervisors need to be trained to
recognize stress symptoms. Officers also need to be encouraged to monitor
their own lives as diligently as they maintain their equipment. If the human
component of a man–machine system gets too far out of adjustment, the
whole system can fail.

Solving a Training Problem by Reduction
of Information Overload and Stress

Every person has an optimal level of activity. Individuals who have to deal
with too much happening too fast tend to freeze and respond in an inappropriate way. Prolonged exposure to conditions in which too much happens too fast results in burnout. At the other end of the spectrum, dealing
with too little, or things that happen too slowly, leads to boredom and an
inability to respond quickly or appropriately to new situations. Prolonged,
unrelieved exposure to boredom results in rustout.

The human system responds in a very specific way to high levels of
stress. Heart rate, blood pressure, and respiration increase; vision and attention are focused on a small set of stimuli (tunnel vision); and the blood
supply is directed toward the long muscles of the arms and legs as the body
gets ready to "fight or flee" (Selye, 1956).

Often situations encountered by law enforcement personnel in the course
of doing their duty can trigger a high stress response. For example, a new
highway patrol trooper driving south on a four-lane road spotted a speeder
going north. He decided to pursue the speeder, turned on his siren, and
got an adrenaline high. He wrecked four cars making a U-turn to go after
the speeding car. This incident led to an agency decision to train troopers
to drive at high speeds, and this decision led to the development of an
Emergency Vehicle Operation Course (EVOC). A human factors analysis was
part of the course development.

An industrial psychologist was called in by the agency as a consultant
(Gettys, Elam, & Davis, 1983). The agency's initial intent was to assign a
pass–fail grade to the troopers taking the course. The grade was to be based
on the subjective judgment of a driving instructor as to how well the troopers
performed in the driving tasks. After analyzing the situation, the consultant

advised a complete change of focus for the course, and a built-in validation procedure for the training. The following plan resulted.

Initial Analysis of the Problem. The agency was advised to study the accident statistics for the previous 5 years to determine what situations were most likely to cause accidents. Next, the driving instructors were challenged to come up with defensive driving techniques to teach troopers to better handle these situations. Several specific situations were identified in this step. Accidents were occurring when troopers lost control of their cars and went into skids (ice, rain, gravel roads, etc.), when troopers engaged in night pursuits (errors in speed or distance judgments, etc.), when they conducted high-speed chases with siren and lights on, and when they had to make quick adjustments (lane changes, stopping at red light, etc.) based on things that were happening around them.

Designing Training to Address the Problem. Based on the analysis of accident statistics, the training program was redesigned. More time was spent in the "skid pan" teaching troopers to react properly to skid situations. Several sessions of "dog–rabbit" pursuit training were included. In these pursuits, with siren and lights all on, troopers (with an instructor aboard) chased another car under very realistic conditions. The chase courses included country roads, city streets, and a specially designed EVOC training course. Also, several specialized training segments were added to the EVOC training. Night pursuit training was added, which gave troopers experience driving at high speeds under nighttime conditions. A reaction task was designed in which a trooper drove down a single line to a choice point, and had to quickly choose one of three lanes based on the color of a signal flashed as he reached the choice point.

Assessing the Effectiveness of Training. Troopers were required to come back for proficiency training 1½ years after completing the initial driving course. Their proficiency was tested on an initial run when they came in for the refresher course. Things that they had "unlearned" (optimal hand position on the wheel, poor performance in the skid tests, etc.) were noted. The effectiveness of the training course could be measured by the number of skills that had to be relearned, or the level of proficiency that was maintained over time.

A second measure of the effectiveness of the program came from monitoring accident statistics before and after training. Initial results indicate that the procedure was effective in reducing accidents.

Training in this case reduced the amount of stress involved in high-speed chases. Troopers got used to the lights and sounds of the siren and to the perceptual demands of high-speed chases in controlled conditions, and this training transferred to their regular job activities on the road.

HUMAN FACTORS AND PERFORMANCE IN LAW ENFORCEMENT SYSTEMS

In earlier sections of this chapter it has been argued that law enforcement agencies need to take human factors into account in acquisition of equipment, training, and monitoring the physical and emotional health of their employees. This section is devoted to the discussion of a system for integrating the various personnel-related concerns for the development and acquisition of equipment and systems. This system is known as MANPRINT (Barber, Ching, Jones, & Miles, 1990; Booher, 1990; Johnson, Rossmeissl, Kracov, & Shields, 1989). MANPRINT is an acronym for **Man**power and **Person**nel **Inte**gration.

A *law enforcement system* is defined as any integrated combination of people, equipment, and working environments. Such systems are created to accomplish specific law enforcement activities within operational, administrative, and management guidelines. Management often has the ability to optimize performance of the system by ensuring that the system is user centered. The Department of Defense has for many years been concerned with the need to improve human performance in military organizations using complex equipment systems. Initially concerned with improving weapon system effectiveness by including human engineers in system design, it was learned that other human factors considerations such as training, the constraints of operational procedural requirements, and tailoring of organizational functions and structures all influenced the ability of military personnel to do their jobs. Failure to adequately take these concerns into account degrade the performance of the people who constitute the system.

The MANPRINT approach has been used in the development of major technology-based systems and the concept is now being transferred to systems that are less technology centered, and exploratory efforts are underway to explore the applicability of MANPRINT concepts to both military and civilian law enforcement organizations. There are four focus areas in the MANPRINT approach: aptitude and training concerns, performance measurements concerns, organization and management concerns, and accountability.

People Performance Affects System Performance

It is evident that both the technology and the user of that technology must complement each other if overall manned system performance is to be successful. A lack of fit between the equipment and its user can create a *performance gap.* A performance gap is the inability of the manned equipment or system to achieve the system performance potential forecast by the hardware and the software alone. Technological advances have brought about the advent of sophisticated communications, investigative, and other law enforcement technology. However, the capabilities of the officers, technicians, and others who are to operate, maintain, and support the equipment have not changed much over time. A police agency, like other organizations, has a fixed pool of personnel at its disposal with finite cognitive and psychomotor characteristics. The number and the knowledge, skill, and ability (KSA) constellation of sworn officers, technicians, and other employees can, therefore, become a limiting factor in the agency's ability to use its technology. An important purpose of a law enforcement MANPRINT program is to influence equipment design and procurement so that technology rather than the employee becomes the limiting factor in achieving the desired operational effectiveness. MANPRINT does this by attending to six human resource concerns: manpower, personnel, training, human factors, system safety, and health hazards, defined here:

- *Manpower:* The number of human resources (officers and nonsworn personnel) required and available to manage or operate law enforcement systems.
- *Personnel:* The aptitudes, experience and other human characteristics necessary to achieve optimal system performance.
- *Training:* The requisite knowledge, skills, and abilities needed by the available personnel to operate and maintain systems under operational conditions.
- *Human factors:* The comprehensive integration of human characteristics into system definition, design, development, and evaluation to optimize system performance. The term *human factors engineering* is used when the focus of human factors is on human–machine–ambient environment combinations. The term *organizational human factors* may be used when the focus is on the performance of the system's individuals or groups within the context of the organizational culture.
- *System safety:* The inherent ability of the system to be used, operated, and maintained without accidental injury to using personnel or others in the proximity of the operating system. In a law enforcement system the term is expanded to include inherent protection against injury arising from hostile activities.
- *Health hazards:* Inherent conditions in the operation or use of a system (e.g., shock, recoil, vibration, toxic fumes, radiation, noise, and the hazards associated with exposure to contagious diseases) that can cause death, injury, illness, disability, or reduced job performance of personnel. The original

concept has been expanded to include conditions hazardous to mental health and functioning. Therefore "fitness for duty" questions may be raised based upon the need to assess either the physical or mental status required for effective job performance.

User Capability Is a Function of Aptitude, Training, and Personality Structure

As expressed here, *user capability* or *skill* is the product of the interaction of the users and training, and those aspects of the user's personality that facilitate or inhibit the acquisition, retention, and wise application of those skills. Aptitude consists of basic abilities inherent in the individual employee and are not readily modified by training. Therefore, the traits that make up the quality called *aptitude* are considered stable over time. The need to identify the traits required for utilization of new technology and the ability to select personnel with those traits is rapidly becoming imperative.

Training refers to a series of activities (e.g., verbal instructions, formal study programs, on-the-job practice, etc.) that enables operators, maintainers, and other users of technology to acquire skill and wisdom in the tasks they must perform to accomplish their mission. Training is most effectively evaluated on two dimensions: completeness (i.e., covered everything the user need to know) and sufficiency (i.e., enough instruction and practice for the user to achieve the acceptable standard of performance).

For our purposes, the term *skill* has at least two meanings: One refers to the occupational specialty (e.g., traffic control, narcotics investigation, patrol officer, SWAT team member, communications technician, secretary, etc.) and the other is the more common use of the term to mean a high level of proficiency. When the term is used to define proficiency, it becomes dependent on (a) the time to acquire mastery of critical tasks initially, (b) the time elapsed since the tasks were last trained, and (c) the methods of training used. As a result, skill is considered unstable over time, due to proficiency decay as a function of time without practice. In this sense, proficiency of employees with known aptitudes and training can be measured at a specific time and place and those time and accuracy scores can be used to predict the level of performance with which other employees with known aptitudes, training, and practice can be expected to achieve.

Operational Performance of Manned Equipment Is Measured by Time, Accuracy, and Reliability

This rule refers to the common sense notion that human performance occurs simultaneously in two dimensions: performance time and freedom from error. Inaccuracy is a measure of error. Measuring either dimension without the other (or measuring them both, but independently) invariably produces a distorted picture of reality; therefore, the need to take both speed and accuracy into consideration is vital in developing equipment system specifications or any evaluation data plan. System defects that might have been disclosed early can be masked if, for example, the system's performance data describes only the time it takes an operator to perform a particular task. Such defective data have been used in the past to argue that any user, regardless of aptitude or training, could perform a particular task within a specified length of time—but the data did not state that the task would be done well (accurately enough to accomplish the system's operational objectives) with a sufficient degree of statistical reliability.

Operational Task Procedures Are Determined by a Mixture of Working Environment, Equipment Design, Organizational Culture, and Administrative Decision Making

Equipment designers and vendors are major contributors to system effectiveness, but their influence is mediated by management when it selects and procures the equipment. The equipment designer (and the equipment purchaser) has the power both to create and to eliminate user performance tasks. A system to perform a particular mission may, therefore, involve very simple equipment and software attended by numerous and highly skilled operators, or highly automated equipment with few operators of much less skill. It is essential that tasks assigned to the user by the designer be within the user's capabilities to perform.

Similarly, an organization's management and the work culture and environment have equal contributions to make to system effectiveness. Management philosophies that have no regard for the users of equipment also tend to ignore the limitations of employees under both normal and stressful working conditions. Managers with this philosophy tend to make their decisions under the assumption that if the company says so, employees have no choice but to adjust to new procedures, equipment, and working conditions. This style of management tends to result in poor morale, providing inadequate training, encouraging or demanding punishing work schedules or assignments, and placing the system at risk of performance degradation. Conversely, alternative management policies have the potential for enhancing the performance of both the users and the system.

Creators and Users of Operational Tasks Bear Significant Responsibility and Accountability for the Effectiveness of Operational Performance

Through its procurement decisions, management has the power to ensure that the designer or vendor takes into account human factors, health and safety, and training requirements. Ordinarily managers are not held accountable for procurement decisions that lead to disastrous breakdowns of equipment or operations. However, the agency itself may suffer in terms of its public relations or in terms of negligence or other tort liability for such failure. Because the designer of equipment has the power to enhance or degrade equipment system performance by the degree of attention given to these factors, the contractors should be given the responsibility and accountability for the field performance of hardware and software they design.

APPLICATION OF MANPRINT IN ACQUISITION OF EQUIPMENT AND SYSTEMS

The Army Materiel Command has prepared a guide that addresses key areas of MANPRINT for nondevelopment (i.e., commercially available) items showing how the MANPRINT process is applied in each phase of the acquisition process. The guide is intended for use in establishing key MANPRINT issues to be included in evaluating nondevelopmental equipment and conducting market investigations and procurement solicitations. The guide stresses total system performance by defining performance concerns, developing MANPRINT issues relevant to those concerns, and preparing questions that address the performance issues (Johnson et al., 1989).

Application of MANPRINT starts with the establishment of a requirement for a new or modified system that may or may not involve equipment. The process of system acquisition is centered about a formal three-phase procedure. The first phase is an assessment of the operability of the system, procedure, or equipment contemplated. Initially, one must build a total system concept in which the means of employment, the people who are part of the system, and the equipment (if any) needed to make the system work are integrated. The total system concept is created by first deriving the performance requirements for the system as a result of the identified need for it. Given the system performance requirements, the doctrine (i.e., when and how the system is to be used, and the organizational, operational, and legal constraints limiting its use) must be thoroughly understood. After the total system is planned, performance requirements are established. If equipment is an integral part of the total system engineering performance requirements, standards and specifications are established. In a parallel effort the human performance requirements are established. They include both the performance of the individuals who will operate and maintain the system and the managerial demands and constraints that must be satisfied. Once both the engineering performance and the human performance requirements have been determined, analytic techniques should be applied to determine whether the system as specified to date is operable. If the analysis findings indicate that it is not, the system concept should be revised or discarded.

The second phase—an analysis of the affordability of the system's manpower, personnel, and training—should be initiated if the first phase indicated that the system is potentially operable. The knowledge, skill, and other abilities required to operate and maintain the system must be determined, and the number of personnel needed to man the system at the level of operation contemplated in the doctrine must be determined and compared to the availability of those human resources. If those requirements cannot be met by existing manpower in the department it may be necessary to hire or contract for individuals who have those qualifications, or to train existing and future employees to operate and maintain the system. If training is contemplated, a training plan should specify training methods such as formal training, short courses, workshops, apprenticeship, or on-the-job training that will be needed. The number of people to be trained and a training schedule for initial and subsequent skill maintenance training should be specified; and the cost of the training, the availability of personnel, and the time requirements should be considered to determine Manpower, Personnel, and Training (MPT) affordability. If the affordability analysis indicates that resources to man the system are not available, the next step is to reconsider the doctrine, employment, design, manpower, personnel, training, or performance requirements for the system.

The third and final phase, system testing, follows a determination that the MPT are affordable. Two types of tests are called for: tests to determine that engineering performance specifications have been met, and ergonomic (i.e., human engineering) tests to establish that people and equipment interact to induce optimal human–machine performance as needed. A third test in which the system is exercised in a real or simulated operational environment is recommended. The performance of the system should then be compared with the system performance, engineering performance, and human performance requirements established during the first phase. If there is an insufficient match between obtained test performance and the requirements it may be necessary to return to an earlier phase of the cycle. If, on the other hand, the match is sufficient, the system may be procured and deployed.

Application of the MANPRINT Approach to Law Enforcement

As part of a pilot study of the feasibility of adapting the MANPRINT approach to law enforcement systems, the Drug Enforcement Administration (DEA) with the assistance of the Army Research Institute, developed and answered a set of questions for a system that integrated two commercially available instruments and a newly developed software package into a system designed to facilitate a particular class of narcotics investigations and operations. The questions listed cover all MANPRINT domains and provided guidelines for developing standards for a novel law enforcement system. These questions may be used as template for the development or the acquisition of law enforcement technology. Appropriately modified, they also may be used for the development or evaluation of proposed law enforcement management systems and operational procedures that are not dependent on a technology base.

Manpower Issues

1. Will the equipment or system (E/S) reduce or increase actual manpower requirements, or will it just convert an existing operator space to an operator space with an increased or changed operational or maintenance burden?
2. To what extent will the E/S increase the workload of organizational maintainers or operators? Can they meet the performance requirements of E/S?
3. Can the remaining agents and others assigned to a case or operation continue if the E/S fails? What will be the impact on the operation if E/S fails?
4. Will the new E/S drive up support manpower requirements?
5. What are the reliability, availability, and maintainability requirements for the new E/S, and will it create a need for additional maintenance manpower or contractual support?
6. What is the manpower requirement to assemble and disassemble the new E/S?
7. How should tasks be distributed among the mission or operation personnel if the new E/S requires tasks they have not performed before the availability of the E/S?

Personnel Issues

1. Will the new E/S be compatible with the quality mix of the current staff? What is the projected quality mix of future users?
2. Will the new E/S require personnel with special skills (operators and maintainers)? Any change in aptitude area requirements?
3. Does the new E/S require special tools and test equipment, and if so can the current and projected personnel use these items?
4. Is a new occupational specialty or additional skill identifiers required?
5. Can the user in the heat of a mission or operation repair the new E/S if necessary?

6. What level of human performance is necessary if the new E/S is to be a success?
7. Are the current aptitude area selection criteria suitable for the projected personnel who will operate the E/S?

Training Issues

1. Will additional training be required to qualify personnel to perform operational and maintenance tasks?
2. What are the training costs and how do they affect the life cycle cost of the E/S?
3. Does the design of the E/S facilitate learning transfer?
4. What are the critical tasks associated with operational and malfunction procedures? Can the software (if any) associated with the new E/S provide a user understandable directions for performance of both normal and malfunction procedures while under operational stress?
5. How many hours of training are required per quarter to keep the operators or the maintenance personnel proficient?
6. What mix of passive training (classroom, demonstrations, etc.), active training (mockups, simulators), and actual experience (induced malfunctions, on-the-job experience) is planned?
7. Will additional cross-training be required?

Human Factors Issues

1. Does the new E/S decrease the interior workspace available to the remaining mission personnel?
2. Where are humans most likely to fail or to commit critical errors in the task sequence?
3. Are critical monitors and switches or other controls readily visible and accessible to operators and to maintainers?
4. What is the measured impact of the new E/S on human performance and reliability?
5. Does the design of the new E/S have user acceptance? Does the new E/S inspire confidence in its workings?
6. Are the technical manuals written in such a fashion that users, during periods of stress, can comprehend the necessary procedures?
7. What, if any, aspects of design induce human error?
8. Where in the task sequence are users likely to be overloaded cognitively or physically?

9. If the new E/S is operated from multiple positions, are identical functional controls and labels available from each position?

System Safety

1. What safety hazards exist in the design or operation of the new E/S?
2. Will operating personnel be protected from hostile activities? What E/S or personnel protection clothing or equipment will be made available in a hostile environment?
3. Will personnel be protected from moving parts? Will they be protected from burns if the equipment contains very hot components? Will they be protected from hazardous substance contact or emissions?
4. What are the safety procedures to be followed?
5. What tasks are required to accomplish emergency procedures?
6. What safety devices are in the design of E/S to prevent personal injury?
7. What information transfer devices (warnings, labels, safety instructions, communication devices, or procedures) are included in the design of the E/S? Do they provide effective prevention?

Health Hazard Issues

1. Will the new E/S design increase the level of combustion products to which the user or maintainer is exposed?
2. Does the new E/S design use any hazardous materials?
3. Will the new E/S expose the user to increased noise levels? Does the changed ambient environment affect the user's physiological or psychological functioning?
4. What are the health hazard probabilities associated with use of the E/S? What are the expected costs associated with long-term health risks?
5. Will the health hazard potential affect the personnel selection policies or the training requirements?

MANPRINT Guidelines Can Be Easily Adapted by Local Organizations

The issues outlined in this section are not meant to be exhaustive, but to make the administrator aware of the manpower, personnel, training, human factors, system safety, and health hazard issues that relate to the acquisition of new equipment or systems in a law enforcement setting. The questions "Does the agency need a gun that shoots more bullets?" "Will we increase our efficiency by buying a faster car?" "Does our agency need a new computer system?" can be answered by gathering data in the six areas identified in the MANPRINT plan, and making a decision based on time, cost, people, and mission considerations.

HUMAN FACTORS AND OPERATIONAL EVALUATION OF LAW ENFORCEMENT EQUIPMENT AND SYSTEMS

The deployment of new police equipment historically has been costly to both the user and the developer. Consequently, there is a need to reduce deployment costs and speed up the deployment of new public safety and law enforcement devices, by ensuring that the tested material is fully compatible with the intended user in the user's own operational environment. The need is being met by the Office of National Drug Control Policy's Counterdrug Technology Assessment Center (CTAC), which established a Technology Testbed program. The program provides an environment to evaluate prototype equipment to improve design specifications before fielding. They allow insertion of new technologies into operational scenarios to assess how those technologies will improve overall operations and performance. All federal law enforcement agencies with a counternarcotics mission were invited to nominate equipment and systems for assessment and to participate in the assessment process. The initial testbed, located at the DEA Miami field office, serves as a model for other testbeds at selected domestic locations (CTAC, 1993). All agencies anticipating use of the equipment are requested to provide operational scenarios in which the testing will be embedded. The test plan is designed to identify limitations of the equipment from an operational use point of view. Both engineering limitations and human factors deficiencies within the simulated operational environment are identified.

A complete testbed procedure should begin with the reidentification of the basic requirements of the agencies that are considering development or procurement of the device or equipment. These requirements should be determined through reviews with the public safety and police communities. Analyses of focus group information, mission statements, and other needs assessment techniques will provide the basis for operational and engineering requirement statements. After the requirements documentation is completed, the performance specifications and the human factors concerns are used to develop an operational evaluation test plan. The plan should include the establishment of a test facility that will permit the equipment to be used in simulated and real-life situations by police and public safety personnel. The evaluations will provide insights into procedural changes and training needed to convert a technologically feasible device into a community inventory item. At the same time they will provide feedback to the developers or procuring officials on enhancements that may be needed to overcome operational limitations and "user unfriendliness" that is likely to inhibit effective use of the equipment.

Extending the Testbed Concept to State and Local Agencies

The CTAC testbed program currently is concerned with assessing sophisticated investigative and communications equipment, but there remains a need for a similar activity that will extend beyond the counterdrug mission of state and local police agencies, and will examine low-tech and high-tech equipment. A movement by former federal law enforcement engineers and human factors psychologists is planned to fill this void. The objective of their activity is to enable all law enforcement and public safety agencies to better consider user needs and capabilities when considering procurement of nondevelopmental (i.e., off-the-shelf) equipment for police and public safety use. A major purpose will be to assess the equipment's engineering design in terms of how it affects the human (user) reliability, ensuring optimization of operational effectiveness of the device or system, maximizing operational safety, and minimizing health hazards associated with its use. The intent is to apply MANPRINT constructs to integrate nondevelopmental items (NDI) into law enforcement systems. This can be accomplished by reviewing and assessing engineering design of NDI devices or systems with reference to human factors (ergonomics), personnel selection, and training trade-offs within the context of operational reality and cost control. The adaption of the CTAC testbed concept to the full spectrum of law enforcement and public safety equipment will offer all police agencies opportunities to:

- Evaluate vendor NDI in terms of its utility within the agency's own operational environment.
- Influence design specification prior to procurement based on testbed experience.
- Determine the need and direction of postprocurement redesign requirements for improvement of operational utility or safety.
- Better assess the reasonableness of reasonable accommodation demands in compliance with Americans with Disabilities Act regulations.

HUMAN FACTORS AND THE AMERICANS WITH DISABILITIES ACT

Earlier in the chapter, there was a discussion of the ways the MANPRINT approach can be used to identify the KSAs and the performance requirements for the human part of any human–machine system. Two pieces of legislation, the Civil Rights Act of 1991 and the Americans with Disabilities Act (ADA), have had a profound effect on the way law enforcement agencies can and should hire, maintain, and retain employees.

Much attention has been paid to changes in testing and other procedures relating to selection of police officers imposed by the ADA, which prohibits an employer or potential employer from discriminating

> against a qualified individual with a disability because of the disability of such individual in regard to job application procedures, the hiring advancement, or discharge of employees, employee compensation, job training, and other terms, conditions, and privileges of employment. (ADA Sec. §12112, 102(a): 42 U.S.C.)

Less attention has been paid by police psychologists to the definition of *discriminate*, which includes inter alia,

> (5)(A) not making reasonable accommodations to the known physical or mental limitations of an otherwise qualified individual with a disability who is an applicant or employee unless [the employer] can demonstrate that the accommodation would impose an undue hardship on [the employer], or

> (B) denying employment opportunities to [a qualified disabled individual] if such denials based on the needs of [the employer] to make reasonable accommodation to the . . . impairments of the employee or applicant. (Sec. 102(b))

Classification of Impaired Individuals

It is clear that police agencies and other employers may not discriminate against disabled but otherwise qualified persons who apply for positions, if the impaired persons request that a reasonable accommodation be made to the disability. The need for police management to be concerned with reasonable accommodations is demonstrated by the fact that within a few months of the implementation of ADA, many employees who had successfully hidden their disabilities from their employers to protect their jobs stopped hiding their disabilities and demanded that their employers comply with the act and make reasonable accommodations to their disabilities (Mathews, 1992). For law enforcement agencies this provision could apply to two sets of disabled or otherwise impaired individuals. The first example might be an applicant for a position who has received an offer of employment subject to a medical examination, and was found to have a disqualifying disability. The second example might involve an already employed officer whose mental or physical condition was questioned, and who was discovered to have a disqualifying disability during a fitness for duty examination. Neither of these two classes of disqualified persons can be denied employment if it can be determined that a reasonable accommodation can be made to their impairments.

Reasonable Accommodations and the ADA

A *reasonable accommodation* is an accommodation that will enable employees to perform the essential elements of a job, or that will enable disabled employees to enjoy the same benefits and privileges that are enjoyed by employees without disabilities (Perritt, 1991). Because there is a wide range in the nature and extent of a disabling condition, and there are also many varieties of job requirements, such accommodations must be made on a case-by-case basis. Accommodations may include inter alia making facilities and workspaces accessible, job restructuring, part-time or modified work schedules, reassignment to a vacant position where the disability is irrelevant, acquisition or modification of equipment or devices, adjustment or modification of examinations, training materials or policies, and provision of auxiliary aids or services.

Reasonable accommodations to all impaired persons whether or not they are employees are also required in public service facilities and public accommodations (see Perritt, 1991, 1992). Title II of ADA calls for equal access to public services and transportation. It also covers requirements for access to public accommodations and commercial facilities and Title IV addresses changes to be made in telecommunications. All three titles impact police operations, facilities, and equipment. Any public place such as a police station (and arguably, even lockups) may have to be redesigned or reconfigured to accommodate both impaired employees and impaired "police clients" who may or may not be in custody. Each police department will need to evaluate its facilities for accessibility by officers, civilian employees, and clients in entry ways, offices, restrooms, locker rooms, signage, and equipment. Such accommodations may be as simple as rearranging furniture, or may call for major redesign of facilities and acquisition of new equipment to accommodate employees. The Building Owners and Managers Association International (BOMA; 1993) identified examples of some of the more readily achievable changes, which are included in the following list:

- Installing ramps.
- Making curb cuts in sidewalks and entrances.
- Repositioning shelves.
- Rearranging chairs, tables, vending machines, and other furniture.
- Repositioning telephones.
- Installing grab bars in toilet stalls.
- Removal of free-standing rugs and high-pile low-density carpeting.
- Creating designated accessible parking.
- Vehicles designed to accommodate impairments, for example, more accommodating access and egress.

- Widening doors and installing accessible door hardware.

The need for such accommodations is not universal, but must be determined on a case-by-case basis (BOMA, 1993). Another example of such an accommodation is a contract procurement by the Treasury Department to provide specialized computer equipment for approximately 5,000 Treasury employees with physical and sensory impairments. The components to be supplied under the contract include software, specially adapted input and output peripherals such as Braille readers and voice synthesis devices (Cox, 1992).

Roles for Psychologists

Occupational psychologists, physicians, and physical therapists may be instrumental in determining the impact of an impairment on job performance. The skills of properly qualified industrial/organizational or human factors psychologists may be applied to a determination of whether a job requirement is an essential requirement by means of job analysis techniques. They also can determine whether or not tasks can be restructured to accommodate the impairment, and assist the agency in establishing or revising training requirements to accommodate impairment.

The model for establishing reasonable accommodations, illustrated in Fig. 22.2, shows the essential role of job analyses in determining what, if any, reasonable accommodations can be made so that ADA requirements can be met. An assertion by an employer that a particular job requirement is essential is not sufficient unless the job or position description has been validated. Validating a job requirement on the basis of content validity requires the completion of a job analysis (Equal Employment Opportunity Commission et al., 1979). Job and task analysis-based performance standards and identification of essential job functions are needed to arrive at a determination that the disability may seriously impact job performance.

There are a wide variety of job analysis techniques that serve a variety of purposes (Harvey, 1991). Not all of them are equally useful for the purpose of establishing a basis for reasonable accommodations. Most job analysis begin with human-factors-based task analyses. Two separate type of analysis are usually recommended, functional job analysis, and ergonomic task analysis.

Functional Job Analysis

Functional job analyses identify and examine each significant task embedded within a specific job; the reasons for conducting the task; and the knowledge, skills, abilities, effort requirements, and working conditions required to per-

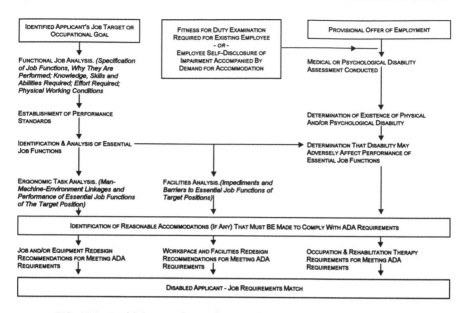

FIG. 22.2. Establishing and complying with ADA "reasonable accommodation" requirements.

form. These are then compared against established performance criteria.
This type of analysis requires intensive data collection from job incumbents
and supervisors (Fine, 1989). A less labor-intensive form of functional job
analysis is Fleishman's Job Analysis System (Fleishman, 1992). This type of
job analysis analyzes a position using a series of 7-point scales that assess
the relevance of 52 cognitive, psychomotor, physical, and sensory and perceptual abilities; 9 interactive and social abilities scales, and 11 knowledges
and skills. A companion book (Fleishman & Reilly, 1992) defines the same
set of abilities, gives examples of tasks and jobs for which the ability may
be a qualifying one, and describes personnel tests that measure the degree
to which a job applicant or employee has that ability.

Both the Fine and the Fleishman job analysis techniques are acceptable
means of establishing and validating bona fide occupational requirements
that may be used to justify or reject prima facie discriminatory personnel
selection decision making. This process may be used to establish legally
viable performance standards for a job, and can provide important inputs
as to which job functions are and are not essential for every job incumbent;
that is, whether the job element should be waived or adapted as a reasonable
accommodation to a disability in compliance with the ADA.

Once a job function is established as essential, and it has also been
established that an applicant's or an existing employee's impairment may
adversely affect his or her performance of those functions, two additional

analyses may have to be performed before identifying what, if any, reasonable accommodations can be made. Additional analyses may need be done to examine in depth how people perform the operations and how they cope with impairments in performing their job.

Ergonomic Task Analysis

Ergonomic task analysis (ETA), performed in coordination with an analysis of the work facility's impediments and barriers, is used to assess the way the environment, equipment, and tool design affect the ability of a disabled individual to provide services safely and effectively within the working environment. A variety of analytic techniques are available to explore the way people interact with the equipment and the work environment (Laughery & Laughery, 1987) and to analyze ways in which human error is caused and dealt with in human–machine systems (Miller & Swain, 1987). An ETA may result in recommended modifications of workspace, facilities, work procedures, tools, and equipment as reasonable accommodations in compliance with the ADA. The human factors literature contains many recommendations and standards for the design of equipment and workspace that optimize the human–machine–workspace links (see, e.g., Department of Defense, 1974; Woodson, 1981). In addition, regulations implementing the ADA provide standards and design guidelines for accommodations related to removal of architectural and transportation barriers and accommodation design regulations imposed by several federal agencies (Perritt, 1991, 1992).

Components of an Ergonomic Task Analysis. An ETA is a multistage process that requires the analyst to:

1. Construct profiles of all significant job functions. This includes consideration of the objective of each activity performed, the equipment used to perform the function, the frequency of performance and performance time, and anything else that may contribute to job-related stress.
2. Conduct task analyses for each job function. This includes identification of the activities performed by personnel, identification of human–machine interactions (i.e., transfer of information and commands between the person and the equipment), and identification of human decision-making requirements. Other activities include identification of critical tasks or concurrent tasks that expose individuals (both impaired and nonimpaired) to impediments to performance, and studying situations that result in accidents, degraded human performance or human–machine system error. It may be important to establish the criticality of the task (i.e., consequences of task error or failures), and a structured interview procedure may be added to assess task criticality.

3. Assess the workload for critical tasks or task complexes. Using established subjective workload assessment techniques (such as time + mental effort + psychological stress loads), study equipment handling characteristics and task-imposed burdens.

4. Assess sources of stress and need for job or task, workspace, facilities, and organizational environment restructuring including:

   a. Workers' knowledge of how to cope adequately or to avoid risk and ineffectual or impaired behaviors. This involves the evaluation of crew education needs, as well as training curriculum design and implementation.

   b. Risk avoidance and reduction skills, including provisions for workers to maintain their skills, and enhance their skills to operate existing equipment.

   c. System operability in light of the workload and risk. This includes an analysis of the design of equipment and operational procedures so that they will be more compatible with human performance capabilities, recommendations of ways to reduce or eliminate error proneness inherent in the design of some equipment, identification of poor human–machine functional allocations, and assessment of the adequacy of feedback and the adequacy of input initiatives.

   d. Identification of personal characteristics that predict risk enhancement or diminishment. These factors might include employee's health deficits, fatigue, schedule pressures, interpersonal conflicts, personal stresses, and workspace and ambient working environments. Recommendations for improvements might include such factors as operator selection, workload redesign, and training options.

   e. Studying the organizational climate as a performance effectiveness enhancement or diminishment factor. Factors of interest might include organizational rewards and punishments for good and poor performance, functional and dysfunctional leadership, and organizational and personal goal conflicts and consistencies.

An ergonomic task analysis and facilities analysis can be useful in identifying both equipment- and facilities-related accommodations and procedural changes that can lead to improvements in the quality of employee performance. It can generate practices and policies that can reduce job-induced stress for both impaired and nonimpaired persons. As a result of this type of study, the employer can be provided with recommendations for modifying equipment design. The "people" part of the organization can generally be improved by following the recommendations for changes in operational procedures, the development of employer performance improvement programs, and implementation of organizational development programs. The job design, workplace, and equipment modifications of targeted positions can then impact the design of individual work hardening programs (occupational training, rehabilitation therapy) to arrive at revised job and performance requirements to accommodate the disabled individual.

An Alternate Task and Facilities Analysis for Situations Involving Accident, Death, Injury, or Property Damage: The Forensic Task Analysis

If the equipment or the procedures that impair performance of disabled persons previously have been involved in an accident resulting in death, injury, or property damage, the analysis of choice might be the forensic task analysis (Kurke, 1991). This process is derived from Bliss' (1979) recommendations for preparation of expert testimony offered in litigations that involve allegations of defective products, defective service delivery, defective human performance, and malpractice. The procedure recommends a system for gathering sufficient information to form an expert opinion as to whether the accident environment or the design of the product or procedures was a proximate cause of the accident. The expert opinion is often derived from a forensic task analysis that reconstructs the series of events leading up to the accident. The forensic task analysis and follow-up activities and analyses seek answers to the following questions:

1. What did the system, consisting of involved parties (victim, operator, service provider), product and equipment and accident environment, and the procedures to be followed intend to do prior to and during the accident?

2. What did each element of the system actually do that led to the accident and its consequences?

3. Did the design of the equipment, working environment, procedures, training, or other safety information transfer procedures facilitate or inhibit the likelihood of the accident or the severity of its consequences? (Did the product, procedures, environment, etc. cooperate with the user or the user's personal characteristics to arrive at the accident? Was the accident an expectable consequence of the design?)

4. What information (training, manuals, labels, warnings, etc.) was or was not available to the victim, operator, or service provider that could have averted the accident or mitigated its consequences? Was there compliance with the training, manuals, labels, or warnings? If not, why?

5. What did the designer of the product or equipment, accident environment, or procedures do to increase or reduce the likelihood of the accident or the severity of its consequences?

6. Did the victim, operator, or service provider have (or lack) any personal characteristics that materially increased or reduced the likelihood of the accident or its expected consequences? Should the designer have taken the likelihood of occurrence of such personal characteristics into account when designing the system?

Answers to Questions 1 and 2 are useful in establishing the facts leading up to the accident and the actual events that occurred. From a human factors point of view, however, the answers to the rest of the questions are more interesting. Questions 3 through 6 relate back to the MANPRINT model. Question 3 refers to the analyses of equipment design and the need to determine that performance was not degraded because the equipment was faulty. Question 4 relates to the requirement that training procedures be reviewed to make sure that information that might have averted the accident was available to the human operator. Question 5 stresses the importance of requiring that the provider of the equipment be held accountable for the product design. Question 6 has two components. On one hand, it emphasizes the importance of developing selection criteria for potential employees and identifying personal characteristics that could influence the likelihood of an accident. On the other hand, it emphasizes the importance of the identification of design flaws, problems, and information transfer and the importance of accommodation in the form of occupational training or rehabilitation therapy for impaired applicants and employees.

SUMMARY

In this chapter we have pointed out several ways in which human factors psychology impacts the day-to-day operation of law enforcement agencies. An old adage says that a chain is only as strong as its weakest link, and in law enforcement, the chain can break if there are significant weaknesses in the human element (the officer), the equipment provided to do the job, or the organization in which the officer functions. The problem of human error was discussed in the context of the interaction of organizational demands and operational requirements, the capabilities of the human operator, and sources of human error or systems error, and several practical examples of situations that might arise were cited. The MANPRINT system was offered as a framework for assessing the need for and the impact of new systems and equipment by analyzing six human resource concerns: manpower, personnel, training, human factors, system safety, and health hazards. Recommendations in the form of specific questions and issues were made for application of the MANPRINT model to law enforcement agencies. The chapter closed with recommendations for using job analysis techniques to identify essential job requirements, and for using this job and task information in compliance with the Americans with Disabilities Act.

REFERENCES

Alluisi, E. A., & Chiles, W. D. (1967). Sustained performance, work-rest scheduling, diurnal rhythms in man. *Acta Psychologia, 27*, 436–442.

Alluisi, E. A., & Fleishman, E. A. (1982). *Human performance and productivity* (Vol. 3). Hillsdale, NJ: Lawrence Erlbaum Associates.

Aschoff, J. (1965). Circadian rhythms in man. *Science, 148*, 1427–1432.

Aschoff, J. (1969). Desynchronisation and resynchronisation of human circadian rhythms. *Aerospace Medicine, 40*, 844–849.

Barber, J. L., Ching, H. L. F., Jones, R. E., & Miles, J. L. (1990). *MANPRINT handbook for RFP development.* Washington, DC: U.S. Army Research Institute.

Besco, R. O. (1990). *The professional performance analysis checklist.* Lakewood, CA: Professional Performance Improvement.

Bliss, W. D. (1979). Defective product design—Role of human factors. In *American jurisprudence: Proof of facts* (2nd Series, pp. 117–147). Rochester, NY: Lawyers Publishing.

Bloom, W. (1961). Shift work and the sleep-wakefulness cycle. *Personnel, 38*, 24–31.

Booher, H. R. (1990). *MANPRINT: An approach to systems integration.* New York: Van Nostrand Reinhold.

Building Owners and Managers Association International. (1993). Americans with Disabilities Act (ADA) compliance. *American Society of Testing Materials Standardization News, 21*(2), 42–45.

Colquhoun, W. P. (Ed.). (1972). *Aspects of human efficiency.* London: English Universities Press.

Counterdrug Technology Assessment Center. (1993, October). *A counterdrug research and development blueprint update.* Washington, DC: Executive Office of the President, Office of National Drug Control Policy.

Cox, C. (1992, December). Coming events in government computer procurement. *Washington Post Computer Showcase.*

Cunningham, J. B. (1990). Twelve hour shift schedules in policing: A review of the evidence. *Canadian Police College Journal, 14*(3), 184–201.

Department of Defense. (1974). *Human engineering design criteria for military systems, equipment and facilities* (Military Standard MIL-STD-1472C). Washington, DC: Author.

Equal Employment Opportunity Commission, Office of Personnel Management, Department of Justice, Department of Labor, and Department of The Treasury. (1979, March 2). Adoption of questions and answers to clarify and provide a common interpretation of the uniform guidelines on employment selection procedures. *Federal Register,* 11996–12009.

Ferguson, E. S. (1992). How engineers lose touch. *Invention and Technology, 8*(3), 16–24.

Fine, S. A. (1989). *Functional job analysis scales.* Milwaukee, WI: Sidney A. Fine Associates.

Fleishman, E. A. (1992). *Fleishman job analysis system.* Palo Alto, CA: Consulting Psychologists Press.

Fleishman, E. A., & Reilly, M. E. (1992). *A handbook of human abilities: Definitions, measurements and job task requirements.* Palo Alto, CA: Consulting Psychologists Press.

Gettys, V., Elam, J. D., & Davis, R. (1983). *Emergency vehicle operations training manual.* Oklahoma Department of Public Safety, Oklahoma City.

Harvey, R. J. (1991). Job analysis. In M. D. Dunnette & L. M. Hough (Eds.), *Handbook of industrial and organizational psychology* (Vol. 2, pp. 71–163). Palo Alto, CA: Consulting Psychologists Press.

Holmes, T. H., & Rahe, R. H. (1967). The social adjustment rating scale. *Journal of Psychosomatic Research, 11,* 213–218.

Huchingson, R. D. (1981). *New horizons for human factors in design.* New York: McGraw-Hill.

Johnson, K. M., Rossmeissl, P., Kracov, W., & Shields, J. L. (1989). *MANPRINT handbook for nondevelopmental item (NDI) acquisition.* Alexandria, VA: U.S. Army Materiel Command.

Johnson, L. C., Naitoh, P., Lubin, A., & Moses, J. (1972). Sleep stages and performance. In W. P. Colquhoun (Ed.), *Aspects of human efficiency.* London: English Universities Press.

Kleitman, N. (1933). Studies on the physiology of sleep, VII: Diurnal variation in performance. *American Journal of Physiology, 104,* 449–456.

Kleitman, N. (1939). *Sleep and wakefulness.* Chicago: University of Chicago Press.

Kleitman, N. (1963). *Sleep and wakefulness* (2nd ed.). Chicago: University of Chicago Press.

Kurke, M. I. (1986). Anatomy of product liability/personal injury litigation. In M. I. Kurke & R. G. Meyer (Eds.), *Psychology in product liability and personal injury litigation* (pp. 3–16). Washington, DC: Hemisphere.

Kurke, M. I. (1988). Aftermath of system safety failure: Lessons to be learned from an expert witness. *Hazard Prevention, 24*(4), 26–29.

Kurke, M. I. (1991). Forensic task analysis. *Statement of litigation support activities* [Brochure Insert]. Alexandria, VA: The Kurke Group.

Laughery, K. R., Sr., & Laughery, K. R., Jr. (1987). Analytic techniques for function analysis. In G. Salvendy (Ed.), *Handbook of human factors* (pp. 329–354). New York: Wiley.

Mathews, J. (1992, November 22). Uncovering a huge, hidden community: Disabilities act reveals more impaired workers—And worry among employers. *Washington Post,* pp. H1, H5.

Miller, D. P., & Swain, A. D. (1987). Human error and human reliability. In G. Salvendy (Ed.), *Handbook of human factors* (pp. 219–250). New York: Wiley.

Mott, P. E. (1976). Social and psychological adjustment to shift work. In P. G. Rentos & R. D. Shepard (Eds.), *Shift work and health* (U.S. Department of Health, Education and Welfare Publication No. (NIOSH) 76-203). Washington, DC: U.S. Government Printing Office.

Mott, P. E., Mann, F. C., McLaughlin, Q., & Warwick, D. P. (1965). *Shift work.* Ann Arbor: University of Michigan Press.

Office of Emergency Operations. (1992, May). *Toward advanced human reliability programs: Structural development considerations for extreme risk environments.* Washington, DC: White House Military Office.

Perritt, H. H. (1991). *Americans With Disabilities Act Handbook* (2nd ed.). New York: Wiley.

Perritt, H. H. (1992). *Cumulative supplement No. 2 to Americans With Disability Act handbook* (2nd ed.). New York: Wiley.

Ray, J. T., Martin, O. E., Jr., & Alluisi, E. A. (1961). *Human performance as a function of the work-rest cycle: A review of selected studies.* Washington, DC: National Academy of Science, National Research Council.

Rentos, P. G., & Shepard, R. D. (Eds.). (1976). *Shift work and health* (U.S. Department of Health, Education and Welfare Publication No. (NIOSH) 76-203). Washington, DC: U.S. Government Printing Office.

Riddell, J. A. (1991). Handgun selection: Rethinking the issue—And the options. *The Police Chief, 58*(7), 30.

Selye, H. (1956). *The stress of life.* New York: McGraw-Hill.

Swain, A. D., & Guttmann, H. E. (1983). *Handbook of human reliability analysis with emphasis on nuclear power plant applications.* (NUREG/CR-1278). Albuquerque, NM: Sandia National.

Woodson, W. (1981). *Human factors design handbook.* New York: McGraw-Hill.

CHAPTER TWENTY-THREE

Strategic Planning

Eugene Schmuckler
Georgia Public Safety Training Center, Forsyth, GA

THE NOTION OF STRATEGY

On a hot, lazy afternoon, a small boy sits barefoot under a shade tree, idly watching a small stream of water from a sprinkler trickle down the street toward him. As tiny rivulets inch their way along the asphalt gutter, they seem to pause at each pebble to build momentum and then push forward again.

Eagerly, the boy grabs handfuls of dirt and builds a small dike that momentarily halts the flow. However, the water slowly wells up in a puddle and edges its way around the barrier. The boy adds more dirt, vainly attempting to outflank and contain the water. As the battle progresses, it becomes apparent that despite the boy's best efforts, he will never prevail. There are larger forces of nature at work.

—Garner (1993)

Larger forces are also being felt within the law enforcement field. Police agencies will find it impossible to remain stagnant and survive. Yet, uncontrolled or unplanned movement can be as counterproductive as stagnation. The police organization needs help in directing that movement (Garner, 1993).

This is an area that can well be served by those engaged in the field of police psychology. As a result, traditional police psychology—which has in the main focused on clinical areas such as pre-employment and fitness for duty evaluations, counseling, and hostage negotiations—will need to redirect its efforts into areas such as organizational diagnosis and development issues (Cummings, 1980; Levinson, 1972) and strategic planning. Recognition that organizational success is not determined by the skills of top management alone, nor by the visible features—the strategy, the structure, and the reward system—of the organization will lead police psychology to examine the work efforts of industrial/organizational psychologists and other management and organizational behavior theorists and practitioners.

Tafoya (1986) presented a chronology of future events expected to impact law enforcement assuming "little if any shift in the present social, economic, educational, political, environmental, and technological trends" (p. 2). According to Tafoya, by 1995 community involvement and self-help (e.g., community policing) in local policing will become common practice in more than 70% of the nation and university and professionally conducted research will have a direct and positive influence on the development of crime reduction strategies. By 1997, state-of-the-art high technology will become the standard for training in more than 70% of all police agencies. More than 70% of all police executives will adopt a nontraditional (proactive or goal-oriented) leadership style. By 2035 private security agencies will assume more than 50% of all law enforcement responsibilities and by 2050 more than 50% of all police agencies will have personnel competent to conduct rigorous empirical research.

THE CHANGING FACE OF POLICE

As we progress to the 21st century we are faced with new realities. We are living in an information-rich society, one that has multiple norms, themes, and styles. There has been a gender redefinition bringing with it a blurring of traditional gender roles. The middle class has been redistributed.

We are seeing changes in demographics within our country. What implications do the changing demographics have on law enforcement selection, training, and day-to-day operations? A number of new issues need to be considered from the sociological, technological, economic, environmental, and political perspective.

Sociologically there is now a demand on the part of the populace that police officers be more responsive. Maddox (1993) suggested that as police administrators in major cities face the reality of inner-city turmoil similar to that experienced by Los Angeles, those in small, rural jurisdictions must not conclude that this situation will escape them. The 1992 riots in Los Angeles sparked a significant increase in ethnic intimidation, ethnic-directed crime, selected hate crimes, and hate group activity. Use of force regulations are leading to searches for nonlethal alternatives. Officers are now found patrolling on bicycles and on foot in order to get closer to the community.

The effects of sociological changes within departments are evidenced by the number of minority group and dual career family members pursuing careers in law enforcement. Law enforcement officers who in the past would remain within the department until the time of retirement now may choose to have two or three occupations outside of law enforcement during the course of their productive work years. Male officers are leaving police work in order to follow their wife's career. No longer is the male viewed as the main breadwinner. The Family Leave Act allowing officers and family members of officers to take time off for medical reasons such as pregnancy now need to be taken into consideration. More women are entering the law enforcement profession. A major reason stems from changing demographics. It is estimated that women will make up 47% of the work force by the year 2000. Whereas the growth in the number of men and women entering the work force has leveled off, the number of men who have retired over the past 30 years has doubled. Agencies need to recognize that working women in their childbearing years need and want accommodations from their agencies when they start, or grow, their families (Kelly, 1993).

Another demographic factor that needs to be considered is that mandatory retirement policies are being challenged with a view to their elimination. Not only will this keep officers working for longer periods of time, but promotional opportunities will be reduced as the incumbents will be forced to stay on the job for a longer time period.

President Bill Clinton has advocated a Police Corps program that strives to enhance the professionalism of law enforcement work through higher education. This notion can only serve to exacerbate problems already existing within many agencies. Until recently, requirements for entering the law enforcement profession were few. However, many states already mandate minimum education and training requirements for police applicants. This, even before implementation of the Police Corps program, is leading to more highly educated officers. Will college-educated officers be more attractive to employers outside the field of law enforcement? At the same time, with a shrinking military, fewer veterans will be available for police work. These nonmilitary individuals will not bring with them the military discipline and unquestioning blind following of directives (Goetz, 1993).

Technologically, the advent of computers and the information highway will impact areas such as robotics and artificial intelligence. Improvements in health technology will bring about an increase in the number of elderly in our population. What demands will this have on law enforcement personnel?

Strategy and Training

The uncertainty of the job market has introduced new economic issues. Terms such as *downsizing* and *rightsizing* are no longer restricted to the private sector. Not only is this reducing the layers of management, it is also pushing authority and decision making as low as possible within the organization. Empowered employees are now making decisions previously relegated to those in supervisory or managerial positions. Successful businesses are concentrating on soliciting input from every corner of their organization concerning every facet of their operation. Many police departments are striving to accomplish this by means of problem-oriented policing. Horizontal management is by no means a panacea. It will force the agency to look at manpower allocation and procedures concerning investigative functions. Sources of funding for training and education will have to be identified (Goetz, 1993).

From the perspective of the environment it is now seen that a number of transnational values will enter into the law enforcement culture. There is an ever increasing number of Latino and Asian immigrants with a commensurate decrease in European immigrants. The dominance of English as a language will wane. The Internal Revenue Service is now printing its tax forms in Spanish and is reviewing the possibility of translating the forms into additional foreign languages. Many training academies now provide courses in "Survival Spanish." Police departments will be forced to recognize that they will encounter that group of individuals identified as "homeless" on a regular basis. This will in turn lead to the development of comprehensive strategies to deal with the social, economic, and constitutional issues surrounding treatment of the homeless (Carter & Sapp, 1993).

Politically there will be the friction between the public and the police. Funding will face stiff competition from other programs as governments face decreasing revenue sources. There is also a redefinition of law enforcement brought about by some law enforcement officers, elected and appointed leaders, and by scholarly studies in which quality of life is being emphasized. Empowerment is being seen within numerous communities. This can be a positive for the agency as empowered citizens take a personal interest and responsibility in their community because they know that they have a say in how their community is governed and policed. Civilian review panels will become more prevalent. For a law enforcement agency a major goal is to preserve and even enhance its ability to respond immediately to true emergencies and find more efficient and effective ways of responding to less urgent calls without disappointing the public in the process (Kennedy, 1993). At the same time the public comes to expect professional police behavior, respectful treatment, maintenance of human dignity, responsiveness, and value added to life. The political influences will carry over to the empowered officers, who, working with empowered community leaders, will demonstrate higher levels of morale because they will feel a sense of pride and ownership in their work.

PERSONNEL CONCERNS

Failure to make the political changes within the department can lead to numerous problems. Examples of these problems include the street officer versus the "brass" syndrome, poor upward communications among rank levels, and an emphasis on negative discipline (Reiser, 1979). Communication barriers in bureaucratic organizations are also perennial problems often linked to system-generated stresses (Reiser, 1974). Currently the selection process is geared toward screening out any disturbed applicants rather than the selection of those with a desirable profile. Little emphasis has been placed on the effects of the quasi-military structure on training, acculturation factors that shape the officer's attitudes and values over time, and the question of integrity. Reiser and Klyver (1987) discussed the need to change from a military model of training, with its emphasis on authoritarian behaviors, to a professional model that focuses on communication skills in problem solving. This of course is quite critical if the agency is to select that individual who can successfully function within a police environment with its shifting emphasis toward human values and resources (Furcon, 1979).

The standard personnel evaluations have looked at the individual with minimal consideration directed toward the organization culture. This culture represents that invisible quality, style, character, or modus operandi that is usually more powerful than the dictates of any one person or formal system. This organization culture "provides meaning, direction and mobilization, a social energy that moves the organization into either productive action or destruction" (Kilmann, 1985, p. 63). Kilmann suggested that in a number of organizations this social energy has been virtually ignored. As a result individuals within the agency seem apathetic or depressed about their jobs. When a new administration is brought in there is the attitude of "here we go again." New programs advocated by the new administration are thus doomed to failure. The culture is also in a state of flux. What has traditionally been a bastion of White males is now being "infiltrated" by females and other minority males. Nevertheless, these White male values still persist (Niederhoffer, 1969). Officers may be called on to handle cases involving sexual harassment and hate crimes similar in nature to those occurring within their own agency.

Looking at the Future

Unfortunately, many police administrators become so preoccupied with current problems that they fail to plan for the future. All too often programs are adopted by law enforcement agencies as a result of having read about them in a professional publication such as *Police Chief* or because a neighboring agency has chosen to adopt this new program. This "me too" approach generally results in a poorly conceived program thrown together in order to demonstrate innovative thinking on the part of the uppermost levels of administration: "The plans of the diligent make only for gain; all rash haste makes only for loss" (Proverbs 21:5). Others adopt programs they consider to be plans. Planning is an active attempt to control outcomes. "It's not a plan if it doesn't illuminate and choose strategic alternatives" (Levin, 1983, p. 30). As a result we see agencies backing away from community-oriented policing programs because they failed to anticipate what this proactive program would do in terms of manpower needs of reactive responses.

To be successful, law enforcement agencies need to engage in long-range planning. Every organization, whether it is in the private or public sector, needs a plan. This is the only way that the agency can answer questions as to its mission, what it will be, and what it should be. The future requires decisions today to make tomorrow happen. Not only must there be a plan but the plan needs to have total agency involvement and understanding (Raichle, 1980). This means that the key people within the agency (sometimes even individuals outside of the agency) see the planning process as important and are willing to invest the time and effort in the process in the way that is visible to the other members of the department.

Strategic Planning

"For want of strategy an army falls, but victory comes with much planning" (Proverbs 11:14). The term *strategy* comes from a Greek word meaning "army leader." According to Bracker (1980) the verb form meant "to plan the destruction of one's enemies through the effective use of one's resources" (p. 219). Strategy became the craft and domain of the warrior.

Miyamoto Musashi (1974) was a renowned Japanese warrior who wrote *A Book of Five Rings* as "a guide for men who want to learn strategy." Musashi compared the way of the carpenter to strategy. The carpenter, like the warrior, must become proficient in the use of his tools, "first to lay his plans with a true measure and then perform his work according to plan" (p. 48). A carpenter would not consider building without first having a master plan of the building. The foreman carpenter needs to be able to take "into account the abilities and limitations of the men, circulating among them and asking nothing unreasonable. He should know their morale and spirit and encourage them when necessary. This is the same as the principle of strategy" (pp. 48–49).

This is the Way for men who want to learn my strategy:
1. Do not think dishonestly.
2. The Way is in training.
3. Become acquainted with every art.
4. Know the Ways of all professions.
5. Distinguish between gain and loss in worldly matters.
6. Develop intuitive judgment and understanding for everything.
7. Perceive those things which cannot be seen.
8. Pay attention even to trifles.
9. Do nothing which is of no use.

According to Levin (1983):

> The *raison d'être* of long-range planning is to create a condition in which top management of the organization takes an active role rather than a passive one; that is the top executives retain the strategic development prerogative within the organization rather than let it get away to the outside, where it can serve only the best interests of others. Another way of saying it: the purpose of long-range planning is to keep management the master of the organization's fate. (p. 15)

This process of determining a uniquely appropriate strategy for an organization is strategic planning.

What then is needed for effective change to take place is for this change to be planned. To quote from the Book of Proverbs, "Schemes lightly made come to nothing, but with long planning they succeed" (15–22). According to Goodstein, Pfeiffer, and Nolan (1986), "Strategic planning is the process by which an organization envisions its future and develops the necessary procedures and operations to achieve that future" (p. 2).

Levin (1983) suggested that the process of determining a uniquely appropriate strategy for an organization is referred to as strategic long-range planning. Strategic planning creates strategy that serves the agency's objectives. Strategic planning is relatively new within the private sector. The reason for its increasing acceptance is that the relative increase in the size of many agencies has led to a need for a greater coordination among organizational activities. A strategic plan allows managers understand how various departments are linked together. A second major reason for the interest in strategic planning is an increase in environmental uncertainty. Events within an organization's context are no longer as predictable as they once were.

Strategic planning is important to managers because it links the goals of the organization within the organization's environment. If the environment of the organization remained constant, strategic planning would be less important to the organization. However, few if any organizations operate in a certain environment. A strategic plan is one that is comprehensive in scope and reflects the overall direction of the total organization or one of its subunits. Steiner (1979) defined strategic planning as the process of determining the major objectives of an organization and defining the strategies that will govern the acquisition and utilization of resources to achieve those objectives.

Strategy is an organization's way of maintaining a positive relationship with its external environment. Strategic planning help makes this happen. It clarifies for the members of the organization and relevant outsiders the goods or services the organization intends to provide, the methods it will use to produce them, and the performance targets underlying these efforts as a whole.

Drucker (1954) wrote: "The future will not happen if one wishes hard enough. It requires decision-now. It imposes risk-now. It requires action-now. It demands allocation of resources, and above all, of human resources-now. It requires work-now" (p. 122).

To be successful, a strategic planning process should provide the criteria for making organizational decisions at all levels and should provide a reference point against which all such decisions should be evaluated (Goodstein et al., 1986).

ENVIRONMENTAL ANALYSIS

The basic process of strategic planning is for management to assess seriously current strategy vis-à-vis organizational objectives, select a strategy, and then implement it through medium-term and short-term action plans. The objective in strategy formulation is to determine for the organization (or individual) a specific course of action uniquely appropriate to:

1. The opportunities available in the environment.
2. The risks associated with those opportunities.
3. The resources available to the organization.
4. The personal values of the organization's leadership and constituency, in particular their preference for risk taking.

The strategic planning process does more than plan for the future; it helps the organization create its future.

Planning to plan is an essential ingredient in the development of a strategic plan. Questions that need to be addressed include: How much commitment is there to the planning process? Who should be involved? How long will it take? What do we need to know in order to plan successfully? Who should develop the data? (Goodstein et al., 1986).

There are four major steps or phases in developing the plan.

1. Process of appraisal. Both the environment and organization are carefully assessed for their future implications.
2. A strategic choice is made.
3. The choice is implemented.
4. The choice is evaluated.

Although strategic planning in the sense of actually implementing this process for the organization as a whole is largely a top management responsibility, managers at all levels must be prepared to participate in various phases of the strategic planning process. The process of developing a strategic plan entails answering a series of questions about an organization and its environment. These questions include:

1. Where are we now?
2. Where do we want to be in the future?
3. How can we get there?
4. What route is best for us?
5. How and when can we implement it?

As can be seen, this is a problem-solving activity and one that provides an opportunity to define or redefine the agency's mission in a time of great environmental challenge and change.

As part of the strategic planning it is necessary to conduct what has been referred to as a *values audit.* This is an examination of the values of the members of the planning team, the current values of the organization, and the organization's culture. This step also involves an examination of the personal values of the individual team members. An officer for whom excitement is an important personal value will envision a different organizational future than will a person who holds security as a high personal value. Likewise, the goals and dreams of an individual who holds professional reputation as a value and is less interested in power will be different from those of a person with opposite priorities (Goodstein et al., 1986).

After the individual values have been worked through, the values of the organization need to be dealt with. As with individual values, any strategic plan that attempts to ignore or is inconsistent with or contrary to the existing organizational values is extremely unlikely to succeed and may well backfire (Goodstein et al., 1986).

Blanchard and Blackwood (1990) indicated that new programs, new technology, and new administrative processes "require changes to organizational structure, policies, procedures and to the values and norms of the people who compose those organizations. It is to be expected that individuals or groups will resist any changes which appear to threaten their self interests. Such resistance must be overcome if desired changes are to become part of the organization's institution" (p. 55). It is obvious that any major change in the way law enforcement is practiced today will pose a threat to members of a law enforcement agency that has adapted to a particular style of policing.

Programs adopted in this manner threaten the officers, and they also fail to take into consideration the organizational culture. Kilmann (1985) pointed out that this culture is separate and distinct from the formal strategy, structure, and reward systems of the organization. He further pointed out that all members of the agency are taught that cultural norms are followed and not questioned. How many new chiefs have vowed that things will be different only to find out that things stay basically the same?

Goodstein et al. (1986) further stated that the audit of organizational values is incomplete without conducting a stakeholder analysis. *Stakeholders* are those individuals, groups, and organizations who will be impacted by the organization's strategic plan. This includes the political bodies overseeing the department as well as members of the community who believe that they have a stake in the organization, regardless of whether or not such a belief is accurate or reasonable.

There are four major elements in the appraisal stage of strategic planning. These include an analysis of:

1. The agency's mission and objectives.
2. Threats and opportunities in the external environment.
3. Managerial values and the agency's culture.
4. The internal strengths and weaknesses of the organization.

Following completion of the values audit the next step in development of the strategic plan is developing a clear-cut statement of the agency's mission and purpose. This entails seeking an answer to what the agency's purpose is: a concise declaration of what purpose or function the agency is attempting to fulfill in society. *Purpose* is defined as "an intention to produce a specific good or service" (Schermerhorn, 1984, p. 149). A statement of the purpose seeks to serve as a guiding philosophy or superordinate goal from which all members of the agency can find direction. This goal lends a sense of unity and direction to an enterprise.

The Mission Statement

In formulating its mission, the agency needs to answer three primary questions: (a) What function does the organization perform? (b) For whom does the agency perform this function? and (c) How does the organization go about filling the function?

This may appear to be an easy task but many agencies have difficulty defining the nature of their operation. A large number of organizations tend to answer the "what" question in terms of the goods or services produced. This is a short-sighted approach that can prevent the organization from seeing new opportunity from growth and expansion and from responding to threats and challenges. The recommended alternative is to answer the question in terms of the customer or client needs that the organization attempts to meet. If an organization identifies itself as meeting certain public needs it will be more sensitive to identifying and treating those needs, more likely to develop new products and services to meet those needs, and less likely to experience obsolescence and decline (Levitt, 1977). Many law enforcement agencies have as their the mission statement "To serve and protect." This mission statement is limited in that it fails to clarify what the agency provides, who its customers are, and what the products or services do for those customers. The New Zealand Police have developed a 5-year strategic plan aimed at combining traditional crime fighting with longer term strategies designed to attack the root causes of crime. The plan was developed following extensive consultation with all sectors of the community, including beat officers. The major strategic goals were listed as an aim to reduce the incidence and effects of crime; to protect property, enhance public safety, and maintain law and order; to improve the safe and efficient use of roads; to implement community-oriented policing; to strengthen public confidence and satisfaction with police services; and to achieve excellence and equity in the management of staff and resources (Harman, 1993). The Saskatoon, Saskatchewan police have as their mission statement, "In partnership with the community, we strive to provide service based on excellence to ensure a safe and secure environment" (Hamilton, 1993, p. 20). Both mission statements help provide action guidelines for all members of the Saskatoon department and are the basis for their community-oriented policing program. The purpose and mission further serve to guide managers in setting official, operative, and operational goals.

As part of defining the agency's mission, goals are determined. These goals specify desired long-run results, as in the case of official goals (an overall reduction in instances of repeat domestic violence offenses), and desired short-run results, as in the case of operative and operational goals. This goal-setting stage is important in that it specifies performance targets for personnel at all levels of the agency. The setting of goals is directly derived from the purpose and mission of the organization.

Identifying the "who" is the second concern of mission formulation. No police agency, regardless of its size, has the capability to meet all the needs of its total constituency. The mission statement requires a clear identification of what portion of the total population the agency identifies as its primary target (Goodstein et al., 1986). After determining what the agency does and for whom, the next step is to decide how these targets will be accomplished. It is at this point that the agency can begin to look at specific programs.

A major function of this stage of the strategic plan is to decide what results will indicate success. A key results area is any area in which the agency must be successful in order to accomplish its mission.

Developing a mission statement is an extremely difficult and time-consuming task, but one that must be completed before moving on to the next step. Developing, editing, and reaching consensus requires skill, patience, and understanding. However, once completed, the mission statement provides an enormously valuable management tool to the agency. It clearly charts its future direction and establishes a basis for agency decision making. An often overlooked phase of strategic planning is the next step, in which each major department of the agency develops its own mission statement. These department mission statements need to be more focused and more limited than that of the total agency, but they clearly must be derived from the agency's statement.

Completion of the analysis of the agency's mission and objectives leads to the next step, which is an analysis of the threats and opportunities in the agency's environment referred to as a strengths and weaknesses of an organization's capabilities and opportunities and threats in the organization's external environment (SWOT) analysis.

Thompson and Strickland (1990) defined and identified a number of strengths, weaknesses, opportunities, and threats.

A *strength* is a distinctive competence, resource, or skill that provides the agency with a competitive advantage in the marketplace. Among the strengths identified are adequate financial resources, a strong and positive image, highly talented managers, and accessibility to quality personnel.

A *weakness* is a negative internal condition that can lead to a lowering of organizational performance. A weakness can be the result of an absence of necessary resources or skills, a deficiency in the development of necessary resources or skills, poor image, high turnover, lack of managerial depth and talent, missing personnel with key skills and competencies, and obsolete equipment.

An *opportunity* is a current or future condition in the environment that is favorable to an organization's current or potential output. This can include an improved relationship with other governmental administrators, additional funding, higher quality applicants, and improved relationships with the community.

A *threat* is a current or future condition in the environment that is unfavorable to the agency's current or potential output. This can include the possibility of consolidation, a radical change in the demographics of the community, changing needs within the community, budget cutbacks, and adverse government policies.

After completing the SWOT analysis, managers are ready to check their agency's existing position and make adjustments that will better prepare the agency for the future. The SWOT analysis is useful for strategic planners in a variety of ways. First, it provides managers with a logical framework for assessing their organization's current and future position. Second, from this assessment, managers can identify a set of alternative strategies. Finally, the SWOT analysis can be conducted periodically to keep managers informed about what external or internal factors have either increased or decreased in importance to the organization's activities.

A SWOT analysis helps managers identify what organizational activities can be realistically achieved over a period of time. However Levin (1983) pointed out that in planning time horizons it is important to keep in mind that: (a) they are not fixed, (b) longer horizons are not always better, (c) planning horizons change over time in response to the rate of change in the environment, (d) different decisions require different horizons, and (e) horizons tend to become shorter as we go further down in the organization. He suggested that in developing a strategic plan an agency needs to look beyond the 4 years in which the mayor or governor may serve: "Planning for long-run organizational needs and changes, for example, in manpower, structure, and training to name but a few, goes beyond four years, if we want to maintain organizational viability and creativity" (pp. 79–80). Governors, mayors, and chiefs come and go, but the agency needs to continue. In fact, a well-developed strategic plan can help offset changes sought by a newly elected politician.

Levin (1983) further differentiated between programs and plans. Community-oriented policing is a program designed to serve a specific purpose. This program is not, however, the strategic plan for the agency. An effective strategic plan for an agency does not need to make reference to a specific program. Instead, the relevant focus of governmental agency planning is on things such as the following:

1. Effectiveness of service. How well is your agency satisfying client demand given the existing constraints? This question asks in fact whether you have a market research system in operation and whether you know how to use some kind of benefit–cost analysis to optimize resource use.
2. Productivity. How effective is your organization in delivering services? Are the delivery procedures cost-effective? Do you measure and compare productivity?
3. Organizational stability and viability. Is your agency organized in the most effective manner given the programs that you implement? Is your organizational structure designed to carry out functions effectively? What is the extent of training carried on by your agency? Is the delegation of authority in your agency sufficient to get maximum decision-making power from the organization?
4. Organizational climate. Do the people in your organization work effectively as a team? Are the procedures adequate? Do you monitor the organizational climate? How do you go about assessing it and identifying problems with it?
5. External relationships. How well does your agency relate to (a) the people who originate the programs you implement, (b) the people these programs serve, and (c) the special interest groups in the environment?
6. Competition. What regulatory, political, and social changes can you see in the environment that will increase the competition that your agency now faces in its "public marketplace"?

Organizational Culture

No strategic plan can be successful if the organizational culture is not examined. This analysis of the agency culture represents the third step in the strategic planning process. The corporate culture is the predominant value system for the organization as a whole. The values of individuals in organizations are subject to the influence of agency culture. This can occur through the hiring process—where people are hired because their personal values are consistent with agency values—and by socialization—where newcomers learn values and ways of behaving that are consistent with those of the agency. This is usually accomplished during the initial period when the new officer is riding with a field training officer. Another way of maintaining the agency culture is by turnover, by which people who do not blend well with the agency culture will leave after approximately 2 years.

Deal and Kennedy (1982) stressed the impact that agency culture can have on an organization's success. By codifying and symbolizing for all to see "the way we do things here," they argued, corporate culture can set a performance tone for the organization. In organizations with strong cultures, everyone knows and supports the organization's objectives; in those with weak cultures, no clear sense of purpose exists.

The corporate culture complements the sense of mission and superordinate goals of the agency. It ultimately affects not only the process of strategy formulation, but also the behaviors and working environments of all employees.

REFERENCES

Blanchard, R. E., & Blackwood, W. O. (1990). Change management process. In H. R. Booher (Ed.), *MANPRINT: An approach to systems integration* (pp. 55–94). New York: Van Nostrand.

Bracker, J. (1980). The historical development of the strategic management concept. *Academy of Management Review, 5,* 219–224.

Carter, D., & Sapp, A. D. (1993, March). Police response to street people. *FBI Law Enforcement Bulletin,* pp. 5–9.

Cummings, T. G. (1980). *Systems theory for organizational development.* New York: Wiley.

Deal, T. E., & Kennedy, A. A. (1982). *Corporate cultures: The rites and rituals of corporate life.* Reading, MA: Addison-Wesley.

Drucker, P. (1954). *The practice of management.* New York: Harper & Bros.

Furcon, J. (1979). An overview of police selection: Some issues, questions, and challenges. In C. D. Spielberger (Ed.), *Police selection and evaluation* (pp. 3–10). New York: Praeger.

Garner, R. (1993, December). Leadership in the nineties. *FBI Law Enforcement Bulletin,* pp. 1–4.

Goetz, F. W. (1993, February). The problem of applying traditional police structure to small police departments. *Law and Order,* pp. 64–66.

Goodstein, L. D., Pfeiffer, J. W., & Nolan, T. M. (1986). Applied strategic planning: A new model for organizational growth and vitality. In J. W. Pfeiffer (Ed.), *Strategic planning: Selected readings* (pp. 1–25). San Diego, CA: University Associates.

Hamilton, S. (1993, December). The Sakatoon experience. *Law and Order*, pp. 20–26.

Harman, A. (1993, December). New strategic plan for New Zealand police. *Law and Order*, pp. 51–54.

Kennedy, D. M. (1993). The strategic management of police resources. In National Institute of Justice, U.S. Department of Justice, & John F. Kennedy School of Government, Harvard University, *Perspectives on policing* (pp. 1–11). Washington, DC: U.S. Government Printing Office.

Kelly, L. (1993, December). The end of the mommy track. *Georgia Trend*, pp. 27–77.

Kilmann, R. (1985, April). Corporate culture. *Psychology Today*, pp. 62–68.

Levin, D. (1983). *The executive's illustrated primer of long range planning*. Englewood Cliffs, NJ: Prentice-Hall.

Levinson, H. (1972). *Organization diagnosis.* Cambridge, MA: Harvard University Press.

Levitt, T. (1977). Marketing myopia. In *On Management* (Reprints from *Harvard Business Review*). New York: Harper & Row.

Maddox, J. H. (1993, July). Community directories. *FBI Law Enforcement Bulletin*, pp. 20–21.

Musashi, M. (1974). *A book of five rings: The classic guide to strategy.* New York: Overlook Press.

Niederhoffer, A. (1969). *Behind the shield: The police in urban society.* New York: Anchor Books.

Raichle, R. W. (1980, March/April). The business of business planning. *Managerial Planning*, pp. 7–10.

Reiser, M. (1974, June). Some organizational stresses on policemen. *Journal of Police Science and Administration*, pp. 156–159.

Reiser, M. (1979). Police consultations. In A. S. Rogawski (Ed.), *Mental health consultations in community settings* (pp. 73–83). San Francisco: Jossey-Bass.

Reiser, M., & Klyver, N. (1987). Consulting with police. In I. B. Weiner & A. K. Hess (Eds.), *Handbook of forensic psychology* (pp. 437–459). New York: Wiley.

Steiner, G. A. (1979). *Strategic planning: What every manager should know.* New York: The Free Press.

Tafoya, W. (1986). *A delphi forecast of the future of law enforcement.* Unpublished doctoral dissertation, University of Maryland, College Park.

Thompson, A. A., Jr., & Strickland, A. J. (1990). *Strategic management: Concepts and cases.* Plano, TX: Business Publications.

Author Index

Subject Index